MANAGING PRODUCTIVE SCHOOLS

_____ *Toward an Ecology*

Managing Productive Schools

Toward an Ecology

Karolyn J. Snyder

Robert H. Anderson

UNIVERSITY OF SOUTH FLORIDA

ACADEMIC PRESS COLLEGE DIVISION
Harcourt Brace Jovanovich, Publishers

Orlando San Diego San Francisco New York London
Toronto Montreal Sydney Tokyo São Paulo

To Helen DeVitt Jones
*Whose friendship and support have
made all the difference*

Academic Press, Inc.
Orlando, Florida   32887

United Kingdom edition published by
Academic Press, Inc. (London) Ltd.
24/28 Oval Road, London NW1 7DX

ISBN: 0-12-654030-6
Library of Congress Catalog Card Number: 85-70463
Printed in the United States of America

CONTENTS

PREFACE

Managing Productive Schools is intended to serve as a guide to the most effective practices surrounding the school principalship. It is particularly geared to those who aspire to become principals, those who currently serve as principals, and those scholars and researchers whose particular academic interest concerns the role of the principal. Our main goal is to provide these audiences with a solid and up-to-date knowledge base regarding productive school management.

Graduate students taking courses in educational administration and supervision will find *Managing Productive Schools* a comprehensive textbook. Seasoned school administrators seeking to augment and expand their leadership skills will find the material superbly suited to their needs. Supervisors and administrators will also find this volume useful in providing an understanding of the ways in which the role of the principal is evolving, an understanding that will serve the goal of greater academic productivity among colleagues in the field.

One of the best-documented conclusions of recent research and experience is that the local principal is in many ways the key person in the educational enterprise. Also well documented is the fact that many principals are awed by the challenges they face, are eager to acquire additional skills, and are grateful for up-to-date, practical advice supported by research evidence. Those who are to become successful school managers must be equipped with a solid foundation that will enable them to face the awesome responsibilities of the principalship with increased confidence and facility. We believe this book provides that solid foundation through its development of essential management concepts.

For some in education, the term "management" may seem less suited to schools than to factories or to business establishments. Similarly, "productivity" is more often associated with agricultural or industrial output than with increments of human learning and development. We have found, however, that the concepts embedded in these terms are wholly relevant to schools, which are, after all, goal-oriented human organizations seeking to produce measurable results (academic products) under the influence and direction of designated leaders.

We have also found that the burgeoning (we are tempted to say exploding) literature aimed at leaders in business and industry (for example, the highly publicized writings of Lee Iacocca, Tom Peters, Robert Waterman, Peter Drucker, Alvin Toffler, Terrence Deal, Allan Kennedy, John Naisbitt, William Ouchi, Rosabeth Moss Kanter, and Richard Boyatzis) has almost total applicability to the work of school administrators. This literature, with its occasional references to schools and their leadership needs, presents the concepts of "management" and "productivity" in positive, useful terms. Perhaps adoption of such terms and enthusiasm for the concepts they represent will help school administrators more forcefully assert their roles as leaders in American society.

The ideas in this book have been brewing since 1977, when a leadership-training model based upon systems theory was first conceived and developed by Snyder. The model sought to blend theories, concepts, and practices from the classical approach known as scientific management, and from the humanistic school of leadership, into a more workable and effective construct for developing schools. The ideas set forth in this work reflect current views of good management, including systems approaches, participation and collaborative decision making, and contingency theory. The latter recognizes both the task and relationship dimensions of work and assumes that leaders will be sensitive to unique and specific conditions in a given situation.

As our early efforts progressed, we developed a series of leadership-training modules, each of which went through successive versions as we implemented our program in numerous school districts and conducted workshops, seminars, and institutes with principals and other school leaders. The final versions of these modules, now 10 in number, have been combined in a companion volume: *Competency Training for Managing Productive Schools.* Readers will find it helpful to refer to the modules as they work their way through this textbook.

The modules in the companion volume focus on 10 competencies essential to effective school management. Three of these are concerned with organizational planning: schoolwide goal setting, work group performance, and individual staff performance. Four deal with staff development, including clinical supervision, work group development, and quality control. Program development (instructional program, and resources development) and assessment of school productivity are topics of the final three modules. All 10 competencies are well-grounded in research and theory, are extensively referenced, and embrace all of the central tasks of productive school management.

During the past five or six years American public education has been in the spotlight as rarely before. Much of the attendant publicity has caused embarrassment for educators. As this book goes to press, however, we sense that the rather shrill tone of printed criticism and public (even legislative) debate is softening as constructive efforts proceed for helping schools to change and develop. A related and major force has been the enormous and welcome increase in published research that focuses on effectiveness and productivity in school settings. One of our special projects has been to collect and review all such studies, partly to keep current in the literature, but also to learn whether research conclusions are consistent with our training program. In the chapters that follow are frequent references to the effective schools research, as it has come to be labeled, and we are delighted that the theory, the assumptions, and the operational components of our approach have been confirmed virtually without exception.

Central to our thinking is that each school is an ecological system. All parts are interdependent, and healthy relationships between the parts can help the school to thrive as an organization. In the opening two chapters we seek to provide a fresh perspective on the principalship and to develop the concept of an ecosystem. We then proceed to examine in detail the various subsystems: leadership (Chapter 3), goals (Chapters 4 and 5), organization (Chapters 9, 10, and 11), and management (Chapters 12, 13, and 14). A theme running through the volume is that each school is a workplace, with both the pupils and the staff in continuous pursuit of new knowledge and new skills. The role of the principal is to invigorate that workplace to enhance both child and adult learning. Another major theme is that the pursuit of goals is a collaborative endeavor. Cooperative work effort is to be especially prized and nurtured. A particular bias of the authors is that productive organizations require team effort and team organization. In our view, one of the most disabling traditions in American schools is the self-contained classroom that discourages interaction and shared learning. We hope this book will reinforce all those professional educators who have taken steps to abandon self-containment and to find ways of working together in the common pursuit of educational excellence. The time is ripe for renewed efforts to implement cooperative teaching in its many possible forms, and we perceive that it is the principal in particular who can inspire and nurture such efforts.

A second companion to *Managing Productive Schools* is a self-diagnostic instrument for principals. The *Personal Perception Profile* enables the respondent to determine the degree to which his or her perceptions of "ideal schooling practices" are matched to the current knowledge base. Diagnostic information from this instrument can aid in planning the pursuit of new knowledge bases and skills.

The ideas in this volume have so many origins and draw upon the work of so many scholars that sufficient acknowledgments are nearly impossible. Perhaps our largest debt is to Fremont Kast and James Rosenzweig, whose use of systems notions to conceptualize the management of business organizations prompted us to make a similar effort in the educational sphere. We are also indebted to those school administrators in the United States and elsewhere in the world who permitted us to implement our training program in their schools and, in the process, make appropriate improvements. We have learned from every author who is cited or quoted, just as we hope our readers will think and act differently after their encounter with our materials. We thank the various professors and doctoral students at Texas Tech University who helped us to improve upon the leadership-training model. We are also grateful for the existence of Pedamorphosis, Inc., the nonprofit organization with which both authors have been associated since 1977 and whose resources made it possible for this work to be done.

Academic Press College Division has been a wonderful partner in the production of the three volumes, and its staff has exhibited the highest professional competence. Deserving of special thanks are Warren Abraham, André Spencer, Gail Tanner, Frank Soley, Iris Medina, and Chris Martin. Our bias in favor of collaboration was strongly reinforced by our work with them. We also received invaluable help from those who reviewed the manuscript: Thomas J. Sergiovanni, Frederick John Gies, James King, and Vernon Hendrix. We hope they will conclude that we took their suggestions very much to heart, and that the final product will please them.

1

Perspectives on the Principalship

Transforming the school into a healthy, vital, and stimulating workplace will probably be the greatest challenge for educators in the remainder of this century. When one considers the schooling task of enabling all students, not just some, to master basic knowledge and skills, the task seems enormous. When one considers the present lifeless patterns found in many schools, the task seems even greater. The blandness, flatness, and lack of intellectual and emotional vigor, which Goodlad (1984) found as pervasive norms in America's classrooms, represent a potential death rattle of the social institution called school. Teachers and students continue to work with amazing tenacity in isolated patterns and are engaged in endless tasks, most of which fail to capture the spirit and inspire productive action. Unless these spiritless work and learning patterns are transformed, schools as we know them will fail in the task ahead.

Researchers have reported convincingly that the principal sets expectations for the school's work culture that either stimulate organizational growth or ensure retrenchment. This book is for those who want to stimulate more productive workplaces in schools. The best that is known about social organizations and practices that enable some organizations to succeed over others weaves its way onto each page of this book. Our purpose is to set forth a conceptual schema, with many practical techniques for leading and managing the most productive school possible. We assume that teachers and principals are partners in this work, as are students and their parents. We further assume, and earnestly believe, that schools can alter ineffective patterns and programs if their people are willing to examine present practices objectively, set new "stretch" goals together, and heed the advice of an increasingly rich literature on the processes of change. The prospect of worthwhile improvements will be

1

all the more enhanced if principals equip themselves to become knowledge-able, dedicated, and skillful managers of such efforts.

Background and Perspective

The twentieth century has been in various ways the most dynamic period in the history of American education. Throughout most of the century, and es-pecially during the most recent quarter century, educators have sought to de-velop effective and varied instructional delivery systems, with the stated goal of enabling every child to develop and extend his or her individual potential. Personalized learning, in fact, has long been a persistent theme of both public and private education. Many political, social, and even economic forces have combined to extend that goal to all kinds of children, including those whose social, ethnic, economic, physiological, and psychological histories caused them to be neglected or overlooked in previous times. The often-stated and unique goal of an adequate education for all children has in recent years be-come a more urgent challenge for teachers and school administrators than ever before. Knowledge and speculation to guide teachers about human growth and development, learning styles and processes, pedagogical ap-proaches, technology, and effective school organization patterns are almost certainly greater than they have ever been. Yet at the same time, there now exist more vexing questions and disturbing uncertainties than most prior gen-erations of educators had to face.

The United States has long occupied a unique place among the nations in its commitment to educate every child at public expense, and also in the faith it placed in education as a means of furthering the nation's growth and well-being. Although many of its educational practices, such as the graded school and emphasis upon classical studies, were borrowed from the dominant European countries, American education pioneered many practices, espe-cially vocational education, and financed and managed itself (through local school boards and local taxes) in new and differerent ways. Partly because of being a decentralized, locally controlled enterprise, and partly because of how American communities developed, education in America generated a pattern of school leadership that earlier rested in the lay citizenry and later became the responsibility of principals and superintendents. In many ways these officials adopted the modus operandi of local business leaders rather than of European school heads and ministry officials.

Inasmuch as local and regional economics and politics, and even social and religious issues, have played such a large role in school district operations over the past half-century, school administrators have also tended to adopt some of the postures and skills of elected public officials. This, we perceive, has helped school districts to survive as important segments of the larger society, but it has seriously impaired their ability to deal with essentially educational issues and to focus upon program improvement. In short, the leaders of American schools have functioned less well as educators than they have as administrators and public officials.

Much of what guides educators in the operation and management of schools derives from scholarship and experience in fields of endeavor other than teaching, particularly business and industry. Similarly, much of the theoretical and practical knowledge about human behavior and tendencies upon which school people draw has been collected or produced in settings other than classrooms and schools. Although strictly education-based research is a rapidly maturing and expanding activity, it remains that school people have long been overly dependent upon, and in some senses the prisoners or victims of, scholars (notably psychologists) whose basic focus is upon questions unrelated to schooling. Furthermore, educational research practices have long been geared to experimental designs that are more appropriate for other sciences and other kinds of human activities. This is due partly to the prevailing research biases in universities, partly to the failure of society to provide adequate research funds for education, and partly to the fact that education has not yet become a full-fledged profession with a solid technology of its own.

If we examine the literatures of school administration, school organization, educational leadership, and educational change and innovation (to mention the topics that are most directly connected to this volume), we discover that until quite recently, many of the authors have had little if any experience in school. In fact, few of the earlier publications even made references to educational applications or examples. The exceptions dealt mostly with nuts-and-bolts topics such as school facilities planning, cafeteria management, and the like. For the most part, educational leaders have found it necessary to borrow and adapt administrative ideas and practices that might be useful in the improvement of education. Sometimes such borrowings and adaptations did indeed prove useful, but sometimes, too, there were disadvantages with which it was difficult to cope.

The emergence of team teaching in the late 1950s as an alternative to protective and insulated self-contained classrooms was a rather dramatic development in American education. One of the greatest by-products of the early training efforts in teaming projects was that teachers, and those concerned with their training, became much more involved in professional exchanges, and in turn became more comfortable about giving and receiving criticism. This proved to be a contributing factor in the recent maturation of supervision as a field of study and development. In particular, clinical supervision—that is, supervision based upon the direct observation of actual events in classrooms (or wherever teachers work with learners)—emerged during the 1950s and early 1960s concomitant with the emergence of collaborative staff arrangements.

During the lively period of educational reform and innovation that began about a decade after World War II, a number of American educators discovered and became enchanted with certain more child-oriented schools in Europe, particularly in the United Kingdom. Although America's love affair with British education, especially those schools that inspired much of the literature of "open education," seems mostly to have run its course, it may be instructive to note that American visitors were especially impressed by the tendency of British school heads to be instructional leaders as opposed to administrators. One booklet, based upon taped interviews with successful school heads, reported that effective leadership grows out of commitment to a well-articulated and functional philosophy, and that these heads regarded themselves primarily "as teacher trainers—as supports for staff, as catalysts, as innovators, as educationists. All gave priority to their role in the classroom, alongside of the teacher, subtly communicating style and philosophy" (Cook and Mack 1971, 11).

We are pleased to observe that in the past two decades, educational administration has made great strides as a field of scholarship, and the topics of educational leadership, organization, and change have come to be much better understood. There are now at least a half-dozen universities, as well as several institutes and centers, in which highly respectable and useful work is under way in these fields. Equally impressive work is being reported from universities and centers in other countries around the world. Furthermore, and as a consequence, the quality of published work by scholars of educational administration has risen significantly since about 1975. It may well be, therefore, that efforts to define and to implement optimal practice will be progressively more successful in the late 1980s and the 1990s.

The authors of this volume have considerable faith in a systems approach to school organization and management, in cooperative leadership and teaching as optimal staff organization patterns, and in clinical supervision methodology as a resource in staff development. The authors also have a deep commitment to those school practices that seek to accept and deal with each child in whatever ways are necessary to help him or her be a successful learner: an educational winner. In the long history of such efforts, the word "individualized" or some equivalent adjective constantly reappears, and over the years specific instructional arrangements have had such labels as activity education, nongradedness, continuous-progress learning, open education, alternative education, and informal education. Even the graded school introduced in the United States in the early nineteenth century, given prevailing assumptions about human motivation and learning, was a well-intended effort to cause greater numbers of children to master the curriculum.

Teaching no longer is the basically amateur vocation that it was for so long, and to become a bona fide professional in education requires far more intensive training and far more supportive in-service conditions than society seems prepared to provide today. All the more reason, therefore, that teachers must "bootstrap" themselves within the most dynamic and growth-producing environment that can be conceived. We dare to believe that a systems approach to school life can provide such an environment.

American Management and Educational Administration

In the early nineteenth century, the German philosopher George Wilhelm Friedrick Hegel developed what is widely known as the Hegelian dialectic: one concept or idea (thesis) always generates an opposite concept or idea (antithesis), and the interaction of these two leads to a new concept or idea (synthesis), which then becomes the thesis in a new cycle.

Within the twentieth century, theories of school organization appear to have gone through an Hegelian cycle. The so-called classical patterns that were popular in the first third of the century emphasized structure and formal relationships. Frederick W. Taylor, known for his "scientific management" ideas, and Max Weber, who studied bureaucratic organization, were among the leaders of this school of thought, which was welcomed by a society eager for more efficiency and willing to let educators incorporate such ideas into the running of schools. Callahan (1962) has provided a very helpful description of this period, during which efficiency literally became a cult.

Coinciding somewhat with the Great Depression that gripped America after the 1929 stock market crash and lasting until the beginning of World War II, classical work patterns came under attack because they overvalued task management and structure at the expense of human factors. Elton Mayo and others who studied the feelings and motivations of industrial workers came to believe that more humanistic approaches to management resulted in higher production as well as high morale. The industrial humanists, whose influence was greatest up to midcentury, soon were joined in education by those who had for some time been working in the cause of progressive education, or who out of similar motivation focused on the people within school organizations and the ways in which they interacted and cooperated. In time, however, the humanistic approach to management also came to be criticized because of a perceived overemphasis upon social and psychological aspects to the neglect of structural and production dimensions of the organization. More recently there has emerged the so-called systems approach which, in the Hegelian sense, represents a synthesis of the classical (thesis) and humanistic (antithesis) approaches. The emphasis currently is balanced equally on the task of the organization and the motivation of its workers.

Management must balance the forces that are results oriented and consider the worker as an important variable. Kast and Rosenzweig (1974), in a landmark work that has greatly influenced our thinking and exerted a major influence upon the model presented in this volume, have taken the concepts of systems theory and translated them into a model of organization and management. In their model, Kast and Rosenzweig view the organization as a sociotechnical system.

> Under this view, an organization is not simply a technical or social system. Rather, it is the structuring and integrating of human activities around various technologies. . . . However, the social system determines the effectiveness and the efficiency of the utilization of the technology.
>
> (p. 111)

We believe that such concepts offer a very useful framework that can and should be used in schools.

The predominant view of educational administration during the first quarter of this century emphasized *scientific management* (Getzels 1977, 4). In schools, Taylor's scientific management concepts and values led to certain schooling characteristics that determined the relationship between pupil and instructor, teacher and administrator. The basic function of school administration was generally to define what was expected of teachers and to ensure that they perform in the most efficient manner. The Taylor model, Getzels notes, was based on a carefully structured four-pillar system of values that included the *work–success ethic* (material achievement); *future time orientation* (time is money), *competitive individualism* (the race goes to the swift), and *Puritan morality* (respectability, thrift, and so on). In an analysis of his own system, Taylor paraphrased scientific management as "task management," suggesting that the *task* concept is its most prominent variable (Taylor, in Sexton, 1970, 6–9). Workers in time came to be viewed as empty organisms responding only to pleasure and pain, reward and punishment, while engaging in job tasks (Getzels, 7).

Max Weber introduced the concept of bureaucratic organization to Taylor's scientific management (Weber, in Sexton, 1970, 41). His assumption was that the ways in which a staff is structured provide the rational means to achieve organizational objectives; various levels of management authority guide decision making regarding efficient uses of staff. Each administrative position has specific amounts of power, salary, and expertise, determined by technical com-

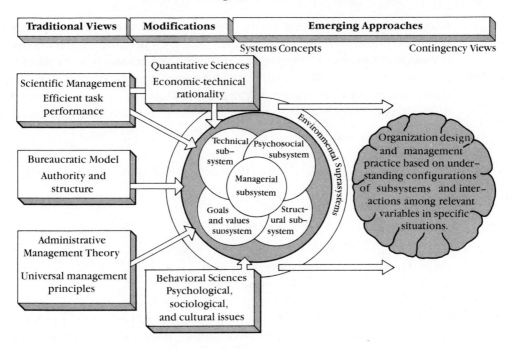

Figure 1.1. Concepts of an Organization: A Century of Ideas. (*Source*: From Fremont E. Kast and James E. Rosenzweig, *Experiential Exercises and Cases in Management*, p. 289. © 1976. Reprinted with permission of McGraw-Hill Book Company.)

petence. Certain rules and regulations specify relationships between administrative officers which define jurisdiction and place in the organization's hierarchy (Hellriegel and Slocum 1974, 50).

Weber's concepts have enabled larger school organizations to develop technical proficiency in efforts to be productive. Clearly defined roles, relationships, hierarchy, and job tasks are strong foundational concepts that guide school organization today. While management authority and job tasks provide a structure to accomplish complex tasks, these concepts as they were defined long ago are inadequate today. Role relationships must be refined to adapt to emerging social conditions. Participatory decision making and group authority must find their way into school organizations so that once again schools reflect social conditions and provide the educational services society needs.

Figure 1.1 provides an overview of the management models that followed Taylor's and Weber's early works. The concepts of efficiency, task structure, bureaucratic organization, and management authority were fine tuned over the next several decades. Eventually organizations lost sight of the worker as an individual, leading to a robot view of worker performance.

In a quest for keys to effective working conditions, many behavioral scientists began examining the worker and the factors of the workplace that stimulated productivity. Mayo's studies in the 1930s precipitated a new era in the study and practice of management and organization. He learned that workers respond not only to management mandates, but also to the ways in which they interact with each other on the job: the logic of sentiment. Subsequently, he made the following assumptions about the worker (Mayo 1945):

1. Man is basically motivated by social needs and obtains a sense of identity through association with others.
2. Man is more responsive to the social forces of the peer group than to the incentives and controls of management.
3. Man is responsive to management to the extent that a supervisor can meet a subordinate's social and acceptance needs.

Social scientists such as Lewin (1958) organized workers into groups where they were urged to share their feelings and concerns about the work environment and about each other. In time it became clear that workers had something besides a specific job skill to contribute to the workplace. They had insights about productivity which, if shared with management, had the potential to increase the organization's productive output, both qualitatively and quantitatively.

McGregor's studies (1960) led to the understanding that two kinds of management assumptions about workers permeate the workplace, each stimulating a different kind of worker productivity. One assumption is that people basically dislike work and consequently need to be told what to do. He called this view Theory X. Another view was that people seek pleasure in their work, and therefore should participate in making decisions about that work. This view was named Theory Y. It was soon learned that management can increase the norms of worker productivity by involving workers in decision making and by organizing them to work within a group context.

To extend the exploration of worker productivity and motivation, psychologists began to study the intrinsic factors that tend to stimulate behaviors in organizations. Maslow (1962) and Herzberg et al. (1959) identified psychological factors that influence performance. Maslow proposed that people operate out of five different levels of personal psychological needs, each level generating a different kind of worker job response. Herzberg categorized workers as either motivators or hygiene seekers. He asserted that motivators are interested in the job *content* and are consequently productive for the organization. Hygiene seekers, on the other hand, tend to be interested in the job *context* and tend to seek satisfaction with the conditions of working.

Both groups of behavioral scientists, those who studied group behavior in organizations and those who studied personal motivation in the work environment, have generated considerable knowledge about workers and about psychological influences on productivity. Eventually managers involved workers more in organizational decision making and also organized them to work cooperatively in a small group context within the organization. The influence of the behavioral scientists on management practice today is considerable. Rather than emphasizing tasks and efficiency, management focuses on the influences of adult learning and productivity in organizations, emphasizing leadership and adult learning theories.

During the same years that researchers were studying workers, others were studying the nature of effective leadership in organizations. Scholars at Ohio State University studied leadership in different kinds of social organizations (Hemphill and Coons 1957). There soon emerged the concept that effective leaders have two different sets of behaviors, both of which are necessary to stimulate workers effectively. Effective leaders are equally strong in initiating a task structure and in worker consideration. This conceptualization blends the task focus of scientific management, and the worker-consideration focus of the human relationship movement. Subsequently, organization scholars, such as Argyris (1964) and Likert (1967) were able to link effective worker behavior (individual and small work group) with effective leader behavior (management of individuals and groups). It was assumed that both sets of behavior (worker and management) act interdependently to influence the health and productivity of the organization.

Likert pursued the question of management behavior in his studies of organizational productivity. He conceptualized that there are four different kinds of operational management systems, each based upon different assumptions about the worker and the appropriate degree of worker involvement. The first system assumes that workers need to be told what to do in order to produce; the fourth system assumes that total worker participation in organizational problem solving and decision making stimulates worker productivity. Systems two and three represent gradual management progression from "no worker involvement in decisions" (system one) to "total worker involvement in decisions" (system four). Likert found that system four was the most productive system, and that this was due largely to (a) management confidence and trust in workers and (b) its patterns of worker co-involvement and participation in decision making. Likert's conceptualization of management styles is useful in that it provides an explicit path for altering norms of productivity by reconditioning worker behavior from patterns found in system one. Eventually management will be able to teach workers to function as participant decision makers (system four) and thereby enhance worker productivity.

The human relations era had less influence upon schools than did the era of scientific management and bureaucracy. Team teaching was a 1950s attempt to organize teachers into work groups to share in instructional decision making. Variations on team teaching began to emerge; team management, for example, enabled administrators to share various schooling tasks. Clinical supervision was another 1950s example of how management attempted to involve teachers in the refinement of teaching practices, through a client-centered classroom observation methodology. Learning specialist teams (which might include teachers, a psychologist, a social worker, and aides) emerged in some schools to study the learning problems of particular students. However, for the most part these grouping and involvement practices within schools were only "permitted" to coexist alongside more typical patterns of role isolation and management decision making. Only now, in the 1980s, are schools coming to understand the importance of group work and involving various roles in decision making about schooling practice.

While the behavioral scientists provided considerable leadership in the field of organization and management during the 1950s and 1960s with their studies and models of human involvement, scientific management practices also matured. Scientific technologies evolved into even more sophisticated theories and principles of economics and technical rationality. Modern management has also developed logical rationalistic models of organizational analysis in the form of microeconomics, operations research, and systems engineering (Newman et al. 1967, 29). Traditional assumptions about management and the worker in these later developments, however, further underscored the widening differences between the behavioral approaches (worker involvement) and the expanding scientific approaches (administrative decision making).

Table 1.1 defines the parameters of organizational practice within each closed-system view of the organization: scientific management and human relations. It is easy to perceive the extremes to which each view developed in its pursuit of organizational productivity.

For a number of years both views and practice of organization and management existed alongside each other. However, scholars began to wrestle with the question of how to merge the best of both views. Scientific management and bureaucracy provide a technology for organizing workers and administrators effectively while focusing on efficient task accomplishment. The individual nontask contributions and psychological needs of workers, however, were virtually ignored. The human relations movement, on the other hand, focused on the added contributions that workers can make if they are organized in groups and participate in decisions concerning their tasks. The task of the organization, however, became blurred as management attended to patterns of worker involvement and consideration. It was time for a synthesis of the thesis (scientific management) and the antithesis (human relations) to emerge, blending together the strengths of both approaches to organization and management.

TABLE 1.1. Outline of Closed-System Strategies

Area	Rational Economic	Human Relations
Objectives	Economically oriented; profit stated in nonhuman terms	Employee oriented; concern for welfare of human, benefit programs. Group help, implementation
Communication systems	Close control; formal channels; concern for and attempt to control grapevine between subordinates	De-emphasis on formal systems, information to all, encourage bypassing; communicate directly; group communications
Control systems	Very close; management-established quotas "countable"; measurable individual incentives and control	Control based on *groups*; peers provide control, social pressures
Decision making	No participation—manager *must* make all the decisions. Technically best decisions desirable	Group participates in decision making; interested more in acceptance of decision than in technical aspects
Structure	"Tall" structure and very detailed regulations; highly organized; authority based	"Flatter" structure; room for groups to form and operate
Leadership styles	Manager makes all decisions and announcements; decisions oriented to results that will provide most economic returns. Autocratic	Leader should fulfill the needs and desires of the group; results emerge from group; group oriented to democratic process
Reward	Economic rewards; tangible, individual incentives	Group incentives economic as well as social; rewards stem mostly from peers; fringe benefits strong

Source: Adapted from Egar Schein, *Organizational Psychology*, 3rd ed. (Englewood Cliffs, NJ: Prentice-Hall, Inc., 1965), 47–56; and William G. Scott, "Technology and Organization Government: A Speculative Inquiry into the Functionality of Management Creeds," *Academy of Management Journal*, 1968, 301–313. Reprinted with permission of Prentice-Hall, Inc. and *Academy of Management Journal.*

Barnard (1938) is credited by many scholars with providing the genesis of such a synthesis in management thought and practice. He asserted that organizational growth necessarily involves both work production and personal forces. The executive function is to coordinate the task production practices while attending to the personal forces of the organization's workers. Consequently, management models began to reflect both task structure and worker involvement, representing responsiveness on the part of management to organizational purpose and also to worker needs.

Bertalanfy (1972) made an important contribution to the new developments in management and organization. He studied various ecological systems in biology in an attempt to identify factors that enable living systems to thrive. He was perhaps the first scholar to conceptualize an organization in an entirely new fashion: a living, growing organism. By introducing the concept of ecology into organizational thought, he built on Barnard's central theme of the five executive functions and developed what he called "general systems theory."

One of Bertalanfy's major contributions was the distinction between an open and a closed organizational system. Traditional theories assumed that organizations function as relative isolates within a social context. Drawing upon concepts of biological systems, he proposed that productive organizations necessarily seek to grow and to interact with their environment continuously, interaction with the environment being the variable that will continuously enable the organization to adjust itself effectively to changing conditions. The closed view of organizations assumes that patterns are predetermined and stable, whereas an open system assumes that the organization can adjust itself continuously by receiving environmental feedback and by developing a capacity to self-adjust.

The concept of boundaries provides additional insight into the difference between closed and open views of the organization. The closed system has rigid and impenetrable boundaries that protect the organization from outside influences and demands for change. The open system, however, has permeable boundaries, and assumes that outside influences provide the necessary direction and energy for growth.

Perhaps the most central concept to an open system view of organizations is "holism." The first law of ecology suggests that everything is connected to everything else (Kast and Rosenzweig 1973, 105). A school, for example, is often viewed as having many separate and independent functions, such as curriculum building, staff development, and teacher evaluation. The systems view, however, suggests to us that in the most productive organizations, separate functions do not operate in isolation, but rather, work interdependently as an energy system to influence total organizational productivity. Systems theory calls for consideration of questions such as: "What will we accomplish together?", "Who will do which tasks?", and, "How will we accomplish our goal?"

Kast and Rosenzweig (1974) were the first management scholars to translate the concepts of general systems theory into a workable management system. In their model, each organization contains five discrete yet interdependent subsystems: goals, management, technical, psychosocial, and structural. Each of these five separate subsystems performs a unique function for the organization, but they tend to operate as a whole and to interact with the surrounding environment. The *goals* and values subsystem provides direction and purpose for the organization; the *technical* subsystem assumes a knowledge base and includes techniques required for task performance; the *psychosocial* subsystem defines individual and group interaction; the *structural* subsystem dictates a division of tasks; and the *managerial* subsystem sees that all subsystem roles, tasks, and technologies work toward the attainment of the organization's goals.

Systems concepts of the organization, Lorsch (1970) observes, move us in a promising direction for tailoring an organization to its environment as well as to the complex needs of its members. The Kast and Rosenzweig model has provided the foundation for the conceptualization of schools as ecological systems as advocated in this book.

The influence of both the traditional and human relations approaches to school organization and management perseveres in schools today, with only a few models reflecting a synthesis of task, structure, production, and human well-being as represented in systems views of organizations. Consequently, schools tend to resemble either a military camp (traditional model) or a summer camp (human relations model). Although the accountability movement of the 1970s and 1980s calls for more attention to student achievement, few schools yet have succeeded in merging the high task structure of accountability, with a collaborative environment that fosters creative thinking and risk taking.

Spady (1977) summed up the past in education by suggesting that schools have held a *maintenance view* of organization and management, with an emphasis on fixed roles and fixed time parameters. The focus of management has rested primarily with student placement and school operations. Schools are shifting, he observes, to a *production view* of the school organization with more of an emphasis on goals and outcomes. Management within the latter view focuses on instruction and learning, rather than on assignment and memos. Our own analysis supports this view and further speculates that the management shift is from maintaining school patterns to nurturing innovative adult performance.

The Changing Role and Context of the Principalship

In the previous section we discussed changes in the field of educational administration in general. In this section we focus attention on the principalship and its recent role changes. While all administrative roles have been altered significantly in the past decade, the principalship has undergone perhaps the most dramatic role change of all. The role shift for principals has been a movement away from priority attention to administration toward an emphasis on managing instructional and organizational growth.

The 1970s decade may well go down in educational history as "The Remaking of the Principalship." Goldhammer (1971), in his national study of the elementary principalship, found that virtually no criteria or rationale existed for the role of principal. A basic conflict existed then among professors, state and federal educators, and principals about role definitions and descriptions. The conflict waged over whether the principal should continue in a relatively passive role as building administrator, or function instead as an influence on teaching practices. Goldhammer further noted that principals lacked expertise in managing a staff, in program planning, and in the kinds of supervision necessary for altering teaching norms.

In a similar analysis, Becker et al. (1971) reported that the lack of knowledge about the necessary strategies for effective change were among the most critical shortcomings among principals. Principals, he observed, feel confident about overseeing routine building operations, but generally lack confidence in assuming a leadership role for improving instruction.

In 1973, Anderson (p. 41), in a book written for elementary principals, concluded that intervention into the instructional process is essential if schools are to alter outdated teaching practices. He observed that

> If we continue to disregard teachers, to exhibit little interest in (or talent for) helping them in their daily classroom activities, to operate on a fraudulent business-as-usual basis while their frustrations multiply, or to remain neutral or aloof while proposals for school improvement (or the actual de-schooling of society) scorch the surrounding air, teachers are likely either to despair or to hold more fiercely to the repertoires they possess. If, on the other hand, we begin to deal with teachers' daily concerns more helpfully, within the framework of a clinical relationship, then as a group they will develop a stronger sense of worth, of basic competence, and of readiness to consider alternative approaches.

In 1974, the Institute for Development of Educational Activities, Inc. (/I/D/E/A/), then the educational affiliate of the Kettering Foundation, continued the role debate about the principalship by sponsoring a series of conferences called the Chautauqua series (Pharis 1975; Houts 1975). Public school administrators from all levels, state and federal agency representatives, and scholars were invited to analyze the growing problems of the principalship. The outcome of the conferences was a call for clearer role definitions for principals with accompanying changes in certification and training. The role definition that seemed to emerge from the conference was that the principal should be viewed as a catalyst in the school's growth process. Clerical work, they argued, should be limited; principals should be given building autonomy and the necessary resources to accomplish school goals.

In the intervening years, a role definition for the "principalship" has surfaced as a priority topic at national and state professional conventions, in local district think tanks, for scholars and researchers in educational administration, and at various conferences on training for administrators.

In Search of a New Definition

The accountability movement that grew to tidal wave proportions during the late 1970s precipitated clarity about necessary dimensions within the role of principal. Many state departments of education and local school districts throughout the country challenged schools to change through such movements as minimum competency testing, back-to-the basics or competency-based education programs. The impact of this strong social force convinced the few wavering experts and skeptical practitioners seriously to insist that principals can and must be accountable for achievement norms in their schools. To that end it was perceived that principals ought to become instructional leaders.

In keeping with social pressures, textbooks on the principalship that emerged in the mid-1970s (Roe 1974; Doll 1972; Lipham and Fruth 1976) all emphasized instructional leadership functions. Several scholars, such as Sergiovanni and Carver (1973) and Kimbrough and Nunnery (1976), however, warned that in addition to managing instruction, principals also must manage a system: an elaborate organization. Simultaneous with new scholarly role definitions, numerous research studies sought to identify new competencies necessary for the changing principalship. Many lists of competencies were catalogued into an exhaustive resource document by Project Rome of the University of Georgia (Pool 1974). To summarize the extensive list of competences, Katz's basic skill categories seem useful. Principals need *conceptional skills* to influence planning, developing, and research; *technical skills* to manage school processes; and *human skills* to involve staff members in decisions about the school's growth process.

In an attempt to resolve the dilemma of role functions, Erickson (1977) made a serious proposal to launch cooperative patterns of research with practitioners in order to remove "the sightless persons on the freeway." He proposed a paradigm shift in educational administration that would address the problems relating to instruction and to student learning outcomes. His proposal sought to establish the necessary relationship between administrative behavior and the productivity of teachers and students.

Research on Effective Principals

In the Erickson spirit, during the latter 1970s the National Institute of Education (NIE) funded several research projects on "school-effects." Researchers (see Austin's summary 1979) observed that successful schools result from the interdependency of certain practices within the school organization. The following characteristics were found to exist in successful schools:

Strong instructional leadership
Program development, planning, instruction
High performance expectations
A belief that all students can learn the basics
A positive climate
Control over school functions, curriculum and program staff
Strong staff support
Support services
Responsibilities for student achievement

Later in the decade Berman and McLaughlin (1978) sought to investigate factors in the successful adoption, implementation, and continuation of school projects. They found that enthusiastic principals are able to marshal support from even reluctant teachers, while a negative principal can discourage supportive teachers. So strong is the influence of school culture, they found, that both principals and teachers together can quietly scuttle or continue a project regardless of district policy. Consequently, the report named the principal "the gatekeeper of change."

In keeping with the Berman/McLaughlin study, a University of Maryland study of 30 Maryland schools (Austin 1979) found that the best schools were run for a specific purpose, rather than from force of habit, through strong principal leadership. Principals set clear instructional goals for the school and spent 50 percent of their time involved in improving teaching. In yet another study, conducted by the Michigan State University Institute for Research on Teaching (Brookover and Lezotte 1979), schools identified as "improving" were found to be clearly different from others in that they set objectives for reading and mathematics achievement. A principal in an "improving school," they observed, was more likely to be the instructional leader and, therefore, assertive in his or her instructional role.

Edmonds (1979) concluded from his studies of successful schools in New York City that there are no good schools with bad principals. A good principal is a necessary (but not a sufficient) condition for a successful school and is likely to be a person who has a firm belief about the central purpose of the school, which is communicated to others. An instructional leader, in Edmonds' view, visits classes systematically and responds to what is seen during those visits.

Several additional studies provide information about what effective principals do. Fullan (1981, 281), for example, found that effective principals become directly involved in what teachers are doing by meeting with them, discussing concerns, and keeping informed about teaching. Several other studies report that effective principals have their secretaries or assistants do much of the routine paperwork so that they can provide instructional leadership (Brookover et al. 1979, 92).

Moreover, in high-achieving schools, teachers are willing to give their time freely to work on school tasks, whereas in low-achievement schools, teachers are willing to give time only if they are paid (Brookover et al. 1979, 115). One indicator of staff commitment to school goals is the extent to which teachers are willing to give of their personal time.

Principals in declining schools, however, appear to be more permissive, to emphasize informal relationships in schools, and to spend time socially with their teachers (Brookover et al. 1979, 100). By contrast, effective principals tend to keep some social distance from their teaching staff. Other researchers report that having good relations between principal and teachers is not enough to increase learning norms in school. However, the ability to work well with people is reported to be the most important asset among [high school] principals (Gordon and McIntyre 1978).

Effective principals tend to use discretion in (1) monitoring what happens in the school; (2) protecting the school from uncertainties; (3) adapting policies to school needs; (4) realizing their personal goals; (5) acquiring power relative to the larger system; (6) adapting the reward system of the district to school needs; and (7) protecting their school from interference in its instructional endeavors (Morris et al. 1981, 217–220).

Effective principals also coordinate, discuss, and advise on instruction, while ineffective principals tend to do none of these (Cohen and Miller 1980). In addition, effective principals offer rewards, resources, and personal interaction with teachers in exchange for compliance and acceptance of a joint responsibility for instructional outcomes. And, high student achievement is found in schools where principals and teachers share a common pedagogical orientation (Bossert et al. 1981, 5).

The Florida Council on Educational Management has recently conducted several studies of principals in an attempt to identify those characteristics that distinguish between high- and average-performing principals (Croghan, Lake, Schroder 1983). What resulted from an analysis of these studies was a list of 19 competencies, which are organized into six clusters:

1. Purpose and direction: proactive orientation; decisiveness; commitment to mission
2. Cognitive skills: interpersonal search; information search; concept formation; conceptual flexibility
3. Consensus management: managing interaction; persuasiveness; concern for image; tactical adaptability
4. Quality enhancement: achievement motivation; management control; developmental orientation
5. Organization: organizational ability; delegation
6. Communication: self-presentation; written communication; organizational sensitivity

The appendix at the end of this chapter describes each competency, along with behavioral indicators. Our perception is that fundamental changes, geared to the newly defined competencies, are being made in university certification and degree programs and also in procedures for the selection, certification, training, evaluation, and compensation of principals in Florida school districts. These changes could eventually influence practices in other states as well.

Current Work Patterns: Another View

Some other researchers have sought to understand the nature of the principal's job without analyzing its relationship to achievement patterns. Both the national elementary (NAESP) and secondary (NASSP) organizations for principals have conducted extensive studies of the behaviors and expectations of principals during these times of changing role definitions. A study of elementary principals by Pharis and Banks–Zakariya (1979, 105) is primarily demographic in nature, illuminating some elements surrounding the role. However, it sheds little light on the principal's changing role. For example, little discussion is found in the report about current role parameters, although the report concludes by challenging principals to define their own role lest other actors (superintendents, state agencies, federal agencies, degree and certification programs, and communities) define it for them. This conclusion is puzzling, since very little information in the 111-page volume deals with role variables, tasks, functions, or definitions. Three exceptions are worth noting, however: (1) the percentage of principals primarily responsible for supervision rose 11 percent from 75.1 percent in 1968 to 86.2 percent in 1979 (ibid., 63); (2) achievement was perceived to have increased since 1968 (ibid., 98); and (3) role problems mentioned related only to deviant student and staff behavior, declining enrollments, and teacher evaluation.

What about the future for elementary principals? The Pharis report concludes that more principals will be male, schools will be smaller, collective bargaining skills will be more sophisticated, and the school's power structure will be changing (ibid., 97). The reader is left wondering what principals actually do, or wish they could do, as school managers.

The study of secondary principals (McLeary and Thompson 1979) appears to be more role focused, labeling future principals as "educators." While goals of educational programs in schools seem not to have changed since a 1965 NASSP study, principals in 1979 perceived that the instructional contexts of programs were significantly different (ibid., 8). Secondary principals generally sought greater autonomy and ways to improve their own performance. Effective principals, it was noted, spent the bulk of their time on program development, personnel, and school management (ibid., 16); furthermore, they wished to spend more time on both program and professional development (ibid., 16). As effective principals tackled their job, they tended to approach problems directly, set high standards, established an open and acceptive climate, and worked to develop new practices in their schools (ibid., 21). Future demands on the secondary principal were likely to include (1) expectations to set school objectives and provide progress reports (to the public); (2) addressing declining enrollments; and (3) addressing new methodologies, technologies, and courses arising from research and social demands (ibid., 56). The report concluded by heralding the importance of developing annual school plans that include a needs assessment, community priorities, and clear reporting systems. Planning skills, it was noted, are perceived to be basic to the successful involvement of others.

Pitner (1981) reports that the work of principals is characterized by (1) a low degree of self-initiated tasks; (2) many activities of short duration; (3) discontinuity caused by interruptions; (4) the superseding of prior plans by the needs of others in the organization; (5) face-to-face verbal contacts with one other person; (6) variability of tasks; (7) an extensive network of individuals and groups both internal and external to the school or district; (8) a hectic and unpredictable flow of work; (9) numerous unimportant decisions and trivial agendas; (10) few attempts at written communication; (11) events occurring in or near the administrator's office; (12) interactions predominantly with subordinates; and (13) a preference for problems and information that is specific, concrete, solvable, and currently pressing.

There seems to be skewing of attention toward organizational maintenance tasks in most schools (Greenfield 1982, 47). The skewing is related to a combination of factors: expectations of superiors; the norms of teachers; dispositions and abilities of principals; the size of the organization and in-school administrative resources; characteristics of the student population; and aspects of the environment within which schools operate. However, effective principals are reportedly able to address their school management tasks in spite of these adverse conditions.

Martin and Willower (1981) found that 60 percent of a principal's time is spent on desk work and in scheduled and unscheduled meetings. More than 65 percent of the principals's time is spent in interaction with or in the presence of others. The job is a highly interpersonal one involving frequent social encounters.

Another study (Peterson 1978) reports that principals engage predominantly in service, advisory, and auditing relationships. They tend not to become directly involved in the work flow at the classroom level. This finding (and also many others) confirms that principals do not become involved to any great extent in classroom observation, curriculum development, and staff development. In short, they are not involved in the core tasks of the school. Women principals, however, are reportedly more likely to function as instructional leaders (Gross and Herriott 1965; Duke, Cohen, and Herman 1981).

Sailey et al. (1979, 32) found four different approaches that principals use in response to their work. There are principals

1. who place high priority on the involvement and support of groups; or
2. who stress the development of teachers through involvement; or
3. who emphasize evaluation and improvement of academic performance; or
4. who stress tight fiscal control and close working relationships with the central office.

The principalship is said to be a highly interpersonal role characterized by a great deal of ambiguity and, hence, latitude for decision making (Blumberg and Greenfield 1980). Principals in smaller schools are involved with students, whereas in larger schools they are more involved with personnel and policy-level issues.

Morris et al. (1982) found from their research efforts that instructional leadership, by any definition, is not the central focus of the principalship. Most of the principal's day is spent on the run and therefore not conducive to ordered decision making. They found that principals devote major amounts of time to school monitoring behaviors, serving as the school spokesperson, disseminating information within the school, and serving as disturbance handler and resource allocator. The 24 principals in their study tended to lead the instruction program indirectly by creating an atmosphere in which teaching and learning can thrive. Direct efforts to train or coach teachers were seldom used.

In an effort to identify what teachers perceive principals ought to do, Hoy and others found that teachers not only respond positively to, but desire, administrative structure in terms of rules and regulations (1977). Moreover, teachers want principals to support and to facilitate their work (Lortie 1975, 199).

In summary, research on the public school principal has found consistently that the principalship is highly interpersonal, full of ambiguous and conflicting expectations, possessed of considerable latitude in responding to situations, and confronted by a diverse range of problems, many of which are out of the principal's direct influence (Greenfield 1982).

Getting from Here to There: Training and Retraining Principals

Complaints about their graduate preparation are legion among principals (Wolcott 1973). As a group, many practicing educational administrators disparage the utility of university training for preparing graduates to face the problems of practitioners (Ourth 1979).

In May 1979, the Department of Health, Education, and Welfare sponsored a national workshop on school administrator training in which the authors participated. A major conclusion of the conference was that administrator training is in a sorry state largely because of the historic unwillingness of administrators and professors to work together. In the workshop summary address, by Anderson, was noted the growing need for all involved in administrator training and administrator effectiveness to collaborate, to join together, and to abandon their traditional patterns of self-containment, of unfettered idiosyncrasy, of entrepreneurial selfishness, and even of self-aggrandizement. In short, a great price has been paid for institutional and personal autonomy. University X continues to operate separately from, and often in obvious competition with, University Y. Professor Smith publishes and consults as a fiercely independent individual, as do Professors Jones, Green, and Brown. This pattern, it was noted, must give way to a more unified approach.

Most states have recently developed or are developing programs through departments of education, regional service agencies, universities, professional organizations, and school districts to provide up-to-date skill-building opportunities for principals. Most of the national professional associations for school administrators are providing regular and timely skill-building experiences.

For example, the National Association of Secondary School Principals (NASSP) has developed assessment centers throughout the country that are designed to identify and develop building principles (Hersey 1982). Twelve skill dimensions (problem analysis, judgment, organizational ability, decisiveness, leadership, sensitivity, stress tolerance, oral communication, written communication, range of interests, personal motivation, and educational values) guide simulation techniques and exercises designed to evaluate these 12 skills. Not only can promising administrators be identified through assessment center techniques, but development suggestions for participants provide directions for personal growth. Training programs have been developed with the Far West Laboratory to enable participants to apply new skills in actual work settings.

Professors of school administration are also presented with a fresh challenge throughout the country. Facing the possibility of being bypassed in the training and certification of principals, Florida's professors of educational administration banded together to respond to changing conditions. Working together with school officials throughout the state, the professors developed a set of competencies within eight clusters, which are designed to build a knowledge base for "high-performing principals," approved by the Florida Council on Educational Management. All leadership departments in Florida's colleges of education, as of this writing, are redesigning their certification programs to correspond to the eight clusters of competencies. The course of training Florida principals has been altered through a series of events involving the legislature, the Florida Council on Educational Management, school district officials, principals and professors, and deans of colleges of education.

We hope and believe that graduate programs in educational administration are in many other cases undergoing significant changes in order to equip principals, superintendents, and other leaders with a solid conceptual–theoretical base for their changing roles. We note that in recent years there has been a notable and welcome increase not only in the number but also in the quality of continuing in-service education opportunities available to practicing school administrators. Some of these deal with the changing roles of school leaders, effective time management practices, curriculum development, teacher evaluation, clinical supervision, labor relations and teacher negotiations, dealing with special children, and staff development. Historically, in the experience of most administrators these sessions have tended to be irregular and uncoordinated. While they responded to needs, they underscored the fragmentation of leadership functions and failed to address the major shift in role emphasis.

Pre-service and in-service education programs, by design, need to provide a more integrated, holistic framework. This is a challenge to be met by universities, administrators, professional associations, and other groups who are pooling their efforts. Likewise, within each school district there are steps to be taken in creating an environment within which principals, central office personnel, and other educational leaders can function more effectively, while at the same time receiving a significant on-the-job training experience. We believe a systems approach to school development would provide such an environment. This is what this book is all about.

Moreover, there is a need for greater emphasis on the responsibility of the superintendent for monitoring principals and providing coaching and assistance when skill deficiencies are present (Yukl 1982, 57). Our hope is that superintendent training programs will increasingly emphasize this aspect of the superintendent's work.

Reflections on Role Transition

If it is true that century-old habits of self-containment are among the causes of ineffective change efforts and of an uncoordinated approach to professional problems, then it follows that all of us in education need to reorient ourselves to work patterns that bring us together. One major consequence of such a reorientation would be a far greater appreciation for *supervision* (role coaching) as a normal and necessary activity. Whenever persons in the same work force become interconnected, and are enabled to exchange thoughts and ideas with each other, it is inevitable that criticisms will pass back and forth. In virtually every other field of work, and especially in the professions, the exchange of criticism (which, by the way, is a neutral word embracing the evaluation of both merits and faults) is seen as a natural and productive element. By comparison, teachers, counselors, and even those former teachers who move into administrative roles tend to be fearful of criticism and tend to resist the idea of being supervised with attendant exposure to critical supervisory feedback.

It needs to be acknowledged that principals face certain inescapable administrative duties. However, we hold that one of the greatest needs in American education is for principals to reexamine their priorities and reconsider how they allocate their time and energy. Textbooks and manuals on the principalship have vainly argued this point for decades, and yet the majority of principals spend their time in maintenance activities at the expense of educational leadership functions. We perceive that this is largely voluntary (it is easier to handle daily trivia than to engage in instructional improvement tasks); that it betrays administration-oriented training (as contrasted with training for supervisory leadership); and that it deprives principals of the opportunity to enjoy a much higher level of professional job satisfaction. We believe that a principal on his or her way home after a successful day in maintenance work (for example, completing the book inventory, solving a bus route problem, providing new projector bulbs, disciplining three students, responding to 10 phone calls from parents, monitoring the lunchroom for an hour, and ordering monthly supplies) does not have as much to feel good about as a principal whose day has included helping a team leader with a team planning problem, conducting an observation cycle on a counseling session, reviewing monthly performance reports from the primary team, meeting with a doctoral student who is doing a study in the school on children's artistic preferences, and visiting four other classrooms to see how the new calculators are being used.

We recognize that bus, lunchroom, discipline, purchasing, and similar problems cannot be neglected; but we are convinced that (1) some of these functions can be delegated to other persons such as a secretary; (2) some, such as disciplining children, are better handled through intelligent classroom management practices at the teacher level; (3) some, such as responding to phone calls, can be largely avoided or at least reduced through improved office management; and (4) some, such as becoming involved with supplies distribution, should never happen to the principal in a well-organized school.

A Paradigm Shift in School Organization and Management

School organizations today seem to be characterized by a growing turbulence and by continuous eruption and disruption. They may be responding to expectations that are well beyond the scope of one social institution (for example, providing breakfast and lunch programs; offering health care; serving as a transportation agency; attempting to offset conditions of poverty and neglect). We have reached the point where schools no longer can continue to accept such an array of social functions without redefining the very purpose and nature of schooling itself. The survival of schools as legitimate social institutions may well depend on the ability of school leaders to reconceptualize, to clarify, and to redefine the purposes and processes of schooling while at the same time adopting organization and management systems that are more likely to foster maximum effectiveness in staff performance.

The task of reconceptualizing the school and its educational service function may best be understood by discussing schooling in paradigmatic terms. Thomas Kuhn's work on *The Structure of Scientific Revolutions* (1970) laid a foundation for understanding the function of a paradigm, and the nature of growth and development. Kuhn suggests that people have always tended to function within a total constellation of values and beliefs about a particular reality. The paradigm within which a group of people lives and behaves (for example, an agrarian society; life on a spaceship) actually governs the behaviors of that group (Kuhn 1970, 23).

Some changes that occur within a paradigm may be mere adjustments or alterations that do not affect the basic governing assumptions (for example, a manual typewriter being replaced by an electric one). A paradigm continues to function for people until sufficient problems emerge that cannot be resolved in the existing paradigm (the necessity for 1,000 first copies of the same letter). Eventually, a crisis, or a series of crises, begins to announce the inadequacy of the present paradigm. Kuhn calls such structural problems "anomalies" (ibid., 52–65). As people begin to search for viable solutions to anomalies, new forms or potential solutions emerge (in this example, memory typewriters). Potential solutions are then tested until an adequate new paradigm unfolds (the word processor). The decision to reject one paradigm (the typewriter) is simultaneous with the decision to accept another (the word processor). Judgments leading to a decision involve strict comparisons of both the old and the new paradigms with existing conditions. A new paradigm, while it is relatively incomplete, is perceived better to resolve acute problems than the old, and consequently human energy shifts from preserving the old paradigm to developing the new paradigm.

Shifting to the education context, it would appear that the major thrusts in reform movements in the past few decades have been to resolve problems (anomalies) within the traditional paradigm of schooling. While our survival instincts naturally tend to protect us from such foolishness or destruction as deschooling society, it may be that the serious lack of engagement by the entire education community, in resolving fundamental schooling problems, is likely to bring on the death of the current public schooling paradigm. To illustrate, Glen Heathers (1972), in his analysis of the 1960s innovations, found that the innovations themselves were developed in response to existing anomalies, and were not the causes of innovation failures. Rather, failure occurred because of the inadequacy of plans for implementing the innovations. Heathers found weak linkages between the aims (individualizing instruction) and the means (packaged learning kits) of the innovations, and also inadequate linkages between means (kits) and accomplishments (increased learning). A more effective combination of factors (goals, means, organizational shifts, in-service and different patterns of supervision and administration) may have yielded quite different results from reform efforts, he surmises, during those creative years.

John Goodlad (1984, 1) concluded from his study of schooling (38 schools; 1,000 classrooms) that

> American schools are in trouble. In fact, the problems of schooling are of such crippling proportions that many schools may not survive. It is possible that our entire public education system is nearing collapse.

He notes further that upgrading schools will best be done school by school, with the principal creating the setting (ibid., 129). Schools must be largely self-directed; this capacity is lacking in most schools largely because principals lack the requisite skills of group leadership (ibid., 276–77).

As principals and teachers continuously experience a bombardment of expectations such as breakfast, IEP's for every child, and programs for the gifted, retarded, handicapped, bilingual, and multicultural, the traditional model of schools (fixed time schedules, fixed student groupings, curriculum, and materials, along with self-contained teaching and managing) will become increasingly incapable of responding effectively to the learning needs of students. The new schooling paradigm requires that a school staff work collaboratively to alter practices to the extent that they become increasingly responsive.

Schools must develop fundamentally different kinds of capacities for meeting the needs of society. What is at stake, however, is the nature of those capacities. A new schooling paradigm can foster either people-determined or technologically determined practices. Technologies of the future have the potential for further estranging workers from finding and nurturing meaningful relationships in the workplace and from entering into meaningful work responsibilities. The choice is ours. We can either permit technologies to shape the processes and outcomes of our schools, a mechanistic/relationalistic paradigm (neo-scientific view), or we can invent human collaborative processes for defining our collective growth priorities school by school, a production paradigm (systems view). Each type of new schooling paradigm is potentially powerful within our society today.

Kuhn provides an important insight into the dilemma of paradigm choice. The transition between competing paradigms cannot be made a step at a time; it must occur all at once or not at all (ibid., 151). Neither proof nor error is at issue. The transfer from one paradigm to another is a conversion experience that cannot be forced. Resistance is inevitable and legitimate (ibid., 152). It is important not to focus on convincing arguments, but rather on a community that sooner or later reforms as a group (ibid., 153). Decisions must be based less on past achievement than on future promise. A community will do all that it can to ensure the continuing growth of assembled data that it can treat with precision (ibid., 170). In the process, losses will be realized and old problems will be banished. The nature of such problem-solving communities provides a guarantee that the problems solved and the precision of problem solvers will mature (ibid., 171). Herein lies the hope for each school community to give shape to a new schooling paradigm.

Spady and Mitchell (1977, 18) provide another perspective in their analysis of power and authority in schools. They stress that "intrinsic," "voluntary," "involving," and "reorienting" mechanisms are the keys to transforming involuntary formal school memberships into committed engagements in the major tasks of the school. Similarly, Boulding, in her challenge to imagine the future, speculates that neither "brainstorming" nor projection of trends will break us out of our technological trap. It is within learning communities that our capacity for transcendence will be reborn (in Bennis et al. 1976, 443). Moreover, in the process of reaching toward the future, Lefton (in Bennis et al. 1976, 458), underscores the need to connect with the past (the old paradigm). He warns that as we transform schooling practices we must connect with our past (the history of each school community) and build upon its uniqueness. Only then are we likely to move beyond mere survival and create more effective outcomes of schooling. The process of reaching toward the future, he notes, is psychological and historical and at the same time aesthetic.

While this book seeks to develop a framework for productive collaboration in schools, the underlying assumption is that schools can transform themselves adequately if they have appropriate knowledge and skills, which are supported by an unwavering belief and commitment to becoming successful together.

The challenge is not for schools alone. In order to meet the current demands of schooling (full student mastery) we must focus on the schooling anomalies as a total education community until new and more viable forms of management, organization, and instruction emerge. We must all participate—scholars, practitioners, publishers, and technologists. Together we can invent, critique, and revise schooling and training practices until a new paradigm unfolds. We must form meaningful partnerships, within schools and across educational institutions and share concerns and goals. Together we can reverse the patterns of lethargy, noncommitment, burn-out and noninvolvement, and provide a synergistic framework of schooling success.

Co-involvement: A Foundation for the New Paradigm

Japanese industrialists have demonstrated that worker involvement in goal setting, work process refinement, and assessment is central to their production achievements (Ouchi 1980). If we assume that co-involvement is essential to organizational growth, then what is the nature of that involvement? Mink (1979, 13) suggests that the process of self-organization in open systems generates an *energy exchange system*. Internal organizational responsiveness, he observes, is maintained through collaboration rather than through imposition by authority, with a work focus on goals, planning, and acting. Creativity, responsibility, and growth are natural outcomes of staff responsiveness to changing conditions as groups focus their energy on goals.

More specifically, co-involvement emphasizes developing staff potential (an ecological process) and results from continuous reexamination of progress. Worker resocialization to a "change" ideology occurs as groups develop the capacity and the willingness to engage continuously in openness of communication, to face problems, and to become involved in solutions, to furnish data, to facilitate inquiries, and to submit ambivalencies and moot points to an empirical test (Bennis 1976, 323). Dialogue allows workers to perceive new possibilities as they entertain movement beyond the present notions of schooling reality. As a result of dialogue, discrepancies between beliefs about schooling are likely to decrease and give rise to a more congruent relationship between new perceptions and actions.

A *paradigm change* then, is not an accumulation process as would be reflected in updating curriculum guides, in terms of what is taught. Rather, a paradigm change is a reconstruction of fundamental assumptions about how curriculum would facilitate fundamentally new definitions (for example, a curriculum reflects what students will master). Moreover, success for schools within the new paradigm results largely from a "promise" of success, rather than from a history of successful practices. The new paradigm will emerge from numerous incomplete and often isolated examples of success, evolving over time.

To abandon the maintenance school paradigm would require, for example, that all educators cease practicing self-containment. Further, it would mean developing and refining flexible work patterns. Hence, schools must cut loose from those traditional practices that either prevent a forward movement or no longer serve our purposes. Attention needs to be given to continuing effective practices and also to developing a capacity for inventing more effective patterns.

The Function of Climate

One of the most useful concepts that emerged out of the human relations era was that of the organizational climate. Flanders (student-teacher interaction), Withall (classroom social–emotional climate), Bales (group interaction), Skinner (behavior modification), Rogers (nondirective teaching), Glasser (classroom meeting), Schmuck and Schmuck (group processes in the classroom), and Brown (confluent education) are a few examples of scholars who in the past several decades have influenced the quality of classroom life and enabled us to describe and measure it. Their contributions have enabled teachers to become more sensitive to the consequences of various teaching behaviors on the learning climate.

The characteristics of school climate are somewhat more blurred, however. Questions have been raised about there being any factor or set of factors that influence the school as a whole. Sarason (1972) concluded, from his sociological study of school organizations, that each school has its own culture, which is predominantly survival oriented rather than goal oriented. Goodlad (1975) contends that school culture was not considered sufficiently in early change efforts. His studies on educational change led him to conclude that the school is the viable unit of change in education. Berman and McLaughlin (1978) confirmed Goodlad's assertion that schools continue to have a strong resistance to change. They observed that principals and their staffs can subvert district change efforts or can successfully develop their own innovations without knowledge or support from the district.

Since a comprehensive model for school change has not yet emerged but only indicators of success, we must look to the field of contemporary organization and management to identify promising practices. This book presents a beginning model that is conceptually, organizationally, and educationally viable, and one in which school climate, staff relationships, collaborative efforts, staff development, teaching practices, and student mastery can be influenced simultaneously.

A systems approach to school organization provides a launching pad for developing ecologically effective educational practices. Organizations, from a systems perspective, are viewed as goal-seeking systems. All technologies, roles, organization, resources, and management practices can be integrally planned to assist the organization in attaining its priority goals.

Conclusion

The principalship is undergoing a radical transformation, emphasizing behaviors that influence instructional practice and school development. However, practices within school districts and within university training programs still largely reflect a school maintenance job orientation. Extensive job retraining of principals is critical for building successful cadres of principals to meet emerging school needs. The transition from a maintenance paradigm to a production schooling paradigm requires that the entire education community become engaged in cooperative research, training, practice, and dialogue about effective school management.

A systems approach to school management and organization provides a conceptual framework for developing the new paradigm. Schooling practices will become increasingly integrated as they focus on specific goals and working collaboratively. Together, the principal and staff can develop a capacity for continuous self-renewal and for achieving productive schooling outcomes.

Appendix A

Florida Principal Competencies: Basic and High Performing

Cluster	Competency	Behavioral Indicators
Purpose and Direction	HP 1. *Proactive Orientation*—Takes the role of being fully "in charge" and responsible for all that happens in a situation or a job. An "internal control" orientation in which persons behave with the full assumption that they can be the "cause" and can move events, create change, and achieve goals. Initiates action and readily takes responsibility for all aspects of the situation—even beyond ordinary boundaries—and for success and failure in task accomplishment. Initiates actions of self and others to learn about the organization and to achieve goals.	1.1 Takes overall responsibility for progress of a group or a task or for obtaining and using resources. 1.2 Initiates actions, proposals, or plans for self and others to accomplish tasks. 1.3 Accepts and portrays personal responsibility for failures/barriers and learns from experiences to overcome potential or real barriers. 1.4 Accepts ultimate responsibility for staff, students, and teachers.
	HP 2. *Decisiveness*—Expresses forcefulness and confidence when a decision is made. A readiness to make decisions, render judgments, take actions, and commit oneself and others regardless of the quality of the decision.	2.1 Expresses little ambivalence about decisions that have been made (but may recognize alternatives). 2.2 Forceful and self-confident in making decisions.
	B 3. *Commitment to School Mission*—Holds a set of values about the school, e.g., welfare of the students, fairness to staff: behavior is consistant with values despite barriers.	3.1 Promotes the welfare of the students. 3.2 Displays a humane concern for the feelings of teachers, parents, and students. 3.3 Takes difficult actions, which may be unpopular, when the welfare of students seems to be at stake. 3.4 Emphasizes the importance of fairness in providing opportunities, distributing priorities, administering discipline, and distributing funds.
Cognitive Skills	HP 4. *Interpersonal Search*—Is able to discover, understand, and verbalize the concepts, thoughts, and ideas held by others. Is not only sensitive to the ideas and opinions of others but behaves to ensure an understanding of the feelings and verbalizations of others.	4.1 Uses probing, repetition to have others describe their own perspectives, ideas, and feelings. 4.2 Is able to discover and understand the ideas and concepts of others—from their point of view. 4.3 Uses summary clarification and paraphrasing to test the accuracy of one's conception of another's perspective, e.g., of a teacher, a student.

(continued)

Cluster		Competency	Behavioral Indicators
	HP	5. *Information Search*—Searches for and gathers many different kinds of information before arriving at an understanding of an event or a problem. Uses formal and informal observation, search and interaction to gather information about the environment. The breadth (number of sources) and depth (what is learned from each relevant source) of information search.	5.1 Gathers information about problems from a variety of sources or events before making a decision or commiting resources. 5.2 Breadth (of the number of different sources) of information search. 5.3 Gathers sufficient information in each essential area searched (both inside and outside the organization) in order to arrive at relevant ideas or concepts. Strives to be well informed.
	HP	6. *Concept Formation*—The ability to form concepts, hypotheses, ideas on the basis of information. Can reorder information into ideas, see relationships between patterns of information from different sources, and can link information separate spacially or over time. A logical process of forming ideas based on information from different sources.	6.1 Develops a concept in order to make sense out of an array of information separated in space or time. 6.2 Finds meaning themes or patterns in a sequence of events or inputs. 6.3 After examining an issue or a problem, insight emerges which is usually labeled and used for diagnostic purposes and for stating cause-and-effect relationships. 6.4 Perceives relationship between important events or links related events into broader meanings (e.g., in In-Basket).
	HP	7. *Conceptual Flexibility*—The ability to use alternative or multiple concepts or perspectives when discussing problem solving or making a decision. Can view a person or an event from different perspectives; can devise alternative plans or courses of action and can visualize the pros and cons of each. Considers information from different points of view in arriving at a decision. The ability to view an event from multiple perspectives simultaneously.	7.1 Views events from different (multiple) perspectives simultaneously. 7.2 In group situations keeps different group members perspectives "on the table" for discussion. 7.3 Conflicting or different views of events are discovered and used in problem solving and dialogue. 7.4 Perspective of subordinates, managers in the person's own unit (e.g., department, school) and significant "others" outside the person's unit and organization are taken into account in planning and problem solving. 7.5 Forms and uses multiple concepts in problem solving and interpersonal and group interaction
Consensus Management	HP	8. *Managing Interaction*—The ability to get others to interact, to stimulate others to work together, to understand each other, to resolve conflict or agree to	8.1 Stimulates others to interact in a group situation. Is able to get another to present and stimulate others to respond.

(continued)

Cluster	Competency	Behavioral Indicators
	its presence, to encourage others to reach mutual agreement. Uses own and others' ideas to initiate and stimulate dialogue between others. To demonstrate good group process and facilitator skills.	8.2 Is able to get others to state their perspectives and then discuss relationships and can motivate the group to move toward mutual agreement. 8.3 Is able to get people from different groups or conflicting groups to engage in dialogue. 8.4 An integrating facilitating role in interpersonal and group situations.
HP	9. *Persuasiveness*—The ability to persuade or influence others through a number of possible means: gaining and sustaining their attention and interest in a group situation; using information or arguments, modeling the behaviors expected; or being direct in specifying what others will do.	9.1 Demonstrates ability to influence or persuade others to support one's ideas or goals. 9.2 May use a variety of techniques; e.g., modeling expected behavior, using information, and expertise or authority, by being directive. Whichever technique is used the operation here is "success in influencing."
B	10. *Concern for Image*—Shows concern for the image of the school via the impressions created by the students and staff and manages these impressions and public information about the school.	10.1 Advertises successes. 10.2 Controls the flow of negative information.
B	11. *Tactical Adaptability*—States the rationale for using particular strategies; e.g., to influence certain groups, tailors style of interaction to fit the situation and changes style if it does not succeed.	11.1 Indicates that an activity will be challenging. 11.2 Tailors one's style of interaction to the audience one wishes to influence. 11.3 Adjusts strategy or adopts a different strategy when one is unsuccessful.
Quality Enhance- ment HP	12. *Achievement Motivation*—States high internal work standards. Verbalizes personal and group goals as a desire to do something better—better feedback or measures of how well self or group is doing; shows frustration in meeting barriers or in response to own or others' mistakes or failures.	12.1 Expresses a desire to do the task better, better than it was done previously, better than others do it, or better according to some objective or subjective standard. 12.2 Makes expectations of high performance, excellence, or high productivity known to others. 12.3 Expresses frustration with barriers to reaching standards of excellence. 12.4 Wants measures of own productivity and performance in order to plot or assess progress.
HP	13. *Management Control*—Devises opportunities to receive adequate and timely feedback about the progress of	13.1 Plans and schedules follow-up for all delegated and assigned activities.

(continued)

Cluster		**Competency**	**Behavioral Indicators**

work accomplishments of others. Follow-up on delegated activities or providing plans for or taking action on feedback of information to others about meeting standards of productivity.

13.2 Monitors the performance of managers and subordinates and schedules reviews.

13.3 Plans and initiates activities which help in observing the work and progress of others—both of individuals and department or grade level.

13.4 Informs others when their work is not meeting standards.

B   14. *Developmental Orientation*—Holds high and positive expectations about others' potential, views developing others as a property of the principal's job.

14.1 Holds high expectations about the potential of other people to develop.

14.2 Works to help others do their job better and uses follow-up in order to develop others.

14.3 Gives support, approval, or recognition for developmental activities of others.

14.4 Instills a value of "developing others" in own staff members.

Organization   **HP**   15. *Organizational Ability*—Sets plans and promotes to accomplish goals. Schedules activities and the use of human and other resources for accomplishing goals. Focuses on time, deadlines, flow of activities or resources on ways to get the job done.

15.1 Makes schedules, budgets own time; shows a concern for time and schedule in exercises and in the simulated role.

15.2 Reviews a task and then plans; e.g., reviews all items on desk or in In-Basket and then proceeds with a plan and schedule. Uses this style in work or simulation situations.

15.3 Establishes priorities, handling important issues first, allocating more time to high-priority issues.

15.4 Organizes the activities of a group in order to develop a logical plan—what will be done first, second, and so forth, meetings and points of communication.

B   16. *Delegation*—Delegates authority and responsibility clearly and appropriately in accomplishing organizational goals. This must be differentiated from organization, that is from the normal assignment of tasks which people routinely do. It is the delegation of a project not currently a routine part of the person's job; e.g., gathering information, developing a proposal or a plan, implementing a project.

16.1 Clearly delegates an activity which is not a routine task. Delegation should specify the authority; e.g., "complete the task and then let us discuss your decision." "Do the initial phase and then check with me before you make a decision."

16.2 Delegates defined activities; e.g., information gathering, planning, implementing.

(continued)

Cluster		Competency		Behavioral Indicators
Communica-tion	HP	17. *Self Presentation*—The ability to clearly present one's own ideas, others' ideas, and information in an open and genuine way. Is able to share ideas with others in an open informative, non-evaluative manner. Effectively uses technical, symbolic, non-verbal visual aids or graphics in order to get the message across.	17.1	Is able to communicate own ideas to others in one-on-one or group situations in a clear, informative manner. The criteria is not persuasion but the degree to which the presentation was understood.
			17.2	Can stimulate others to ask questions about own issues.
			17.3	Is able to present in a way which is not interpreted as "demanding conformity" or control.
	B	18. *Written Communication*—Clear, concise and properly structured written communication.	18.1	Meaning clearly expressed in memos and letters.
			18.2	Adequate vocabulary.
			18.3	Correct spelling and punctuation.
			18.4	Sentence and paragraph construction appropriate and correct.
	B	19. *Organizational Sensitivity*—The awareness of the effects of one's behavior and decisions on other people and other groups in and outside the organization.	19.1	Tactful written and oral responses to others in and out of the organization.
			19.2	Keeps persons in the organization informed when information received is relevant or could be relevant to them.
			19.3	Considers the position, feelings, and perspectives of others when planning, making decisions, and organizing.

HP—High Performing
B—Basic

Source: Florida Council on Educational Management, Tallahassee.

2

The School As an Organization: Toward an Ecology

The Social Context of Schools

The 1983 report of the National Commission on Excellence noted serious weaknesses and deficiencies in American schools, and offered various proposals for reversing the alleged decline in the quality of schooling. Among the remedies offered up by this and other major reports on schooling in the early part of this decade were an extension of the school year, lengthening of the school day, increasing homework requirements, paring down curriculum electives, providing merit pay for teachers, evaluating teacher performance more rigorously, offering tuition tax credits, and permitting prayers in the schools. While some of the proposed solutions deserve implementation, others are naive and even absurd. In our view, the significant improvement of American education can come about only if three changes are made: (1) radical revision, in the direction of lengthier and more extensive preparation, of statutes and standards governing the education and certification of teachers and administrators; (2) substantial increase in the resources made available by taxpayers and also by other agencies to the enterprise of public schooling; and (3) a major shift, along the lines proposed in this book, in the ways that schools are organized and managed.

The central issue for school officials is to invigorate the organizational work context for teachers and students, where productivity is expected, nurtured, and reinforced. Moreover, the ways in which people work together toward specific goals will determine the kinds of teaching and learning that a school produces. Our claim, in brief, is that the work context of schools can and must be altered for teachers and students before new achievement norms can be realized. The work environment, which includes role expectations, organizational climate, role relationships, staff development, and supervision, influences how people work and the results from their work. The present outdated organizational structures of schools can and must be altered radically. Stimulating staff productivity is today's school management challenge.

Lessons from Industry

In sharp contrast to the recent proposals for improving schools, the work context itself receives the primary focus in successful Japanese companies and excelling American companies. Management ensures that employees understand and accept corporation goals, job parameters, and role development expectations. In addition, management provides a work environment for employees that fosters and reinforces group productivity, risk taking, creative ideas, and high levels of performance and productivity. In so doing Japanese management has gone well beyond "participation patterns" found in productive companies in earlier decades. "Delegation" of tasks for group decision making appears to be the work norm to be studied.

The Japanese industrialists, and a growing number of American businesses, attribute their corporate success to basic work-group patterns and to group decision making. Adopting a cooperative work ethic, employees are assigned to work groups where they share in the production of their task assignment. During their work, the group regularly critiques work patterns, resolves work problems, and makes recommendations for ways in which technology ought to be refined. Workers are skilled for a task individually, but they strive collectively to study their work pattern and to improve its design and results.

Peters and Waterman (1982) found similar work patterns in the most successful Fortune 500 companies in America. They observed, again, that the basic organizational work pattern is the group. Ten-person work groups form for a specific task. When the task is completed, the group dissolves (1982, 113). Groupings of employees tend to be brief, evolving in response to the growing needs, problems, and new product development of the company. Workers volunteer for assignments and talk out problems and possibilities in efforts to complete tasks. In brief, the excellent companies have developed a capacity to evolve and to learn from their experiences continuously, and to grow and adapt to changing conditions. The evolving task groups are the basic building block of excellent companies (1982, 126).

Naisbitt (1983, 200) in his analysis of current trends in American society, reports that there is an observable shift from representative work patterns to participatory decision making. There is a growing disdain for old-fashioned hierarchical structures in favor of a networking approach to work, in the form of (more lateral) quality circles, workers' rights groups, and participatory management. Naisbitt notes that decentralization is the great facilitator of social change; furthermore, the new kind of leader is a facilitator rather than an order giver (1983, 129). Networking practices foster self-help among workers, information exchange, improved productivity, and shared resources. In addition, networking provides a form of communication and interaction that is suitable for an energy-scarce, information-rich future.

Research on effective schools has generated findings that support the trends of participatory management (social trends), continuously evolving work groups (in excellent companies), and shared responsibility (in Japanese industry). Research on successful schools reveals that collaboratively defined school goals, cooperative work patterns, and shared decision making are the work norms. Moreover, no study that we reviewed mentioned any effective characteristics of management or organization other than "cooperative." (See Chapter 3 for details on effective schooling research.)

The lone wolf principal and the isolated teacher are like dinosaurs from another age. Production sharing is the only form of work activity that organizations throughout the world find successful today. We need to rid our schools of isolated work patterns and, instead, inspire in teachers a sense of shared purpose and shared success in redefining schooling outcomes and work patterns.

A problem for educators in the next several decades will be to define what is and what is not the business of schools. In recent years schools have become the dumping ground for all varieties of societal functions. If schools are to succeed in the student achievement business, then a staff will need to be given more latitude in determining how that will occur. The "extras" during the school year absorb considerable staff energy and divert attention away from the central issue of schooling. Schools need to attend to their central mission if they are to survive.

A schooling agenda that focuses on student-achievement-for-all is the purpose for which this volume is written. To that end, we have defined parameters for how the principal manages, how teachers instruct, and how students learn. Our basic assumption is that 95 percent of existing schools can develop the capacity to become viable and productive social institutions that foster optimal growth. This assumption can become operationalized if the conditions are right; that is, if (1) school goals are defined, (2) school needs are assessed (cognitive and affective), and (3) appropriate leadership and programs are developed and implemented. We further assume that

1. dynamic leadership and a strong commitment to develop the optimal school are essential;
2. all members of the school community can develop and share a common vision and set of beliefs about what is optimal;
3. given a direction, the entire school community can participate in defining annual improvement priorities and action plans;
4. the staff can be provided with an appropriate growth environment, including
   a. organizational groupings that foster continuous involvement and interaction
   b. multiple growth opportunities
   c. coaching, feedback, criticism, and support for performance;
5. student programs will reflect the beliefs and priorities of the staff, and foster mastery of expected competencies for all students.

The purpose of the first part of this chapter is to explore the social context of schools and to address the essential variables in a productive school organization. In the second section, a model will be presented for conceptualizing the essential variables in a school (subsystems), and to define the general functions for each subsystem and the nature of its interdependence with the other subsystems. Following this chapter, which presents an ecological approach to schooling, each subsystem will be further developed in the form of concepts and methodology.

A Paradigm Shift for Schools

The survival of schools as legitimate social institutions may well depend on the ability of school leaders to reconceptualize and redefine the purposes and processes of schooling. We have reached the point in education where we can no longer impose new sets of requirements or services on schools without having to redefine the very nature of schooling itself. Attention to school effects began perhaps with Goodlad's earlier analysis (1975) of the school organization culture as the focus for change. We now realize more clearly that a reconceptualization of the school must take into account the interactive effects of school leadership, school organization, management and instruction, and the school's unique history. Moreover, school improvement must be viewed holistically if we are to alter work patterns and learning norms. All school functions must work in a given direction of organizational growth to influence specific developments.

Reconceptualizing schooling may best be understood by discussing it in paradigmatic terms (discussed initially in Chapter 1). A paradigm is an accepted model of how things function best, not in the sense that the paradigm is complete and replicating, but rather that it is an object for further articulation and specification. Changes *within* a paradigm are adjustments and alterations that do not affect the basic paradigm assumptions. An emerging paradigm is relatively incomplete, but is able to gain acceptance because it is better able to resolve acute problems than other paradigms. Success in an emerging paradigm is due largely to the *promise* of success that can be discovered in selected and incomplete examples (Kuhn 1970).

A paradigm change is not a cumulative process, but rather a reconstruction of fundamental assumptions and concomitant practices. The rules of the schooling game become altered to the extent that practitioners relate to each other in collaborative arrangements. What precipitates a paradigm change? A crisis, or series of crises, precipitates a series of attempts to resolve certain existing and emerging problems (anomalies). Cracks (or anomalies) in the current paradigm must be resolved by the new paradigm if it is to survive as a viable alternative.

The systems model for a productive school, which is defined and developed in this book, provides an attempt to give definition to the emerging schooling paradigm. However, an emerging paradigm is incomplete. We urge that a holistic approach to resolving the problems (anomalies) with the old schooling paradigm be given careful consideration by educational practitioners, scientists, and theorists, both separately and collectively. A new schooling paradigm is evolving, to be certain. Our purpose is to provide specific parameters to guide in its development.

Both administrators and teachers are experiencing a transition from the old ways of schooling to a more effective set of practices. There is a growing sense that schools need to become increasingly productive. Let us consider a few characteristics of the old paradigm. Within it, conditions in the schools have been considered relatively certain and predictable. "Education" for a student has been thought to result from a fixed number of days, years, and courses spent and acquired in school. Teaching, learning, and administering have best been accomplished when all roles functioned efficiently alone in predetermined patterns.

Sensing that the constraints of fixed conditions, programs, and role responsibilities and relationships no longer serve their function well, many teachers and principals are devising more flexible approaches to schooling. Within the new production paradigm, all conditions, programs, and role relationships will be considerably more flexible as school staffs respond to an increasingly complex clientele and public. "Education" will result from individual mastery of concepts, attitudes, and skills, rather than from fixed programs and amounts of time. Further, work with and among all roles will be largely collaborative.

Let us consider the apparent paradigm shift from another perspective. In the last century, schools were expected to sort out and to process learners for various layers in the work force. Consequently not all students were expected to respond successfully to all that schools provided. It was presumed that blue-collar workers, for example, required different kinds of knowledge than white-collar workers. Only in recent years has the public begun to require the same kinds of academic success for all students. Consequently, schools are now expected to ensure that most students achieve at higher levels of proficiency. School professionals who were prepared for the maintenance role of sorting and programming students now are seeking ways to enable all students to become winners. A new kind of schooling age is inevitable, and the foundations of one paradigm (sorting students) are beginning to give way to the new (mastery for all).

Further, in the old paradigm, teachers focused primarily on the content of what was to be learned. It was assumed that somehow students would learn the content. In the new paradigm, teachers will center their attention on the learning process itself and on the challenge of how to cause certain learning (content) to occur. For principals there is an equally fundamental shift in job focus. In the past, attention has been given primarily to the smooth operations of student and staff assignments, of numerous instructional and social programs, and of school building services. In the future, staff development will become a daily focus as teachers become skilled in new instructional methodologies and technologies and in collaboration on instructional tasks. Further, the principal, rather than the superintendent, supervisor, or consultant, will become the leader and shaper of school development activities, using the resources of outside professionals as needed.

Consequently, this book is about the work life of principals as they grow with and into the new paradigm of schooling. This book should be viewed as a guide for restructuring the work environment in schools so as to influence the direction of school growth and also the results of teacher and student performance. Our purpose is to enable principals to become effective instructional leaders and managers of productive staff performance. The Dutch educator Elizabeth Rotten spoke to the central issue when she said:

> Our work, which starts out from the child, but which really means work on ourselves, on the adult world around us, has, so it seems to me, barely begun. It deserves all our effort, our undivided devotion, and all our genuine wisdom.

(This relevant analysis was delivered in 1927 in a personal message to friends, one of whom shared it with us recently.) It behooves principals, therefore, to borrow from their experiences, values, knowledge, and visions of the optimal school, and to seek ways to improve the quality of work life in school.

Another clue to a crack in the old paradigm relates to outdated organizational patterns. The days of viewing schools as static, unchanging organizations are past. All forms of social life are increasingly complex. Social and business institutions reflect complexity and ambiguity as they seek to grow and to prosper. It is normal, rather than exceptional, for school organizations, like other organizations in our society, to have many of the following characteristics:

A turbulent environment
A complex goal and evaluation orientation
Increasing diversity in values and life-styles
Increasing size and complexity
Mushrooming accumulation of knowledge
Multiple technologies for knowledge integration
Computerized information systems (Kast and Rosenzweig 1974, 617–618)

The survival needs of adapting to the society and achieving goals are especially problematic for schools. There is a compliance atmosphere among schools with regard to new legal regulations. There remains, however, a strong resistance to the spirit of fundamental change at the local school level. Furthermore, while many schools today have broad philosophical goals, seldom do goals function as guides for practice to any significant extent. Consequently, organizational growth strategies must be designed in such a way as to influence the school's inability both to be goal directed and to respond significantly to pressures. The old practices of bypassing the principal and focusing on changes in teaching practices will continue to fail in the new paradigm. The channel for altering instructional norms and levels of achievement is through the *principal* who redesigns and manages the work patterns of teachers.

If a school is to respond successfully to its students, who reflect a changing society, then most assuredly instruction and learning will necessarily need to be altered continuously. An active formal and informal dialogue process among staff members lies at the very center of a school's capacity to become a self-renewing school (Schmuck et al. 1977, 158). Continuing dialogue reflects group needs, values, wants, and preferences and pursues ways in which these can be addressed. Skillful group interaction draws out these articulations (needs, wants, preferences) and attempts to integrate them with overall school improvement directions. The creation of formal and informal groupings tends to draw out goal articulations and to match them with organizational goals.

Lessons from Successful Schools

In recent years numerous studies have been conducted on effective schools in search of the variables that relate directly and indirectly to student achievement. For example, the National School Public Relations Association (Tursman 1981) reviewed several reports and concluded that successful schools have strong administrative leadership, high expectations for students and teachers, a positive school climate, and community support. Similarly, sociologist Wynne (1980) examined 167 schools of all types and levels, in relation to student achievement, and concluded that good schools are such because principals and teachers like and respect their students, expect them to achieve, expect them to behave in an orderly way, and put education before all else. Bad schools, on the other hand, are chaotic, lack a sense of purpose, and lack authority over what teachers and students do.

Perhaps the most well-publicized study of effective schools in recent years has been Edmonds' project in the New York City schools (1979, 15–23). He identified five factors as probable determinants of academic success in certain elementary schools: (1) strong administrative leadership, (2) school climate conducive to learning, (3) classroom emphasis on basic skills and instruction, (4) optimistic teacher expectations of pupil ability, and (5) ongoing assessment of pupil progress.

A summary analysis of effective school variables points out that for those schools that have clear goals and action plans, there exist strong leadership and high expectations for goal attainment; instruction based on sound principles of learning; school communities committed to their task; and, the school staff that has a sense of control over their collective destiny.

Williams (1974) analyzed the characteristics of self-renewing schools in California and also noted that active staff involvement in dialogue, decision making, and action has the power to alter the effects of apathy and indifference, and to facilitate the renewal process. Dialogue, decision making, and action are the processes for stimulating productivity. The model presented in this book defines more clearly what successful principals do and how work is organized to influence teaching and learning.

Lessons from Open Organizations

Mink, Shultz, and Mink (1979) observe that organizations in general, not merely schools, are being challenged today because of their inability to respond flexibly and appropriately to the needs of employees, the environment, and students. To survive organizations need to be based on principles of adaptability, rather than predictability, so that they can respond adequately to shifts in a changing social environment. The open organization is one that is open to feedback, pressures, and needs, and consequently remains adaptable.

Mink et al. describe the open organization as an "energy exchange system," one that functions as an integrated whole that has unity and coherence. Unity of purpose, and internal and external responsiveness are central to organizational productivity and occur as a result of a clarified concensus of priorities. Collaboration, they observe, is the key to internal responsiveness. To remain open and healthy, workers must collaborate continuously in decision making and problem solving. Likewise, leaders must be able to focus energies on achieving goals while involving organizational members and external constituents in contributing to organizational efforts. Further, the organization must develop a capacity for data-based feedback and problem solving by using outside specialists and internal feedback mechanisms.

Toward Productivity

In the past, many educators have tended to reject a production view of the schooling process, believing that producing automobiles cannot be compared with student achievement. However, in recent years society has begun to hold schools accountable for student achievement results. Several court cases won by parents, whose children were graduated from high school as illiterates, have caused educators to take a fresh look at their responsibilities and to once again consider a production model: it may ultimately be the most humane approach to productive schooling.

In Japanese industry, where collaboration among management and workers is the norm and where production is among the highest in the world, "trust" accounts for the high level of employee commitment and loyalty, and, in turn, for the astounding levels of industrial productivity (Ouchi 1981). Internal work groups, referred to as clans, provide intimate associations in which workers become engaged in economic activity toward common goals. Understanding comes from an open expression of skepticism through a process of debate and analysis. Trust links workers together as they ask tough questions and work together on solutions. Trust, involvement, communication, and high expectations are central to work patterns in organizations that are managed similarly in the United States (which Ouchi refers to as "Type Z" organizations). By changing organizations, rather than individuals, social structures can integrate the worker more fully into the life of the organization. As a result, Type Z American business is organizing industrial clans to accomplish organizational purposes.

Literatures of "open" organizations and Type Z organizations both focus their attention on "purpose" and the ways of interacting to attain purpose. Formal organizational charts, outlining roles and responsibilities, are secondary to the dialogue and action processes perceived to be essential in productive

TABLE 2.1. The School Ecosystem

Characteristics	Maintenance Paradigm	Productivity Paradigm
Role group relationships	Hierarchical	Collaborative and cross role groups
Design	Based on function and assignment	Based on goals and function
Work patterns	Individual tasks: permanent	Group tasks: temporary and permanent
Design duration	Static, permanent. Based on function set pattern	Fluid, evolving. Based on organizational needs. Changing groups
Planning	Function/defines individual plans	Group action plans guide individual plans
Response patterns	Closed response patterns to external and internal pressures	Open and adaptive to external and internal pressures for growth

organizations. Systems theory likewise de-emphasizes organizational structure and focuses its attention on goals, functions, and processes necessary for self-renewal. Attention to the structure of the school will facilitate changes in teaching practices and in schooling outcomes.

One of the major tasks for schools is to address pressures adequately from external sources while tending to their own ecological needs. The external and internal pressures on a school must be balanced continuously in order to generate rapid growth. Likewise, learning from work experiences is a continuous task. Consequently, healthy school organizations will be in a constant state of flux, that is, in a fluid state seeking a balance between pressures, performance, and productivity.

Table 2.1 outlines differences between organizations that are closed to the environment and to change, and those that are open, adapting, and growing.

Given that in today's context many organizations are finding more success with fluid work arrangements, we turn to the concepts of systems theory for more direction.

A Systems Approach to School Organization

The systems literature, which has greatly matured since the early 1940s, stimulates a way of thinking about schools while we develop a new schooling paradigm. Schools can now be viewed as growing and maturing systems, in which all parts are related in an interdependent, interrelated fashion. The concept of an "open" system allows for schools to correct themselves through various adaptive devices that are developed to respond to feedback. In this way the school as a system remains in a continuous state of transformation (a necessary ingredient for growth in the natural biological world).

A review of the systems literature suggests that healthy organizations today

1. require strong, contingency-style leadership;
2. establish their own goal set;
3. organize into numerous temporary and permanent subdivisions;
4. develop staff performance standards;
5. provide team leadership;
6. develop collaborative patterns of problem solving and decision making;
7. require individual growth plans;
8. provide continuous staff supervision;
9. provide continuous growth opportunities;
10. design and implement a management control system for goal attainment;
11. evaluate all forms of organizational performance.

Systems concepts about organizations are descriptive of the ways in which functions, tasks, and roles all relate to each other. A life flow exists in healthy systems in which all forces are working toward a common goal and are constantly responding to feedback, needs, and aspirations. Perhaps it will be useful to the reader to explore concepts inherent in a healthy growing organization, referred to here as a system.

There are at least two words with which every American has become familiar in recent years, neither of which was in common use a decade ago. One of these, ayatollah, could not even be found (at least by us) in English dictionaries published before 1980. The other, ecology, belonged primarily to biology professors and their students. As humankind has suddenly and belatedly become concerned about the spoilage and depletion of the earth's limited resources, worry about our planetary ecosystem has dramatically increased and all of us are sharply aware of the relationship that exists between each segment and all of the others. Pollution of the atmosphere, whether blatant (as when factories arrogantly dump poisonous wastes into streams or the air) or unexamined (as when automobile owners prior to the 1970s cheerfully cruised around for recreation), has become a vexing world concern, and the habits of individuals and of nations are undergoing profound changes—with even more profound changes in the offing.

The word "ecology" therefore has a generally negative meaning in many conversations. However, bionomics is also a positive field of study, and the healthy balances found in nature can provide constructive models to guide humankind in its search for a safe, pleasant, productive existence. It is in this frame of reference that we choose to pursue the analogy of ecosystems in our search for safe, pleasant, and productive schools.

An Ecosystem Analogy: The Beehive

In administrator training programs that we conduct, we sometimes introduce the concept of school ecology by inviting the participants to "brainstorm" for several minutes about one of the ecosystems found in nature, such as an ant colony or a beehive. In one workshop recently, the leader wrote the word "beehive" on the top of a large easel pad and asked the group, "What are some of the qualities, characteristics, or features of a beehive that come to mind?" Within less than three minutes the pad was filled with the following words or phrases:

Bees
Climate
Workers
Environment
Pollen
Wax
Architectural design (of hive)
Division of labor
Sex chamber for reproduction
Cooperation
Self-contained
Threatened (by bears, by men)
Reacts to danger—stingers are weapons
Busy—lots of activity in motion—in and out
Peaceful
Different ranks (queen, workers, drones)
Scouts
Highly organized
Labor distribution—each does personal job
Differentiated
Common goal
Mutually supportive

Teamwork
Needs water
Hive self-made (can be)
Different parts: throne room, honey storage, comb nursery (eggs), cells
Skillful builders
Social
Communications (dance message)
Gets crowded—groups leave
Like a city
Weatherproof (strong)
Sanitary (clean)
Different task specializations
Interdependent
Honeymaking (goal-oriented)
Pollination
Functions smoothly
Needs outside food source (flowers)
Where queen goes hive goes
Workers attend the queen; gather pollen and process nectar, and defend hive
Everyone has a clear responsibility
Ratio of workers to drones

Population control (queen principle)

Weather hazards (hail)

Sweet taste

Social structure

Nonworkers booted out

All necessary functions are assigned

Cannot function without each other

Organized in chambers

Definite goals

Workshop participants quickly began to perceive the ways in which the bee-hive thrives. The next question was, "What facilitates the survival of beehives, a system which is millions of years old?" The following list emerged:

Hive Survival

Organization

Communication

Queen

Operator/worker

Climate

Flowers

Pesticides

Predators

Education of bees

Resistance to include number of bees

Roles and tasks defined

Dedicated

Goals and purposes—keep species alive; reproduce; find food for themselves; give us food

Cooperation—working together to produce

Structure—hierarchy, continuity

Social dance—an announcement of where certain flowers are

Reluctant to give up product unless treated kindly

Reproduction of bees

Wax

When the group was presented with the task of making a transference of bee ecosystem and survival concepts to a school, the following items surfaced:

School Productivity

Goals

Structure—roles and organization

Communications network

Knowledge about school organization and teaching

Discipline—consistent, self-disciplined control for teachers and students

Response to the internal and external environments

Student productivity

Learn how to adapt—how to say no

Roles of queen, drone, workers: analogy to school roles

After the group refined its list, the following ecological concepts emerged as those important to school survival:

Goal-oriented activity

Role expectations

Relationship to the larger environment
A communication process
Total worker participation
Interdependence
Survival behaviors: response to feedback

Perhaps not so amazing is that system theorists describe growing, healthy systems with similar concepts (note the similarity to those concepts just mentioned that describe a beehive ecosystem):

Systems Concepts

Interrelated	Has a spirit—a life flow
Intersupportive	Dynamic as opposed to static
Balanced	Evolving
Dependent	Turbulent
Interdependent	Structured
Self-contained	Changing
Responsive	Parts tuned into the whole
Purposeful—has a direction	Parts working toward end of the whole
Goal oriented	
Identifiable parts	Sustaining

Central to the ecology of an organization is its unrelenting attention to purpose. With a purpose constantly in view, people are organized in various groups to accomplish numerous tasks. Work is intensive, interactive, and interrelated as each group attends to a portion of the tasks that relate directly to the central purpose. The organization modifies its patterns continuously as it responds to feedback and pressures and constantly seeks a steady state between chaos and lethargy. Growth is the dynamic that enables the organization to remain continuously vital and relevant to its constituents. Shared participation in the dynamics of an organization's growth provides the energy exchange system for remaining vital.

Systems Concepts Defined

In this section are found selected systems concepts which we perceive are ever present in the school's development process. Full understanding of these concepts will enable a principal to facilitate appropriate forces as the school develops.

A dynamically growing, evolving organization functions in ways that are fundamentally different from the kind of system that strives to maintain practices as they have always been, and to prevent pressures from influencing alterations. Therefore, it is important that the reader understand the concepts that are basic to school growth and that form the foundation of an ecological approach to schooling.

Closed systems are those that perceive they are self-contained and deterministic. Traditional management theories assumed a closed-system view of organizations by concentrating largely upon internal operations and functioning independent of their environment. Closed systems are becoming increasingly dysfunctional.

An *open system* is in a dynamic relationship with its environment, receiving various inputs and transforming the inputs to produce certain products. The open system is in continual interaction with its environment and achieves a "steady state" of dynamic equilibrium (its energy) while it retains the capacity for work or energy transformation (Kast and Rosenzweig 1974, 109).

The systems approach to organization and management, which emphasizes *adaptive mechanisms,* calls for the system to develop a wide variety of technology (rather than a limited amount) and thereby avoid organizational failure. When an organization is capable of more differentiation in its responses, and as it becomes more elaborate and more highly organized, its versatility increases and it has much better prospects of finding at least one way for dealing with each of the unique problems it confronts. Having available a great variety of alternative approaches is, in fact, an almost indispensable element in an organization's survival today.

One of the terms associated with systems theory is *boundary management.* The underlying concept is that each system, such as a school, is separated from the suprasystem (such as the total school district or the municipality it occupies) by boundaries that must be maintained or managed in ways that protect the interests of the system (school). The phrase "protecting one's turf" is better known than the term boundary management, but we prefer the latter because it suggests a greater openness and a greater willingness and ability to permit and encourage the two-way exchange of ideas, services, materials, and persons between the system and other components of the environment. We perceive that the ways school leadership people manage boundaries, both boundary problems and boundary opportunities, have a strong impact upon the quality of life and productivity within the boundaries.

Interface is the point of contact between one system or subsystem and another involving many transactional processes for transfer of energy, materials, people, money, and information (Kast and Rosenzweig 1974, 114). Schools interact with each other in an exchange of services, with other agencies in exchange of resources, and with a central office in exchange of expectations. The point of transaction, called interface, can be potentially negative, neutral, or productive, depending on a school's capacity to grow and to maintain its vitality. Managing boundaries and interface with other systems are vital for healthy organizational development.

Feedback mechanisms provide the system with a means of balance in its growth process. Both positive and negative feedback enable the system to keep on its course by adjusting to environmental conditions (ibid., 117). Feedback is central to growth and productivity.

Equifinality is a concept that suggests that the final results of transformation may be achieved under different conditions and in different ways. The closed system, which operates on cause-effect relationships, operates on the assumption that there is one best way. The open system goes beyond cause-effect simplicity, and achieves its purpose in numerous ways under varying conditions (ibid., 118–119). Diversity and multiplicity are the norms in a growing, dynamic organization.

Some writers in the field of systems theory refer to the concept of "steady state" or *dynamic equilibrium* as a desirable condition. What it implies is that systems need to be able to maintain stability, while at the same time adapting to environmental changes, thus continuing to perform effectively. Historically, and especially in the present, schools have generally locked themselves into too stable a pattern and have been incapable of responding to either changing internal or external forces. Stability without movement is an impossible goal for schools in today's context. Balancing growth activities and stabilizing practices generates the healthy state: the dynamic equilibrium.

For the most part, except when anti-intellectuals or other critics bully the schools into a mindless, retrogressive "back-to-the-basics" approach, the pressures upon schools from the outside create greater complexity and call for more complex and varied responses than schools usually are able to provide. Teaching healthy and normal children, whose native language is English and whose families provide a favoring environment (good nutrition, good medical care, strong adult role models, wise child-rearing practices) is sufficiently challenging to keep even outstanding teachers on their toes. However, when schools seek to deal with children whose health histories, family backgrounds, language, and other characteristics require many different pedagogical approaches on the part of teachers, the traditional school program simply collapses and individual teachers suffer defeat, frustration, and burnout. To strive for dynamic equilibrium in this event though more difficult is absolutely necessary for schooling success.

The *function of management,* from a systems perspective, is to maintain dynamic equilibrium. Management diagnoses the situation and adjusts the organization to contain the following characteristics:

1. enough stability to achieve goals
2. enough continuity to ensure orderly change

3. enough adaptability to react to change
4. enough innovativeness to be proactive when conditions warrant

Control, a concept and action fearsome to many educators, is an essential variable in an organization's growth. Control refers to the regulation and co-ordination of activities and of results so that goals will be accomplished. Perhaps if the control mechanisms were functioning effectively, school activities would not divert the staff into numerous disconnected assignments. As Toyota controls for the new production of Coronas and Corollas, so goal attainment in schools requires control on activities to enable the staff to eliminate irrelevant or non-goal-related tasks from their pattern. Control is always used in relation to goals, and in the systems approach school goals are collaboratively defined. Therefore, control is also collaborative in nature and is viewed as a healthy necessity in accomplishing an ideal. The champion skier, pianist, and scientist all eliminate many potentially useful activities in their schedule so that they can excel in one certain direction. So also must schools control for their given and chosen priorities.

A Systems Model for School Productivity

With the foregoing brief orientation to basic systems concepts in hand, it is now time to consider implications for schools. We find it helpful to view the school as its own ecological system, such as a beehive. While each school functions within the larger context of the school district, and within the broader community, the school has a self-contained existence. The life forces of the school, ecologically speaking, are its own particular expertise, experience, and culture. While its general purpose is to cause learning to occur effectively and efficiently, each school has its own perceived state of the art and its own particular sense of where it wants to be. Most schools are similar in a general sense, but each has its own ambience, its own unique mix of people, its own history, and its own value set and traditions. Furthermore, even a slight change in the overall pattern, such as the retirement of a particular teacher or the adoption by the school board of a new art education program can radically alter the ambience and the quality of school life. Other more major changes, such as the replacement of an authoritarian principal or the adoption of a different pupil-evaluation system, can have an even more powerful impact on the school's culture. Americans have recently had ample experience with the impact upon schools of deteriorating neighborhoods, racial tensions, fiscal crises, court-ordered busing, and similar societal forces to appreciate how much the nature and well-being of schools, and the children served by them, can be influenced by the surrounding environment (for which we use the term "suprasystem").

In a systems-oriented school, teachers and principals together decide on school improvement targets for the year, and subsequently define action plans for achieving those goals. A collective sense of purpose generates an energy exchange system among the staff and enables the staff to respond creatively to problems and to opportunities in the school improvement process. Specific improvement goals provide parameters for how the school staff engages in tasks.

The school has multiple schooling factors to consider as it works toward goals. We propose that all factors (for example, program development, parent involvement, staff development) belong to one of five major schooling categories. The school's ecosystem (see Figure 2.1) contains six separate but interdependent subsystems which serve a specific function for school productivity. To illustrate the concept of subsystems, the cognitive, affective, and behavioral learning trichotomy (Bloom 1956; 1964) enables teachers to separate and plan for learning activities more effectively in each of the three domains of learning, thereby enhancing total learning results. Actual learning occurs not only in one domain, but, rather in all three domains, either sequentially or simultaneously. Planning learning experiences for the separate domains, however, can enhance the probability of effective total learning of a skill or concept. Likewise, the six subsystems of the school enable teachers and principals to plan for the effective functioning of each dimension in the school's production process. Each subsystem plays a vital role. Each is separate, and yet the six systems function interdependently in the school's development process.

The school-development *goal subsystem* provides the specific direction for improvement in a given year or set of years. Goals tend to generate a collective sense of purpose that nurtures the ecology of a school. Development goals reflect the staff's perceptions of schooling needs (for example, parental involvement; improving the math program) as well as external demands on the school (for example, IEP's for all special students). The two sets of pressures, external and internal, are synthesized by the staff and translated into development goals. By defining goals cooperatively, the staff is far more likely to be committed to achieve the goals than if goals were assigned. In Figure 2.1, we emphasize the goal subsystem, referring to it as the heart, the honeycomb, the subsystem that provides direction for all other subsystems. In Chapter 4 we will explore the function of collective values and beliefs in determining development goals. In Chapter 5, specific methodology for staff collaboration in the determination of goals will be presented.

The *educational leadership* and *management subsystems* provide the vision and the inspiration for reaching toward certain educational ideals. In ad-

SUBSYSTEMS

Environmental Suprasystem

Figure 2.1. The School As an Ecosystem

dition, they provide the structure for facilitating and ensuring staff productivity. The *educational leadership subsystem* is presented in Chapter 3. The research on effective schools and organization provides a rationale for ten leadership competencies for productive school management. Emphasis is given to specific planning, development, and evaluation tasks that result from effective leadership and provide direction for school development.

More generic management practices are discussed near the end of the volume (Chapters 12, 13, and 14). The skills of planning, supervising, controlling, and evaluating are the management functions that permeate all schooling activities and provide a generic structure for ensuring that goals are achieved. Employment of specific management practices can greatly increase the effectiveness of educational leaders and, further, will contribute to significant gains in staff performance. Thus, the emphasis in the management subsystem is on managing and controlling staff performance (rather than on building maintenance).

The *organization subsystem* (addressed in Chapters 6 and 7) provides concepts and procedures for organizing the staff in a variety of ways. A goal dispersement model is discussed that guides task assignments and school activity in general. We will examine how teams, task forces, committees, councils, and other arrangements can serve either a temporary or a permanent function for the school.

In Chapter 8 we will examine the *performance subsystem,* which classifies the various roles and responsibilities of individuals and groups. Expectations and standards of performance are defined for teachers, team leaders, department heads, directors, assistant principals, and principals each of whom plays a specific role in school development. With role standards and expectations carefully defined, it then becomes possible for individuals to make explicit performance plans. These plans provide a basis for staff development, for clinical supervision (especially between and among peers), and for the school's overall evaluation activities.

The *program subsystem* explores learning in schools (Chapter 9). Adult learning is no less important a concern for the principal than is student learning. In general, the term "staff development" is used as a label for activities designed to increase the knowledge, skills, and other attributes of the adults who work with students; and terms such as "student learning" are used when referring to the benefits that are intended to accrue to children and youth when the educational program is under way. Although we are well aware that student learning is what the taxpayer is buying, and while we agree that the cost-effectiveness of schools must be determined by examining student, rather than teacher, growth, we nonetheless believe that student learning ultimately depends largely on the quality of teachers' performance. Therefore, in this volume our focus is primarily upon how to bring adult performance to the highest possible level.

The staff development program (Chapter 11) which is part of the program subsystem in the school, is determined by priorities generated within the goal subsystem. If parent involvement is selected by school staff as one of the year's goals, teachers may need retraining and re-orientation with respect to the ways that parents might enter into the program life of the school. If the time has come for major overhaul of the school's art curriculum, then various art experiences as well as curriculum revision technologies must be featured for the entire staff.

Staff development activities are determined in part by action plans of various work groups and individuals. For example, the primary team might perceive a need for better oral language training. Similarly, the performance plans that are developed by individual teachers, such as Sally Benson's resolve to do a better job with parent conferencing, help to indicate appropriate staff development experiences that are needed. In Sally's case, for example, the principal might help her to find some useful readings on conferencing, or to attend a workshop on evaluating and reporting pupil progress at the regional service center.

Student learning, another dimension of the school's program, is a function of planning, teaching, and learning activities. An instruction system is presented in Chapter 10 that discusses the state-of-the-art and specific concepts within five categories of instruction: curriculum selection; diagnosis and evaluation; program planning; classroom management; and teaching and learning. The five instructional categories, while planned separately, function as a unit to influence student achievement.

All six of the school's subsystems are integrally linked and interdependent; each subsystem performs a specific function for the school. Moreover, each subsystem must be organized and managed so that the goals of the school are realized. However, all subsystems are not equal in importance. We place the goal subsystem at the very center of the organization because we recognize its supreme importance. Yet, in some sense each of the other subsystems is also essential to the school's survival. Figure 2.2 summarizes the basic nature of each school subsystem. The external school boundaries are fluid today rather than rigid. Consequently, the staff needs to be continuously responsive to the pressures emerging from the school district, the community, and various private, state, and federal agencies.

A home is considered effective today if all of its various systems function well for its owners. If the heating system quits in winter, or if the basement develops a leak, the house as a unit cannot function at full capacity until those problems are resolved. Likewise, a school without a focused staff development program will falter, whereas one with a staff development program designed around school goals is far more likely to increase its productivity. The authors' intent in organizing this book around the six subsystems is to stimulate and enable principals to develop each subsystem well, and thereby realize total increases in productivity norms.

Shifting from a maintenance paradigm to a production paradigm is a developmental process. The atmosphere must be conducive to school growth, or anticipated results are likely to be aborted. Consider the following six prerequisite conditions. First, the staff must make a strong commitment to the goals of the school and to the ways in which they need to be organized to achieve school goals. Second, the staff will work more productively if it has been given an orientation to the concepts of school ecology. Third, each staff member should have a strong sense of control over the knowledge base within his or her field of competence, and be keenly aware of the unique contribution he or she makes to overall school development. Fourth, each work group member should receive information about the backgrounds and potential contributions of other staff members to make necessary linkages with fellow team members. Fifth, sufficient opportunities should be provided for teams to meet together regularly to plan, implement, supervise, and evaluate their programs. Sixth, it is necessary for the principal and all team leaders to remain knowledgeable about school plans and activities and to ensure that all groups are fulfilling their responsibilities.

The principal creates the essential conditions that favor collaborative efforts

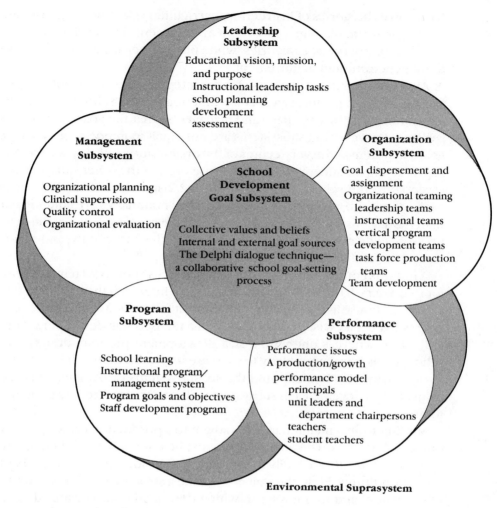

Figure 2.2. School Ecosystem Variables

and that establish control over anticipated schooling outcomes. It is crucial for the individual principal to have a genuine commitment to school development and to exhibit that commitment regularly and consistently. One conclusion that can be drawn from recent research on innovative programs is that principals must themselves have not only a strong but also a *visible* commitment to the school's program, and possess knowledge and understanding of how people work together productively. Principals need social engineering skills that will help the staff to achieve schooling goals each year, and they must allocate sufficient and appropriate resources so that school programs can flourish.

Each school has its unique strengths and weaknesses that must be understood in planning for school growth. Likert (1967, 148), in his studies of numerous organizations and their ability to accomplish goals adequately, noted that the following characteristics or conditions that differentiate the human assets in an organization, tend to influence the quality and success of the organization:

1. level of intelligence and aptitudes
2. level of training
3. level of performance goals and motivation to achieve organizational success
4. quality of leadership
5. capacity to use differences for purposes of innovation and improvement, rather than allowing differences to develop into bitter, irreconcilable, interpersonal conflict
6. quality of communication upward, downward, and lateral
7. quality of decision making
8. capacity to achieve cooperative teamwork versus competitive striving for personal success at the expense of the organization
9. quality of the control processes of the organization and the levels of felt responsibility that exist
10. capacity to achieve effective coordination
11. capacity to use experience and measurements to guide decisions, improve operations, and introduce innovations

Peters and Waterman (1983) also report a number of excellent characteristics in many Fortune 500 companies that would have strong implications for schools as they grow and seek to become increasingly productive. There is a *sense of family* within the organization. A spirit of camaraderie and belonging is generated, for example, by telling and retelling the success stories of its people. The emphasis continuously reinforces that "our people are our primary resources." There is a continuous effort on the part of management to keep workers "built up"; this is accomplished by continually sharing and telling the myths that evolved over time in the company.

Many successful companies have been built on the concept of a small *team organization.* Employees work alone at times but always within the context of a small work group where team plans guide individual performance. As workers function within their own group *informal communications* are used for resource exchange with other groups. Team plans and reports are limited to one page rather than extensive documents to enable significant energy to be task directed. Essential goals and results are all that is reported to management, but the essential goals tightly control the rather loose and informal working patterns, relationships, and continuous exchanges. Emphasis is given to productivity goals and results.

Peer reviews are conducted regularly and replace individual performance evaluations. Managers of successful companies have learned that peers know far more than management about each other and are less likely to "snow" one another. The objectives in peer reviews are to critique and recommend modifications and also to applaud and reinforce accomplishments. Hence, the organization's ecology receives vital internal feedback.

Positive reinforcement occurs through various forms of "hoopla" in successful companies. Myths about the values of the organization guide what accomplishments are recognized. Exemplary performance is recognized daily, weekly, and monthly in celebrations of all kinds, some of which are formal ceremonies and others of which are more informal outings. Awards are given regularly as individuals and groups excel in producing. Successful managers in these companies are effective listeners of consumers and workers and regularly make necessary adjustments in work patterns. The primary characteristic of effective managers is that they *transmit purpose regularly and consistently.* Often companies have a theme, such as "Service is our business," which permeates all dimensions of work life.

Successful companies reflect an *ecological spirit.* Workers function in groups around a specific purpose in the organization's goal structure. Work goals tightly control a rather informal pattern of work relationships and provide the major thrust for continuous interaction, exchange, and production. Management listens, reinforces the central mission continuously, and recognizes and applauds accomplishments. Workers, together with management, review each others' performance and provide the energy for directing and redirecting performance. In a real sense, the company belongs to the workers because they are its major resource.

Conclusion

Schools can become transformed into thriving social agencies for society as their workers develop the capacity to work together and to define regularly the next tasks in their school development mission. Working together around certain goals, refining conditions, and adjusting to changing environmental expectations is the work norm in a productive school.

In the following chapters, each subsystem will be developed more fully, providing the reader with selected and pertinent concepts and specific methodology (see subsystem characteristics in Table 2.2). As the reader engages in each chapter's content, new insights will emerge as well as specific ideas for creating ecologically sound work conditions in a school. In addition, methodologies for developing each subsystem will be introduced, some of which may be new while others are familiar. Our intent is to reinforce exemplary practices that now exist in schools and to introduce concepts that will strengthen the subsystems, each with its cumulative effect on school productivity.

TABLE 2.2. A Systems Approach to School Organization and Management

Subsystem Dimensions	Maintenance Paradigm	Production Paradigm
1. Educational Leadership Subsystem		
Leadership vision	Provided by central office	Personal mission
Knowledge base	Manage personnel, students, and building functions	Manage staff performance and student learning
Role functions	Organize and control school order	Lead, plan, and develop staff performance
Leadership goals	Increase efficiency	Increase effectiveness
Commitment	Perform as expected	Attain educational ideals
2. Goal Subsystem		
Pervasive values	Stability, efficiency, predictability, security, vagueness, tradition	Responsiveness, growth, problem solving, uncertainty, adaptability, risk taking
Goal sources	Administration/school board/ state and federal agencies	All school community members plus external forces
Goal focus	Global-age ideals, traditional practices	Measurable, definable/priorities and objectives
Goal decisions	Central administration	The entire school community; the principal
Function of goals	Provide general guidelines	Provide specific staff performance parameters
3. Organization Subsystem		
Role group relationships	Hierarchical	Collaborative and cross role groups
Design	Based on function and assignment	Based on goals and function
Work patterns	Individual tasks: permanent	Group tasks; temporary and permanent
Design duration	Static, permanent; Based on function Set pattern	Fluid, evolving Based on organizational needs Changing groups

(continued)

TABLE 2.2. (continued)

Subsystem Dimensions	Maintenance Paradigm	Production Paradigm
Planning	Function defines individual plans	Group action plans guide individual plans
4. Performance Management		
Role performance standards	Job descriptions	Categorical performance outcomes
Planning	Personal/informal	Organizational and individual Negotiated goals
Development	Personal counseling	Training Clinical supervision Job enlargement
Motivation	Assignment expectations Autonomy	Goal focus Achievement recognition Development tasks
Control	Evaluation	Periodic management reviews/ positive reinforcement and/or correction
Evaluation	Observation assessment	Goal based Measured results
5. Program Subsystem For Students		
Objective	To complete the course outline	To master certain skills/ concepts
Focus	Grade level content; program objectives vary with each teacher; course outline	Specific learning objectives based on district standard and diagnosed need
Evaluation	Students receive grades: A,B,C,D,F	Degree of mastery
Outcome	Students promoted or not promoted	Objectives mastered
For Staff		
Objective	To provide information	To provide staff selected school goals based on growth experiences
Focus	Defined by central administration	Selected needs as dictated by school and work goals
Evaluation	General: like or dislike	Degree to which the program facilitated anticipated growth
Outcome	Number of required hours of staff development fulfilled	Increased staff knowledge and skills in relation to goals
6. Management Subsystem		
Planning	Staff/student assignments, facilities, maintenance, supply and equipment, inventory and budget	Goal focus for the school; task assignments to work groups; strategies for supervision and control

(continued)

TABLE 2.2. (continued)

Subsystem Dimensions	Maintenance Paradigm	Production Paradigm
Supervision	Inspection visits by principal that provide data for teacher evaluation	Regular and systematic inclass coaching of teachers by peers and administrators/supervisors Facilitates skill development
Control	Problems are addressed as needed: crisis orientation	Regular assessment of progress toward goals by work groups and administration; feedback utilized
Evaluation	Staff evaluation by the principal; judgment about teacher cooperation with administration and ability to control students	Assessment by work groups and administration of progress toward goals; of achievement gains; of program effects on performance

3

Educational Leadership Subsystem

The principal has been described as the "gatekeeper" of change, whose active support or lack of support influences the degree of success with any new program or innovation in a school (Berman and McLaughlin 1978). Many researchers have summed up the significant influence of principals by referring to them as the "key" factor in school success.

The purpose of this chapter is to present a task model for leading the school development process. The leadership tasks are organized into clusters of planning, staff development, program development, and evaluation. A strong research base exists to support each task cluster. The research also provides perspectives on the nature of effectiveness within each task. Selected research findings and systems theory concepts are further synthesized into ten competency statements. These provide a focus for the specific concepts and methodologies presented throughout this volume.

The ten school leadership tasks are viewed as primary mediating variables for creating favorable ecological conditions within a school. The six subsystems presented in the previous chapter are static conceptual organisms that require manipulation of some sort. We have organized this text around the subsystems; the leadership tasks are developed within each subsystem chapter. That is, those tasks that influence the effectiveness of a particular subsystem are presented in that chapter in the form of methodology. Our intent is to provide options for the ways in which each subsystem can be influenced by the principal and the leadership team. Within the planning, developing, and assessing task structure, the effective principal provides goal-based leadership for altering learning norms and increasing adult productivity in an ecologically sound environment.

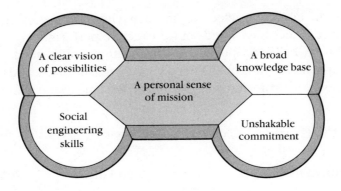

Figure 3.1. Requisites of the Principalship

The Work Context of the Principal

The possession of leadership skills and strong command of educational concepts alone do not make a great school leader. Volumes have been written
about leadership, enough to suggest that certain qualities or approaches can
enable one skilled person to be more effective than another. While this book
presents concepts and methodologies for providing effective school leadership, we believe that the person providing leadership must also bring certain
qualities to the task.

Let us consider the requisites in Figure 3.1 for effective school management.
Even more than in years past, today's principal must have a clear vision of what
a school ought to be, and a keen sense of how a particular staff can work toward
that ideal. Similarly, success depends upon the principal's personal knowledge
base in learning, teaching, organizing and developing work groups, and managing people. In addition, a principal must possess skill for enabling groups to
work productively toward common purposes. Knowledge, skills, and a clear
vision must be attached to a strong commitment to coach the staff while it
works toward new ideals of schooling. And last, an effective principal must
have a personal sense of mission in a particular job, a mission that is communicated continuously to the staff, students, and parents in a variety of forms.

In addition to the generic requisites noted in Figure 3.1, an effective principal must have certain cognitive, affective, and behavioral characteristics to
become successful. Just as basic beliefs, attitudes, and skills about sailing, for
example, are essential for racing a sailing boat successfully, we believe that
certain prerequisite beliefs and attitudes prevail for someone to master effectively school leadership skills and subsequently manage a productive school.

Note the cognitive, affective, and behavioral requisites in Table 3.1. These illustrate a necessary mind-set for effective performance.

Burns (1978) proposes that organizations today need "transforming" leadership which builds on the need for personal meaning and creates institutional purposes. Transforming leadership is dynamic in the sense that leaders throw

TABLE 3.1. Cognitive, Affective, and Behavioral Requisites for Effective Principals

Cognitive Requisites	Affective Requisites	Behavioral Requisites
1. A belief that all students can achieve what is expected if the schooling conditions are appropriate	1. Openness to the ideas, influence, and recommendations from staff, parents, and students	1. Ability to listen to and value the ideas of others
2. A belief that the staff and principal together can transform schooling practices sufficiently to alter learning norms	2. A sense that one can and must guide collaborative activities	2. Ability to create a work climate that will motivate staff members
3. A belief that collaborative staff decision making in planning, action, and evaluation will facilitate greater school productivity than will administrative decision making and work isolation	3. Motivation to alter the school's learning norms	3. Ability to provide leadership in group problem-solving meetings
4. A belief that goals are an important guide for the performance of individuals and groups	4. Openness to ideas for altering the organizational structure	4. Ability to provide counsel to individuals or groups
5. A belief that continuous staff development (through in-service and on-the-job coaching) is the primary job task of the principal	5. Motivation to share leadership responsibilities with selected staff members	5. Ability to listen to the public and to involve them productively in school improvement tasks
6. A belief that individuals can work more productively in a group context		

(continued)

TABLE 3.1. (continued)

Cognitive Requisites	Affective Requisites	Behavioral Requisites
7. A belief that student achievement is the most important measure of school productivity		
8. A belief that the quality control of staff performance is an essential in altering work norms		
9. A belief that the staff learns daily		
10. A belief that continuous staff dialogue is a critical practice in altering a school's norms		

themselves into a relationship with followers who feel elevated by it and often become more active themselves, thereby creating new cadres of leaders (Peters and Waterman 1982, 83–85). Building organizational purpose involves transforming people from neutral technical units into participants who have a particular set of characteristics, sensitivities, and commitments. To institutionalize is to infuse an organization and its workers with values beyond the technical requirements at hand. In so doing, the organization becomes changed from an unimportant force for workers into a source of personal satisfaction. The institutional leader, in this sense, is an expert in the promotion and protection of certain values.

Given a basic orientation to the job and a set of related knowledge and skills, the principal must consider the social context of the school. What are the school's norms as they relate to learning, to teaching, to organizing, and to relating to parents? What are the forces already at work for school improvement, and what are those that might retard growth?

Figure 3.2 identifies the forces that influence a principal's decisions for school growth and for the plans necessary to achieve that growth. An accurate assessment of context factors, along with plans for school growth, determine

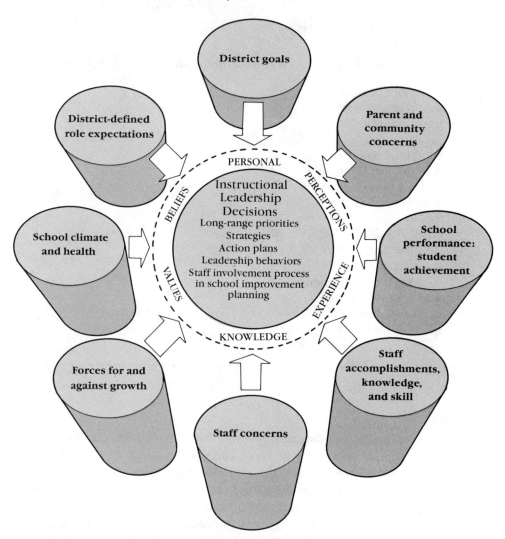

Figure 3.2. Influences on Instructional Leadership Decisions

in large measure a principal's success with school development. Forces and conditions external to the school, as well as conditions within the school, influence leadership decisions.

Significant changes in the functions of school leadership also require a shift in purpose and in orientation to job tasks. The necessary vision, knowledge, role orientation, goals, and commitment of leadership persons must be suited fundamentally to a production paradigm for schools. Leadership emanates from a personal sense of mission and extends the mission by involving the staff in planning and managing school development. Greatness in leadership is the

TABLE 3.2. The Educational Leadership Subsystem

Subsystem Functions	Maintenance Paradigm	Production Paradigm
Leadership vision	Provided by central office	Personal mission
Knowledge base	Manage personnel, students, and building functions	Manage staff performance and student learning
Role functions	Organize and control school order	Lead, plan, and develop staff performance
Leadership goals	Increase efficiency	Increase effectiveness
Commitment	Perform as expected	Attain educational ideals

capacity to enable ordinary people to accomplish extraordinary feats (see Table 3.2.).

In the maintenance paradigm, direction for a school is provided by central administration; the knowledge base for job success has to do with personnel, program, and building administration; and the leadership function is to obtain and maintain order and to increase efficiency in ways that are expected. In the new paradigm, however, leadership will spring from a personal sense of mission for a school and will focus on managing performance to increase staff effectiveness and attain educational ideals.

A Model for Productive School Leadership

The leadership model presented in this volume defines the principal's primary role functions as they relate to school productivity: orchestrating collaborative school improvement planning; developing staff and programs; and achieving and assessing anticipated schooling results. The maintenance functions usually ascribed to the principal, involving such matters as scheduling, transportation, supplies, and meals are to be managed differently, and preferably by others. Such functions represent secondary tasks, whose purpose it is to maintain a smooth-running operation; they do not serve to alter the norms of school productivity.

For the past eight years we have been developing a leadership training program around a comprehensive school management model. The model, summarized in Figure 3.3, employs a systems approach to the management of a school organization. A key assumption is that all four parts of the management model are interdependent. Another is that the process is cyclical, proceeding

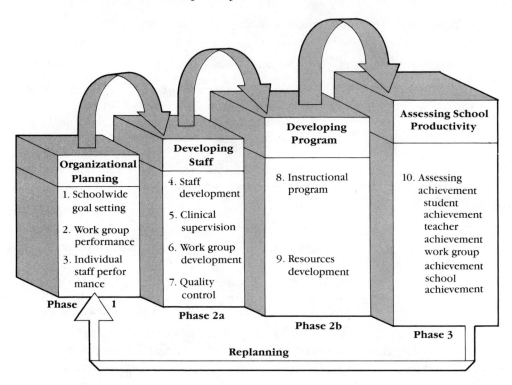

Figure 3.3. Ten Competencies for Productive School Management

from planning, to two dimensions of development, to assessment, and then back again to replanning, redevelopment, reassessment, ad infinitum. It will be noted in the figure that 10 task areas, or competencies, of management are identified: Phase 1, (planning) has three components; Phase 2a (staff development) has four; Phase 2b (program development) has two; and Phase 3 (assessment) has one component of which there are four parts.

Considerable support for the model design exists in the various research literatures of business, schooling, and the social and behavioral sciences. An analysis of approximately 200 studies provides beginning parameters for productive school planning, development, and assessment activity. Moreover, collaborative work patterns in organizations throughout society today provide the critical dynamic for the process that can invigorate school work life, and produce new norms of work results.

In the following paragraphs are the themes we found from research studies in the 10 model dimensions for school planning, development, and evaluation. It is these beginning themes that provide task and process directions for school development activities. Our intent is to provide a picture of ideal adult work life found in productive schools and other agencies in the mid 1980s. The statements from the 200-odd studies that led to the summary paragraphs that follow can be found in Appendix A of this chapter.

Organizational Planning

1. School Planning

In effective schools, teachers and principals translate collective concerns into specific achievement-oriented school improvement goals. Improvements are planned by the entire staff in response to needs and changes in the school environment. Collaborative decision making creates a healthy school climate, which tends to foster a sense of community. Cooperative dialogue, decision making, action, and evaluation characterize effective programs. Goal structures tend to be complex while goal tasks are dispersed to a web of both permanent and temporary work groups. Purpose and order for schooling activities result from collaborative goal definitions. Responsibility for total program success is shared by the entire staff.

2. Team Planning

In effective organizations individuals work in the context of both permanent and temporary work groups. Effective schools develop creative approaches for grouping teachers into working teams. Members collaboratively set goals, specify means of goal attainment, assign responsibilities and determine evaluation criteria. Authority for success is delegated to the team, where collaborative decision making and creative problem solving foster both group cohesiveness and productivity. An interchange of ideas among teachers occurs regularly and permeates school life. Team success seems to hinge on the leader's ability to maximize member assets.

3. Individual Performance Planning

In successful organizations a high level goal orientation exists for individual performance that is linked to the organization's goals. In successful schools, both school and teacher goals tend to guide teacher performance. Role expectations are clear and teachers are held accountable for student performance in effective schools. A goal structure for performance discharges responsibility for contributions to organizational success, and provides a framework for work activity, skill development, supervisory feedback, and performance evaluation.

Staff Development

4. Staff Development

Staff development programs that are school based and linked to improvement goals are the most effective. In successful schools, staff development is viewed as an essential to improvement efforts, and is planned by teachers and principals together to address skills that are transferable to the classroom.

Small group activities and experimental learning are the most influential growth activities in training programs. Readiness, planning, training, and follow-up coaching are all essential elements for staff development programs that are directed to improvements in teacher performance.

5. Clinical Supervision

In effective schools principals conduct frequent formal and informal observations to coach teachers in their development of instructional skills. "Effective teaching" behaviors guide supervision practices as principals and teachers seek to improve teaching, and subsequently, raise the levels of student achievement.

In successful schools teachers are able to transfer new skills to classroom use when peers, supervisors, and principals are trained in coaching skills and use them. Teachers prefer and are influenced by peer coaching in the form of observing and critiquing, and their performance is influenced positively through continuous self-confrontation and feedback.

6. Work Group Development

A group orientation to school work is characteristic of effective schools. Teachers plan programs together and make buildingwide articulation decisions with the principal. An effective manager uses networks and coalitions to solve problems and accomplish tasks. Principals initiate and sustain group participation; the group provides a context for active involvement in, and healthy criticism of, the school development process. Work groups become learning centers for teachers as they share, plan, act, and critique progress on tasks together. Each member participates actively on productive teams.

A productive staff is cohesive, has a unity of purpose, and shares concerns for program improvements with its members frequently. A spirit of staff cooperation and satisfaction permeates effective schools.

7. Quality Control

In effective organizations, a quality control process that is goal focused keeps workers on planned tasks, improves work group effectiveness, and influences organizational success. Responsibility, reinforcement, and recognition are the most effective motivators for improved performance. Collegial control processes that provide data-based monitoring and intervention are the most effective and the most satisfying forms of performance management.

In successful schools, principals control a complex web of staff interactions. The staff is held accountable for results, individually and collectively, in a supportive atmosphere.

Program Development

8. Instructional Management

In effective schools, principals communicate a system of instructional standards to teachers, coordinating schoolwide curriculum and instruction. Teachers plan and carry out programs together, providing a climate of high achievement expectations for all students.

Ninety-five percent of all students can master expected skills and knowledge if the learning conditions are supportive. The instructional program is characterized by adaptability and consistency, and by clear and timely instructional cues, reinforcement, correctives, and feedback. There is active student participation in learning activities.

In successful schools teachers are able to alter outdated methods of instruction and to adopt new practices when the expectation for such change exists, and where teachers frequently exchange ideas and support each other in the instructional improvement process.

9. Resource Development

Making productive use of resources is central to effective organizational productivity. Principals of successful schools plan for, organize, and distribute resources to their staffs; resource management is tied to school goals. Effective principals are able to secure adequate material and human resources in spite of seeming constraints. District resources are used to augment the instructional program.

Many schools become uniquely successful from the effective involvement of a particular community business. High levels of parent or community involvement tend to facilitate student achievement. Involved schools have a greater awareness of community issues. Involvement results in increased satisfaction between parents and the school. Parent and community participation in school projects reduces alienation, creates trust in the schools, and facilitates project success.

School Evaluation

10. Assessing Achievement

Schoolwide Evaluation
Principals of successful schools develop a schoolwide accountability model. Measures of schoolwide productivity are evidenced in student achievement gains, work group productivity, and staff behavior and performance. In successful schools the staff uses data-based feedback (internal and external to the school) and staff experiences for problem solving and adjusting to conditions. Students in effective schools are recognized for their accomplishments.

Team Evaluation
Work groups in effective organizations are measured against organizational goals and standards of group productivity. Effective teams evaluate their own progress. Rewards and recognition for success are shared with effective teams by managers.

Teacher Evaluation
Successful schools have staff performance reviews by principals. Performance assessment that is based on a combination of individual and organizational goals influences performance positively. Teachers trained in observation techniques believe that evaluation is more helpful than do untrained teachers. Job assignment, working hours, and traditional evaluation procedures produce *no* noticeable change in performance, whereas awards for excellence, worker visibility, and new opportunities influence performance positively. High teacher morale is the chief teacher characteristic in assessing effective schools.

Student Evaluation
Successful schools are characterized by continuous evaluation of student progress. The greater the involvement in assessment by the principal, the higher is student achievement. Feedback on progress is useful when standards exist for achievement and where principals have high expectations. Student academic self-concept and self-reliance tend to be high in effective schools. Student achievement increases with teacher satisfaction and with the goal emphasis of principals, especially women principals.

Transforming School Management

Over the next several decades we expect that the errors, half-truths, and/or verities in the preceding summary statements will come into sharper focus. For the moment, each sentence *seems* to be well supported in the literature, and therefore it makes sense to pay it some attention. Abundantly clear is that when principals and their staffs apply their collective energies to all four clusters of activity, the transformation of schools from outdated and unproductive environments to vibrant and productive workplaces becomes much more probable. Since it is to the principal that we ascribe the most important role in school tranformation efforts, it has been our intent to develop clearer definitions of the job tasks necessary to invigorate a school staff and to transform work results.

The task is to cause teachers to work not harder, but smarter. Cooperation and support must be garnered from and with a staff regarding continuous school development for improvement efforts to succeed. To provide a beginning direction for that challenge, we have identified 10 school management competencies. Each competency grows out of the growing research themes noted earlier, and is supported by sound theory on productive management that reflects the 1980s workplace. With the task in mind of stimulating a productive work context, consider the following competency statements. Each of the 10 competencies is further described by 10 behavioral indicators; see Appendix B of this chapter.

School Management Competencies

Organizational Planning Cluster

1. *Schoolwide Goal Setting.*   Establish annual school development goals through administrative assessment and selection and also through total staff collaborative decision making.

2. *Work Group Performance.*   Designate school work groups, both teaching teams or departments and task forces, to which are assigned school goal objectives and action-planning responsibilities.

3. *Individual Staff Performance.*   Establish and operationalize a teacher performance system that includes performance standards, individual goal setting and action-planning procedures, performance monitoring, due process procedures, and evaluation.

Staff Management Cluster

4. *Staff Development.*   Develop and operationalize a school program for staff growth that emphasizes new knowledge and skills that are necessary for the successful attainment of school-development goals (school, work group, individual).

5. *Clinical Supervision.*   Develop and operationalize a peer and supervisory clinical supervision program for all teachers and teams, where performance feedback and correctives are provided weekly.

6. *Work Group Development.*   Establish a healthy work climate and develop work group skills in action planning, creative and productive group communications, problem solving, and decision making.

7. *Quality Control.*   Establish and operationalize a quality control system for work groups and individuals that includes progress reports and plans, and conferencing and supervisory plans.

Program Management Cluster

8. *Instructional Program.*   Establish and operationalize an instructional program that reflects up-to-date research on teaching and learning, and that guides teaching improvement efforts in the following areas: curriculum implementation; student diagnosis and placement; program planning; classroom management; teaching; and learning.

9. *Resource Development.*   Facilitate staff productivity in work groups and provide the necessary resources for making the school an increasingly productive unit.

Assessing Achievement Cluster

10. Establish and operationalize a set of school evaluation procedures to assess student achievement gains, teaching team and task force productivity, individual teacher performance, and total school productivity.

Relationship of Leadership Tasks to a School's Subsystems

The 10 school management tasks of planning, staff and program development, and evaluation are designed to direct the active process of school development. Each task functions as a facilitating force to activate each of the six school subsystems. Figure 3.4 illustrates the general relationship of management tasks to the six subsystems.

The *leadership subsystem* is driven by the principal's personal plan for school development. The *goal subsystem* is driven by collaboratively defined staff and administrative goal setting activities (competency 1). The *organization subsystem* is driven by group workers being responsible for selected per-

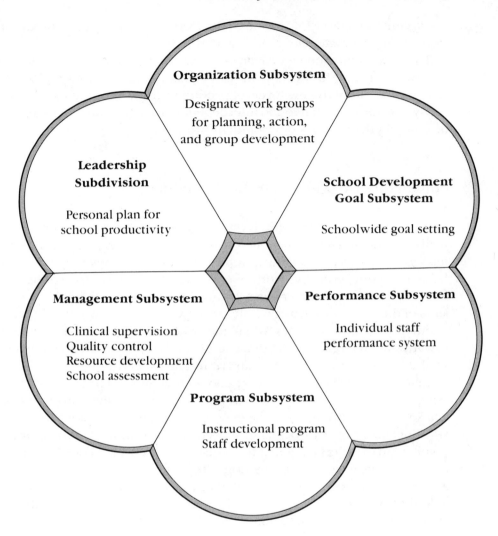

Figure 3.4. Relationship of Leadership and Management Tasks to the School's Subsystems

manent schooling tasks and temporary tasks (competency 2). In addition, attention to group development enables workers to perform more effectively in their tasks (competency 6). The *program subsystem* is driven by the school's instructional program (competency 8) and by the school's staff development program (competency 4). The *performance subsystem* is driven by program that guides individual performance within the context of a school's development plan (competency 3). The *management subsystem* is driven by four tasks: clinical supervision, resource development, quality control, and school evaluation (competencies 5, 9, 7, and 10).

The subsystems and tasks define concepts for guiding school management practice. Together they enable the principal to stimulate a staff and to successfully lead a school to new levels of productivity for its students. All tasks and subsystems are interactive and interdependent, each stimulating a different dimension in the school's development process.

Stimulating Growth of the Work Culture

The concept of school culture is one that can fight the problems posed by the well-documented phenomenon of loose coupling (Morris et al. 1982). Changing schools requires changing groups of people, their knowledge, activity, and behaviors. Moreover, the work of each part of a school necessarily must be interdependent with other parts. In an ecologically sound workplace, the results of the organization as a whole far outweigh the results of individuals. An additive principle operates when the school functions as a cohesive unit toward shared targets. Collective energy tends to invigorate the individual, as well as corporate work patterns, and results far exceed individual productivity.

Given a shared goal context for cooperative work, and given certain planning, staff development, program development, and evaluation practices, how can schools be developed to the extent that productive work patterns are institutionalized? For a principal to succeed in altering work norms, far more is involved than announcing that the collaborative era has arrived and proceeding as if it were welcome information to the staff. Several theoretical constructs are useful in conceptualizing the different involvement patterns that will enable success to build. Several questions need to be addressed simultaneously in seeking to identify management involvement patterns.

How Does Work Culture Evolve?

Consider the postulate that "behavior is learned." Consider also that "organizational behavior is learned in organizations" (Luthans and Kreitner 1975). If this postulate is true, then the current work patterns of a school were learned in school, and are now reinforced and maintained by administration. If management now perceives that new behavior patterns are necessary, then adopting new work norms becomes a learning process for the organization, rather than a mandate.

The central concept within this schema is that behavior norms can be learned through instruction, practice, reinforcement, and time to master. The learning process of a school and its work culture can be stimulated through teaching, reinforcement, and maintenance behaviors on the part of management, while workers practice and learn together. The growth of a work culture and the learning of individuals are similar. Yet, for a work culture to alter its work patterns, pervasive attitudes, habits, and traditions must be considered. Time is essential for learning and practicing together, for correcting, adopting, and inventing patterns. New work norms can be established in the workplace called school through collective learning, work reinforcement, and maintenance patterns.

How Are Work Culture Patterns Altered?

Change theorists have provided important clues for altering practices in organizations, such as involving users in planning, and developing action plans that specify strategies, time lines, and responsibilities. Essential to the success of change programs is the involvement of affected workers in planning the change process.

Lewin (in Bennis, Benne, and Chin 1969) provides essential guidelines for anticipating success as workers participate in planning change. He suggests that the first stage, *unfreezing,* is critical to any forward movement. During this period, expectations are clear about the direction of the organization. Time and opportunity, however, are provided for workers to question, doubt, explore, and become introspective about the direction and nature of the change. Questions must be addressed, such as, What is the worst that will happen? What is the best that will happen? Am I/are we capable of succeeding? Do we believe a change will work?

The next level of the change process is *teaching and learning* the new patterns. Time must be planned for workers to try, to correct, to discard, to fail, and to succeed. Given success with the learning/adapting process, workers will be eager to define and select those patterns and practices that they want to build on for years to come.

The last stage is referred to by Lewin as a *refreezing* stage. Following a major change and adaptation to new work conditions, selected patterns must be reinforced, maintained, and institutionalized. Rather than anticipating the refreezing period as a long period of time, it must be considered relative. Within the refreezing period, expectation must be given that continuous modifications are normal and desirable.

What Kinds of Worker Involvement Patterns Are Productive?

Any work context has some workers and groups of workers that are different from the norm. Some are systematically more productive, while others are systematically less productive. Hersey and Blanchard (1977) have developed a particularly useful guide for anticipating the kinds of worker involvement patterns that will be successful. Varying leader responses to varying levels of worker task maturity provide important contingency guidelines.

For those groups and individuals who are the most immature in relation to a given work behavior, the appropriate leader behavior is to *tell* workers what to do and how. For those who are less immature, the leader task is to *sell* the workers on what and how. For those who are relatively mature, the leader task is to *participate* with workers in deciding what and how. For those who are the most mature, successful leader behavior is to *delegate* the what and the how.

If a principal's objective is to stimulate the entire work culture, a careful analysis of current worker maturity levels will lead to a variety of leader involvement patterns. Moreover, no one work culture is all productive or all unproductive. In some schools, a principal will necessarily use a balance of telling, selling, participating, and delegating. In other schools the leader necessarily will participate with and delegate changes for most work groups. In other schools, a successful leader necessarily will tell and sell the changes to most groups. An understanding of maturity levels within a particular work context will enable principals to respond appropriately to different levels of involvement. If success is the leader objective, providing appropriate involvement parameters is likely to stimulate worker cooperation.

How Can Principals Stimulate Individual Workers and Groups?

Although a great deal is known about individual worker stimulation in business and industry, little is known about adult worker motivation in schools. However, in 1967, Sergiovanni replicated Herzberg's study of workers who are hygiene seekers (concerned about work conditions) and workers who are motivators (concerned about organizational growth) with a group of teachers. He found that virtually the same kinds of motivators existed for teachers as did for workers in industry. The most important stimulators were identified as achievement, recognition, and responsibility.

Rather than focusing attention upon teacher concerns such as hours, class size, and duties, principals are likely to realize far more payoff for their schools with a different emphasis. Those teachers who will contribute to a school's development in significant ways will respond with increased responsibility and recognition. Rather than merely paying Master teachers more for their excellence, for example, schools need their expertise to influence the work culture. Along with the Master teacher label, we need to add responsibility as a contingency variable. Schools will profit from our best teachers serving as team leaders, where they can influence instruction and program norms, or as task force leaders, where our most pressing problems are resolved.

Moreover, the cultural noise of the school workplace ought to be teacher achievement and recognition, rather than failure, fear, inadequacy, and judgment. Teachers ought to work together to the extent that they achieve new levels of professional competence together, and be recognized for those successes routinely.

By sharing responsibility with the most capable staff, creating the conditions for professional innovation and achievement, and by recognizing success in numerous ways, principals are likely to observe the transformation of apathetic behaviors to those that are creative and entrepreneurial.

Conclusion

The challenge of impacting and invigorating the school workplace has been developed around the concept of work culture. Partnerships among agencies and within schools are key variables for altering the inert direction of the work life found in most schools. Shared decision making among the professional staff about the "what" and "how" of school development provides the foundations for a productive work ecology. Moreover, a focus on learning as a corporate way of life enables a school staff to plan to work and to succeed together. Adapting to changing conditions, and critiquing each others' process and results, provides a growth expectation for a staff to stretch its limits continuously.

Altering outdated work cultures in schools is not only essential to the survival of schools, it is well within our reach. The first task of school management is to create the conditions whereby a staff will want to alter their work patterns, and then to involve them in varying degrees in planning, development, implementing plans, and realizing success.

Given the necessity for co-involvement in work cultures, certain theoretical constructs are helpful in understanding the nature of success in varying school cultures. If we are able to unlock the puzzle of changing gross work patterns in schools, as well as identifying beginning change variables, we will generate useful knowledge for stimulating productive work environments.

APPENDIX A
Research and Observational Support for Each Competency

Competency 1

Schoolwide Planning

Ackoff 1974. Participation decreases employee resistance to innovation due to motivational properties inherent in participative decision making.

Araki 1982.   Teachers are more satisfied when the principal's leadership is participative.

Armor et al., 1976.   The change process involves collegiality in effective schools.

Austin 1979.   Effective schools function for a specific purpose during a given period of time.

Bennis 1976.   Change comes from groups who face problems and become involved in solutions.

Bentzen 1974.   Staff dialogue, decision making, action, and evaluation processes exist in improving schools.

Berman and McLaughlin 1980.   The entire staff is involved in decision-making efforts.

Brookover and Lezotte 1979.   School goals, a schoolwide social system, healthy school climate, and school management are characteristic of effective schools.
Teacher dissatisfaction with unproductive practices creates a productive tension with existing conditions.

California DPE 1980.   Effective schools have a sense of educational purpose. Improvement programs are designed to meet needs.

Collins 1980.   Teams of teachers and principals share responsibility for the total program.

Duffy 1980.   Productive schools have school improvement goals.

Edmonds 1979.   The principal demonstrates strong administrative leadership. The school atmosphere is orderly.

Educational Research Service 1982.   Involvement of citizens in long-range planning procedures generates better educated citizens and more trust in schools.

Fosmere and Keutzer 1971.   Interpersonal goal setting in a new high school improves climate and interpersonal behavior.

Fullan 1982.   Goal clarity about the essential changes is important to success.

Georgiades and Guenther 1981.   Teachers perceive that collaboration is important in setting school goals, sharing strategies, and seeking subject-area articulation between grades.

Glenn 1981.   Effective schools have explicit goals.

Goodlad 1975.   School improvement must be planned by those who are affected: the school staff. School change is planned jointly by staff and principal in successful schools.

Heathers 1972.   Change must be user-initiated and originate out of needs; it must be planned by the administration, staff, parents, and students.

Kanter 1983.   Building blocks in the most productive companies are: departures from tradition; a galvanizing event (or crisis); strategic decisions (articulation of a clear direction); individual prime movers (who remain steadfast in pushing toward the dream); action vehicles (procedures for achieving goals).

Klausmeier 1982.   Staff plans for improvement are related to changes in student outcomes.

Levine and Stark 1981.   A schoolwide approach to improvement exists in effective schools.

Lewin 1958.   Group discussions develop support for change, decisions, and solutions.

Lieberman and Miller 1978.   The principal transforms individual concerns to collective concerns. Schools adapt to improvements developmentally. Conditions for school improvement are motivated by the principal.

Likert 1967.   Worker participation in setting goals and appraising results is a characteristic of most effective organizations.

Lipham and Fruth 1976.   Principals foster cooperative decision making, intragroup coordination, and systematic planning. Involving parents in planning leads to broad-based support of objectives.

Mann 1957.   The greater the degree of worker involvement, the greater the positive organizational change.

McLaughlin 1978.   The principal and staff mutually adapt the change process to each other and to conditions in the entire school culture.

Miller 1980.   Teachers engage in developmental activities in improving schools.

Mink et al. 1979.   Open organizations are energy exchange systems that adapt to the changing needs of staff, students, and the external environment. A unity of purpose exists in effective organizations.

NASSP 1979.   Principals set school objectives and develop annual school plans. Collaboration is the work norm between staff and parents.

Newman 1981.   A sense of community permeates productive schools.

Odiorne 1979.   The purpose and aim of an organization determine its quality and style of life.

Peters and Waterman 1982.   Excellent companies focus on tangible results, rather than programs, in launching performance improvement thrusts. They identify one or two specific short-term goals for which the ingredients for success are already in place.

Phi Delta Kappa 1980.   Successful schools have specific school goals. Participatory decision making is a norm for teachers and the principal.

Purkey and Smith 1982.   There is staff concensus on school improvement goals.

Rand Study 1979.   The more comprehensive the plan and the more complex is the innovation, the more likely it is to succeed.

Rutter 1979.   The whole school is treated as an element of change. A school ethos that is a quality of life; expectation of student success; staff concensus on values and aims creates a healthy school climate.

Schmuck et al., 1977.   In a self-renewing school, continuing dialogue, skillful interactions, and goal articulations are characteristic.

Schmuck, Runkel, and Langmeyer 1969.   High-school faculty goal setting improves attitudes; innovations increase.

Spady 1977.   Involvement of staff in reorienting experiences is key to power and authority.

Spady and Mitchell 1977.   Involving and reorienting mechanisms are keys to committed engagements for transforming schools.

Vallina 1978.   Parents and staff are involved in planning program improvement.

Vanezky and Winfield 1979.   Successful schools have an achievement orientation. Instructional efficiency is a schoolwide goal and work effort.

Weber 1978.   School climate is conducive to learning. An atmosphere of purpose, order, and pleasure exists in effective schools.

Williams et al. 1974.   Self-renewing schools have continuing dialogue, skillful interactions, and goal articulations.

Wynne 1980.   The staff and community support a common sense of purpose. The staff respects students and expects them to achieve. Students behave in an orderly way.

Competency 2

Work Group Planning

Adizes 1977.   Teamwork is key to management success.

Anderson 1979.   Effective teams have both long- and short-range plans.

Austin 1979.   Teachers work together over time to achieve common work objectives.

Bentzen 1974.   Solutions to school problems often reside in the staff; peer groups work on solutions.

Berman and McLaughlin 1980.   Collegial planning is characteristic of successful change efforts.

Bragg and Andrews 1973.   Goal setting in hospital work groups leads to improved productivity and attitudes.

Brookover and Lezotte 1979.   The principal has a collegial working relationship with teachers in effective schools.

California DPE 1980.   Principals and teachers practice shared decision making and shared planning.

Collins 1980.   Teachers share task assignments.

Cook 1982.   The success of quality circles depends on shifting power, authority, and decision making to the circle level.

Deal and Kennedy 1982.   Work organization in the future is likely to have four striking characteristics: 1) small, task-focused work groups, 2) economic and managerial control over its own destiny, 3) interconnected with larger entities through computer and communications capabilities, and 4) bonded into larger parts of the company through strong cultural bonds. This structure is referred to as "atomized organization."

Deutsch et al. 1971.   One-half of all scientific contributions have been made by teams in the latter part of this century.

Doss and Holley 1982.   Teachers collaboratively develop and implement group plans in effective schools.

Edmonds 1979.   An administrative team plan is generated for improving reading schoolwide.

Fullan 1982.   Specified means of implementing goal targets is critical to success.

Ginnell 1974.   When dental teams are cohesive, they can assume highly complex tasks and produce creative results. Teams plan for implementation.

Glenn 1981.   Joint staff planning is characteristic of school improvement efforts.

Goodlad 1975.   Teachers work cooperatively on school improvement tasks in achieving schools.

Hellriegel and Slocum 1974.   Effective organizations organize goal tasks around principles of role differentiation and integration. Authority is delegated to the lowest level for decision making and task achievement.

Hyman and Cohen 1979.   Teamed teachers are better able to handle complex tasks than isolated teachers. Teams need an administrative structure for sharing their expertise.

Kanter 1982.   The most successful innovations are derived from cross-department contributions. The matrix organization structure is the most effective.

Kast and Rosenzweig 1974.   Decision making and problem solving are collaborative. Open organizations have adaptive mechanisms.

Lathan and Yukl 1975.   Goal setting helps people gain control over their activities and positively influences performance.

Lawler 1964.   The way in which an organization is structured affects job satisfaction. The small organizational unit correlates with job satisfaction.

Levine and Stark 1981.   Staff planning occurs among and within grades.

Lieberman and Miller 1978.   A change in the school requires the cooperative efforts of teachers. Principals lead groups of teachers.

Likert 1967.   The quality of communication and decision making, and the capacity to achieve teamwork in subgroups, influence organizational success.

Lippitt 1979.   Improvement in the quality of work life depends on goal clarity and work responsibility.

Maier and Maier 1957.   A structured discussion procedure increases concensus and improves discussion and decisions.

Mink et al. 1979.   Collaboration provides the organization's energy exchange system.

Morse and Reiner 1956.   Participation in decision making increases the level of work group productivity.

New York State, Case Study 1974.   Administrative effectiveness depends greatly on teamwork.

Ouchi 1981.   A team is a concentrated form of ownership; worker collaboration in refining work technologies and in activity toward goals. The major task of a quality circle is to study and improve the work group's productivity for its part in the organization's success.

Peters and Waterman 1982.   Small groups are the best organizational building block of excellent companies. Effective new product teams range in size from five to ten persons. Teams consist of volunteers, are of limited duration, and that set their own plans for achieving results are the most productive. Chunking is a vehicle for enhanced efficiency and for adaptation and survival.

Rowe 1981.   Team selection of evaluation criteria for assessing team productivity leads to increased productivity.

Rutherford 1979.   Team teaching flourishes in effective schools because it is more productive for teachers and students.

Thompson 1967.   Brainstorming is effective in generating ideas and ensuring that important ideas are not overlooked.

Trisman 1976.   Interchange of ideas among the staff is a regular occurrence in successful schools.

Vallina 1978.   Effective schools launch creative approaches to school organization.

Competency 3

Individual Performance Planning

Ackoff 1974.   High expectations in performance goals are influential in determining subsequent performance.

California DPE 1980.   Teachers are held accountable for student performance.

Cummings and Schwab 1973.   If performance standards are expressed in terms of behavior, they can guide staff training and supervision.

Drucker 1982.   The key to worker productivity is to demand responsibility and to direct behavior toward contributions rather than effort.

Hackman and Lawler 1971.   Responsibility for making decisions concerning one's job is a prerequisite for applying a skill. Job autonomy, variety, identity, and knowledge of results are positively related to productivity.

Kanter 1982.   Innovating managers assign key players to leadership roles and involve them in key decisions.

Kast and Rosenzweig 1974.   MBO improves communications, increases understanding, utilizes abilities, promotes innovation, and integrates individual worker goals.

Knezevich 1973.   MBO is the system that enables an organization to achieve organization goals and results: MBO discharges responsibility through specific worker engagement in the organization's goals.

Lathan and Yukl 1975.   Goal setting positively influences performance for the organization.

Lieberman and Miller 1978.   There is a linkage between school and teacher concerns that guides performance.

Likert 1967.   High levels of performance goals influence organizational success.

Locke 1968.   Goals are important determinants of performance.

Luthans 1981.   Skill variety, task identity and significance, autonomy, and feedback all relate to employee satisfaction.

McGregor 1960.   Worker incorporation of personal goals into work settings facilitates productivity.

Mink et al. 1979.   Work energy is focused on achieving the organization's goals.

Odiorne 1979.   MBO goals include regular responsibilities, major problems, and needed innovations.

Ouchi 1981.   In Japanese companies, trust exists between co-workers and management who ask tough questions and analyze and debate productivity issues.

Phi Delta Kappa 1980.   Role expectations are clearly communicated to staff in successful schools.

Reddin 1970.   MBO achieves congruence between job performance and organizational goals by identifying performance targets. MBO focuses management efforts; motivates workers; strengthens relationships; provides a coaching framework; and eliminates weak appraisal.

Rogers 1973.   The mature individual does not hold his or her values rigidly, but is continually changing. Freedom, responsibility, and self-understanding promote personal growth.

Sergiovanni and Carver 1973.   People who are "motivators" rather than "hygiene seekers" hold promise for producing school success efforts; motivators attend to school goals.

Skinner 1980.   The consequence of behavior reinforces the continuation or elimination of behaviors.

Competency 4

Staff Development

Armor et al. 1976.   Topics for in-service are determined by teachers. Staff development programs require long-term support.

Berman and McLaughlin 1978.   Principal involvement in workshops with teachers enhances change.

Brookover and Lezotte 1979.   Teacher decisions are key to staff development effectiveness.

California DPE 1980.   Ongoing in-service is tied to the instructional program.

Clauset and Gaynor 1982.   Principals are able to implement programs of supervision and training that raise teacher skills and expectations in ways that are transferable to the classroom.

Coleman 1976.   Experimental learning is likely to be used after training. Implementation of change is more likely if in-service is conducted by local staff.

Edmonds 1981.   Teacher decisions are key to effective staff development programs.

Ginnell 1974.   Training in how to achieve collectively is related to success and productivity.

Glenn 1981.   Staff development activities are essential to school improvement efforts.

Hall and Loucks 1978.   Teachers adapt to change developmentally over time.

Harris 1980.   Teacher involvement and planning in staff development is related to overall satisfaction with in-service programs. Training that is linked to school and teacher goals is the most effective.

/I/D/E/A/ 1971.   Small-group adult learning promotes growth in higher cognitive development.

Joyce and Showers 1982.   Staff development programs can cause 25 percent of participants to implement the concept and/or methodology of the training program. School-based programs with teacher involvement in planning are the most effective. Programs relate to teacher goals; teachers participate in shared activity. The most effective in-service includes theory, modeling, practice, feedback, and coaching. Coaching is essential for skill transfer to the classroom.

Levine and Stark 1981.   Effective staff development programs are building-specific.

Lieberman and Miller 1978.   Staff development efforts are remedial or an approach to change. They are always linked to school goals in achieving schools.

Little 1981.   Interaction of teachers with principals occurs in effective staff development. Teacher–administrator planning teams correlate with effective staff development programs.

McLaughlin 1978.   Teacher decisions are key to effective staff development programs.

Miller and Wolf 1978.   Staff development efforts are linked to school improvement goals.

Phi Delta Kappa 1980.   Staff development focuses on specific school outcomes in successful schools.

Reddin 1970.   MBO identifies development needs.

Tikunoff, Ward, and Griffin 1979.   Released time for participants is associated with effective staff development.

Vanezky and Winfield 1979.   Staff development is schoolwide and closely related to the instructional program.

Wood et al. 1982.   Readiness, planning, training, implementation, and maintenance are essential elements in school-based programs.

Wood and Neil 1976.   A clinical approach to in-service holds promise for changing practice.

Wood and Thompson 1980.   School-based programs, where administrators help in planning or conducting programs, tend to be more successful than those involving consultants.

Competency 5

Clinical Supervision

Anderson 1979.   Members of effective teams observe and critique each other.

Berliner 1982.   Teachers and administrators frequently observe each other teaching, and provide useful feedback on teaching.

Berman and McLaughlin 1978.   Follow-up and assistance by principals to workshop practices enhances changes in performance.

Bessent et al. 1968.   Classroom observation is an important element of staff development for helping teachers.

Blumberg 1980.   Teachers seek assistance from other teachers far more often than from superiors.

Boyan and Copeland 1974.   Supervisors trained in clinical supervision skills are able to help teachers improve significantly in a number of critical teaching behaviors.

Brookover and Lezotte 1979.   Supervision is conducted in reading and math in the effective schools studies.

Cawelti and Reavis 1980.   Attitude changes, high levels of openness, and increased accepting behaviors result from clinical supervision practices. High frequency of supervisory visits correlates with high rating of supervisory service by teachers.

Clauset and Gaynor 1982.   Principals are able to implement programs of supervision and training that raise teacher skills and expectations in ways that are transferable to the classroom.

Edmonds 1982.   Principals conduct frequent formal and informal collegial encounters regarding classroom instruction, based on systematic observation and analysis; "effective teaching" is the standard.

Freer 1983.   Teachers do not perceive that they profit from instructional improvement dicta but do profit from someone who is willing to function as a partner in exploring alternative approaches. Improvement does not occur unless the climate fosters trust, modeling, and feedback.

Fuller and Manning 1973.   Self-confrontation and feedback with a focus, fosters behavior change.

Goldhammer, Anderson, and Krajewski 1980.   Clinical supervision is a goal-oriented methodology for performance coaching.

Goldsberry 1980.   Collegial assistance influences teacher performance positively. Colleague consultation (teachers) fosters leadership development, direct classroom support, and increased colleagueship among teachers.

Guditus 1980.   Pre-conferences improve reliability of observer ratings.

Harris 1980.   Guided practice and feedback for teachers occur most often in school-based in-service programs.

Joyce and Peck 1977.   Teachers and administrators believe they learn a great deal from sharing in feedback sessions.

Joyce and Showers 1982.   If teachers are coached, new skills can be developed and transferred to the classroom. Coaching follow-up of training ensures performance changes.

Joyce and Showers 1982.   People need feedback on their own behavior to make efficient use of learning experiences. Role coaching enables 98 percent to adopt the concepts taught in training.

Levine and Stark 1981.   Supervision is based on student achievement outcomes in basic skills in effective schools.

Lieberman and Miller 1978.   Principals reward teachers for new efforts in successful schools.

Competency 6

Work Group Development

Armor et al. 1976.   Program coordination and interaction among teachers guide problem-solving practices. Teachers share flexibility in modifying and adopting instructional approaches. Frequent informal consultations permeate school life.

Armstrong 1977.   Time is provided for effective groups to understand their roles, expectations, and the management function.

Aspy and Roebuck 1974.   Teachers in healthy interpersonal situations in schools are more apt to change and to transmit the interpersonal behaviors to classrooms. Teachers with "high" interpersonal skills have lower pupil absenteeism, higher achievement, fewer discipline problems, and more parent involvement.

Berman and McLaughlin 1977.   Everyone shares the commitment for articulation and adaptation of programs in successful schools.

Boyatzis 1982.   An effective manager verbalizes a need for cooperation and thereby creates a group identity. The manager uses networks and coalitions to solve problems and accomplish tasks, and functions as a coordinator and conduit for exchanges between groups.

Managing group process is significantly related to effectiveness as a manager. Groups are a basic element in managing human resources. Task groups are formed, collaboration is facilitated, and groups are helped to build identity and pride.

Brookover and Lezotte 1979.   Teachers frequently discuss and work on assessment objectives. Achievement test results are discussed at faculty meetings. Weekly faculty meetings include discussion on progress toward objectives.

Cohen-Rosenthal 1982.   Work groups provide schooling for adults. In the process of working in groups, adults accomplish their tasks and learn from each other.

Doss and Holley 1982.   Staff members collaborate to develop and implement schoolwide programs.

Ellett and Walberg 1979.   Rapport between staff and administration is positively related to student achievement.

Friedlander 1974.   Team development activities affect member attitudes and behaviors positively.

Fullan 1982.   Quality work relationships grow out of open communication, support, interaction, assistance, collegiality, and trust.

Glenn 1981.   The staff participates in joint planning in effective schools.

Griffin 1982.   The principal structures readiness activities for group work through support systems, expectations, assistance, and rewards. Staff members work across role sets, participate in decision making about the school, and tend to discover their own expertise through work engagements with others.

HEW Safe Schools Study 1978.   Teacher groups that are satisfied and cohesive and agree with the principal are characteristic of effective schools. Effective schools are supported by the central office staff.

Hoover 1978.   Group-oriented philosophy is characteristic of successful minority schools.

Little 1982.   Principals are responsible for initiating and sustaining effective group participation through resource provisions, release time, job requirements, and evaluation. Group work structure provides a context for active participation in shaping and critiquing the school improvement process. The staff tends to engage in frequent exchanges and observations about teaching practices.

McLaughlin 1978.   Work groups are the learning centers for teachers as they participate in regular meetings for sharing, reporting, helping, and learning.

Maier 1973.   Group productivity hinges on leader ability to maximize group assets and minimize liabilities.

Maier and Maier 1957.   Managers can learn skills to facilitate group dialogue by posing problems and encouraging sharing.

Naisbitt 1982.   Cooperation, exchange, and interdependence are central to success in the information age.

New York State, Case Study 1974.   Staff satisfaction is traced to behaviors of an administrative team. All-day aides are preferred over part-time aides; they are better able to establish team relationships with teachers. A friendly, cooperative atmosphere produces few grievances and low turnover. Faculty staff relationships in effective schools reflect a "spirit of cooperation."

Nolan 1977.   Principals structure time for teachers to plan together, become involved in group planning, and make themselves available to individuals.

Purkey and Smith 1982.   A productive staff has unity, commonality, and collegial relationships. There is a sense of being a member of a group. Collaborative planning between teachers and administrators occurs frequently.

Rutter 1979.   Cooperative, concerned interaction is typical among teachers in exemplary schools. Group decision making is related to achievement.

Schein 1969.   The two main purposes of group work are problem solving and decision making, which are accomplished through problem formulation, posing solutions, examining consequences, planning actions, and evaluating results.

Schmuck et al. 1977.   Effective work groups make decisions for member responsibilities; each member participates in articulating expectations for performance and future outcomes.

Schmuck, Runkel, and Langmeyer 1969.   Team development activities increase staff productivity.

Stodgill 1959.   Group achievement depends on morale, integration of group structure, and productivity.

Thelen and Dickerman 1961.   Groups progress through four stages as they grow toward productivity: individually centered; frustration and conflict; attempted consolidation; productivity and problem solving.

Woodman and Sherwood 1980.   A goal setting–problem solving approach to team building is most effective.

Wynne 1980.   Group decision making is related to program coherence.

Competency 7

Quality Control

Boyatzis 1982.   At the core of every manager's job is the requirement to make things happen according to a plan. Competent management competencies include efficiency orientation, proactivity, diagnostic decision making, and concern with impact. Subordinates are given feedback on their performance, help in problem areas, along with counseling and advice.

Cohen 1981.   Effective schools are tightly managed; the staff is held accountable for results.

Drucker 1982.   Assignment control causes knowledge workers to be productive.

Duke 1980.   Principals employ troubleshooting mechanisms for anticipating and resolving problems.

Glenn 1981.   Principals and teachers monitor student discipline. A supportive atmosphere exists for the staff.

Heathers 1972.   A feedback process for renewal is necessary for effective change programs.

Hellriegel and Slocum 1974.   Control standardizes performance and limits authority at various levels.

House 1973.   Effective management provides a path to worker goals.

Kanter 1982.   The flow of communication is horizontal in the most effective organizations.

Levine and Stark 1981.   Principals are supportive of teachers in effective schools.

Lieberman and Miller 1978.   Principals keep a complex web of interactions under control.

Likert 1967.   Quality of the control process influences organizational success.

Luthans and Kreitner 1975.   Goals and evaluation control behavior. Adult behavior in organizations is learned behavior.

Madden 1976.   Principals have management skills in successful schools.

McBer and Co. 1982.   High-performing principals demonstrate a sense of control over school practices, the ability to recognize patterns, to perceive objectively, and to analyze effectively. These principals show evidence of their commitment to quality through focused involvement in the change process.

McFarland 1974.   In the absence of quality control, individuals tend to stray from plans or orders.

McMahon 1972.   The amount of control operating in an organization is directly related to its effectiveness.

Michael 1981.   Feed-forward control systems allow for planning the future.

Miles 1980.   Principals engage in data-based monitoring and intervention in successful schools.

Morris 1981.   A principal's relationship with teachers is collegial in "more satisfying schools."

NASSP 1979.   Principals control and maintain activity within allowable limits; maintain dynamic equilibrium through goal focus, orderly change, adaptability, and innovativeness. Control regulates the process of growing.

Peters and Waterman 1982.   An excellent company acts and then learns from what it has done; it learns from its mistakes. It experiments, makes mistakes, finds unanticipated success, and permits new strategic direction to emerge. The adaptive corporation learns how to kill off dumb mutations and invest heavily in ones that work. Management's most significant output is getting others to shift attention to desirable directions.

Rowe 1981.   Monitoring of work productivity improves effectiveness.

Sergiovanni and Carver 1973.   Reinforcement, responsibility, and recognition are the greatest work motivators.

Skinner 1980.   Teachers employ a system of positive reinforcement; they praise accomplishments, and reinforce achievements.

Competency 8

Instructional Management

Anderson 1973.   Intervention into the instructional process is essential to alter outdated practices.

Austin 1979.   Principals participate in the instructional program and in teaching. A system of instructional adaptability and consistency exists in effective schools.

Bloom 1976.   95 percent of all students can master what the school expects if schooling conditions are favorable.

Bragg and Andrews 1973.   Students in cooperative learning groups gain in liking group mates, in helping behaviors, and in liking the experience.

Brookover and Lezotte 1979.   There is an assumption that all can master reading and math goals in effective schools. The principal is the instructional leader.

California DPE 1980.   Reading for required mastery is managed by the principal.

Coulson 1977.   Principals communicate viewpoints about instruction to teachers, and participate in decisions about instructional planning, material selection, and evaluation.

Edmonds 1979.   A climate of high expectations for all students exists in effective schools.

Glenn 1981.   Principals and teachers have high expectations for all students in successful schools.

Klausmeier 1982.   Teachers set subject area goals together, develop plans, and carry out plans to achieve goals.

Levine and Stark 1981.   Coordination of curriculum, instruction, and testing exist in effective schools.

Little 1981.   Teachers engage in frequent concrete talk about teaching practice.

Lortie 1975.   Implementing new teaching skills and behaviors depends significantly on teachers working together to exchange and support.

Lysakowski and Walberg 1982.   Instructional cues, participation, reinforcement, and corrective/feedback produce effects that place systemically instructed groups at over the 80th learning percentile.

Madden 1976.   The principal in effective schools has instructional skills. Teachers apply learning principles.

Marcus et al. 1976.   Administrators in effective schools communicate a point of view concerning teaching practice.

NASSP 1979.   Effective secondary schools address new technologies, methodologies, and courses rising from research and social demands.

Trisman 1976.   There exists a focus on the basics, with small group instruction in successful schools.

Vanezky and Winfield 1979.   Strong buildingwide curricular leadership, instructional adaptability and consistency, along with efficient implementation of the instructional programs, exist in effective schools.

Weber 1971.   Individualization in reading is managed by the principal in successful schools.

Competency 9

Resource Development

Armor et al., 1976.   High levels of parent-school contact exist in effective schools.

Austin 1979.   A satisfactory parent–teacher relationship exists in effective schools.

Barsky 1975.   Principals in effective schools learn how to cut through red tape, generate alternative funds, and learn of resources before other colleagues.

Bloom 1976.   Parental involvement in language and social science activities are the most effective types of parental involvement in learning.

Brookover and Lezotte 1979.   Less overall parent involvement exists in effective schools with higher levels of parent-initiated involvement.

Corwin 1973.   Community-school support is correlated positively with innovativeness.

Crosset 1972.   Parents observe reading groups and use additional materials at home. Training parents in sets of behaviors increases English scores.

Drucker 1954.   Making a productive enterprise out of human and material resources is the most important management function in an organization.

Duke, Cohen, and Herman 1981.   Principals are able to secure adequate resources even though confronted by fiscal stress.

Edmonds 1979.   Resources are tied to school goals in effective schools.

Edmonds and Frederikson 1978.   Family background neither causes nor precludes mastery.

Fantini 1979.   Involvement of parents as tutors and aides is a leverage for new program success.

Glenn 1981.   Principals provide planning resources and people resources in effective schools.

Goodson and Hess 1975.   Parents as teachers produce gains in student IQ in successful schools.

Gordon 1979.   Parent impact models are positive when planned, structured, have an educational focus, and include working at home on learning tasks with children.

Gross et al. 1974.   Program development by community/staff is characteristic of effective schools.

Hoban 1982.   Citizen involvement in long-range planning creates more trust and a healthier attitude toward schools.

Hobson 1976.   Direct parent involvement in a child's program raises achievement norms.

Ingram 1979.   Participatory parent and school problem solving influences achievement. Home–school communication is the largest variable in effective school–community relations.

Joyce 1978.   Parent councils effectively translate local needs. Participation reduces alienation.

Kanter 1982.   Rewards for performance include increased budget for projects.

Lipham and Fruth 1976.   Increased interaction and involvement of home-school relationships occurs in successful schools.

Loughheed et al. 1979.   Team building improves problem-solving capacity for parent councils, and fosters productivity.

Love 1977.   Adopt-a-school program(s) raise achievement levels. Parents and students are trained to turn off home TV sets and monitor homework in effective home–school programs.

Madden 1976.   Volunteers in math are used in effective schools. District support services are used and there is access to materials outside the classroom in effective schools.

Miles 1980.   Attention to political stabilization in the community is a primary task in planning/implementing new programs.

NASSP 1979.   Effective secondary schools provide progress reports to the public.

Niedermayer 1979.   Parents are trained for teaching reading to their children.

Reagan 1977.   Adopt-a-school programs raise achievement norms (industry and local school).

Vallina 1978.   Effective schools have an awareness of community issues due to school–community communications systems.

Weber 1971.   The principal helps organize and distribute resources in successful schools.

Competency 10

Assessing Productivity

School-Level Evaluation

Brookover and Lezotte 1979.   There is recognition of student success and achievement of basic objectives in effective schools. Achievement is tied to the school's social system. Principals assume responsibility for the development of an accountability model.

Edmonds 1982.   Changes in student achievement, organizational design, and teacher and administrator behavior are all measures of school improvement.

Kanter 1982.   Change is constant and viewed as normal in the most "entre-preneurial" companies.

Kast and Rosenzweig 1974.   Negative and positive feedback enable an organization to adjust to conditions.

Likert 1967.   A capacity to use data and experiences to improve operations influences organizational success.

Mink et al. 1979.   The school staff uses data-based feedback for problem solving that is internal and external to school.

Work Group Evaluation

Anderson 1979.   Effective teams evaluate both short- and long-range results.

Cook 1982.   75 percent of quality circle recommendations presented to the management of American industrial firms have been used.

Kanter 1982.   Managers share rewards and recognition with subordinates in effective organizations.

Ouchi 1981.   A culture of group cohesiveness results from productive work relationships.

Peters and Waterman 1982.   Peer reviews exist in excellent companies, where groups report their progress, and are critiqued and recognized by peers from other groups. Peer reviews replace individual performance evaluations.

Exemplary performance in excellent companies is recognized daily, weekly, monthly, and annually. Celebration and ceremony permeate the work culture as desired achievements are applauded.

Rowe 1981.   Work groups measured against group productivity and objectives for the organization are characteristic of effective organizations.

Teacher Evaluation

Brookover and Lezotte 1979.   High morale among staffs is characteristic of effective schools.

Coulson 1977.   Review of teacher performance is conducted in successful schools.

Duffy 1980.   High morale is characteristic of effective schools.

Edmonds 1981.   High morale is characteristic of effective schools.

Kanter 1982.   Abundant rewards, worker visibility, and opportunity to do more challenging work in the future influence performance.

Abundant rewards exist in the most innovative companies and include visibility, opportunity for more challenging work, and bigger budgets for projects.

Lawler 1971.   Incentive systems are more satisfying than wages.

Martin 1975.   Teachers trained in systematic observation techniques believe that evaluation of themselves is more helpful than do teachers untrained in observation.

McGregor 1960.   Performance appraisal can influence goal aspirations through integration into the organization's goal structure.

Morris 1981.   Principals are a key factor in teacher satisfaction in high-achieving schools.

Murnane 1975.   The higher principals' ratings of teachers, the higher is student achievement.

Odiorne 1979.   Appraisal based on standards of performance and goals carries a value for results.

Porter and Lawler 1968.   Performance that leads to rewards will lead to satisfaction to the extent that the reward is valued; intrinsic rewards are more directly involved in the performance-satisfaction relationship.

Vallina 1978.   There is greater involvement of principals in instructional assessment in higher achieving schools.

Student Evaluation

Araki 1982.   Student achievement increases with teacher satisfaction and the goal emphasis of the principal.

Armor et al. 1976.   Students who are evaluated in reading achievement tend to achieve more than other students.

Brookover and Lezotte 1979.   Academic self-concept and self-reliance are high among students in effective schools.

Clauset and Gaynor 1982.   No sustained improvement can occur unless student progress is monitored and assessed longitudinally. Feedback is useful for planning only if there are standards for assessment.

DeGuire 1980.   Frequent assessment of student progress exists in effective schools.

Duke, Cohen, and Herman 1981.   Students achieve better under women principals.

Edmonds 1982.   Measures of student achievement as a basis for program evaluation are used in effective schools.

Gigleotti and Brookover 1975.   Principals' expectations for student performance are higher in achieving schools.

Glenn 1981.   Students who are assessed in reading and math achievement show achievement gains.

Trisman 1976.   Students assessed in reading achievement show achievement gains.

APPENDIX B
Competency Statements and Subset Skills

I. Organizational Planning Cluster

1. School-Wide Goal Setting

COMPETENCY 1: *Establish annual school improvement goals through administrative assessment and selection and also through total staff collaborative decision making.*

Emphasis is given to the involvement of all faculty members in a process of establishing annual school improvement priorities. Many factors influence goal decisions, such as state mandates, district requirements, available resources, staff interests, and perceived needs. The outcome of the collaborative goal-setting process is a set of school improvement priorities.

Competency Subsets
1. The principal identifies school improvement targets each year.
2. The entire staff is involved in identifying school improvement targets.
3. Data about school productivity are gathered and analyzed by the staff in identifying school improvement goals.
4. The staff is well informed about how school goals are determined.
5. Staff members feel free to express concerns about school problems.
6. Feedback from parents influences goal decisions.
7. Parents and students participate in selecting school improvement goals.
8. Collaborative decision making about school goals leads to active participation in school improvement efforts.
9. The staff is clear about the relationship between school goals and their work activity.
10. School improvement goals are subdivided into tasks.

2. Work Group Performance

COMPETENCY 2: *Designate school work groups, both teaching teams or departments and task forces, to which are assigned school goal objectives and action-planning responsibilities.*

School goals are dispersed by the school's leadership council to appropriate teaching teams and task forces for planning and action. Each work group analyzes the ways in which it can best work toward the attainment of goal(s), and subsequently defines work objectives, tasks, responsibilities, resources, and time lines.

Competency Subsets

1. A leadership team identifies work groups (teaching teams and task forces) necessary for accomplishing school goals.
2. Staff members are assigned to teaching teams or departments to work cooperatively.
3. The expected results of work groups and task forces are clearly defined.
4. Staff members work in groups for attaining school goals.
5. For each work group there is a designated leader with well-defined responsibilities.
6. Work group leaders receive training and coaching in leadership skills.
7. Work group members assume responsibility for specific tasks.
8. Work group plans include references to objectives (goals), a time line, resources, and group responsibilities.
9. Work group plans are approved or disapproved by the principal.
10. A master plan of goal-related activity is developed for the school.

3. *Individual Staff Performance*

COMPETENCY 3: *Establish and operationalize a teacher performance system that includes performance standards, individual goal setting and action-planning procedures, performance monitoring, due process procedures, and evaluation.*

Each faculty member develops annual performance goals and plans that reflect school priorities, various teaching and work group responsibilities, and personal interests.

Competency Subsets

1. A set of performance standards guides teacher performance.
2. Teaching expectations correlate with the characteristics of effective teaching (as identified by research).
3. Teachers set annual performance goals.
4. Individual teacher goals link closely with school goals and their work group responsibilities.
5. Individual teacher goals emphasize intended contributions to the school's development.
6. Individual staff members develop a plan for accomplishing their goals.
7. Teachers are supervised regularly to assist them in achieving their goals.

8. Teachers submit plans for, and reports of, their accomplishments.
9. Teacher performance is monitored periodically to ensure appropriate behavior.
10. Teacher performance is evaluated in relation to goals.

II. Staff Management Cluster

4. Individual Skill Development

COMPETENCY 4: *Develop and operationalize a school program for staff development that emphasizes new knowledge and skills that are necessary for successful attainment of school improvement goals (school, team, individual).*

Given the rapid growth through research in knowledge about instruction, staff members need to update their own knowledge and skills continually. The focus of school-based staff development is on staff growth as it relates to school priorities and also to individual performance goals. Programs are planned to reflect school growth priorities and to foster the adult learning process.

Competency Subsets
1. The school's staff development program grows out of school improvement goals.
2. Teachers are involved in developing the staff development program.
3. Staff development plans grow out of individual staff performance plans as well as work group action plans.
4. Staff development programs reflect research on effective teaching and schooling.
5. Supervisory activities provide teachers with feedback on their performance.
6. Staff members frequently develop new instructional materials.
7. Staff groups organize themselves around work goals.
8. In-service programs address the cognitive, affective, and behavioral dimensions of adult learning.
9. The staff development program facilitates adult learning.
10. Staff development programs provide goal-related information and opportunities to build new skills.

5. Clinical Supervision

COMPETENCY 5: *Develop and operationalize a peer and supervisory clinical supervision program for all teachers and teams, where performance feedback and correctives are provided monthly (weekly).*

Teachers can improve their teaching effectiveness through feedback and reinforcement from skilled observers. Emphasis is given to skill development in observation cycle activity (contracting, observing, data collecting and analyzing, and feedback conferencing). It is assumed that clinical supervision will provide a coaching mechanism to enable teachers better to attain their instructional goals.

Competency Subsets
1. The purpose of supervision is to develop more effective teaching skills.
2. Teachers receive regular feedback on their teaching performance.
3. The supervision of teaching is related to annual work goals.
4. Use is made of a teacher observation cycle that includes a preobservation conference, observation, data collection, analysis, and a feedback conference.
5. Data collected during classroom observation are based on goals for the supervisory session.
6. Supervision helps to bridge the gap between actual teaching and the characteristics of effective teaching (as reported in research).
7. The focus of a classroom observation tends to relate to lesson objectives and outcomes.
8. Supervision focuses on the results of planned activities, rather than activity itself.
9. Teachers regularly observe and assist each other in some systematic manner.
10. Following each supervisory session, teachers understand their success and also areas for improvement.

6. *Work Group Development*

COMPETENCY 6: *Establish a healthy work climate and develop work group skills in action planning, creative and productive group communications, problem solving, and decision making.*

The working relationships among and within groups of staff members, students, parents, and administrators determine the work climate of a school. The emphasis in this competency is to become skillful in helping work groups to develop skills in communications, planning, and decision making.

Competency Subsets
1. Staff and parent work groups plan strategies for attaining their task objectives.
2. In staff work groups, all members typically are expected to participate in tasks.

3. All members share their concerns about, and their ideas for, improving group productivity.
4. Staff members work together in many formal and informal ways.
5. Staff members critique each others' ideas and actions.
6. Staff members provide feedback and correctives to each other.
7. Leadership decisions include staff concerns and recommendations.
8. Principals and teachers exchange concerns and recommendations continuously.
9. Staff work groups consider novel strategies for improving their work.
10. A high degree of trust exists among teachers, principals, parents, and students.

7. *Quality Control*

COMPETENCY 7: *Establish and operationalize a quality control system for work groups and for teachers that includes goal-based observations, conferencing, and periodic progress reports.*

To ensure that goals are attained, the performance of work groups and individuals must be monitored and supervised. The emphasis in quality control management is on those processes that motivate performance as well as those that provide leaders with sufficient data for planning assistance and/or intervention actions.

Competency Subsets
1. Staff work groups report periodically on the results of their activity and on future plans to the principal.
2. Individual teachers report periodically on the results of their activity and on future plans (to the team leader or the principal).
3. Group leaders observe and review the performance of each member.
4. The principal reviews and critiques the performance of work groups.
5. Group members periodically review and critique each others' performance.
6. The behavior patterns of groups are shaped in part by the feedback, correctives, and reinforcement they receive.
7. Monitoring individuals and groups reinforces and/or corrects behavior patterns.
8. School goals guide the monitoring of individual and group performance.

9. Changes in work activity are the result of group decision making.
10. Group reflection on activity guides modifications in plans.

III. Program Management Cluster

8. *Instructional Program*

COMPETENCY 8: *Establish and operationalize an instructional program that reflects up-to-date research on teaching and learning and that guides teaching improvement efforts.*

The presence of a design for managing the instructional program influences the norms of achievement. Attention should be given to six basic areas of instruction that contribute to the success of the program: curriculum objective selection; diagnosis; program planning; classroom management; teaching; and learning processes.

Competency Subsets
1. Instructional programming is guided by the school's curriculum objectives.
2. Instructional programs are planned around the diagnosed readiness of learners.
3. Instructional programs are planned cooperatively by teachers.
4. Classroom management decisions focus on program goals, materials, time, student movement, teaching logistics, and recordkeeping.
5. Students know what is expected of them in classrooms.
6. Teachers reinforce desired learning behaviors in pupils.
7. Students are provided with adequate time for learning.
8. Students work frequently in cooperative learning groups.
9. Teachers provide students with feedback and correctives to facilitate mastery.
10. Students participate in planning for their own learning experiences.

9. *Resource Development*

COMPETENCY 9: *Facilitate staff productivity in work groups and provide necessary resources for making the school an increasingly productive unit.*

Resources are selected for the purpose of enhancing the productivity of a school's goal-seeking efforts. Attention should be given to the responsibilities of managing work groups, as a resource, and providing external resources in support of staff work.

Competency Subsets
1. Work groups are assisted by the principal.
2. Resources are identified and utilized that will facilitate work group productivity.
3. School leadership coordinates the identification and utilization of various human resources.
4. Resources are identified for assisting work activity.
5. Students are used as resources in school improvement efforts.
6. Resources from community members, businesses, and industries are identified and utilized to facilitate school productivity efforts.
7. The school budget is designed around school goals.
8. Work groups share resources with other groups.
9. School leadership provides nonmonetary resources to work groups and individuals.
10. The school leadership staff is a resource to work groups.

IV. Assessing School Productivity Cluster

10. Assessing Achievement

COMPETENCY 10: *Establish and operationalize a set of school evaluation procedures to assess student achievement gains, teaching team and task force productivity, individual teacher performance, and total school productivity.*

Evaluating progress, within a planning and developing context, involves the measure of results of all performance areas: evaluating teacher performance (based on goals, observation and additional data, and results); and school performance (based on measures of school climate and student achievement). Evaluating activities focus on school/team/individual goals, on standards of performance, and on development activities. The outcomes of evaluation provide a foundation for planning the next year's school improvement plans, development, and evaluation activities.

Competency Subsets
1. School goals provide the basic framework for school evaluation procedures.
2. Individual staff members are evaluated according to results in relation to performance goals.
3. The evaluation process identifies the results of performance.
4. Individual staff members evaluate themselves in relation to their performance goals.
5. Work groups conduct a formal self-evaluation.
6. Evaluation is based upon performance observations as well as other data.

7. Student evaluation is based on measures of achievement.
8. Evaluation of school productivity involves assessment of a cluster of outcome measures: school improvement goals; team and teacher work goals; and student achievement.
9. Leadership evaluation by the staff is based on the extent to which the school leadership facilitates staff productivity.
10. School climate is assessed in relation to characteristics that are conducive to staff productivity.

4

The Goal Subsystem: Concepts

The educational mission of schools in American society, though often expressed in terms that are very general and even vague, changes very little from decade to decade. Each generation hopes that schooling will provide its young with the information, the skills, the values, and attitudes that will help to preserve and to improve the nation while equipping each individual boy and girl to lead a productive and satisfying adult life. Increasingly society has also charged the school system with other (than educational) missions, such as providing transportation, food service, medical and psychological assistance, recreation outlets, public athletic and musical entertainments, and many other services that distract the professional staff, cut into available resources, and divert energies from the basic educational mission. In addition, for reasons totally beyond the scope or control of schools some of society's most serious problems (such as urban decay, inequitable distribution of wealth, increases in criminal behavior, drug addiction and alcoholism, radical changes in family life, and economic instability) invade the schools in direct as well as indirect ways and make it more difficult for teachers to pursue their basic work.

Even in the absence of these counterforces, maintaining high-quality educational programs is difficult and challenging work. As knowledge (subject matter) grows exponentially, as individual differences among children become more vivid, as technology introduces new options and challenges, and as research yields more and more information about human development and learning, every educator finds it both necessary and possible to make perennial changes in what is taught, how it is taught, and under what surrounding conditions it will be taught. No school, however glorious its past or lustrous its reputation, remains immune to this obligation or untouched by various forms of obsolescence. *Every* school, as we perceive it, must accept the need for con-

106

tinuous self-improvement, and develop means for ensuring that growth and improvement will occur. This textbook, we earnestly hope, provides guidelines for such activity.

To pursue the goal of continuous school improvement requires intelligent and candid assessment of existing strengths and weaknesses, re-examination of the fundamental values and aspirations that direct the school enterprise, definition of the highest priority improvements that are needed, and the charting of a course for action. In this chapter, and the next, our plan is to consider the role that is played by the goal subsystem in connection with such pursuit.

In his analysis of practices that seem to be succeeding within American culture today, Naisbitt (1982) observes that successful companies are driven by a longer range strategic vision that precedes and influences annual strategic planning (pp. 94–95). In the course of his discussion are cited several companies that "reconceptualized the business they are in." Two examples are the Singer Company, which moved away from the declining market for sewing machines and became an aerospace company, and Sears, Roebuck and Company, which moved into consumer financial services as its retailing effort reached a plateau. These and other examples confirm Naisbitt's argument that reconceptualization must be a constant process within the institution:

> . . . the hard work of colleagues rigorously questioning every aspect of an institution's purpose—and the questioning of the purpose itself. The purpose must be right, and it must be a shared vision, a strategic vision.
>
> (p. 94)

The specific purposes of this and the succeeding chapter are (1) to establish a conceptual base and a rationale for school goals, and (2) to present a methodology for defining school improvement goals collaboratively. We will begin by discussing the function of goals for the school's growth process. Next, the principal's role as value shaper is explored as it relates to identifying specific school improvement goals. The concept of staff collaboration in defining school goals is further explored as it relates to the initial stages of the school improvement process. The ensuing chapter is devoted to the Delphi Dialogue Technique, a specific methodology for eliciting concensus on a strategic vision and on growth targets for a year at a time.

Rationale for a Goal Orientation to School Development

During the past 20 years school districts have sought to define goals and develop five-year improvement plans in order to meet state requirements, as well as to produce better schooling results. Only recently schools are coming to perceive that redefining goals in itself can be a useful force in moving schooling practices out of yesteryear and into tomorrow. Having merely complied with state mandates for improvement plans for years, many schools now are sensing the power that is present within a goal orientation to school improvement.

To develop a rationale we shall discuss various forces without and within school organizations and their influence on what schools practice and produce. First, we examine briefly several forces that influence the direction of organizations throughout American society. The goal focus of organizations has shifted considerably in recent years to become increasingly responsive to society. Secondly, the principal's function as the school's value shaper provides a unique perspective on the school's work culture and its products.

Next we discuss the often-elusive practice of identifying school goals and how they are and can be defined collectively. Assessing the school's growth needs is a crucial diagnostic dimension of goal setting, although the assessment task need require only a minimal amount of staff energy when compared to the planning task ahead. Before setting goals it may be important to understand the impact of selected goals on each part of the school subsystems, as well as the impact on total school productivity. The discussion of these five related variables and their impact on the school's development plan provides a foundation for actual planning methodology, discussed in the next chapter.

A Social Perspective

A social perspective is necessary to guide the pace and direction of planning practices in schools. Very clear signals of possible disaster await public schooling unless administrators are able to read the signals and to transform outdated practices and results quickly (Goodlad 1984). Education Secretary Terrel Bell's report, *A Nation at Risk,* claimed that the basic purpose of schooling has been lost and along with it the high expectations and discipline needed to attain those purposes. His commission noted several indicators of the risk of continuing our educational system as it now exists. For example, American students, in recent international comparisons of achievements, never rated first or second, and often rated last among industrialized nations. Further, about 23 million American adults are addressed as functional illiterates. The average achievement of high school students on most standardized tests is now lower than 26 years ago. SAT scores have shown a steady decline from 1963 to 1980. To provide a social context for assessing the decline, the report went on to mention that business, industry, and the military spend millions of dollars annually in remedial training programs in the basic skills for their workers.

Many schools in all states have made many major attempts at renovation in recent years. Those efforts of renovation need to continue and to become increasingly more effective in transforming the school as a workplace for both staff and students.

Excellent companies in our society are driven by a few key values, in which workers are given considerable space to take initiatives in support of those values (Peters and Waterman 1982, 72). The notion of "a few key values" provides a clue for educators. A former superintendent in Hightstown, New Jersey, John Hunt, successfully launched a 10-year district improvement campaign by consistently drawing attention to his banner: "Our job is to cause learning to occur."

As was noted earlier, schools in recent years have provided many peripheral services for their communities; considerable energies have gone into making those programs work. It is time to retreat and to define or affirm the central purpose of schooling: for example, to prepare youth for productive roles in society. Such a purpose requires constant attention to the knowledge, skills, and experiences necessary to cause this specific kind of learning to occur. We must recognize the business of schools and then devote our full energies toward making schools increasingly productive toward that end for society.

Newly defined goals can be a first step in a new direction, but in themselves are not sufficient. What is required is "transformational" leadership; that is, the principal and leadership team must become the value shapers, the exemplars and the makers of meaning for the staff (Peters and Waterman 1982, 82–85). Transforming leadership occurs when key persons engage with each other to operate on higher levels of motivation. Individual interests become fused as power bases (administration and teaching) become mutually supportive of a common purpose.

The inbuilding of purpose in organizational life involves transforming individuals and groups from neutral, technical units, into participants who have a particular dedication. The principal as the transformational leader is the expert in the promotion and protection of core values.

As we have noted, several industries have made significant alterations in their purpose when, sensing their potential demise, they looked around and asked the question, "What business ought we to be in?" The railroad industry, however, is a different story. Not long ago Pennsylvania Railroad was considered the best managed institution in our country. In addition, railroading was the largest industry in the U.S. economy. Because the railroad people failed to redefine their purpose as a transportation business that moves goods by air, truck, and ship, as well as by rail, we have witnessed the actual demise of the railroad industry (Naisbitt 1983, 85–86). Society needed the kind of transportation options that the railroad industry was not prepared to provide.

It is critical that school staffs also address the basic question, "What business ought we to be in for society today?" After a central value has been established, a plan must be developed for how the staff will focus on those few central values in every activity. Moreover, the staff must define a few measurable goals for improving school productivity in that direction each year. Long- and short-range development plans provide a basis for creating a dynamic school organization. After plans are made and put into operation there must be continuous attention to purpose through feedback mechanisms that propel a school toward excellence.

The first consideration in planning for school development is to determine who makes which goal decisions. In the past, school boards and central administration typically have defined goals, incorporating feedback from parents, teachers, and principals. In the future, full-fledged staff participation in actual school goal decisions will occur to a greater extent. Naisbitt (1983, 159–188) observed that one of the ten main trends in our society is the shift from representative decision making to participatory decision making. A shift in decision-making patterns translates on the job front into a rejection of old-fashioned hierarchical structures, in favor of an approach represented in quality circles and participatory management. Decision making, as we noted in the previous chapter, reflects the participatory approach. Teachers and principals together define specific improvement goals in successful schools, and organize work collaboratively toward selected ends.

The function of goals for organizational growth is to enable workers to emerge from the random activity trap and to work productively toward selected purposes. Every organizational goal that is selected also represents many others that are rejected. Goals are far more than words; they are road maps to new destinations. They represent selections from among numerous possibilities concerning how workers will be productive. Goals function to provide clarity for performance and to enable a staff continuously to reorganize to accomplish organizational tasks.

If there ever was a time to tap human resources in schools it is now. The knowledge and experience of every staff member are needed to serve as a collective catalyst for transformation if schools are to become productive enterprises for society. Just as doctors and lawyers are prevented from performing outdated practices, so must educators be. Teachers must be made aware of what researchers have found that works in schools, and then principals must insist that today's knowledge base become the only legitimate base for defining goals, tasks, and work patterns.

Table 4.1 outlines the nature of goals in productive schools. Values, goals, and decision making in the past were based largely on vague traditions about society and about the general function of schools. Given increasing clarity about schooling for an information age, schools will be able to define more clearly the productive outcomes anticipated from staff efforts.

TABLE 4.1. The Goal Subsystem

	Maintenance Paradigm	Production Paradigm
Pervasive values	Stability, efficiency, predictability, security, vagueness, tradition	Responsiveness, growth, collaboration, problem solving, uncertainty, risk taking
Goal sources	Administration/school board/ state and federal agencies	All school community plus external forces
Goal focus	Global/vague ideals, traditional practices	Measurable, definable/ priorities and objectives
Goal decisions	Central administration	The entire school community; the principal
Function of goals	Provide general guidelines	Provide specific staff performance parameters

The Principal's Role As Value Shaper

The focus on a few key values lets everyone know what is most important. A few key values, driven by a few goals and work objectives, enable a staff to keep focused in their activity and to become increasingly productive. Naisbitt (1982, 65) reports that when Rene McPherson took over Dana Corporation, he threw out 22½ inches of policy manuals and replaced them with a one-page statement of philosophy focusing on productive people. Later, he was nearly fired when he told his workers what their sales and profits were and how they stacked up against other plants. However, this very act of comparison against an external norm became the practice that led to Dana's success. A few key values about productive people, along with several goals and objectives, were combined with results-oriented feedback to workers.

What does society value about learning, instruction, school organization, and management? What is valued about schools in general? Moreover, what do educators value about these same dimensions of schooling? What is the nature of an individual and an organization's value system as it relates to school growth and to collective productivity? Rokeach (1973) defines a value as an enduring belief that a specific mode of conduct is preferable over another.

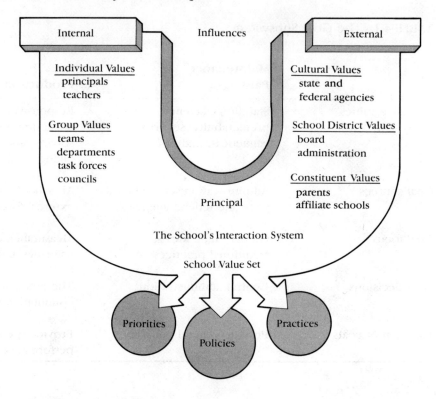

Figure 4.1. The School Value Set

School work norms build on individual value sets and form a standard for performance, solutions, choices, and decisions. One familiar example is the prevailing, yet regrettable, preference for the self-contained classroom over team teaching in a flexible larger space. Kast and Rosenzweig (1974, 155–156) identify five levels of values that must be considered: values held by the individual; values held by small, informal, and formal groups; those (composite) values that are held by the organization; values held by constituent groups of the task environment; and cultural values held by the total society.

Figure 4.1 illustrates the internal and external value sets of a school and the interaction system that must be organized to establish consensus about goals and practices.

In schools, individual values that affect the personal/professional behavior of teachers include attitudes toward reward or punishment, attitudes toward various types and varieties of children, and convictions about appropriate social behaviors. Some teachers, for example, feel that discipline is best achieved by praising and endorsing appropriate behavior, and ignoring negative behavior. Others believe that negative behavior should be punished; among these, there are some who condone corporal punishment. As members of groups, such as an elementary school staff or a junior-high departmental unit, teachers also generate and agree upon group values. It is possible, with respect to discipline, that such a group of teachers might reach consensus on the use or the avoidance of physical punishment. Their value decision might or might not be consistent with the values (and therefore the policies) of the larger organization, which is the school or the school district. These values are heavily influenced by attitudes that prevail among the constituent group that is the parents, or within the larger society.

There are few universal values, except of the most general sort. In New Jersey, for example, the state can revoke the professional license of any teacher who punishes a student in any physical manner. By contrast, in other parts of the country (for example, Texas) paddling as a form of punishment is regularly practiced in some schools with the full support of parents and community members, teachers, and even the students. Some parents, in fact, become disturbed when school officials refrain from physical punishment, their strong conviction being that sparing the rod spoils the child. We (the authors) much prefer the New Jersey policy and the research-based value system that undergirds it. We have also experienced uncomfortable value conflicts as we have confronted this issue with some of our Texas friends. Sometimes the research evidence concerning the consequences of positive and negative reinforcements, once understood by a school staff, will help to resolve such conflicts.

For us an even more basic value conflict can arise with respect to educational expectations. Some teachers are guided by biases, prejudices, misconceptions, and misinformation about the achievement potential of certain types of children. They find it very difficult to work in situations where, as they perceive it, few of the children have a reasonable chance of significant success. The literature of self-fulfilling prophecies in education is now familiar enough, so that the disastrous consequences of negative predictions are well known. A related, though less well-publicized research conclusion, as confirmed by Bloom (1976), is that only a very small percentage (5 percent at maximum) of children are literally unable to succeed in schools. Our frequent references to 95 percent, in parts of this text, are a constant reminder of the affirmable fact that 95 percent of children can be educational winners, under the right conditions. We yearn for the time when all teachers in all schools will embrace this view within their value system.

Value conflicts, when they arise, cannot easily be ignored. Sometimes differences can be reconciled or negotiated, with skillful leadership providing the energy, the information, or the mechanism that is needed. At other times, compromise and/or reconciliation may be impossible, at least for the moment. The movement in the 1960s that led to "free schools" and other kinds of alternative schools provides a case in point. Following unsuccessful attempts to incorporate their values into existing school value sets, many teachers and parents withdrew from public schools to form their own schools. Today, many of those once seemingly "radical notions" of learning (for example, active student involvement and peer learning) can be observed in many public schools, and value conflict is less likely to occur.

How can principals manage differing values sets when they conflict within their school community, especially when cultural diversity is becoming more prized? Similarly, how can a principal manage the diversity of values in a given school community and at the same time attempt to derive consensus regarding school improvement priorities, policies, and practices?

One principal developed a plan for shaping value conflicts within the community. Many parents wanted open space and team-taught instructional environments for their children; some wanted self-contained classrooms; and other program structures with varying characteristics were also suggested. A task force of parents was appointed by the principal to resolve the issue of learning environments. They were directed to propose a plan for multiple learning environments that could be supported by research and also by parent preferences. The task force proceeded with its charge and subsequently proposed that the school be organized into six different learning environments. Subsequently, the six environments were developed by the staff, with student placement resulting from staff and parent negotiation. The result of this strategy to address value diversity was that after six months of operation, when given the opportunity to change their placement, only a handful of the 600 students and their parents requested a change.

This story demonstrates how a principal can function as a value shaper and resolve school community conflict. Research findings about effective learning environments provided a standard for parent involvement in resolving community conflict about its school. Williams (1974) found startling evidence from his study of eight California schools that supports the outcome of the preceding story: the degree of value diversity within a school community has little to do with a school's success. The difference between successful and unsuccessful schools has more to do with the ways in which value diversity is incorporated into the school's planning, action, and reflection processes in the form of problem-solving activities. Engineering dialogue around value issues is critical to the school's success for the community, parents, students, and staff.

Through a valuing process, the school community can clarify its purposes for each year and provide an order for its activities. Influences and pressures need to be synthesized and prioritized by the staff. The productivity paradigm provides a context within which a staff can analyze pressures and make recommendations for annual school priorities.

Complex school environments can be managed and controlled as they increase their own capacity for responding to changing schooling conditions. The relationship between existing arrangements and emerging forces for change must be identified and analyzed almost daily so that schools can respond effectively. With each new set of pressures, whether internal or external, a decision must be made as to how best to realign priorities. Decisions about "how best to respond" to pressures belong to the entire school family, which has a sense of owning the problem. The entire group, too, examines the new pressures and defines the relative importance of each to the process already in motion.

External forces are growing more powerful in their influence on schools. Complexity is not a disease to cure, but rather a phenomenon to address, manage, and control. Examples of external forces that prompt alterations in school practice follow.

1. Federal legislation and guidelines (for example, P.L. 94–142: the school must provide personalized programs for all special students within the regular education classroom)
2. State legislation and guidelines (for example, many states have taken a strong stand on meeting the needs of bilingual, handicapped students, or gifted and talented students)
3. Community culture (for example, a continuum of values regarding language ranges from "English is the only American language and that's all that should be taught in our schools" to, "We must provide appropriate learning experiences (multilanguages) so that all children will succeed in school")
4. School district goals (for example, "A meaningful educational plan will be developed for each child, with emphasis given to the needs of special children")
5. Parental values (for example, many parents believe that if schools told children what to do, as they used to, students wouldn't have the learning problems they have today. Other parents may value that their children need to learn how to take personal responsibility and participate in making decisions about their own learning program)

Schools have a wide range of response choices, which directly influence their capacity for growth. It must be recognized that pressures for change are the vital sources for the growth of any school. Public Law 94–142, for example, will probably go down in history as one of the most far reaching, beneficial, and necessary statutes in the history of American education. Initially it caused shock waves among educators, and prompted schools to scramble in their efforts to comply with the new regulations on providing individualized programs for children with special needs. Schools that continued to ignore their obligation to special students spent negative energies in scheming ways to subvert the process. Pressures to conform only to the spirit of making individual provisions for all students, however, only increased staff frustration. Consequently, schools that neglected their responsibilities became further frustrated as they continued to deprive students of learning opportunities that are their right. In the reverse, those schools that accepted the problem as a new opportunity for student success, proceeded with implementation and in doing so developed a stronger sense of control over their destiny, in working not only with special students but with *all* kinds of students.

Generating the School's Value Set

See again Figure 4.1, which suggests that the various internal and external value influences must be processed with the principal's assistance through the school's interaction system, after which policies, priorities, and practices can be determined. To illustrate, value questions surface as the staff increases in their collaborative efforts. Many begin to ask "What is legitimate for teachers to be spending time on during school hours?" Many teachers believe their job is to teach children all day. Value problems emerge, however, as teachers begin to develop new teaching and learning options that require more preparation and planning time than previously. Hence, values need to be examined in the light of changing conditions. Additional value questions about student grouping, time use, and teacher responsibilities will naturally change as teachers attempt to organize more effective learning experiences. Substantive changes in school practice either precede or follow a team's exploration of current values.

Rogers' (1973) work on the valuing process provides important insights for conceptualizing value issues in relation to the individual staff member. "The mature individual," Rogers observes, "is one who does not hold his values rigidly, but is continually changing." He further notes that "a healthy person continuously practices a valuing process (becoming)." He describes this process as "letting oneself down into the immediacy of an experience to sense, clarify and explore all its conflicting and/or complex meanings." This kind of continuous valuing is effective, Rogers indicates, to the extent that a person is *open* to exploring that experience.

If the school staff is to engage in a valuing process, thereby becoming continuously relevant, experiences must be provided regularly to enable individual students and staff to explore and reflect on what is happening. In doing so, the school community will learn to ask tough, embarrassing, potentially explosive questions in order to clarify, understand, and act more intelligently.

Principals also behave in response to their own convictions or beliefs about what ought to happen. England (1967) noted that the *values* of individual managers caused them to channel staff behavior in a given situation. Personal values and perceptual screening were found to influence the decisions that managers made in England's study in the following areas:

1. their perception of situations and problems
2. decisions and solutions
3. views of workers, groups, and their interaction
4. organizational and individual success
5. ethical behavior
6. acceptance or resistance to organizational pressures and goals

We perceive that the belief system and value orientation of the principal is the primary influence upon the direction of a school. Research studies have shown that most principals tend to be authoritarian and traditional in their orientation to life. Unless the question of a principal's values and beliefs is addressed, no matter what advice comes from the central office or the community, many schools will continue to reflect the past. Furthermore, principals are likely to be ineffective in improving instructional practices in their schools until values about their role are altered and they perceive (and come to believe) that their intervention, especially in the form of coaching instructional processes, can lead to improved instruction. The routine tasks of purchasing, budgeting, and inventorying will otherwise remain the top priorities for principals and therefore go undelegated. Further, if principals show little interest in discussing value questions with their staff, and even less interest in addressing diversity, then no federal, state, or local pressure is likely to be strong enough to alter local school practices. Individual school leadership values must be explored and subsequently applauded or challenged. Left unchallenged or bypassed, maintenance-oriented leadership will, in all likelihood, persist.

Defining Collective School Goals

The goals toward which each school staff directs its energies derive from many sources. The larger American society, through various state and federal mandates, provides a rather broad definition of what schools ought to be emphasizing in the educational program. Locally there are numerous forces that bear upon program goals, through the voices of community leaders, school board members, parents, and, of course, members of the professional staff. Individual perceptions, value systems, and aspirations combine to produce possible school goals, all of which are filtered through the school community interaction system before some of them become the school's goal set (see Figure 4.2).

Little is known about the actual approaches most schools use in defining

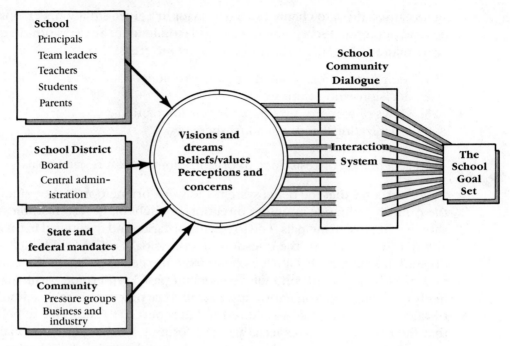

Figure 4.2. School Goal Variables

their goals. The following practices for establishing goals, however, can be observed in many schools throughout the country:

1. District goals, unilaterally determined, are dispersed to the building level for implementation purposes; or
2. District goals are assigned to principals in the form of job *targets*; or
3. Principals identify and announce building improvement priorities for a given year to the staff; or
4. Teaching teams and departments determine their own growth needs and improvement targets for the year; or
5. Individual teacher goals are established by the principal and teacher jointly; or
6. Goals are established by the entire school community to reflect schoolwide team/group and individual concerns for improvement.

Is there a best way to establish school goals? The school community already acts as a force for or against change, and we know that ownership of work goals correlates with commitment and responsibility in organizations. Due to the complex relationship between organizational goals and personal commitment, worker involvement in organizational goal setting is important and no truly "best" way can exist without it.

The overwhelming conclusion from research is that individuals gain a sense of belonging and usefulness when they participate in decisions influencing the direction of their organization. Likert (1967) stressed that subgroups within organizations tend to be motivated through worker involvement in decision making. The function of subgroups in the productive life of a school is necessary for two reasons. First, small groups provide individuals with many opportunities for meaningful involvement. Furthermore, subgroups provide legitimate and manageable avenues for total participation in the life of a school. The energy exchange and the commitment that emerges from working for shared purposes are forces that can transform a school.

We are persuaded that establishing school goals occurs best by organizing the staff into small groups. Individuals can explore, invent, and decide upon collective priorities together. Goals that emerge from groups result from a continuous bargaining–learning process, to which Kast and Rosenzweig refer as a "learning–adapting system" (1974, 158). Goals are not to be viewed as chains that inhibit action, but rather as desired states toward which a group progresses. In the process of defining school goals, new perceptions are formed of problems and possibilities. Moreover, as staff values shift and change, so also will goal definitions. The staff's learning–bargaining system results from a continuous conscious response to changing conditions and translating perceptions of next steps into goal definitions.

Schmuck et al. (1977, 158) observe that effective group bargaining includes the following four elements:

1. a continuing dialogue about individual needs, values, wants, and preferences, and about ways in which these can be realized within the organization;
2. skillful group interaction that draws out ideas and recommendations and attempts to integrate them with overall district goals;
3. the creation of formal/informal groupings to draw out emerging goal articulations, and match them with subsystems and organizational goals;
4. time taken during discussion of present and proposed subsystem or organizational goals, to ascertain their congruence with individual interests and values.

The role of the principal in establishing school priorities therefore is threefold: (1) to announce district goals to the staff and their implications for practice; (2) to define specific schooling targets for improvement that are based on

Figure 4.3. The School's Goal Set Cluster

a personal assessment of school productivity; and (3) to organize the staff in such a way that collective concerns can be translated efficiently into goals. Figure 4.3 illustrates the sources of the school's goal set.

Given complex influences on school goals, the staff must recognize external expectations, define their collective concerns for school improvement, and define how they will blend all pressures into a manageable set of improvement targets for the year. Response to district level, parent, and principal expectations will take the form of "how." Response to staff priorities is one of selecting the "what" as well as the "how." The "whats" and "hows" then become the school's goal set and action plan for a given year. Table 4.2 illustrates the level of staff decision making for establishing school goals in one hypothetical situation.

An analysis of various pressures for growth will point to ways of responding to each set of expectations. Several expectations might be reduced to two goals, for example

Goal 1   The school will design and implement a program to increase learning norms of gifted and talented, and bilingual students.

Goal 2   The school will develop a program to increase communications with, and the involvement of parents, students, and staff in the school's development process.

TABLE 4.2. Levels of School Goal Decisions (Samples)

Expectations (What)	Staff Decisions (How)
District Goal Each school will develop a program for gifted and talented	A task force will develop a plan for identifying and providing for the growth needs of creative, intellectual, and leadership gifted students in our school by February 1
Federal Guideline The needs of bilingual students shall be met within the school	A bilingual education plan shall be developed by November and implemented by January 30 to increase learning norms of the school's bilingual students
Parents' Survey Increase the involvement of parents in decisions about each child's program	To develop and implement a plan, at the team level, for parent involvement regarding each child's program and progress
Principal's Goal To design a program for greater parent and student involvement in school decisions	To develop a parent involvement program, and a student involvement program that includes their ideas and work contributions
Staff Goal To design a means for effective communications among and within teams in order to enhance total school productivity	A task force will develop three mechanisms of schoolwide communications Each department will develop a plan for increasing communications with parents, other teams, administration, department students, and colleagues

The staff, working collectively, makes decisions about *how* concerns will be resolved for the school. Decisions include programs and plans to be developed, designed, defined, identified, selected, and applied. School goals identify results that are specific, measurable, and attainable. Goal decisions do not include projects out of the realm of their control, such as, "build a new gymnasium." Recommendations for such improvements can be made, however. Staff goal decisions reflect areas in which they have a degree of control, and in projects where they are the major workers.

The focus is on factors that either directly or indirectly relate to instruction and learning. Legitimate areas for staff goal decisions include

school climate
school organization
staff performance/skills
learning programs
curriculum
instruction/instructional processes
supervision
leadership and management
staff development
parent involvement
accountability

Who Participates?

In every dimension of our society, we are witnessing the need for people to have a direct voice in decisions that influence their lives. In past years school administrators made most decisions about what teachers do; teachers planned how to carry out policy. As schools become more collaborative in work style, the administrator–teacher decision hierarchy will become increasingly flat. More work decisions will be made together, in a cooperative effort to improve practice.

Possible arrangements for schoolwide goal setting reflect either natural (existing) groups or cross-group teams that are organized specifically for the goal-setting activity. In the junior high and senior high schools in Anchorage, where we trained all principals and their teams in cooperative goal setting, various forms of grouping arose. Some schools used department structures; some organized new cross-department teams. Others elected to involve only interested teachers during the first year with the process. Consideration needs also to be given to the role of students and parents in goal setting. It may be that students and parents will be invited to become involved only after teachers feel successful with collaborative goal-setting practices.

Existing teaching teams, grade-level groups, departments, or other natural groups (for example, east-wing teachers) can be organized for goal-setting purposes. In all cases, the principle of "effective size" should be followed: five to eight persons per group. Listed here are several typical group options. Each alternative includes one member who serves as group representative to a central leadership group.

Option A: *The teaching/administrative staff*
Teams of teachers are the base unit for school goal setting, with the team leader representing the team on the school-level coordinating body (e.g., school council; administrative team).

Option B: *Teachers and parents*
The team is the base unit for school goal setting. All teachers plus representative parents form the work group. The team leader represents the work group to the school council.

Option C: *Teachers, students, and parents*
Representative team students and parents work together with teachers to define team goal recommendations. The team leader represents the team to the school council.

Option D: *Separate teaching teams, student teams, and parents*
Each role set (teachers, parents, and students) assesses its own role concerns as a working group. Following an assessment of school needs, group members (parents, students, and teachers) share their ideas, and a team recommendation for the school's goals is developed. Either the team leader or a representative teacher, student, and parent will represent the team on the school council.

Assessing the School's Growth Needs

Organizations that spend more than the necessary time and effort in a needs assessment process often run out of energy before the improvement activities begin. We have witnessed time and again that staff members, parents, and students often know exactly what next should be improved. Through a quick, structured dialogue process, those concerns and recommendations can be shared, classified, and translated into specific improvement goals.

We recommend that for "Year One" the staff select its school improvement targets without a lengthy needs assessment. In subsequent years, a more thorough approach utilizing (for example) school achievement scores, and parent and student surveys can add depth to the goal-setting process. The first time around, usually such thoroughness is unnecessary. Peters and Waterman

(1982, 149), for example, found that excellent companies can select quickly those growth targets that seem most obvious to everyone. Typically, the goals represent projects that require little difficulty in accomplishing, rather than others that might require more effort. "Quick hit" task forces often can be identified to tackle a problem or an innovation for organizations, a practice that eliminates paperwork and enables work to be done. One senses from Peters and Waterman that excellent companies look like exploding atoms, continuously identifying new tasks, completing tasks, and again identifying new tasks that surface.

The keys to success in goal setting and planning are clarifying problem areas and planning manageable resolutions. The forward motion of defining purpose and taking prompt action enables a staff to eliminate or ignore perceived restraints, and plunge into creative, energy-packed, productive activity.

The school's subsystems (organization, program, performance, and management) may provide useful lenses in identifying areas most in need of improvement. Listed here are possible goal areas within each subsystem.

Organization Subsystem

differentiation of roles (teaching team)
integration of roles (task forces)
leadership roles (leadership council)
team roles
power and influence patterns
student groupings

Performance Subsystem

role definitions
performance standards
individual needs
motivation
team productivity and cohesion
instructional behaviors
instructional management systems

Program Subsystem

student learning needs
curriculum objectives
curriculum development
curriculum implementation
program planning
staff learning needs
staff development program

Management Subsystem

organizational planning
staffing
problem solving
control
monitoring
evaluation

To illustrate the relationship of central values to goals and how these can be translated into improvement targets, let us consider what happened in 1980 in the East Oak Cliff subdistrict in the Dallas Independent School District where one of the authors served as a consultant. First, the administrative staff of the subdistrict set down the following statement of the mission (vision) to which the enterprise would be dedicated.

Mission/Vision

To raise the achievement norms in East Oak Cliff by providing a superior alternative to the quality of education traditionally offered to black and/or poor students across the nation.

Next, the administrative staff selected three particular aspects of the mission on which to concentrate.

Three Major Thrusts

Creating a school community climate that affirms education and the black, brown, red, and yellow experiences in tandem with the Euro-American experience;

Implementing a more effective delivery system to ensure mastery of basic academic and social skills;

Developing a community outreach and involvement program that maximizes the home–school partnership.

The staff then set down "priority foci" for the immediate biennium.

1980–82 Priority Foci

Goal 1: *Pluralism*

To develop corporate knowledge and a conceptual understanding of cultural pluralism, and to employ culturally pluralistic strategies for all programs in the governance of the schools and the subdistrict.

Goal 2: *Mastery learning*

To come to a conceptual understanding of mastery learning, and to employ mastery learning strategies in the governance of the schools.

Goal 3: *Governance*

To ensure effective implementation of the governance system (school and subdistrict) as a self-correcting and self-renewing process.

Goal 4: *Direct instruction*

To increase the quantity and quality of teacher/student interaction in order to facilitate more effective and efficient instruction/learning.

Goal 5: *Language development*

To develop a body of corporate knowledge, based on the nature and function of language, to be used in the development of instruction and curriculum program parameters.

With this master plan established, the central office then began to involve the principals in the district growth effort. They sought first to have themselves trained in the concepts and practices inherent in each goal statement. Pursuant to this bootstrapping staff-development effort, the central office staff and the principals sought to develop a common conceptualization for each goal area. Eventually they developed a series of "we believe" statements to which all were earnestly committed.

The process of defining collectively the substance and examining the implications of each goal area is extremely important. It helps to clarify underlying values and beliefs, deal with value conflicts, ensure a broad base of understanding, and simplify the subsequent definition of standards for determining successful achievement of the goals. If this important step is bypassed, numerous and loosely coupled definitions or perceptions of the "substance" of each goal could lead to weak results. What was sought in the "we believe" activity was a common understanding of performance outcomes. To illustrate, the following "we believe" statements were developed for the *mastery learning goal* (Goal 2).

1. Ninety-five percent of East Oak Cliff students can learn what we have to teach, given the right conditions;
2. The outcome-based curriculum must define what we have to teach/what kids must learn;
3. Learning/mastery requires a continuum of skills and knowledge;
4. Both students and parents should know what is to be learned;
5. Appropriate diagnosis is the central task in teaching for mastery;
6. Diagnosis is antecedent to prescription;
7. Teaching for mastery requires program planning in cognitive, affective, and behavioral domains;
8. Instruction must provide appropriate cues and directives, reinforcement, participation, and application of what is learned.

Our perception is that the careful, step-by-step analytical process that was followed in East Oak Cliff provided a much more solid foundation for translating values into goals and goals into an action plan than is possible in less thorough, Band-Aid-type approaches. The 40-plus "we believe statements" that were generated overall not only made the project dimensions crystal clear, but also served as the common language—the common dream—of those who were involved.

Now that the possibilities inherent in the process have become somewhat clearer, let us, in effect, back up to earlier stages of the planning for school development.

Planning Considerations

Following the identification of general improvement areas, various questions will surface to guide actual goal development. The following questions may be useful in preparing for extensive data gathering and analysis (Myers and Koenigs 1979).

1. Whose needs are being assessed?
2. What types of data will be gathered?
3. From whom will the data be collected?
4. How and by whom will the data be collected?
5. What are the procedures for data analysis?
6. What are the activities to be influenced by the data?
7. What are the procedures for interpreting or drawing inferences from the data analysis?
8. What arrangements are made to detect future changes in the data?

Illustration of Process

In our work with one particular school, we developed a staff needs assessment process at the end of one school year that served to guide the school goal-setting process the following fall. The process evolved in the following stages:

Stage 1:   a personal analysis by each teacher of progress toward the school's original mission (which had been clearly defined)

Stage 2:   a personal identification by each teacher of school weaknesses in that regard

Stage 3:   within each teaching team, a sharing of individual perceptions and a selection of priority concerns

Stage 4:   a total school analysis of team-identified concerns

Stage 5:   individual and team recommendations for improvement emphasis

Stage 6:   synthesized recommendations and a schoolwide action plan for resolving major areas of concern

Stage 7:   a personal assessment by each teacher of growth needs as they relate to the selected major concerns

This needs-assessment process produced the following general goal areas:

1. Program development that focuses on mastery levels
2. Principles and methods of classroom organization and management

3. Planning a program to meet the needs of gifted and talented students
4. Team organization and management concepts and procedures
5. Schoolwide curriculum development procedures
6. Develop a media program for visitors

As the staff considered the organizational arrangements best suited for addressing these goal areas, several options emerged: (1) a seven-day summer workshop, (2) product-oriented task forces, (3) in-service workshops, and (4) materials development sessions. Specific responsibilities were then assigned to the three teaching teams, seven vertical curriculum teams, various task forces, individuals, and the school's leadership council. Action plans subsequently were developed in each of the previously mentioned subgroups so that concerns and issues could be resolved.

Several pitfalls can be avoided in defining school goals. We advise principals to

1. *Direct teachers to focus on goal areas for which they can assume work responsibility* (not: build a new middle school building; get more money for materials);
2. *Set improvement goals that influence learning* (not: decrease teaching hours per day; develop a teacher lunchroom);
3. *Set goals that are achievable within one to five years* (not: individualize all instruction; ensure that all students learn according to their learning style in all subjects);
4. *Set a reasonable number of achievable goals* (two to five, not 10).

School goals guide the entire organization, as an ecological entity, toward a specific collective purpose. The identification of collective priorities is a prerequisite for individual commitment to collaborative tasks, and ultimately for building a productive school. It also announces the school's broad mission and its annual improvement priorities to the outside world (the school district, community, state and federal agencies). Such goals are more likely to be attained if they were defined collaboratively by the entire school community including representative parents and students. Collective priorities provide a shared framework for all planning and action in a given year.

Once defined, broad goals are translated into tasks for work groups. Three other levels of organizational goals exist to enable a school to *reduce uncertainty* in relation to planned actions.

1. The coordinating level identifies operational mechanisms for linking team and task force activities to the school's general mission, and for assigning additional work groups. The school's leadership council makes decisions regarding the objectives for each work group, staff assignments, and control procedures.

2. The operating level is the cooperative work level. Each work group (teaching team, vertical curriculum team, task force, council) reviews its assigned objectives and prepares action plans, time lines, and responsibilities for attaining school goals. The work group level becomes the focus for supervision, monitoring, and control activities in the goal attainment process.
3. The individual level operates within the context of a work group and the personal responsibilities assumed in team plans. The emphasis in individual performance is upon contributions to work group success. Staff motivation and commitment will be high when there is a good match between personal and organizational goals.

Following the development of the school's goal set, work-group action plans must be developed at the decision levels noted previously. Key activities, individual responsibilities, time lines, resources, and assessment processes are identified as each group develops a framework for its activity.

A word of caution is needed regarding the function of goals and their relationship to action plans and to goal attainment. Comprehensive planning is only half the battle in the goal attainment process. Being responsive to emerging conditions, pressures, and problems is equally important. Plans, and even goals, must be continually revised to reflect changing conditions. Strict adherence to original plans, policies, and procedures can cause work groups and the school organization to become rigid. Plans should serve as means rather than ends. Merton (1957, 199) has observed that goal displacement, or ignoring the official goals and returning to former priorities, occurs if the organization members retreat from the complexity that is involved in organizational growth and change. It is therefore critical that members of all goal levels (schoolwide, coordinating, work team, individual) develop skills for continuously critiquing and analyzing present conditions in order to reaffirm or revise plans. *Responsiveness to existing conditions* is the key variable in the school's ability to grow and to be continuously productive.

Impact of Goals on the School's Subsystems

An appropriate linkage of the goal set to the school's organizational design and to its activity is essential to the school's ecology. School goals that are linked to teacher actions have the potential for offsetting the disappointing change efforts of the past decades. Glines (1978), lamenting the usual failure of school change efforts, has likened the school to a medieval castle. Little progress, he notes, has penetrated the school's outdated operation, because of the wide moat (successful resistance) that encircles to protect it. Probably the slow growth phenomenon is due to time-worn patterns of low-level participation in decision making, outdated patterns of staff and student organization, and continuous unexamined use of ineffective instruction and learning practices.

School goals that have been defined collaboratively have the potential for controlling conditions so that the school community grows in specific directions. If this be the case, school improvement goals can influence all subsystems of the school. To illustrate the potential influence of goals on all subsystems, let us simulate that influence using the following goal:

Hypothetical Instructional Improvement Goal

To provide instruction that links individual student interests, needs, and learning styles to the following: (1) learning outcomes, (2) active student involvement in learning, (3) appropriate teacher coaching, and (4) student mastery.

Effects on the Organization Subsystem

Working toward a goal of individualizing instruction, a staff needs to examine its organizational patterns. It must plan for more flexible uses of time and provide for a wide range of student groupings. Further, the staff may decide it can make better use of its own resources by deciding to work in teams. As teachers address the inherent complexity in renorming instruction, a variety of approaches for sharing students, space, materials, plans, and role functions will emerge.

Effects on the Performance Subsystem

Teacher performance practices in schools have remained relatively unchanged in the last half-century. If teachers make a commitment to individualize instruction, a psychological shift will occur as teachers alter groupings, instruction, and learning practices. The psychological shift results in tossing away the attitudes of "I can be all things for all my students," or "If they don't get it, they're not paying attention" (a maintenance paradigm), and prompts a different perception: "If he/she doesn't master a skill I must develop instructional techniques to facilitate and guarantee expected mastery."

Teacher performance in the ecosystem context is measured in terms of observable growth in altering outdated instructional patterns and in contributions made to the school's development, within a team context. Teacher performance standards and evaluation must be designed to match changing beliefs about instruction, to link the school's goal set, and to individual teacher responsibilities.

Effects on the Program Subsystem

Commitment to personalizing learning requires developing a scope and sequence of skills that include cognitive and affective learning expectations. Preparing instructional programs for whole-group learning, such as "all 10th grade math students are on page 212 today," will cease to exist.

The 1977 National Science Foundation study (Weiss 1977) and Goodlad's study of schooling (1984) both have concluded that whole-group learning remains the norm in American schools. To change this norm, teachers must ask fundamentally different instructional questions as they seek to determine the "what," "how," and conditions for optimal individual learning.

Similarly, professional development activities for teachers must focus on the skills of accurate student diagnosis. Teacher skills in diagnosing the learning levels, emotional and social needs and strengths, and learning styles and cognitive processing styles of students account for 65 to 75 percent of the variance in learning, according to Bloom's study on school learning (1976). Helping teachers to be at least twice as accurate as before in their diagnosis of student readiness, and then helping them to link diagnostic data to program planning and to instructional strategies that facilitate mastery learning, could therefore help them to become at least twice as successful as they have ever been.

Effects on the Management Subsystem

The primary function of management is to ensure that all staff and student activities and practices support and facilitate the goal attainment process. Progress needs to be reinforced and monitored. Resource linkages need to be provided and evaluation must be conducted to measure the results of student and staff performance at all levels. Teacher motivation, monitoring, and evaluation all must act as enabling functions to increase staff productivity.

Conclusion

Like all other organizations, schools need clearly defined and well-conceived goals to provide a sense of purpose for all the activities in which teachers and students engage. Within a production paradigm, anticipated outcomes must be well understood and highly valued by all concerned. The principal plays a key role in helping to generate the school's value set, in bringing all personnel resources into the tasks of goal definition, and in linking goals to the various subsystems of the school.

In the next chapter is proposed a specific methodology, to which we have given the name Delphi Dialogue Technique, which has been designed to ensure that there can be total staff involvement in these all-important activities.

5

The Goal Subsystem: Methodology

The Delphi/Dialogue Technique

In the previous chapter we discussed school goals as the central organizing mechanism for the school. Goals help to define tasks, activities, and responsibilities; help in designing staff development and instruction programs; and provide parameters for the school's quality control and evaluation activities. The principal's role is that of value shaper for the school and chief architect in engineering collaborative decisions about school goals.

In this chapter, attention is given primarily to a methodology for organizing a total staff decision-making process for school goals. Referred to as the *Delphi/Dialogue Technique* (DDT), the four-part methodology we have developed is intended to promote total staff involvement in the making of goal decisions.

The Delphi/Dialogue Technique grew out of our work over several years with hundreds of school principals who expressed concern about how school goals are established and what happens to them after they are defined. The process is primarily conceptual in nature, and therefore adaptive to numerous cooperative situations. It is methodological, however, in that an actual step-by-step process is presented.

Before we describe DDT operationally, it may be helpful to review some of the characteristics of educational goals, the generation of which is DDT's function.

Goals: What Are They?

In the classic syllabus for Ralph Tyler's influential course in curriculum and instruction at the University of Chicago (Tyler 1950, 3), the words "purposes," "goals," and "objectives" all appear in the very first paragraph as essentially interchangeable terms, although Tyler then elects to use the word "objectives" more consistently than the other two. Another example is the famed trilogy of taxonomies of educational objectives by Benjamin S. Bloom and his colleagues (see Bloom et al. 1956). Bloom attempted to classify instructional goals by arranging them in subsets for which the word "objectives" is generally used.

Tyler, Bloom, and most other scholars use words such as "objectives" to connote the explicit formulations or statements by educators of the ways that students are expected to be changed, with respect to either thought, feeling, or action, during the educative process.

Craig (1978, 25) views objectives as general problem statements that reflect future conditions. To her, objectives include the situation or condition, of people or an organization, that will exist in the future and that is considered desirable by members of the organization. A Phi Delta Kappa (undated) publication, by contrast, indicates that *goals* should be specific, measurable, and linked to a specific time frame. Lipham and Fruth (1976, 101) distinguish between goals and objectives by suggesting that *goals* describe general states or behaviors that a unit (school or school district) will attempt to achieve, while *objectives* refer to specific skills, behaviors or outcomes that the program will achieve. In this view *goals* are general and broad in scope and usually are longer range than objectives. *Objectives* focus more on shorter range targets and are narrower in scope.

In this book, although at times the distinction between goals and objectives will be less evident, we will use the term *goal* to refer to a broad statement of a major outcome that is desired over a period, let us say, of one to five years. We will use the term *objective* to refer to subgoals, each a shorter range, smaller scale, more explicit outcome that is sought as an aspect of goal attainment. Further, we agree with the following criteria, which apply to both goals and objectives:

1. They must be stated in language that is easily understood, *specific* in its implications, and free of generality or ambiguity.
2. They must refer to a specific outcome or *result*.
3. The outcomes (events, conditions, activities, or other consequences) to which they refer must be *measurable* or otherwise verifiable.
4. The outcomes to which they refer must be *realistically attainable*.
5. They must be attainable within a specified *time frame*.

In summary, the goals and objectives to which any group or individual commits energy must be *clearly stated; results centered; measurable; attainable; and time bound.*

Schoolwide (organizational) goals, such as will be generated by the Delphi/Dialogue Technique, will belong to all of the individuals and groups within the school, and no one person or group carries the entire responsibility for their attainment. Various parts or pieces of each broad goal, in the form of objectives, will become the responsibility of separate groups or individuals through the dispersement process described in Chapter 6. The achievements of these various groups, in the aggregate, will lead to attainment of the broad, school goal. Here is an example of how a goal might be approached:

School Goal

To develop (first stage, 1986–1987) and implement (1987–1989) a mathematics program within each teaching team, based upon diagnosis of each learner's affective readiness, cognitive readiness, learning style, and needs/interests.

Work Group Assignments

1. *Task force for in-service development*

   Objectives: 1986–1987: (a) Sponsor two-week workshop on mastery learning, summer of 1986. (b) Conduct workshops, fall and spring semesters, on motivation, learning style, and cognitive processing. 1987–1989: Conduct workshops and technical assistance clinics in response to implementation concerns of teachers.

2. *Leadership Council*

   Objectives: 1986–1987: To develop a planning model for teaching teams to use in linking diagnostic data with curriculum guides and available resources. 1987–1989: To develop a math program management guide for use by team leaders.

3. *Teaching Teams* (preprimary; primary; intermediate)

   Objectives: 1986–1987: (a) To utilize a complete diagnostic battery in inventorying the learning styles, interests, self-concepts, and math mastery levels of all students by March 1. (b) To practice using the planning model for linking diagnostic data with curriculum guidelines. (c) To develop more flexible grouping patterns for math instruction. (d) (Upper-level teams) To train students in self-diagnostic techniques, mathematics. 1987–1989: Implementation objectives to be developed during spring and summer 1987.

4. *Inventory development task force* (1986–1987 only)

   Objectives: To select or develop, by mid-December 1986, a battery of diagnostic instruments for learning styles, interests, self-concepts, and mathematics mastery levels.

5. *School math coordination committee* (K–6)

   Objectives: 1986–1987: (a) Complete the inventory of all mathematics instructional resources begun last spring. (b) Examine district curriculum guides in math, as preliminary to developing a mastery-specific guide for our school. (c) In October, visit the Emerson School in Hale County (a model mastery learning program). 1987–1989: Assist in coordination and monitoring as implementation proceeds.

Conceptual Framework

The methodology presented on the following pages is a combination of several known approaches to decision making and problem solving. Two outcomes of the Delphi/Dialogue Technique are (1) goal decisions, or definitions, and (2) concensus about selected goals. The process is designed to encourage dialogue among staff members in such a way that individuals view themselves as major actors in the school's development and decision-making process. First we will examine the origin of concepts central to DDT.

The Delphi Approach to Forecasting

A forecasting tool was developed more than 20 years ago by the Rand Corporation. It was dubbed the Delphi Technique, presumably in tribute to the forecasting skills of the oracles in ancient Delphi, Greece. The technique has proven useful to futurists and planners in a wide variety of corporate, military, and government agencies. The technique involves a series of probings of experts' opinions, which are systematically refined until a general consensus is achieved (Hellriegel and Slocum 1974). Through an initial questionnaire, estimates, predictions, or statements about specific possible or probable events are generated. The identities of the experts are concealed from each other while responses are summarized and then recirculated to each respondent. In a second round, the experts consider the forecasts of their anonymous peers and have an opportunity to provide revised estimates of certain event probabilities. Again, the collected responses are referred back to each respondent who is asked to justify his or her forecasts, if they do not fall somewhere near the median. Finally, in a typical cycle, the justifications for nonconsensual predictions are fed back with the request for further appraisals.

As can well be imagined, many variations of the Delphi Technique have been developed; and there are elaborate extensions possible. Sergiovanni and Carver (1973, 237–239), within a chapter on educational decision making, present the technique for gathering majority, as well as minority, opinions from school constituencies, through a series of four questionnaires. The technique is said to be particularly useful in gathering ideas and opinions from many sources ordinarily not available to the school.

The Delphi Technique, and various offshoots of it, provides a process for involving all significant members of an organization or classification to participate in several stages of decision making regarding specific issues. Whether they are all in the same building or spread out over the country, all contribute through individual questionnaires or ballots, and a centralized system for data analysis helps each successive stage of participation to have a higher level of meaning and importance for those involved. The top-down syndrome that characterizes many school organizations can thus be modified or avoided with the Delphi Technique.

However, one major problem exists when the Delphi Technique is used as a tool for deriving staff consensus about goals: virtually no dialogue occurs in the process. Participants do not interact with each other, or have an opportunity to probe, challenge, and persuade, except in an impersonal, indirect, and largely invisible manner. In effect, the Delphi Technique fosters consensus through isolation. Therefore, we have selected some of the advantages of the technique while correcting this perceived serious weakness for a within-school context.

Dialogue

Staff dialogue is perhaps the central most important variable in altering norms of school productivity. For this reason we have sought to structure the dialogue process for obtaining consensus on goal decisions. Increased worker communication and total participation are two trends that Naisbitt (1982, 22–24; 159) predicts will permeate every segment of our culture. Formal and informal communications among and within groups enable organizations to increase their growth rate and to remain vital. By continuously assessing "where we are" in relation to "where we want to be," dialogue enables workers to become critical decision makers in achieving goals.

Freire's (1971) analysis of pedagogical oppression is helpful in understanding the function of dialogue in the growth of any group. He observes that critical reflection is a group practice that allows people to assess their present reality. It is assumed that all persons are capable of looking critically at their world through "dialogical" encounter with others. Dialogue enables a group to develop an objective distance from their reality in order to understand it more fully. Distancing occurs when criticism is the expected model of conversation and where transforming action results from dialogue. This kind of conversation is based on an assumption that the human vocation is to act upon and to transform one's own world. In so doing, people are able to progress toward a more full and rich life, both individually and collectively (Freire 1971, 12–13).

From this perspective, its staff, through continuous critical reflection, can transform a school into a more meaningful institution. If the professional goal of a school is to increase learning norms through collaborative staff responsibilities, then the production process must include continuous tough-minded dialogue and examination of progress. Vitality and productivity are achieved by establishing and maintaining a collective critical consciousness.

Delphi and Dialogue

We have blended together the strengths of the Delphi Technique (individual reflection, nomination and prioritizing) with dialogue (shared analysis through collective consciousness). Both individual and group reflection and dialogue can be structured for deriving goals. The *Delphi* Technique enables each individual to probe his or her own experiences and to recommend schooling improvements. The *dialogue* process provides a structure for group interaction. Perceptions of school problems and possibilities will emerge and lead to a staff consensus about a vision and each year's goals. Together, the Delphi and dialogue processes ensure that each individual has a voice in shaping new directions for a school.

The Delphi/Dialogue Technique Methodology

The Delphi/Dialogue Technique (DDT) includes a four-round cycle that is repeated until consensus emerges for school goals (see Figure 5.1). Round one in the cycle is a *total staff* meeting designed to elicit staff selection, through dialogue, of two to four general categories for school improvement (for example, school climate, math program, parent involvement). In round two, *each staff member* reflects privately on current conditions and identifies concerns about each selected goal category, then prepares recommendations for specific corrective action. In round three, individuals meet in *groups* or *teams* of five to eight members to share their individual recommendations. The outcome of the small group session is to define a goal recommendation for each school improvement category. Then, in round four, representatives (one from each group) and the principal meet together as a *council.* Their purpose is to share group recommendations and to evolve one representative school goal recommendation for each category. At the completion of round four, all individual recommendations will have been synthesized into one goal for each category (see Figure 5.1).

The foregoing explanation is of the briefest possible cycle. Often, more dialogue and compromising of positions are required before a result with which everyone is happy can be achieved. Rounds three (group) and four (council)

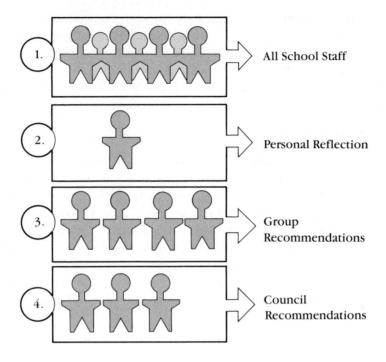

1.   All School Staff

2.   Personal Reflection

3.   Group Recommendations

4.   Council Recommendations

Figure 5.1. The Delphi/Dialogue Technique

may have to be repeated from one to three times, during which each group reacts to goal developments and refines and alters them until total staff consensus emerges.

In Figure 5.2, the four rounds of DDT are further elaborated to illustrate the goal-setting process. This shows how the process progresses from a large group meeting, to individual reflection, to small group dialogue, and finally to council recommendations for school goals.

Round One: School Community: Dialogue

The purpose of round one is to select several areas or categories for school improvement within a one- and/or five-year time frame. Through structured activities the principal guides a staff in identifying those areas that most urgently require school improvement.

At first, teachers typically identify administrative or housekeeping improvements, such as longer lunches for teachers, more aides, and smaller class size. Some of these are obviously beyond the power of teachers to provide; others can be identified as "quick fixes" and are listed separately, with a promise that effort will be made to solve several of the problems immediately.

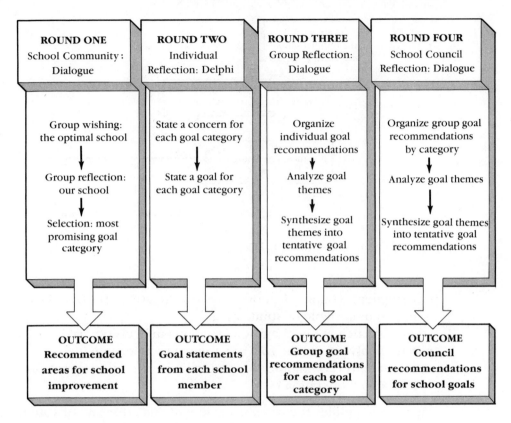

ROUND ONE School Community: Dialogue	**ROUND TWO** Individual Reflection: Delphi	**ROUND THREE** Group Reflection: Dialogue	**ROUND FOUR** School Council Reflection: Dialogue
Group wishing: the optimal school ↓ Group reflection: our school ↓ Selection: most promising goal category	State a concern for each goal category ↓ State a goal for each goal category	Organize individual goal recommendations ↓ Analyze goal themes ↓ Synthesize goal themes into tentative goal recommendations	Organize group goal recommendations by category ↓ Analyze goal themes ↓ Synthesize goal themes into tentative goal recommendations
OUTCOME **Recommended** **areas for school** **improvement**	**OUTCOME** **Goal statements** **from each school** **member**	**OUTCOME** **Group goal** **recommendations** **for each goal** **category**	**OUTCOME** **Council** **recommendations** **for school goals**

Figure 5.2. A Goal-Setting Process

It is important to establish realistic parameters for selecting goal areas. Legitimate areas for staff decision making are twofold: (1) those areas that either directly or indirectly influence learning, and (2) those areas in which the staff can in fact become the workers and decision makers. For example, teaching hours and class size relate neither directly nor indirectly to learning nor to areas of teacher decision making. Further, a new gym might be desired, but staff involvement in construction of the gym is not feasible. Staff recommendations need to be considered, but these are not categories for their active involvement and productivity. The following goal areas relate more directly to learning and to staff involvement:

organization (how the school is organized)
learning (how students learn in school)
instruction (how teachers teach)
curriculum (the learning program)

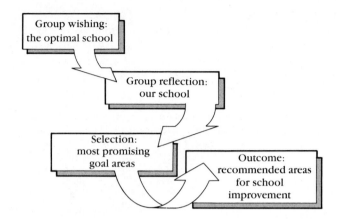

Figure 5.3. School Community: Dialogue

environment (communications; physical climate, and how it can be made
   more comfortable or stimulating)
student participation (the role of students in decision making)
parent involvement (the role of parents in school activities)
accountability (communications regarding learning outcomes, progress,
   and school operation)

Figure 5.3 outlines the process for identifying areas and/or categories for
school improvement in round one.

Step 1: Group Wishing

The principal engages the entire school community in warm-up activities for
goal setting. The first task requires each individual to dream and to "brood
about" the optimal school. Next, individuals are asked to share aloud "I wish"
statements regarding the optimal school. The principal writes "I wish" ideas
on the easel paper, which serves as a springboard for generating other ideas.
Brainstorming and wishing promote group understanding of the range as well
as the complexity of schooling values, ideals, and concerns.

Wishes about the ideal school, among literally thousands of possibilities,
might include

summer courses on a bus
yearlong learning programs
student project teams
learning in the community
studying in France
science experiences at Dow Chemical Labs

    every student viewed as gifted and talented
    involvement of the over-65 "community members" as community part-
      ners
    building and selling a house

Why have a wish/dream session? More conventional and logical approaches to planning typically rule out the exploration of wishes, dreams, and creative imagination. Perceived impossibilities tend to immobilize people, so that they become bogged down in the immediacy and practicality of the situation. When encouraged to dream a little, a group is often able to go beyond existing constraints and to envision more wonderful possibilities. Typically, dream sessions do in fact produce a very attainable image of an ideal school, one that is well within the reach of any community.

A technique that we have found useful when conducting wishing and dreaming sessions is to encourage participants to wish for things that are so far out that others might regard them as irresponsible or even outrageous. We find groups are more able to let loose when "irresponsible" wishing is permitted, thereby enabling them to move beyond low expectations and awareness of obstacles. "Irresponsible" wishing in a group context loosens people up, and enables them to fly beyond the moment and tap their often-buried dreams and hopes, along with their basic values and ideals, about learning and schooling. Upon examination of seemingly irresponsible responses, we have been impressed time and again with how participants sense new potential, invent solutions to old problems, and consequently come up with ways to break out of old traps. Thus, this first step in goal setting can enable the participants to define for themselves a qualitatively new kind of future.

Step 2A: Group Reflection: Large Group Option
The second step in round one is to examine the school's strengths and weaknesses as they relate to generated wishes about the optimal school: "What is our school like *now,* in relation to what we have said we value/want?" Shared group perceptions often clarify problems quickly and enable new perceptions of problems to emerge. Relevant school data should be considered in describing the school's current state of the art. Data from the following sources can assist in this analysis session: (1) student achievement scores, both norm and criterion referenced; (2) student/parent/staff attitude scale results; (3) external and internal studies of program design and implementation; and (4) studies of other school needs relating to organization, technology, materials, and staff development.

To foster quick and productive dialogue in a large meeting, small groups can be organized to analyze one school area (e.g., instruction, parental involvement) within a limited amount of time. Results of the subgroup can be shared with the group as a whole.

Dialogue at this point serves three functions: (1) to clarify individual perceptions of specific issues; (2) to foster shared communication and understanding around shared experiences and responsibilities; and (3) to identify areas of concern that might otherwise go unattended. The outcome is a listing of school strengths and school weaknesses. An example follows.

Areas of Strength	Areas of Concern
Team organization	Lack of a good scope and
Healthy school climate	sequence for curriculum
Strong parent advocacy	Collaborative teaching practices
Teacher commitment	Personalizing learning
Individualized math program	Parent involvement
Large number of visitors	Accountability processes
Large number of student teachers	(effective?)
Mainstreamed special education	Classroom management
students	procedures
Strong team leadership	A program for visitors
	An organized program for student
	teachers
	Staff work overload
	Low reading scores
	No music and art program

Step 2B: Group Reflection: Multiple Small Groups Option

An alternative to the whole-group task discussed previously would be to generate ideas for school improvement through a series of small-group brainstorming and prioritizing activities. Prior to brainstorming for school improvement areas, involve the entire group in a series of warm-up brainstorming activities:

In groups of three to five persons, list the many possible uses of some familiar item (such as bottle caps, rubber tires, steering wheels, safety pins). Time: One minute. Rules: One recorder; generate fanciful ideas; no discussion; no censoring.

Request groups to count their responses. Recognize the group with the largest number of ideas. Have them read their list, then applaud.

Repeat with one or two more warm-up brainstorming exercises, they activate the mind and stimulate group productivity. The playfulness of warm-up sessions creates a nurturing environment for tough decision making.

Next, get down to more serious business. Request that groups generate as many school improvement ideas for your school as is possible in one minute. Invite the group with the largest number of ideas to share their list; applaud. Invite one or two other groups to share items from their lists. If it seems that the process generated a fair number of interesting suggestions, proceed to the next stage. If not, repeat the process once more.

Next it is important for each group to cluster the generated ideas, then label and identify several areas for school improvement. We recommend the following process:

1. Assign groups to discard nonsense ideas, cluster their ideas into similar groups, and then label those groupings. For example,

$$
\text{Cluster 1} \left\{ \begin{array}{l} \text{parent involvement} \\ \text{communications} \\ \text{instruction techniques} \\ \text{staff development} \\ \text{student involvement} \\ \text{mastery learning} \end{array} \right\} \text{Cluster 2}
$$

   Cluster 1 may be labeled "Parent and staff participation"
   Cluster 2 may be labeled "Learning to teach for mastery"

2. After the groups have completed their discarding, clustering, and labeling tasks, invite them to select the two most important ideas on their list. As they share their selections with the total group, record their ideas. *Note:* By having small groups generate and prioritize ideas, you as leader never need to synthesize an excessively long list of ideas.

3. The leader then invites the large group to cluster and label the total group of selections. Groups often will have similar labels, and therefore patterns will emerge and appear to be obvious from group reports.

4. Invite the large group to select clusters and blend ideas until final improvement areas emerge (one to four). Discuss, share opinions, and finally vote on the final areas that will become the focus for defining specific parameters in the next three rounds.

Having identified several categories for school improvement (for example, parent and staff participation; learning to teach for mastery), the staff is ready for round two, individual reflection. The principal prepares forms and a time table to complete round two.

Round Two: Individual Reflection: Delphi

In a typical group discussion, the ideas that usually get on the record are those presented either by group extraverts or by the older or more seasoned staff

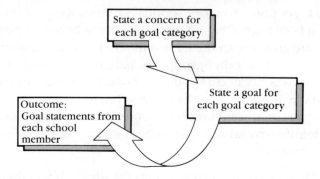

Figure 5.4. Individual Reflection: Delphi

members. To ensure that actual school goals reflect everyone's recommendations, we have designed a personal reflection step. As noted in Figure 5.4, each individual, during private time, reflects on the goal categories identified in round one. The task is for each person to identify concerns about the goal category (for example, student learning and involvement) in his or her school, and then to translate those concerns into a specific recommendation for corrective action: a goal. Each staff member prepares to shift psychologically from a static or complacent complaint mode to an action mode by making a recommendation. Personal reflection prepares each individual to participate in round three because of preplanned recommendations. Note the example in Figure 5.5 of Donna Morris's personal reflection on the student learning and involvement goal category.

Round Three: Group Reflection: Dialogue

The objective of round three is to generate one recommendation for each goal category that represents the ideas and concerns of individual members. Sharing perceptions and concerns in a group context raises new questions and generates new insights into a particular problem. Consequently, as the individual recommendations are shared and as the group works to synthesize them into one team recommendation, several important things happen. Each member, because he or she has prepared, becomes more willing to share important ideas. Secondly, as group members share, discuss, and cluster ideas, each person's ideas are refined, altered, or expanded through dialogue, and a group consciousness begins to emerge. Figure 5.6 outlines the steps of round three as the group progresses from the level of individual ideas to a group recommendation. Conversation seldom is sequential if left to flow undirected. A leader can guide the group from individual ideas to group ideas by leading an idea-organizing, idea-analyzing, and idea-synthesizing process. Figure 5.7 outlines a logical order for group dialogue.

Round Two: Individual Reflection

Goal Category: Student Learning and Involvement

Teacher's Name: _Donna Morris_ _____ Goal Category:_1_

My Concerns: _As teachers we talk a great deal about individualizing instruction, but the greatest amount of our energy goes into thinking about what we do, not what the students do. We need to shift our emphasis and focus more on learning needs and learning styles of students Considerations for what we do as teachers should follow naturally._

My Goal Recommendations:

To develop schoolwide procedures for teachers to:

(1) assess student learning needs, learning styles, rates and cognitive processing styles.

(2) observe the learning process while students are engaged in planned activities.

(3) develop a repertoire of instructional techniques to match learning styles, teaching styles, and desired program learning goals.

(4) evaluate instructional programs in relation to the observation & assessment data of school learning process & outcomes.

Figure 5.5.

Figures 5.8 to 5.10 illustrate the nature of a group's dialogical process. In Figure 5.8 the team develops procedures for *organizing* individual ideas into lists that can be analyzed. The team may divide its labor by delegating subgroups to work through the ideas in one or two goal areas. The purpose of

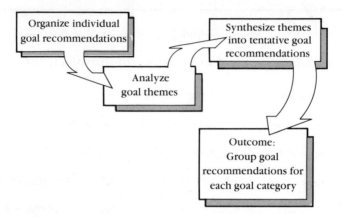

Figure 5.6. Group Reflection: Dialogue

this step is to list each person's recommendations until all ideas are represented.

Following the organization of all responses, the group must *analyze* the ideas and identify certain themes. The group consciousness that emerges is as important as the goal statements. First, the team groups together similar items and explores their meaning in order to label each group. For example, in Figure 5.8, numbers 1, 7, and 12 (indicated by asterisks) link together and may be labeled "Develop contracts to include diagnostic data and student responsibility." Numbers 2, 4, and 6 (indicated by dots) could be grouped under

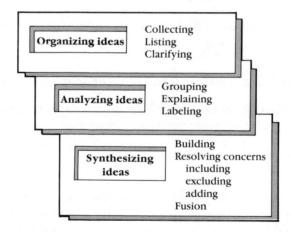

Figure 5.7. A Dialogical Process

Round Three: Team Reflection

Goal Category 1: Student Learning and Involvement (stated)

Main Ideas

* 1) Student Responsibility
* 2) Individualized Programs
  3) Peer tutoring
* 4) Traning and diagnostic procedures
  5) Developing recordkeeping system
* 6) Inventorying student interests
* 7) Designing learning opportunities that reflect style, rate, processing need, and interest data
  8) Varieties of grouping size and function
  9) Flexible use of time - free up the schedule
  10) Team teaching - balancing our resources
  11) Observe learning and teaching behaviors
* 12) Involve students in planning

Figure 5.8.

"diagnostic/prescriptive teaching." Remaining items would follow in a similar pattern.

A second task in analysis is to consider possible items that might belong to goal categories other than the ones being analyzed. Members may decide that "team teaching," for example, belongs to a goal category other than "learning" such as "instruction" or "organization". The theme "record-keeping systems" may belong under a "classroom organization" category along with "grouping" and "use of time." Figure 5.9 illustrates how one group clustered several ideas and gave them new labels.

The process of *synthesizing* many ideas into one new idea enables the group to sift all labels/themes into one or two goal statements. For example, "diagnostic/prescriptive learning" may suggest merely a cognitive focus and not include the variables of style, rate, processing, and interests. Thus, the act

Round Three: Categorizing Goal Themes

Goal Category 1: Student Learning and Involvement

Main Ideas:	Labels/Themes:
I.	**I.**
1) Student responsibility	Develop contracts to
7) Designing learning oppor-tunities that reflect style rate, processing need, and interest data	include diagnostic data and student responsibility
12) Involve students in planning	
II.	**II**
2) Individualized programs	Diagnostic/prescriptive
4) Training and diagnostic procedures	teaching
6) Inventorying student interest	

Figure 5.9.

of critically analyzing themes becomes the key to resolving concerns. The resulting goal hybrid includes all that is important to the team at a given point in time. Figure 5.10 illustrates the result of synthesizing all ideas and identifying inherent themes.

The team is now ready to participate in round four, school council reflection. The team identifies a representative (or one is identified by the principal). His or her task is to share the team's recommendation at the school council level, and to work as a member of the council to establish all-school goal recommendations.

Round Three: Team Goal Recommendations

Goal Category 1: Student Learning and Involvement

To develop learning programs that take into account learning, mastery, needs, rates, interests, style, and processing tendencies, and which involve students in the selection of specific activities for developing responsibility and mastery.

Figure 5.10.

Round Four: School Council Reflection and Decision Making: Dialogue

A representative from each goal planning team joins a new team, the school council, with the principal as team leader. Their task is to share their group's recommendations and to evolve one council goal recommendation for each category that represents all groups' concerns. As team leaders share and refine ideas, perceptions of problems and possible solutions are modified again through a mutual exchanging/learning/adapting process. The goal is for all groups to become winners and none to become losers as team leaders work together to blend ideas into a new, refined goal.

Figure 5.11 outlines the council's task in round four, which is the same as that for the team level in round three:

Organizing ideas (Figure 5.12) Team representatives share their team goal recommendations with fellow council members. The council may then work as a whole or divide into subgroups as it works on separate goal categories. Team recommendations in each group are listed by "main idea" and clarified.

Analyzing ideas (Figure 5.12) Group ideas are clustered and analyzed in search of emerging themes.

Synthesizing ideas for goal recommendations (Figure 5.13) Following the grouping/labeling activity, themes are probed and ideas are rephrased until new goal statements emerge. Figure 5.13 illustrates what evolved from dialogue after the council identified "student planning," "program planning," and "mastery focus" as themes.

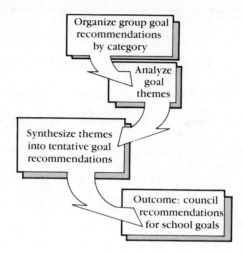

Figure 5.11. School Council Reflection: Dialogue

Round Four Complete: What Next?

After the first DDT cycle has been completed, the tendency is to want to announce the goals as complete and developed by consensus. However, it is critical that each team have the opportunity to react to and refine the council's

---

Round Four: School Council Reflection

Goal Category 1: Student Learning and Involvement

Team Main Ideas:	Themes:
• *Student Project Groups*	• *Student Planning*
• *Peer Instruction*	• *Program Planning*
• *Diagnosis*	• *Mastery Focus*
• *Needs Assessment*	
• *Mastery Learning*	
• *Program Planning*	

Figure 5.12.

Round Four: Council Goal Recommendations

Goal Category 1: Student Learning and Involvement

Given a commitment to a mastery approach to learning, an assessment of individual learning needs, styles, rater, and interests will serve as the basis for program, planning, learning, and student choice.

Figure 5.13.

recommendations. *Consensus* on goals is critical to success; consequently, rounds three and four probably will need to be repeated until genuine consensus emerges. New insights for all participants will have occurred throughout the first cycle; those insights need to be incorporated into final goal statements.

A second cycle allows for all participants to have another opportunity to clarify, revise, refine, and prioritize the final goal statements. Furthermore, a second cycle offers a mechanism for rethinking original ideas in light of new insights that were gained along the way. No one individual remains the same in their thinking throughout the process if true exchange of ideas has occurred. Dialogue stimulates a process of group thinking.

In the repeated cycle, round two (personal reflection) may be omitted if it is perceived that teams are already sufficiently responsive to each team member. Whatever re-entry point is selected, it must be understood that the purpose of the second cycle is to flesh out new thoughts that emerged during the first round.

The repetition of rounds continues until consensus is achieved and each individual and team is willing to make a 100 percent commitment to the attainment of stated school goals. The recycling mechanism prevents avoidance games that are often expressed in such comments as, "Well, I don't have to do that task because I didn't agree with the idea originally." The cycle repetition process requires a more professional response ("I will because I agreed to") by the entire school community, before the goal-setting process is complete.

After Goal Setting, What?

After school goals and their parameters have been clearly defined and the commitment of the entire staff has been obtained, decisions need to be made regarding responsibilities for the goal attainment process. Such decisions can be made by the principal, school council, and/or all of the staff. Examples of such decisions might be as follows:

School Goals	Planning and Action Responsibilities
1. to develop specific plans for implementing a school reading lab	vertical reading team (one representative from each teaching team) materials development workshop
2. to develop a schoolwide communication system	school leadership council principal (daily bulletins)
3. to develop staff skills for providing personalized instruction for those children who are performing below expectations	teaching teams in-service task force
4. to develop teacher skills in diagnosing learning styles	in-service team (utilize consultants) teaching teams
5. to coordinate record keeping and reporting system in math	task force teaching teams vertical curriculum teams
6. to begin Phase II of the program for gifted and talented students	gifted and talented task force
7. to develop a cohesive and productive school climate	school leadership council teaching teams
8. to involve curriculum planning	teaching teams

Principals may elect to use the checklist provided here to plan and organize schoolwide goal-setting activities.

The Principal's Checklist for a School Goal-Setting Activity
Prior to Goal Setting (Round One)

☐ 1. Assign individuals to gather data and report briefly to the staff on student test scores, district priorities, the results of surveys, and other relevant information.

☐ 2. Prepare goal-setting work groups:
Team members
Team leaders

Council members

Goal-setting process facilitator

☐ 3. Prepare goal-setting forms for rounds two, three, and four.

Begin Goal Setting (DDT)

☐ 1. Review district goals and your goals
☐ 2. Report data results of surveys and tests [see (1) above]
☐ 3. Review DDT goal-setting format (rounds one through four)
☐ 4. Begin DDT process

In the next chapter on the organization subsystem, we will discuss the process of identifying tasks and work groups to produce elements inherent within each goal. The groups in the following list make various kinds of decisions regarding the school improvement process. The basic principle of goal dispersion is to delegate decisions to the lowest work group capable of making certain decisions.

SCHOOL DECISION SETS

Principal Decisions

Several school improvement priorities

Selection and role assignments: teams; leaders

Goal-setting process

School organization

Planning processes; teams/organization and instruction

Budget and space allocation to teams

Student selection

School Decisions: Goals

Reporting system

Evaluation system

Curriculum implementation

Behavior management

Council Decisions

Goal dispersement process

Staff development program

School organization

School communication system

Space allotments

Team Decisions: Organization and Roles

Objectives

Program

Space use
Time
Resources
Staff
Groupings

Conclusion

A collective vision of the ideal school provides the driving force for planning and action. Each year new strategic goals are identified by the staff as the next steps toward achieving that ideal. The principal provides leadership and control for goal-setting activities and for goal statements.

It is critical that high standards be applied to the goal-setting process. Research and theory about productive organizations, schools, and teaching must guide staff decisions. Staff ignorance should be prohibited from influencing goal decisions. The principal creates the conditions for productive goal decisions. On the other hand, the staff is the genuine expert group in knowing the conditions of a school. Their ideas and concerns provide significant resources and energy for school development.

Additional considerations for the principal include deciding which areas are legitimate for staff decision making. Parameters need to be defined for productive staff involvement. Another question relates to how best to prepare the staff for collaborative activities. The goal-setting process presented in this chapter occurs at a school level after each team or department has developed comfort and skill with a smaller version of DDT. The staff may need to be inducted into schoolwide collaboration through a series of smaller, successful experiences in collaborative decision making.

With reference to a schoolwide needs assessment, several practices are useful to define the "next steps" in school development:

1. Personal interviews may be conducted with selected students, teachers, parents and administrators;
2. An analysis of *test data* will reveal obvious areas for program improvement. A more detailed analysis may illuminate instructional problems by level or area within the school;
3. Analysis of a *parent survey* will point out specific areas that may be important to include in the goal-setting process;
4. A staff survey may point out areas of concern in categories such as diagnosis, problem solving, program planning, cooperative learning, and communication.

Other means of obtaining specific feedback on school successes and problem areas include contacts and/or conversations with individuals or groups, sometimes by mail or phone. Questions can address concerns about specific or general schooling practices, experiences, perceptions, and attitudes. The intent is to search for significant response patterns in order to develop a coherent picture of the school. Feedback should be synthesized into a useful form and provide input into the school's goal-setting process.

After corporate goal decisions have been made for the distant future, and for the year at hand, questions about how to organize to accomplish goals are appropriate. In the next chapter we present the rationale and methods for organizing the staff into both permanent and temporary work groups.

6

The Organization Subsystem:
Organizing Work Groups

Perspectives on School Organization

Its organizational structure is the central nervous system of a school. When it is functioning properly it permits the organization to perform a variety of related motions and activities simultaneously (Sergiovanni 1979, 55). Perhaps the most noticeable change for schools in a production paradigm will be the ways in which work is accomplished. Cooperation and collaboration are the cornerstone concepts of an effective school as well as a productive business. Consequently schools will be organized around the values of collaborative action. Furthermore, organizational behavior in schools will shift from rather loose arrangements with vague objectives to numerous clusters of goal-specific activities. Table 6.1 identifies basic features of school organization in the maintenance and productivity orientations to schooling.

Our discussion of school organization begins and ends with group activity. The school staff is organized into various work groups on the basis of goal-related tasks.

In this chapter we begin discussing the school's organizational structure first by reviewing the ways in which schools have been organized in the past. Understanding why decisions were made in the past will release us from restraining traditions and enable us to make new decisions for the future. Next, we shall discuss school organization concepts in a production-oriented school, in which we set forth the concept of both permanent groupings (teaching teams) and temporary groupings (task forces). The concepts of task forces and team

TABLE 6.1. Organization Subsystem

Characteristics	Maintenance Paradigm	Productivity Paradigm
Role Relationships	Isolation among and within role groups	Collaborative arrangements
Performance	Activity-oriented events Competitive	Goal-oriented events Cooperative
Orientation	Diversity of goals Fragmentation Arbitrary decision making	Uniformity of goals Coordination Goal-related decision making
Accountability	Limited responsibilities Individual effort	Shared responsibilities Group effort
Organizing Mechanisms	Isolated roles Discrete functions	Temporary work groups: problem resolution Permanent work groups: primary job tasks

teaching will both be developed as they relate to school productivity. In the last section of this chapter, attention is given to skill development for work groups and to the various strategies that principals can employ to enable groups to become increasingly productive. Hence, this chapter provides a rationale for assigning staff members to both permanent and temporary groups. In addition, it presents many useful techniques for developing group work skills for effective teams and task forces.

The Worker-in-Isolation Paradigm

Of the major institutions that are found in modern American society, schools are among the most simple in their organizational pattern, even though they address extremely complex problems. In a given community a century or so ago could be found the family doctor, the family lawyer, the independent farmer, the independent storekeeper, the one-room schoolteacher, the independent craftsman, the preacher, the small manufacturer, and various other persons or small groups of persons, pursuing their livelihoods within an uncomplicated framework. This is not to say that their lives were easy or that their work was not highly challenging, but rather to point out that each pursued his or her goals in relative independence and without much interaction with workers within the same vocation.

Early Patterns of School Organization

As communities expanded and society changed, particularly in the ways foods and goods came to be produced and distributed, complex organizations emerged and workers functioned within a much more complicated framework. Even doctors, lawyers, and preachers, despite the personal nature of their services, gradually adopted organizational patterns (within clinics, hospitals, large law firms and large churches) that permitted greater specialization and worksharing and also required more interaction and integration. To some extent this also became true of educators, especially in the larger school districts where central administrative headquarters were established; but for the most part, teachers themselves continued to function as they had in the little red schoolhouse.

Specialization within schools did occur, and a certain amount of worksharing became common, but especially when compared with large hospitals or with business-industrial models, school organization models remained relatively simple.

For reasons that appear to have been largely accidental (as opposed to deliberate, based upon well-conceived pedagogical theory), and due to habits that had become well established during the era of one-room schools, school architects in cities simply recreated such schools by placing classrooms, one alongside the other, along connecting corridors under the same roof. A major breakthrough in the early nineteenth century was the graded-classroom arrangement, which separated the vertical school program into annual segments, and which was designed to make it easier for each teacher to master, and to carry out, the work of that section of the program identified with his (or, more likely, her) grade. Inasmuch as teachers in those days had very little training and received practically no supervision (as opposed to judgmental inspection), being able to specialize at just one or two grade levels made it more likely that a teacher would in time develop a clear understanding of both goals and ways to achieve them.

Secondary schools developed more complex organization patterns and also received greater financial and other support than did elementary schools. The graded pattern was a less dramatic innovation at the secondary level because a hierarchical curriculum already existed in a sense. However, the major organizational invention in secondary schools, borrowed from universities, was departmental organization. Each teacher was responsible for being the master of only one or two disciplines, except in the very small schools where such a luxury was less possible. Departmental organization also led to a highly desirable invention, the department chairperson, which greatly increased the number of persons within the secondary school charged with various leadership and coordination functions. The grade-level chairperson in elementary schools was and is a version of the secondary-school departmental leader, but the pattern rarely developed to a point where sufficient leadership time and energy became available.

Within most school districts the central office, staffed by specialist workers responsible for services to individual schools, developed a relatively complex bureaucratic organization. Over time, as boards of education were faced with numerous state and federal regulations, pressures from outside groups, and complicated management tasks, the resources of central offices were increasingly diverted from their services-to-schools tasks, toward district-survival tasks. It is not generally acknowledged by superintendents and board members, since taxpayer pressures for efficiency and economy seem to be greater than for high-quality services, but the central office in modern school districts more often resembles a military war room than a research and development center, and usually less than half of the budget for central office personnel and operations has the intended impact on instructional activities in the schools. This is not necessarily the fault of the central office people, since, after all, they are responding to the needs of the school district's leaders. But it is a fact that causes us to concentrate all the more heavily on how to help individual schools "make it on their own."

Within schools the prevailing delivery system is the self-contained teacher, such as a third grade teacher with 29 boys and girls or a secondary school Spanish or mathematics teacher with five classes a day involving three separate preparations. In perhaps one-fifth of American schools the delivery system has been modified so that one or another form of collaborative teaching takes place. Most elementary schools also include on their rosters a few specialists who supplant the regular teacher, for example, a counselor or librarian or reading teacher. Happily, for both normal and exceptional children, P.L. 94-142 and other federal programs have, in recent years, also brought special education teachers into the schools to work in close partnership with regular teachers. Thus the term *self-contained* does not have quite the same meaning that it may once have had in describing elementary teachers.

The same is true at the secondary level, where various specialists supplement each other or collaborate in various patterns. Wherever in this book we refer to self-contained teachers, however, we refer to the prevailing independence, and lack of significant professional interconnections with other teachers, that characterizes the working life of most elementary and secondary teachers, especially with respect to actual "teaching."

Efforts to alter and improve school organization have been going on ever since 1848, when graded student organization was adapted from Germany in Boston's Quincy Grammar School. Monitorial schools, platoon schools, the Dalton Plan, the Winnetka Plan, the Cooperative Group Plan, Dual Progress Plan, ungraded schools, team teaching and unit organization, multi-age and family groupings, Individually Guided Education, house plans, open education, alternative schools, differentiated staffing—these and other terms remind us of the unceasing effort to find "right" patterns of horizontal and vertical school organization within philosophically sound and technically practical organizational frameworks. In the 1980s, though the terms may have been discarded or modified, the essential features of many of these patterns are surviving or evolving into slightly different forms. In particular, the focus remains upon making schooling more productive, providing more efficiently for individual learning, and exploiting the advantages of human collaboration.

The Graded School

Although the introduction of graded schools in the mid-nineteenth century brought with it some notable advantages, the assumptions about child growth, development, and learning upon which graded structure was based were very primitive and in fact had more theological than pedagogical underpinnings. "Good" children who were conscientious and obedient would assuredly learn. "Bad" children, slothful, and/or mischievous, would fall into difficulty. Books about teaching, as well as books for use by children, were highly moralistic and supported the view that school failure was in fact a failure of virtue. As more enlightened and realistic views of pupil capability and motivation were propounded, the good–bad explanations gradually gave way, but alas, the mechanics of the graded school remained strongly entrenched. Even after a century of progress in understanding how and why children respond to schooling as they do, teachers and administrators remain unashamedly loyal to a graded structure that is altogether inconsistent with current knowledge. Teachers in most other countries remain similarly narcotized by graded customs and traditions. This is one of the great anomalies in a world where nearly all other human-service professionals pay at least some attention to knowledge about how human beings (their clients) grow and prosper.

What follows may seem an unfair caricature, but we are convinced that it reflects reality. Educators (teachers, administrators, professors) who support gradedness with its customary self-contained classroom arrangement tend to believe (1) that children of every age level are, in the final analysis, similar to each other in potential for learning, except perhaps for motivation; (2) that teachers work more comfortably and efficiently by themselves; and (3) that the purpose of schooling is to ensure that every child reaches or achieves specified learning goals, level by level, that have been predetermined by the school system in an allotted amount of time. Through the system of gradedness and self-containment, they believe, schools can check achievement and classify children according to their success or failure within normed expectations.

The graded school uses a variety of means to ensure standardization of programming and learning.

1. Competitive marking system: Students recognize their relative position within the class and grade level; teachers record progress in terms of levels of success
2. Periodic report cards: Parents are given coded clues to their child's progress according to normed expectations
3. Parent/teacher conferences: Sometimes these take place as a supplement to report cards or to resolve particular problems
4. Pass vs. fail: Teachers determine whether the student has successfully learned the graded curriculum. Consequently, the child is either promoted to the next grade or required to remain in the present grade
5. Ability/achievement groups: Each child is placed, especially for reading, in a group of students presumed to have equivalent skills and to be capable of proceeding at a similar pace
6. Content of curriculum: Content is organized by grade level, based upon normative data for the entire national population
7. Closed-room approach: The teacher, an isolate, paces the entire curriculum according to the needs of the class in general

With respect to the seventh point, it should be acknowledged that in some schools where the graded approach is followed, teachers do in fact work within teams of some sort. In our experience, however, cooperative teaching almost always results in a softening of the lockstep graded approach to children because the teachers can be more flexible in curriculum organization, pupil grouping, and responding to the needs of children above and below the related grade level.

Assumptions Made About Children

It is assumed that all children in graded classrooms can function at relatively the same level, learning in basically similar ways as their peers. It is further assumed that deviant behavior results from poor motivation, unfortunate home conditions, or other problems within the child. When a child fails it is usually perceived as the child's fault, rather than as the failure of the school system to provide an appropriate learning situation.

Organizational Structure of the School System

Students in graded schools are grouped by age starting at age 5 or 6:

an elementary school usually has kindergarten (age 5) through grade 6 (ages 11 and up)

a junior high school usually has grade 7 (ages 12 and up), grade 8 (age 13), and, sometimes, grade 9 (age 14)

a high school usually has grades 10–12, for youth age 15 and above

Sometimes the school district determines a different organizational configuration, for example, the elementary school may include only K–4 followed by middle school, grades 5 and 6; junior high school, grades 7 and 8; and high school, grades 9–12.

Individual Differences in Graded Schools

These are believed to exist primarily in personality and in learning rate or ability. Students read from the same books, are assigned work on the same level, and are evaluated by comparison with other children's work. Higher level students are discouraged from advancing too far ahead of the class, while slower students are rushed in order that everyone can engage in class activities of the same sort.

Teaching Methods

In graded schools methods are fairly uniform. The elementary teacher, responsible for all subjects, limits pupils by spending most of the time on areas the teacher knows best and prefers. Secondary teachers take their classes through one textbook, chapter by chapter, and all pupils are on the same time table. Teaching methods are limited primarily to lecture, question-and-answer, and test. Pupil progress is reported in grades on report cards and is based largely on tests. Grade-level books, star charts, IQ tests, achievement tests, and teacher discussions all contribute to actual grades.

Children's performance is based on a numerical or alphabetical marking system such as

$$A = 90–100 \qquad C = 70–80 \qquad F = \text{below } 60$$
$$B = 80–90 \qquad D = 60–70$$

Age-Level Assignments

One of the most fundamental problems in graded schools, which is especially evident in the first grade and again in the first year of the junior high (or middle) school, is that it attributes equivalent educational readiness to all children who happened to be born within a given calendar year. The "five-year-olds" who are accepted into kindergarten in 1986 because they were born between September 1 of 1980 and August 31 of 1981 are all assumed to be a relatively homogeneous group for all of whom a particular sequence of developmental and readiness activities will have approximately equal value. Ignored is that some of them have spent almost 20 percent less time on earth than their older classmates, or that some were playing chess with their grandfathers while others their age weren't yet speaking in sentences.

Fortunately, kindergarten teachers are usually patient, flexible, child-development-oriented, and relatively immune to pressures for measurable scholastic achievements in their classes. In September of the year the children officially become "six-year-olds" (despite a 364-day spread), however, the evil pressures begin to bear down hard. Even more cruel, in our opinion, are the things that happen to some of the so-called "twelve-year-olds" when they enter the fiercely standardized world known as seventh grade. Quite possibly the rapid development of special education programs, especially after enactment of P.L. 94-142, was one of the most powerful recent forces in weakening the stranglehold of graded thinking and practice. Mainstreaming of special children within a framework that accepts great individual differences as an opportunity rather than a nuisance, has a salutary effect on teachers as they reconsider their approach to "normal" children. Furthermore, teachers with special education training help their colleagues to know more about the diagnosis and treatment of various learning disabilities, and their prescriptive approach to learning sets a new standard for instruction.

Alternative Arrangements

Following is an effort to suggest the many different organizational patterns that have emerged in recent decades and that can be found in many schools throughout the country. In sum, they illustrate the profession's earnest attempts to shed old assumptions and norms, and to develop more enlightened and suitable patterns of working and learning.

Organizational Schemes

Team teaching
Nongradedness
Educational parks
K–12 groupings
Differentiated staffing
Units/houses
Alternatives
Mini-schools
Magnet schools

Curriculum

K–12 scope and sequence
Individualization
Outcomes or objectives
  oriented
Programs for career
  education, handicapped,
  the gifted and talented,
  and retarded
Core programs

Instruction

Programmed instruction:
  IPI and PLAN
Discovery
Process systems: IGE
Learning centers
Materials centers

Learning

Different styles, rates, and
  thinking processes
Informal and formal
Values oriented
Human relations
Continuous

Media centers
Small group, large group
Choices and options
Technology

Individualized
Cognitive, affective,
   behavioral
Cooperative peer groups
Mastery learning

Teachers

Staff development
Accountability
Competencies
Clinical supervision
Evaluation

Schools

Open space
Flexible spaces and
   furniture

It would be gratifying if we could report that these efforts, commendable and varied as they are, are leading to significant changes and gaining in widespread adoption. However, recent studies of prevalent practice suggest that the conditions we attributed previously to graded, self-contained classroom arrangements have changed very little. The Rand study (1979) and the more recent reports by Goodlad (1984), B. Tye (1985) and K. Tye (1985), have confirmed that most teachers still work alone professionally with classes (30 or so students) whose members read the same texts and complete the same tasks as their classmates. It therefore is a challenge to "sell" more flexible and appropriate arrangements to school staffs.

We hope the reader understands by now some of the authors' reasons for preferring that pupils be placed in situations where (1) they are able to interact with other children whose ages, backgrounds, and talents cover a larger spectrum than is usually found in a unit-age classroom, (2) they are not oppressed by the machinery and the psychological atmosphere that characterize literal gradedness, (3) they are in regular contact with an organized group of teachers (as contrasted with one self-contained teacher), and (4) they have claim to adequate space and varied instructional resources. Children who work and live under such conditions are, in our opinion, specially fortunate.

Not only children, however, benefit from such organizational arrangements. We perceive that stimulation of *teacher* growth and enthusiasm is another goal that can be met through adopting appropriate environmental structures. There is value in placing each teacher in a work situation that permits him or her to make full use of existing skills and talents while also having opportunities to develop new skills and talents and to profit from constant professional interactions with peers. In this volume we therefore address attention to collaborative teaching arrangements. We also focus, throughout, on ways to link teachers together in the various activities of planning, development, and evaluation.

No discussion of optimal organizational patterns would be complete without reference to questions of size. In recent years, budget constraints have caused educators once again to strain for research evidence in support of smaller class sizes, and in some communities with declining enrollments they have faced similar pressures to defend the cost effectiveness of small schools. No easy answers are to be found, despite the "prevailing wisdom" of educators to the effect that about 25 is an appropriate number of pupils in a class.

The Carnegie Council on Policy Studies in Higher Education, in examining problems of youth crime and unemployment, recently made some recommendations that included a reduction in the size, and changes in the structure, of American secondary schools (Carnegie, 1980). Goodlad (1984, 360), concludes from his study of schooling that elementary schools of 300 pupils and secondary schools of 500 (several schools within a school) pupils are the most productive. In keeping with several other recent reports, the Carnegie group proposed that high schools should not only be smaller, but should allow for more diversity and provide more options, including modification of compulsory full-time attendance to allow for more work experience. Gottfredson and Daiger, in a Johns Hopkins University Report (1979) concerned with making schools more safe, concluded after analyzing 600 schools that schools need to be made smaller, especially at the junior high level, and that teachers should have a small number of students with whom they are in regular contact. Of interest is that they did not propose smaller class sizes, but rather, sought to reduce the rotation of students. Even more significant from our perspective is that the researchers called for a high degree of cooperation between teachers and administrators, as well as the provision of more adequate resources for teachers and the development of clear, firm, and fairly administered rules to govern student behavior.

Two kinds of size questions seem critical—one about the most appropriate ratios that should exist between teachers and students, and the other about the nature and magnitude of the overall environment in which teachers and students are housed. Subsumed under these are intriguing questions about (1) the numbers and types of other students with whom various kinds of students can profitably interact; (2) the numbers and types of teachers and other adults in the school context, with whom such students can profitably interact; (3) the optimum administrative arrangements, including types and numbers of decision-making adults (such as principals), for students at various levels; and (4) effective ways of subgrouping students within classes or units to achieve specific purposes.

Vertical Patterns

There appears no longer to be the rather heated debate of a decade or two ago, about the optimal pattern of school unit organization. In those days, when the middle school alternative to conventional junior–senior schools was much discussed, where best to locate grades five, six, and nine became a troublesome question for some communities. Familiar patterns such as K8-4, K6-2-4, K6-2-3, K6-6 were joined by newer patterns such as K5-3-4, K4-4-4, as well as some odd alternatives (K5-1-3-3, K6-2-1-3) that were spawned in peculiar administrative, legal, or political situations. Throughout this period and continuing to the present, it seems that no compelling evidence has emerged to support one or another pattern above others from an educational, physiological, or psychological point of view. What has been confirmed, however, is that the specific unit arrangement is much less important as a factor in student growth and development than is the quality of life (and hence the learning opportunity) provided within each of the units within the sequence. A sixth-grader or a ninth-grader can be totally happy or totally miserable, within any one of the possible organizational schemes. A student can be happy or miserable within one of the units in the sequence and have an opposite experience in one of the other units. It all depends, in the final analysis, upon the ability and willingness of the staff to provide, each year in the child's life, the environment and opportunities that make sense for that child during the year.

Arrangements that Foster Maximum Growth

Although the call for smaller schools probably makes sense, we believe it is possible to make schools more comfortable for students and more responsive to their needs, even when the schools are relatively large. Larger schools have a distinct advantage over smaller schools in at least one respect: they usually are provided with the various specialized physical facilities and special personnel that are necessary in order to provide a full range of curricular and human services. It costs more per student for a community to provide small schools with suitable libraries, physical education facilities (and instruction), auditoriums, art rooms, science laboratories, counseling offices, and the like.

On the other hand, larger schools can overwhelm students and often students feel that they are insignificant, unnoticed, and unloved members of a huge organization. They also tend to feel totally unconnected with the principal and others in authority. These problems can be handled by mechanisms such as the "learning community" in an elementary school or the "house" in a secondary school. Several thousand schools organized according to the model labeled Individually Guided Education (IGE), for example, bring together a manageable number of pupils in the custody of a cross section of the teaching staff functioning as a team and occupying a physical area within the school that is essentially self-sufficient. Most IGE schools are elementary, although a fair number are middle schools and senior high schools. Usually such schools are coordinated by a leadership team, known as the Program Improvement Council (or some equivalent term), in which the principal, unit leaders, student representatives, and others set basic school policies, analyze school operations, seek to ensure attainment of school goals, and coordinate staff improvement programs.

Secondary schools utilizing a "house" plan of organization follow a similar pattern. A house can be comprised of pupils from one grade level, (for instance, ninth grade), or, preferably in our minds, it can be a mixed-age unit, which, in effect, makes it a school within the larger school. Houses can be organized to include at least one teacher from each major discipline, or they can be set up more narrowly within one or two disciplines. Students usually spend a substantial fraction of their time in the house with their house teachers, and also venture into the larger school for specialized classes such as art, homemaking, commercial courses, and the like.

A major advantage of such arrangements is that each unit or community can make many of its own program and management decisions, and the team or house leader becomes in effect the principal in the experience of the students. A general and useful precept of school administration is that the decision-making professional in each child's life ought to be immediately familiar with that child and his school history, and in turn should be a familiar and visible person to the child. One reason for preferring smaller schools is to make it more possible for the principal to have direct acquaintance with each student under his or her jurisdiction. A way to honor this notion in larger buildings is to delegate more of the principal's role responsibilities to unit leaders.

An alarming consequence of financial cutbacks and school closings in many hard-pressed school districts has been a reduction in leadership services and an increase in the numbers of teachers for whom principals carry supervisory responsibility. When principals carry heavier loads than they should, not only the pupils suffer but also the teachers. A disturbing 1979 report from Educational Research Services, Inc., utilizing 1978–1979 data, showed that the mean number of pupils per principal was 622, ranging from 440 in very small systems to 706 in large systems (ERS 1979). The same report showed the mean number of teachers per principal to be 31.2, with the range between 24.4 to 34.1. From such reports, in which admittedly the existence of house plans or team organization is not readily identifiable, we conclude that much more needs to be done to ensure that factors of size will not detract from the creation and maintenance of a comfortable and productive family-type atmosphere.

There are not many studies to guide schools in knowing how many students to bring together in a continuing school relationship, but experience with house plans and team teaching over more than a generation has provided some useful clues. One strong message from such experience is that self-contained classes of the usual 25 to 30 in number, and especially classes that remain more or less intact over several consecutive years, tend to create and preserve stereotyped reputations for its members (Nancy is always the best reader, and teacher's choice for prized assignments; Carl is the class clown; Melanie is always shy and withdrawn; John is the star athlete, perennial team captain; and so on). Social mobility is limited, cliques tend to live on, children find few surprises in the behavior or the growth of their classmates. The myth of a well-integrated family, happily living together, has failed of research verification.

In IGE and similarly organized schools, however, where the basic family unit is from three to six times larger, it has been found that social, educational, and other benefits exist for children. Stereotypes are less common, partly because the situation is more complex and it is less possible for a Nancy or a John to dominate every situation. For that matter, every child belongs to a much greater number of pupil groups within which friendships and recognition become possible. Carl finds several friends who meet his needs, and to whom he is able to present a different personality. Melanie, too, may open up as a greater variety of stimuli or opportunities present themselves. Since there are also several teachers in the situation, at least one of whom has a natural ability to work with students like Carl and Melanie, there is much less danger of a child suffering because of the mind-sets and tendencies that teachers often unwittingly possess in self-contained situations.

With respect to numbers, it would seem that two collaborating teachers (with 50 to 60 pupils) is a much better arrangement than 1:25 or 30 each, although when three or more teachers combine their efforts, the benefits (per teacher and per child) are even greater. As the number of teachers exceeds *five,* however, three problems emerge: (1) greater difficulty for the children in affiliating with the larger number of teachers and fellow students, (2) more complications in keeping track of students and in coordinating the daily/weekly program, and (3) more time spent by the adults in communicating and working with each other. As a general rule, then, it would seem that teams of three to five teachers are to be preferred. When conditions seem to call for six or seven teachers to collaborate, it may therefore be best to break up into two subgroups.

Being a teacher involves more than just the "teaching" that is done in the classroom in the presence of boys and girls. It involves all kinds of preparations, including the all-important goal-setting activities discussed in Chapter 4, and it requires working with other teachers (parents, citizens) in the pursuit of various projects related to the school's programs and services. It also involves participating in district-sponsored or voluntary staff-development activities, and, of course, attending various meetings that relate to the general welfare of the total school district.

Concluding Comments

School organization in the twentieth century has been dominated by staff isolation and student gradedness. Numerous attempts have spotted the path of progress that sought to connect teachers with each other in work patterns, and students with age and grade groups other than their own.

To illustrate the severity of the current problem in schooling, Sizer (1984) asserts that high schools will not change without a complete overhaul of the structure, methods, and goals. There is no serious way to improve high schools without revamping their structure, the organizing framework. The unproductive organizing structure of modern high schools dates from the late nineteenth century and persists today; it is remarkably consistent across all regions of the country and across public and private sectors. This organization, Sizer challenges, no longer serves its purpose and must give way to new, more productive patterns before high schools will be capable of reversing their low levels of success.

As we move into the late 1980s, there is little doubt that we will witness the demise of the maintenance paradigm of role and grade isolation organizationally. In a production paradigm, groups will emerge as the dominant work pattern for adults and students, linking professionals to each other in productive ways and students with other ages and abilities for greater achievement, resources, skills, and energy. Collaboration, the central concept in future school organization, nurtures and channels growth for all.

School Organization: A Collaborative Work Context

Principles of Effective Organization

Drucker in one of his recent books, *Managing in Turbulent Times* (1980), proposed that the concept of "production sharing" is necessary for the *transnational* production of goods in today's global economy. To illustrate, he suggests that the last pair of shoes you bought may have started out as an American cow. The hide, however, was probably tanned in Brazil and sent through a Japanese trading company to the British Virgin Islands and Haiti for the shoe uppers and soles to be made. Then the parts were perhaps shipped to Jamaica where they were worked into shoes and shipped throughout the world for sales (ibid., 101–102). Production sharing, in this sense, makes high demands on shoe design and quality control of labor efforts. The demands on management are equally high for planning, organizing, integrating, and coordinating transnational production.

In education, coordination and cooperation have also gone well beyond the classroom and into virtually every corner of schooling. Educators are at last recognizing that collaboration is a necessity for effective school leadership, and for people and/or program development in schools. While schools do not produce shoes or children, they are in the business of producing certain kinds of learning outcomes for all students. As never before, schools are being held accountable for results by communities and states. Job sharing at all levels is critical for meeting the schooling challenge.

Teachers or other personnel can no longer be managed as if they were assembly-line workers. Drucker calls professionals in today's organizations "knowledge workers," and proposes that knowledge be endowed with responsibility, or else it becomes irresponsible and arrogant (1980, 190). With little money, a great deal of creativity, and some risk taking, all school professionals can become involved at a qualitatively higher level of participation in the schooling enterprise.

We must assume that multiple collaborative arrangements are essential throughout the field of education for managing and instructing staff members; for developing materials; for researching influences on school achievement programs; and for creating models of schooling capable of launching schools well into the twenty-first century. The trends of school productivity must be reversed and practices must be eliminated that hinder progress, while simultaneously those practices that now enable educators to be productive must be recognized.

Role expectations for all educators will shift to a "results" orientation. Hence, the practices of role planning, coaching, monitoring, and evaluating will become vital for all roles. Assessment of performance also will shift from analyzing "practice" to analyzing results. Teachers will not be able to raise learning norms in schools alone. They need to link formally with other teachers to share in teaching and also to link with other roles outside the team for additional resources. As more stringent role expectations are defined, teachers and others will need to work in various kinds of groupings to accomplish their purposes.

Let us assume, then, that in the years ahead, all role occupants in schools will work together for various purposes and interface with those in other roles for additional resources. In our discussion of the school's ecosystem (Chapter 2), we briefly discussed certain concepts that are central to a systems approach to organization and management: boundary management, subsystem interaction, dynamic equilibrium, and differentiation. Now it seems appropriate to examine several additional concepts that bear more directly upon the organization and how it functions.

Persons who serve as leaders of schools have many opportunities to influence or determine the way schools shall be organized. From many scholarly literatures, especially the most recent literature of systems approaches, and from practical experience come many ideas to guide the leader in such efforts. Few if any of these ideas are absolutely applicable, since every school (or other human enterprise) is unique in some ways and therefore requires or invites unique organizational arrangements.

By way of definition, organizational structure refers to the established relationships among component parts of the system (Kast and Rosenzweig 1974, 207). Formal relationships, procedures, and compensation are planned structures for organizing tasks and controlling for goal accomplishment. Among the absolute concepts is that *all organizations are goal seeking* and must arrange themselves so that goal attainment is facilitated. Also universally true is that organizations exist within an external environment to which they must continuously adapt. In the case of schools, seeking to be in harmony with a society that is in considerable turmoil is a difficult task, and requires a very complex and differentiated set of responses and services. In "open" systems, characterized by role differentiation, one of the problems for administrators and managers is to strive for *"holism"* (another word not yet in many dictionaries), that is to say, helping the separate parts of the organization to exist as an integrated totality. Within the analogy of an ecosystem, this means regarding all of the subsystems as parts of an entity that is more productive *because* each part plays its supporting role.

Organization theory has spawned, or at least appropriated, another useful word, *"feedback,"* which refers to the data that are fed back to participants in ways that enable them to determine the progress that is being made toward goal attainment. In complex situations, feedback is essential nourishment for success and also for survival.

Among the more respected conclusions from the literature of organizations and groups is that workers are both more satisfied and more productive when they have appropriate opportunity to *participate in the decision-making process.* Such participation helps the worker to feel a greater sense of "ownership" of the resulting goals, and ensures that he or she will understand those goals and appreciate why those goals have been decided upon.

Delegation of authority, so often nonexistent within a school, is essential to productivity in open systems. Authority is the permit to carry out a duty. Delegation of responsibility develops subordinate self-reliance, initiative, and decision-making abilities. It is recommended as a rule of thumb that authority be delegated to the lowest level at which there is sufficient competence and information for effective decision making and task achievement (Hellriegel 1974, 109–110).

To break the school staffing pattern of worker isolation, structured interaction about matters of immediate educational concern must be introduced. *Dialogue,* which is more than conversation, occurs between two or more people who engage in reviewing, reflecting upon, and critiquing past experiences in order to act more effectively in the future (see Freire 1971). Dialogue is a combination of listening to one's own thoughts and those of others and also sharing perceptions, solving problems, and probing ideas collectively. During dialogue, understanding is likely to increase as new insights are formed. In the process of joint struggle with a problem, a sense of community is born. Moreover, trust is built that guides future collaborative actions and functions to transform the present situation into a new reality.

The concepts noted thus far have been drawn from scholarly literatures and have been underscored by experience. They are further underscored in the success of the Japanese industrialists. Japan's progress is to be applauded and also studied for clues to potential success in schools. That the Japanese learned the basic concepts for their success (working and making decisions in groups) from Americans is, at the least, embarrassing. While analysis of Japanese methodology uncovers certain cultural differences that cannot be translated in America (for example, in Japan a person works a lifetime in only one company), there exist certain concepts which can be adapted to American society that warrant our consideration (Ouchi 1981). Note the following:

Organizational culture of trust.   Successful Japanese companies focus on organizational productivity needs and individual needs simultaneously. Consequently, the organization emphasizes involvement of workers in the refinement of the design and the manufacturing process. Everything important happens as a result of teamwork. The Japanese organization is a "consent" culture that changes slowly. Any change involves worker decisions and addresses the deep-rooted values and beliefs of the organization.

Individuals are integrated into the organization as a result of holistic relationships. That is, trust, involvement, communications, and high performance expectations form the basis for organizational work patterns. Furthermore, all work patterns spring from corporate philosophies, which include organizational objectives, operating procedures, and the constraints placed on the organization by the environment. Goals and the co-involvement of culture members guide productivity; productivity gains stem from improved coordination of individuals and work rather than from increased effort.

Teamwork.   The fundamental plant group in Japan is the team, which takes responsibility for all activities related to its function. The team, which represents a concentrated form of ownership, is either formal, or special (organized to solve particular problems), or invisible (rises to meet a continuous need).

Moreover, team objectives take precedence over individual objectives; likewise, no individual credit or blame is given. Collectivism emerges from group work, causing people to work well together and to encourage better efforts. In fact, team-building activities as such do not exist. Rather, a culture is created to foster interpersonal subtlety and intimacy; group cohesiveness results from productive working relationships.

The team assumes responsibility for many things, including selection of the team leader, job assignments, peer evaluation and control, absenteeism, record keeping, scheduling, budget, and evaluation. Likewise, sharing work decisions with management lies at the heart of team success. The team systematically shares in locating and solving problems of its own productivity and coordination, thereby contributing to the improvement and development of the enterprise.

The concepts drawn from systems and other literatures and from Japan's success story all provide educators with basic principles for reorganizing schools in subgroups around purposes and for organizational growth. Subgroups within the organization are essential for its systematic and effective accomplishment of assigned tasks. Organizations that foster collaboration are more likely to be successful in achieving their goals than those in which separate individuals function on isolated tasks.

These concepts present a rationale for considering school organization in terms of staff groupings. Schools need to develop the capacity for collaboration within productive groups. Tasks can be delegated to numerous teams where individuals participate in reflection, planning, and action. Success depends on group skill in developing trust and openness, in reacting to feedback and in developing a sense of community with itself as a team, and within the whole of the school. Our purpose in discussing organizational concepts is to provide guidelines for successful community building in schools. It is our hope that the reader will be persuaded to abandon practices of role isolation of every sort and to seek out numerous ways to link people together in formal and informal patterns for greater school productivity.

We view the principles presented in the following as "givens" in organizing a school. The intent is to unleash the creative energy of the entire school staff.

Principles of Effective School Organization

As we consider principles for organization, it seems appropriate to focus on the mission of schools: to raise the norms of productivity and learning. In an analysis of the change process (or innovations) in the 1960s and 1970s, Heathers (1975) asserts that to be effective, change or development programs must

1. be user initiated
2. originate out of user needs
3. be planned by a mix of administrators, staff, students, and parents
4. be planned for implementation
5. include feedback for renewal purposes
6. include the values of program users

Organizing Principle 1.   *Users must be involved in the planning of any growth process.*

Productivity seems to be a key organizational concept of the 1980s. As has been noted earlier, Japan attributes its production success to the involvement of every worker in a group for purposes of action, work reflection, and refinement (Ouchi 1981). In a sphere closer to home, Deutsch et al. (1971) reports from a study of conditions favoring major advances in social science, that one-half of all scientific contributions made in the latter part of this century have been made by teams of social scientists. Moreover, it seems likely that teams will be the main source of major advances in years to come.

Organizing Principle 2.   *A productive school climate, no matter what degree of value diversity exists, results from group dialogue, decision making, and action.*

To support the concept of user involvement in planning growth programs, Williams et al. (1974), in a study of self-renewing schools in California, found that active involvement in the process of dialogue, decision making, and action can alter the negative effects of value diversity and, further, enable a school staff to become productive. Williams also observed that groups with value diversity in "renewing" schools were able to resolve conflicts and to produce a climate favorable to school growth by becoming involved in planning and dialogue.

Organizing Principle 3.   *Productivity is more likely to result from groups of people working together on a particular task, than from individual efforts, due to the synergistic explosion of energy and ideas.*

Hellriegel and Slocum (1974, 124) discuss two ways for organizing activities: differentiation and integration. *Differentiation* occurs both vertically, by chain of command (for example, principal, team leader, teacher, aide) and *horizontally,* by function, product, and location (for example, a team of teachers for 14 to 17-year-old students). Differentiation enables the school organization *to specialize* in a wide variety of ways in order to provide optimal learning resources for students. *Integration* of activities is achieved by linking individuals from various differentiated teams for a particular *short-range purpose* (for example, a task force to develop an up-to-date record keeping system for all students in science). The purpose in integration is to minimize the amount of total effort expended by the organization on a particular task, and to concentrate efforts in a small work group that produces for the organization as a whole (for example, a program for gifted and talented students, a schoolwide social studies curriculum/program, a reading lab for all students, a parent work program, or a school visitors' program).

Organizing Principle 4. *Small group involvement tends to generate a greater clarity of purpose, a greater coordination of efforts, and greater trust to work together productively.*

Small units in schools that involve each member in a meaningful way tend to produce a climate of trust among group members in school leadership. Furthermore, grouping for a purpose tends to eliminate the unclarity and misconceptions that permeate large group efforts. A recent NIE study of school violence (*Education USA,* January 28, 1980) concluded by urging educators to make schools smaller so that more personal learning climates for both students and teachers could develop, ones in which there would/could be a high degree of cooperation and trust. Goodlad (1984, 310) supports this recommendation.

Organizing Principle 5. *Organize a school into permanent groupings for specialized ongoing purposes and into temporary groupings to complete short-term tasks for the entire school.*

A basic principle of effective organization is to subdivide the staff into various kinds of work groups for the purpose of productive collaboration. The principles noted here include user involvement in planning; dialogue among workers; task-oriented groups; trust and task clarity emerging from small groups; group differentiation and integration stimulating holistic growth; and productive group size of five to seven persons. All principles describe elements found in effective organizations. Kanter (1982) observes from her analysis of productive companies that a matrix organization is the most often used. Workers are grouped for more permanent tasks, and grouped again across team lines to work on short-term tasks.

Organizing Principle 6. *Five to seven people is an optimal small work-group size.*

The question of *organization size* cannot go unnoticed. Management literature abounds with recommendations for the span of management control not to exceed seven subordinates. Yet schools remain in gross violation of basic principles of organizational productivity with 35:1 and 150:2 ratios. Span of control is defined as "a limited number of subordinates who may be supervised effectively by any single manager" (Graiconus 1937, 183–187). Several companies and scholars have attempted to link the span of control principle to behavioral science findings. Productive group size is the major behavioral variable that can guide span of control decisions. Hellriegel and Slocum (1979, 108–109) noted the following guidelines:

1. Member concensus is most easily reached in groups ranging from five to seven in number.
2. As group size increases beyond seven, members feel less directly involved in the task's success.
3. Member satisfaction is related to opportunity for participation in the decision-making process.
4. As the group becomes larger, the leader exhibits more structure and directive leadership behavior because of the difficulties of coordinating the efforts of a large group.

In summary, organizing a school requires consideration of several basic principles. Workers must be involved in planning, which effects their work. Value diversity among group members can be resolved productively through dialogue, decision making, and action. Groups are more productive than collections of individuals. Small group work fosters clarity of purpose and member trust. Two kinds of basic work groups serve the functions of a growing organization: permanent and temporary. The most productive size for work groups is five to seven members.

Permanent and Temporary Work Groups

Productive organizations are those in which work occurs in groups for a wide variety of permanent and temporary organizational purposes. Permanent groups are those that specialize in a particular function over time for the organization. In schools, departments such as science and music or interdisciplinary teams (6- to 8-year-olds, 11- to 13-year-olds) are examples of groupings that *specialize* in a particular curricular or age level teaching focus. These groups provide a special function for a school that is not addressed anywhere else. Temporary, or integrated, groups are those that are organized for a particular short-term purpose and are dissolved when the task is completed. Task forces, such as a math curriculum task force K–6, or a gifted program design task force for the high school, illustrate the short-term nature of the task and, in addition, the integrating nature of the task for the school.

Organizing Around Tasks

One way of viewing the two kinds of staff groupings is to consider the concept of the warp and woof in fabric. In weaving a fabric, the threads that run lengthwise comprise the warp, and the crosswise threads comprise the woof. In common parlance, "warp and woof" connotes the underlying, cohesive structure on which something is built. We find this metaphor to be useful in conceptualizing school organization (see Figure 6.1).

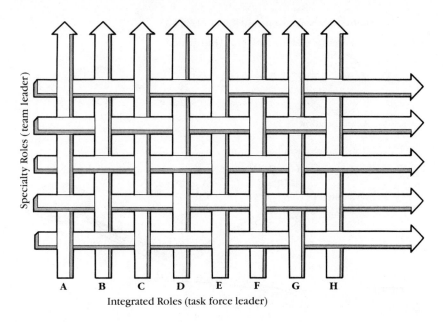

Specialty Roles (team leader)

A   B   C   D   E   F   G   H

Integrated Roles (task force leader)

Figure 6.1. Warp and Woof: Weaving the Fabric of School Growth

The warp can be viewed as specialized groups or instruction teams, as shown in arrows A, B, C, D, and E. These groups/teams might be subject-matter teams, so that A is the English team, B is the social studies team, C is the mathematics team, and so on. In an elementary school, A might be the preprimary team, B the lower primary (grades one and two), C grades three and four, and so on.

The crosswise threads, the woof, can represent the various specialty teams or groups to which the teachers from any one of the instructional teams (A, B, C, D, and E) are assigned, and through which the other growth needs of the school are met. The woof might include

The leadership team: headed by the principal and including the team leaders or other designated representatives of the teaching groups. This team is the "cabinet," the policy-making, decision-making, coordinating body that enables the total school to function more effectively

Production teams: committees, work groups, or other units with assigned responsibilities, such as production of a video program for visitors to the school

Curriculum development teams: teams assigned to coordinate the school program (for example, K–6, K–12, 7–12) usually within content areas. A mathematics team in an elementary school, for example,

Role Differentiation and Specialization

Purpose: Administration and Instruction

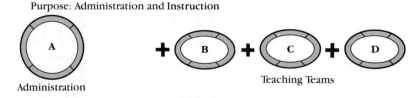

Administration   Teaching Teams

Role Integration

Purpose: Ad Hoc Problem Solving

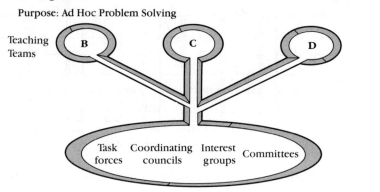

Figure 6.2. The Organization Subsystem

could include one math-responsible delegate from each grade or unit-level, and the team's job would be to see that the math program, K–6, has good flow, continuity, and validity

Councils and study groups: teachers, and perhaps parents or others from outside the school, concerned with review and analysis of questions, topics, problems, or concerns

Task forces: groups on special assignments of schoolwide interest, for example, a task force that includes teachers and other citizens to develop a schoolwide program for creatively gifted students

Figure 6.2 illustrates the differentiated and integrated nature of both kinds of groupings: ad hoc, and administrative and instruction.

Responsibility for the pursuit and accomplishment of goals is distributed throughout the organization. Some goals can be pursued in various ways by two or more groups. On the other hand, certain goals may become the exclusive responsibility of one group or another. The principal, as chairperson of the leadership team, occupies the central role that relates to all groups. Listed in the following are some of the potential differentiated and integrated groups that can be formed for a particular purpose.

Kinds of School Work Groups

1. subject area teams
2. leadership teams
3. instructional teams
4. vertical curriculum teams
5. task forces (to produce a product)
6. planning teams
7. schoolwide goal-setting teams
8. training teams
9. social functions committee
10. outside school activities group
11. evaluation task force
12. human relations committee
13. parent advisory group
14. faculty advisory group

Figure 6.3 illustrates the specific arrangement that one school leadership team developed to accomplish different tasks that grew out of their school's goals.

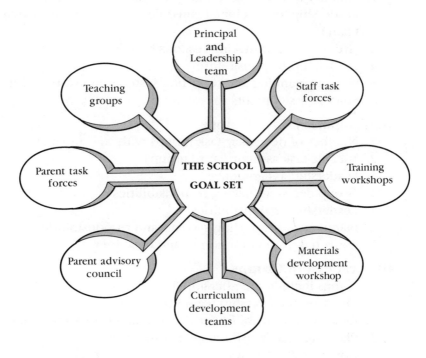

Figure 6.3. Goal Dispersement Model

The management task (actual decisions may involve the leadership team) is to determine the number and size of permanent teaching teams, and to plan for temporary work groups. Planning for organizing involves a number of considerations:

1. the size of the entire school staff
2. optimal task group size of 4 to 7
3. leadership strengths among staff
4. staff teaching strengths and school needs
5. number of needed task forces
6. necessary training in group problem solving and planning and group leadership

After the basic organizational structure has been determined, a tentative plan is made for deciding who belongs to which permanent group and temporary group, and also for outlining group responsibilities and leadership assignments. Final plans ideally are made with staff involvement in decision making. In summary, the plan for school organization includes the following decisions:

I.　Permanent Teaching Groups
1. Number of teaching teams with accompanying staff assignments
2. Leadership for teaching teams (determined by the principal or the team)
3. Group decision-making responsibilities
4. Leadership responsibilities
5. Specific planning and reporting systems and responsibilities
6. Student assignments to teams

II.　Temporary Task Groups
1. Number of necessary task groups with staff and assignments
2. Specific task assignment to groups
3. Leadership assignments
4. Group decision-making responsibilities
5. Leadership responsibilities
6. Planning and reporting systems and responsibilities
7. Expected project outcomes and deadlines

III.　Leadership Groups
Decisions include membership for
1. The school leadership team (council)
2. Council responsibility for the teaching teams and task force
3. Planning and decision-making processes
4. Communications systems
5. Leadership group for task forces

Clarifying Terms

Of the various kinds of association, partnership, and experience sharing that are possible for two or more teachers, teaming carries with it a connotation of thinking and acting together in some officially sanctioned manner. Let us summarize the various kinds of staff groupings in a school. When teachers are organized into a *teaching team,* they then together carry out all the functions of planning, executing the plan, and evaluating that they would otherwise do separately. The term *leadership team* generally applies to a collection of designated leaders (principal, assistant principal, department or unit leaders, and so on) who convene officially in order to make schoolwide plans and decisions. A *discipline team* in a middle school or high school will be a group of teachers selected in some officially approved manner to deal with certain kinds of referred pupil behavior problems. A *vertical curriculum team* will consist of designated representatives of each school level (preschool, primary, intermediate, middle school, secondary) responsible for seeing that the (language, science, mathematics, art) program K–12 has appropriate cohesion and continuity. A *planning team* will be a group assigned to a specific planning function for the school's overall benefit. Another kind of a team is what we choose to call a *task force:* a group responsible for completing a specific task or resolving a school problem, such as development of a public relations package for the school, designing a program for gifted and talented children, or working out a better pupil record-keeping system.

In all such team activities, teachers have an opportunity not only to join in the larger scope of school activities but also to grow professionally through interaction and exchange. Oddly, skill in working with colleagues is itself a growth need of most teachers, despite the fact that teachers ordinarily regard such skills as an important part of what they are seeking to contribute to the students in their classes. Many teachers apparently fail to see the irony in their own resistance to collaboration. Fortunately, such resistance seems to be lessening in schools throughout the country, and therefore a leadership/management system geared to collaborative endeavors will probably be more welcome in the decade to come than it would have been earlier.

In the last several decades attention has been devoted to the teaching team organization, especially in IGE schools. While many schools were organized around teaching teams, little mention was made of the various other groups that emerged out of necessity to address certain needs, such as integrated teams (Lipham and Fruth 1976). This chapter attempts to build onto the concepts of the multiunit school by suggesting that such units are one type of team essential to school productivity. Initially the work of each team is based on goals, some of which are assigned or selected from the school development goals, and others of which emerge from team needs. Other work falls to those staff members from any team who are interested in resolving a particular problem.

Goal Dispersement Activity

The task of organizing a staff into permanent and temporary work groups grows out of goal activity decisions: What groups are required to accomplish the selected school goals? As a general rule, each school goal probably will require three to six different work groups to complete parts of the entire goal. School goals generally are sufficiently comprehensive to require more than one work group to complete discrete tasks within the goal.

The following is an illustration of goal dispersement. A school in Texas with which we worked selected four improvement goals for a given year. The principal and the leadership team then identified the tasks inherent in each goal. It was determined what kind of work group was needed to complete each task, either a teaching or a task force. After the types of work groups were identified for each goal, the leadership team translated the identified task into a work group objective. Note the example that follows.

Goal Dispersement: A Sample

Selected school goals. In this example we will refer to the following four schoolwide goals:

1. To develop a schoolwide *communications system* that will foster greater organizational effectiveness, increased cross-team collaboration, and enriched program development
2. To develop a continuous improvement process whereby *teachers improve their skills* for causing student mastery
3. To develop a *system for student involvement* in school organizational life and in personal program development
4. To plan team-taught, personalized learning *programs* that are *based on diagnosed* mastery level, affective needs/interests, learning style, and cognitive processing style

Group objectives and responsibilities. Responsibility for each of these four school goals was dispersed to various groups within the school.

School Goal I: Communications System
(Dispersed to one group)

Leadership Council
Task Objectives
To produce a staff weekly news sheet of events, needs, responsibil-

ities, resources, and so on as they relate to the activities of the following:

> leadership council
> the teaching teams
> task forces

To organize vertical curriculum teams to develop a schoolwide curriculum that is outcome/mastery oriented

To organize task forces to develop three identified products:

> record-keeping system
> reporting system
> audio/video public relations program

To coordinate schoolwide in-service programs and materials development workshops that are based on needs

School Goal II: Instructional Skill Development
(Dispersed to three groups)

In-service Task Force
> Task Objectives:
> > To conduct workshops on peer supervision, observation technology, the elements of quality instruction, and mastery learning
> > To videotape segments of instruction for staff analysis and improvement recommendations

Teaching Team A
> Task Objectives:
> > To observe each other, collecting data on the four-variable effectiveness (Benjamin Bloom's construct)
> > To plan for the use of the four instruction variables in team program plan
> > To critique each others' instruction plans as they relate to quality instruction/mastery learning variables

The Principal
> Task Objectives:
> > To observe formally each teacher at least four times per year and to informally assist teachers in developing "quality instruction" expertise

School Goal III: Student Involvement
(Dispersed to all teaching teams)

Each Teaching Team
> Task Objectives:
> > To develop a team student council that will organize student task forces as they relate to team life

To develop a student advisory system to ensure personal growth
and well-being

To develop a planning model for regular student input into program
focus, design, and learning alternatives

To develop a contract system for individual planning and evaluation
in each program area

School Goal IV: Diagnostic-Based Instructional Programs
(Dispersed to four groups)

In-service Task Force

Task Objectives:

To conduct workshops in diagnostic procedures that include the
following topics:

learning style

program interests

cognitive processing style

mastery level

motivation

Council

Task Objectives:

To develop a planning model for teaching teams to use in linking
diagnostic data with curriculum parameters and available resources

Teaching Team B

Task Objectives:

To diagnose all team students in the following areas by March 1:
learning style, interests, self-concept, and mastery in major curriculum areas

Inventory Development Task Force

Task Objectives:

To develop an inventory for all teachers to use that diagnoses student interests, strengths, motivation, and self-concept; successful
history

In the preceding example we have sought to demonstrate how the responsibility for goal accomplishment can be distributed among various staff working groups. After goals have been dispersed to teaching teams and task forces,
in the form of task objectives, the work of the school is ready to begin. In the
next two sections we shall discuss more fully the concepts of work in task force
and teaching team arrangements.

The following checklist will guide the principal's decision-making tasks for
translating school-development goals into specific task objectives for staff
work groups.

Organizing Tasks

The Principal's Checklist

After School Goals are defined

- ☐ 1. Define the work groups necessary to complete the goals defined
- ☐ 2. Assign specific objectives to each work group
- ☐ 3. Introduce an action planning process for all groups to use
- ☐ 4. Negotiate and approve team plans
- ☐ 5. Designate due dates for team action plans
- ☐ 6. Designate due dates for periodic team reflection, with reports and new short-range plans being sent to you

Your Job as team coach

- ☐ 1. Observe teams planning or working, or individuals working on team plans
- ☐ 2. Conduct conferences for performance feedback and correctives
- ☐ 3. Provide resources to teams in terms of ideas, materials, experts, and dollars
- ☐ 4. Recognize exemplary performance publicly
- ☐ 5. Plan your supervision of each team, providing the necessary on-the-job coaching

Task Force: The Ad Hoc Work Group

Peters and Waterman (1983, 125–134) found that excellent companies have the capability to get their arms around almost any practical problem and "knock" it off. They give the term "chunking" to this action-oriented work group. Chunking means simply breaking things up to facilitate organizational fluidity and to encourage productive action. While a "chunk" is similar to more familiar terms (task forces, teams, skunk works, quality circles), they seem never to appear on organization charts. Yet chunks are the most visible part of an "adhocracy" that keeps the company moving.

The small work group is the most visible chunking device, an eight- to ten-member work group that takes initiatives for getting a task accomplished. The optimal size of a chunk is seven, which consists of volunteers for a limited duration who set their own goals and plans for productive action. This kind of task force, different from the kind that produces 100-page reports, is a remarkably effective problem-solving tool. The duration of a task force typically is four months, and it is pulled together rapidly. Documentation of efforts is minimal and follow-up action typically is swift. In this way excellent companies solve and manage thorny problems and spur new kinds of action and attitudes. Climate and culture must treat ad hoc behavior as more typical than bureaucratic behavior of permanent work groups. Underlying seemingly unstructured and chaotic environments of task forces lie shared purpose, internal tension, and a competitiveness that makes these cultures "tough as nails."

The task-force approach will take on new vitality in years to come as schools develop the capacity to resolve problems creatively through ad hoc task forces. By organizing volunteers from any and every team to work on a problem common to all teams, the energy system of the school literally explodes with new vitality. People resolve their own corporate problems and in a sense take charge of their own destiny.

Let us return to the hypothetical school goals in the preceding goal dispersement sample and review how goals were dispersed to permanent and temporary work groups. Goal IV, which addressed diagnostic-based instructional programs, was dispersed to two permanent teams (the Leadership Council and Teaching Team B) and to two temporary groups (in-service task force and inventory development task force). We shall develop the concept of chunking by demonstrating the function and process of the first task force.

The function of the in-service task force is "to conduct workshops in diagnostic procedures that include learning style, program interests and motivation, cognitive processing style and mastery level." The task force is comprised of eight staff members who elect to work on this particular task. For each workshop, the work group will need to identify and contact trainees, plan the program with each trainee, and conduct and evaluate the workshop. Task force members may decide to divide their labors so that each workshop is planned and implemented by subgroups of two persons. Therefore, while the task force responsibility as a whole is to provide four workshops, each person on the task force develops only one workshop with one other team member. After their task is complete the group will disband and join other task forces as the school progresses in its development process.

Other ad hoc groups that grow out of a school's goal set might include task forces to develop K–12 curriculum documents, record-keeping systems, student evaluation systems, report cards, a video tape for public relations purposes, a gifted and talented program, school musicals, a spring festival, a special olympics, a reading lab, math lab materials, curriculum file in each content area, media center, adopt-a-school program, and so on.

The ad hoc group formed at any given moment reflects decisions of the staff to work on priority problems. Staff members volunteer for a task force, participate in minimal planning, and then act cohesively and productively to complete the task effectively for the school. Task forces may well provide the school with a source of vitality that solves basic problems and propels a school well into the future.

Teaching Teams: The Basic Work Group

The work organization of the future is likely to have four striking characteristics: (1) small task-focused work units, (2) economic and managerial control over its own destiny, (3) interconnected linkages with larger entities through computer and communications capabilities, and (4) bonded into larger companies (school within the district) through strong cultural bonds (Deal and Kennedy 1983, 183). The term given to this structure is "atomized organization" to emphasize how small, flexible units are linked to the corporate whole like molecules.

The new form of organization will be more effective for four reasons, assert Deal and Kennedy (1983, 184):

Studies demonstrate that people are more effective when they are in control of their destinies. Pay will be linked directly to performance

Peer group pressure is the single most powerful motivating force

Strong cultures are more easily built in smaller units, which will behave more cohesively and achieve higher productiveness

Computer and communications links will be cheaper than layers of middle management for bonding individual units

For schools, the basic work task is *instruction* for various populations. Conceptualized and developed first at Harvard University in the mid-1950s, team teaching provides the basic work structure for schools of the future. Although historical scholarship has provided perspective and demonstrated that the idea of collaborative teaching endeavor has many antecedents (not only in America but elsewhere) over time, a rather special spirit of pioneering excitement prevailed in those American universities, including Harvard, whose staff members participated in various research and development activities related to team teaching prior to 1961.

One of the best known of the pilot projects at the elementary school level was sponsored jointly by Harvard and the Lexington, Massachusetts, Public Schools. The apparent success of this project and of similar projects across the nation, led to the initiation in 1961 of a special training program (known as the Harvard–Lexington Summer School) designed to provide experienced teachers and administrators with a carefully supervised introduction to those processes of planning, teaching, and evaluation with which teams of teachers are concerned.

The team teaching project in Lexington was begun in 1957 and continued (under a generous grant from the Ford Foundation) through the 1963–1964 school year. In a brief span of seven years, stimulated in considerable measure by the Lexington project, the idea of team teaching became well established as a viable alternative to the traditional patterns of self-contained classrooms. Significant literature was produced, including two books (Shaplin and Olds 1964; Bair and Woodward 1964) by persons from Harvard and Lexington, and although (as is still true) much work remained in defining and implementing the best possible models, there was a growing confidence in the merit of team teaching across the land.

Early Conceptualizations of Team Teaching

Basic definitions of team teaching have been offered so widely in the literature (especially in the Shaplin–Olds volume), that it would be wasteful to repeat them here. However, it might be helpful here to include a 10-point summary prepared in mimeo form by Anderson at Harvard–Lexington in 1963.

1. *Team teaching may exist in a variety of patterns, some involving loose or informal cooperation or collaboration, and some highly formalized.*

2. *Teams of teachers engage jointly in planning, teaching* (that is, implementation of the plan), *and evaluation* (that is, appraisal of the plan and how it was carried out). All three aspects are assigned great importance. What may be unique to most newly involved teachers, and probably the most emotionally loaded, is the emphasis upon full-scale and relentless evaluation. In the typical school situation, few teachers engage in continuous evaluative exchange with professional colleagues; therefore participation in evaluation sessions is likely to have a rather dramatic impact on staff.

3. *Team organization theoretically allows for unusual variety in the assignment, scheduling, grouping, and location of pupils.* It permits many patterns and sizes of instructional groups to be organized. It allows for teacher specialization while at the same time compelling (or at least attempting to compel) an integration of the total program for each child. It makes possible the relatively economical use of supplies and resources, physical spaces, and nonprofessional adult assistants.

4. As (2) above implies, *team organization has built-in "supervisory" potentialities ("supervision" here meaning influencing the professional performance of a teacher through discussion, observation, and related procedures).* Team teaching permits supervision through group work and cooperative efforts within the context of the working situation and is facilitated by direct observation of the performance of the individual on the job. It therefore offers opportunity for leadership to those career teachers with talents in the supervisory (and/or exemplary and inspirational) area, while at the same time

providing a nourishing and stimulating atmosphere within which beginners and other teachers can work.

5. *Team teaching is not in itself a methodology or a system for instructing.* It is, rather, a stimulant to the analysis of instruction and to the development of needed technologies. In particular, it should lead to the invention and/or development of useful strategies vis-à-vis large-group teaching, small-group teaching, and so-called independent learning.

6. *Team teaching,* similarly, *is not a curriculum system* as such. Rather, it tends to stimulate reexamination of existing curricula and the creation of new curriculum approaches. Such developments are independent of team organization.

7. *Teachers are by training and/or disposition unaccustomed to the patterns of small-group adult interaction characteristic of team teaching.* The literatures (mostly from fields outside education) dealing with social structure, social organization, communication systems, reward systems, leadership, morale, and the like have not yet been sufficiently translated into operational guidelines for instructional teams.

8. *Team teaching can at this stage be regarded only as primitive,* and it remains for theories and procedures to be further developed before the long-range usefulness and applicability of team teaching can be adequately examined. Heathers has rightly indicated that (a) almost all accomplishments to date belong to the design stage (that is, the planning and engineering of suitable team models); (b) none of the theoretical models currently being treated has yet been fully implemented (that is, there are still discrepancies between what is and what is intended); (c) the development and evaluation of team teaching is being impeded by a general failure to apply appropriate research strategies to the stage of design, the stage of implementation, and so forth; (d) the tendency of proponents (or for that matter, opponents) to argue the merits (and demerits) of team teaching, especially in advocating widespread dissemination and adoption, is therefore premature and unfortunate. Many years of exploratory development will be required, and more suitable techniques of research and evaluation must be utilized.

9. *Though little reliable research is yet in the record,* the directors of pilot projects have reported their experiences with enthusiasm and optimism. The extent to which team teaching as such explains the reported outcomes is still very unclear. Tentatively, however, it may be stated that *team operations are feasible*; children appear not to suffer disadvantages (personal-social-emotional, and academic)

asserted by theories favoring the self-contained classroom; participating personnel, including adults as well as children, offer largely affirmative testimonial opinions; various improvements in curriculum, supervision and administration appear to be stimulated by team operations. Of particular interest are certain indications that the pupil-guidance function is pursued more effectively, at least for children at the extremes of the continuum, when several adults share information and responsibilities in the guidance area.

10. *Team teaching has certain built-in characteristics that facilitate in-service staff growth.* It is also dependent upon adequate external (pre-service and in-service) training of the staff in the fundamentals of instruction, in emerging theories of learning, in the generic goals of education, in group processes, in teamwork, in roles of specialization (content oriented, methodology oriented), and in evaluation. Persons of such training are now almost nonexistent, and a major problem for the profession is to increase their supply.

Pitfalls and Hopeful Signs

With roots in the work of John Dewey and others, team teaching was a product and a part of the major educational reform movement that was launched in the 1950s. Credit for much of the early work belongs to the Fund for the Advancement of Education (Ford Foundation), to at least nine universities (Harvard, Wisconsin, Chicago, Claremont Graduate School, Wayne State, New York University, George Peabody Teachers College, Hawaii, and later, Stanford), and to about 50 school systems that were engaged in pilot projects. A major figure in the early development of secondary school team teaching was J. Lloyd Trump, who was secretary of the Committee on Staff Utilization of the National Association of Secondary School Principals.

Another aspect of the larger reform movement, the use of paraprofessionals as part of the school work force, proved to be a good connecting link with team teaching and in fact was partly responsible for the gradual use of the term "differentiated staffing" in the literature of team teaching. That literature reached its peak by 1970, although it is of interest that into the 1980s teaming seems to be accorded matter-of-fact acceptance within the general literature, and continues to receive far more endorsement as an organization option than does its antonym, the self-contained classroom.

Team teaching generated numerous configurations, most of which are informal. Few models of administratively engineered team teaching organizational arrangements have survived the 1960s and early 1970s; most of the surviving models were teacher initiated. Middle and senior high schools have readily institutionalized the department (a team) focus, many departments resembling the size of an elementary school.

Nevertheless, schools remain organized virtually as they were midcentury. For elementary schools, principals manage large numbers of individual teachers, some of whom choose to team together for their own purposes. In middle and high schools, teachers are organized more formally into subject area departments, with one teacher assuming administrative duties and program control functions. One might assume that all schools are significantly different in organizational design from one level to the next; that is, elementary teachers teach all basic subjects to thirty students while middle and high school teachers are responsible for teaching one subject to 125 or more students. However, the differences in organizational function are negligible after that. Teachers in virtually all levels, except in rare exceptional schools, actually plan alone, teach alone, and assess student progress alone, and rarely work on all-school productivity tasks.

We hypothesize, therefore, that role isolation is still the dominant work pattern for teachers for the following reasons: (1) administration has provided low expectations for the outcomes of teaming; (2) teachers have received insufficient training in collaborative communications and work processes generally, and in team teaching specifically; (3) the team typically is given no authority over individual teachers, either with regard to their participation in team efforts or in the individual teaching; (4) few reward systems exist to motivate teachers so they can succeed in team teaching, and work through problems and changes; and (5) teachers receive little or no coaching in the teaming process; therefore when skills are developed they emerge in a hit-or-miss fashion.

To our surprise and delight, a 1979 report out of Stanford University notes that although many educators and citizens believe that teaming is dying out, it is an innovation that persisted into the 1970s. Elizabeth Cohen, a researcher at Stanford's Center for Educational Research, notes that the center has been studying teaming in elementary schools since 1968. Technological conditions and the growing complexity of instruction, along with the influence of open-space architecture, have in her view prompted teachers to turn to collaborative arrangements, despite some of the problems and frustrations that are sometimes involved. Her other observations include that (a) teachers are rarely provided with the training necessary to take advantage of teaming; (b) isolated teachers have more difficulty handling tasks of complexity than teamed teachers; (c) many teams are temporary or prove to be unstable, but new ones spring up to replace the ones that disappear; (d) few principals realize that teams require explicit policies and support from the administration (for example, help with policies to deal with discipline, help with leadership techniques, and provision of planning time). Her overall conclusion is that *teachers need a structure for sharing their expertise,* and despite the problems, "when it's done with proper support, teaming is the best low-cost innovation I know to improve complex instruction" (Saily 1979).

Another researcher, William Rutherford, conducted a two-year study supported by the National Institute of Education involving interviews with 1,200 teachers in school districts where teaming is used. Rutherford notes that despite the lack of attention to it in journals and forums, teaming "continues to flourish" (Rutherford 1979, 29), and that despite various concerns (such as time management, changed relationships with students, and intrateam relationships) teachers tend to support it because it is effective for them and their students.

Rutherford and others have observed that team teaching is hard to define because there are so many varieties of it. It may be useful, therefore, for us to discuss and define the concept later in this section, and further to offer what we regard to be an ideal version worth working toward.

How Teams Work Productively: Clues from Non-Education Models

As we educators look around, we observe virtually every other profession functioning collaboratively. For example, in hospitals, team responsibilities are essential to caring for the sick and injured. Doctors, nurses, technicians, and others carry out functions within role sets (doctors or nurses) and across role sets (doctors–nurses–technicians). Imagine the impossibility of one person attempting full responsibility for even one patient, let alone 30. Virtually all role sets are interdependent.

The high levels of industrial productivity in Japan have caught our attention due to the claim that quality circles are the key to Japanese success. In quality circles (QC) workers are organized with others into work groups for the purpose of

1. contributing to the improvement and development of the organization;
2. respecting humanity and building a happy, bright workplace for meaningful work; and
3. displaying human capabilities fully and eventually drawing out infinite possibilities (Ouchi 1981, 265).

How do the circles work? From two to 10 employees are assigned to a permanent circle in which everyone's work is related to the others' in some way. The task of each circle, headed by a foreman, is to study the problems of production and service that relate to their work. Workers select a problem area and then suggest steps that need to be taken to correct it. Results of the study are implemented within the circle; recognition is given to successful implementation, for example, through a plant newspaper. If particularly innovative, the project might be nominated for a plant award.

Quality circle members notice all the little things in the organization that influence work success. One challenge for management is to provide both training and on-the-job coaching to employees, in group work skills, including collaborative decision making. Another is to delegate to the circles the power and authority to influence changes in their organization and the technology of work. It is the management sharing of power with employees, combined with significant training, that has marked Japan's innovation.

Management journals in the United States today are filled with articles and studies on how QC has been implemented successfully in American industries. However, a major hurdle for Americans is to determine *whether to* and *how to* shift management from a top-down authority pattern in developing materials and services, to a shared pattern of decision making, where ideas are expected to generate from the bottom as well. In industries where top management has shifted its power-control pattern, QC circles are effective; where power has remained top-down, little impact is felt within the organization from QC activity.

The QC circle concept has been implemented with some degree of success in such companies as Ford Motor Co., Honeywell, General Electric, Bank of America, and 3M (Cook 1982, 4). Cook notes that in addition to profit organizations, many service organizations throughout our society have also expressed varying degrees of interest in circles. Cook, who is the editor of *Training and Development Journal*, observes and also warns that successful implementation of circles depends on shifting power, authority, and decision making to the circle level. Middle management, he observes, provides the greatest stumbling block to implementing effective circle organization. Unless middle managers perceive workers' participation as a resource, circle effects are likely to produce little that is useful to the organization. Given support and leadership by middle management, QCs can contribute significantly to organizational productivity. In fact, Cook cites a study that shows that 75 percent of the solutions presented to management in the United States have been implemented.

What can schools learn from quality circles to improve the quality of life in our schools, as well as the productivity of teachers? Drucker (1982, 113) observes that today's workers are "knowledge workers" who demand responsibility for making contributions. He asserts that the key to worker productivity is to demand responsibility and to direct behavior toward contributions rather than effort. He warns, however, that to make workers productive requires "assignment control" because results are often hard to measure (ibid., 115).

We propose a rather bold approach to school organization that will cause both teaching and management to become more reasonable in scope, and more effective in results. We propose that schools be organized into permanent teaching teams, each team with the responsibility as well as the authority to produce certain levels of student achievement. Accountability for student achievement should be placed at the level where teaching occurs (the team) and where groups of teachers can assume joint responsibilities for certain results.

Team Teaching in the Current Context

The teacher who works within a team does not lead a more difficult professional life or work toward different goals for children than does a self-contained teacher. The teacher in a team does not have to sacrifice meaningful interactions with children or abandon a unique and worthwhile pedagogical style. A common misconception is that teachers lose their individuality when they merge their activities with other teachers. On the contrary, opportunities for personal satisfaction and growth are far greater within the team context than in the isolated classroom. Furthermore, the goals that the school has for its learners remain the same, and neither parents nor the community expect the results of schooling to be qualitatively different in team-organized schools from conventionally organized schools. That the delivery system is organized in a rather different way, and that there is greater presumed flexibility in a team arrangement might cause parents to hope for somewhat greater (as opposed to different) results. However, teachers in teams and self-contained teachers both hope for the same kinds of student outcomes. Similarly, the budget for a team-organized school is not necessarily greater or smaller than that of a conventional school with the same adult and pupil population, and one could expect in either school to find pretty much the same institutional resources (such as books, maps, microscopes, and supplies). The building custodian will not necessarily be any grouchier or any happier in one or the other setting, the food services personnel will not necessarily deal with different opportunities or problems, and counselors or administrators do not necessarily have a harder or easier time of it.

Stated another way, teachers in teams seek to accomplish, collectively, what an equal number of self-contained teachers seek to accomplish independently. Whatever belongs to the role of teacher belongs also to the role of team teacher. However, the self-contained teacher ordinarily has limited obligations and opportunities for collaborating with colleagues, with the various dimensions of task sharing and communication that collaboration fosters, whereas the teamed teacher has many such obligations and opportunities.

There are at least *nine functional aspects of teaming,* and the extent to which all nine of the following can be found in a given situation will signify how completely team teaching has been implemented.

1. *Long-range plans* for the instructional program (that is, the curriculum, or a major portion thereof, for which all of the co-involved teachers share responsibility) have been developed jointly. All of the team members share a distinct sense of ownership of, as well as commitment to, the long-range plans (and related goals) that are to be pursued.

2. *Short-range plans* for the instructional program (that is, the elaborate amplification of each successive portion of the long-range program), similarly, have been collaboratively developed. Team members participate at least weekly in formulating more immediate objectives. Over time, all team members become reasonably conversant with the specific daily plans and professional repertoires of their colleagues. As a result, it would be relatively easy for any team member to step into a colleague's teaching shoes in an emergency.

3. *In-depth discussions and critiquing* of individual teacher plans occurs for each member at least once each month. Example: In Tuesday's team planning session, Miss Jones presents the detailed lesson plan she has prepared for use on Thursday afternoon with her math group. The ensuing discussion reinforces many of Jones's ideas but provides some helpful advice as well. For everyone, the discussion raises levels of pedagogical consciousness. Next Wednesday, Mr. Green's plans for a lesson on soil samples will be on the agenda.

4. The members of the team often engage in *co-teaching*, which involves two or more of them in the same lesson or sequence of lessons.

5. *Members of the team,* whether or not co-involved in certain lessons, frequently *observe each other* at work with children, taking notes (as appropriate) of the ways plans are working out, materials and resources are serving their purpose, students are responding to the elements of the lesson (and to the teachers), and goals are apparently being accomplished. Such observations are desirable not only because of the helpful feedback that can be provided to the observed teacher(s), but also because of the insights that can be gained by the observer and translated into his or her teaching.

6. *Short-range evaluation,* for example of instructional sequences and units recently completed, is conducted by all members of the team.

7. *Long-range evaluation* of the entire program is similarly conducted by all members of the team.

8. The entire team sits together, as often as appropriate, to *review individual pupil progress.* Ideally, this is done for every pupil for whom the team has responsibility, and often enough so that the experiences of every member of the team with that child become a part of the

record and better educational prescriptions can be designed for him or her.

9. All of the *materials* and *resources* that are used in the program, including classroom floor space, *belong to everyone on the team,* and territoriality is avoided.

The foregoing list could probably be expanded, especially to include some of the attitudes (especially of willingness to share, and to accept criticism in good spirit) and communication skills that need to exist if a team is to function well, but this list of nine conditions or aspects not only seems basic, but indicates the various procedural dimensions that can be identified in full-fledged teaming. We might add that there are at least three other characteristics often found in teams:

1. *Designation of leadership* in some formal manner. Many teams operate well without designated leadership, or with a rotating parliamentary-type chairperson, but on the whole it has usually seemed desirable to appoint a leader with a certain degree of authority and responsibility during a designated period of time.
2. *Role specialization,* which calls for various members to function as specialists. This is, of course, a built-in condition in interdisciplinary teams.
3. *Differentiated staffing,* for example with aides or clinical assistants serving as support personnel.

Teaching teams that are found in secondary schools are usually organized within a single subject or discipline, although occasionally one finds teams that embrace two or more disciplines, such as math–science or language arts–social studies. Multidiscipline teams are more common in middle schools, and are in fact the rule in elementary schools. Especially in the latter, teams also are multigraded, encompassing several adjacent grade levels (e.g., grades four, five, and six). There are several inherent advantages in such arrangements, one of which is that the curriculum can be more responsive to the needs of learners. Another is that vertical continuity can more easily be ensured when the same teachers work with a group of pupils over several successive years.

Teachers whose entire histories have been linked with self-contained classrooms may need a considerable reorientation, especially psychologically, if they are moving into a team. Fortunately, most teachers do not find it especially difficult or traumatic to make the adjustment, although various habits have to be discarded or modified and several new habits need to be formed. In most cases, teachers new to teaming appear to find considerable satisfaction and even excitement in discovering new sources of stimulation, assistance, and sense of achievement. There is, further, a synergistic dimension when several teachers pool their ideas and talents, and many popular aphorisms ("two heads are better than one," "many hands make light work," "in union there is strength") come to have practical meaning for the collaborating professionals.

Especially in view of the emphasis schools place on cooperation and sharing on the part of children, team teaching offers a better and more applicable work model for children than does self-contained teaching. When teachers in their own work behaviors are providing examples of sharing and collaborating, this is certain to make an impression upon the youngsters. Among the modeling behaviors will be included mutual goal setting; shared problem solving; helping and assisting; open and continuous communication; application of specialized talents for benefit of the group; and joint decision making and adapting to changing needs and situations. In a healthy team, leadership is situational, and invention and compromise are frequently necessary to keep the program moving forward. Individual talents are respected, as are individual needs and limitations, and each member is accepted for what he or she is best able to contribute. Children observing and working with a healthy team cannot help but be positively influenced.

There are certain advantages in a team approach for promotion of the school's educational program. When there are several professionals involved, and especially if they work with a fairly large number of students, access to a large number of parents can be had more readily and less effort is required of the staff. Only one member of the team needs to be involved, for example, in the preparation of messages to parents, or in presenting programs or explanations to parents in PTA meetings or other assemblages. Similarly, one member of the team can represent the others at in-service sessions, schoolwide or systemwide conferences, or planning meetings. The team's representative can easily share with colleagues the results of all such activities; and in view of the responsibility implicit in representing colleagues, that person is likely to make sure that the team follows through with the various tasks that grow out of those activities.

Team-Level Decisions

As a relatively permanent specialized group within the school organization, the teaching team has various decisions to make that influence its functioning as a unit, and consequently, its actual teaching. The teaching team, while it is a subsystem of the school's organization, is, in a sense, its own ecosystem with its own goals, organization, performance system, program for students, program for staff, technology, and leadership and management. The decision sets that follow can guide the teaching team in planning its organization and its growth.

Team Improvement Goals

Each teaching team has its own improvement goals that reflect assignments from the school goal set (for example, Team A may want to develop new materials for its math program, while Team B develops a new program for parent and community volunteers in the classroom). Each team, like the school, is responsible for goals that influence school life beyond team boundaries and at the same time must be responsible for growth needs within the team. After improvement goals are defined the teaching team uses the action planning system (presented later in this chapter) for determining its action course for the year.

Team Organization

Various ways exist for organizing teaching teams into productive groupings of students and teachers. The special interests and talents of team members, the diagnosed skills and needs of pupils, the spaces and other resources available, the schedules of specialists who are available to work with the team, and other factors will be taken into account as the team decides how it wants to establish spatial and instructional territories, pupil subgroups, program time tables, and other organizational dimensions. Also necessary to decide will be the responsibilities to be shared by all members, versus responsibilities to be borne by particular individuals. How to use parent volunteers or other aides; when and where to hold team meetings; what to do about meeting professional development needs of members (for example, through peer supervision); and related matters will also be topics for group decisions.

Some organizational functions, such as team leadership and management, may be assigned to one person. Other areas, such as program assignments and supervision require several persons working together. All functions mentioned are important for team growth and are usually addressed by teams in some fashion. If left unplanned, however, the function may hinder team productivity. If planned, the likelihood of the function contributing to team productivity is great.

Instructional Student Groups

Though the recitative, total-class arrangement apparently prevails in American schools, even after a half-century of exhortations about more individualized forms of instruction, there appears to be greater and greater acceptance of the need for more one-on-one arrangements and for more patterns that bring small numbers of learners together for specific purposes.

It remains appropriate for pupils sometimes to be assembled in aggregates of 20, 30, 50, 150, or even larger numbers, especially when some sort of information is being made available (as in listening to a lecture, watching a demonstration, viewing a film or TV program, or hearing progress reports from fellow students). Large-group instruction of this sort is economical of time and of resources, and to some extent it helps to reinforce each child's membership in the larger community. As long as the large-group experience is demonstrably appropriate, in at least some way or ways, for each participant, teachers need not hesitate to sponsor such activities.

For purposes of discussion or other interactive modes of learning, however, numbers above 10 or 15 are highly inappropriate. Especially in secondary schools, teachers who are accustomed to conducting "discussions" in classes with more than a dozen or so students usually find this view hard to accept, since the norms of their experience are deeply rooted over time; but the fact is that the usual such discussion rarely provides benefits to more than a fraction of the class. We think that a teacher with 40 available minutes and 24 students can accomplish more by spending 20 minutes each with two groups of twelve, if the discussion mode is the chosen delivery system.

Classroom discussion is sometimes likened to decision making, since one reason for discussing a problem or topic is to come to some sort of conclusion about it. It seems probable that over the centuries, perhaps even reflected in the fact that Jesus Christ had 12 disciples, men have determined that a dozen is an effective number for the accomplishment of certain purposes. Judicial systems generally employ not more than 12 persons on a jury, for example. Recent data from social-psychological research suggest that member consensus is most easily reached in groups ranging from five to seven in number. As group size increases beyond seven, the research indicates, members feel less directly involved in the task's success. Observations of participating behavior also confirm that there is more and better participation in discussions when the number of discussants is within the five-to-seven range. Above 12 or 13 it is difficult for all participants to remain actively involved.

In passing, it might be acknowledged that it is *sometimes* advantageous to have as many as 12 or 13 participants in a discussion, especially where the information base is thereby enlarged beyond that possessed by a smaller number of persons. On a whole, however, member satisfaction in discussion and decision-making groups is related to opportunity for participation, and also to the extent to which the members' needs for affiliation and goal attainment are satisfied. This argues for smaller rather than larger discussion groups.

There is another type of pupil grouping that often occurs in schools, and this has to do with collective effort to create some sort of a product. Working groups of this sort may include class committees, task forces, laboratory project groups, or other aggregates of students with a common responsibility. Sometimes such groups are as small as three or four. Research evidence suggests that about six is a good number for a working and interacting group, with eight as probably the maximum if the group is to function well.

A pattern of pupil grouping to which we are particularly loyal, involves the deliberate mixing of children from two or more adjoining age levels. This arrangement is variously called mixed-age, multiage, multigrade, or (as in England) family grouping. Especially when multiage grouping occurs within a multiunit or team-teaching organization, so that the total number of available children allows for a wide variety of homogeneous and heterogeneous subgroupings, being continuously in the company of classmates whose age and life experience differs from one's own can be enormously beneficial both socially and academically. Ever since the famed Torrance (California) Plan demonstrated that the older as well as the younger children benefited from multigraded grouping, and especially in light of very favorable experience with multiage teaching teams, educators have been hard pressed to justify separating children into unit-age, intentionally homogeneous groups.

In a very real sense, our current preference for multiage class/team grouping reflects at least one advantage that was enjoyed in the Little Red Schoolhouse: older and/or more advanced pupils served as models and tutors for the younger and less advanced, and there was a family atmosphere within which interdependence was accepted in good spirit. Also, teachers sought to organize some parts of each day around topics, problems, or activities in which children of varying abilities could find some educational values for themselves. This learning-together, sharing-together, helping-each-other atmosphere is often lost in the single-age, single-grade classroom, where competition sometimes takes over and teachers make less effort to plan activities that fit a wide range of interests and abilities.

Another advantage of multiage arrangements is that they give children several types of leadership-followership opportunities, and in the process they extend the range of personal friendships. We prefer having *three* ages together, for instance, grades 1–2–3 and grades 10–11–12, because this permits a greater range of skill-learning groups. A very bright six-year-old, for example, could be grouped for math instruction not only with seven-year-olds but also, as appropriate, with eight-year-olds (and vice versa for a slow-developing eight-year-old), with minimum social labeling. However, let us postulate a two-year pattern: grades 1 and 2 together, grades 3 and 4, and grades 5 and 6. Note that a first-grader in year one will connect not only with other six-year-olds, but also with seven-year-olds. In year two, his age group will be joined by a new group of friends who spent last year in kindergarten. On the playground and in the corridors there will continue to be friendly exchanges with former older classmates who are now in the grade 3–4 unit. In year three, he rejoins these former older classmates. In year four, he is rejoined by former younger classmates, and so on.

In such situations, it is much easier to arrange for grade acceleration of a very advanced pupil (since all he or she has to do is advance with existing older classmates) or to "hold back" a child who needs an extra year's time to master grade-level basics (since all he has to do is stay for a third year with existing younger classmates). This arrangement also ensures that advancement to junior high school will be less perilous, because a nucleus of former older classmates and friends will be there to offer assistance.

In secondary schools, almost any subject area can be multiaged to include skill level variations as well as interest area variations. Learning in a context of mixed age grouping prepares the secondary school student for the mixed age learning that follows schooling: the workplace. Learning is a lifelong activity as is learning within an organizational context. Multiage experiences reflect realities in the work world and precondition a student to work with the differences and similarities in people, which have little to do with age.

For these several reasons, we would like to see all American elementary schools adopt a multiage pattern. Middle schools, too, find that multiaging increases the school's ability to meet the wide-ranging needs of their students.

Individual Staff Performance

Each adult team member is responsible for both teaching and team organization assignments. Eventually the team leader must know all that Susan is responsible for and the areas of responsibility for Tom, Jean, and Bill. While the team has plans to accomplish its various functions, each individual will plan for his other individual performance yearly, monthly, weekly, and daily. The strength of the team emanates equally from team dialogue and plans, and individual performance within the team context. It should also be noted that a teaching team member will have responsibilities to task forces and other work groups outside the teaching team, bridging gaps that can emerge from teams working in isolation from other teaching teams and from total school needs.

Team Program

Team programs vary greatly from school district to school district; from school to school; and from team to team. On some elementary teams, all teachers may decide to teach reading and math, and specialize in other subject areas. Other teams may decide to have math/science and language arts/social studies subteams. Junior high/middle school and high school groups may decide to divide responsibilities within a discipline (science) in various ways, or to link math/science or language arts/social studies teachers and students together. Other schools may organize around a number of students (400) and provide a program for those students.

Whatever program assignments result from school and team decisions, there are guidelines that can be helpful in the planning sequence. It is recommended that one team member be responsible for the success of math, for example, for the entire team. However, teammates must share in some math program decisions. We recommend dividing up responsibility so that there is continuous program interaction, feedback, and refinement. The *team* generally makes broad program recommendations and decisions. The *program specialist* does the detailed work and presents plans to the team for feedback, refinement, and dispersement of teaching responsibilities. The *individual teacher,* who, for example, teaches math, but is not the team specialist, receives the general plan and prepares for his or her part in the instructional program. The following list provides a more detailed outline of team/specialist/individual responsibilities in program planning.

Guidelines for Team Program Planning Decisions

Team-level program planning decisions

1. Assign responsibilities to individuals for program planning in each curriculum area
2. Assign responsibilities for teaching, both program areas and student groups
3. Review and finalize detailed program plans developed by specialists
4. Determine general diagnostic procedures: levels of mastery, learning styles, interests, cognitive styles, problems
5. Determine general learning outcomes for each program area
6. Determine record keeping and reporting procedures
7. Define general uses of space, materials, people, time, and resources
8. Supervise instruction, providing feedback correctives and reinforcement
9. Evaluate program effectiveness in each curriculum

Curriculum specialist level planning decisions (math, reading, etc.)

1. Develop a learning scope and sequence
2. Develop broad program time lines for planning and teaching
3. Collect and assign instructional materials
4. Provide the team with updated knowledge on teaching in the particular program area
5. Recommend cognitive and affective diagnostic procedures for initial diagnosis for placement
6. Design basic team programs in the assigned curriculum area for cognitive, affective, and behavioral development
7. Recommend types of student groupings for each program and methods for determining groups
8. Develop specific objectives for each program for all learning levels
9. Determine instructional options, student choice options for various student groups
10. Develop procedures for student planning

11. Prepare program time lines and staff responsibilities for each program

Individual teacher level decisions (non-specialist)

1. Participate in team program planning meetings
2. Select teaching assignments based on personal strengths and team needs
3. Develop a detailed learning program that fits into the team's general program plan for the assigned students
4. Conduct a needs survey
5. Select or develop specific objectives for the assigned students
6. Develop classroom management procedures for assigned students
7. Plan for and assist in student planning activities
8. Provide instruction to facilitate student mastery
9. Request and also provide peer observation and feedback in areas of concern
10. Provide feedback to the specialist and to the team on program implementation process and results

Team Technology and Administration

Who reports to parents? Who records student progress? What are the student discipline procedures? What budget plans need to be made for next year? What kinds of instruction systems or supervision will be used? Many decisions that are administrative or technical in nature are necessary to the success of the team. Depending on the teaching loads of team members, administrative responsibilities can be assumed by one or by many team members to ensure team success.

Leadership and Management

Teams find various ways to assume responsibility for leadership. Some teams elect leaders for a year or rotate leadership responsibilities by the month. Leadership responsibilities from other teams are assigned to them by the principal. The method used to determine leadership potential often depends on the perceived maturity of the group to make intelligent decisions. Whichever method is used, the functions must be fulfilled for the team's productivity to be realized. Note the leadership functions listed in the following.

Team Leadership and Management Responsibilities

1. Team-level goal setting and action-planning activities
2. Staff organization
3. Team planning and problem-solving procedures
4. Implementing team plans
5. Instruction and learning progress

6. General student groups
7. Team's budget
8. Results of plans and programs
9. Team-wide student achievement gains
10. Team growth needs
11. The team's instructional progress

Teaching in teams requires more than shared decisions about teaching. The team identifies its own growth and production needs as one organization or subsystem. In addition, the team organizes for effective utilization of team strengths, plans for the numerous factors that influence student achievement, and communicates decisions to various school officials and to parents. The effectiveness of a team lies in its ability to function productively and cohesively as an ecological unit within the school context.

Listed here are the variables that influence teaching team productivity. The responsibility of the team is to address each as it bears on action plans and to work toward its goals within the uniqueness of its own learning community.

Influences on Team Productivity

1. School and team goals
2. Specialized and integrated team roles
3. Individual and collective beliefs
4. Collective resources
5. Principles of learning implemented
6. Principles of instruction implemented
7. Learning program design
8. Individual and collective experiences
9. Individual and collective performance
10. Technologies
11. Management planning, supervision, and control
12. Continuous evaluation

Giving Teams a New Sense of Vitality and Purpose

The concepts presented in the following pages are still embryonic and they may be filled with legal problems. However, within the basic model lies the spark that may generate productive renewal for teams within a school. We propose that every teacher be assigned to a teaching team (or department) of three to eight members each, with an assigned team leader. The primary purpose of the team is to produce certain levels of student growth collectively

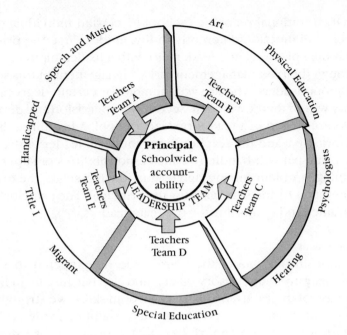

Figure 6.4. A School-Based Production-Sharing Model

within each school year (see Figure 6.4). The new twist is this: the principal will negotiate with each team for the degrees of measurable achievement it can expect to produce in a given year (using standardized test predictor scores for planning). Then, the principal will delegate to the team the necessary power and authority to plan to develop professional skills and programs, and to organize and teach to accomplish their goal. Evaluation of the results, in this view, would be a team responsibility; individual worker evaluation occurs within the team context, in cooperation with the principal. Evaluation questions, such as Did the team meet its goals? To what degree? What were the strengths of the team? Weaknesses? What are suggested next steps? provide specific feedback for team growth.

Implications for Role Responsibilities

Principal
No longer responsible for direct supervision of 30 or 100 individual teachers, the principal in a team-organized school directly coaches, supervises, and plans with the perhaps 6 to 12 team leaders or department heads. Together this group forms the leadership team for school planning, solving school problems, and making decisions that affect the work life of the school as a unit.

Organizational planning (school level) and individual planning (teaching level) will function differently in this model. First, the principal shares organizational planning and leadership with a leadership team, working with and through them on management tasks. Management in this sense is shared with subgroup leaders who are accountable for certain degrees of school productivity within their own team. Secondly, supervision and performance planning tasks are shared in a team-organized school. A less direct line exists between the principal and the teacher, since the team leader under the supervision of the principal will handle routine responsibilities of supervision (coaching), training, problem solving, and evaluation. In a sense, the team leader serves as an assistant to and surrogate for the principal. The principal, in turn, functions as trainer and counselor for the team leaders.

Team Leader

Because in our model the team leader is expected to serve in part as an administrative/supervisory officer, and also because team leaders are selected because of their extraordinary classroom skills, we strongly recommend that team leaders should receive financial recognition in their roles. This might take the form of a stipend above base salary, or an upward-step adjustment; also, many districts put their team leaders on a lengthier contract so that they can engage in planning work during the summer. Usually, too, the daily classroom-teaching loads of team leaders are reduced at least slightly, so that they can more easily attend to administrative/supervisory functions. Given a slight degree of authority over, and considerable professional responsibility for, their team colleagues, team leaders guide team productivity for the year. Translated into specific behaviors, the team leader, in collaboration with team members, is responsible for organizing team planning, dividing team labor, assigning students, organizing space, solving problems, clinical supervision, determining staff development needs, and assessing work processes and results.

In addition to collaborative tasks, the team leader also conducts teacher planning sessions, clinically supervises teachers regularly, and requires quarterly progress reports and plans as they relate to a teacher's annual performance plan. The team leader, with the principal, also conducts performance evaluation conferences with individual teachers. These tasks do not prohibit the principal's involvement in individual teacher planning, supervision, and evaluation. However, the structure does permit more meaningful involvement of the principal, on a request basis by the team leader or teacher.

Teacher

No longer a role isolate, the teacher participates in all team decisions and actions as a partner in team production pursuits. Together the teachers in a team develop a culture that reflects the ways in which they best can share their talents. A particular advantage of teaming is that all of the students belong to all members of the team, although a portion of each team will be assigned to individual teachers for counseling purposes. Teachers and students all belong to a community that develops its own patterns for meeting growth needs. Subgroups, for example, in skills teaching, provide for at least as much person-to-person interaction as occurs in self-contained classrooms.

Teaching in this model results from team decisions about who teaches what, to whom, and for how long. Supervision of teaching occurs as teachers observe and coach each other under the team leader's guidance. Responsibility for evaluation shifts from the principal to the team leader, who is intimately aware of daily patterns, and who knows the results of teacher activity. Teachers view the team leader as their immediate instructional leader and coach.

Special Teachers

With decreasing federal, state, and local dollars challenging the future of special programs, creative approaches are necessary in assigning special teachers. Within the proposed team structure for achievement, productivity, and accountability, special teachers can augment team practice in several ways. One option is for all special teachers (for example, Title I, migrant, special education, art, music and P.E.) to form a separate team. Within this model the regular teams would contract for the services they need in order to meet their productivity goals. The team leader would then negotiate with specific members of the special team for measurable contributions [goal(s)] to team productivity. Special team individuals would then be evaluated by the principal, with input from team leaders, on the basis of results delivered to each team. Thus, a direct line would be established between each team and specialists whereby goals would define expected results and thereby link special teachers directly into the productivity–accountability chain.

The Team

Plans for development and teaching responsibilities are made by the team as a unit. Periodically, the team monitors its own progress and critiques the performance of individual members in relation to goals. Planning, action, and reflection are the basic activities of the team in its production efforts. The concept of peer reviews holds promise for raising individual member performance to new norms.

In summary, team teaching decisions and responsibility sharing include the following dimensions:

1. leadership functions
2. team operations and policies
3. communications and responsibilities for reporting pupil progress, student management, and parental involvement

4. program planning
5. teaching assignments
6. planning, problem solving, decision-making policies and methodologies
7. use of space/use of time
8. materials development and utilization

Production sharing and accountability at the team level: can it work? We believe that if teachers (knowledge workers) are given responsibility for achieving certain student outcomes collectively, in groups of workable size, schools can develop the capacity to alter many current problems. Archaic teaching practices will be altered by teams in their efforts to become more effective. Supervision and evaluation practices are likely to be specific and to trigger vital teacher growth. Moreover, staff development activities are more likely to influence practice if keyed to team goals. Teacher burnout trends will be reversed as teams plan for, succeed in, and are recognized for their collective achievement outcomes.

Conclusion

David Johnson (1981), who has studied cooperative student learning in schools with his brother, Roger, identified the group characteristics, listed here, that enhance individual learning. If these principles work for students in a group context, might they not also facilitate teacher growth in teams? Our answer to this question is "yes." Cooperation promotes more/greater/higher

effective exchange of information
facilitation of each others' achievement
tutoring and sharing of resources
trust among students
emotional involvement and commitment to learning
utilization of resources of other students
achievement motivation by nonstudents
lower fear of failure
peer acceptance and support
peer pressure toward achievement
divergent and risk-taking thinking

School organization in the years ahead will include various permanent and temporary groups whose work has both a direct and indirect effect on student achievement. An ecological organizational design will engage teachers in collaborative teaching teams and task forces, where individuals assume responsibility for portions of the school's tasks. The small group will dominate school work life as teachers function together on tasks that link to selected school improvement priorities. The concepts of holism, synergism, cohesiveness, dialogue, conflict, trust, sharing, responsibility, flexibility, alternative planning, time lines and accountability, will all take on new meaning as groups develop skill in accomplishing tasks together. Professional life is likely to rise to new levels of concern, skill, and productivity in a climate of openness, feedback, growth, and accountability. In the production paradigm, group collaboration will generate greater accomplishments for schools, as teams aim at increasing levels of student achievement.

Given a basic group work structure, teachers on teaching teams and task forces will require regular assistance in a variety of ways. In the next chapter we will pursue many ways that the principal can become a resource to work groups, helping them to develop proficiency in collaborative efforts.

7

The Organization Subsystem: Developing Work Groups

Schools historically have devoted neither time nor effort to building a capacity for working productively in groups. Research on successful schools, however, points out that patterns of collaboration permeate the life of such schools through a common goal focus, continuous dialogue, shared decision making, planned action, and periodic reflection and feedback. In this chapter, attention is given to ways in which the principal can facilitate work group productivity. We begin by discussing the dynamics of groups and the ways in which dynamics can be controlled to facilitate group success. Next we pay specific attention to four intervention strategies for team development: (1) requiring and helping groups to plan, (2) helping groups to conduct productive meetings, (3) helping them develop communication skills, and (4) helping them to solve problems creatively. Figure 7.1 illustrates the interrelationship of group work skills and group productivity.

Principles of Productive Work Groups

The concepts developed in the literature of group theory provide a context for conceptualizing the life of a school work group. We explore the concepts of work group definition, function, size, structure, growth phases, productivity, and achievement as they relate to productive groups.

Definition of a Group

Group theorists have concentrated on many and various aspects of the group phenomenon. Some scholars are able to discuss group phenomena at length without presenting a specific definition; others specify group characteristics.

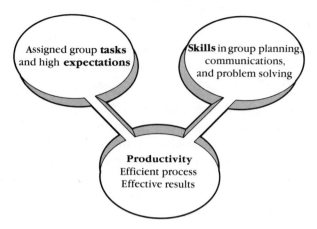

Figure 7.1. The Productive Work Group

Several other scholars define groups in terms of perceptions or cognitions of group members; motivation and need satisfaction; group goals; group organization; interdependency of group members; and member interaction. Stogdill (in Sexton, 1970) provides a broad framework by suggesting that a group is a system of various kinds of inputs, mediating variables, and outputs.

We have selected a group-goal approach for discussing the context for developing work groups. The school work group is defined as a collection of five to eight persons who are organized to accomplish specific objectives cooperatively for the school, within a specific amount of time.

Group Function

The function of a group, according to Bennis et al. (1976, 46), is to facilitate some kind of change: a function that relies on the participation of group members; trust in the proponents, advocates, and leaders; and clarity about the change. A group is described more in terms of activities than outcomes. Bennis observes four functions: data gathering (what's happening now); feedback (what is needed/desired); action (development of a new program); and assessment (what worked and how can it be improved?). Several other theorists view the function of groups by describing them in terms of task functions (the product outcome desired; Benne and Sheats, 1948) and maintenance functions (supporting mechanisms that facilitate group productivity; Bales 1950).

We view group function in terms of producing a product or a change for the school that relates to its goal structure. Participation of all group members is critical to its healthy functioning, as are member trust and clarity of purpose.

Group Size

As group size increases beyond seven or thereabouts, there are both positive and negative influences on individual performance (Hellriegel and Slocum 1974, 376–377). As group size increases,

1. more demands are made of the leader;
2. the group tolerates more direction by the leader;
3. active members are more dominant in interaction;
4. ordinary members tend to reduce their participation and therefore there is less exploration and adventure in the discussion;
5. group atmosphere is less intimate;
6. it takes longer to make decisions; and
7. rules and procedures are more formalized.

Group Structure

Another factor influencing group productivity is the compatibility of group members with respect to their knowledge and also their skills for achieving the assigned task. Compatibility can either enhance or restrict group productivity. While group members need not be personal friends, it is important for group productivity that group membership be selected on the basis of a best guess about member compatibility. It must be kept clear that goal accomplishment is the objective, not conflict resolution capability.

Group Roles

Group productivity hinges on the ability of the group to work through individual differences toward the attainment of a group's purpose. Maier (1973, 422–428) observes that productivity depends on the leader's ability to maximize group assets and minimize liabilities. The deficiencies in any group, according to Maier, are not with individual members, but with processes used to elicit effective group functioning. The following factors can serve either as liabilities or assets depending on leader skill: disagreement (necessary for innovation; depends on climate of acceptance); conflicting interests (cooperation grows out of mutual interests); risk taking (groups are more willing to take risks than individuals); time requirements (group productivity requires more time than individual work); and minority opinions (influence group decisions if protected and when facts favor it).

Growth Phases

Each group grows in certain predictable phases. Group theorists are in general agreement that there are three to five phases in group life. However, scholars differ in the way those phases are defined. Our own experience with groups connects best with the ideas of Stock and Thelen (1958). They describe four phases that seem appropriate for work groups in schools:

1. the group defines direction on task problems
2. the group concentrates on task problems
3. group conflict decreases effectiveness
4. group productivity and member cohesiveness emerge

In our work with groups in schools, we have observed five distinct phases of group development, similar to Stock and Thelen's, that enable groups to become productive.

Stages of Group Growth

1. Introduction—awareness
2. Planning and initial implementation
3. Conflict regarding process
4. Refinement of task ideas, process, and role definitions
5. Group productivity

The primary challenge for a work group is to channel its energies toward completing the task successfully. Group activity often stops altogether when conflict, a state that is inevitable in a group's growth, appears. The ability of members to work through (not avoid) problems and emotions relating to the task, will determine in large measure the actual productivity of the group. As a general rule, avoidance of conflict will prevent productivity and cohesiveness, whereas constructive exploration of the conflict followed by resolution will generate greater understandings and cohesiveness, and lead to expected productivity.

Group Productivity

Cohesiveness is a product of time spent together and of achieving success, although group failure can also sometimes bind group members together. Scholars of group productivity also refer to other factors that increase or decrease group cohesiveness:

Factors Increasing Cohesiveness	Factors Decreasing Cohesiveness
groups provide status and recognition for members	disagreement over the ways to solve group problems
attack from the outside	unpleasant experiences resulting from group membership
favorable evaluation of the group by outsiders	failure of the group to move toward its objectives
personal attractiveness of members to one another	dominating or self-oriented behavior on the part of group members
intergroup competition	intragroup competition
opportunity for interaction	

Stogdill (1959) developed a theory of group achievement that focused on productivity rather than behavior. Cartwright and Zander (1968) refer to this theory as a systems approach to groups due to Stogdill's emphasis on member inputs, mediating variables, and group outputs or achievements. *Inputs* include member performances, interactions, and expectations. *Mediating variables* refer to the group's role structure. Group achievement (*output*) is characterized by productivity (changes in expectancy values of members resulting from work), morale (degrees of freedom from restraint in working toward goals), and integration (degrees to which a group can maintain its structure and operate under stress).

Facilitating Group Productivity

The guidelines that follow grow out of an assessment of group dynamic concepts and our experience in working with many school groups. Principals and teachers will need to spend considerable energy in the coming years learning from and teaching each other how to work productively in groups. Consider the following recommendations for facilitating productive work in groups.

Facilitating Rule 1: Keep the group size small and the task clear.

Research on group productivity has led management theorists to advise a span of control from four to eight persons. Principals often report difficulties in managing 20 or more teachers. As we have noted, the problem can be resolved easily if teachers are organized into teams and principals then work primarily with team leaders. Setting up committees, task forces, and other small-size work groups, with whose chairpersons principals can deal, also helps to reduce the span of a principal's control. At the teacher level, similarly, having a manageable number of colleagues with whom to interact in each work situation makes it more likely that work can be accomplished efficiently. Equally important is that the nature of tasks to be performed should be crystal clear to all involved. The less complexity, especially for short-run tasks, the better. The more obvious the outcomes that are expected or sought, the more certainly the activity can be designed and pursued.

Facilitating Rule 2: Be sure the group understands who is responsible for what.

Enormous amounts of time can be wasted when groups are unclear about either their task set or their decision set. In the hierarchy of school systems, some decisions are made

1. by administrators above the level of the building principal (therefore the principal, unless he or she elects to negotiate the matter, accepts the decision);

2. at the building-principal level (the principal determines, and teachers, save for negotiation, accept the decision);
3. by the principal after staff input (the principal invites discussion and is influenced by teachers' views);
4. by various co-involved participants (principal, teachers, and perhaps even parents and/or students negotiate a decision collectively); and
5. by teachers (to whom full authority for the decision has been delegated).

One of the keys to a principal's success, especially from an administrative point of view, is knowing how to avoid confusion or conflict about which decision set is operative at any given moment. If the teachers proceed to make a decision about something that is, in the end, within the province of higher authority than theirs, an awkward or even dangerous situation could result. The principal's veto, for example, could damage teacher morale and reduce mutual trust. It is much better, we believe, for everyone to understand that the principal has full responsibility for certain types of decisions and on other matters, the teachers have either an influencing role or full responsibility.

Facilitating Rule 3: Require group action planning.

Action planning accomplishes two things: it forces a group to define a course or a blueprint for action; and it provides management with specific information and enables the principal to work effectively with the group toward productive ends. We believe that principals should insist that all groups, after having defined their goals (see Chapter 4), set down a plan for goal attainment. In most situations the action plan need not be comprehensive and detailed, otherwise busywork could dilute the available energy. A bare-bones approach that identifies at least six action dimensions is needed:

1. key activities or events along the way
2. individual responsibilities
3. available resources
4. time lines to be followed
5. monitoring procedures to be used
6. evaluation procedures to be used

It is the principal's responsibility to see that action plans are made and to critique and approve each plan before activity begins. For experienced groups, the principal's review might be perfunctory, but until groups demonstrate considerable skill in action planning it is wise for the principal to monitor the process closely. Good action plans lead to productive work efficiently pursued; shoddy plans can lead to enormous waste and failure.

In effective groups, most of the actual work is done by individuals or pairs, and the total group meets only as necessary to define general parameters, receive and discuss progress reports, create new approaches, and/or evaluate completed work. There should be a good fit between assigned tasks and members' interests or talents. It is also important to be sure that all members carry their fair share of the load.

Facilitating Rule 4: Help groups to cope with conflicts and move toward productivity.

Many team efforts fail due to a general lack of knowledge about how groups work. In the literature on the growth cycle of groups one theme is consistent: groups naturally pass through a stage of conflict before becoming productive. In seasoned groups, when conflict arises it is addressed productively and creatively, and work soon resumes. In novice groups, however, the presence of conflict often debilitates a group and causes it to become dysfunctional. Without the knowledge of natural stages in a group's development, many workers may give up prematurely and conclude that group tasks are not practical.

Effective leaders can teach skills for confronting and addressing disagreement. One myth that group members need to abandon is the belief that the best idea "wins." In productive groups, ideas are viewed as seeds to be nurtured by all members and refined until a workable "hybrid" idea emerges from group dialogue. In such a context, many ideas can be said to have "won." Building on each other's ideas is basic to group productivity.

Facilitating Rule 5: Structure group progress assessment and reporting.

Administrators often have difficulty envisioning how best to assist a group in its production efforts. Informal verbal checks are typical procedures for monitoring group progress. A structured periodic reporting system can provide additional useful information. Such a practice provides the work group with "must times" for reviewing progress, for deciding on new strategies, and revising plans. Furthermore, a periodic report and short-term plan provide the administrator with tangible clues for how best to intervene and provide resources and assistance to the group. The team will benefit more from targeted assistance than from random verbal checkups.

Periodic reporting and planning need not be lengthy or complex. *A report* on the past short time period need only include the objective and the results of activity (one page). *A plan* for the next several months need only include the objectives and new activities, resources, responsibilities, and any requests for assistance (one page). A simple plan and report offers the administrator a view of the group's perspective and provides clues for assistance and resources.

Given basic guidelines for facilitating group work, what are the specific interventions that can increase group productivity? Let us consider four global categories for team intervention.

Team Intervention Strategies

In this section on team development, attention is given to the principal's intervention role in work group activity. Emphasis is placed on assisting groups in team planning, productive team meetings, communications skills, and creative problem solving (see Figure 7.2). We can assume that all groups require careful management, and at times they also require targeted intervention. Figure 7.3 outlines the basic intervention process that can be used in all four of the interventions discussed. A group's goals provide the context for identifying group needs, resolving a problem, implementing a new plan, or assessing progress. As the principal considers one or several of the intervention strategies, a generic process will be used in helping a group: identifying a need, recommending a solution, planning for implementing of the solution, and assessing the impact of the solution on group productivity.

Intervention I: Group Action Planning

The most helpful intervention a principal can provide is a planning structure for each work group. In an action plan the best route is mapped for achieving the group's goal(s). Plans help a group to eliminate or avoid nonproductive activities and select the most useful for achieving results. Action plans provide the basic context for individual work and further ensure that all activity links to school goals. In a sense, plans are guideposts along the path to goal attain-

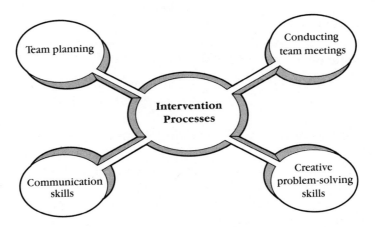

Figure 7.2. Team Development Intervention Processes

Figure 7.3. The Principal's Intervention Cycle

ment. Figure 7.4 outlines the basic decision variables in a simple, workable action plan.

Many considerations are useful in the planning process as the group maps out its course of action. Examples of planning considerations include

essential activities
optimal activities
constraints (such as time, legal, and funds)
strategies for various actions
balance of team labor
intervening to remove roadblocks
facilitating forces
outside resources (human, financial, material)
implementation/dissemination strategies

The following action plan of one team is provided to demonstrate the parts of a basic plan and to illustrate its direct link to a school goal.

Action Planning for a Teaching Team: A Simulation

School Learning Goal.   To increase student achievement levels in math by developing processes and procedures for identifying student interests, levels of mastery, needs and learning style, and for translating these data into personalized learning programs by May 1987.

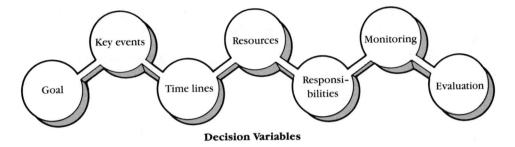

Decision Variables

Figure 7.4. Action Planning Model

Team Goal.   To assess the learning styles, needs, interests, and mastery level of each team student in math, and develop programs that incorporate collected data by April 1987.

Action Planning I: Select Key Events

In a short span of time, using a brainstorming technique, team planners generate a list of both possible as well as seemingly impossible activities. Initial playfulness enables a group to break through perceived restraints and limitations, into potentially more satisfying and productive results.

By establishing an "I wish we could" atmosphere, planners can generate a long list of possible procedures for attaining their goal. Out of a lengthy list, desired actions are selected and might include some of the following strategies:

1. Be trained in diagnosing student learning styles
2. View a videotape on learning styles
3. Ask the university professors about various style inventories
4. Make up our own inventory for assessing needs
5. Observe students in regard to their thinking style
6. Develop a system for recognizing and categorizing cognitive style
7. Diagnose all team students
8. Develop learning outcomes in all curriculum areas
9. Develop a record-keeping system to record diagnostic data (mastery levels, style, interests)
10. Form a schoolwide task force to develop a mastery-outcome-based curriculum
11. Develop videotapes for other school district teachers, training them in diagnosis and planning procedures
12. Conduct a workshop on planning programs for mastery

13. Conduct observation and feedback sessions on team members regarding the effects of our plans on students

The team selects the most promising ideas as their key activities or events in accomplishing their objective.

Team Key Events (examples)

1. Identify instruments that diagnose learning style, rate, interest, and mastery
2. Plan in-service for training and diagnosis
3. Diagnose all team students
4. Identify and/or develop a record-keeping system
5. Suggest to the school council the formation of outcome-based curriculum development teams for mastery learning to be formed
6. Explore ways to translate data into learning programs
7. Prepare a manual for diagnostic procedures for other teachers

Action Planning II: Define Time Line

Viewing the entire year (or several months) as the available time span, each selected activity is then planned in relation to beginning dates, benchmarks and completion dates.

Key Events

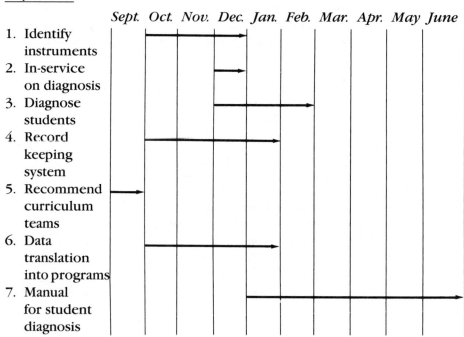

	Sept.	Oct.	Nov.	Dec.	Jan.	Feb.	Mar.	Apr.	May	June
1. Identify instruments										
2. In-service on diagnosis										
3. Diagnose students										
4. Record keeping system										
5. Recommend curriculum teams										
6. Data translation into programs										
7. Manual for student diagnosis										

Action Planning III: Identify Resources

The team's next task is to speculate about potential human, material, and financial resources. *Human resources* might include the services of retired people, industry, big and small businesses, parents, city agencies, and school neighbors. *Material resources* might include free, discarded, or inexpensive items that community businesses and agencies can provide; or surplus materials, materials that can be made available. *Financial resources* might include donations from business, income from fund-raising projects, dollars reallocated from other program budgets, and grants from federal and state agencies as well as from private foundations and local philanthropists. Note in the following how the teaching teams matched resources to their key events.

Key Events	Resources
1. Identify diagnostic instruments	University professors; curriculum office; consultants
	Library books and periodicals
2. Provide in-service on diagnosis	One of the above consultants
3. Diagnose team students	Our team staff
4. Develop a math record-keeping system	Library readings; university; central office; consultants; friends; national and professional organizations
5. Consult with math curriculum team	Leadership council and content area teachers on each teaching team
6. Translation of data into math programs	National consultants—university professors and doctoral students; other professional specialists; readings
7. Develop manual for teachers	The team staff

Action Planning IV: Team Member Responsibilities

Actual work is done by individuals, not groups. Assigning task responsibilities allows several different group activities to occur at one time. Furthermore, the practice of delegation ensures that each key event is accounted for and that each team member assumes a specific responsibility. An important outgrowth of delegation is the strong team bond that emerges; individual actions are directly related to team plans, and results are shared as they relate to the team's objective. In the following, note the team's objective as well as the team's delegation of responsibilities.

Key Events	Team Member Responsibilities
1. Diagnostic instruments	Joan and Ken
2. In-service	Joan and Ken
3. Diagnose students	Joan, Ken, Jim, Susan, Alice
4. Record-keeping systems	Joan
5. Curriculum team	Susan, Alice, Jim
6. Data translation into programs	Susan, Alice, Jim
7. Manual development	Joan, Ken, Jim, Susan, Alice

Action Planning V: Monitoring the Plan

To ensure that individuals are accomplishing assigned tasks, action plans need to be monitored by the team as a whole as well as supervised by the principal. The team's monitoring system enables it to correct its own patterns. The team leader provides a checkup system and a format for resolving problems that occur along the way. Similarly, the leader is accountable to the school for team progress toward school goals.

It should be noted that an action plan rarely is implemented exactly as it was developed. The normal changing nature of school environments and conditions suggests that a plan is only a "best guess" about what will work. Actual plans, then, are guides that might be altered along the way. The team leader needs to guide, coach, assist, and control actions, keeping in view the goal(s) toward which the team strives. Plans made in September are speculative, and October and February activities become clearer as the year progresses. Consequently, original plans are to be viewed as beginning expectations, with the understanding that refinements and additions will occur throughout the year.

The principal needs to be aware of *actual* progress periodically, in order to determine ways of assisting the team. We have found a quarterly report and planning system to be useful for monitoring and controlling progress. The system requires approximately 30 minutes a month (or each quarter). We assume that periodic team reflection on progress is a prerequisite for team productivity. Following a team's reflection session, the team leader prepares a one-page progress report such as the one that follows.

First Quarter Progress Report and New Plans

Key Events	Progress	Plans
1. Identify instruments	One professor identified for cognitive style	Develop our interest inventory Analyze cognitive style inventory

	Dunn LSI instrument located and distributed to team	Recommend developing a math scope and sequence for determining mastery level this year
2. In-service workshop		We need to identify someone to conduct a workshop in various diagnostic procedures
3. Diagnose students		In January begin LSI
4. Record keeping	Math professor has a system he'll share with us	We need to locate math record-keeping systems from service centers and other school districts

Action Planning VI: Goal Completion and Evaluation

Goal attainment is usually not a final product delivered at the end of the year. Rather, it usually occurs in a series of benchmark activities. Note the completion of one team's learning goal in the following.

Team Evaluation at End of Project

Team Learning Goal and Analysis: The team has learned a great deal about the varieties of ways to find out how to assist students in their personal, social, and intellectual growth. The workshops on learning style, record keeping, and program planning each gave us a productive start in planning for learning variables. However, we feel in need of additional training and actual practice in diagnosis and feedback. Cognitive style diagnosis is much more complex than we anticipated; no scholars seem to agree on what is cognitive style. We have decided therefore to table that objective until next year. We need to make our own translation of Professor Jones' record-keeping system for our math program. In addition, we sense that the system we develop may be useful to other teams. We would like to coordinate our work in this regard with the other teams by means of a task force. We feel we are on the right track; our students will learn more if we provide the appropriate targeted learning experiences. Listed here is an outline of our accomplishments.

Key Events	Results
1. Instruments	Six instruments located
2. In-service workshop	Training in LSI (learning style inventory)
	Designing an interest survey
	Grouping students after math pretest
	Math record keeping
3. Student diagnosis	Interest inventory conducted in November
	LSI conducted in December
	Math pretest conducted in January
4. Record-keeping system	Workshop in January
	Our own workshop to design the system
	Record-keeping system developed in April
5. Curriculum development teams	We are pleased with the progress of each of our vertical curriculum teams in designing program outcomes
6. Data translation	We have begun to plan programs based on data, but need more help in this area
7. Develop the manual	The first draft was completed in May and is ready for dissemination

Intervention II: Conducting Productive Team Meetings

The "meeting" is the albatross in the work world of schools. In this section we will discuss the varieties of meetings and their functions, and how they can aid, not hinder, a group in its quest to be productive. Figure 7.5 outlines the varieties of team meetings that can be useful to a work group. The focus of all meetings is the group's goal set. Team meetings can be two hours, one-half hour, or 10 minutes in length. A stand-up meeting of five minutes also is a quick and efficient way to make team decisions on less profound matters.

Goal-Setting Meeting

To begin, the team needs to discuss its task assignment(s) and determine the implications for organizing and planning. All group activity grows out of a goal definition, whether delegated by the principal or developed by the team. The

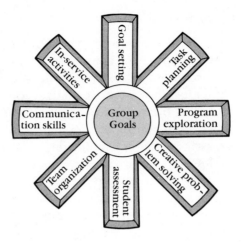

Figure 7.5. Types of Team Meetings

results of group activity are spelled out in the plan as definition is given to the task.

Several themes have emerged as we have worked with groups. Staff members report that they learn to listen to each other as they seek to clarify goals. New insights emerge as members begin to recognize the views of other members. A kaleidoscope of ideas surfaces as members share perceptions and modify their own views. Ideas literally leap out as individuals find commonness of purpose. The opportunity for negotiation and synthesis emerges as individuals evolve a group spirit. Out of dialogue grows a sense of what needs to be achieved, which in turn leads to goal definitions. Goals provide the rationale for all team and individual activity. *When intervention is needed, the principal can assist in clarifying goal expectations and helping the group to develop clarity about its task.*

Task-Planning Meetings

After goals are defined, as our preceding example illustrates, the team specifies key events, time line, resources, and responsibilities. The action plan becomes the pivot for group action as well as for periodic discussion. Meetings around plans and progress provide opportunities for incremental assessment, refinement, and correction. Since the plan is the team's best guess as to the most efficient/effective route to their goal, dialogue around plans is useful in rechanneling or reaffirming the direction of activity. *When intervention is needed, the principal can assist the team in exploring its options and making decisions for future activities.* Making efficient decisions by concensus is a typical group problem.

Program-Planning Meetings

The team decides on global goals and directions for the program, and approves or makes recommendations for the plans of content area specialists. Each individual teacher provides leadership for at least one curriculum area. Individual plans and activities grow out of team decisions and provide energy for accomplishing program objectives. Consequently, program planning at the team level concerns decisions about the overall program, delegation of curriculum responsibilities, assignment of teaching duties, discussion of progress, and assessment of results. Actual work is carried out by individuals. *When intervention is necessary, the principal can assist the teams in clarifying decisions about the program and the roles of specialists and teachers.* Clarity about decisions and the function of the team in program planning can enable a team to make more efficient use of its meeting time.

Problem Exploration Meetings

Conditions in schools change continuously due to influences from students, parents, central administration, the principal, and from the natural growth idiosyncrasies of each group. A team needs to develop skill in identifying problems as they arise, probing causes and consequences, and defining solutions. Most problems are easy to resolve if identified and addressed quickly. Patterns of similar problems lead a group to develop policies. *When intervention is needed, a principal can assist a team in identifying and resolving the problem and in developing team policies to correct problem patterns.*

Creative Problem-Solving Meetings

Often, problems that arise in group life are more extensive and pervasive. Deeper rooted problems require a different kind of group attention. By creating a specific block of time, a group can explore the problem briefly and then spend the major portion of time inventing creative solutions to nagging problems. By using analogies, metaphors, and excursions, a group can often identify creative solutions to problems. Structured playfulness in some meetings permits groups to resolve problems in novel and satisfying ways. *When intervention is necessary, the principal can act as facilitator for a problem-solving meeting.*

Team Organization Meetings

Every group has members with particular interests and skills that will be useful in goal pursuits. The team decides how to divide team responsibilities so that all goal parts are accounted for. It is important that everyone is clear about who is responsible and accountable for which tasks. One person should assume the leadership responsibility for providing team planning, organizing, supervising, and evaluation structures. Left unassigned, these essential management tasks will go unattended and the group will easily drift from its agreed-upon course. Consequently, examining role responsibilities, expecting accountability, and conducting periodic reviews are important practices for group success. *When intervention is required, the principal can assist a team to understand the nature and consequences of their organizational problems and to identify corrective measures.*

Communication Skills Meetings

Being able to listen, to contribute, to build, to negotiate, and to evaluate together directly relate to the group's ability to produce. From time to time it may be useful for a group to assess its skills in communicating, to identify strengths, problems, and to take "next steps" in improving communication skills. For those who perceive that their ideas are rarely considered, or who feel ignored by the group, sharing problems can enable the group to tap its total energy more productively. Often team members are unaware of communication problems, and sharing perceptions can enable a group to progress more effectively. A team may periodically plan a communication skill-building meeting, where new knowledge and techniques are presented to the group for trial and consideration. Periodic communications meetings can clear the air and enable the team to proceed more efficiently. *When appropriate, the principal can teach and provide other resources to the team in its communication skill-building efforts.*

Student Assessment Meetings

The primary outcome of teaching team activity is to cause learning to occur for students. Regular assessment meetings, each for the purpose of discussing certain students, enable a team to learn more about the students to plan more effectively for their growth. Teachers derive greater clarity about the team's strengths and weaknesses in providing learning experiences. Student assessment meetings should occur regularly for correcting immediate problems and also for serving as a barometer for program effects on randomly selected students. Outcomes of these meetings will influence plans, decisions, and role responsibilities at all levels of team life.

   When appropriate, a wide variety of district specialists can assist the team in planning effective programs for certain students. The more extensive use of resources a team employs in student assessment meetings, the more likely are the programs to precipitate desired outcomes.

In-service Activities Meetings

An effective team identifies its own development needs and plans ways to grow. In-service meetings provide opportunities for teams to gain new knowledge and skills for achieving their goals effectively. While other school or district workshops may provide general help, in-service at the team level should be keyed to task objectives. *The principal can assist in identifying in-service tar-gets and also in identifying resources for in-service.*

The principal's intervention role in all nine types of team meetings is to ob-serve, to lead, to coach, to provide resources, and to teach. Each team meeting provides a useful mechanism for intervention into the team's ecosystem. Left to themselves, group members can become productive if they use the guide-lines presented in this section. The principal, however, can add significant en-ergy to team growth by reinforcing, motivating, correcting, and revising per-formance norms through careful observation and intervention into team activity.

The Process Observer.   One way a group can design its own self-help is by nam-ing a group member to be a process observer, or by inviting an outsider to play that role. As group processes are observed at selected meetings, a team can learn important information about its communication and interaction pat-terns. For example, one person may be dominating group meetings while oth-ers may be too intimidated to question the troublesome patterns. An observer can provide useful feedback to the group in the form of descriptions of *ob-served behaviors* and recommendations. By learning about its own dialogue process, a group can quickly eliminate dysfunctional practices and develop more useful patterns.

Building a Meeting Agenda

Two factors are important in building an agenda: (1) team members make rec-ommendations; and (2) the team leader (and principal, when appropriate) plans items that key into team productivity problems and opportunities. The two sources for agenda items are synthesized by the team leader and the actual agenda is developed.

Each team develops a procedure for agenda building. Some teams have a suggestion box; others have a posted sheet of paper where members list items for the agenda. Prior to the meeting, the team leader prepares the agenda, se-lecting relevant items for the next meeting and relegating others to another, more appropriate meeting.

Understanding the function of different types of meetings can aid a work group in its growth activities. The principal can use the meeting as a source of intervention and provide timely, specific help to a growing team.

Intervention III: Communication Skill Building

The ability of a group to accomplish its purpose depends largely on the ca-pability of its members to communicate with each other effectively. Interper-sonal communications are the cornerstone for effective team planning, problem solving, action, reflection, and evaluation. Consequently, intervention into the communications dimension of group life in all probability is necessary for most school work groups. Few teachers have had formal training in communications or group dynamics. Further, the history of role isolation for most teachers as students and as professionals has prevented them from learning the essential skills for cooperative production. Consequently, attention needs to be given to a conscious awareness of communication processes, both those that are effective and those that are not.

Problem-solving and planning meetings often are characterized by confusion about the problem at hand and about the expected outcomes of the meeting. The resulting mazelike meeting environment is further complicated by poor listening and idea-building skills among group members. The four communication skills, shown here, are designed to foster group cohesiveness for effective cooperative analysis, invention, and idea refinement.

Communication Skills

Listen to group member ideas
    Practice in-and-out listening
Paraphrase someone's idea
    State what you thought you heard
Build on others' ideas
    State: what you like
           a headline
           what you need to know
           an extension
           other options
Be critical of final possible solutions
    State your concerns
    Refine solutions

In-and-Out Listening

The ability of group members to listen, to hear, and to understand the contributions that others make directly influences the group's productivity. *In-and-out listening* is a technique that enables group members to listen to others (out-listening) while recording their own thoughts (in-listening) without losing the idea. This technique enables members to develop the skill of timely introducing an idea to the group. The bulldozer effect of "never mind the rest of your idea, listen to mine," is minimized, and collective invention is fostered through in-and-out listening.

People think at approximately six times the rate at which one speaks; consequently, individuals have plenty of time to listen to others for ideas, clues, and possible solutions, while simultaneously recording their own ideas. When the appropriate moment emerges, a recorded idea may appear appropriate to the development of a group solution.

Paraphrasing

Communication is enhanced as perceptions are clarified. Once communication channels are cleared, new ideas can be added or refined. Group participation is nurtured as members build, add on, or refine someone's contribution. The open-ended statements illustrated here are examples of the kinds of paraphrasing that foster collaborative invention.

1. "This is what I hear you say: _____."
2. "What I like about your idea is _____, but my concern is _____."
3. "I like the idea and I wish _____."
4. "My guess is that _____."
5. "I need to know _____."
6. "I think your headline is _____."

Paraphrasing helps the other person to understand whether what you heard is what he or she was trying to say. Also, it communicates to the other person that the idea (good or bad) is worth exploring; it is valued. The paraphrased person is consequently motivated and remains in the dialogue. Group participation is further reinforced as people attempt to refine each other's contributions, and to be sure they are understanding each other's statements.

Idea Building

At several points in a meeting, and usually after numerous ideas have been generated, the group needs to select those ideas that appear to be most promising and to refine them until workable solutions emerge. As illustrated in Figure 7.6, contributions usually range from irrelevant to precise (Prince 1976, 46). Initial ideas seldom are precise, yet many suggestions hold promise for becoming workable solutions. Rather than waiting for the perfect "gem" to be delivered, group members can expect that most ideas will fall well below a level of precise solutions. The group begins its idea-building process somewhere along a continuum. As members express what is good about an idea, concerns are identified and ideas are refined until optimal solutions are sculptured.

Critical Analysis

Prior to decision making, a group needs to develop the capacity to state concerns and to problem-solve ideas until workable ideas emerge. A serious problem can develop if group members withhold their concerns in an effort to be cooperative. If reservations about a final solution or plan are not voiced during decision-making moments, potential pitfalls will go unnoticed and problems

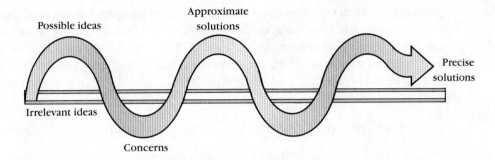

Figure 7.6. The Idea-Building Process

will inevitably emerge in the implementation phase. Reluctance to be critical is referred to as "groupthink," a disease to be avoided as much as possible.

In order to overcome the groupthink tendency, time must be set aside specifically for playfulness and idea generation, with another block of time reserved for tough-minded refinement of ideas until workable solutions and plans emerge.

The following characteristics have been found in groups that generate effective solutions to problems:

1. The leader encourages each member to be a critical evaluator.
2. All group members should be impartial in the early stages of deliberations.
3. At every meeting someone is assigned the role of devil's advocate.
4. Outside experts are invited in and encouraged to challenge views of key group members.
5. After consensus is reached, a follow-up meeting should be held (time permitting) in order to allow "second thoughts" and residual doubts to be aired (Janis 1971, 76).

The building process involves a step-by-step reinforcement of an idea or strategy until concerns are resolved and the resulting solution or plan is satisfying to all members.

The Principal's Role in Communication Skill Building

The principal can intervene productively in several ways into the communicating patterns of a work group. As a process observer, feeding back behavioral events to the team, the principal provides useful information and insights about the group's communication patterns. As *coach,* he or she can reinforce those communication patterns that are particularly useful to the group, and also point out areas in which the group needs to develop skill. As *teacher,* the principal can train groups in communication techniques (in-and-out listening, paraphrasing, idea building, critical analysis). The intervention objective is to enable the group to communicate more efficiently and effectively. This can be accomplished by making the group members aware of their own patterns, providing new knowledge, and coaching them to greater levels of proficiency.

Intervention IV: Nurturing Creativity in Group Work Sessions

Teachers are faced with increasing odds today as they attempt to solve educational and organizational problems in schools. Conflicting expectations, combined with the constraints of money, time, and teacher contracts provide a complex setting for solving school problems. The traditional approach to problem solving in schools tends to block natural tendencies toward invention. The typical approach, as noted in the first column, is restrictive because of its limiting characteristics. A more creative approach (second column) is likely to generate solutions that are more effective in the long run because they are more likely to resolve fundamental problems.

Typical	Creative
order	speculation
correctness	options
control	building
certainty	playfulness
undirectionality	deviations
fixed classifications	alterations
judgments	richness
expected answer	irrelevancy
detail	
precision	

The traditional method for generating solutions to school problems is guided by group norms that dictate logical behavior. Restricted by obvious and safe solutions, group members often produce mediocre or simplistic solutions to complex problems. If groups are to produce other than mediocre solutions, they must learn how to function within an environment that not only fosters invention but encourages it as a daily routine. Creative thinking is apt to generate playfulness and seemingly irresponsible hunches. Often those ideas that seem almost dangerous have within them appropriate concepts which may evolve into creative and powerful solutions or plans. Furthermore, creative thinking is likely to "snowball" when a balance of invention and analysis is employed.

Important to effective problem-solving meetings is a balance between logical or restrictive ideas and those that are more creative and playful. A certain amount of time should be set aside during a problem-solving meeting for creative thinking. In the creative problem-solving process presented on the following pages, three distinct phases are simulated: (1) analyze the problem (logical–rational); (2) generate multiple possible solutions (creative–illogical); and (3) refine ideas until they are workable (logical–rational).

Problem-Solving Technique A: Brainstorming

Brainstorming is the most simple form of generating numerous creative ideas. In one or two minutes a group (5 to 8 persons) can identify a remarkable number of ideas. The purpose in brainstorming is strictly to generate ideas. There is no discussion of ideas, nor are judgments made. A short span of time (about two minutes) is designated for free thinking about a certain subject.

In any team meeting, a member can request two minutes of group time for brainstorming a problem area. The entire staff can be divided into groups of five to generate ideas around a specific topic (for example, ideas for student leadership; experiences in social studies; ways to develop more student responsibility). The person requesting the two minutes may collect as many as 100 ideas from the total group effort. After the meeting the ideas can be sorted by the requesting teacher and potentially useful ideas selected.

The leader of a brainstorming session imitates an auctioneer. The purpose is to elicit comments from the groups. A cardinal rule in brainstorming is to respect and record *every* comment or suggestion, and to encourage a spontaneous and uninhibited flow of thought. Groups are usually surprised and pleased by their collective knowledge and creativity, and the exercise produces material on which further discussion or action can be built.

Often after a list has been developed, the group wishes to organize and classify the responses. During this stage, ideas that are less useful can be tactfully ignored, reworded, subsumed under a related idea, or otherwise passed over. The more powerful ideas, which become the psychological property of everyone, become the useful products of the exercise.

A good rule in brainstorming is to soft-pedal the authorship of specific ideas. If, for example, Jack Jones contributes one of the most acceptable or useful ideas in a brainstorming session on how to get parents involved in decision making (for instance, he suggests they serve on school task forces), later it is generally better to refer to "the excellent task force suggestion" rather than to "Jack's idea about task forces." Jack will be well enough aware that this was his idea, so he gets sufficient reinforcement anyway through what is said. By praising the idea rather than connecting it with Jack, the leader (or whoever offers the praise) helps everyone else to regard the idea as a group accomplishment.

Often brainstorming has not only an intellectual but also a humorous dimension, and the process is fun for the participants. Sometimes persons who were virtual strangers only a few minutes before begin to see each other as colleagues and friends. Listed here are actual samples from groups with whom we have used the brainstorming technique.

Problem: How to Relieve Group Tension

Brainstormed Solutions

Humor—tell a joke	Take a break
Give ridiculous solution or ideas	Table it
Deal with personality of uptight person	Drop it/bring up another idea
	Take excursions
Egg them on; let them laugh, too	Force field analysis
Body language	Walk around the building
A touch	Get soda
A sound	Have a party
A gesture with historical meaning	Play pin the tail on the donkey
Tears	Stop and brainstorm
Stop and bring someone in	

Problem: Improving Team Relationships

Brainstormed Solutions

Give and take	Excursions
Giving and accepting criticism and praise	Body language
	Human feelings
Sharing of ideas	Want trust
Building on ideas	Take risks
Discussions	Respect
Picture, books	Sensitivity
Brainstorm	Care

Problem: Building Trust

Brainstormed Solutions

Becoming vulnerable	Honesty and truthfulness
Confidence	Disclosure
Depend on someone	Will keep a confidence
Believing that they want the best for me	Accept weakness, strengths
	Emphathetic
Openness	Open
Risk and acceptance	Show respect

Problem: How to Develop Reward Systems for Students

Brainstormed Solutions

Praise	Body language—nonverbal
Points	Special privileges—day off
Goodies, treats	Child's choice
Bank accounts	Book to take home
Recognition	Teacher's day off
Henry's donuts	Hug, pat

Following are procedures for leading a brainstorming session. The procedures begin with brainstorming but extend to include activities for developing selected ideas into useful strategies.

Guidelines for Brainstorming in Small Groups

Purpose: To generate numerous ideas for improving *our* school/program, as it relates to an ideal.

1. Prior to the brainstorming for school improvement areas, involve the group in a series of warm-up activities.

> In groups of 3 to 5 persons, list the many possible uses of, let us say, a truckload of bottle caps, or a warehouse full of red pencils.
>
> Time: One minute
>
> Rules: 1 recorder; generate fanciful ideas; no discussion; no censoring
>
> Request groups to count their responses. Recognize the group with the largest number of ideas. Have them read their list, then applaud.
>
> Repeat with one or two more warm-up brainstorming exercises; they activate the mind and stimulate group productivity. The playfulness of warm-ups energizes the group for the serious tasks to follow. Other warm-up ideas: rubber tires, steering wheels, safety pins, ax handles.

2. Request that groups generate as many improvement ideas as it is possible to imagine in one minute. Then reconvene the entire membership and invite the group with the largest number of ideas to read its list aloud. Applaud. Invite one or two other groups to add some unique ideas not mentioned by the first group; applaud.

List Group Priority Ideas

> Request groups take another *x* minutes privately to examine their list and select the two most important ideas on it. Next, as they share their selections with the large group, record their

ideas. *Note:* By having small groups generate and prioritize ideas, you, as leader, never need to synthesize an overly
long list of ideas.

*Separate Administrative Tasks from Instruction and Learning-
Related Tasks*

Many teacher concerns focus on improvements that are administrative housekeeping concerns, such as lunch lines for
teachers and hall duty. Request the group to identify administrative "quick fixes" and list these on a separate easel pad.
Promise to solve several of the problems immediately.

Cluster Ideas

Continuing to work with the entire group, invite them to consider linking together several (remaining) similar or compat-
ible ideas. Work on the list with the group until two or three
major groupings or clusters of ideas emerge.

Label Ideas

Invite the staff to label the idea clusters (for example, communication, student involvement, mastery learning).

Select Final Solution Areas

Now the crucial step: Invite the group to select from the larger
list, one to four final school-improvement areas. Discuss, share
opinions, and finally vote on the areas that will become the focus for planning.

Problem-Solving Technique B: Creative Processes

Often a team needs to explore a problem more fully and to invent new solutions prior to making decisions. The group creative problem-solving technique presented on the following pages is useful when a group wants to develop more creative responses to a problem or wants to understand the
problem itself more fully.

Group Roles

Effective group solutions and decisions depend to a large extent on the ways
in which three critical group tasks are conducted: process leadership, idea generation, and idea and solution critiquing. Prince (1970) found from studying
thousands of groups in problem-solving meetings that these three tasks are typically assumed either by one person or by all group members. Due to a lack of
clarification regarding specific role responsibilities, group members often become frustrated and withdrawn and, consequently, meeting outcomes tend to
be less than satisfying. To overcome a tendency toward role confusion and low
energy/low productivity, Prince suggests that the task responsibilities be divided among all group members. The *leader* assumes the responsibility for

guiding the group through the problem-solving process. The *client,* a selected problem expert, bears the major responsibility for the problem, providing background information and criticism until workable solutions emerge. The remaining *group members,* relieved of process and critic functions, are free to generate ideas until workable solutions emerge. Prince's categories assisted us in developing a model, whose key elements in the three group roles are as follows:

Leader Tasks (Process Manager)

to keep the group on task
to encourage listening
to encourage paraphrasing
to nurture idea building
to match group ideas to client concerns, building toward solutions
to keep "tuned in" to client clues for direction to record all participant
    ideas

Client Tasks (Problem Expert and Critic)

to define the problem to the group
to offer information, clues and reasons
to select useful ideas
to guide the direction of new ideas
to be tough-minded
to reinforce group contributions
to inform group members of their useful process contributions

Group Member Tasks (Idea Generator)

to practice in-and-out listening
to generate ideas, wishes, and solutions
to respect others' ideas and build on them
to ask for information
to speculate
to be playful
to trust your hunches and instincts
to be yourself

The leader's task is to work for the client and with the group so as to maximize group resources and produce workable problem solutions.

Key Points

1. Learn the steps in creative problem solving.
2. Protect each speaker. Assure his or her chance to express thoughts, ideas, and solutions. Protect the dignity of each contribution.

3. Keep the entire group involved and its energy level high. Don't let one or two dominate.
4. Acknowledge contributions. Be sure that all ideas are written down.
5. Keep the group on target, guarding against the natural tendency to digress.
6. Check with the client frequently as to whether the discussion is moving in a helpful direction.
7. Keep the ideas coming and ensure that group members build on each others' ideas.
8. Guide the process from one creative problem-solving step to the next. Use your instincts.

The leader will have done the job well if all group members become actively involved with the client's problem throughout the session and if the client is able to identify workable solutions and "next steps."

The client's (problem expert) *task* is to be the problem expert, explaining the problem and giving the group feedback throughout the session.

<u>Key Points</u>

1. State the problem as clearly and concisely as you can. Be sure to tell the group: What is the problem? Why it is a problem? What has been done about it so far? What would you like the group to do for you?
2. Keep the problem statement as short and simple as it can be and still provide the necessary information.
3. Steer the group's efforts. You are the problem expert and its judge for possible/workable solutions. The group is there to help you, so feel free to let them know what sort of ideas are helpful.
4. Appreciate the group. They're trying their best to help you. If an idea seems unlikely to be useful, first say what you like about it, then provide direction for the discussion.
5. Keep a clear focus on the problem before the group.
6. Sum up by telling the group what you've gained from the session and what you plan to do next.

The client will have done his/her job well if the leader and group respond to your continuous cues and generate ideas in your desired direction and if the entire group helps you continuously until workable solutions are developed.

The group member's task is to work for the client and to help him or her find a solution for the problem.

<u>Key Points</u>

1. Be sure that you understand the client's problem and what he or she wants from the group.

2. Stay tuned into the client throughout the session. Focus on what the client needs.
3. Let your imagination range over many ideas. Generate relevant as well as irrelevant ideas. The client will be the judge.
4. Be aware of the group. Listen to and build on others' ideas.
5. Work with the leader. He or she may occasionally need input from the group as to the next step in that particular problem-solving session.

The group member will have done his or her job well if the client arrives at new insights and perspectives about his or her problem and if the client identifies workable solutions to the problem and "next steps" following the problem-solving session.

Creative Problem-Solving Stages

The creative problem-solving process is divided into three distinct stages, each having its own purpose and process:

Stage One: Problem analysis
Stage Two: Idea generation/speculation
Stage Three: Idea fusion (see Figure 7.7)

Stage One: Problem Analysis (limit to 10 minutes)

During the first stage the client presents the problem, briefly describing the discrepancy between what exists and what is desired. The problem expert provides a limited amount of background information and reports what has been

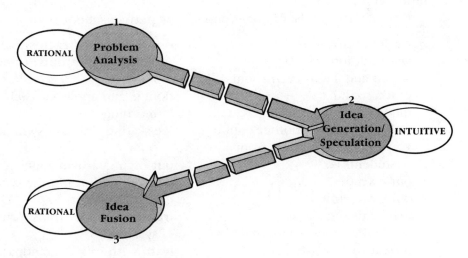

Figure 7.7. A Group Creative Problem-Solving Process

done about the problem. The expert then defines the problem in simple terms and states what is expected from the problem-solving session.

The following guidelines can be used by the client:

Identify discrepancies between what is desired and what actually exists
Describe what has already been tried for solving the problem
Define the problem in simple terms

At the end of the problem analysis stage, group members should have sufficient information about the problem to begin generating ideas toward a workable solution. You are ready to begin stage two.

Stage Two: Idea Generation and Speculation (limit to three-fourths of the total allotted time)

During the second stage the task is to set a playful environment for generating ideas, one that supports and nurtures speculation. Judgment is suspended as the leader guides participants through the following three phases to generate multiple solutions to the problem at hand.

First Phase.   During the first phase of stage two, participants "blow up" the problem by redefining it in terms of wishes. People are encouraged to be seemingly irresponsible, to dream of wild, absurd, and even illegal solutions to the problem. This can occur by prefacing ideas with either, "I wish that ____," or "I want to figure out how ____." As people listen to ideas, new possible solutions surface in a snowball effect. Communication channels remain open as the leader guides the process of group members generating ideas. The client can provide additional direction by saying, "I wish the group would speculate more on that idea."

Note the dream list of one group for the perfect school environment:

carpet entire school
air-condition school
stereo and TV in each room
piped sound
murals on all walls
visit a school in another country
you can't tell teachers from
   students
our own pets
our own garden
field trips once a week
assemblies once a month
retreat to New Mexico
three weeks school/four weeks
   break

one teacher for each student
no lunch or bus duty; catered
   lunches
donuts and apple for each
   morning
ice-skating rink and swimming
   pool
our own guardian angel
work sometimes in the city
   courtroom
travel on all city transportation
   systems
learn with lots of grandparents

Second Phase. During the second phase of stage two the leader takes participants on one or two excursions, looking at the problem in a seemingly related context. For example, the problem of diverse community pressures on the school can be analyzed by exploring the world of transportation: How does community pressure affect urban transportation? How does transportation affect the urban community? Group members generate all kinds of possible solutions as the leader records suggestions and keeps the energy level high. To illustrate how various forms of transportation meet different client needs, the following concepts may emerge:

> Each form of urban transportation has its own system of management control
> Each form of transportation serves a different segment of the community
> All forms of transportation coexist to meet collective community needs

As group members "play" with concepts borrowed from the world of transportation, further excursions reveal new dimensions about pressure releases.

1. *Analogy:* A commuter train is to daily travel as a daily plan of activities is to learning.
2. *Metaphor:* Teacher-developed materials often become the underground curriculum, providing a rapid access to meaningful learning activities.
3. *Image:* I can imagine a child having free passes on any kind of learning program so that he or she can progress to desired locations in the manner that makes most sense.

Sample excursions are listed here to provide the reader with ideas on how excursions can be useful to a group for unfreezing mind-sets. Excursions unblock the mind as ideas flow free in a structured, related situation.

Sample Analogy

Classroom noise level seems like	*Ideas for problem solutions*
building construction	use rubber ear muffs
Six Flags	sponge-soled shoes
herd of cattle	separate noisy/quiet activities
running a motor	place signs "quiet," "at work"
freeway traffic	time for noise

Sample Images

Places where relationships can develop

spaceship	train trip
camping trip	stranded on an island

Prairie Dog Town   Cypress Gardens
underwater   Animal World

Underwater world is like

little ones getting eaten by big   water transmits sound
  ones   info sharing—Dolphin/warning
balance   systems
exchange   adaptation to depth—physically
traveling by schools or groups of   self-preservation—sting—own
  fish   built-in protection
plants provide what fish need   spacing—cavities, etc.
sunlight

Sample Free Association

Underground space

lack of light   tunnels
making more space   lowered ceiling
how to get there   throw out dirt
furniture   use natural cavities
digging—walls

The excursion options listed in Table 7.1 are useful for speculation sessions. Participants play with the ideas in a free form until enough ideas surface that have potential for being fashioned into workable solutions.

TABLE 7.1. Excursion Options

Kinds of Excursions	
Analogy	"A cocoon is like a school because _____."
Metaphor	"The queen bee entered the classroom."
Imaging	"I can imagine a child having his or her own private plane and being able to fly to any part of the world that is of interest at any time."
Word Association	Child—spring—bud—vase—rose—peddles—bike
Personal Analogy	"I am a car going into the repair shop. I feel I'm about to be exposed."
Essential Paradox	Active kids in a noiseless classroom.
Guided Fantasy	"Imagine you are a butterfly just leaving the cocoon. Where will you go?
Absurd Solution	All kids should have their own free lifetime ticket to anywhere.

TABLE 7.2 Excursion Worlds*

Organic Worlds	Inorganic Worlds	Other Worlds
Biology	Physics	
Sports	Mineralogy	Science Fiction
Fashion	Chemistry	Computers
War	Mathematics	Noise
Botany	Astronomy	Pollution
Medicine	Machines	Finance
Theatre	Rocks	Archaeology
Animals	Geology	
Politics	Oceanography	
Art	Architecture	
Comedy	Aeronautics	
Criminology	Transportation	
Witchcraft		
Exploration		

* (*Source:* Prince 1970, 225)

Excursions often tend to be more fruitful if, during the planning session, the leader and client select the kinds of excursions that appear to generate the most promising solutions to the problem. Consider the list of possible worlds in Table 7.2 for exploring imaging, free association, analogies, and other processes. The task is to relate the problem at hand to another world, for example, individualizing instruction may be similar to a car in an auto repair shop. The leader then has the group free-associate processes that happen to a car while it is in a shop.

Third Phase.   During the third phase of stage two, the client selects those ideas that appear to hold the most promise as workable solutions. Participants begin to build on these ideas as the client acts as group critic. The task of critic is to provoke the group to refine "possible" solutions until they become potentially useful. For example, the group can explore how each form of transportation exists to meet different kinds of needs, such as:

commuter trains transport suburbanites to and from work and business
subways provide low-cost, high-speed transportation to many parts of the
    city
buses offer low-cost travel for short distances
cabs offer high-cost, quick, door-to-door travel
airplanes provide high-cost, fast linkages between cities
cars provide high-cost, convenient, door-to-door transportation

Stage Three: Idea Fusion (limit to 10 minutes)

The last stage in creative problem solving requires that group members, and particularly the client, be tough-minded about the feasibility and workability of the suggested solutions. The client's task is to identify the most promising solution (remembering that none are perfect initially) and to "loose-fit" it onto the problem. For example, the client may ask the group to explore how the numerous needs and options regarding transportation can apply to the school problem of providing various kinds of learning environments. The group generates possible solutions while the client guides the direction for developing a workable solution. Note the final solution of one group to their problem with student learning style differences.

> Parents and teachers will form a task force to identify the following kinds of knowledge and information relating to individual learning styles and the influence of the classroom environment:
>> Different kinds of learning styles and preferences among children
>> The nature of a learning environment conducive to each particular learning style
>> Existing options for designing learning environments and instructional methodologies for meeting different learning styles
>
> The task force is requested to make certain recommendations to the school's coordinating board for providing optimal learning environments for all students.

The reader may want to try the three stages in group creative problem solving. The problem stated in the following can be given to a group to solve. Give them 10 minutes to develop a solution prior to any information about the three-stage problem-solving process. Analyze their results and then try the three-stage process as described.

A GROUP PROBLEM-SOLVING ACTIVITY

> Pretend that one member of your group has been recently appointed to the principalship of a 600-pupil elementary school. Her predecessor resigned because he was unable to cope with conflicting parental values regarding optimal learning environments. One powerful community group wanted to continue improving the options for learning in flexible spaces. Another group, with a great deal of support from the board of education, wanted to limit learning options and return to a more traditional approach of assigning each child to one teacher.
>
> The task of the new principal was to resolve the problem of conflicting educational values and expectations in such a way that student learning needs were met and parental concerns resolved.
>
> In a group, appoint a school principal and determine the roles for each

group member (parent, teacher, student, etc.). In the next 30 minutes develop a hypothetical plan of action for resolving parent concerns, and at the same time meeting student learning needs.

In summary, the three-stage creative problem-solving technique enables a group to identify a problem quickly and to spend considerable time and effort in structured speculation activities. Most promising solutions subsequently are selected and refined until a workable solution surfaces. Figure 7.8 provides a guide to the leader, client, and team members in using the creative problem-solving process.

A group can tap its collective logical and intuitive responses by structuring time for problem analysis, idea generation and speculation, and idea fusion. In some meetings all three stages of the problem-solving process will be useful.

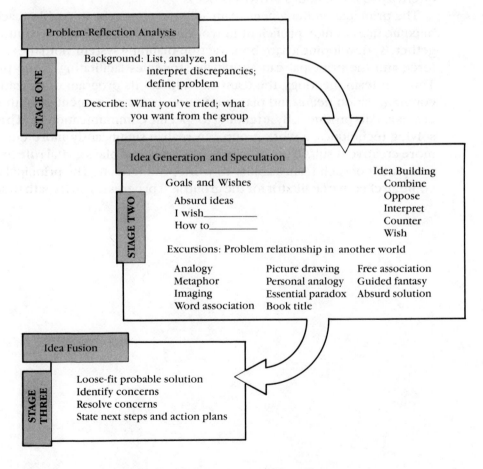

Figure 7.8. Creative Problem-Solving Process Flowchart

In others, only one of the three stages may be necessary to break the patterns of logical thought and enable the group to move on to decision-making tasks. Hence the three stages presented here are to be viewed as optional techniques for groups in making creative and tough-minded decisions.

Conclusion

School organization in the future will resemble a beehive more than a series of separate cocoons. Teachers will be organized into teaching teams and task forces to carry out the school's teaching functions and for solving its most pressing problems. Both teaching teams and task forces will be goal oriented rather than activity oriented and will be more tightly accountable for their productivity in the school's growth process.

The principal will engineer team skill development to enable teachers to become increasingly proficient in working productively and accountably together. By developing a bare-bones action-planning system, both the team/task force and the principal can anticipate strategies facilitating group practice. Through team meetings, the team can address its program organization and communication needs and plan continuously for refinement of both its processes and its products. By attending to specific communications and problem-solving techniques, a work group can realize significantly more energy and more creative results from its efforts. The principal plays a vital role in the development of each team's ability to work productively. The principal can become an effective facilitator for the group as it progresses on its path to success.

8

The Performance Subsystem

Individual role performance and role relationships in education have remained virtually unchanged over the past 50 years or more. As has been noted in previous chapters, the attitudes of mind and the working habits of most teachers hark back to the days of the one-room schoolhouse, where each teacher worked in isolation and carried the entire instructional burden for the children in his or her charge. The initial developments of cooperative teaching and differentiated staffing, in the mid-twentieth century, represented the first large-scale attempts to link teachers together so that, among other advantages, they could learn from each other and enlarge their professional/technical repertoires. While team teaching has received mostly a grudging or apathetic response, it is heartening that cooperative arrangements are slowly spreading. Significantly, the importance of professional collaboration is underscored in the research on effective schools. It is also reinforced by developments in the industrial world, where Japanese and American experiences have shown the benefits of worker affiliation within a group work structure. A major message in this book is that greater school productivity can be expected when more effectiveness is being made of human and material resources. Drucker, observing that management's most important function is resources utilization, notes that of all resources available, "man" is the only one that can grow and develop (1954, 12). Hence, effective adult performance in schools is much more complex than the mere development of an evaluation system. Evaluation practices tend to function as a restraining force for teacher development on the job. Furthermore, there is little evidence that teacher evaluation practices correlate to any extent with student achievement. Management research, however, has found that when performance evaluation is linked with the goals of the organization and of the worker, evaluation tends to provide a specific feedback func-

TABLE 8.1. Performance Management: Paradigm Shift

Practices	Maintenance Paradigm	Productivity Paradigm
Role performance standards	Job descriptions	Categorical performance outcomes
Planning	Personal/informal	Organizational and individual Negotiated goals
Development	Personal counseling	Training Clinical supervision Job enlargement
Motivation	Assignment/expectations Autonomy	Goal focus Achievement/recognition Development tasks
Control	Evaluation	Periodic management reviews/positive reinforcement and/or correction
Evaluation	Observation assessment	Goal based Measured results

tion and subsequently shapes behavior to influence the organization's productivity (Odiorne 1979; Knezevich 1973; Reddin 1970; Lathan and Yukl 1975).

Table 8.1 provides a comparison of performance management in the maintenance and the productivity paradigms. In the former, job descriptions provide general parameters for performance, and a general structure for role evaluation. The new era calls for goal-based performance, which is linked with certain role standards of excellence. The intent of a performance system within the productivity paradigm is to develop talent, in relation to an overall mission and goals, rather than to label talent according to general criteria. Evaluation assesses the extent of effective development for the organization.

The purpose of this chapter is to present a framework for designing effective performance systems for all roles within the school. The model provides guidelines for developing each dimension of a performance system and illustrates the concepts through a system that we designed for a school in Texas. Figure 8.1 outlines the planning, development and evaluation dimensions of a performance system for teachers.

The chapter will begin with attention to problems with traditional performance systems in schools. Role theory provides certain concepts that illuminate the interaction within and across roles, and with the nature of current role problems among teachers and administrators. Management-by-objectives (MBO) is the most powerful practice in industry for integrating individual performance with organizational goals. We will discuss the origins of MBO as well

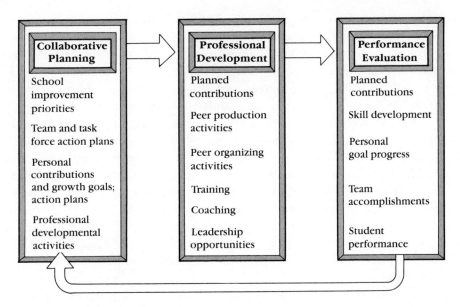

Figure 8.1. A Systems Approach to Teacher Performance

as later developments, as a foundation for the performance system model that follows. Attention also is given to the dismissal issue as it relates to work productivity. The thrust of a performance system is role development as it relates to the productivity of a specific school. The concepts within the performance system model are generic and can therefore be adapted to any school for any role. Our attention throughout this chapter, however, is primarily on the role of teacher.

Traditional Role Performance

The Problem

Confusion about role expectations troubles teachers and principals alike. It is certain that schools are in changing times, but little definition exists for each role group as each adjusts to new expectations. Merton (1957) defined social status and roles as the building blocks of a social structure. *Status,* he notes, describes the norms of a position. For example, teachers work in a certain kind of situation (classroom), have certain kinds of training (B.A. or B.S. in education), and receive a certain income for services (for example, $12,000 for beginners). *Role* refers to various performance expectations within a group. All teachers, for example, are planners and instructors. A *role set* includes a grouping of those with the same role definitions, such as a group of teachers (for example, science teachers) with similar job expectations.

The last decade has seen an upheaval and increasing strain in all three of these social mechanisms. Goode (1960) observes that role strain springs from a combination of sources: (1) demands of role performance; (2) ambiguity within the system of expectations; (3) conflict of allocation across members of particular sets; (4) problems across a status set (all the life roles of one individual). Current demands for workshops on burnout and concern with contract negotiations are but a few clues to the role strains that exist in the nation's schools. Fortunately, we perceive that there are a few tangible ways for reducing role strain and creating environments for higher productivity among all of the school's role sets.

Teacher role strain exists because of problems within role status. Teacher training and pay are both inadequate as teachers now are expected to shift from large-group, norm-referenced, grade- and group-bound instruction, to that which is individually oriented and requires diagnosed, multi-optional, alternative, flexible, and mastery-oriented instruction. The former roles of guardian, lecturer, dispenser, disciplinarian, and evaluator are less effective today than in the past and are examples of practices belonging to the maintenance paradigm. These practices will be less useful in the productivity paradigm. In time the role strain will be resolved as job parameters and training are more clearly defined and executed. The teacher roles of diagnostician, program designer, coach, leader, and counselor will surface as more effective role behaviors in the future. New kinds of training and better pay can also offset role strain somewhat. However, role strain will continue to dominate schools until teachers are provided with clear standards of new expectations along with the continuous training that is required for new role practices.

The basic problem with the role set of teachers is that they have rarely been organized into formal groups to provide services for schools. A functioning role set has only existed as an informal collection of individuals. In the years ahead the role set of teachers and other roles will be characterized by organized group functions for each role set. Teachers often are resistant and fearful of working cooperatively with their peers; and principals tend to ignore the problem or possibility altogether. If teachers were organized formally into groups with group productivity expectations, and were provided with training in group efforts, much of the role set strain in schools today would dissipate. Perhaps with new and clear role definitions, and with explicit group productivity expectations, the fears of collaboration will give way to bursts of shared energy.

The challenge for school district officials today is to provide new and clear role expectations for all role sets, not merely one. In the innovation years of the 1960s and 1970s, attention was given to teachers alone. Even though the principal now is receiving more attention as a key to school success, little definition has surfaced regarding the new tasks, functions, expectations, and training. A challenge for the education community is to attend to the many job dimensions of principals as well as of teachers. Further, attention must be given to definitions of department chairpersons, team leaders, and assistant principals as well. A change in any role set influences all other sets. The productivity era will require new role definitions for all role groups in schools and the addition of team leaders in elementary schools.

Schools need to design and institutionalize a performance system for developing talent, one that reflects current knowledge about specific role performance and about organizational influences on adult performance. In so doing, there necessarily will be an exchange of assumptions from

role isolation $\rightarrow$ a group work context

role generalization $\rightarrow$ standards of productivity

effort focus $\rightarrow$ a results focus

job protection $\rightarrow$ skill proficiency

personal interest $\rightarrow$ goal-based tasks

individual deficits $\rightarrow$ individual contributions

In a recent workshop in Texas, over 100 administrators identified the issues they felt related most to teacher performance. The items mentioned not only inform us of the concerns of principals, but also amplify the degree to which evaluation is the major thrust in conceptualizing teacher performance.

teacher evaluation instruments
criteria for evaluation
time management for supervision
conference techniques
techniques for giving feedback
techniques for data analysis
the affective dimension of performance
the value premise in evaluation
placing students with ineffective teachers

The current preoccupation among principals with the evaluation dimension of performance underscores the need for a far more holistic view of adult performance in schools and the function of evaluation. Let us examine performance issues briefly as they relate to school productivity, role expectations, adult learning, evaluation procedures, and contract negotiations.

Issue One: School Productivity

Pressures to increase student performance have precipitated a flurry of activity in an effort to hold schools accountable for student performance. State departments and school boards, in their effort to assist in this task, however, further thwart the school improvement process by employing a deficiency focus in teacher improvement plans. A deficiency emphasis may correct gross performance problems, but it does not promote the school and teacher improvement process. Further, an "individual teacher" approach to performance does relatively little to foster schoolwide organizational productivity and, instead, tends to overburden the school's already heavy activity load. Rather, teacher improvement targets need to be identified in relation to selected organizational improvement priorities, and to standards of teacher performance. Performance must be viewed holistically, within the school's growth context if it is to function as an influence on student achievement.

Studies continue to stress that collective activities among workers generate greater work results than isolated work activities, greater energy, and a stronger commitment. Teacher performance plans that relate directly to the school's improvement priorities and to team objectives tend to elicit contributions to school development. A "contribution-to-school-goals" mind-set emphasizes growth; deficiencies are addressed effectively in the context of productive work.

The Phi Delta Kappa study (1980) of exceptional urban schools found that staff evaluation was one of several factors not even critical to school success. However, the study did find that staff development programs that focused upon specific school outcomes contribute effectively to altering learning norms. The study goes on to recommend that school improvement processes focus on specific goals and on increasing resources for attaining those goals.

In conceptualizing staff performance, attention must be given to the several practices that influence behavior changes. School goals and group plans are the springboards for individual performance and it is within this goal context that performance is judged, and also is planned and developed. We assume that each individual staff member belongs to a work group and is expected to make specific contributions to group productivity. Guideposts such as role standards or school/team goals provide the direction for performance and for evaluating effectiveness.

A corporate framework influences the design of individual performance systems. Rather than concentrating on a worker's deficiencies, the Japanese mind-set, for example, provides a much more nurturing context for performance.

Trust and intimacy among workers and management are central to organizational productivity (Ouchi 1981, ix). Fear, hostility, doubt, and punishment only contribute to organizational decline, notes Ouchi; they do not translate into increased productivity. As principals and teachers consider the challenges that a particular year presents, certain performance goals are considered, negotiated, and defined. Management needs to invite interaction and dialogue about performance expectations and to use these as a guide for planning, developing, and evaluating staff. Responsibility must be given and assumed in a climate of trust that is combined with collective decision making. Common goals provide the cohesion necessary for group productivity and accountability, and high-quality performance results from a continuous refinement of work processes and learning programs.

Issue Two: Role Expectations and Responsibilities

Expectations for the role of teacher are changing dramatically. Yet, a wide gap exists between what is now known regarding effective teaching and the teaching patterns found in most schools. Because of teaching research in the past decade, which has focused primarily on teacher behaviors that correlate with achievement, relatively certain effective teaching patterns are beginning to emerge. We are able to state, for example, that *diagnosis* of student readiness accounts for considerable variance in student mastery of a particular concept or skill. Diagnosis no longer is an optional teacher task; it is critical to achievement. Students learn best in a nurturing *climate* (Edmonds 1979, 15–23), and in one that is *high* and realistic in *expectations* (Brophy and Good 1974). Furthermore, mastery results from appropriate and effective *instructional cues* and *directives, reinforcement, correctives,* and *feedback* (Bloom 1976); and from sufficient *time, interactive learning experiences* (Stallings 1980), and *cooperative learning activities* (Johnson 1981). Moreover, student mastery is influenced by *personal motivation* and a strong *self-concept* (Rogers 1969).

Nevertheless, performance expectations for teachers in most schools are little more than a vague hope that teachers will "figure out" how to improve instruction. Teaching expectations rarely relate to research on effective practices but rather resemble the norms as they have been established in the past. Typically there exist rather rigid, graded programs, geared to standardized and graded textbooks and offered within inflexible time frameworks (class periods, semesters, grade-per-year organization). The usual patterns of diagnosis, motivation, reinforcement, and correctives are geared to graded standards, rather than to need, and to a basically competitive environment associated with the bell curve. It is our contention that a teacher performance system must be designed to shape new kinds of teaching behaviors in order to alter instructional norms. Traditional evaluation systems have neither the power nor the intent to transform teaching behavior.

The State of Georgia (*Education USA,* July 16, 1980, 319) defined 14 competencies for teachers in planning, classroom procedures, and interpersonal skills, and required teachers to demonstrate mastery of these within a three-year period. Another system categorized competencies into the following groups: productive teaching techniques; positive interpersonal relationships; organized and structured classroom management; intellectual stimulation; and out-of-classroom behaviors (Manatt et al. 1976). Popham (1973) suggested another approach by proposing three teaching evaluation categories: (1) achievement of instructional objectives with diverse learners; (2) selection and generation of definable objectives; and (3) detection of the unanticipated effects of instruction.

Whichever teacher performance categories are selected or developed, it is important that they be linked to *current* knowledge about the teaching/learning process. An appropriate selection of categories, which narrows and defines expectations for teachers, will unleash staff energy and commitment in a desired direction. If teachers remain uncertain of expectations, however, a sense of job unmanageability will continue to ensure burnout and prompt more teachers to leave education for other, more certain jobs.

All roles performed within schools can and must be provided with a specific set of results-oriented standards (a productivity orientation). There exists no perfect set of standards that can be used in all schools; however, any results-oriented, research-based set of role standards will provide efficient role clarity to teachers. Role clarity in combination with school improvement priorities can stimulate even the mediocre teacher to become exceptionally productive.

Issue Three: Adult Learning

Learning has been conceptualized in schools primarily as a phenomenon that happens to students. In the last decade the notion of teacher and administrator/supervisor growth has led to a flurry of workshops, courses, and seminars sponsored by various educational institutions. The problem with most of these sessions, however, is that they are largely restricted to information sharing. Perhaps this is due to a general belief that adult learning results primarily from listening. However, adult learning occurs in a wide variety of experiences that include workshops and courses, and extend to on-the-job experiences. When principals realize that they have 180 days to motivate staff learning, rather than 5 or 10 district-allotted days, far more growth will be realized for the school. Hence, evaluation-only approaches to adult performance fall far short of the range of possible influences on adult learning. In the future, each year's growth process will begin with goals and include all learning experiences in the school, including performance evaluation.

Luthans (1975, 12) claims that all organizational behaviors are learned in an organizational setting. This notion suggests that teacher behavior that now exists in schools has been learned and reinforced in schools. Changes in behavior norms will occur only when different expectations exist and where management views every day as a learning opportunity for adults. The principles of reinforcement and contingency management (which Luthans calls "Organizational Behavior Modification") can nurture daily growth and alter work practices in schools. Skinner (1980) further recommends that schools employ systems of positive reinforcement for adult workers by praising accomplishments and recognizing achievements. Goal-related achievements tend to reinforce performance in the desired direction. Given a climate of recognition for new, more desired behaviors, those teachers who remain resistant and/or ineffective will tend to seek other employment, almost unnoticed.

Issue Four: Evaluation Procedures

Research on effective schools reveals virtually nothing about current teacher evaluation practices that correlates with student achievement gains, and yet, a large proportion of district development activities are focused on devising new teacher evaluation instruments. When considering the adult learning process, there seems to be little capability within instruments, if used alone, to alter behavior patterns. Yet the search for the perfect evaluation instrument continues to drive school districts. This current preoccupation is grossly disproportionate to the cluster of factors that influence adult learning and productivity. More appropriate performance questions include: What is the purpose of evaluation? Which performance results are to be assessed? What are the standards of performance? What is the goal context within which evaluation occurs? And, will performance-based merit pay and increases in salary alter the quality of performance?

Concern for teacher evaluation has generated a wide variety of state codes, local policies, and procedures. Various persons within school districts have been designated to evaluate teachers within a range of guidelines and standards. Zirkel (1978) studied the public laws on teacher evaluation in many states and found there to be a general lack of unanimity with regard to current evaluation practices. The scope of evaluation, he observed, ranges from global competencies to measures of actual student progress. Evaluation procedures range from checklists and ratings (the majority) to goal-oriented methods (a few). In over one-fourth of the states, school board members themselves evaluate teachers, while in the remainder of the states, teachers are evaluated by an entire spectrum of school administrators. Moreover, in some states all professionals are evaluated; in others, only nontenured teachers are assessed with the frequence of evaluation ranging from annual assessment to once every three years. Haefele (1980, 349–353) also found that the focus for evaluation is varied throughout the states and includes a combination of measured student achievement gains, formal and informal observations by supervisors, student ratings, and teacher exams. While it is not clear how inclusive are the Zirkel and Haefele studies, there seems to be a lack of consensus among and within states and within districts on the procedures and policies for teacher evaluation. In fact, purposes and outcomes do not appear to be an issue in the minds of most evaluation system designers. Questions about performance outcomes are virtually unasked in most redesigns. Moreover, job descriptions generally describe what teachers are to *do,* not the *results* of their performance.

The extensive research on performance in the business and industrial workplace suggests to us that evaluation practices *can* stimulate worker learning and productivity and function as a correlate of organizational success. To become more effective, schools must shift their attention from global measures "following" performance to identifying role standards and an organizational goal context "before" behavior. By shifting attention from "after" to "before" performance, actual behavior can link directly to organizational purpose through a goal structure. Evaluation in this sense measures the results of what management and worker agreed upon before performance began.

Issue Five: Contract Negotiations

A recent Rand Study (1979) of organized teachers found that the most dramatic gains that have been made through contract negotiation practices relate to reducing class size. Moreover, policy decisions regarding assignment, transfer, length of school day, and in some cases, teacher evaluation methodology have also been a focus in contract negotiations. However, such gains, the study reports, have not produced any noticeable gains in the quality of services provided in classrooms. While teacher influence in management decisions could potentially lead to problems with federally mandated programs, for example, the study shows that in many cases more harmonious and productive relations resulted from teacher involvement, perhaps because of the perceived disinterest among school administrators regarding the substance of many educational programs. Researchers suggest that teacher commitment to reform can be strengthened through involvement. At the least, collective bargaining may have produced a higher quality of performance among teachers than was anticipated by critics.

How, then, can contract negotiations fit into the scheme of a school's ecological growth process? In many recent workshops we have conducted for school administrators, occasionally the president of the local teachers' professional organization has been present. Their assessment of the workshop often suggested to us that principals are perceived as not wanting teachers to innovate or to work together. In addition there is a perception that principals know little about teaching and learning. If this is accurate, perhaps there is some reasonable justification for the pattern of classroom visits only once a year for the purpose of evaluation. Perhaps contract negotiations will ultimately precipitate greater management involvement in the instructional improvement processes. Perhaps contract negotiations also will help to create the necessary atmosphere for collaboration.

Sergiovanni and Carver (1973, 80–85) suggested several ways for administrators to climb out of the negotiations "trap." Using the Herzberg model of worker motivation, they observe that current negotiation practices are geared to the "hygiene seeker" (the type of worker who is chronically dissatisfied with the work environment) who is interested primarily in private goals and realizes little satisfaction from corporate accomplishments. Such a person is unlikely to translate negotiated achievements into school improvement behaviors. At best, only their dissatisfactions will be resolved for a period of time.

The "motivation seekers" (task-oriented workers), on the other hand, hold the greatest promise for contributing significantly to school improvement efforts. Primary attention needs to be given to the needs of motivation seekers rather than to hygiene seekers. Sergiovanni and Carver urge principals to attend to school goals, tasks and accomplishments, and to the natural enthusiasm of the "motivation seekers." Further, motivation seekers who work effectively on their tasks need to be recognized for their accomplishments, given added responsibilities, or advanced. Perhaps, higher standards of staff performance will enable schools to focus more on student achievement issues and less on working conditions.

It is our contention that the constraints placed on principals by negotiated contracts will dissolve as a school develops a capacity for shared decision making about the larger issues of schooling. Cooperative attention to achievement, learning, and teaching results will lift the entire staff to a higher level of dialogue and will result in far greater productivity for the school than has been realized in the adversarial practices of the past decades. Both teachers and administrators have gained some advantage during the battles over conditions; the time has come, however, to proceed into a new era of dialogue and activity around central schooling issues.

A performance system for a school will necessarily include role standards for teachers, team leaders, assistant principals, and principals. Role expectations for nonprofessionals will evolve in time after the new definitions for professionals are in operation. A first consideration in discussing performance systems is the nature of a goal based system. Numerous research studies cite a goal orientation to performance as the most effective base in linking performance to organizational productivity. For insights into problems and opportunities in goal based systems, let us consider developments within the field of management-by-objectives.

Management-by-Objectives (MBO)

Lippitt (March 1979, foreward) observes from studying organizations in general, that improvement in the quality of working life depends in part on the goal orientation, definition and responsibility for the work itself. "For more than 20 years people have been falling in and out of love with the MBO idea. . . . Yet despite a decade of obituaries, it continues to grow more persuasive and has become almost orthodoxy in management" (Odiorne 1979, 326). Why does MBO continue to intrigue school administrators?

MBO is not only a management methodology, but also a philosophy that suggests that *purpose* and *aim* are important in determining the quality and style of life in an organization (Odiorne 1979, 17). Odiorne (1979, 42–44), defines MBO as a system under which management and subordinates talk about job goals until agreement is reached. During dialogue, job results are defined for selected goals, as well as the assessment process itself. Knezevich urges that the organizational framework be added to individual goal-setting practices (1979, 5). MBO is a system of operation, he observes, that enables the organization and its personnel to identify, move toward, lock onto objectives, and manage effectively for results.

Early research showed that effective MBO programs accomplished the following organizational outcomes:

> improved communications
> increased mutual understanding
> created more positive attitudes about evaluation
> helped in utilizing abilities
> promoted innovations
> integrated individuals and organizational goals (Kast and Rosenzweig
>   1974, 173)

An error made by many schools in adopting MBO was paying attention solely to the individual worker and the goals that were expected to result from individual worker performance. However, and more importantly, MBO is a methodology for *managing* workers toward specific organizational results. MBO success requires teamwork between management (principals and team leaders) and workers (teachers) throughout the school improvement process (not merely the beginning and end of a work cycle), where opportunity exists for influencing teachers in a certain direction.

MBO, thought by many administrators to be one additional burden in an already overloaded job, is actually a replacement for other kinds of management. It is another way of discharging responsibility for performance results (Knezevich 1973, 3). The objective in MBO is for individuals to work not harder but smarter (Reddin 1970, 86). The intent is to achieve congruence between job performance targets for all roles that will facilitate organizational productivity. Furthermore, the MBO process provides a mind-set of looking forward rather than backward (Reddin 1970, 195). Note the following benefits of MBO to all status sets:

Subordinate Benefits

(teachers, team leaders/department chairpersons)

> knowledge of what outcomes are expected
> specific performance measurement
> clarified authority
> increased job satisfaction and responsibility

Superior Benefits

(principals and team leaders/department chairpersons)

> motivation for subordinates
> strengthened role relationships
> a coaching work framework
> weak appraisal methods eliminated (ibid., 198)

Organization Benefits

(schools and teams/departments)

> managerial effectiveness becomes a central value
> management efforts focused on results
> coordinated effort facilitated
> objective reward criteria provided
> profit (achievement) potential provided
> advancement potential provided
> development needs identified
> growth facilitated (ibid., 199)

With the potential for individual growth so high, why, then, has MBO failed so often? Reddin, who wrote about MBO in 1970, observed general MBO pitfalls in organizations, which also apply to schools (Reddin 122):

1. lack of commitment
2. top managers not involved
3. poor implementation methods
4. little coaching and assistance
5. no follow-up
6. objectives handed to subordinate
7. creative goals stifled
8. fuzzy top policy

9. overemphasizing appraisal
10. making it mechanical

Job Descriptions Versus Role Standards

The purpose of a job description is to define general role activities. *Job descriptions,* however, tend to provide only general guidelines for performance and suggest an "activity" approach to a job. Schools exemplify the activity-trap syndrome today as teachers focus on peripheral duties (for example, counting lunch money, planning 45-minute periods, grading papers, attending PTA, completing report cards, attending meetings). Hence, goal displacement results from a job description orientation to performance by its continuous attention to activity. Moreover, job descriptions enable workers to focus on portions of a role that are of particular interest and to hide, so to speak, in the activity whirlpool. Job descriptions themselves provide suggestions, activities, and responsibilities defining job *input* areas (activities and tasks; what to do). Time and the results of performance are virtually impenetrable and extremely difficult to assess when viewing activity.

Further analysis of the problem reveals even more subtle failures of a job description orientation to performance. Research has pointed out that the average boss and subordinate are caught in the activity trap and consequently fail to agree on expected *outputs* (Odiorne 1979, 44–48). Because of this failure, disagreement results in major subordinate problems and, further, the boss and subordinate fail to agree on how performance should be improved. Consequently, few changes in the way things are done tend to emerge from performance reviews that are guided by job descriptions.

Role standards are only slightly different in appearance from job descriptions, but are fundamentally different in their effect on actual performance. A job analysis can reveal categorical areas necessary for effective performance of any role. Standards emerge from a job analysis and define the areas in which effectiveness is expected. Consequently, the worker is able to shift from an *input focus* (productivity measures as indicated in standards). However, measuring effectiveness is difficult and problematic to most managers. Kast suggests that the measurement of performance include both effectiveness (the degree to which goals are accomplished) and efficiency (use of resources in the attainment of goals) (1974, 174). A goal focus provides a necessary framework for evaluation. The challenge in designing standards is to determine categories for effective performance. Reddin suggests that areas should be defined in terms of effectiveness dimensions (1970, 30–34), and suggests the following:

Effectiveness Areas

subordinate (setting performance goals)
innovation (develop new methods or systems)

project (group production)
development (personal skill development)
system (response to the school or district)
co-worker (productive relationships)

MBO offers an effective antidote to the job description activity-trap syndrome, by building into management an unremitting attention to purpose (Odiorne 1979, 48–50). Consequently, conflict and ambiguity decrease as objectives become clear. MBO aids teachers to internalize school goals, and performance improves as individuals become clear about their job objectives. Consequently, individual performance should improve overall organizational performance, and at the same time increase the levels of staff participation in school growth. Goals that are agreed on prior to actual performance tend to facilitate congruence between actual performance and school improvement. Both actors have the same script, thus enabling the quality of performance to improve.

Principals become less frustrated over the multitude of school activities when teachers function within an MBO system. A central school improvement thrust provides a general focus for all role performance whereas MBO provides a goal-hook into each team and individual teacher. The job planning session for each individual defines specific expectations for performance results and, in addition, provides a necessary framework for staff development, clinical supervision, monitoring, and evaluation. A goal and results orientation to performance enables a principal and teacher to sort out and select activities that relate to goals; expected results provide the necessary structure for assessment.

Odiorne offers the following guidelines for successful MBO in the 1980s (1979, 74–76; 326):

1. Management by objectives is a system of managing, not an addition to the manager's job.
2. The manager who adopts management-by-objectives as a system of managing must plan to drop some of the more time-consuming vocational hobbies. Thus, the *learning curve* for the subordinate is the *delegation curve* for the superior. Your former hobbies become responsibilities of the subordinate.
3. The system of management-by-objectives requires a behavior change on the part of both superior and subordinate. Subordinates move in a more results-oriented fashion because they know what are their goals.
4. MBO requires changes in the way things are done, and requires some advance commitments.

We are convinced that MBO will enable principals to develop more successful schools by linking teacher performance more directly to the school's growth needs. Ouchi (*St. Louis Dispatch,* March 16, 1981) observes that U.S. companies are like Tinkertoys: we insert, add, and subtract parts without altering the organizational structure. For those principals who are flooded with responsibilities from serving breakfast and giving health examinations to providing after-school classes, there is hope. MBO provides a method for altering the school organization as it is needed, and for ignoring pressures for activities that have little to do with selected school priorities.

A Systems Approach to Performance

The primary function of management is to increase the job results of other people. Job behaviors are learned in the organization; consequently, management is concerned primarily with appropriate behaviors and the results of performance as it relates to organizational purposes and to priorities. An efficiency issue for performance today is producing more and better with less; the effectiveness issue focuses on the congruency between activity and results, as it relates to goals. Therefore, management must define expectations for efficient and effective performance and focus on results-oriented behavior.

In Part I of our performance Linkage System (see Figure 8.2), the annual process of planning performance is outlined for all role sets. *Annual goals* are established, for example, between teacher and principal (or team leader/department chairperson) as they relate to role standards, to school priorities, and to personal contributions and growth needs. *Action plans* are de-

Figure 8.2. A Performance Linkage System: Part I

veloped subsequently (not a part of negotiations), outlining the sequence of key activities, resources needed, and time lines. During the *implementing* stage, workers engage in planned activities during which contributions are made to the school's growth, and achievements are realized. Throughout the year, and at the end of the performance cycle, each worker assesses progress made toward goals and *replans* for the subsequent year.

A major error in many school MBO systems is the singular focus on individual planning. Individual performance occurs within a work context that is influenced by the work climate and by factors that either facilitate or retard individual growth. Consequently *organizational functions* must be designed to facilitate personal productivity and school productivity simultaneously. Note the following organizational functions contributing to productive performance:

> school and team goals
> role performance standards
> a staff development program
> clinical supervision
> monitoring
> performance evaluation

School goals and team plans provide the context for planning and assessing annual performance. *Standards* (written in effectiveness/results terms) define the general categories for work results. *Staff development* programs grow out of school/team/individual plans and provide new knowledge and skills. *Clinical supervision* serves a coaching function that is critical to skill development. Periodic *monitoring* corrects and reinforces trends in performance, while *evaluation* judges the results of all the previous activities. Together these practices provide a comprehensive context for effective performance (see Figure 8.3).

In designing a comprehensive performance system for all role sets, many considerations are important to the effective management of performance: outcome categories; school goal context; the planning system; the training/coaching systems; the monitoring system; and the evaluation system. Let us consider each function as it defines the context and parameters of performance.

Performance Outcome Categories

For each role set, performance expectations are examined in terms of behaviors (not activities) that are necessary for organizational productivity. Necessary behaviors are synonymous with competencies and are defined in terms of

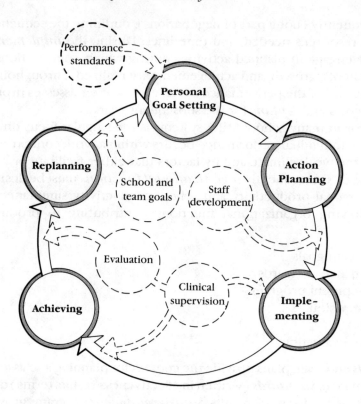

Figure 8.3. A Performance Linkage System: Parts I and II

essential categories. Hall and Jones (1975) describe a competency as a description of effective performance that is based on the acquisition, interaction, composite building, and application of a set of related knowledge and skills. Hence, performance categories define expected categorical competencies (not attributes or activities).

The role sets of teacher, department/team leader, assistant to the principal, principal, and student teacher are each conceptualized in relation to certain integrated role behavior sets that are necessary for effective performance. Figures 8.4–8.7 convey a message that all designated performance areas are essential to effective performance.

The Teacher Role Set

The teacher role set is defined as that which is most directly responsible for student achievement gains. Likewise, the teacher is viewed as a member of a teaching team where students, programs, space, and time resources are all group properties and group responsibilities. Thus, the teacher effectiveness areas assume that teacher collaboration is a work norm (see Figure 8.4). Spe-

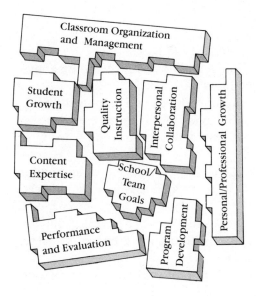

Figure 8.4. The Teacher Role Set

cialists, such as music, art, physical education, and special education teachers, form a team of their own and assume responsibility for student achievement on all teams within their domain. Role categories for teachers include quality instruction, classroom management and organization, program development, interpersonal collaboration, professional growth, content expertise, and measured student growth.

Each performance category has a list of indicators that provides clarity for each subsystem.

Teacher Performance Standards
1. Instruction that fosters individual student mastery
   A. Improve existing instructional modes
   B. Diagnose student readiness, interests, and learning styles
   C. Participate in peer and administrative observation and criticism
   D. Develop competence in additional instructional models
   E. Provide appropriate cues and directives, reinforcement, student participation, and continuous feedback and correctives to students
2. Management of classroom organization for effective learning
   A. Group students in a wide variety of ways to facilitate the learning process

B. Develop systems for
   1. personal student goal setting
   2. identifying learning interests and levels
   3. moving students through and to various learning activities
   4. recording student achievement data
   5. developing student independence and responsibility
C. Implement the school behavior management policies
D. Provide a work climate that facilitates learning

3. Program development
   A. Develop learning programs that correspond to curriculum expectations and to student learning needs in assigned academic areas
   B. Define learning outcomes as they relate to intellectual development, self-concept and motivation, competencies, social responsibility, and social interaction
   C. Monitor and evaluate each unit of study upon completion

4. Student growth
   A. Conduct a needs assessment for each individual program
      1. cognitive, affective readiness; interests
      2. learning style and cognitive style
   B. Plan a personalized instructional program that grows out of general program plans
   C. Provide cues and directives, reinforcement, feedback and correctives as necessary
   D. Conduct continuous assessment of learning outcomes
   E. Provide advisory services

5. Content mastery
   A. Demonstrate an adequate, up-to-date working knowledge base for your teaching assignment that reflects sound theory, current research and personal reflections on past teaching experiences

6. Personal/professional growth
   A. Plan for personal growth, as it relates to school goals. The following formats for learning can guide your planning: readings, workshops to attend, workshops to present, visitations, task forces, graduate courses, seminars, demonstrations, and presentations

7. Collaborative productivity
   A. Participate in productive team program planning and implementation
   B. Share team responsibilities
   C. Resolve conflicts directly
   D. Work enthusiastically toward team goals

    E. Share knowledge and skills

    F. Participate in school improvement task forces, materials development, program development, leadership responsibilities and tasks

In negotiating performance goals, the teacher and supervisor (principal or team leader/department chairperson) synthesize performance categories and school goals, and define targets of personal contribution and innovation, as well as growth needs.

Department/Team Leader Role Set

The role of team leader is defined in relation to the management of group productivity. Role standards are similiar to that of the principal but are written in terms of managing team productivity. The designation of the specific role expectations noted here reflect the needs of the teaching teams in one elementary school. The role standard subsystems are generic enough to be used by middle, high school, and college-level department heads; only the category indicators would change. Performance areas include team leadership and management, team organization, team program development, team instructional planning, staff development, student development and evaluation, personal planning, parental involvement, and boundary management (see Figure 8.5).

<u>Department/Team Leader Performance Standards</u>

    1. Team leadership and management

       A. Conduct annual team goal setting and action planning

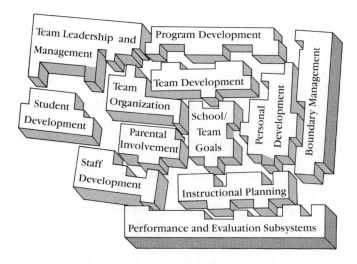

Figure 8.5. The Department/Team Leader Performance Standards

   B. Develop patterns of communications and decision making
   C. Coordinate team activities
   D. Monitor and control team programs
   E. Evaluate team goal attainment process and outcomes
2. Team organization
   A. Assign roles and responsibilities for the most effective and efficient use of staff resources
   B. Coordinate student groupings
   C. Define the functions of team space
   D. Coordinate the team schedule
   E. Develop a management system for student/teacher movement, performance, and accountability
   F. Provide team and individual planning time during the school week
   G. Plan for parent involvement
3. Team program development
   A. Plan programs in the following (or selected) academic areas to meet individual learning needs, desires, and goals
      1. language
      2. math
      3. art
      4. music
      5. physical education
      6. social studies
      7. science
   B. Conduct continuous evaluation of team programs
      1. student learning outcomes
      2. staff performance
      3. staff specialization
      4. program design
4. Team instructional planning
   A. Develop multiple instructional techniques to foster maximum learning
   B. Match instructional techniques to program goals and to differing student learning styles
   C. Add new instructional techniques/modes to the team repertoire
   D. Involve team members in observation cycles to analyze, critique, and improve existing patterns of instruction
5. Staff development
   A. Identify staff growth needs
   B. Locate appropriate resources for staff growth needs
   C. Plan for effective involvement of available resources

     D. Involve team members in planning staff learning programs
6. Student development and evaluation
     A. Identify student individual learning needs/goals: cognitive, affective, behavioral
     B. Plan for individual student learning needs/goals in all school defined program areas
     C. Plan for student learning goals with parents
     D. Develop individualized record-keeping systems
     E. Foster intellectual, physical, social growth, development of self-concept and independence, and responsibility for one's learning
     F. Evaluate individual learning outcomes, using such information for new planning
     G. Involve students in team activities and team planning
7. Personal planning
     A. For team improvement
     B. Time management
     C. Delegating responsibilities
     D. Professional growth
8. Parental involvement
     A. Develop a program for parent participation in student learning goal setting
     B. Develop a program for parent involvement in team program planning and implementation
9. Boundary management
     A. Represent team concerns to the school leadership council
     B. Communicate team concerns to the council and principal
     C. Participate in schoolwide planning and problem solving as guided by the project director and principal
     D. Resolve parental concerns
     E. Plan for the involvement of community resources

In negotiating performance goals, the department/team leader considers school and team goals, in relation to performance categories to analyze leadership challenges for the year. The goal structure further reflects the particular contributions of the leader to that team's success and productivity.

Assistant to the Principal Role Set

This role is conceptualized in our model as one that performs all administrative maintenance functions necessary for smooth school operations. Seven effectiveness areas are outlined: financial record keeping, buildings and grounds management, pupil transportation, auxiliary services, student control, schoolwide student record keeping, and personal growth, (see Figure 8.6).

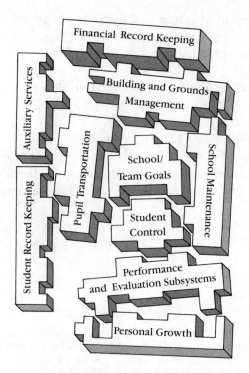

Figure 8.6. Assistant to the Principal

<u>Assistant to the Principal Performance Standards</u>
1. Financial record keeping
   A. Purchasing
   B. Inventory
   C. Bookkeeping
2. Administration of building and grounds
   A. Building maintenancc
      1. supervision of custodians
      2. planning and scheduling of improvement and maintenance tasks
   B. Supplies and equipment management
      1. storage
      2. repairs
      3. inventory
      4. acquisition/purchase
3. Pupil transportation
   A. Busing routes—coordination with central office
   B. Student assignment to buses
   C. Field trip arrangements

4. Auxiliary services
   A. Food services: supervision of lunchroom program
   B. Supervision of health services
   C. Substitute teachers: daily routines
   D. Special duties
5. Student control
   A. Work with unit leaders to develop a schoolwide behavior management program
   B. Implement and monitor student behavior management program
6. Student records
   A. Maintain a system for student record keeping to include
      1. grades or other data on pupil progress
      2. health information
      3. transfer information
      4. special services recommendations
   B. Manage the student enrollment and transfer program
7. Personal growth
   A. Develop weekly action plans for managing tasks and time
   B. Plan ways in which to grow professionally

Negotiations with assistant principals involve an analysis of the kinds of maintenance required in each category to assist the school in its development and in its smooth operations.

Student Teacher Role Set

The student teacher role is similar to the teacher role. The description for each category, however, reflects expectations for a brief training period, such as eight weeks of half-day teaching. The student teacher is assigned to a teaching team (not to an individual teacher) and works with the entire team. Specific goals for each performance subsystem grow out of team priorities and needs. Categories include quality instruction, classroom organization and management, program development, measured student growth, content expertise, personal and professional growth, and interpersonal collaboration (see Figure 8.7).

Student Teacher Performance Standards
1. Quality instruction
   A. Develop an instructional technique for each of the following
      1. small skill groups
      2. large group presentations
      3. small task groups
      4. individual consultation

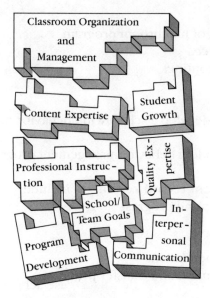

Figure 8.7. The Student Teacher

B. Participate in two peer observation cycles, one as an observer and one as the teacher observed

C. design learning centers to correlate with team program needs

2. Classroom organization and management

A. Participate in team decision making and planning for grouping students that will take into account learning needs, styles, rates, and desired program outcome

B. Participate as a team member in developing student management systems that foster personalized learning and reporting

C. Participate as a team member in planning the use of instructional space

3. Program development

A. Participate in planning the team's instructional program, assuming a major responsibility for one area of the program

4. Student growth

A. Conduct individual needs assessments in relation to your area of specialization

B. Plan, implement, and evaluate a personalized learning program in your area of specialization

5. Content expertise

A. Select one area of curriculum based on team needs for which you will provide expertise and assume a major responsibility

6. Personal/professional growth
   A. Plan four specific ways, in addition to school-based experience, in which you will expand your knowledge and increase your skills in teaching and teaming
      1. readings
      2. workshops
      3. school visitations
      4. seminars
7. Interpersonal collaboration
   A. Participate as a member of the teaching team, sharing your knowledge and skill and assuming responsibility for parts of the team's instructional program
   B. Meet weekly with your cooperating teacher to plan and assess your involvement in the instructional program

When viewed together, all role sets provide a unique function in school productivity. In this sense they function interdependently to raise achievement norms.

School Goal Context

The school's goal structure provides the necessary context and targets for individual performance; at the same time it enables the school to determine who does what. The school/team/individual linkage for goal responsibilities enables the school to achieve success in a planned, rather than a haphazard, fashion. (See Chapters 4–7 concerning goals and organization for additional information.) Individual staff members negotiate performance goals in terms of their contributions, rather than deficiencies, to school development each year.

In the following list are the goals that were developed in a school in Texas that illustrate the context for performance activities for all school role sets for a particular two-year period. Each role set established personal goals in relation to school goals that were filtered through role categories.

School Goals

1. To establish annual school goals and action plans
2. To develop a technology for identifying student learning needs and planning for their growth
3. To become more knowledgeable and skillful in using various instructional methods and materials
4. To participate in schoolwide instructional improvement by being clinically observed and observing other teachers

5. To develop a schoolwide curriculum scope and sequence in reading and language arts
6. To develop a schoolwide record-keeping system to monitor and report individual student progress in reading and language arts
7. To increase communications and effectiveness in team planning, teaching, and assessment
8. To engage each child in multiple activities that promote exploration, divergent thinking, and discovery at his or her own rate

The Planning System

Individual Goal Setting

The role standard categories mentioned in the previous section provide the framework for merging personal role responsibilities with categorical contributions. The teacher, for example, prepares for goal setting by identifying commitments made to the school's development by teams and task forces, and reflects on past accomplishments and assesses personal growth needs. The principal and team leader plan for the teacher's goal-setting conference by assessing past accomplishments, school needs, and assessed individual teacher growth needs. Prepared for dialogue, the principal/team leader and teacher identify perhaps four contributions/growth goals, using the role standards framework. Effective goals, the reader will recall, will be measurable, specific, results centered, attainable, and time bound. A rule of thumb in writing goals is to avoid the use of certain unquantifiable terms such as increase, decrease, maximize, minimize, satisfy, and optimize.

Odiorne (1979, 83) provides a guideline to assist managers in preparing performance objectives. He suggests that each person set three kinds of goals: (1) a goal for regular responsibilities of the position; (2) a goal for major problems that need to be resolved; and (3) a goal for innovations needed for more effective operations. A principal or team leader may decide on the number of goals in each category, remembering that goal setting is a forward-looking process that is conducted by imperfect people in an imperfect world. The goal-setting negotiation represents a "best guess" about future conditions.

A range of performance levels exists for every goal when defining desired results. Since work conditions change daily it is important to define pessimistic expectations, realistic expectations, and optimistic expectations (Odiorne 1979, 123). Since there is no one role that controls all the variables influencing schooling results, it is important to establish a general sense of what can be expected, with the results being weighed against current conditions. The pessimistic to optimistic range provides a frame of reference as the teacher, for example, works toward goals and is subsequently evaluated.

A key to successful performance lies in the up-front nature of goal setting that identifies indicators of attainment as well as management commitments. Odiorne (1979, 108–116) offers for consideration a number of rules for goal writing that were generated by a dozen directors of management development, MBO administrators, and executives from twelve organizations who have used MBO techniques for many years and have found their MBO programs successful. The following is our summary of their cumulative advice.

What Makes the Best Kind of Goal?

1. Do not stress the obvious.
2. Every goal you accept means you have rejected some other goals.
3. A mistake in goals will produce a mistake in activity.
4. Goals are most useful when stated as indicators.
5. Goals can reflect real effectiveness or apparent effectiveness.
6. Force a measurement, and if it does not work out, drop it.
7. If your goals will make your boss uneasy, back off.
8. If goals are conditional, state the conditions.
9. Side effects cannot always be predicted in detail.
10. Imagined side effects should not be allowed to stop goal setting.
11. Experience is a pretty good teacher, and experienced goal setters set better goals.
12. The business environment is always part of reality-based goal setting.
13. Goals that are routine will not excite anybody.
14. Low confidence means low goals; high confidence means high goals.
15. Good goals create the resources to produce them.
16. It is a good idea to pick a goal to command resources.
17. The goal setter is an important part of the quality of the goal.

The reader may want to practice applying these criteria by analyzing the sample performance goals in Figure 8.8. The reader will note that one goal is established for each effectiveness area; however, there are actually only three separate goals when they are grouped into broader categories.

In the goal-setting conference it is important to define ways in which the results of performance will be measured. Note the indicators of attainment mentioned in Figure 8.8 plan, and also the ways in which the principal (or other leader) intends to facilitate Donna's successful performance.

A performance plan such as Donna's grows out of a negotiation over what is expected by a certain point in time. For some teachers, a principal and/or team leader will need to extend a teacher's preplan. For others, principals will limit the plan's scope. The focus and level of expectations depends on teacher readiness and existing skills. No two teachers will develop similar plans; each plan is designed according to needs, commitments, and responsibilities.

Annual Performance Goals

Name Donna Morris   **Team** The Arts

Subsystem I: Instruction for Mastery

Goals	Indicators of Attainment	Principal/Team Leader Responsibilities
Define and develope proficiency in 4 instructional techniques by May 1 Demonstrations Learning Contracts Peer teaching	Classroom observation Student inventory Learning outcomes	Identify books Identify teachers worth observing Observer critique

Subsystem II: Classroom Organization and Management for Effective Learning

Goals	Indicators of Attainment	Principal/Team Leader Responsibilities
Group students to increase their time-on-task by March 1	Increase in "P" ratio scores	Develop workshop on diagnosis Observe with the "P" ratio instruments

Subsystem III: Program Development

Goals	Indicators of Attainment	Principal/Team Leader Responsibilities
Develop a K-6 art scope and sequence by April	A curriculum stating learning outcomes	Conduct monthly curriculum work groups Provide art and curriculum writing specialists Critique product

Subsystem IV: Student Growth

Goals	Indicators of Attainment	Principal-Team Leader Responsibilities
Develop and implement system for mastery in all art programs by October	Planning system operating effectively	Provide student planning system options

Figure 8.8.

Subsystem V: Content Expertise

Goals	Indicators of Attainment	Principal/Team Leader Responsibilities
By January 30, identify 10 ways that art can be a springboard for learning in non-art classrooms	Report to principal Reports from teachers	Assist in locating conference books Subscribe to art journal

Subsystem VI: Collaborative Productivity

Goals	Indicators of Attainment	Principal/Team Leader Responsibilities
By May 1, implement three art instruction programs that will link students together around art theme	Student survey Teacher survey	Conduct planning sessions between art teacher and team leader

Subsystem VII: Personal/Professional Growth

Goals	Indicators of Attainment	Principal/Team Leader Responsibilities
Identify and implement three new concepts for teaching art in cooperative student work groups	Observation data Increase student achievement	Observe learning and critique

Figure 8.8. (cont.)

Action Planning

Following a goal-setting conference, specific plans are made by each worker, mapping out their scheme. Plans are not constraints, but rather are lighthouses to keep a worker goal focused during work activity. The action plan "puts feet" on the goals and provides a context for both performance and supervision throughout the year. Planning is an intellectual activity that precedes action and identifies the perceived best course. For example, if Donna plans to focus on "cues and directives for learning centers" in January, then that is the month when supervisory resources, feedback, and correctives can be most useful to Donna's development. An action plan is more than getting in gear and going.

Performance Action Plan

Name *Donna Morris*

Subsystem I Goal   Develop and Define Proficiency in Four Instruction
Techniques by May 1

Action Steps	Sept.	Oct.	Nov.	Dec.	Jan.	Feb.	Mar.	Apr.	May
RE: Demonstrations									
1. Observe 3 Demonstrations	X----	-X-X-							
2. Develop criteria for demo.			X						
3. Be observed 3 times			X------	-X------	-X				
4. Assess effectiveness					X		X		X
RE: Learning centers									
1. Locate books on L.C.	X								
2. Observe 3 L.C.s		X------	----X------	-X-----					
3. Develop criteria for effective L.C.s					X				
4. Develop 3 L.C.s per month						X----	--X-----	-X	
5. Evaluate effectiveness							X-----	-X-----	-X
RE: Contracts									
1. Review the literature				X					
2. Talk with 3 Teachers effectively using contracts					X				
3. Experiment with contract development						X			
4. Develop criteria								X-----	-X
5. Utilize student assessment								X-----	-X
RE: Peer teaching									
1. Observe P.T. in nearby school						X			
2. Talk with teachers observed						X	X	X	
3. Talk with own peers									
4. Develop strategies for P.T.									

Figure 8.9.

It is a specific allocation of time to a specific set of tasks for a specific purpose. Note the key elements below and Donna's action plan for her first goal (see Figure 8.9).

<u>Strategies for Accomplishing Goals</u>

key events/activities
resources
responsibilities
a time line

The Training/Coaching System

The rate at which research is generating new knowledge about schooling is awesome. Consequently, continuous training and coaching are vital to the development of all role sets. It has been common in the past for principals to leave teachers virtually on their own from September to evaluation time. However, training and coaching throughout the year have far greater potential for affecting achievement norms than does evaluation. Hence the two practices of training and coaching are viewed as the transforming agents for all roles between plans and assessment.

One of the school goals toward which Donna is working indicates that the staff will become more knowledgeable and skillful in using various instructional methods and materials (see school goal number 3 on page 273). Donna's own first performance goal indicates that she wants to become proficient in demonstrations, learning centers, student contracts, and peer teaching. The school's training/coaching plan addresses both needs by focusing on the plans of Donna's work group. The team leader synthesizes individual plans and charts growth needs; all team leaders, together with the principal, subsequently plan the school's development program.

The Monitoring System

Monitoring the implementation of plans, and keeping teams and individuals on course, is a management task that occurs throughout the year. Monitoring may be akin to inspection, a control function that is necessary for producing desired results. The monitoring process identifies problems, calling for a management response by team leaders and principals. Further, monitoring highlights performance successes and provides opportunity for recognition and reinforcement. Performance monitoring requires both a formal and an informal information exchange system. Accountability is a two-way exchange system:

Teacher Progress Report

Teacher: *Donna Morris*

Quarter: *First*

Subsystem 1: Quality Instruction

Objectives: Develop Proficiency in Demonstrations and Learning Centers

Activities

1. Observed 3 teachers in demonstrations and 1 in learning center

2. Developed criteria for demonstrations

3. Read 2 books on learning centers

Outcomes

1. I have a sense of an effective demonstration but need to develop more clear cues about next steps and to involve learners in problem solving re: demonstration concept/skill

2. I am having a difficult time locating effective learning centers in action

Figure 8.10.

Quarter: *Second*

Subsystem 1: Quality Instruction

Objectives: Develop Proficiency in Demonstrations, Learning Centers, Contracts

DEMONSTRATIONS

1. Work on cues and student problem posing

2. Involve 2 teachers in classroom observation-feedback

LEARNING CENTERS

1. Locate 2 more effective learning centers to observe

2. Study learning center books and select 1 curriculum area in which to begin a learning center

CONTRACTS

1. Browse the bookstore and library for readings on contracts

2. Locate professors at universities who use contracts

Figure 8.10. (cont.)

management to worker (this is what I observe; here are a few alternatives), and worker to management (this is what we've accomplished; we need help with this). The two-way exchange recognizes two sets of professional responses and provides opportunity for continuing the organizational growth process. (See the discussion on quality control in Chapter 14 for further detail.)

Teacher participation in the monitoring system involves a quarterly one-page report (see Figure 8.10) on goal-related activities, with mention of notable outcomes and requests for assistance. Based on an assessment of progress and conditions, plans are made for the next quarter. The report and plan together provide the principal/team leader with the teacher's perceptions of past activities as well as future needs. Thus the intervention path is kept open, allowing the principal to provide necessary resources and to require alternate routes to goals. Listed in Figure 8.10 are Donna's progress reports for the first quarter and her plans for the second quarter as they relate to her first goal. The principal considers whether her reports and plans adhere to annual action plans, and how progress can be recognized, assisted, and/or corrected in the second quarter.

Principal and team leader responses to the monitoring process grow out of formal and informal exchanges and observations, and from an assessment of what is necessary at a particular moment in the goal attainment process. After an assessment of the past, the principal and team leader plan for next steps in teacher development and motivation. Listed here are several monitoring activities, designed to steer the school organization toward its selected goals.

Monitoring Activities

individual reports and plans
informal observations
conversations
group reports and plans
interviews
conferences
data collection

The Evaluation System

Evaluation systems used in schools today fall far short of measuring the adequacy of professional performance. A major flaw with most evaluation systems is a lack of adequate performance standards. The effective teaching research phenomenon has begun to generate knowledge about patterns of teaching behavior that facilitate learning. These patterns enable school districts to identify standards for acceptable teaching performance. An evaluation system that measures the extent to which desirable teaching behaviors are demonstrated consistently is likely to stimulate productive teaching performance. A trend in the performance literature suggests that measuring the *results* of performance, in relation to standards and goals, influences the individual and the organization in productive ways. A standard- or goal-based evaluation system communicates organizational values about the expected results. Standards and goals set up a value system thereby guiding the useful evaluation of performance results.

Note the evaluation of Donna on the results of goal number one (see Figure 8.11). Her accomplishments are the recognized results from a wide variety of information: classroom data, informal conversations, and observations, and from an analysis of various reports. The area mentioned to be in need of attention resulted from many observations. Recommendations for next steps grew out of an assessment of the results of accomplishments. The value placed on the total goal resulted from Donna's total achievements.

Evaluation differs from monitoring in that it seeks to determine not only the completion of tasks but also the quality of performance and therefore the extent to which goals are actually accomplished. Evaluation deals with end products and their relative adequacy; it serves to identify partial, as well as com-

---

FORMATIVE/SUMMATIVE EVALUATION

Name _____ Donna Morris _____   Date ____ 4/8 ____

Evaluator _Jerry Willis_ _____

Subsystem 1 _____ Instruction _____

Goal
To develop proficiency in 4 techniques:
      Demonstration
      Learning centers
      Contracts
      Peer teaching

Accomplishments
Donna was successful in developing minimum proficiency in 3 of the 4 techniques: demonstration, contracts, and peer teaching; and developing criteria of effectiveness for each technique.

Areas in Need of Attention
Donna's cues and corrective mechanisms in all three areas need further attention.

Recommendations
1. Due to her particular success with demonstrations, Donna should be listed as exemplary and serve as a model for other teacher observations.
2. Due to the extensive involvement in 3 techniques, it is recommended that skill in learning centers be postponed until next year.

Figure 8.11.

plete, achievements and also nonachievements. Assessment helps to identify problem areas and provides a basis for making recommendations for the future. In a sense, evaluation is the activity that provides direction for the next round of goal setting. It is not only the end product of one cycle but the front-end activity of the succeeding cycle. Evaluation therefore concerns itself with the quality and the clarity of established goals, with the appropriateness of the organizational structure, and with the roles that have been defined. Evaluation is a dynamic force in the life cycle of the organization, and must necessarily employ the whole range of evaluative devices, some quantitative and others qualitative.

Viewed within the school growth context, evaluation becomes a measure of success as it relates to specific goals. Evaluation is an assessment that springs from goals, results, formal data, formal and informal observations, reports, problems, deviations, and needed improvements. In a sense, evaluation is a stepping stone to the future that follows an assessment of the past and an interpretation of what is needed. Rarely does performance evaluation dwell on personality, punishments, and reprimand, and if it does, only as these areas relate to the results of the goal attainment process. Thus, evaluation is not merely a linear analysis of performance results measured against plans. Growth factors of the individual and the school, coupled with a value-driven assessment of the worth of results, lead to final assessment and recommendations.

Termination and Due Process Supervision

At least 95 percent of performance evaluations result in relative success, if the teacher development system is effective. What about the five percent (or so) of teachers who need either major correction or termination? Reports from principals and supervisors have consistently indicated that judging the competency of teachers is one of their major problems. Regularly, such groups are told that guidelines need to be developed that define the process of establishing a record of incompetence, the lack of which is the major stumbling block in termination procedures.

Most authorities agree that the most effective behavior of principals in such situations is to conduct numerous, well-documented observations. Further, principals must prepare ample evidence of their attempts to assist the faltering teacher well in advance of actual termination. Ineffective management practices have led to pro-teacher court decisions in termination suits. Principals tend to lack documentation of the problems or of provisions for remediation.

Courts consider a variety of data to support either retention or dismissal of teachers (Thomas 1980, 27). Consideration is given to (1) whether incompetence can be corrected; (2) whether adequate time has been provided for correction; (3) whether dismissal is warranted; and (4) whether sufficient data are available.

If a principal perceives that a teacher is inadequate in achieving stated goals or is not performing according to standard expectations, notification must be given with time and assistance provided for correcting deficiencies. The Performance Linkage System (see Figure 8.3) provides a guide for acceptable performance growth: nearly all of the problems or deficiencies of a substandard teacher will fall within one or another of the system categories. Also, interconnections between problems can be more readily identified when the system diagram is consulted. As the principal or other administrator/supervisor comes to perceive that a given teacher's performance and potential may be dangerously below expectations, then the regular, optimistic performance management system must be abandoned in favor of a "due process" system. Due process is a legal term for those actions that a court of law will expect an employer to have taken, in a serious effort to help a questionably effective teacher to succeed, before a decision to terminate may be regarded as proper. Also implied by the term is that adequate records will be assembled over time, both to confirm that help and direction was provided and also to prove that performance is indeed below standard and therefore a probable detrimental force for children within the school.

In a well-managed, systems-oriented school, due process is almost a natural way of life for *all* teachers, and ample evidence would exist concerning the growth-inducing efforts under way as well as the effectiveness of each person. Even in excellent situations, however, switching out of the normal mode into a due process mode will require major adjustments on the part of the principal (and supervisory colleagues) as well as the teacher(s) involved. For one thing, a correction plan needs to be set in place, with a time table calling for certain changes to have occurred by specific dates. Documentation intensifies, and the principal plays a more directive role. No ambiguity is permitted with respect to the technical, procedural, stylistic, or other changes expected in the teacher's work behaviors.

Most of the time, it is to be hoped that due process supervision will help the teacher to overcome the perceived weaknesses and, eventually, to return to the normal cycle, again in good standing. Due process supervision in such cases pays rich human dividends and protects the school's long-term investment in the teacher(s) concerned. Sometimes, however, the dismissal of the teacher is a necessary final outcome. The courts, whose ultimate concern after all is for the children being taught, will support such dismissals when the good faith and

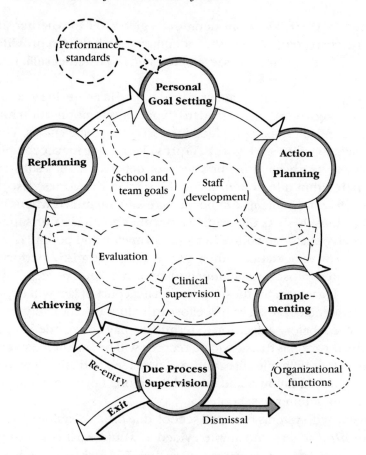

Figure 8.12. A Performance Linkage System and the Due Process Dimension

skillful effort of the school leaders is clearly in evidence. Figure 8.12 illustrates the relative nature of due process to the regular performance cycle.

On the following pages our due process model is presented to illustrate the nature of planning, assistance, and evaluation for those whose performance is inadequate.* Figure 8.13 outlines the procedures in due process supervision.

To demonstrate the process, a simulation will be used. Helen Green, a primary teacher, persists in using outdated modes of instruction, especially in math lessons. Consequently, her six- to eight-year-old students have performed poorly on achievement tests in the past, and the pattern continues.

---

* Note: Ours is a general model, and the reader is cautioned that collective bargaining agreements, state laws and regulations, or local policies in any given situation may require different or additional procedures.

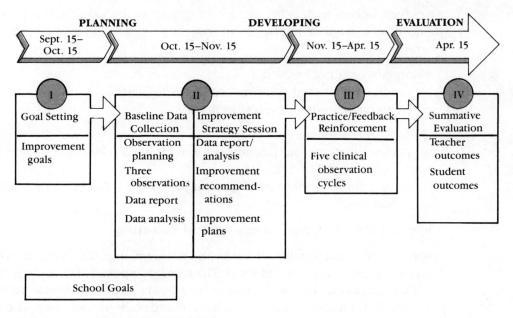

Figure 8.13. Due Process Supervision

Helen has not adopted any current instructional strategies for math concept development for her primary age students. Helen continues to use whole-class assignments, which for all students are found on the same page of the math book. She tends to chastise sternly those students who are unable to perform at a certain level of difficulty. It has been documented that training programs, on teaching strategies, following coaching activities precipitated no changes in her performance. Hence, the principal has informed her that termination is possible and that due process supervision will commence immediately. During the due process period she will have an opportunity to alter her teaching practices.

Stages in Due Process Supervision

Stage 1: Analysis of the School-Goal Work Context

One school improvement goal for the year in Helen's school was to alter achievement norms in math; there had been a steady decline over the past several years. While other teams and individual teachers were making adjustments to their programs and teaching strategies, Helen remained steadfast in continuing the patterns she had used for years. Hence, objectives developed for Helen during due process supervision were (1) to develop several alternative strategies for students to develop math concepts at their level of mastery, and (2) to develop a student management system to foster effective independent learning.

Summary of School Goals

    to improve student learning outcomes in math
    to increase student interest in math

Helen's Due Process Goals

    to develop numerous learning options for math concept development at each level of difficulty
    to develop a student management system that fosters independent learning

Stage 2: Baseline Data Collection and Planning

A supervision team was appointed by the principal to gather data and to assist Helen over the next several months. The team, composed of Helen's principal, two teachers, and a supervisor, planned to observe Helen during math class and to collect data on salient teaching behaviors and student responses. Their next task was to synthesize the data and to develop a plan of intervention for Helen. Data from the three data collection observations are presented in Figure 8.14.

During the data collection period, the team members were formulating ideas on the probable causes for Helen's resistance to change. Further, they began to perceive which teaching behaviors needed to be altered during the probation period. Helen was to develop options for learning math concepts at the various readiness levels of her students. Further, Helen was to plan programs in which students worked together and took some responsibility for their progress.

Figure 8.15 outlines the analysis of Helen's problem by the team of observers and sets forth several strategies for altering her instructional patterns. The plan provides Helen with a framework for improvement within a given period of time. During the practice period (stage 3), Helen will be observed and coached by the same team and will be expected to seek out additional resources for targeted changes.

Stage 3: Practice and Feedback

During the intervention period, Helen will receive four or five coaching sessions, in the form of complete observation cycles (discussed more fully in Chapter 13). The intent is to recognize and to reinforce observable and targeted changes, and to assist Helen in the next steps during the intervention period.

Figure 8.16 illustrates the outcomes of two coaching cycles. Helen has developed several learning options; and, most students appear to be working on

---

SUMMARY OF OBSERVATIONS

Observation I Data Report

Student learning activities included

    writing in math packets
    small group instruction

10 of the 25 students were off-task 60 percent of the time observed
Teacher drilled students on number facts

Observation II Data Report

Students worked at three levels of difficulty in relation to whole number operations
Students were off-task 15 minutes of the 30-minute observation
Student interaction was permitted only when students were with teacher

---

Observation III Data Report

---

6 students took a post-test
6 students were off-task
10 students worked on packets
Teacher demonstrated the concept of unequal sets
Students with the teacher circled unequal sets of objects on paper

---

Figure 8.14.

expected tasks. However, there remain several problems with the management system that require Helen's attention.

Stage 4: Summative Evaluation

At the end of the probation period, the principal reviews the growth plan, recommendations, and the evidence of growth during the intervention period. In Helen's case, the continuous coaching enabled Helen to progress beyond her present behavior norms. The fear of change had prevented Helen from trying new teaching strategies. The observation team, however, was able to work with her one step at a time, to reinforce appropriate changes and to recommend modifications. Helen was better able to provide her students with a math program designed for their levels of need. Further, she was gradually able to introduce optional learning activities within each level of difficulty. Hence, it

DATA COLLECTION RECORD SHEET

Baseline Period

Teacher __Helen Green__   School __Johnson Park__   Year _____1985-1986_____

Age group__6-8 year olds__

SCHOOL/TEAM/INDIVIDUAL GOALS: To improve student learning out-comes in math. To increase student interest in math.

RELATED PRINCIPLES OF LEARNING AND INSTRUCTION: Students need multiple opportunities to explore math concepts concretely and with othe students. A program must provide numerous learning options, a process for nurturing independent and cooperative learning with continuous practice and feedback.

TARGET BEHAVIORS TO BE ALTERED BY MARCH 1, 1986: (1) Develop numerous learning options for math concept development. (2) Develop a management system that fosters independence, continuous practice, challenge, and feedback.

Date/Observer	Data Report	Intervention Strategy
3/17/86 P. Haven	Student learning activities limited to writing math packets and small group instruction 10 of the 25 students were off-task 60 percent of the time observed	Develop learning activities at various stages Plan to use machines and space in alternative ways Develop management system to include pre/post test and learning options for student selection in relation to specific math concepts
4/26/86 P. Haven	Students working at three levels of difficulty 8 students off-task 15 minutes Student interaction permitted only when students were with teacher	Reconsider the use of only 3 levels of learning and how this might connect to problem of 8 off-task students Plan co-learning activities. Involve students as teachers

Figure 8.15.

DATA COLLECTION RECORD SHEET

Intervention Period

Teacher __Helen Green__   School __Johnson Park__   Year ____1985-1986____

Age group ___6-8 year olds___

SCHOOL/TEAM/INDIVIDUAL GOALS: To improve student learning outcomes in math. To increase student interest in math.

TARGET BEHAVIORS: 1) Develop numerous learning options for concept development 2) Develop a management system that fosters independence, continuous practice, challenge, and feedback.

INTERVENTION STRATEGIES: Tasks: Develop learning activities at various stations. Technology: Plan to use machines and space in alternative ways. Program structure: Develop management system to include pre/post test and learning options for student selection in relation to specific math concepts.

Date/Observer	Data Report	Intervention Strategy

4/20/86
B. Kliff
	Learning options included
	  packets, 3 learning
	  station activities, and
	  small group interaction
	5 out of 25 students
	  wandered
	20 out of 25 were on-task
	4 students questioned
	  what to do next
		Develop plan for meeting
		  needs of wandering students
		Work out problems with the
		  management system
		Develop group learning
		  activities

5/21/86
B. Kliff
	23 students on-task
	2 small groups:
	  1 teacher/instructor
	  1 activity (student)
	3 students reading library
	  books
	6 students asked teacher
	  questions of what to do
	  next
	5 learning stations
		Study management system
		  gaps and refine
		Identify problems with
		  students reading

Figure 8.16.

was determined that Helen was now able to continue teaching under "normal" conditions, with periodic coaching for feedback and corrections.

What if Helen had not progressed as planned? Two assumptions can be made about the lack of growth in certain directions. The first possibility is that the teacher is intellectually or otherwise incapable of performing expected tasks. In such a case, the teacher needs to be coached into another job or profession. The second possibility is that the teacher is not interested in changing and essentially refuses to perform as expected. In such cases, sufficient evidence now exists to begin preparing for termination proceedings, and (subject to legal, regulatory, or other requirements in the specific local context) to establish cause for dismissal. The burden of proof as we see it rests on the effectiveness of the due process supervision cycle: the goal framework (stage 1), evidence of the problem (stage 2), assistance (stage 3), and the final data and judgment (stage 4).

Due process supervision is a technique that enables a school to keep its focus on school productivity. The goal framework provides the context in which performance is judged, either adequate or not adequate, corrected or terminated. Attention is given to organizational priorities throughout the process with the intent being to correct individual performance so that it makes a necessary contribution to school productivity.

Conclusion

Managing performance is the primary activity of the principal. By using outcome-stated role standards and a school goal set, the principal is able to engage in coaching and facilitating staff success throughout the weeks and months of a given year. Individual performance goals and action plans provide specific clues to principals for training and continuous coaching. The same goal set guides periodic inspection (monitoring) and also evaluation judgments at the end of the year. Further, the goal structure provides an organizational standard for engaging in due process supervision, and prevents principals from spending months preparing a case against one unproductive teacher. In essence, a goal-based system keeps everyone focused in their work and subsequently enables the school to increase its norm of productivity. The school's ecological characteristics in fact provide a continuous standard for planning, developing, and assessing staff performance.

9

The Program Subsystem: A Learning Focus

In the school's instructional program is the very essence of the schooling process. Considerable attention has been given in recent years to the gross inadequacies of school programs to produce levels of acceptable student achievement. In this book we have sought to establish the nature of influences on instructional programs that are derived from the school's leadership and management practices, goal structure and organization, and adult performance system. Now we will discuss dimensions of the instructional program itself, providing guidance to principals for developing and managing programs that ensure student mastery.

Figure 9.1 outlines the relationship between the school's instructional program and student achievement. The several external and internal school influences on program design, on teaching, and on achievement are also noted. In other chapters of this text we have presented the ways in which many of those influences can be altered effectively by the principal and teachers. In this and the following two chapters the key concept is learning, and we examine the nature of both students and staff programs that have the power to influence learning norms.

There exists a strong relationship between the knowledge and skill levels of the staff and the instruction they provide. For this reason we view continuous adult learning as the key to altering student achievement norms. It is our contention that the functioning knowledge base of the staff relates directly to the patterns of learning that result from the school's program.

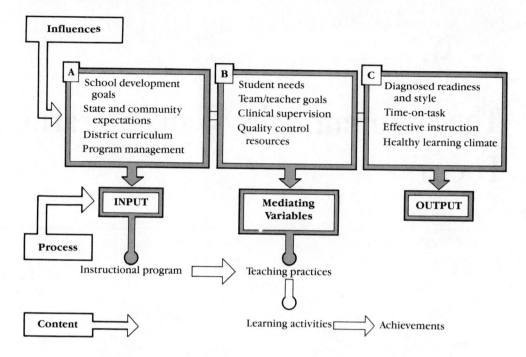

Figure 9.1. Influences on Learning

Learning in this chapter is discussed in generic terms for all people anywhere. In the next two chapters we focus on the nature of school learning for both students and staff. Primary attention is given to the student's learning program, which is presented in five discrete dimensions of instruction: curriculum selection, diagnoses of readiness and style, program planning, classroom management, and teaching. Finally, we describe the adult learning program for the staff as it relates to the five instruction tasks, to school development goals, and to the adult learning process.

Our basic assumption about school learning is that most students can learn all that the school expects if the schooling conditions are appropriate. That is, students will learn (1) if they are placed in programs based on *readiness* levels (not grades), (2) if program content is of *interest* (not illusive), (3) if students *participate actively* with others (not passively), (4) if students are given appropriate knowledge of *expectations,* positive *reinforcement,* and *correctives,* (not dictates), (5) if they are *coached* (not merely graded) until mastery occurs, and (6) if they are given sufficient *time* to succeed. Unfortunately, these conditions do not prevail in most schools. Goodlad's study of schooling (1984, 123–124) offers a snapshot of instruction and learning norms that is gleaned from 1,000 classrooms in 38 schools. Consider the current learning conditions:

1. The dominant pattern of classroom organization is a group to which. the teacher most frequently relates as a whole.
2. Each student essentially works and achieves alone within a group setting.
3. The teacher is the central figure in determining the activities, as well as the tone of the classroom.
4. The domination of the teacher is obvious in the conduct of instruction.
5. There is paucity of praise and correction of students' performance, as well as of teacher guidance in how to do better next time.
6. Students generally engage in a rather narrow range of classroom activities—listening to teachers, writing answers to questions, and taking tests and quizzes.
7. The variety of teaching techniques is greatest in the lower elementary grades and least in the secondary school years.
8. Large percentages of students appear to be passively content with classroom life.
9. Even in the elementary years there is strong evidence that students do not have sufficient time to complete their lessons, nor do they always understand what the teacher wants them to do.

In summary, Goodlad reports that "there was increasingly less use of teacher praise and support for learning, less corrective guidance, a narrowing range and variety of pedagogical techniques, and declining participation by students in determining the daily conduct of their education" from early elementary school to senior high school years (p. 125).

The gap between optimal conditions and those that exist in many schools has been clearly established by Goodlad, Sizer, and others. We firmly believe, however, that the principal, working together with the staff, can alter outdated instruction norms through a commitment to student mastery and by implementing instructional practices that facilitate rather than restrain learning.

Table 9.1 outlines many of the essential differences found in school programs within the maintenance and productivity paradigms. Practices for students and staff are discussed in relation to objectives, task focus, evaluation, and outcomes in both the old and new paradigms. The emphasis from a maintenance perspective is on general activity, whereas in a productivity orientation, the emphasis is given to certain results for all students.

TABLE 9.1 Program Subsystem

For Students	Maintenance Paradigm	Productivity Paradigm
For Students		
Objective	To complete the course outline	To master certain skills/concepts
Focus	Grade level content. Program objectives vary with each teacher. Course outline	Specific learning objectives based on district standards and diagnosed needs
Evaluation	Students receive grades: A, B, C, D, F	Degree of mastery
Outcome	Students promoted or not promoted	Objectives mastered
For Staff		
Objective	To provide information	To provide staff-selected, school goal-based growth experiences
Focus	Defined by central administration	Selected needs as dictated by school and work goals
Evaluation	General: approval or disapproval	Degree to which the program facilitated anticipated growth
Outcome	Number of required hours of staff development fulfilled	Increased staff knowledge and skills in relation to goals

About Learning

Learning theories provide conceptual models for interpreting, discussing, and planning for school learning. A variety of theoretical perspectives equip teachers and principals with an assortment of workable models for creating solutions to learning problems and challenges. Some theories focus primarily on students, while others concentrate on adult learning in the workplace. Nevertheless, the reader should consider the broad implications of all concepts presented. Since the turn of the century, critics and scholars have sought to challenge many of the prevailing assumptions about learning and the function of schooling. Dewey (1916, 163–164), for example, fought for a view of school learning that involved active student participation. The Dewey movement rejected the mind-building (Herbartian) view of learning that then dominated schooling. Dewey contended that learning is an active process rather than passive; it involves far more than mere understanding and acceptance of answers. An experience itself is insufficient to precipitate learning; persons need to "undergo," to reflect, in order to alter perceptions that are inherent in an experience. Learning essentially is a problem-solving activity. Dewey's philosophical precepts about learning provided a stage on which learning theorists later developed principles of cognitive, affective, and behavioral learning.

Cognitive theories now influence our beliefs about how new concepts are formed and how information is learned and retained. *Motivation theories* help us to understand the many factors that influence our desire to learn. *Personality theories* probe psychological styles and health factors that influence one's ability to learn and to perform. The *behaviorists* study observable patterns in performance and provide important information about shaping behavior. Together the cognitive theorists, motivation and personality psychologists, and behavioral scientists probe the major elements of learning (cognitive processing, motivation, self-concept/style/interests, and behavior/skill). When viewed as one cluster, learning theories provide us with a holistic understanding of human growth.

Cognitive Learning

Gestalt Cognitive Psychology

Cognitive theory provides insights into the nature of perceiving, knowing, and believing. The early Gestalt psychologists believed that various elements or influences interact on the cognitive structure in a nonlinear fashion and spontaneously spark new insights. These nonlinear elements tend to generate new perceptions and conceptualizations about a certain reality (see Figure 9.2). Kohler (1969) perceived there to be a noncognitive dimension to insight as well. He contended that insight is a direct awareness that is experienced not only intellectually, but also emotionally. Insight occurs in leaps that defy logic, and results from the cumulative interaction of hunches, information, and interests that are focused on a particular problem.

The insight-gaining process has important implications for instruction. Since the natural learning process is nonlinear and results from a variety of cognitive, affective, and/or behavioral experiences, the teaching task is to develop potentially powerful learning experiences of the sort that will involve the entire cognitive structure and generate desired new insights. The early cognitive psychologists also paved the way for understanding the importance of dialogue in the learning process. Interaction with persons, ideas, or machines provides a critical and pivotal opportunity for new insights and for cognitive structures to be reshaped.

Lewin (1942) expanded on the concept of cognitive influences on insight,

Figure 9.2. Insight

and proposed that a variety of elements in one's cognitive map are the critical influences to insight. He observed that changes occur in perception and behavior as a result of the ways in which an individual addresses the various influencing forces within his or her sphere (cognitive field) of influences. Negative forces tend to retard change or growth, while positive forces tend to facilitate change. An individual's process of problem solving or controlling negative and positive forces tends to determine the nature of a cognitive change.

Lewin's view of cognitive growth suggests that teachers ought to assist learners to reduce restraining forces and to nurture facilitating forces. That is, new cognitive insights and learnings are likely to occur through problem-solving activities that involve the learner's personal sphere of influence.

Later, Festinger (1957) sought to determine the precipitating factors to insight, that is, why changes in cognition (insight) occur unpredictably. The concept of "dissonance" emerged from his work as the variable that appears to trigger cognitive attention to a particular problem. As a problem surfaces and becomes personally important, an individual has a choice: either to dismiss the problem (cease probing), or to entertain the problem more fully (heighten probing). Festinger further hypothesized that any "non-fitting" cognitive element (dissonance or contradiction) forms a pressure to resolve the apparent conflict between self-concept and cognition. Dissonance, the trigger in the problem-solving process, is considered to be both healthy and necessary for altering cognitive constructs about a certain reality. Dissonance ought to penetrate classrooms regularly as a strategic mechanism to stimulate interaction and problem solving, in all subjects.

In more fully developed models, cognitive learning occurs within psychological parameters through interactional processes. During interaction a person gains new insights or changes old ones (Bigge 1971, 198–242). Learning in this sense is a reorganization of insights that results in changes in skills, knowledge, attitudes, values, and beliefs. Rokeach, a social psychologist (1968), proposed that a person's cognitive construct includes beliefs, values, and attitudes; a change in any one of these alters the construct as a whole. In this sense, learning results from a cluster of influences that alter attitudes, values, and beliefs simultaneously. An example of the total impact of reflection on experiences which alters a construct is found in the "yes, there-is-a-Santa-Claus" construct versus the "no, there-is-no-Santa-Claus" construct.

What are the implications of cognitive psychology for school learning? Those activities that engage students in problem posing/solving experiences are more likely to engage the cognitive growth process. As problems are probed through the stimulation of experiences, reflection, and interaction, new insights are formed about a specific reality and tend to nurture the cognition formation process. Consequently, learning activities that engage the student/teacher actively have the greatest power to stimulate cognitive growth.

Cognitive Processing

More recently, psychologists and physicians have studied the component parts of the brain to learn how various brain dimensions facilitate learning and thinking. It has been generally concluded by scholars that at least two distinct brain thought processes exist in humans. The *right brain* responds to emotions and relationships, and is the seat of holistic thinking patterns, creativity, and imagination. The right brain processes information through intuitive leaps in a holistic fashion (Springer 1981, 44). The *left brain,* however, is the seat of logic and verbal language and is concerned primarily with linear activities involved in reading, writing, and organization. Each side of the brain serves a unique function for an individual. A balance of right and left brain functioning is an ideal capability; however, individuals tend to prefer one way of processing information to another. Table 9.2 is an adaptation of Paul Torrance's work (Springer 1981, 44), and outlines the characteristics of right and left brain tendencies.

A challenge for teachers and principals is to balance right and left brain activities. Schools tend to respond primarily to left brain needs and tendencies, virtually ignoring the contributions and needs of the right brain. For those in-

TABLE 9.2 Left and Right Brain Dominance Characteristics

Left	Right
Intellectual	Intuitive
Remembers names	Remembers faces
Verbal instructions and explanations	Demonstrated, illustrated or symbolic structures
Prefers solving problems by breaking down into parts, then approaching the problem sequentially, using logic	Prefers solving problems by looking at the whole, the configuration, then approaching the problem through patterns, using hunches
Planned and structured	Fluid and spontaneous
Prefers established, certain information	Prefers elusive, uncertain information
Primary reliance on language in thinking and remembering	Primary reliance on images in thinking and remembering
Prefers talking and writing	Prefers drawing and manipulating objects
Multiple choice tests	Open-ended questions
Prefers work and/or studies carefully planned	Prefers work and/or studies open-ended
Prefers hierarchical (ranked) authority structures	Prefers collegial (participative) authority structures
Controlled feelings	More free with feelings
Auditory, visual stimuli	Kinesthetic stimuli (movement, action)
Logical problem solving	Frequently uses metaphors and analogies
	Intuitive problem solving

(*Source*: Adapted from Judy Springer, "Brain/Mind and Human Resources Development" in *Training and Development Journal* 35 [August 1981], 44. Reprinted by permission of American Society for Training and Development, © 1981, all rights reserved.)

dividuals who have a left brain dominance, schools foster achievement more easily; those who function best in right brain patterns have necessarily force-fitted their learning mode and rarely work in a fashion that is most comfortable. A schooling practice of fostering left brain functioning has had its deleterious effect on many students. Occasionally, right brain dominant persons have not achieved well in schools; some have even been assigned to classes with a disability label. It is important that classrooms and schools of the future provide opportunities for both right and left brain contributions and tendencies. Further, schools must develop a capacity to reinforce both types of brain functioning for all individuals.

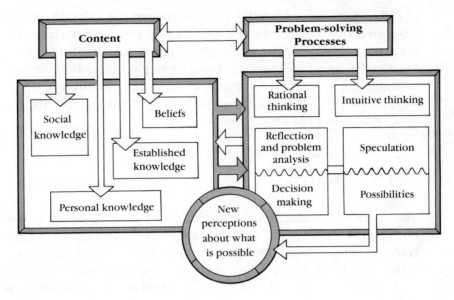

Figure 9.3. Cognitive Domain

In summary, early scholars believed that cognitions result from new *in-sights* and new perceptions about reality. Later, Lewin proposed that the ways in which an individual manages restraining and facilitating *forces* within his or her own cognitive field determine the direction and outcome of insights (personal problem solving). Festinger added a specific dimension and hypothesized that "*dissonance*" tends to provoke resolution to a dilemma. More recent theories, however, have shifted attention to the various brain functions in problem solving. The brain hemispheres have been explored in attempts to understand how persons work through their dominant cognitive modes to process and arrive at new knowledge.

Cognitive theory has developed to a level that has broad implications for school learning activities. Cognitive learning occurs in different patterns for everyone and results from a personal desire to resolve certain dilemmas. Further, learning occurs best for some through sequential, structured, learning activities and for others through more open-ended challenges. The dominant variable in all learning, however, is a personal drive to know. Current understandings of how cognition is formed suggest that teachers must vary learning tasks and problem structures so that the anticipated cognition can occur efficiently and result in mastery.

Figure 9.3 outlines our conceptualization of the content and processes of the cognitive domain. The *content* that triggers new cognitions is a combination of social knowledge (driving a car), established knowledge (water boils at 212°), personal knowledge (I know how to sail a sloop), and beliefs (I believe men and women are equally capable; women have had to struggle for equal opportunities). The *processes* necessary for personal knowing are thinking and dialogue processes. Problem solving requires both rational and intuitive thought processes. It is relatively certain, nevertheless, that the content and processes of the cognitive domain interact in unpredictable ways to foster new understandings about reality.

Affective Learning

The affective domain includes personal psychological factors that influence both cognition and behavior. "Affective" is generally defined as a psychological term pertaining to or resulting from emotions or feelings rather than from thought. Motivation and self-concept are among the aspects of knowledge that typically are considered "affective." It seems useful to our discussion to consider those dimensions of human growth that trigger action and thought.

Human Motivation

Often referred to as the psychological process effecting behavior in a given direction, motivation seems to be central to the precipitation of human action or growth. Hellriegel and Slocum (1974, 304) refer to motivation as an intervening variable that cannot be seen or heard but which directs behavior.

The concept of motivation has been virtually ignored in schools, both for students and for adult workers. At best, motivation has been equated with coercive practices on the part of teachers and administrators in attempts to solicit compliance. Motivation, however, is a personal dimension, that which activates personal behavior. An outsider (teacher or administrator) can manipulate events in such a way as to trigger, inspire, and stimulate behavior in a certain direction; but an outsider cannot motivate another person.

The study of human motivation originated in the adult work setting. Hence, our discussion of basic motivation concepts begins with adults; interpretations extend to students. We assume that motivation is a dimension central to human learning, and therefore it has broad implications for all who learn and work in schools.

In the early years of motivation theory, personal motivation was conceptualized as a "drive state" which is activated when there is an urge to move *away* from something undesirable. Later, scholars came to perceive that motivation can also be an urge to move *toward* something desirable. Mayo's studies of the psychological factors influencing worker productivity (1933) prompted a major turning point in thought about human motivation. Since

Mayo's Hawthorne studies, the field of motivation has included a "drive state" which activates behavior *toward* something desirable. It is now believed that psychological factors tend to stimulate behavior in either direction, becoming an internal energizer toward or against something.

Luthans and Kreitner (1975) categorized the developments about human motivation into three schools of thought: content theories, process theories, and behavior theories. Maslow (1962) and Herzberg (1959) exemplify *content theory* in that each defines specific psychological factors (content) that stimulate behavior. Maslow, for example, found that people tend to function at one of five particular levels of need until they feel secure enough to progress to the next level.

The *process theories* of motivation include Hull's drive theory and also Festinger's cognitive dissonance theory. Each proposes that a cognitive factor stimulates a drive to make a personal choice. Hull's early work (1943) proposed that motivation is a product of drive and habit (effort $= D \times H$). *Drive* is the energizer that determines the intensity of behaviors. *Habit* reflects personal choice of learned behaviors. Hull's drive theory served as a theoretical base for the later development of motivation cycles (needs $\rightarrow$ drives $\rightarrow$ goals), and his theory further links cognitive factors (drives and incentives) as motivators for behavior (habit). Festinger's theory (1957) is also categorized by some scholars as a motivation theory due to the motivating function of dissonance to cognitive development. Dissonance provokes an individual either to engage actively in solving the problem or to withdraw from the problem altogether.

Behavioral theories assume that an internal response controls behavioral responses to an outside stimulus. A critical stimulus following a response signals which kind of behavior will elicit positive reinforcement. Skinner's reinforcement theory (1953) led to the concept that the consequences of a behavior act as a stimulator either to repeat or to eliminate the behavior.

The content, process, and behavioral approaches to motivation indicate how broad is the potential range of psychological stimulation on human behavior. Whether the stimulation begins with knowledge, feeling, or behavior is not the most important consideration for educators. The central issue is how to manipulate the classroom and school work environment so that people become motivated (want) to act in productive ways for themselves and for the workplace of rooms and schools.

In the following several pages we discuss five specific theories of motivation. Our purpose is to help the reader to understand alternative approaches to human motivation, and consequently develop a repertoire of concepts for motivating teachers and students. With an understanding of several approaches to motivation, the reader will be better equipped to manipulate events favorably for many different situations and to realize desired increases in motivation for school growth activities.

The Influence of Affiliation

Researchers in the Hawthorne plant studies (Mayo 1933) were efficiency experts who were seeking to understand the relationship between working conditions, hours, and other methods of stimulation to worker productivity. In the first study they provided new lighting for the experimental group and no change in lighting for the control group. The result of experimentation was that *both* groups increased their levels of productivity.

Not expecting outcomes such as this from their study, the researchers went on to explore additional behavioral considerations in the workplace. They next studied women who assembled phone relays. The researchers improved working conditions by scheduling rest, providing lunch, and a shorter work week. As was expected, productivity increased. However, when the new altered conditions were withdrawn and the old conditions prevailed, work rose to a new high, rather than regressing along with conditions.

Gradually the research team began to understand the functioning dynamics in the experiments that they engineered. Because the women in the experimental group were considered a "group," there emerged a sense of affiliation and of personal competence and achievement. Moreover, the researchers soon came to perceive that women produced more in a group context where congenial and cohesive relationships could evolve. The Mayo team concluded from their studies that the *single most important factor relating to worker productivity was the interpersonal relationship that emerged on the job.* Moreover, it was believed that when informal groups of workers identified with management, productivity rose and with it, a feeling of competence and a sense of mastery over the job and the work environment. Researchers also observed that when the group felt their own goals were in opposition to those of management, where supervision was low, and where there was no significant worker control over the job or the environment, productivity remained low.

Gradually the concept of worker affiliation and involvement in organizational life infiltrated the American workplace. Today, worker collaboration is a norm in most social and business organizations in America. While schools have made various attempts to group teachers and students, the predominant work pattern of role isolation persists (Goodlad 1983). Yet sufficient evidence exists for validating worker affiliation and collaboration to urge principals to establish work norms in schools that function around small group adult work and small group learning. Worker and learner isolation patterns do not contain sufficient power to stimulate sufficient productivity in schools. By establishing formal affiliations, principals are likely to stimulate staff and students' performance to higher levels of engagement and productivity.

The Influence of Motivators and Motivation Seekers

Herzberg's motivation theory (1959) provides another important perspective on worker motivation. He found from his studies of accountants and engineers in Pittsburgh, that two kinds of on-the-job stimulants exist. Job satisfiers are related to job content, whereas dissatisfiers are related to the job context. Out of his studies emerged the two-factor theory of motivation. The satisfiers were labeled "motivators" and the dissatisfiers were called "hygiene factors." Workers were categorized as one of two types of workers: motivators or hygiene seekers. Hygiene seekers, Herzberg observed, are interested primarily in working conditions factors; when problems are resolved with the conditions, worker productivity does not necessarily increase. Only the motivators, those who are interested in the job content, actually contribute to organizational productivity.

An interpretation of Herzberg's theory is that *hygiene factors prevent dissatisfaction but do not lead to satisfaction or to productivity,* whereas *motivation factors stimulate worker performance and satisfaction.* Herzberg's theory has stimulated considerable controversy as to the meaning of the two factors on job performance. However, several interpretations can be made. First, satisfaction with the job context only prevents dissatisfaction; it does not stimulate productive behavior. The job or task itself is that which has the potential to motivate human behavior. Further, those persons who are concerned primarily with working conditions are far less likely than those concerned with the job to behave in productive ways.

A study conducted in schools by Sergiovanni (1967) reinforces Herzberg's findings. It was learned that teachers fall readily into the hygiene/motivator categories. In addition, certain job content reinforcers act as stimulators to motivate teachers. Table 9.3 identifies the different characteristics of motivation seekers and hygiene seekers, identifying those job factors that are of major interest to each group of workers.

Figure 9.4 lists factors that tend to act as satisfiers and those that act as dissatisfiers, and further describes the consequence of each set of factors on worker performance.

In studying the two factors among teachers, Sergiovanni found that interpersonal relations with students and with peers are the two greatest dissatisfiers (see Figure 9.5). If problems are resolved for teachers with the relationships dimension of the job, they will tend to be more satisfied. However, mere satisfaction with work relationships is unlikely to translate into productive behavior. By resolving hygiene problems, principals can create the conditions for job motivators to stimulate behavior in a certain direction. Moreover, the

TABLE 9.3. Differentiating Hygiene Seekers from Motivation Seekers

Motivation Seekers	Hygiene Seekers
1. Emphasize the nature of the task.	Emphasize the nature of the environment.
2. Are primarily committed to the goals of the school or profession and work to pursue these goals.	Are primarily committed to private goals or extraschool goals and work for rewards from the school which help to pursue or purchase these nonschool or nonprofessional goals.
3. Show higher, but not unlimited, tolerance for poor hygiene factors.	Intermittent but chronic dissatisfaction with aspects of the work environment such as salary, supervision, working conditions, status, security, administrative policy, and fellow workers.
4. Show less reaction to improvement of hygiene factors.	Tend to overreact in satisfaction to hygiene factors.
5. Satisfaction is short lived when hygiene factors are improved.	Satisfaction is short lived when hygiene factors are improved.
6. Milder discontent when hygiene factors need improvement.	Tend to overreact with dissatisfaction when hygiene factors are not improved.
7. Realize great satisfaction from accomplishments.	Realize little satisfaction from accomplishments.
8. Genuinely enjoy the kind of work they do.	Show little interest in the kind or quality of work they do.
9. Profit personally and professionally from experience.	Do not profit personally or professionally from experience.
10. Have positive feelings toward work and life.	Generally cynical toward work and life.
11. Belief systems are sincere.	Prone to cultural noises—i.e., take extreme positions that are fashionable, superficially espouse management philosophy, act more like top management than top management does.

(*Source*: Thomas Sergiovanni and Fred D. Carver, *The New School Executive: A Theory of Administration* [New York: Harper & Row, 1973], 85. Reprinted by permission.)

greatest job motivators for productivity among teachers are achievement and recognition.

The two-factor theory suggests that principals can realize increases in staff productivity by analyzing their management tasks and determining which are

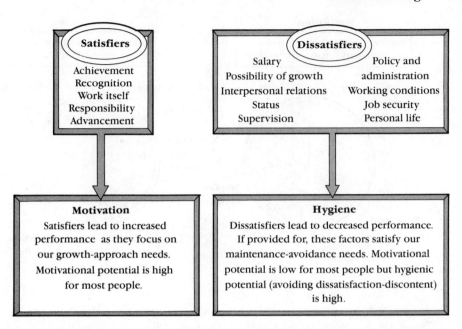

Figure 9.4. Satisfiers and Dissatisfiers (*Source*: Adapted from Thomas Sergiovanni and Fred D. Carver, *The New School Executive: A Theory of Administration.* [New York: Harper & Row, 1973], 71. Reprinted by permission of Harper & Row, Publishers, Inc., © 1973.)

most likely to stimulate productive work. By resolving concerns for work conditions, the principal merely prepares the environment for certain new tasks, a necessary prerequisite to work stimulation. However, *teacher achievement and recognition are the job motivators that are most likely to stimulate actual productive behaviors.* Further, teachers who tend to respond best to job content considerations are far more likely to behave in productive ways for development of the school's programs. Consequently, continuous attention to teachers' contract problems, to teacher dismissal procedures, and to discipline procedures is likely to create only a neutral ground. Subsequent attention to teacher development and to program development with a focus on teacher achievement and recognition is necessary for stimulating productive teacher behavior.

The Influence of Personal Needs

Individual teachers and students have varying levels of psychological needs that influence their degree of engagement in activities and the quality of performance. Maslow's theory of motivation provides clues for levels and types of management expectations of individuals. Maslow's hierarchy of needs (1962)

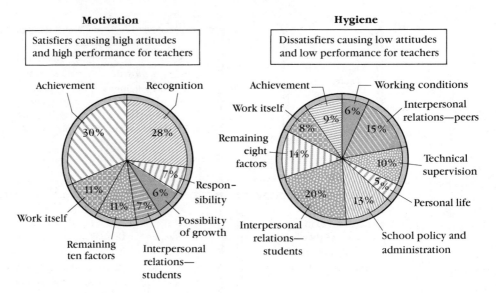

Figure 9.5. Comparison of Satisfiers and Dissatisfiers for Teachers (*Source*: Adapted from Thomas Sergiovanni and Fred D. Carver, *The New School Executive: A Theory of Administration* [New York: Harper & Row, 1973], 76. Reprinted by permission of Harper & Row, Publishers, Inc., © 1973.)

suggests that *motivational needs are hierarchical in nature.* He hypothesized that once needs are satisfied at one level, a person seeks to function at the next level of need. In this sense, once the needs of one level are satisfied, there is little or no motivation to continue functioning at that same level; a higher level is more desirable.

Little research exists to support the concept of five levels in a need hierarchy, and researchers have not verified that satisfaction at one level will lead to activation of the next level. Consequently, many scholars have been critical of Maslow's theory. Yet, the model remains one of the most discussed views of human motivation. Perhaps for many, the concept of varying levels of worker needs is sufficient to continue prompting managers and scholars alike to explore the varying levels of worker stimulation needs. Figure 9.6 illustrates the levels of motivation in the work context, using Maslow's hierarchy of needs as the basic model.

For principals the hierarchy provides a conceptual framework within which worker stimulation can be planned. Some may never need to function at each level, and instead skip a level. To illustrate an orderly fashion through all levels, teachers who perceive that the school environment is hostile and unsafe both emotionally and psychologically are unlikely to be motivated to initiate professional interests. When basic safety needs have been met, and persons per-

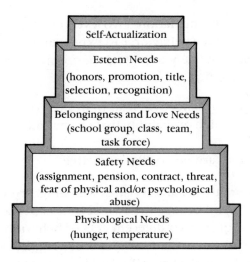

Figure 9.6. Hierarchy of Work Motivation

ceive they belong to a group, then there is personal and psychological freedom to pursue activities that will enhance the sense of belonging (next level).

Likewise, if organizational expectations of teacher performance reinforce safety level behaviors (contract negotiations), the school is unlikely to realize, in its work output, the potential energy existing within the staff. However, if job expectations stimulate and reinforce worker involvement in school development activities, teachers are more likely to function at a higher need level and consequently contribute qualitatively more to school development. Staff involvement in decision making, for example, has within it the power to stimulate greater staff productivity.

The Influence of Expectations

Researchers are in general agreement that high teacher expectations correlate with gains in student achievement. It would seem that when teacher expectation levels are raised, students tend to perceive that they have the ability to achieve at higher levels. Consequently, students perceive that they not only have the ability, but task engagement is likely to be successful. Hence, students not only put more effort into learning activities, but expectation also stimulates individuals to behave in more effective ways.

Vroom's model of motivation, expectancy theory (1964), is useful for exploring the nature of stimulation that triggers several levels of behavior. Expectancy theory hypothesizes that motivation is a process of governing *personal choice* among behavior options. Motivation occurs when an individual perceives engagement in an activity as being worthwhile at two different levels of psychological expectation. Two levels of expectations act interdependently to motivate worker behavior: (1) expectancy and (2) instrumentality.

Individuals are likely to be high performers, according to Vroom's theory, if they perceive that

1. high performance will lead to desired outcomes;
2. there is a high probability that efforts will lead to higher performance; and
3. outcomes are personally attractive.

If one of these three characteristics is missing, Vroom asserts that performance will not be high because the two sets of expectations function interdependently and require two different sets of behavior. Motivation in this view is equated with the expectation times the strength (valence) of that expectation, or $M = E \times V$ (see Figure 9.7). To illustrate, teachers might engage in cooperative program planning (first level engagement) if they perceive that a cooperatively developed program, when taught, will increase student achievement. That is, teachers might engage in the first activity (planning) if they perceive there will be a payoff (learning) from the second activity (teaching).

Ability functions as another variable in motivation. For example, if a high school science teacher perceives that she or he does not have the ability to teach math to freshmen, the teacher is unlikely to engage in cooperative math planning (1) and math teaching activities (2). Perception about one's ability influences actual performance ($P = M \times A$). Figure 9.8 illustrates the interactive nature of motivation and ability on performance.

Vroom's theory provides a conceptual context within which principals can examine their expectations of teachers. Consider this: If increased student achievement is an administrative expectation, then teachers need two levels

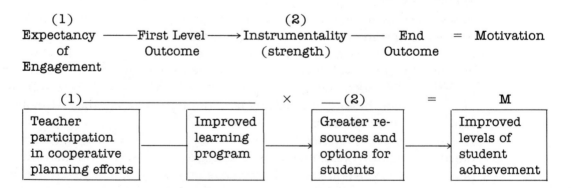

Figure 9.7. Applied Expectancy Model ($M = E \times V$)

$$P \quad = \quad (1 + 2) \quad \times \quad (3)$$
$$\text{Performance} = \text{Motivation} \times \text{Ability}$$

Performance		Motivation		Ability
Effective planning and cooperative teaching	=	Increased levels of student achievement	×	Skills in cooperative planning and teaching efforts

Figure 9.8. Performance Variable ($P = M \times A$)

of consideration. They are more likely to engage in cooperative planning and teaching to achieve the administrative goal if they (1) come to understand (knowledge) the relationship between cooperative planning and teaching and achievement, and (2) perceive they have the ability to plan and teach successfully in a cooperative manner. In the past, there has been a trend among administrators to tell teachers what to do at a general level. By sharing the rationale for a new set of expectations, and ensuring that teachers have the appropriate skills, teachers are more likely to become personally motivated to perform in new ways.

The Influence of Personal Goals

In the past 25 years, researchers have identified goals, both personal and work, as perhaps the single most important stimulants for worker productivity. Researchers and scholars alike report that *goal-based performance* systems tend to achieve congruence between personal interests and increased work productivity (Odiorne 1979; Knezevich 1973; Reddin 1970; McGregor 1960; Ivancevich 1976; Ackoff 1974; Locke 1968; Lathan and Yukl 1975).

The function of goals in the workplace is to stimulate new norms of work productivity. Hersey and Blanchard (1977, 23–24) describe the motivating situation as a drive such as hunger (see Figure 9.9).

Cummings and Schwab (1973, 22) hypothesize that motivation and ability are not interdependent. *Ability* is a relatively stable capability factor, whereas *motivation* represents the dynamic of how vigorously individual capabilities are displayed in an activity. To illustrate, a college dean was recently informed by his president that he would attend a workshop with other deans on communication in organizations. Since this dean himself conducts workshops on that very topic, he was not motivated to engage as a relative novice in workshop activities. Motivation intensity might have been high, however, if he were invited to conduct that same workshop, or at least to participate in the planning. The dean's professional goals were to assist others in learning about communications. The university realized negative output from the dean in its de-

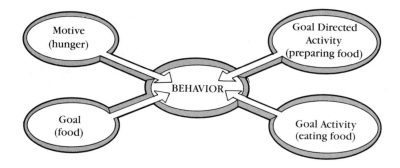

Figure 9.9. A Motivating Situation (*Source:* Adapted from Paul Hersey and Kenneth Blanchard, *Management of Organizational Behavior: Utilizing Human Resources.* [Englewood Cliffs, N. J.: Prentice-Hall, Inc., 1977], 24. Reprinted by permission of the publisher.)

velopment activities. By linking with his goal structure, the university might have benefited from his knowledge and skills.

House (1973) developed the path-goal theory of worker motivation. The assumption is that *worker productivity is likely to increase if management actually assists the worker in achieving his or her work goals.* Teacher and student activity systems that are goal based tend to circumvent inappropriate uses of time and energy. As a consequence of worker/student engagement in goal setting, more interested and motivated behavior results. Continuous helpful management intervention along the path to worker goals provides regular stimulation and reinforces the appropriate direction of worker behavior.

In summary, motivation is a personal response to opportunities for task engagement. *Affiliation* with other workers acts as a stimulator to produce at higher work norms. The job *motivators* of achievement and recognition provide workers with the necessary stimulation to continue performing at certain high levels. Individuals function at various levels of *psychological need.* When principals and teachers interpret those levels appropriately, teachers are more likely to behave in satisfactory ways. Personal *expectations* of the outcome of certain behaviors, and perceived levels of ability, tend to influence the levels of motivation for task engagement. *Personal work goals* provide an opportunity for self expression in the workplace and tend to stimulate behavior in an appropriate direction. Affiliation, job motivators, psychological needs, expectations, and personal goals are all variables that principals can manipulate in their efforts to increase performance levels. The five theories presented provide a set of options for decision making about stimulating teachers and students.

Self-Concept and Psychological Health

Until recently, personality theorists believed that normal persons with unchanging personality patterns were stable and therefore healthy (Mischele and Mischele 1973). With little or no evidence to support the stability concept, scholars now are studying discontinuity as a necessary and healthy growth-producing variable.

In his studies of personality, Rogers (1973, 220–224) observed that freedom, responsibility, and self-understanding tend to promote personal growth or change. In his view, the stable person, or conformist, tends to develop feelings of personal inferiority or inadequacy, demonstrating a lack of openness and freedom. The noncomformist, on the other hand, tends to be more autonomous, self-contained, open, and also more spontaneous and confident in thought and action. A confident or healthy person, therefore, exhibits commitment to personal goals and is more open to taking risks to achieve goals.

A short visit to any school or classroom can reveal how administrators and teachers foster or inhibit growth in self-concept. Does the environment expect teachers and students to explore ideas and actions, and does it value spontaneity and nonconformity? Or, are there expectations for teachers and students to continue in the same patterns as they have been for years? Are expectations for students and teachers predictably the same from year to year, or is there an expectation for teachers to grow and change and consequently alter and refine instructional practices continuously?

Self-concept grows as role expectations for teachers and students continuously change and expand. Expectations for growth can stimulate individuals to engage in new activities if they perceive that a personally desirable outcome will result from such engagement. If levels of teacher or student productivity are expected to develop continuously, the school environment must be supportive of and provide safety, reinforcement, recognition, and personal as well as organizational payoff for engagement in development activities.

Figure 9.10 outlines our conceptualization of the affective domain, which identifies goals and styles as the personal factors influencing behavior. Motivation sparks personal planning and action, whereas self-concept, values, and personality influence personal styles and the quality of performance. Together goals and styles interact to increase or decrease personal action in a given direction, influencing levels of personal motivation.

Behavioral Learning

Studies of human behavior began formally with Watson's break from the Gestalt psychologists, with attention to internal cognitive phenomena. By focus-

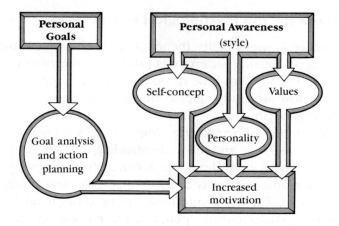

Figure 9.10 Affective Domain

ing on that which is observable (behavior), the behaviorist school of psychology was born.

Initially the focus of behavioral study was on the stimulus–response connection, with an emphasis on the causes (stimuli) of behaviors. Eventually, Skinner hypothesized that the consequences, not the stimuli, operate to reinforce the continuation or the elimination of certain behaviors. A contingency chain, as shown here, prompts behavior.

Cue → Behavior → Consequences

A *cue* informs an individual that certain *consequences* will follow certain *behaviors.* Eventually Skinner was able to demonstrate that new behavior can be learned by systematically managing the consequences of a behavior through schedules of reinforcement.

Luthans and Kreitner (1975), who are management scholars, work with behavior management concepts in adult organizations. They contend that *all organizational behavior is learned.* If organizations are clear about which behaviors are the most productive, then the adult learning process can be managed on the job by predicting, directing, and controlling the cues–behavior–consequence chain. The implications for school administrators are to concentrate on managing specific kinds of adult behavior rather than school activities. Figure 9.11 outlines a behavioral management cycle that principals may find useful in eliciting certain staff behaviors.

Staff behavior changes can be made through on-the-job learning and teaching by attending to that which is observable, and creating a desirable chain of events. Learning can be facilitated by focusing on observable *behavior.* The principles of behavior management widen the management repertoire for fa-

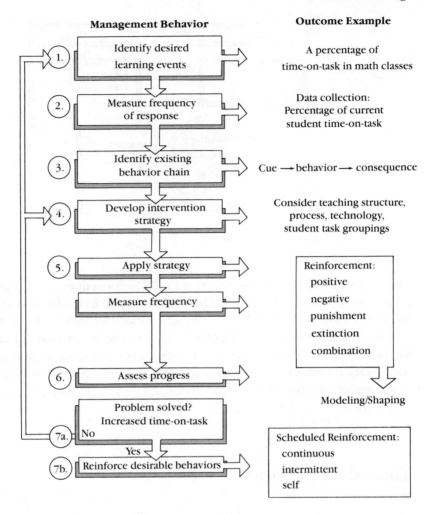

Management Behavior

Outcome Example

1. Identify desired learning events — A percentage of time-on-task in math classes

2. Measure frequency of response — Data collection: Percentage of current student time-on-task

3. Identify existing behavior chain — Cue → behavior → consequence

4. Develop intervention strategy — Consider teaching structure, process, technology, student task groupings

5. Apply strategy

Measure frequency — Reinforcement:
positive
negative
punishment
extinction
combination

6. Assess progress — Modeling/Shaping

7a. Problem solved? Increased time-on-task — No

Yes

7b. Reinforce desirable behaviors — Scheduled Reinforcement:
continuous
intermittent
self

Figure 9.11. Behavioral Contingency Management (*Source:* Reprinted from "The Management of Behavioral Contingencies" by Fred Luthans and Robert Kreitner, in *Personnel*, July-Aug. 1974, p. 13. © 1974 by AMACOM, a division of American Management Associations, New York. All rights reserved.)

cilitating staff growth. A school can virtually eliminate practices that reinforce undesirable behaviors (punishment/embarrassment). More effective results can be accomplished through an analysis of the consequences of undesirable behavior. Strategies for desirable change in practice can be designed and facilitated. Patterns of positive reinforcement elicit far more lasting evidences of desired behavior than does punishment or ignoring undesired behavior.

Likewise, by actually managing behaviors, principals will provide teachers with more correctives and feedback. Teachers are far more likely to develop student behavior management skills if they are reinforced in the same way.

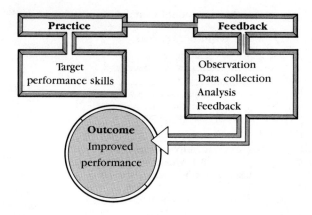

Figure 9.12. Behavioral Domain

Noticeable achievement increases are a likely consequence of a behavior management approach to learning. Often attention to behavior and managing the consequences are the only effective teaching alternatives for principals.

Figure 9.12 outlines a conceptualization of the behavioral domain. Practice of a given skill, combined with feedback and correctives on performance, are necessary for effective skill development, either cognitive or behavioral. The outcome of effective practice and feedback is the desired performance or new behavior.

Concluding Comments

The cognitive, affective, and behavioral domains all contribute unique dimensions to the learning process. The *cognitive domain* generates new insights and perceptions through linear and nonlinear cognitive processes and as a result of interaction. Cognitive style preferences tend to guide the choice one makes. The *affective domain* prompts individuals to act in certain ways (motivation) that appear congruent with self-concept, and which are of interest personally. Psychological health is likely to continue if individuals, over time, act in ways that are self-renewing and self-developing. The *behavioral domain* focuses on observable behavior and enables individuals to develop skills through practice, feedback, and reinforcement.

The three learning domains always act as a unit (cognitive/affective/behavioral) on human growth. When examined individually, each cluster of theories offers the educator numerous possible approaches for facilitating desired

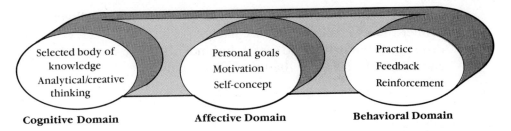

| Selected body of knowledge Analytical/creative thinking | Personal goals Motivation Self-concept | Practice Feedback Reinforcement |

Cognitive Domain   **Affective Domain**   **Behavioral Domain**

Figure 9.13. Learning Variables

learning. Figure 9.13 provides a summary of learning in each of the three domains which interact to foster changes in performance.

School Learning: Mastery for All

In the 1960s, Jerome S. Bruner proposed what seemed to many educators at that time a wild notion—that any subject can be taught to any child in some honest form (1973, 424). Bruner's belief challenged the very foundations of thought regarding what should be taught at each school age. Furthermore, Bruner called attention to *teaching* as the schooling problem rather than *learning*. If students (learners) can learn relatively anything at any time, then the task for teachers is to focus on "how" to cause the learning to take place. Bruner's bold assertion questioned and challenged the guarded practice of organizing curriculum content logically to present to students, who may or may not be interested or ready. Given Bruner's view of what is possible, the task for educators began to shift emphasis from teaching subjects to facilitating desired learning.

During those same years, Bloom and his colleagues at the University of Chicago were developing the concepts of mastery learning. In 1976, Bloom published the results of a 13-year-long study of learning in 37 different countries. He concluded that 95 percent of all students can master all that is expected of them if the schooling conditions are favorable, that is, students receive appropriate diagnosis, placement, and quality instruction. Bruner's theory (all students are able to learn anything) was supported by Bloom's extensive research on what actually occurs in schools under favorable conditions. Both theoretical and practical postulates (that all can learn what is expected) challenge educators today to create, to control, and to manage the kinds of schools where almost all sudents can and do succeed. If we act intelligently upon the Bruner/Bloom challenge, we are likely to eliminate illiteracy and intellectual dropouts in our nation and create the kinds of schools that produce productive and learned citizens for the twenty-first century.

New Views of the Learner

Bloom (1978, 564) observes that during his career, educators have been preoccupied with several different, basic assumptions about the learner. The first construct, which guided Bloom's early research and still guides much practice in schools, is that "there are good learners and there are poor learners." Learning, according to this view, has highly predictable characteristics. Consequently, various tests can predict school achievement levels for each student. Ability is viewed as a highly stable trait, about which schools can do very little. This view of learning led to the schooling practices of grading, tracking, and selection. Once a particular ability is determined, a student is placed in skill groups and classes that remain virtually unchanged during a given year or the student's entire schooling career.

In the second construct, "there are faster and there are slower learners" (Bloom 1978, 564). This view of the learner (proposed by Carroll earlier) assumes that most students can achieve equally high levels of learning in a school subject if sufficient time and help are available. It is assumed that learners have varied rates of learning, and, when provided adequate time, all can achieve equally. The implications are to alter and even eliminate the use of aptitude and intelligence tests to predict levels of success and student placement. Secondly, school time ought to be conceptualized as a flexible variable in which all students do achieve. Many time-flexible versions of nongraded school organization grew out of this view of learning for it defined flexible organizational parameters in which all students can achieve over time.

Bloom proposes that the third construct, which grew out of his research on the second construct, will remain a challenge for the remainder of this century. He asserts that "most students become very similar with regard to learning ability, rate of learning, and motivation for further learning, when provided with favorable learning conditions (1978, 566). This construct questions the good-poor and faster-slower constructs mentioned earlier; it also suggests that these characteristics can be altered for greater student success if schooling conditions are favorable.

Figure 9.14 outlines Bloom's theory of school learning (1976, 11), which is based on construct three. The assumption underlying the theory is that *95 per-*

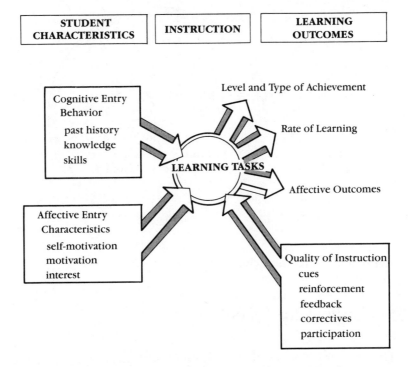

Figure 9.14. Major Variables in the Theory of School Learning (*Source:* Adapted from Benjamin Bloom, *Human Characteristics and School Learning.* [New York: McGraw-Hill Book Company, 1976], 11. Reprinted by permission of the publisher.)

cent of all students can learn what is expected if the schooling conditions are favorable. The favorable conditions, he observes, are cognitive readiness (a student's cognitive entry behaviors); affective readiness (a student's affective entry characteristics); and effective teaching (quality instruction: cues and directives; participation; reinforcement; and feedback and correctives). These three conditions work together interdependently (readiness and teaching) to foster student mastery.

In the next decade schools can alter and eliminate those practices that provide damaging or less-than-favorable conditions for student mastery. Bloom proposes that several practices are alterable and these should guide research and practice in the years ahead (Bloom 1980, 382–385). The variables that can be altered in schools are (1) time-on-task, (2) cognitive entry, (3) formative testing, (4) teaching, and (5) home involvement (see Figure 9.15). These five practices provide a sound structure for schooling alteration in the decades to come, along with additional factors that Bloom and other researchers are now finding to be important to school learning.

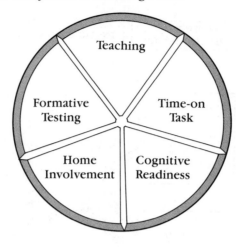

Figure 9.15. Alterable Schooling Variables

Implications for Schools

The challenge to create schooling conditions that will enable all students to succeed is indeed awesome. However, we believe that many of the bad habits and restraints to learning that now exist in schools can be eliminated, and conversely, facilitating procedures and practices can be introduced into the classroom environment. For far too long teachers have accepted the fact that many children fail to achieve, and have explained away poor results by placing the blame (poor attitude, insufficient effort, hopeless family situations, poor learning potential) on the learners rather than on themselves and their modus operandi. Too many teachers feel that so long as they present the material ("cover the textbook," for example) for that grade level or course, they have done their duty. There are teachers, however, who recognize that Bloom and others have pointed the way to a much more honest, practical, and exciting way of viewing human potential for achievement. They realize that there is not only room for improvement in daily instructional practice, but there is also great opportunity to enjoy previously unimaginable success and satisfaction.

Figure 9.16 illustrates how instructional practices could be altered in order to attain the ideal teaching/learning environment. The area within each of the two circles represents the total instructional time available to each teacher in a given year. Since each school year has about 180 days, each embracing about 5.5 hours instructional or instruction-related time, the circles symbolize about 1,000 hours. If all of the things the children experience during those 1,000 hours could be identified as pedagogically excellent (state-of-the-art instructional technology) and also philosophically sound (an "ideal" curriculum for American children), educators would surely be among the most productive, satisfied, and honored people in society. The left-hand circle, representing this attainable ideal, gives educators a goal to strive for, and in the best of all worlds the right-hand circle, representing what is generally happening in American classrooms, would overlap it 100 percent. In actuality, however, only a part (area 1) of what goes on is consistent with the best that we know. Whenever it is discovered that teachers are functioning in this best-possible category, their work should be reinforced and rewarded in all possible ways.

Another fraction of the time (area 2), children experience instruction that falls a bit short of the ideal but all the same is fairly worthwhile. When teachers are functioning within this category, encouragement and assistance should be offered to fine-tune their pedagogy in the direction of best-possible practice.

During a third, and in our opinion the largest, fraction of time (area 3), children experience instruction or activities that waste their energies and produce little of enduring value. We are troubled, as we visit classrooms, to observe how often pupils are simply "in storage," doing trivial things or waiting for something more important to happen. Much energy, too, is going into learning things of little short-range or long-range value, including materials that might once have been worth learning (*Silas Marner* is a favorite example) but now need to be replaced with more relevant materials. Teachers who complain that there is too little time to teach important things should be encouraged to approach the problem by axing all the *un*important things that now clutter the day.

Note, finally, there is a fourth area in Figure 9.16 representing practices that are actually harmful and counterproductive. Examples include materials within the curriculum that distort history, provide false or misleading infor-

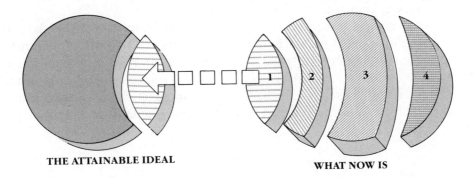

THE ATTAINABLE IDEAL   WHAT NOW IS

Figure 9.16. Altering Instructional Practices. Area 1—Current "ideal" practices. Area 2—Practices that are *almost* what they should be. Area 3—Harmless but nonproductive practices. Area 4—Harmful or conterproductive practices.

mation about the world and its many subpopulations, tend to reinforce racism or sexism, or gloss over certain of the less pleasant realities of human social and political behavior. Other examples include many of the things teachers do, in the name of assessment, that generate unhealthy competitive attitudes and grade mongering. It includes the frequent use by some teachers of sarcasm, or the tendency of others to "put down" children at the cost of their motivation or self-esteem. It even includes some of the overemphasis upon certain dubious "rules" of grammar, for instance, which may be irrelevant or inapplicable more often than they are useful; upon boring and repetitious exercises in language or mathematics that thwart pupil interest; and upon homework assignments that are nothing more than compulsory activities. Principals and teachers should be constantly on the watch for ways to eliminate area 4 practices, to reduce areas 3 and 2, and to enlarge area 1 to the point where it clearly dominates each day's work.

Conclusion

In this chapter we have sought to establish a conceptual framework for adult and student learning in the school workplace. If schools are to produce different learning norms from the past, then school leaders necessarily will bring to bear all they now know about learning that impacts on working and learning.

Cognitive learning is a nonlinear process that draws upon past knowledge and relies on problem solving to evolve new understandings about a reality. Affective learning is goal directed and draws on a person's psychological health and values as he or she is stimulated to want to know. Behavioral learning requires practice and feedback of certain skills. Together cognitive, affective, and behavioral learning interact in a dynamic fashion that enables a person to grow in many dimensions.

Learning for workers and students in school necessarily needs to draw from cognitive, affective, and behavioral experiences. Bloom has demonstrated that almost all students can master what schools determine if readiness is diagnosed and used in placement procedures, and if time allotments and instruction facilitate full mastery. The challenge to principals is to design work and learning environments that nurture growth and stimulate development in natural, nonlinear ways.

10

The Program Subsystem: Student Learning

Schools have always planned instructional programs for students. Society now is placing pressure on schools to do far more, however; schools are expected to *ensure* certain learning norms for all students. In the traditional practice of planning programs, the focus was on teaching. The new emphasis is on learning, with an assumption that teaching is to vary in ways that facilitate and even guarantee mastery.

The old view of instruction (planning programs and teaching subjects) had its origins in Herbartian beliefs about the learner which prevailed through the nineteenth century (see Bigge 1971, 45–46). Central to Herbart's view was the belief that a student's mind is merely an aggregate of contents that results from a person's having certain ideas presented to him. All perception is a process of relating new ideas to the store of old mental states. Herbart recognized three stages of learning: (1) sense activity, (2) memory, and (3) conceptual thinking or understanding. The real task of instruction is to implant knowledge in order to form a mental background (an apperceptive mass). The teacher in this view is an architect and builder of minds, and hence, of the characters of students, while presenting knowledge and information. The reader will be interested to learn that Herbart lived from 1776 to 1849. The problem is that Herbartian views of learning and teaching still dominate schooling practice in the twentieth century.

Research, theory, and experience in the twentieth century have altered those dated beliefs for many. More educators now believe that teaching is a set

323

of facilitating behaviors that enable students to master certain concepts or skills, rather than acts of dispensing knowledge. The outcome of teaching today is learning for all, a view that rejects the "blame-the-student" attitude to which many still cling when facilitating mastery becomes difficult.

A Systems Approach to Instruction

In an attempt to cluster essential instructional acts, we developed a model of interdependent teaching tasks (see Figure 10.1). The model identifies five sets of decision-making tasks that act interdependently to influence learning: curriculum selection; student diagnosis and evaluation; program planning; classroom management; and teaching and learning. The model provides a language system and a conceptual framework around which principals and teachers can discuss and refine instructional processes. All teaching decisions can be placed

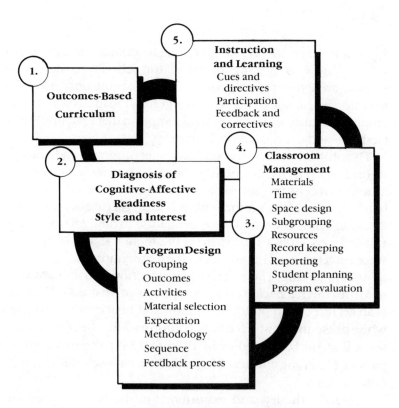

Figure 10.1. A Systems Approach to Learning and Instruction

somewhere within the five-part system. The first four tasks are planning decision sets, and the last task is actual teaching and learning.

Research on Effective Teaching

In the pages that follow we present an analysis of the research on effective teaching, using the model in Figure 10.1 as a lens for the study. The research pattern of studying correlates between instruction categories and achievement is relatively young; however, sufficient knowledge now exists to produce a beginning direction for improving teaching efforts.

Review of Effective Teaching Studies

Teacher Task 1: Selecting Curriculum Objectives

Armor
1976   Objectives guide teaching in reading.
Bloom
1976   Explicit learning outcomes are the foundation of a student mastery program.
California DPE
1980   Objectives guide teaching and learning activities in reading.
Edmonds
1979   Basic skills objectives guide instruction in effective programs.
Glenn
1981   Basic skills objectives are the focus for instruction in effective programs.
Levine and Stark
1981   Objectives (reading and math) guide teaching activities.
Lezotte and Brookover
1979   Objectives (reading and math) guide teaching practices.
Trisman et al.
1976   Objectives guide teaching in reading.
Weber
1971   Specific objectives (in reading) directed instruction in successful programs.

Research Summary: Curriculum Outcomes
In successful schools, specific learning objectives provide the foundation for achieving and measuring student achievement. Objectives also direct instructional program planning and implementation.

Teacher Task 2: Student Diagnosis and Evaluation

Bloom

1976   Diagnosis of appropriate cognitive and affective entry levels accounts for 60 to 70 percent of the variance in mastering a specific task.

Brookover and Lezotte 1979; Anderson et al. 1982; Duffy

1980   Three Michigan studies where an assessment system is used for student placement in effective programs.

Dunn

1981   Diagnosing learning styles and planning programs around data increase learning.

Edmonds

1979   Monitoring of student progress occurs in effective programs.

Levine and Stark

1981   Coordination of curriculum, teaching, and testing exists in effective programs.

Weber

1971   The evaluation of student progress directs teaching decisions.

Research Summary: Student Diagnosis and Evaluation

In effective instructional programs, diagnosis of student cognitive readiness and affective characteristics accounts for a significant amount of the variance in mastery. Diagnosis of learning styles, and planning programs according to test data enhance achievement. Diagnosis and evaluation data are used for student placement and subsequently guide instructional planning and teaching.

Teacher Task 3: Program Planning

Brookover and Lezotte 1979; Anderson et al. 1982; Duffy

1980   Three Michigan studies where teachers have control over teaching decisions in effective programs.

Glenn

1981   Joint teacher planning is characteristic of successful programs.

Levine and Stark

1981   Grade-level teacher decision-making is characteristic of effective programs.

Vanezky and Winfield

1979   Joint teacher planning occurs in successful programs.

Weber

1971   Cooperative teacher planning occurs in successful (reading) programs.

Research Summary: Program Planning
The primary characteristic of teacher involvement in program planning is that it occurs cooperatively, with teachers having control over many teaching decisions.

Teacher Task 4: Classroom Management

Armor
1976   Effective programs are found in orderly classrooms.

Brophy
1982   A key to effective classroom management is prevention: advance planning, communication of expectations, monitoring, and selection of purposeful academic activities.

Brophy and Putnam
1979   Effective classrooms are characterized by effective management.

California DPE
1980   Record keeping and time allocation are characteristic of effective programs.

Edmonds
1979   An orderly classroom atmosphere is characteristic in effective schools.

Emmer, Evertson, and Anderson
1980   Teachers establish and maintain an activity system; get started quickly; anticipate misbehavior; and stop misbehavior early in effective schools.

Glenn
1981   Effective classrooms set guidelines for student discipline.

Good
1979   Teachers have management abilities in effective classrooms.

Kounin
1970   Teacher creates, maintains, and restores conditions that foster effective learning.

Levine and Stark
1981   Adequate materials are available in successful programs.

Rutter
1979   There are student management guidelines for behavior in effective high schools.

Research Summary: Classroom Management
In effective classrooms, teachers plan, manage, and monitor an orderly student learning activity system. Effective classroom management includes guidelines for student behavior, record-keeping systems, and adequate learning materials.

Teacher Task 5(a): Teaching

Armor
1976   Teachers have high expectations of students in effective programs.

Berliner and Tikunoff
1976   Teachers monitor learning; are optimistic and reactive-corrective toward students.

Block
1970   Feedback and correctives lie at the heart of the mastery process.

Bloom
1976   Teacher cues and directives, reinforcement, feedback, and correctives are adapted to student needs.

California DPE
1980   Teachers have high expectations of students in successful schools.

Doyle
1980   Teachers monitor and provide variety in pace and activity and intervene in the learning process in successful programs.

Doyle
1981   Teachers structure academic tasks in successful schools.

Duffy and McIntyre
1983   Teachers monitor student progress and are reactive and corrective.

Gage
1978   Teachers provide a high degree of structuring in effective programs.

Gage
1978   Teachers provide praise and acceptance, are indirect, and solicit ideas in effective classrooms.

Glenn
1981   Teachers have high expectations of students in effective programs.

Levine and Stark
1981   Teachers gear instruction to high-order cognitive skills in successful programs.

Lezotte and Brookover
1979   Teachers believe that all children can learn, in effective programs.

Lysakowski and Walberg
1982   Instructional cues, participation, reinforcement, and corrective/feedback produce effects that place systematically instructed groups at over the 80th percentile in learning.

Three Michigan Studies
(Brookover and Lezotte 1979; Anderson et al. 1982; Duffy 1980)

Teachers have high expectations of all students.

Rosenshine

1979 In successful programs, learning goals are announced; low-order questions are asked; teachers control learning goals, pacing, and materials, and provide immediate monitoring and feedback.

Rosenshine and Furst

1973 Teacher clarity, variability, enthusiasm, and task orientation are characteristic of effective instruction.

Rutter

1979 Teachers provide feedback and correctives, high expectations, and praise in successful schools.

Trisman et al.

1976 High student expectations and small group instruction are characteristic of effective schools.

Van Wagenen and Travers

1963 Direct interaction with learning materials and the teacher produces higher levels of achievement than merely listening to or watching.

Vanezky and Winfield

1979 Teachers display adaptability and consistency in effective programs.

Weber

1971 Teachers have high expectations for all students in successful programs.

Wright and DuCette

1976 Students who feel they have control over their successes and failures achieve more in open approaches to teaching than in direct instruction. Students who feel their success or failure is due to forces outside their control respond best to direct instruction.

Research Summary: Teaching

Teaching in successful classrooms is characterized by high learning expectations for all students and a task orientation to instruction. Teaching is adaptable, structured, filled with variety, and based on specific learning goals. Teachers structure both high- and low-order cognitive activities; instruct in both small and large groups; are interactive with students; and, in general, intervene in the learning process, providing reinforcements and correctives.

Teacher Task 5(b): Learning

Berliner

1982   A high success rate is especially important for young children and slow learners.

Berliner and Tikunoff

1976   Student engagement in learning activities is a characteristic of effective schools.

Bloom

1976   The amount of student participation (time-on-task) correlates with the amount of achievement.

California DPE

1980   Student progress is monitored for low achievers especially.

Doyle

1980   Engaged student time-on-task correlates with achievement gains.

Doyle

1981   Students are provided with ample opportunity to work successfully in effective schools.

Glenn

1981   There is a supportive atmosphere in effective classes.

Hyman and Cohen

1979   Mastery students master more objectives in a given time period than nonmastery students. Increases in time-on-task cause gains in achievement.

Johnson and Johnson

1981   Cooperative learning is more effective than competitive and individualistic learning for any task.

King

1981   A task focus exists in effective classrooms.

Peterson

1979   High-ability students do better in a small group approach than in a large group with direct instruction. Low-ability students do better in large group than in small group instruction settings.

Peterson, Janicki, and Swing

1981   Students improve their own learning by teaching other children, the benefit being greater to "teacher " than to "learner." High-ability students tend to stay on-task more in small groups.

Rosenshine

1979   Sufficient engaged time-on-task correlates with achievement gains.

Rosswork

1977   Inducing students to set specific learning goals can lead to performance increases.

Rutter
1979   Successful schools have active learning and high degrees of student responsibility.

Sagotsky, Patterson, and Lepper
1978   Students taught to self-monitor and to record daily progress show increases in achievement and study behaviors.

Sharon
1980   Cooperative learning and high cognitive skills correlate with increased achievement.

Slavin
1980   Cooperative learning is good for low-ability students for solidarity and relationships. Student team learning is an effective example of cooperative learning.

Slavin
1980   Teams, games, tournaments improve quantity and quality of contact among team members inside and outside classrooms.

Stallings
1980   "Interactive" time-on-task correlates with achievement gains.

Watts and Anderson
1971   Questions requiring application of principles result in greater achievement than recalling information.

Weber
1971   Teachers individualize instruction in successful programs.

Research Summary: Learning

In successful classrooms, learning occurs within a supportive atmosphere, where students work in both small and large groups, in individualized learning activities, as well as in cooperative learning and peer tutoring arrangements. Interactive learning is a primary characteristic of successful school environments. Students have ample time and opportunity to master skills; and, in addition, students assume high degrees of responsibility for their learning by participation in setting their own learning goals, actively applying program principles and concepts, and monitoring their progress.

To summarize, successful classrooms are characterized by the following practices:

identified *learning objectives*
diagnosis of learner readiness and style preceding and throughout the program
instructional *programs* that are designed cooperatively by teachers

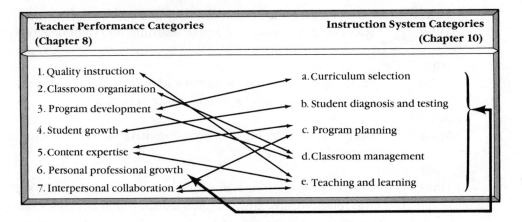

Figure 10.2. Relationship of Teacher Performance Categories to Instruction Tasks

an *activity system* that specifies parameters for student behavior, and focuses on learning goals and which is controlled by the teacher

interactive *instruction* that provides appropriate expectations, reinforcement, and corrective/feedback; and which organizes students
into various types of groupings for work

learning activities that *engage the learner actively* with peers and
teacher, and which require degrees of student responsibility for
success

In the following section of this chapter, the five teacher task sets are further
discussed to provide additional concepts and methodology. The principal
should read each section with the purpose of identifying patterns in instruction that are most likely to facilitate learning. The instructional management
task (the principal's role) involves five interdependent processes: (1) to inform teachers of effective practices, (2) to require that programs designed for
students reflect research findings, (3) to coach teachers as they develop proficiency in each decision set, (4) to monitor achievement patterns in each program, and (5) to assist teachers with program modifications.

Figure 10.2 illustrates the relationship between the categories of teacher
performance that were discussed in Chapter 8 and the dimensions of the instruction system presented in this chapter. Why is it necessary to discuss two
separate sets of performance categories involving teachers? The reader will
note that the performance categories (Chapter 8) are stated in terms of teacher
performance outcomes and extend beyond teaching to include work with
other staff members. The instruction system focuses on the tasks (not outcomes) related only to the teaching functions of the role. For example, certain

performance outcomes can be expected each year in relation to professional growth (6); the results of that growth, however, influence all five categories in the instruction system (a through e). Another example of the ways in which the performance system extends beyond the instruction system is found in the interpersonal collaboration category (7). Working with other staff members includes teaching (e) and planning instructional programs (c), but extends beyond the instruction system to include other responsibilities. Five teachers may form a task force to develop a new record-keeping system for the school's science program or a schoolwide student tutorial program. Consequently, the teacher performance system should be viewed as a comprehensive statement of teacher responsibilities; the instruction system directs attention to the teaching tasks of the role.

Our contention is that the process of revitalizing instructional programs involves principals and teachers working together to alter instruction and learning norms. The five-task model of instruction provides a useful framework for that dialogue and action.

What is the nature of the principal's responsibilities for the school's instruction system? It may be helpful to use the analogy of an effective football coach. The coach works with the team prior to the season, throughout each practice session, during each game, and in every postgame analysis. Likewise, effective instructional leaders will engage their teachers in continuous and active dialogue, training, peer and supervisory coaching, and critical analysis of and about teaching and the results of teaching.

Teacher Task Set 1: Curriculum Selection

The involvement of teachers in district curriculum development varies widely from district to district, and from state to state. The variance is due not so much to specific administrative decision-making preferences but rather to general indecision about curriculum, its function in a school, and principal-teacher responsibilities for curriculum work.

During the last quarter century curriculum activity has been extensive in school districts, universities, research and development centers, and publishing houses. It would seem as though schools by now would have a very clear sense of obligations to curriculum development or selection, and to implementation control practices. Our own experiences with thousands of principals, however, support what was learned in Goodlad's study of schooling: there exists a general lack of clarity among administrators about curriculum, its function, and staff responsibility (Klein 1980). Klein's report specifically notes that many curriculum guides tend to confuse goals, objectives, performance objectives, content, and activity, often within the same guide, undifferentiated. Goals or objectives frequently exist for both teachers and students within the same document. Some guides recommend the Mager format for stating objectives but fail to follow that advice throughout the document. Many other curriculum guides discuss materials in specific terms, stating pages and correlated materials in other texts. Curriculum content itself is treated extensively, ranging from broad topics to specific items. Few guides actually separate methodology for teachers from activities for students.

Also, time is addressed in curriculum documents primarily as a specific allocation per subject area, rather than as a gross period within several years during which students can master concepts and skills. The concept of individualization or mastery is virtually ignored. Rather, many curriculum guides provide suggestions for teachers on methodology and focus on student outcomes only by inference. Only a few guides are prescriptive in nature and written in the form of objectives (Klein 1980, 5–7).

One senses from the report just mentioned and from visiting many school districts that assumptions about curriculum, its function, and principal and teacher responsibility are all rather loose. Given the general lack of clarity concerning educational purposes, there is little wonder that problems persist with regard to achievement results from the schooling process.

To offset the many problems that are consequences of vague curriculum designs and implementation practices, the Texas Education Agency in 1983 launched a statewide effort to develop one standard curriculum. The documents developed are intended to provide school districts with descriptions of essential learning objectives in each curriculum area. Rather than providing a comprehensive approach to each area, the documents specify a bare-bones approach to curriculum. Essential learning objectives will comprise the focus for statewide testing, which is conducted annually in several grades in all Texas schools.

This landmark effort on the part of the state of Texas provides a basic teaching and learning standard for each school district. Schools are then free to select any materials and methods for achieving those objectives. In addition, locally developed programs and thrusts will continue to exist; the state will control only for basic learning outcomes.

In the following section, we will briefly discuss several working definitions of curriculum, including our own. It is our hope that principals and teachers will explore specific implementation issues (not development) that will lead to responsible control patterns in schools.

Definition of Curriculum

Tyler (1950) developed the first widely circulated definition of curriculum which is still used by many educators today. He recommended that a curriculum (a document) must contain four elements: (1) *objectives* (which state purpose); (2) *means* (which suggest educational experiences and time lines); (3) *organization* (which provides a conceptual design or scope and sequence of skills and concepts); and (4) *evaluation* (which measures the degree to which purposes were met).

In a later assessment of his own model, Tyler (1977) recommended adding another dimension, which would interact with the other four: "the active role of the learner." The role of the learner, neglected by most earlier discourses on curriculum development, now ought to play a central role, according to Tyler. He noted further that the selected curriculum objectives should be (1) important for students in order to participate constructively in society, (2) sound in terms of the subject matter itself, (3) in accord with the philosophy of the institution, and (4) of interest or meaningful to the learner. Since student interests are often stimulated in other parts of their life experience, the school and community need to be linked in numerous interdependent configurations so that practice in a skill as well as initial learning can be provided to augment the mastery process.

Social pressures on schools to ensure mastery for all students in the basics, have precipitated considerable action from educators. Competency-testing programs which many states developed are one attempt to hold schools accountable for what they produce. Is this phenomenon not another example of an anomoly in the maintenance paradigm? Traditional teaching practices were adequate for the sorting task of schools. However, as society has begun to require mastery for all students, teaching also will have to be altered. The competency testing movement was an attempt to control what schools produce. However, testing does not address the central issue of purpose; this is a curriculum issue. Until states and districts decide which outcomes schools will produce, control practices are likely to generate no different schooling results than in past decades.

Competency-based education, a term used by many to describe the curriculum and operational dimensions of a learning outcome-based approach to schooling, offers additional insight. Competencies are indicators of successful performance in real life role activities (Spady 1978). However, competencies involve far more than the ability to perform effectively in a given situation; they involve dimensions of cognitive structuring that can be addressed tangibly and successfully in schools. Competencies involve real life roles, success in which requires coping with ever-changing social conditions. Further, competencies are formed complexly in persons as capacities are tapped and nurtured; developing competency is rarely a mechanical manipulation of logically ordered acts. Proponents of competency-based education are calling for fundamentally different kinds of learning than can result from a traditionally designed curriculum. For example, in real life, who diagrams sentences? Schools remain largely subject bound in curriculum and instruction. Yet the demonstration of a competence, such as conducting a research activity, requires a complex configuration of knowledge, concepts, and skills and is developed adequately only if the experience is provided and repeated sufficiently.

How does the broad challenge of developing human competence become translated into curriculum decisions? A school district first must develop a set of learning outcomes for students that is stated as standard learning measures for various age groups (for example, 5 to 8; 8 to 11; 11 to 14; 14 to 18). Second, that standard must then be communicated to principals and their teachers, along with a set of procedures for responsive and accountable implementation. In this sense, a standard is a prerequisite to a control cycle (for example, Sony TV design and subsequent production). A curriculum standard and a quality control system both are necessary for effective learning for all students.

Perhaps the reason "successful schools" are effective in altering learning norms has little to do with the basics. Perhaps these schools are successful because of an effective curriculum design and control system. The point to be made is this: Schools must define the learning outcomes they expect and then control for those ends. Our objective in discussing curriculum is not to recommend a particular approach for developing curriculum, but rather to point out that the field is confusing at best. Curriculum decisions need to be made locally and then controlled for desired outcomes. Publishing houses do not provide implementation controls; schools must control for the productivity they select. The challenge for principals is to control school life in such a way that the curriculum guides instructional practice and controls for specific learning outcomes.

Managing Curriculum Implementation

The curriculum serves as the standard for guiding teacher planning for learning and for measuring teacher effectiveness in fostering expected learning outcomes. *Curriculum* is defined in this volume as *the district standard for student mastery at various age groupings* (for example 5 to 8; 8 to 11; 11 to 14; 14 to 18) *in selected bodies of knowledge, selected personal and interpersonal growth competencies, and selected cognitive and behavioral skills.* Many districts have already developed a content-oriented curriculum that embraces cognitive and behavioral skills, but we see the addition of personal and interpersonal competencies as necessary since isolated knowledge and behavioral skills are important only as they relate to the social work world and to the community and family of individuals. Another assumption is that schools should prepare citizens to behave as mature, self-confident individuals who relate in productive ways with coworkers, and community and family members. Thus, we urge that personal and interpersonal competencies be added to school program expectations, along with the more measurable cognitive and behavioral outcomes.

Levels of Decision Making

Implementing and translating a district curriculum into instructional programs requires a clear understanding of who makes which decision. *District-level* curriculum decisions define the broad scope and sequence of cognitive, affective, and behavioral outcomes in each curriculum area, stating the age benchmarks for mastery. *School-level* curriculum decisions define the more specific program parameters for all teaching teams in a given year. For example, all levels may decide to study the same three cultures, each focusing on a particular emphasis as they relate to the curriculum outcomes and to the interests of particular age groups. Or, the school's coordinating council may decide that each teaching team will make its own separate curriculum selections and program designs. Another year the school may decide to have a theme for the entire year, into which curriculum objectives are fit to meet specific learning needs. In summary, a school considers the curriculum as a skeleton around which different teams plan learning programs.

The *team level* coordinates or selects program themes for the year, choosing curriculum objectives as program foundations for specific measurable learning. To illustrate, let us suppose the social studies curriculum for 7- to 9-year olds contains 24 learning outcomes. Team members assign particular outcomes to certain months, building learning objectives into specific programs in a planned way, and repeating them periodically over the three years or so that students are on the team.

Let us consider one example. Suppose a team of 9- to 11-year-old students expressed a strong interest in the Indians of North and South America and their migrations. A typical outcome-based curriculum makes no specific mention of mastering knowledge about a particular group of Indians. Nor is there an expectation for students to learn the entire social history of every group of Indians that ever lived in North and South America. More often an outcome-based curriculum states that students must be able to compare the ways in which various people throughout history have adapted to their environment.

Student-level decisions regarding curriculum objectives relate to individual choice about program topics and kinds of learning experiences. A student's personal plans specify learning activities and *how* selected objectives will be mastered. Students can be assigned to next-level objectives efficiently during a particular unit if a record-keeping system is in place. The curriculum objectives, not program objectives, are then recorded on a student's permanent record to indicate experience with and final mastery of each curriculum outcome, in every program area.

The *principal's role* in curriculum implementation is to guide teaching teams in the kind of planning that is responsive both to the district's curriculum objectives (high school English; middle school math), and to the particular needs of students. Teachers develop an annual plan for teaching assigned curriculum objectives. The principal then monitors team progress through team reports, observation, and records of student mastery. Following each unit of study, the team critiques its program strengths and weaknesses in relation to student mastery levels and builds in recommendations for improvements. Team plans and operations may need to be revised considerably if achievement is lower than anticipated. Curriculum implementation actually occurs at the level of instruction.

Beyond the Curriculum

Defining curriculum parameters has been a major school district task during the past decade. Yet, many curriculum guides tend to confuse rather than guide teaching by mixing learning objectives, instructional options, resources materials, and content (Klein 1980). Further, by concentrating on the basics, a student's school day is dominated by isolated assignments, tasks, and tests that have little transfer potential into the real social world. An enormous amount of effort has been directed at developing programs and practices that will raise achievement norms. Consequently, with the prevalent narrowness of conceptualizing the causes and effects of learning, students tend to be defined in terms of test results and placement, primarily in the basics of reading comprehension and mathematics.

In the decades ahead, schools will need to develop the capacity for producing specific learning results, and at the same time develop more breadth in programs so students are prepared adequately to function as skillful persons in an increasingly complex adult work world.

The Challenge: Preparing Students for Life Roles

For several years the authors have been proclaiming that three goal categories need to exist in any school program. Fundamental *competencies* provide students with established knowledge about how the world is conceptualized now, as well as how it was in past centuries. Upon existing knowledge bases, learners build their own understandings of how the world works and how they fit into that world. *Practical wisdom* is that personal quality that transcends paragraph comprehension, for example, and enables a student to weigh options and to make moral and social decisions. Building ego strengths, which develops through social interactions and personal accomplishments, must become a teaching priority day after day. Personal autonomy grows out of successful experiences in making decisions and addressing consequences. Students need opportunities for making important social decisions, either through simulation, active roles in school life, and/or through community projects. Practical wisdom grows out of guided practice in life decisions, experiences, and consequences. Consequently, school learning in the future will necessarily resemble real life experiences, rather than unrelated book assignments.

A *capacity for pleasure* is a goal category virtually ignored by many and nurtured only by a few. A basic human need is to derive pleasure from personal, family, work, and social exchanges. If there is little or no joy in a person's life, that individual merely exists. To kindle or even rekindle, a sense of joy and pleasure, schools must provide experiences that tap the imagination and the bodily senses, and make students aware of numerous resources. Finally, schools must instill in students a genuine enthusiasm for and optimism about the future. The latter most certainly grows out of a personal sense of worth and the knowledge and skill necessary to be successful.

Many curriculum specialists, aware that the world is changing at a spectacular rate and influenced by the "futures" literature, are eager for the curriculum to be so designed that young people will be well prepared to cope with, and thrive under, conditions not now predictable. We perceive that if schools provide children with a solid and fundamental body of currently valid knowledge, if they help children to make practical use of their knowledge and skills in wise ways, and if they foster an upbeat, optimistic view of the opportunities that life presents, they will have done a great deal to prepare young people for whatever surprises and challenges lie ahead. Another way to think about preparing children for the future is to consider certain capacities worth cultivating:

Problem solving.   The capacity to comprehend, accept, and deal with problems is essential to all life roles. Schools can provide continual experiences in genuine problem solving, either simulated or real. The capacity in problem solving ought to be nurtured throughout a student's schooling under careful teacher coaching. The mindless experiences of "complete the questions at the end of the chapter" are no longer adequate to developing capacity for solving real life problems; such experiences are only a beginning to a more complete end.

Self Learning.   This capacity enables individuals to become effective lifelong learners. Some people are more successful if they read first and then engage in an activity. Others need a demonstration or an experience prior to reading. Knowing personal success patterns enables learners to make effective decisions about future involvements, some of which may determine life role success or failure.

Occupational Choice.   Ability to make vocational role decisions is essential to the future well-being of all students. Far too little useful guidance is given to make students aware of work options and the kinds of personal decisions that are required prior to selecting a career. Some futurists suggest that most workers in future years will have at least three or four careers during their lifetime. A huge gap exists between the simplicity of career guidance in schools and the complexity of job skills and knowledge required in most work roles. Consequently, information must be made readily available to students at all age levels about the numerous work options in society, and the schooling routes to those roles. Equally important is personal knowledge about particular skills and the match between those tendencies and skills required for various jobs or professions. To make intelligent choices, students need knowledge about work options, assessments of their own preferences and skills, and knowledge about the paths necessary to obtain a job in a chosen field.

Collaboration and Interpersonal Relations.   Future forecasters tell us that the ability to work productively with others is essential to work success. Perhaps the greatest visible change in schools of the future will be in the ways adults and children exchange patterns of role isolation for patterns of working together within and across roles. Students must be provided with numerous and continuous cooperative work patterns to learn how to work productively with others. A schooling life of cooperative experiences is critical for building this capacity.

Capacity for Pluralism.   It would seem that social attitudes toward working with different groups of people have shifted dramatically in recent years. When our forefathers arrived in America, the social goal was for all nationalities to shed their uniqueness and become one people: Americans. However, the mood in our country has changed somewhat so that we now value various cultures maintaining their differences while becoming American. Consequently, the one goal in each classroom most certainly must shift from sameness and norming group values, to learning, understanding, appreciating, and working with cultural differences. Our task is not to melt down but rather to bend flexibly and blend in efforts to collaborate productively.

Computer Literacy.   The social world has exploded with technological capabilities far beyond imagination a decade ago. Students will need to become skillful in operating computers of all kinds and in developing programs for their work tasks.

Aesthetic Breadth.   Life is neither logically ordered nor unidimensional. The arts have permeated all cultures as the symbol systems that express their rich meanings. The arts are basic forms of human expression in all cultures; however, in the American culture the arts have almost been excluded from schools.

"Reading" a manual on sailing a boat may be sufficient for mere survival. However, reading the history of travel throughout time, reading about the development of sailboats, and/or seeing plays, or listening to music that describes the wonders and frustrations of sailing may inspire different kinds of sailing activity and purpose.

Eisner (1980) draws attention to the arts as basic in schools. He notes that "the potentialities of the human mind do not develop isolated from a fertile environment, but in interaction with it" (p. 14). People learn to see aesthetically by being given the opportunity to look artistically. People learn to hear musically by learning how to listen to rhythms and melodies. The ability to use a symbol system such as in the arts, makes another contribution to understanding the world. Through the arts we see how the world looks; through music how it sounds; through history how it was in the past; through physics how it was constructed; and through poetry how it expresses the ineffable (Eisner 1980, 4–5). The arts must become integrated into all school programs providing students with the basic riches of the cultures and allowing them to develop their own aesthetic response dimensions.

Concluding Comments (Task Set 1)

Curriculum learning objectives guide the bare essential planning for student achievement. Schools can provide far more by developing programs where fundamental knowledge is mastered and where students develop practical wisdom as well as a capacity for pleasure. In addition, schools need to develop in their students a capacity for problem solving, for self-learning, for making occupational choices, for collaborating with others productively, for working effectively with those of different cultures and colors, for operating computers, and, finally, for developing personal breadth and depth from aesthetic symbol systems. Schools that incorporate these additional basics into their programs are likely to produce the most capable and the most skilled members of tomorrow's society. Perhaps the happiest, too!

Teacher Task Set 2: Diagnosis of Learner Readiness and Style

"Diagnose" is a verb that means to identify, determine, distinguish, pinpoint, or recognize characteristics that are idiosyncratic, individual, peculiar, and/or proper. Further, diagnosis refers to the process of determining the nature or characteristics of an organism through detailed description and examination for classification.

Diagnosis has been practiced for some time by school psychologists and special educators who have sought to identify particular problems. However, the task of diagnosis has been virtually absent from the regular classroom, existing only in the form of global levels of skill development. In the past several decades the practice of diagnosing more particular learning attributes and characteristics among normal students has seemed more and more worthwhile. Our belief is that in the decades that follow, the practices of diagnosing student readiness and style will become more sophisticated and capable of streamlining the school learning process.

Bloom's research (1976, 169) provides new insights into the centrality of readiness to skill mastery. He found that 65 to 75 percent of student success depended on their readiness to learn a particular task. Fifty percent of the variance in learning is due to cognitive readiness (as it refers to the availability of requisite entry behaviors), and 25 percent of the variation is attributed to affective entry characteristics (referring to the interests, attitudes, and self-view of the learner while engaging in a learning task). Only 25 percent of the variation in mastering a skill is due to the quality of instruction provided to the learner. Teacher training and practice in schools, however, is based on a reverse assumption: most of the variance in learning is attributed to the quality of teaching or to stable learner characteristics. Bloom's work tells us that such an assumption is wrong: the most perfect instruction presented to learners who are not ready will predictably fail to foster mastery of the desired task.

Recent studies of effective teaching support Bloom's findings on the importance of teacher diagnosis for student mastery. Weber (1971) noted that the evaluation of progress was critical to mastering next steps in reading. Levine and Stark (1981) report that coordination between teaching, curriculum, and testing is central to effective learning in math and reading. Moreover, three Michigan studies (Brookover and Lezotte 1979; Duffy 1980; Edmonds 1981) all observe that an assessment system is critical to student mastery; Edmonds (1979) also notes that monitoring progress is an important variable in basic skills mastery. While most of the studies just mentioned were conducted in urban elementary schools in the basic skills, the centrality of diagnosis to achievement in all studies is worthy of attention and action.

The tasks of diagnosis are complex, far more complex than determining whether James has the prerequisite skills to master multiplication tables. Learning is a reorganization of insights into the cognitive structure of one's total life space. Perceptions and new understandings are born out of cognitive readiness and are built on the entire life space schema of interests, self-concept, personality, and learning style. To diagnose James's readiness for multiplication tables, therefore, requires an understanding of his affective characteristics and also his learning style preferences and patterns. Adequate diagnosis requires an understanding of James's characteristics, and an ability to classify and translate diagnosed data into productive learning tasks. *Diagnosis, then, is a set of examination procedures used to determine levels of cognitive readi-*

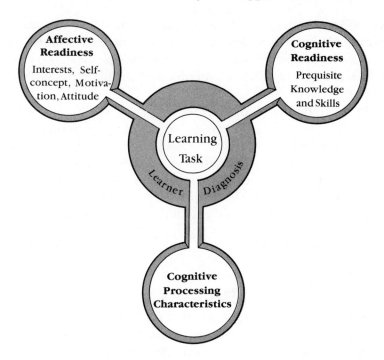

Figure 10.3. Learner Diagnosis Variables

ness, personal psychological characteristics of the learner (motivation, interests, self-concept), *and also learning style preferences and tendencies.*

In this section we discuss diagnosis by exploring cognitive and affective dimensions of readiness (see Figure 10.3). In addition, *learning style* is discussed as it relates to processing information cognitively and to styles of responding to environmental stimuli. The purpose in exploring both readiness and style dimensions of learning is to expose the reader to the breadth of readiness and style variables and their complexities for understanding the dual nature of the diagnostic task.

A problem may exist for principals in that many teachers mistakenly perceive that they do in fact diagnose regularly, and have little need for additional ways to diagnose. However, the literature reveals that the procedures teachers regularly use are personal and idiosyncratic. Research has failed to generate even descriptors of what processes teachers use (Gil, March 1980, 3). Moreover, there is lack of evidence that teachers demonstrate skill in diagnosing even reading problems, which is generally their "strongest suit." Classroom teachers lack comprehensive and effective strategies for data gathering and analysis; and teachers also differ in how much data they collect in order to diagnose students. Further, teachers tend to lack information-processing strategies for gathering data and for diagnosis. Consequently, they tend to be global, nonspecific, and incomplete in their approach and results. The virtual absence of training in diagnosis and of models of diagnosis in use leads us to conclude that teachers are relatively unqualified to diagnose and to plan instruction based on needs (Gil, March 1980).

In an attempt to learn whether diagnostic skills could be easily learned and applied by teachers, Gil and others at Michigan State University designed a training program. Their conclusion was that teachers can be trained successfully in diagnostic model strategies and remedies; and, in a relatively brief span of time, teachers can develop consistency in their diagnosis of and prescription for learning (Gil et al., January 1980). Let us now examine the complex dimension of diagnosis as we currently understand the field.

Cognitive Readiness

Global Measures

Students who are passed from one grade or course to the next are presumed to have mastered at least minimal cognitive requirements of that grade or course. However, the courts are filled with lawsuits initiated by parents against school districts for failing to teach their children minimal skills. Courts have tended to support parents and their indication of the failure of schools to guarantee certain learning outcomes within grades and courses. The back-to-the-basics movement and tough promotion standards are backlash attempts to demand a correction in schooling practices. School achievement scores on standardized tests have emerged as a central measure of schooling success. While many clamor for more than the basics, a public focus on the basics is likely to continue until achievement norms are raised everywhere for all students.

Global measures of achievement by grades and schools serve two purposes: (1) to identify program strengths and weaknesses by pinpointing areas in need of alteration or applause, and (2) to assign students to general skill groups for similar levels of instruction.

Standardized tests provide a teaching staff with a norm for *diagnosing* their *programs* and learning results against a national norm. Test results are descriptive in that samples of universal concepts are tested and reported in aggregate terms. Moreover, standardized tests enable a staff to assess pupil progress in groups and to assess which concepts and skills are mastered. Global measures of student achievement are useful in decision making for program modifications and new program design, for necessary instructional materials, and for assessing instructional effectiveness.

Criterion-referenced tests report the *degree of student mastery* in comparison to a defined standard. The district's program typically describes in more detail the nature of learning outcomes it expects from each program. Popham (1977, 259) advocates local development of criterion tests, for only then can local program emphasis be measured. Criterion-referenced tests monitor learner performance and determine whether mastery has been achieved. The emphasis is not on "poor," "satisfactory," "good," or "excellent" ratings, but rather criterion tests report mastery versus nonmastery against the district standard.

Both norm-referenced and criterion-referenced tests provide a dual check system for a school. The norm-referenced tests provide indicators of school performance in basic skills as measured against a national norm. Criterion-referenced tests provide indicators of local program effectiveness as well as measures of group mastery. Both measures are barometers for identifying strong and weak programs, and, in addition, assist teachers in assigning students to various levels of program difficulty.

Individual Measures

Individual diagnosis permits teachers to assign students to appropriate levels of program difficulty, especially in the basics, and subsequently to teach for mastery.

Many programs, such as math, foreign languages, beginning reading, and physics, require a sequence of learning tasks. Diagnosis of prerequisite skills for sequential learning tasks is relatively simple. Generalized entry measures can be determined, for example, through tests of reading comprehension and arithmetic processes.

Following diagnosis of a student's cognitive entry behaviors, continuous formative feedback measures are necessary during the learning process to enable a student to master a task and to proceed to the next level. If each task is mastered, the mastery of subsequent tasks is more or less routine. If initial tasks are not mastered prior to assignment to the next task, learning becomes increasingly difficult, and the gap becomes increasingly wide between entry behaviors and assigned tasks. There is a predictive relationship between cognitive entry behaviors and achievement, for cognitive entry behaviors are causal links in accounting for achievement (Bloom 1976, 68). Entry behaviors are descriptive of a learner's history; those same behaviors are alterable through remediation. If a student is diagnosed as not quite ready, the teacher's task is to remediate until entry skills are mastered; only then is the learner ready to proceed with identified task assignments.

Early achievement in school has a powerful effect on later achievement in school. In a review of studies Bloom (1976, 39–40) notes that two-thirds of the variance in eleventh grade achievement was predictable from third grade achievement; 81 percent was predictable from the seventh grade. In the first grade, children with a large vocabulary have considerable advantage over others in learning to read (an entry behavior). Likewise, in arithmetic, the knowledge of numbers acquired earlier appears to be a consistent predictor of achievement in first grade arithmetic (p. 45).

The task for a principal and staff is to select or develop tests that measure cognitive entry behaviors for all courses. Textbook publishers have become increasingly helpful in recent years, but are still relatively unclear about defining *prerequisites* of courses, such as the prerequisites to algebra, to physics, and to first grade reading.

Affective Readiness

Observation of a student often yields reasonable estimates as to the affective condition of the learner, with respect to a specific task, to schooling in general, to peers and adults, and to himself or herself. Interests, motivation, attitude, and self-concept all are more or less observable, and all have some relative influence on achievement. Affect is another causal link in determining learning and accounting for educational achievement (Bloom 1976, 104).

Bloom (1976, 104) analyzed learner affective entry characteristics as they relate to three aspects of schooling: (1) subject-related affect, (2) school-related affect, and (3) academic self-concept. Only 10 to 17 percent of the variation in a learning task is due to the positive or negative affect a student has toward a particular subject. However, 20 percent of the variation is accounted for by the student's perceptions of failure or success in school learning tasks in general. Over time, approval and disapproval by parents and teachers results in either a positive or negative attitude toward school.

Academic self-concept (ASC) accounts for up to 25 percent of the variation in school learning after the elementary period. ASC, Bloom notes, is the strongest affective measure in predicting school achievement. It is an index of a student's perception of himself or herself in relation to the achievement of other learners in the class, and is based on feedback through grades and tests by teachers, parents, and peers about school work. Academic self-concept is cumulative, correlating with achievement only after the elementary grades. This finding strongly suggests that attitudes toward self emerge over time and result from a history of success or failure, or disapproval. ASC correlates more highly with teachers' grades than with achievement scores; the cumulative effect of such judgments is an academic self-concept.

The importance of the academic self-concept to mastery suggests that teachers provide numerous and continuous opportunities for success and recognition. High achievement increases positive affect which in turn influences achievement; low achievement decreases positive affect which depresses achievement further (p. 103).

Self-concept in general is developed through interactions with persons who are important to a student, interactions influencing future behavior (Brookover 1964). Self-concept in general can be altered through changes in academic performance and academic self-concept.

Altering Affective Characteristics

Growth is far more complex than working toward a goal. Attitudes about the goal, about the learning context, and about self all influence the level of motivation and ultimate success. Maslow (1962) observes that growth takes place when the step forward seems more joyous and satisfying than the previous gratification with which a person may have become familiar or bored. The new experience is self-validating. We grow forward when the delights of growth and the anxieties of safety are greater than the anxieties of growth and the delights of safety. Assured safety permits higher needs and impulses to emerge and to grow toward mastery. Only under the impact of danger, threat, failure, frustration, or stress does the learner regress or fixate. Safety for growth is essential.

Assessing the affective characteristics of a learner can reveal the safety level and concomitant readiness for particular learning activities. Note the following informal and formal diagnostic procedures (adapted from Gephart et al. 1976, 96–97, reprinted by permission of Phi Delta Kappa, Inc.,© 1976):

1. *time*—the amount devoted to a task is often a reflection of interest
2. *verbal expressions*—to elicit preferences can be assessed by using Likert scales, semantic differentials, and opinionnaires
3. *fund of information*—a certain kind of student task may reflect attitude and be observable over time
4. *reaction time*—to certain tasks or decisions may indicate either a positive or negative interest
5. *written expressions*—provide a self-revealing record about the structure and dynamics of a person's life. Analyze autobiographies, diaries, records, letters, journals and compositions to identify attitudes
6. *sociometric measures*—indicate social preferences and distances
7. *observations*—of behavior provide cues to attitude and self-perception
8. *specific performance*—can demonstrate certain affective characteristics directly

9. *simulation*—provides worthwhile information about affective dimensions
10. *dialogue*—with a learner gives both overt and covert clues to interests, motivation, and self-concept

Additional inventory options include open-ended inquiry, use of interest inventories, forced-choice preference (Kuder Preference Record and Minnesota Vocational Interest Inventory), observation of free play, analysis of artwork, observation of selection, notice attentiveness or distractability, and observing decreases or increases in attendance, vandalism, drug use, home problems, and peer and school problems. By using a network of assessment techniques, a picture can be identified of a learner's relatively stable affective characteristics as they relate to motivation, interests, attitudes, and self-concept. After diagnosis, the next teacher task is to translate collected data into a plan for either remediating or reinforcing affective entry characteristics.

Instructional Responses

If a student has a history of failure or frustration in relation to school learning, either specific or general, the obvious teaching objective is to alter the student's self-perception. Listed here are a few options for reversing negative self-images and preparing a student psychologically for success:

1. Identify student interests and incorporate those into skill-specific learning experiences.
2. Identify a student skill that is unrelated to the curriculum. Invite the student to teach the skill to other students and teachers.
3. Identify prerequisite learning tasks, and reinforce and recognize success for each step toward mastery.
4. Assign nonlearning task responsibilities, and reinforce and recognize desired performance.
5. Assign students to learning teams where peer coaching and task completion occurs cooperatively.
6. Assign students to nontask work groups where cooperative working is expected.
7. Assign a student to tutor a younger student in an area of either difficulty or expertise for the older student.
8. Invite the student to share skills, either old or new, with others.
9. Organize group work where students learn the following collaborative skills:

    to listen to others

    to accept and respect others

    to understand others

to identify and express one's feelings
to become aware of the feelings of others
to experience being accepted by peers
to recognize commonalities
to explore oneself in a context (Berman and Roderick 1977, 173–174)

By altering the patterns of both actual and perceived failure a student is able to begin a winning pattern. The teacher's task is to diagnose affective characteristics and to create an environment whereby affective deficiencies are altered and become positive motivators for student success.

Learning Style

Cognitive style and learning style are concepts that describe how different individuals process information and also respond to environmental stimuli. Learning style cuts across readiness and skill levels and describes individual response patterns that remain relatively stable over a lifetime. Scholars focus on one or many dimensions of style and tend to describe differences and similarities in different ways. Styles help to explain the qualities that guide a person's approach to learning in any situation.

Learning style appeared in the research literature as early as 1892 (Keefe 1979, 4). Researchers were interested in finding the one best perceptual mode for increasing learning. By 1947 Allport coined the term "cognitive style," referring to the adapting influence of personality types. During the 1940s and beyond, Thurston, Guilford, Asch, Witkin, Holtzman, Gardner, and Kagan all developed conceptualizations of how cognitive styles predictably guide a person's response to situations. Learning style and cognitive style focus attention on the ways in which people process and respond to experiences.

For our discussion, two categories have been arbitrarily designated for describing cognitive processing and environmental responses: the former an internal response pattern, and the latter an external response pattern.

Cognitive Processing Characteristics

The focus of cognitive psychology is on the processes by which sensory input is transformed, reduced, encoded, stored, recovered, and used (Singer and Gerson 1979, 222). The manner in which a person engages in various processes is a major determinant of individual differences in acquiring a skill.

Guilford (1967) observed that only a small number of 120 intellectual processes that he has identified are used in schools. Traditional classroom activities typically are "convergent," that is, they rely primarily on memorization, simple recall, deductive reasoning, and simple application of known facts. Very little in schools requires "divergent" thinking, that is, generation of information, variety, and creativity.

A characteristic problem for right-brain-dominant students, for example, is the persistent teacher use of multiple-choice tests. Right-brain-dominant students tend to view every answer as possible if modified slightly; and no answer as perfect. The left-brain-dominant-student, however, can more readily distinguish a "best" answer. Consequently, the left-brain-dominant student is at an advantage because he or she is taking a test in a preferential style. The right-brain-dominant student will succeed better in essays, verbal activities, or demonstration kinds of testing situations.

The diagnostic task is to identify the dominance or preference of each student and then to design learning and testing options in a variety of ways. No person ever functions only out of the left or right hemisphere, however. Right-brain persons often develop skill in the left brain activity of planning, for example, to balance the nonlinear patterns of their dominant cognitive responses. Left-brain-dominant persons often develop skill in music or art to develop their right-brain potential and to add richness to the left-brain tendencies. Each individual needs to develop a balance between hemispheres and profit from their separate contributions to the functioning of the whole person.

Cognitive style, rather than learning style, refers to information processing tendencies or habits representing the learner's typical mode of perceiving, thinking, problem solving, and remembering (Messick and Kogan 1963). Letteri (1977) observed that a significant relationship exists between a child's cognitive style and his or her ability to perform in school. Listed here are several approaches to conceptualizing cognitive styles.

Impulsive Versus Reflective Thinkers (Jerome Kagan 1964).   Impulsive thinkers are those who have a fast conceptual tempo and tend to respond quickly. Reflective thinkers are those who prefer to evaluate answers in more detail and to give only correct responses.

Analytical Versus Thematic Thinkers (Kagan 1969).   Analytic thinkers are uncomfortable with open-ended questions but delight in responding to questions step by step. Thematic thinkers thrive on the global aspects of issues and often are frustrated by a step-by-step approach.

Field Independence Versus Field Dependence (Witkin et al. 1977).   People have a tendency to perceive either analytically or globally. The field independent person makes judgments independent of field constraints while the field dependent person is influenced by the context. The dependent person tends to be people oriented, uses social cues, and is less analytical. The independent person is nonabstract and impersonal, and provides his or her own structure.

Conceptual Differentiation Versus Compartmentalization (Gardener and Schoen 1962; Messick and Kogan 1963). Those who conceptualize differentially tend to conceive of things having many properties, rather than a few. Compartmentalizers are inclined to place concepts in discrete and often rigid categories.

Cognitive Complexity Versus Simplicity (Harvey et al. 1961; Scott 1963). A highly complex style is multidimensional, attracted to diversity and conflict, while a low complexity style prefers consistency and regularity.

Diagnosing Cognitive Style

The field of cognitive style is still relatively new. Consequently, few instruments exist to measure cognitive style, and those few that exist are inconsistent in their findings. For example, Thompson, Finkler, and Walker (1979) conducted a study of five cognitive style tests to determine their relationship to college student achievement and other student characteristics. The result of their study revealed that only the Group Embedded Figures Test (GEFT), which is a group bipolar measure of field independence/dependence, demonstrated consistent and meaningful relationships to the choices of college majors and the grade point average. None of the other measures related consistently to educational outcomes.

Until the field of cognitive style becomes more mature, the task for the principal and teacher is to become generally aware of student differences in processing information and to offer a wide variety of learning options for all cognitive styles. As was mentioned earlier, Fitzgerald (1977) reorganized her 600-pupil elementary school on the basis of diagnosing student field independence and dependence tendencies. Students were assigned to six different kinds of instructional settings on the basis of test results and conferencing with parents, teacher, and student. After six months of the program only a handful of parents wanted their children reassigned; a useful match was made between style and learning environment.

The following example provides guidelines for conceptualizing learning activities for the two brain preferences (McCarthy 1981). This example illustrates different kinds of teacher decisions based on cognitive style differences.

Left-Brain Mode

Primary   Phonics, decoding, breaking down words into parts

Intermediate   Lecture on the stages of insect growth

Middle School   Lecture on probability, sample space, odds, and so on

High School   Lecture and readings on socioeconomic problems, intellectual currents of the period

Right-Brain Mode

Experience stories, context clues, configuration clues	*Reading*
Give partners their own live grasshoppers to observe; include drawing assignments, naming their grasshoppers, and so on	*Science*
Have the children test each other for ESP, using the Duke University cards and guestimating the cutoff for probability of ESP ability	*Mathematic Probability*
Groups plan a trip West on horseback: maps, supplies, obstacles, campfire conversation. It is 1850. (Use newspapers on microfilm 1845–1850 in area libraries.)	*Social Studies*

Environmental Preferences

Many arguments are launched over appropriate environments and appropriate behavior. Some believe "appropriate" means no extraneous sound, low light, cool temperature, and working at desks. Others define appropriate environments as bustling with activity, bright light, warm temperature, and working on the floor, chair, or whatever fits the mood. Many others prefer neither the first nor second example noted, but rather prefer a different configuration of those same environmental conditions.

Gregorc (1979) defines learning style as "distinctive behaviors which serve as indicators of how a person learns from and adapts to his environment. . . ." He further notes that every environment places demands upon individuals for adaptation. Learning styles are both hypothetical constructs and accessible characteristics that can guide teachers in unlocking "best fits" between a person's style preferences and the teaching/learning conditions.

Dunn and Dunn's (1975, 77–81) inventory describes four discrete attributes of learning style, one of which identifies elements of environmental preferences. They note that sound, light, temperature, and design are all elements of the environment that cause varied responses from learners.

Concluding Comments (Task Set 2)

Determining and then acting upon the readiness and style characteristics of the learner can account for the major variance in student achievement. Cognitive readiness for a set of tasks can be learned in general terms through standardized and criterion-referenced global measures, and in specific terms by discussing particular prerequisite skills. Affective readiness is most critically measured in procedures to reveal academic self-concept, which can be formed and altered in the classroom. The ways in which students process information, problems, and experiences are indicators of style strengths in the learning process. Adapting programs to cognitive dominance, particularly to right and left brain preferences enhances the probability of student mastery. Environmental preferences also influence how and the extent to which learners attend to their tasks. Diagnostic information can aid a teacher in planning a best fit between program content, type of learning activities, and environmental conditions and the achievement gains that are anticipated.

Teacher Task Set 3: Program Planning

Program planning for many teachers is little more than following the outline in a textbook. If programs are to reflect learning needs and interests, however, instruction requires far more than assigning students to prepackaged programs. A connection must be made between the learning standards (district curriculum) and the needs and interests of certain students. Our contention is that teachers are the decision makers in program planning, linking curriculum objectives with student needs and a program of study, some of which may be standardized materials.

Research in program planning reveals one consistently effective practice: cooperative teacher planning. Beyond this basic variable, little is known about what elements constitute an effective plan. Hence, the process presented in this section functions as a guide to conceptualizing the planning task.

The first planning question is to determine the differences between the curriculum and the program. The function of the *curriculum* is to guide teacher planning for *student learning outcomes.* Curriculum objectives tend to be broad, rather than specific, but describe learning outcomes nevertheless. The *program* defines ways in which students will master the general outcomes. An analogy might be to again consider the curriculum as the skeleton, whereas the program is the muscle, flesh, and life force that enables the objectives to have meaning for students.

As an example, let us use again the group of elementary students interested in Indian migration throughout North and South America. The teacher task would be to select basic curriculum objectives that can be met in the process of learning about Indian cultures. The elements in the program plan would

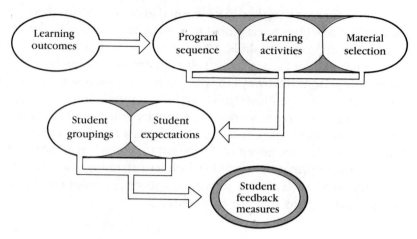

Figure 10.4. Learning Program Design Variables

include the activities, materials, methodologies, student expectations, and sequences that link the program theme (Indian migration) to the particular curriculum objectives. Figure 10.4 outlines basic program planning elements, each of which will be discussed briefly in this section.

Variable 1: Learning Outcomes

Curriculum objectives specify general *learning outcomes* rather than instructional plans. In making program decisions teachers plan experiences that are likely to connect student interests and needs to objectives within a context of viewing a particular set of concepts. Skills are not learned effectively in isolation from real life experiences; the relationship of skills to an immediate purpose stimulates learners to engage in activities.

The term *program objective* refers to a cluster of learning expectations that might evolve from only one curriculum objective. Figure 10.5 outlines the relationship of program objectives to the curriculum, the program, and the learner.

Objectives are not isolated learning expectations, but rather a cluster of expectations that relate to a standard, to the group, and to individuals within the group; all are interrelated and interdependent.

Writing objectives is difficult conceptually, even though the outcomes may seem clear. Davies (1981, 137) provides a useful approach to conceptualizing "objectives." He suggests three parts: *Conditions* identify the specific context of learning, that is, the parameters and limitations. *Performance* identifies the particular behavioral manifestation of learning within a particular program

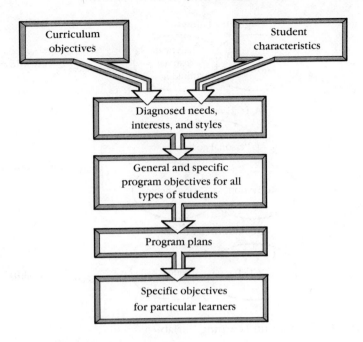

Figure 10.5. Program Learning Objectives

content. *Criterion* defines the quality and specifies standard procedures, or the degree of accuracy or time constraints.

Objectives for each domain.   Learning results from a set of activities that engage cognitive (knowledge), affective (motivation), and behavioral (skills) dimensions of human growth. Program objectives must address all three dimensions. As general and specific program objectives are written, the needs of each learning domain can be addressed adequately using the guidelines in Figure 10.6.

Variable 2: Program Sequence

The next task is to conceptualize the many parts of the program and to sequence the parts into time parameters. The program might be planned for four weeks, each week focusing on one of the program dimensions. After decisions have been made about the general program plan and sequence, learning activities can be identified. It is important to consider a general learning process when defining sequence. Learning requires more than going through various activities; activities must be selected that seem likely to facilitate the mastery process at each stage.

Learning is a process that occurs sometimes in clearly identifiable steps, and

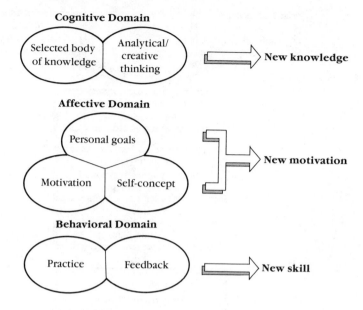

Figure 10.6. Program Learning Variables

at other times in quantum leaps. One cannot anticipate when the leaps will occur and for whom. Therefore, it is important to plan activities that will facilitate an incremental growth process. Not every student will need to experience all of the planned activities for mastery to occur; some will need more or less than others.

Variable 3: Selecting Learning Activities

To prepare the activities for a program that go beyond reading the text, writing papers, and listening to the teacher, many other options should be considered for engaging the learner.

Group Investigation

Student task groups study various aspects of the program.

Laboratory Approach

Individual students manipulate materials and explore environments to increase their understandings and skills in a specific area.

Learning Center

Instructional display areas where educational tasks are organized for the learner with specific objectives in mind, along with established procedures for tasks and for evaluation.

Simulation

Teachers conduct problem situations and/or games for students in which pupils play roles and respond to relevant but "safe" situations with an eye toward subsequent transfer of learning.

Discovery

Guided discovery can provide an opportunity for students to practice analyzing and solving problems through individual and group inquiry.

Performance-Based Learning Activity Package

Learning activity packages enable students to achieve learning outcomes through a set of sequential individual paper-and-pencil activities.

Independent Study (IS)

A strategy for individualizing instruction, IS encourages full use of a wide variety of situations and resources.

Group Building Project

Group responsibility for designing one product together teaches skills of cooperation and shared productivity.

Student-Designed Learning Center

Students study one dimension of the program for the purpose of teaching other students to learn certain concepts. A set of criteria guides students as the plan for an effective learning center: pre- and post-tests, activity sheets, materials, maps, 3-D demonstrations. Students become both learners and teachers during the class project.

Student-Designed Learning Stations

Given a specific focus, students design miniclasses for peers in their specialty area. Students develop a presentation, learning activities, use audiovisual materials, and provide posttests in their learning station.

Discussion

Students profit from sharing ideas and entertaining the ideas of others. Discussion with teacher and/or peers allows individual concepts to become refined and expanded.

Drill and Practice

Students engage in a repeated activity to enable them to retain specific information.

Role Play

Situations are designed to enable students to act out a role according to a basic script. This aids in the understanding of human problems and dilemmas.

Debates

Activites are designed to permit students to study and defend a particular position against those with opposing views. This kind of experience aids in understanding the complexities of human problems.

Lecture

A presentation provides students with basic information that will aid in subsequent learning activities.

Games

Games allow students to pool abilities and knowledge while working and competing with given concepts. Group decisions are often better than individual; the process promotes cooperation as well as healthy competition and also practice and skill building with given concepts.

Audiovisual Materials

Technology provides alternative modes for gathering information and solving problems for a limited number of students.

Computer Instruction

Computers provide specific predefined information as well as opportunities for skill building and problem solving around a particular concept or task.

Teachers consider all the ways students can learn about social conditions of the Incas and Mayans, for example, economic conditions, political conditions, and scientific conditions. The group can brainstorm and analyze a list of possible activities and select the most feasible for a particular study.

Variable 4: Selecting Materials

A problematic task for teachers is selecting specific instructional materials other than the basic text to help develop concepts and skills. The practice of materials selection needs to facilitate learning and address learning styles and readiness levels.

Materials that can function as teaching/learning tools can be gathered from other areas in the school (science lab, library, shop, gymnasium), from donations from local businesses and industries, and from common household items students themselves can bring in. Student skill building can also be enhanced through the use of computers, audiovisual equipment, art supplies, and so on.

The selection of materials ought to be based on a principle of balancing book learning with activity learning, balancing right- and left-brain activities, and balancing real life problems with conceptual understandings.

Variable 5: Selecting Student Groups

One of the most striking features of the research on effective teaching is the power of cooperative student task groups to facilitate growth. Cooperative learning among students is more effective than individualistic or competitive activities for many kinds of learning outcomes (Johnson 1981). Cooperative student work groups are likely to replace many of the lonely, unstimulating, and "flat" learning activities in classrooms.

Teachers generally gear their instruction to the total class (Wright 1980, 185–187). Students rarely work on different levels or from different instructional materials, and they tend to work in isolation from peers, most of the times from materials selected by the teacher. Little, if any, grouping for instruction and individualization occurs in classrooms. Students function as independent learners who are dependent on teachers for most of the necessities of classroom life. And yet research provides clues that cooperative learning groups promote far greater achievement than competition, isolation, and individualization. Johnson (1981, 7) reports from his analysis of 122 studies comparing the relative effects of cooperation, competition, and individualistic effort, that cooperation is considerably more effective in promoting achievement and productivity. These results hold for all ages and all subject areas for tasks involving concept attainment, verbal problem solving, categorizing, spatial problem solving, retention and memory, motor performance and guessing-judging-predicting. He further notes that cooperative learning experiences promote greater cognitive and affective perspective taking and are more related to high levels of self-esteem and psychological health, than are noncooperative experiences.

Teacher planning for instructional grouping requires assessment of student needs levels and interests, which are subsequently translated into program task groups. Some groups are formed for skill building and probably should be homogeneous. Other groups are formed around interests and learning styles; again there is an element of homogeneity. In assigning other groups, however, it is important to consider the positive effect of grouping by different ability. Swing and Peterson (1982, 271) found that the various achievements of high- and low-ability students especially were facilitated by learning in small heterogeneous groups. Consequently, groups in general should reflect a range of abilities, skills, and interests.

Grouping students depends on a number of interacting variables that are isolated for particular purposes throughout a unit or course of study. If coop-

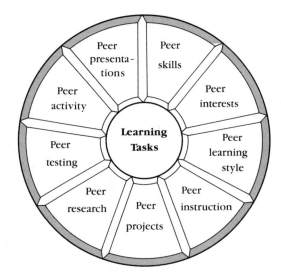

Figure 10.7. Student Groupings

eration is the new international worker norm, then student groupings should provide skill-building opportunities for students to work productively with each other. Figure 10.7 outlines several grouping options: skill, interest, learning style, projects, peer research, testing, activity, and presentation.

Variable 6: Define Student Expectations

Human learning is motivated primarily by personal interests and goals. It seems reasonable to assume, therefore, that students in school ought to practice making choices within a structure of options. Furthermore, if self-concept is built by making correct choices and succeeding in those choices, then choice making ought to become routine for students. However, the majority of students surveyed in Goodlad's study of schooling (Wright 1980, 115) reported that they played no role in classroom decisions regarding what they did or learned. Selection was offered to students more often in nonacademic courses, however, than in the academic courses.

Planning for student performance is far broader than deciding "what" students will do. Specific learning results are the objective for all instructional activities. What, then, are the learning outcomes expected for each group, for each task? If teachers want students to make choices, they themselves need to be clear about the parameters for student choice. Program decisions necessarily fall into a number of categories (see Figure 10.8).

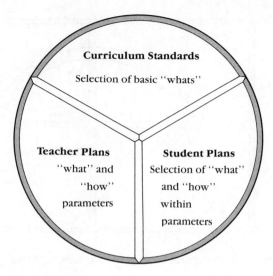

Figure 10.8. Program Decision Levels

Student Contracts

One of the most useful mechanisms is the student contract. A contract is an agreement between a student and teacher that specifies what will be learned, tasks to accomplish, and deadlines. Each party makes certain decisions; the teacher defines choice parameters and the student selects or identifies specific choices for individualizing learning. Volumes have been written about how to prepare contracts; however, contracts often become merely a teacher information sheet given to the entire class. Used appropriately, contracts can guide student performance at various levels and for various purposes in a manner that fosters responsibility, independence, cooperation, and success.

Contracts can be conceptualized in four stages and prepared according to teacher perception of the degree of structure required for a student to become successful. Some students flourish if given minimal guidance, while others would fail under the same guidelines. A contingency approach to decision making provides a useful framework for selecting choice options in a contract (see Figure 10.9). Some students require a high degree of structure to succeed. Others require less structure to succeed. In the converse, too much structure restrains some students, while too loose a structure causes some to become immobilized.

A student's need for high or low structure has little to do with intelligence, ability, or mastery level. The determining factor is the student's learning style. Some learners need greater degrees of structure than others, a characteristic that remains relatively constant throughout a person's lifetime. A teacher who

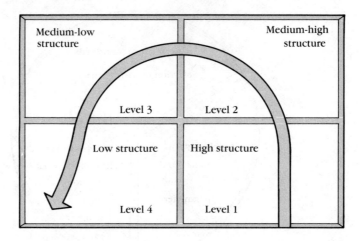

Figure 10.9. Task Structural Variables: Learning Style Requirements

is observing for cues to structural needs will soon determine which students succeed with which kinds of structure. The following list outlines teacher contract decision levels for each kind of learner.

Student Needs for Structure

1. High Structural Need Students
   Teacher Decisions:
       set all objectives
       list all learning activities
       decide materials
       assign student groupings
       define time lines
       provide feedback
       define evaluation criteria

2. Medium-High Structural Need Students
   Teacher Decisions:
       set all objectives
       list all learning options; student selects several
       list all materials; student selects several
       recommend student groupings
       define time lines
       define evaluation criteria
       teacher/student joint feedback

3. Medium-Low Structural Need Students

Teacher Decisions:

 set most objectives and work criteria
 list learning parameters
 identify major resources
 suggest work group actions
 suggest time lines
 teacher/student/peer feedback
 negotiate evaluation criteria

4. Low Structural Need Students

Teacher Decisions:

 negotiate objectives and work criteria
 negotiate learning options
 delegate resource identification
 delegate work group preference
 negotiate time lines
 delegate feedback resource/provide feedback
 negotiate evaluation criteria

Planning for contracting can appear awesome unless guidelines are used. Typically a teacher can plan four to six levels of contracts rather than 30. Once students receive their level contract they can make their decisions and request teacher approval. Peers can assist each other in providing feedback and correctives while they individually plan their contract. Teachers act only as a final negotiator. After signatures (student and teacher) have been signed, duplicate copies are made. The student uses the contract for daily planning; the teacher uses it for monitoring performance. Consider the following teacher tasks:

1. Determine the objectives for the contract period.
2. Decide the type of contract to be used: levels 1, 2, 3, 4. A responsive teacher adapts learning contracts to fit pupils with both low and high structural needs.
3. Construct the four levels of a contract, incorporating the following six elements:
   a. behavioral objectives
   b. evaluation procedures
   c. resources to be used
   d. tasks or activities to be completed
   e. additional events, checkpoints for student progress
   f. deadlines for task completion

Variable 7: Selecting Student Feedback Measures

Teachers provide feedback and correctives least well of all the instructional variables. Planning for a variety of feedback measures can offset the probability of inadequate teacher response. Listed here are a few examples of feedback options. Selection depends on the learning activity and the perceived response of the student to the feedback measure.

Periodic testing provides information both to student and teacher about learning concepts already mastered.

Peer critique provides immediate peer insight into the quality of progress.

Self-correcting materials provide instant feedback on the quality of work results.

Tutor critique provides outside response to student progress.

Group critique permits a work group periodically to assess its own progress toward its goals, allowing each member to participate in criticism.

Aide critique provides adult perspective on work results.

Self-critique causes periodic reflection of progress.

External adult critique allows outside experts or nonexperts to provide candid feedback on the results of activity.

External peer critique permits students to engage both in analysis of others' work and also to be assisted by a peer group.

"Which" method is selected is not the vital issue; selection itself is critical. Multiple feedback mechanisms are essential for correcting both work patterns and their results, and also for reinforcing and recognizing exemplary performance.

After program decisions have been made for the new unit of study, the entire teaching team critiques and refines each of the seven program plan variables (learning outcomes, program sequence, learning activities, materials selection, student groupings, student expectations, and feedback measures). The result of effective planning is an identifiable plan of learning outcomes, learning options, and expectations. The next task is to make classroom management decisions that will effectively permit students to engage in selected activities in such a way that fosters optimal mastery.

Teacher Task Set 4: Classroom Management

The primary objective in classroom management is to gain and maintain high student involvement in productive activity (Doyle 1981) by establishing a student task system. The focus of classroom management is academic tasks, for that which students learn is a function of tasks performed. The task system guides planning for the structured management of classroom life while teachers guide learning.

In the past, primary attention has been given to teaching activities, rather than to learning tasks. Any disruption in teaching activity has been considered a student behavior problem. In a learning task system, numerous activities are planned to anticipate the variance in learning needs and styles and to best-guess the type of tasks that will facilitate mastery. Hence, the focus of classroom management has shifted from managing deviant behavior to managing a learning task system.

Our assumption is that classroom management is the teacher function that bridges program plans and learning outcomes. Classroom management decisions translate plans into tasks and allow teachers and students to engage productively to facilitate learning. In this sense, a task system enables a teacher to gain the active cooperation of students during the hours of teaching and learning. Figure 10.10 outlines the management decisions, illustrating the interdependent relationship of planning, organizing, motivating, supervising, controlling, and evaluating performance.

The concept of managing students implies that a series of events will occur in a planned manner. Deviant behavior signals to a teacher that modifications in the management system are required for gaining student cooperation. The object of the management function is to design classroom activities so that

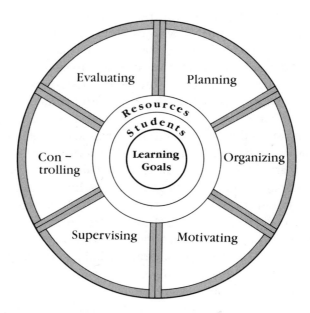

Figure 10.10. Classroom Management Tasks

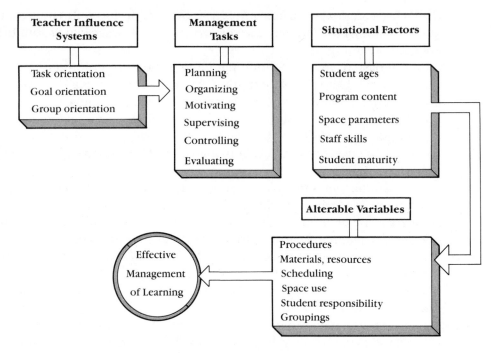

Figure 10.11. Classroom Management Context Variables

maximum learning can occur. Behavior disruption is viewed as a flaw in the management plan, not a flaw in the learner. The learner will respond appropriately when conditions are conducive to his or her learning. The teaching task is to develop options for creating an environment conducive to learning.

We will review selected studies of classroom management to identify known management factors that link with achievement. Each section of the classroom management model is discussed as it relates to student learning. Managing students occurs within a particular social context, however. Consequently, teacher planning, organizing, motivating, supervising, controlling, and evaluating tasks are unique for each situation. The effectiveness of a particular management plan is determined by the degree to which a teacher is able to gain student cooperation during the learning activity. Effective management results from a careful analysis of the context and a corresponding management plan. Figure 10.11 outlines a conceptualization of the context for designing a classroom management plan. Teacher influence systems, management tasks, and situational factors each influence the choice, as well as effectiveness of selected plans (alterable variables).

During teaching/learning episodes, teachers give consideration simultaneously to managing instruction, managing groups, and managing individuals within groups. The managing task is complex, requiring continuous reinforcement or alteration of plans. Actual management is not divided into discrete tasks, such as were outlined in Figure 10.10; rather, it requires immediate teacher responses to situations, drawing from one or several of the management tasks categories. Thus, the six tasks should be viewed as a cluster of variables that are interdependent in influencing the learning process; actual classroom management maintains the conditions for learning.

The Planning and Organization Tasks

The classroom management plan enables students to engage productively in activities. The management plan addresses the question, "What is the plan for implementing the program?" Considerations are given to student behavior expectations, space use, staff roles, use of resources, and a time line. The plan reports how, when, and where students and teachers will interact with each other and with other resources to accomplish specific tasks. Activity structures vary in the extent to which they elicit and sustain cooperation (Doyle 1979, 66). The teaching challenge is to select content, arrangements, and activities that are most likely to elicit the cooperation of the greatest number of students. Appropriate use of this strategy reduces the monitoring load in managing the classroom.

The essence in gaining student cooperation is to connect alternative courses of action (activities) with states of nature (student motivation) in order to facilitate learning outcomes (Doyle 1979, 48). If learning is to result from instruction, then student cooperation must be sustained. To ignore this fundamental concept is to fail to understand the essence of an effective learning environment.

What, then, is the concept of "classroom" if cooperation is the teacher's management task? Goodlad (1979, 401) describes the learning context in ecological terms. Cooperation is gained, he contends, not by passive student compliance with regulations, but rather through shared goals, space, and programs.

Planning for student behavior is a critical variable in managing classrooms. If the teacher places emphasis on the program and the student behaviors necessary for successful performance, a message of purpose and order is communicated to students, which tends to influence their behavior. Successful classroom management begins by creating levels of order and work involvement at the beginning of the year. Three factors have been found to be effective in initial phases of the year: (1) getting started and moving as soon as possible, (2) anticipating and heading off misbehavior, and (3) becoming aware of misbehavior early and stopping it (Emmer, Evertson, and Anderson 1980). Teachers need to anticipate appropriate behavior within programs. In addition, they must communicate their plans and expectations to students throughout the teaching and monitoring activities.

During instruction, some activities place greater demands on teachers for stopping misbehavior. Bossert (1979) found that teacher-centered activities such as recitation or lecture require more effort to stop misbehavior than student-centered activities such as small group work. Recitation activities place teachers at the center of control and cause them to rely more on commands than on personal influence. The greater the student involvement in activity, the easier it is to control behavior through personal interactions.

Workable, clearly defined rules are also characteristic of effective classroom management (Emmer and Evertson 1980). More effective teachers typically have expectations about student call-out, movement around the room, and talk among students, which they translate into procedures for managing behavior. Rules are particularly effective if students perceive them as facilitating successful accomplishment of their own goals (Cohen, Intili, and Robbins 1979). Good and Brophy (1978) recommend that rules be phrased in qualitative terms, rather than in "do's" and "don'ts," and that they be flexible to changes in the situation. A minimum number of qualitative rules will help students to remember the spirit of orderly behavior and enable them to make best guesses for changing situations.

Organizational considerations need to be given to the logistical dimensions of program implementation. The major part of classroom management involves active teacher decision making, which focuses on setting up a functional physical environment, matching curriculum and instruction with student needs, and establishing efficient routines for handling daily housekeeping matters (Brophy 1982, 21). The following list identifies several of the organizational considerations in establishing effective classrooms.

Organizational Decisions

1. *Instructional materials:* types, titles, sources, acquisition variables
2. *Time line of events:* introduction, learning blocks, benchmarks, special events, culminating activities
3. *Subgroup membership:* Student assignment: skill groups, project groups, leadership groups, activity groups
4. *Resources:* People: community members, business, district staff or students, teams. Materials: space, time, and equipment
5. *Record keeping and reporting:* curriculum expectations, diagnosed needs, unit mastery outcomes
6. *Student planning:* Elements of choice: program expectations, student interests, diagnosed needs, choices, and requirements

Transition from one activity to the next often signals the relative effectiveness of a classroom management system. Kounin (1970) found that transitions between activities in effective classrooms were brief and orderly. Teachers who enjoy the cooperation of students are able to accomplish whatever they need to do with minimum time and effort.

Motivating Tasks

Earlier it was noted that human motivation springs from a "desire" to engage in an activity and the belief that such engagement will be successful. Student planning for their involvement in the program provides an opportunity for students to express interests and make choices within a given structure. Student planning is perhaps the greatest motivator for student engagement in tasks, along with positive reinforcement.

A system of consequences that are contingent on certain behaviors, or performance, requires clear identification of acceptable performance in relation to the learning goals. The motivating task is to maintain student engagement in meaningful learning tasks. Reinforcement of appropriate behaviors is likely to increase the frequency of appropriate behavior. However, it is not possible to determine in advance which reinforcer will in fact shape a specific behavior for all students. Some reinforcers have no effect at all in some situations, and yet are quite effective in others. Hence, a reinforcer can be viewed as *anything* that will increase the frequency of a behavior.

Praise is unlikely to reinforce unless it is sincere and adapted to the specific accomplishments in question. Praise must also be adapted to preferences of the individual, and specific in describing what the student did that was praiseworthy (Brophy and Putnam 1978, 53).

Helping students to set and meet personal goals, especially difficult goals, is more effective than monetary incentives in producing high levels of performance (Rosswork 1977). So important is goal setting to students that high school students, in a study conducted by Ware (1978), ranked the opportunity to reach a personal goal first out of 15 potential rewards. And further, rewards such as peer esteem and symbolic recognition were ranked above teacher praise and several other categories of concrete rewards.

Self-reinforcement is especially effective for students who are deficient in achievement motivation. Self-reinforcement techniques are taught to students whereby they recognize and reinforce themselves for progress in achieving their goals (Brophy and Putnam 1978, 73). This phenomenon illuminates one of the advantages of contract systems. Students can set manageable goals and then recognize their own accomplishments throughout the contract period. The key to motivating students in the task system, then, is to involve them in making choices regarding the nature of their involvement.

Supervising and Controlling Tasks

After the management system has been designed and organized, and students have planned their activities, the remaining management tasks are to supervise and control environmental conditions to ensure success. Without effective supervision and monitoring, well-designed plans may not yield desired results. Perhaps the most difficult and most time consuming management task is ongoing supervision and monitoring.

Effective managers keep track of how students are progressing and whether they completed assignments according to the task focus (Emmer and Evertson 1980, 15–16). Ineffective managers tend not to circulate among students during seatwork, and thereby diminish their ability to monitor accurately. Effective managers punish less and are more likely to involve students in their own behavior change, for example, through use of contracts (Brophy 1980).

Teachers often become aggressive because of their inability to cope with specific student behavior. They become harsh when they are unaware of options for altering deviant behavior. Public corrections cause students to lose face, which causes them in turn to become aggressive. Private corrections, however, enable the teacher and student to work out the problem without fear (for teacher and student) of other student reactions. In the same view, individual commands are far more effective than group commands in altering deviant behavior (Lasley 1981).

Academic feedback acts as a stimulant for future actions. Higher amounts of academic feedback and more substantive academic interaction are associated with higher student engagement (Filby 1978). On the other hand, discipline-related feedback is negatively related to engagement rates. Not only is an academic task orientation important to initiating student engagement, but the task orientation is the supervisory-monitoring focus for maintaining task engagement.

Contingency management, which involves principles of reinforcement, enables certain students to maintain their task focus. Systems of consequences usually have several components (Emmer and Evertson 1981). Desired behaviors are clearly identified; students are given subsequent feedback; consequences that are rewarding are used consistently; and undesirable behavior is clearly specified. Students are given specific feedback, and punishment is made contingent on inappropriate behavior. Consequences are effective in managing behavior when used systematically.

The practice of punishment is effective only in limiting undesirable behavior; it does not promote appropriate behavior (O'Leary and O'Leary 1977). Punishment should be used sparingly and teachers should provide alternative means of getting positive reinforcement. Brophy and Putnam (1979, 60) argue that punishment is likely to be effective only when used as a last resort method within a larger problem-solving approach that stresses positive methods. Punishment is likely to be more effective when it follows immediately after a transgression, or when it comes early in a sequence of undesired behavior (Brophy and Putnam 1978). To conclude, punishment is only a partial solution. After the inappropriate behavior has been stopped, a plan for appropriate behavior needs to commence, followed by regular positive reinforcement.

Behavior modifiers are useful in some situations as a transitory solution. Token systems are effective in some situations, for they allow for individual differences in response to various reinforcers, and they allow students to exercise some choices in how they spend accumulated points. Tokens may include physical tokens or symbols that act as an orderly record-keeping system. Contingency contracting allows teachers to make special arrangements with selected students, for it places emphasis on student responsibility. Contracts are useful because they provide a way for students to be responsible for their own time at school (Brophy and Putnam 1978, 69). Contracts often include certain student responsibilities and they provide a needed structure for students who are easily distracted.

Record keeping is a continual process that involves both the student and teacher in accounting and reporting individual growth and learning progress. The purpose of an independent record-keeping device is to encourage student responsibility while keeping the teacher apprised of student task accomplishment. The devices used for record keeping indicate which tasks the student has undertaken and how much has been accomplished. While records show what the student has done, they also help in planning for future learnings.

The teacher and the student share responsibilities for maintaining the records. They also decide which record-keeping instruments and procedures to employ. Record keeping cannot be separated from evaluation; the function of record keeping is to report what has been accomplished. Evaluation tells how well it has been accomplished.

The Evaluating Task

Evaluating the effectiveness of a classroom management task system occurs within the context of assessing achievement gains. The relative student achievement gains provide a broad indicator for determining the effectiveness of the task system. Assessment of learning outcomes provides the context clues for assessing the effectiveness of the task management system.

The process of evaluation occurs in relation to program goals. If there is no goal or objective in mind for the assignment of a task or activity, then it is difficult to make a judgment as to whether or not anything has been accomplished. Students must perceive goals as *purposeful* and *personal* and then they must be involved in planning and setting goals for themselves. In evaluating the task management system, several considerations are appropriate. For example, consider the following:

Program design content integration: assessment regarding such factors as relevance, interest, timing (note: strengths and weaknesses)

Learning outcomes: assessment regarding outcome relevance, measurability, and accomplishment (note: strengths and weaknesses)

Learning environment organization: assessment of space usage patterns in relation to facilitating program

Key events and time line: assessment of relevance of activities and the appropriateness of time allotments

Staff responsibilities: assessment of adequate use of staff strengths, as well as the quality of staff performance in sharing program responsibilities

Student progress reporting system: assessment of the feasibility of the reporting system adequately to communicate learning progress to students and parents

Resources: assessment of strengths and limitations of resources employed/not employed

Task management system: assessment of the feasibility of selected learning tasks and activities to nurture desired learning outcomes

Student record-keeping system: assessment of the feasibility of the record-keeping system adequately to monitor and record student progress

Concluding Comments (Task Set 4)

In summary, effective classroom management is a cluster of management activities that function interdependently to keep students optimally engaged in the learning task system. *Planning* and *organizing* for task involvement include decisions about the varieties of tasks, student grouping for tasks, and a time line of events. Plans also include decisions about student involvement in planning. *Supervising* and *controlling* student engagement in tasks is most effective when teachers are involved continuously in learning activities with students, and when teachers provide positive reinforcements for appropriate task behaviors. Teachers can vary procedures, resources, time, space use, and student groupings as the situation requires modifications. The goals of the program and the task system are the focus for teacher supervision and control as they seek to maintain student cooperation. *Evaluation* processes help to identify the dimensions of the management system that are effective or less than optimal in maintaining student engagement in tasks. This kind of evaluation is distinguished from program evaluation in that its focus is on the management of student engagements in the task system. Together the management tasks function to engage and maintain students in learning activities so that expected learning outcomes will be realized.

Teacher Task Set 5: Teaching for Mastery

Until the beginning of the 1970s, little was known about teacher characteristics or teaching behaviors that were causal links to student achievement. In the early part of the decade, Rosenshine and Furst (1973) and Dunkin and Biddle (1974) reported consistent relationships between two teaching variables and student achievement: a businesslike approach to teaching; and teaching clarity and enthusiasm. A new approach to the study of teaching was launched: identifying causal teaching behaviors in the learning process.

In the decade following, the National Institute of Education funded extensive studies that sought to examine correlates of teaching and learning. The early studies were conducted primarily in urban elementary schools, and in basic core subjects. Those early studies have since been replicated in junior and senior high school settings, providing an emerging clear picture of teaching variables that influence achievement, some of which are appropriate to all age groupings, and others of which are singularly effective.

Brophy (1973, 3–4) summarized a number of correlational studies and arrived at several generalizations about teaching behaviors that influence achievement.

1. *Teachers make a difference.* Certain teachers elicit more student learning than others, and this success is tied to consistent differences in teaching behaviors.
2. There appear to be no generic teaching skills, but rather *clusters of behaviors* that consistently relate to achievement gains.
3. Teachers are successful who define their role in terms of instruction that relates to specific students.
4. Effective teachers organize and maintain a *classroom environment* that maximizes productive learning activity and minimizes transactions, confusion, or disruptions.
5. *Direct instruction* is an effective teaching strategy in the early grades when mastery of basic skills is the goal.

More *interaction* among students and with teachers is important in upper grades, where there is more need for a higher level cognitive activity, more student autonomy, and more concentration on academic activities. However, direct instruction is effective in the upper grades for students who are anxious and dependent, and who are easily distracted, low in ability, and low in achievement motivation (Brophy 1979, 410–412, 414).

From our own review of teacher effectiveness studies, several additional teacher behaviors or characteristics have surfaced that correlate with achievement gains. The most consistent theme among researchers is that *high teacher expectations,* an affective variable, translate into student success. Another theme focuses on the nature of teacher expectations: *cues* and directives; *goals* and clarity about the expectations; and learning procedures. Teacher praise and *reinforcement* encourage learner success, while *feedback* and correctives tend to guide learner activity toward mastery. One senses from the research reports that successful teachers expect students to achieve and then provide a specific structure to nurture student mastery against the expectations. In no study we reviewed was there support for learner isolation from peers and teachers in the learning setting. There was, however, a strong sense that student interaction with teachers and peers was a key variable in a structured and nurturing learning environment.

The effective teacher not only plans and organizes for learning, but is a highly interactive and intervening facilitator throughout classroom life. Effective teachers are similar to effective coaches: they organize the game plan and then are highly visible manipulators of events and behaviors in pursuit of winning the game.

In this volume we have elected to discuss teaching within the framework provided by Dollard and Miller, and Bloom. Significant supporting research provides the justification as well as the validation for using the four-variable teaching model for discussing, examining, and improving teaching. Consequently, we will discuss (1) cues and directives, (2) participation, (3) reinforcement, and (4) feedback and correctives, and how they provide a conceptual and practical model for managing teaching.

One cannot, however, expect to realize effective teaching in a nonsupportive classroom environment. A nurturing climate designed by the teacher(s) is essential for effective teaching. We begin the discussion of teaching by examining classroom climate factors. Then we will explore more fully the interactive nature of cues, participation, reinforcement, and feedback, followed by a brief discussion of each teaching variable.

Classroom Learning Climate

One of the most fundamental concepts in education is that pupil learning is influenced by the climate or environment within which the learning occurs. The physical environment, over some elements of which teachers have a degree of control, can have either positive or negative effects upon a learner's receptivity to the planned educational program. Such factors as the size and design of the classroom (or other instructional) space, the nature and the amount of noise, color patterns, heating and lighting, available furniture and equipment, and the child's ability to fit into and have some control over the physical setting, will influence that child's sense of engagement and belongingness. More significant as environment elements, however, will be the other human beings with whom the child shares the learning area, and with whom the child interacts in the course of each day. Interactions with the teacher(s) in the environment are in many ways the most powerful of the forces that impinge upon the child's ability to grow, in various dimensions, and to learn; and analysis of the teachers' behaviors in such interactions is often a fruitful approach in efforts at improving learning.

Most assumptions about classroom learning are geared to the premise that children seek and need to find security and significance within the educational group to which they belong. Given personal security within the group setting, children can make more effective use of opportunities to develop skills in problem solving, decision making, hypothesis testing, communications, inquiry, venturing, and coping. Learning how to deal with individual and interpersonal anxieties and how to accomplish tasks that grow out of group activity is among the prime needs of children that schools are expected to meet.

Research on the classroom as a social system (Withall 1977) confirms that group members (pupils) are unable to deal adequately with substantive problems *if* anxiety and/or individual feelings of inadequacy are produced or perpetuated in the group situation. Teachers need to assume a "facilitative role that entails encouraging the development of skills of group members for satisfying individual security needs and achieving the group cohesion with which to complete the task" (p. 168).

If teacher behavior during learning activity influences the climate and subsequently the achievement, what then are the behaviors most likely to be effective? Two types of behavior provide substantive assistance: proactive and reactive (Roehler and Duffy 1981, 8). *Proactive assistance* is that which is planned, objective driven, and characterized by active instructional intervention into the learning process. Moreover, proactive assistance is motivated by a belief in the learner's ability to succeed—a belief that is communicated to the student. Teacher cues, highlighting, modeling, drill, and recitation are examples of how the teacher intends to assist students in the learning process. *Reactive* assistance is distinguished from proactive assistance by spontaneous responses to the student during learning activity.

A healthy learning climate is both planned (proactive) and spontaneous (reactive) as teachers assist in the mastery process. There is insufficient evidence, however, to affirm that teachers are, on the whole, succeeding in these facilitative functions. Teachers need assistance in learning how to engage in and demonstrate some "fairly simple interactional skills. These include the learner's participation in decision and policy making; honoring and capitalizing on learners' inputs; and thoughtfully attending to learners' comments, questions, and objections, and communicating a fully acceptant attitude to each learner"

(Withall 1977, 168). Among the most common and observable forms of such communication is talk: how teachers talk to children.

It seems likely that the overwhelming majority of classroom teachers are in general agreement with the premise that a "good" and nurturant classroom climate can enhance learning. Most teachers, as we have observed them and gleaned from their conversations, try to relate to their pupils in ways that foster trust, respect, and caring. An environment characterized by these concepts enhances the probability that learning will occur and students will enjoy a more robust view of themselves as persons as well as learners. However, many teachers, by virtue of their personalities or their pedagogical habits, seem prone to violate these values as they work day by day in classrooms. Often there is a discrepancy between the actual climate that a teacher's words (and associated nonverbal behaviors) may be creating, and what the teacher hopes or believes is happening. With the help of an instrument such as the Withall Social-Emotional Climate Index (SECI), a supervisor or colleague can provide a teacher with useful feedback on the climate he or she produces, as well as guidelines for creating the most conducive climate for student learning.

Teaching Behaviors

Models of school learning, such as that enunciated by John B. Carroll (1963), call for teachers to take the aptitude and prior educational history of each learner into account, to make appropriate provisions for learning experiences, to organize the learning experiences within a suitable time frame, and to utilize evaluation procedures that help both the learner and the instructor to assess results and plan future experiences.

The components of quality instruction (Bloom 1976) include the *cues* or *directives* that are provided to the learner, the opportunities that are provided for the learner to *participate* in appropriate experiences, the *reinforcement* that the learner receives for productive activity, and the *feedback/corrective* mechanisms that operate to inform the learner of progress being made and alternatives that are needed. All of these components are essential, and all are more or less under the control of the teacher.

Elements within each of the four instructional behaviors are summarized in Figure 10.12. Note the interactive nature of the four instructional behaviors. The behaviors, in a sense, are a system that, when provided effectively, impact as a unit on the mastery process and its results. That is to say, all four variables are essential in effective teaching. The absence or ineffectiveness of any one behavior influences the impact of instruction on the learning process. The following list indicates samples of ways in which teachers can plan and provide each instruction variable.

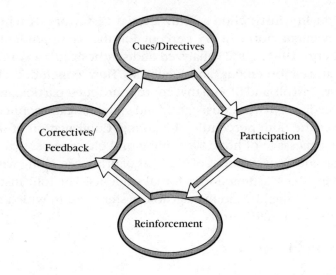

Figure 10.12. Instruction Cycle

Samples of Effective Instructional Behavior

1. *Cues/Directives*
   contracts: individual/group
   learning center procedures
   chalk board directions
   student leader/teacher verbal
   cues
2. *Participation*
   materials
   peer tasks
   small group skills
   student/student
   student/teacher
   produce a product
   practice
   ask/answer
   questions
   demonstration
   reading/writing/production
   teaching
3. *Reinforcement*
   verbal/nonverbal
   recognition
   self-correcting materials
   achievement
   peer
   awards
4. *Feedback and Correctives*
   self-correcting materials
   self-evaluation
   peer observation
   teacher/student conference
   grades
   teacher notes
   verbal messages

Bloom reported to us in a professional conference in 1981 that teachers involved in more recent comprehensive study demonstrated that they could alter the 50 percent norm of achievement significantly by being trained to employ mastery learning techniques (diagnosis, appropriate student placement, and quality instruction). With altered behaviors, teachers realized a new achievement norm of 85 percent for the same students. Lysakowski and Walberg (1981; 1982) analyzed and synthesized 54 studies of cues, participation, reinforcement, and feedback. They concluded along with Dollard, Miller, Carroll, and Bloom that appropriate cues, participation, reinforcement, and feedback, when consistently and systematically applied, can place groups at over the 80th percentile of learning. Confirmation of this magnitude provides a message of hope for schools and classrooms: that through an examination and improvement of four sets of practices, along with diagnosis, teachers can alter learning norms for all students. The four instructional variables provide a tangible and manageable system within which to alter instruction patterns and their results.

Cues and Directives

The precision and the clarity of the information and instructions provided to learners by the teacher have long been regarded as important variables influencing achievement. The early work of Rosenshine and Furst (1973) suggests that if one teacher's instruction is clearer than another's, students of the former will do better on tests than students of the latter. Subsequent research has attempted to address the question, "What skills are necessary in providing clarity?" (Cruickshank, Myers, Moenjak 1975; Kennedy, Cruickshank, Bush, Myers 1978; Land and Smith 1979; Hines 1981).

Once a teacher has determined that the time is at hand for the learner(s) to begin, or to continue, a particular activity or task, the next teaching behavior is to make known to each learner what is expected. In the terminology selected by Bloom, we speak of providing cues and directives to the learner. As used in the theater, the word "cue" refers to words or signals used by a director, prompter, or fellow actor to cause a particular speech or action to take place. Sometimes the term also refers to a hint, a reminder, or a clue that enables the person who receives the message to approach the task with an accurate understanding of what is involved in that task, or at least how to begin. The term "directive," by contrast, carries an implication of more authoritative behavior by the teacher. Expectations are set forth, time lines and procedures are provided, and information is offered regarding work parameters.

Cues and directives must satisfy two related sets of conditions: they must be clear to the students, and they must elicit intended responses (Levin and Long 1981). After receiving instructional goals, a student develops a standard of performance, and subsequently acquires information until the standard is attained (La Porte and Nath 1976). When students are told merely, "do your best," they set performance goals below their capability. On the other hand, when students are required to master a maximum number of goals, their incentive as well as their learning increases.

Cues and directives are used not only to begin a particular activity or sequence but also at many subsequent stages in the learning process. They can be provided verbally, either by being spoken by the teacher or by appearing in some written form. Cues can also be nonverbal, as for example, in the body language of the teacher or in visual, tactile, kinesthetic, or even olfactory stimuli that are provided. Cues can be very subtle or they can be very intense. They can be either *abstract* or *concrete.* They can be presented only once, or they can be repeated thus gaining in *intensity.* Cues can be more or less *meaningful* to each student, depending upon such factors as strangeness versus familiarity, or complexity versus simplicity. Among the conclusions of recent investigations into the usefulness of cues is that *variety* is desirable in order to make certain that the guidance needed by many different kinds of learners will in fact be available to all of them (Bloom 1976, 115–117). Another conclusion, though very tentative, is that about 14 percent of the variance in pupil achievement is accounted for by the qualities of cues (ibid, 119). It would seem that this percentage can be increased as teachers, with the help of supervisors, become more skilled in analyzing the nature, the strength, and the meaningfulness of the cues they are providing to individual students.

Student Participation

As Bloom and others define effective instruction, the quality and the amount of pupil involvement in appropiate tasks have an important bearing on results. The "model of school learning" developed over 20 years ago by John B. Carroll of Harvard University has provided a useful theory upon which various instructional approaches (notably Bloom's Mastery Learning Program) have been based, and which has stimulated a great deal of research concerning "time-on-task." Carroll noted that the degree of learning is reflected in the relationship of the amount of time actually *spent,* to the amount of time *needed* to learn (Carroll 1963). Carroll noted further that opportunity to learn and perseverance in the learning activity are elements of the time spent, whereas aptitude, quality of instruction, and ability influence the time required for learning to occur. Bloom expanded upon these constructs by focusing specifically upon the learner's cognitive and affective readiness, on the one hand, and upon the nature of the instructional situation, on the other. Readiness as defined is meant to include how the learner *feels* about a prospective learning task given his self-definition and his interests, and also how well his prior learning has equipped or prepared him to approach that task.

The reports and summaries of effective teaching research point out that school learning is complex, and, consequently, time-on-task activities require multiple learning options. For example, researchers report that time-on-task is the variable most significantly linked with achievement. Rutter (1979) identified active learning and student responsibilities as correlates of achievement. Berliner and Tikunoff (1976) and Doyle (1980) talk about student engagement in tasks as a correlate of achievement. Stallings (1980) found that interactive time-on-task correlates more highly with achievement gains than noninteractive, strongly supporting the concept of pupil team learning (or colearning) and suggesting important new approaches to time-on-task research.

Concern with time-on-task has two dimensions. First, human energy is precious and time is finite; therefore it is important for children to make the best use of the time they spend in school. Wasted time is not recoverable. Second, there appears to be a strong correlation between time spent concentrated on task, and consequent learning that takes place. Put another way, children who make the best possible use of appropriate amounts of time, toward the accomplishment of educationally significant tasks well suited to their needs and interests, end up as successful learners. While this is not an earth-shaking discovery, since we may safely assume that "sticking to the task" has been an approved behavior in school settings for many centuries, it nonetheless deserves strong emphasis at a time when off-task behavior seems to have become excessive.

Since each child's day in school includes many different kinds of activities, time-on-task can be observed in many different contexts. The teacher up front, directing a whole class activity, is one common context. A class divided into various groups, each engaged in a particular activity (either on its own, or with occasional teacher participation), is another. Said to be the most common pattern, accounting for 60 to 75 percent of instructional time (AASA 1982, 39), is seatwork. Other patterns include individual instruction, mastery learning, and peer interaction. Data concerning the on-task or engagement rate within each context can be very helpful to teachers, not only for clues to the effectiveness of each arrangement but also for clues to the overall instructional management plan.

Some studies have revealed that seatwork is one of the least productive arrangements, even though it makes it possible for the teacher to work with individuals and/or small groups, or to complete routine managerial duties. Furthermore, even when they walk around the room or keep a vigilant eye upon the class, teachers are generally unable to tell how much the children are attending to their assigned tasks. Some research suggests that 70 percent time-on-task is the usual average in seatwork situations, as opposed to 84 percent in whole-class instruction (AASA 1982, 39–40). Data collected by an observer whose vigilance is continuous can help a teacher to know how well a seatwork situation, or a whole-class activity, or one of the other possible arrangements, appears to be working out.

Overt behavior, however, is not always a reliable indicator of the things that may be happening inside a child's head. As teachers we have taken children on field trips to museums, zoos, farms, and factories, and invariably there have been youngsters on the trip who seemed almost totally disinterested, uninvolved, or distracted. However, back at school, to our astonishment, some of these seemingly off-task youngsters became veritable encyclopedias about the exhibits, or the animals, or the factory layout. Sometimes a child who was seen to be reading a book on the field trip bus turns out to have observed more about the area through which the bus travelled than children who, apparently more faithful to the teacher's instructions, kept their faces at the bus windows. Within the classroom, too, a youngster who seems to be daydreaming or fooling around with stuff from his pockets, sometimes turns out to have been very much intellectually involved with aspects of the task, and to have used the time productively. Often, too, a child who at one moment is sitting quietly and who is not apparently filling out an exercise sheet or pursuing the lesson materials, turns out to have been thoughtfully considering the material at hand.

Conversely, behavior that on first glance seems to be on-task may upon closer inspection be totally unrelated to what the teacher intends to occur. Therefore, observers must be careful to watch for appropriate clues, over sufficient time, before concluding that child X is on task and children Y and Z are off task during a given observation.

Elapsed time (the total of time required by a child to achieve mastery) and time-on-task (the extent to which time is "put to good use") are two different time variables about which teachers need information as they manage the instructional program. Time-on-task within a given class period is probably easier to observe and measure than is the appropriate allocation of time for various tasks. It is obvious that in many situations some children are able to complete the task much faster than others, in which case they may be observed to be off-task during the latter part of the period. Similarly, some who are feverishly on-task may well be in trouble because too much is being expected of them within too short a time frame.

Mastery learning approaches are built upon the "timeliness" of each event in the instructional sequence, as well as upon the allocation of appropriate amounts of time to each instructional step. Our concern is primarily with helping teachers to know how much of the allocated time is being put to apparently good use. How much time it will or should take for a given individual to master a certain skill or body of knowledge is not easy to determine in advance, and teachers are constantly engaged in a process of trial and error, child by child, as they seek to plan and manage classroom learning activities efficiently. Assistance in that process, by an observer who can report the extent to which each child or group of children was apparently focused upon the assigned task, can be extremely helpful to teachers.

Some useful clues have been reported from effective teaching studies to shed light on what works to keep students on task and continuously achieving. Increases in achievement have been correlated with the practice of students setting their own learning goals (Rosswork 1977). Further, when students are taught to self-monitor and record daily successes, increases in achievement have been observed (Sagotsky, Patterson, and Lepper 1978).

Teachers also can realize increases in student achievement by planning learning activities that motivate and stimulate student response in a wide variety of ways. In addition, by monitoring, reinforcing, reacting, and correcting throughout classroom time, teachers can learn to increase productive time for students. Interaction among peers and with the teacher is the optimal classroom learning mode. A variety of grouping situations with various levels of student responsibility all have the potential of influencing the nature of student engagement and the learning that results.

Reinforcement

Reinforcement practices are now so much a part of the teacher/scholar repertoire that it is difficult to locate a discussion of core concepts or even recent research validating its importance. Our guess is that Skinner's work provided a foundation of concept, practice, and sufficient research and scholarly attention, that the importance of reinforcement, practice and its significant role in learning permeates the teacher effectiveness reports.

Bloom tentatively reports that appropriate reinforcement accounts for six percent of achievement variance, based on studies dealing with group reinforcement (1976, 120–121). Let us examine a few basic principles of reinforcement theory to provide a backdrop for recent findings from successful classrooms.

Most learning theories agree that reinforcement is a necessary accompaniment to the learning process (Hilgard and Bower 1966). Skinner's work has perhaps been the most influential in eliminating punishment from classrooms and providing more effective strategies for positive reinforcement. With punishment, student misbehavior dramatically drops off, but only temporarily. The behavior subsequently reestablishes itself. Skinner found that systematic reinforcement of a desired behavior often resulted in lasting patterns. Hence, educators translated the concepts of behavior modification through incremental positive reinforcement strategies into several dimensions of classroom life.

Behavior is strengthened, maintained, and weakened by its consequences, a behavioral contingency. Skinner (1969, 7) identified three elements of a behavior contingency: (1) the occasion upon which a response occurs, (2) the response itself, and (3) the consequences. The interrelationships among them are the contingencies. Behavioral control involves the management of contingencies (Luthans and Kreitner 1975, 44). Four behavior modification strategies have emerged: (1) *positive reinforcement* (reinforcement of the desired response, such as praise) (2) *negative reinforcement* (elimination of a negative response, such as withdrawal) (3) *punishment* (punishers that decrease undesired responses, such as admonishment) and (4) *extinction* (elimination of any response to a behavior, such as ignoring).

The success or failure of a particular reinforcement strategy depends on the timing of the contingent consequence. For example, some students may require regular and consistent praise for individual successes; others may require only intermittent recognition. Some students may benefit from systematic withdrawal of negative factors (for example, time at the crisis center); others may never require negative reinforcement. A few students require admonition to help them dramatically to alter their patterns. Punishment often produces an immediate response, which then needs to be followed by positive reinforcement when the desired behaviors are demonstrated. Ignoring certain undesirable responses is likely to cause those responses to cease. If extinction is followed by continuous and then gradual positive reinforcement when the desired behavior is demonstrated, behavior can be managed successfully.

The principles of reinforcement apply to managing social behaviors in the classroom, as well as learning behaviors. The focus in this section is upon how reinforcement facilitates the learning process. Bloom (1980) defines reinforcement as the extent to which the student is rewarded or reinforced in his or her learning. The teacher effectiveness research points to two kinds of reinforcement that facilitate achievement. Rutter (1979) observed that successful teachers provide *praise* to their students. Teachers also monitor student progress and are *reactive* and *corrective* toward students (Berliner and Tikunoff 1976). Further, teachers control learning goals by pacing and providing immediate monitoring (Rosenshine 1979; Doyle 1980). Other studies noted that students monitor their own progress (Sagotsky, Patterson and Lepper 1978), and also reinforce concepts by teaching other students (Peterson, Janecki and Swing 1981).

Peer relationships also reinforce learning outcomes. Interaction among peers is more frequent, intense, and varied than with teachers. Peers learn attitudes, values, information, social patterns, social roles, and acceptable behaviors from each other (Johnson 1981). Cooperative learning activities, consequently, are more effective than those that are individualistic or competitive, in promoting and reinforcing information exchange, tutoring, sharing, trust among students, greater emotional involvement, and commitment to learning. Further, cooperative learning promotes higher levels of self-esteem and psychological health than individualistic or competitive strategies, a variable fundamentally important to academic success.

In the various social sciences as they deal with human behavior, one of the most basic assumptions is that people, and in fact all animals, require and value the psychological reinforcements provided through affirmation, approval, praise, rewards, and other types of satisfactions that are "earned" through succeeding in a particular activity. In the school context, teachers provide students with many different kinds of encouragement, or try to arrange the learning experience in ways that ensure that signals will be given to the learner when things are going well. The provision of such encouragements and rewards is regarded as essential to motivate the learner and ensure his or her continuing participation in the learning process.

A great variation exists among teachers with respect to the types of reinforcement employed, the frequency and the timing of (their) reinforcement behaviors, and the amounts of reinforcement provided to different individuals in their classes. Sometimes teachers provide extrinsic rewards (food, toys, games, stars, money) to children. More often they use verbal expressions, or their nonverbal equivalents, to indicate approval or disapproval. Sometimes teachers find ways to arrange for reinforcements to reach a child by way of classmates or other adults.

Some principals have found it useful, during staff meetings or workshops, to ask teachers to discuss with each other the many different kinds of reinforcements they try to use in their classes. Such discussions can help teachers with relatively limited repertoires of reinforcement devices to become aware of other possibilities. Most researchers who have explored this topic have concluded that teachers need a great deal of help in expanding their repertoires, especially those who deal with learners who come from a wide variety of cultural and social backgrounds (Bloom 1976, 113–114; 119–121).

A major challenge for teachers, as already implied, is that children bring many different histories, interests, and values into the classroom, and they do not respond all in the same ways to the reinforcements teachers habitually provide. Furthermore, not only the *type* but the *amount* of reinforcement needed by children will vary considerably, and teachers need to be made constantly aware of their relative success in meeting this challenge.

Feedback and Correctives

Feedback and correctives are the very core of mastery learning. As a tennis coach provides continuous feedback and correctives to a beginning player or a professional, so the teacher provides a student with information regarding both progress and next steps on the way to mastery. Without the feedback/ corrective teaching variable, we can expect to see the "normal" learning curve continue. With effective feedback and corrective patterns, teachers can expect *all* students to master 80 to 90 percent on final tasks. That is, feedback and correctives enable 80 to 90 percent of all students to master appropriately assigned tasks. And, as students proceed under a mastery teaching framework, successive amounts of feedback and correctives will gradually lessen.

Learning results from multiple sequential efforts, each trial representing either a success or a failure. The learner requires a constant flow of information either to confirm each success or to indicate each error or difficulty that blocks success. One of the teacher's most important roles in the learning process is to arrange, either through personal efforts or through the materials, for the learner to receive feedback that prompts the learner to continue and strengthen correct procedures and to modify or eliminate procedures that pose difficulties. In other words, the process of providing feedback and suggesting correctives where needed enables the learner to make continual adjustments in the ways learning tasks are pursued.

Bloom suggests that the provision of feedback and correctives has a major positive impact upon the amount and quality of learning, especially when corrective procedures are provided quickly where they are needed so that errors are not compounded. One of the major conclusions from the studies of mastery learning is that a system that provides feedback to the teacher and to students can reveal any errors that are being made shortly after they occur. If appropriate correctives are promptly introduced as needed, the learning program can move forward with a minimum of errors and consequent positive learning effects (Bloom 1976, 212).

Summative testing, which typically results in the only feedback students receive, offers a judgment about the extent to which a student has mastered a task. Most often, students are assigned a task and graded on their results. Summative judgments in this sense are final, and are not viewed as information for a student to use en route to mastery. Formative testing, by contrast, serves a different function: it provides an information exchange on the road to mastery regarding progress. Feedback assumes a standard of performance and provides evidence of progress and corrective procedures (Levin and Long 1981, 15–16). Consequently the feedback/corrective process causes a teacher to shift emphasis from final-judgment behaviors to helping behaviors in the mastery process.

A significant amount of research supports the feedback/corrective process, a practice that only a few teachers employ regularly. Rutter (1979), Berliner and Tikunoff (1976), Stallings (1980), Rosenshine (1979), and Block (1970) all report that feedback and corrective teacher behaviors are positively correlated with achievement. So powerful is this set of behaviors that Bloom asserts that feedback and correctives enable students to arrive at a mastery status of 80 percent. Cues, reinforcement, and participation account for perhaps 20 percent of the variance in learning; the addition of feedback and correctives raises the influence to 25 percent. The presence of feedback/corrective behaviors near the end of each task will enable 80 percent of the students to have the necessary prerequisite skills for the next task. In a mastery process students build on skills with fewer gaps between tasks if teachers provide feedback and correctives during each task.

Zahorik (1968), found 180 different types of feedback behaviors, but observed that teachers only use 15 of them. Many of these are criticism behaviors that hinder the learning process. Feedback and corrective behaviors that are approving in nature are likely to improve learning and performance. The literature seems clear: if students are deprived of standards, feedback, and correctives, some may learn well, but many will accumulate errors and achieve much less than they might. Feedback, followed by opportunities to make alterations, significantly improves the chances for success.

Models of Teaching

In the coming decades it will be increasingly important to assist teachers in moving beyond the norm of direct-instruction behaviors. Bruce Joyce has identified 80 distinct models of teaching being used throughout the country, each of which facilitates mastery of some identifiable outcome, and each of which is based on some defendable theory of learning and developing. Joyce (Joyce, ASCD 1978) categorized the models into four distinct families, each focusing on a unique dimension of human growth:

1. *Social-interaction models* focus on processes by which students learn to negotiate their reality. The emphasis is on relationships and how to develop interaction skills and to work productively in society.
2. *Information-processing models* focus on how students handle various types of environmental stimuli. Some models focus on problem-solving skills and others emphasize concepts and information derived from academic disciplines. The emphasis in all models is placed on social relationships and self-development through intellectual functioning.
3. *Personal models* focus on self-development, emphasizing the processes by which individuals construct and organize their reality. Concern in these models primarily is for an individual's emotional development, helping students to develop healthy relationships with others and with their environment.
4. *Behavior modification and cybernetic models* emphasize changes in observable behavior that result from efficient shaping of behaviors through reinforcement and by sequencing learning tasks. Behavior modification is the term applied to teaching models in this family, due to an emphasis on changing observable behavior.

As principals work with teachers to develop their skills in climate building, cues, reinforcement, participation, and feedback, they can also draw on this rich array of effective teaching models, all of which employ Bloom's four instructional variables. As classroom life reflects transforming action in the decades ahead, it is our fervent hope that emphasis will be given to teacher development in the four basic skills of quality instruction, and in addition, that educators will make a commitment to varying the lifeless nature of classrooms and the norm of direct-instruction behaviors. Perhaps as we learn how to facilitate mastery for low achievers in our nation's schools, we will proceed in the development of the teaching profession. The Joyce models of teaching provide a sound conceptual basis for helping teachers to branch and to develop a variegated repertoire of effective teaching behaviors. Learning occurs differently for each kind of social, cognitive, personal, and skill need. Teachers need expertise in a variety of targeted models of teaching so that their students can be nurtured in all dimensions of their cognitive, psychological, behavioral, and social growth.

Conclusion

Teaching includes a cluster of instructional behaviors, all of which function interdependently to influence the learning process. Curriculum objectives provide a district standard for achievement at several benchmark years, (for example, grades 3, 6, 9, 12) throughout the schooling process. The teaching task is one of accountably ensuring that students master selected portions of the curriculum during a particular year. Selection of appropriate objectives guides student diagnosis. What are the various levels of student readiness and style?

Instructional activity should be based on general objectives, levels of student readiness, and interest. The program provides an interest context in which mastery of objectives will occur. The classroom management task system provides a mechanism for translating plans into tasks, and guides the teaching and learning interactive engagements.

Teaching activities are those interactive exchanges that facilitate learning in the task system. The objective is specific learning, rather than task completion. A climate conducive to exploration during tasks is essential to mastery. The teacher creates a climate of expectations, which sets a tone for task engagement. The behaviors of providing cues, reinforcement, and feedback function interdependently to guide the mastery process for all students.

The instruction system provides a language system and specific content for principal–staff dialogue about instruction tasks. Each of the five task clusters provides a potential source of problems and strengths. These clusters can guide instructional improvement efforts to the extent that teaching norms will be altered and function effectively to facilitate mastery.

11

The Program Subsystem: Staff Learning

Staff development in this volume is viewed as a cluster of staff learning experiences that are designed to raise selected norms of staff competence. The staff development model we propose is ecological in nature and situation specific.

Researchers recently have begun to identify salient features of effective programs. Fendley and Harris (1980) from the University of Texas report that the most effective Texas staff development programs are those that are school based and designed by the school staffs to meet their needs. A number of other researchers in recent years have reported that when staff development programs are linked to the school's goals and developed cooperatively by teachers and principal(s), those programs are correlated with gains in student achievement (Glenn 1981; Lieberman and Miller 1978; Miller and Wolf 1978; Levine and Stark 1981).

To illustrate the nature of cooperative skill development within a specific context, let us look at how the medical profession and its various subprofessions carry out and coordinate their functions. The authors had occasion to observe the assistant dean of a large medical school and became conscious of the urgency with which medical professionals regard in-service education. The number of hours spent by physicians and surgeons in daily study averages about two. Doctors turn not only to seminars and conferences but also to printed materials, cassettes, and innumerable charts and records that help them to remain in touch with developments in their field. The biggest problem faced by medical people, aside from the psychological burden of caring for human lives, is to remain current; and in a field as dynamic as medicine, it is all but impossible to do so. One wonders what might happen to teacher performance if the pursuit of new knowledge would become even half as earnest an activity for school teachers and administrators!

During a tour of medical school classrooms and teaching laboratories, the authors saw how at least one university has turned medical training from a competitive enterprise into a cooperative one. Not so long ago, it was fairly common in medical schools to assume that only a certain percentage of students admitted would survive the rigorous and demanding experience of a professional education.

In this particular university, however, the faculty's goal was to help as close to 100 percent of the students as possible to succeed in the program. The faculty worked on the assumption that if the admission process was sufficiently careful and if student motivation was sufficiently intense, the great majority should, with faculty help, be capable of successfully completing the program. Students were encouraged to work together as learning teams and share note taking. Student use of tape recorders in the classroom was standard procedure. In some courses, students compiled a textbook from their own notes and from materials provided by the instructor. Since each student contributed to the volume, it had immediate and practical value for him or her.

Even at the outset of his or her career, the physician is encouraged in habits of collaboration, cooperation, and concern for mastery of knowledge within a nurturing atmosphere that maximizes his or her prospects of success. There is no such thing as a self-contained physician, nor is there temptation to develop a posture of functioning entirely on one's own. This posture, which is so rampant and so destructive within the *teaching* profession, is simply incompatible with the goal of providing the best possible care for patients. We believe that the implications of such cooperative skill development techniques also apply to the goals of staff development activities in schools.

Staff Development Clusters

As we explore the parameters of teaching development within the school context, let us consider four different kinds of teacher growth activities in schools (see Figure 11.1). *Training* includes all areas in which the staff perceive, or are made aware of, a need for new knowledge and skills. *Clinical supervision* provides an in-class observation and feedback system for teachers as they develop skills related to their goals. Several actions require their collective efforts through task forces where they may *produce* various schoolwide procedures,

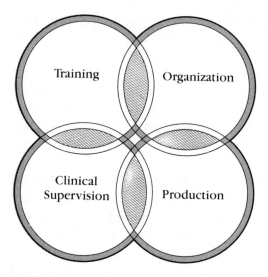

Figure 11.1. Staff Development

materials, or programs. Several improvement areas naturally lead to staff exploration in the various ways to *organize* themselves and students.

In each of the four development clusters, teachers participate actively toward accomplishing school improvement priorities. In the training and clinical supervision clusters, teachers are active learners of new knowledge and skills, and the refiners of instructional practice. In the production and organization clusters, teachers actively contribute as initiators, leaders, critics, explorers, inventors, and producers. In combination, each teacher shares his or her individual expertise, interests, and energy as all grow toward new norms.

A Simulation

To provide a conceptual context for planning staff learning programs, a simulation has been developed to stimulate your thinking further about an ecological context for adult growth. Suppose 30 people were to agree on a sailing trip from San Francisco to Honolulu, which would provide a group adventure and would require all to participate in a service role during the trip. The conditions for the trip would be as follows:

A ship is available, with a captain and three sailors, at a nominal fee
All other labor and nonsailing supplies need to be supplied by the group

Food, entertainment, and custodial services are to be planned by the
    group of 30
Sightseeing will need to be planned
Money will need to be raised
Responsibilities will need to be shared according to some plan

During the initial planning meeting, group members decide that the following tasks will be assumed by various work groups:

Task Groups	Objective
Budget and finance	To raise funds and manage expenditures
Food preparation	To plan, prepare, and serve all meals
Custodial services	To plan and care for all nonsailing maintenance functions
Recreation	To plan and provide for all types of recreation and entertainment during sail
Communications	To provide for all ship and land communication needs of the group
Sightseeing	To plan for and make arrangements for all land trips
Management	To coordinate all activities

Each person volunteers for a task group. Each group develops an action plan for their task responsibilities, outlining key activities, resources, responsibilities, and time lines. Each group shares its plan with the elected management team, whose function it is to coordinate activities for the trip.

Many learning needs grow out of plans as work group members recognize their collective knowledge and skills. The following list illustrates the learning needs the group then identifies.

Crew Learning Needs

Training	*Organization*
buying and serving food in large quantities	conduct surveys
	solicit funds
maintaining nonsailing dimensions of a ship	sightseeing stops and arrangements
management functions/procedures on a ship	events and messages for communication
	communication networks on a ship

Supervision	*Production*
meals	a budget and control process
maintenance activities	recreation program
communication procedures	a communication program
sightseeing arrangements	a menu
recreation program	

Each work group, in cooperation with management, needs training and coaching from the staff and from outside experts as well. Resources might include experts to provide *training* and trip members to provide *feedback* on the adequacy of the service provided. The *organizing* and *production* activities are those in which work group members learn in the process of assuming their task responsibility, service, or function. All individuals will develop new knowledge and skills in the course of performing their group function while either working on their task assignments or interacting with experts and other trip members.

Continuing this line of thought, at no time would the entire group be trained or coached on the same information or skill (except on how to live on the particular sailing vessel). Each group needs different kinds of knowledge and skills to accomplish its function effectively; to expect all trip members to attend all training sessions would be to add an unbearable stress factor to the whole group and to its objective. The combination of personal motivation and commitment, along with new knowledge, actual performance, and feedback on a specific function, serves as the skill-building activity cluster for the sailing group.

School-Based Staff Development

Staff learning in a school setting is similar to the sailing analogy just described. Given clear work group goals, tasks are assigned, action plans made, and growth needs identified and provided.

The staff improvement model described in the following pages presumes that all staff development activities are integrally linked to school goals, to individual staff performance goals, and to the learning process. Likewise, staff learning occurs through a combination of four sets of experiences: *training, organizing* ventures, *production* projects, and clinical *supervision.* Important to the success of the staff development program is the quality of leadership and instruction that is provided for each set of learning experiences. A staff development program of this sort is likely to increase school effectiveness and

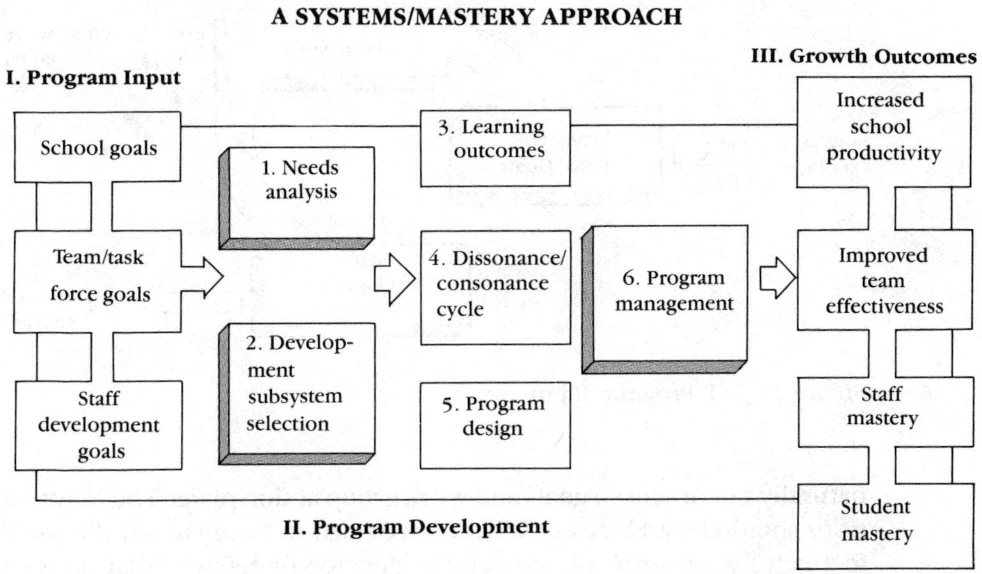

A SYSTEMS/MASTERY APPROACH

I. Program Input

III. Growth Outcomes

School goals

1. Needs analysis

3. Learning outcomes

Increased school productivity

Team/task force goals

4. Dissonance/ consonance cycle

6. Program management

Improved team effectiveness

Staff development goals

2. Development subsystem selection

5. Program design

Staff mastery

II. Program Development

Student mastery

Figure 11.2. Staff Performance Improvement Model: A Systems/Mastery Approach

efficiency, and at the same time facilitate staff mastery of skills necessary for effective collaboration and instruction.

In this chapter we will discuss the ways in which staff development needs are identified and met. The greatest attention is given to designing the staff development clusters noted previously. As a result of defining needs, a school can expect certain kinds of schooling outcomes to result from its staff development efforts.

Figure 11.2 outlines the three parts of a staff performance improvement model. "Program Input" (part I) identifies the goal structure for the staff development program. "Program Development" (part II) identifies the planning tasks and procedures for designing an effective learning program. "Growth Outcomes" (part III) identifies the results that can be expected from the effective implementation of a goal-focused staff development program.

Program Input: The School's Goal Set

The purpose of a staff development program, within an organizational framework, is to equip workers with the necessary knowledge, skills, and experiences to accomplish their tasks. A school's staff development program grows

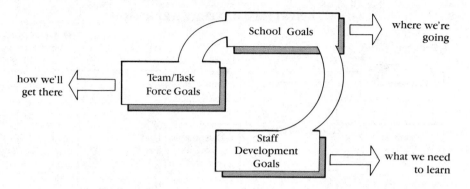

Figure 11.3. I. Program Input

naturally out of school goals and work group action plans. The following questions should be addressed: What do we need *to know* to get the job done effectively? What *skills* do we need to develop or refine? What do we need to *produce*? What do we need to *organize* differently? Figure 11.3 outlines the functions of the goal structure for designing staff development programs.

An analysis of a list of school goals and objectives will enable leaders and workers to identify the most obvious growth needs. The school improvement goals and task assignments listed on the following pages were discussed earlier in the organization subsystem (Chapters 6 and 7). They are presented again to illustrate the nature of a school plan to the staff development program.

School Improvement Goals

1. To develop a schoolwide *communication system* to foster greater organizational effectiveness, increased cross-team collaboration and enriched program development
2. To develop a continuous improvement process whereby *teachers improve their skills* in providing instruction for mastery
3. To develop a *system for student involvement* in school organizational life and in personal program development
4. To plan team-taught, *personalized learning programs* that are based on diagnosed mastery level, affective needs/interests, learning styles, and cognitive processing styles

Dispersement of Goals to Teams and Task Forces

School Goal I: Communications System

Leadership Council

OBJECTIVES:

1. To produce a *weekly news sheet* of events, needs, responsibilities, resources, and so on, as they relate to the activities of the

a) leadership council
b) three teaching teams
c) task forces
2. To organize *vertical curriculum teams* to develop a schoolwide curriculum in language arts and reading that is outcomes/mastery oriented
3. To organize *task forces* to develop three identified products
    a) record-keeping system
    b) reporting system
    c) audiovisual public relations program
4. To coordinate schoolwide *in-service programs* and materials development workshops that are based on needs

School Goal II: Instructional Skill Development

In-service Task Force

OBJECTIVES:

1. To conduct workshops on peer supervision, observation technology, the four elements of quality instruction and mastery learning
2. To videotape segments of instruction for staff analysis and improvement recommendations

Teaching Team

OBJECTIVES:

1. To observe each other, collecting data on the four-variable effectiveness
2. To plan for the four instruction variables in team program plans
3. To critique each others' instruction plans as they relate to quality instruction variables

Leadership Team

OBJECTIVES:

1. To formally observe each teacher four times and to informally assist teachers in developing "quality instruction" expertise

School Goal III: Student Involvement

Teaching Team

OBJECTIVES:

1. To develop a team student council that will relate to team life
2. To develop a student advisory system to ensure personal growth and well-being
3. To develop a planning model for regular student input into program focus, design, and learning alternatives

4. To develop a contract system for individual planning and evaluation in each program area

School Goal IV: Diagnosis-based Instructional Programs

In-service Task Force

OBJECTIVES:

1. To conduct workshops in diagnostic procedures that include the following:
   a) learning styles
   b) program interests
   c) cognitive processing styles
   d) mastery level
   e) motivation

Council

OBJECTIVES:

1. To develop a planning model for teaching teams to use in linking diagnostic data with curriculum parameters and available resources

Teaching Team

OBJECTIVES:

1. To diagnose all team students in the following areas by March 1: learning styles, interests, self-concept, and mastery in major curriculum areas

Inventory Development Task Force

OBJECTIVES:

1. To develop an inventory for all teachers to use that diagnoses student interests, strengths, motivation, and self-concept; success history

Based on an analysis of goals and plans, many needs can be identified as goal-based staff need areas and can provide the basic framework for designing the staff development program. Staff needs have been listed for each school improvement goal as follows:

I. **Schoolwide Communication System**
    1. produce a weekly news sheet
    2. organization procedures for gathering and writing news
    3. organize curriculum teams, K–6, for language arts and reading
    4. produce a schoolwide language arts and reading program
    5. produce a record-keeping system for reading and language arts
    6. produce a public relations program

II. **Teaching Skills for Mastery Learning**
1. training in peer supervision and mastery learning
2. produce a videotape of instruction
3. practice peer and supervisory observation and criticism
4. adapt quality instruction variables to learning programs

III. **Student Involvement Activity**
1. organize student councils
2. organize a student advisory system
3. produce a model for student participation in program development
4. develop a student contract program

IV. **Personalized Learning Programs**
1. training in diagnostic procedures
2. develop a planning model for incorporating diagnostic information into program planning
3. develop diagnostic instruments
4. diagnose all students using new procedures

The next task is to prioritize needs and to plan a learning program for areas of priority concern.

Program Development and the Learning Process

The task in program development is to design activities so that learning and development needs are met. Not all staff members will become involved in every program, for learning opportunities are provided only *to meet a need.* Figure 11.4 outlines the six layers of program development, including a management dimension for staff development. The first activity is to determine priority staff needs.

Needs Analysis

A general survey, by work groups, of growth needs provides a general sense of the most obvious growth needs of the total staff in a given year. The leadership teams may have additional perceptions of staff growth. Other needs assessment techniques can generate more in-depth information about development needs.

Interviews with team and task force leaders provide additional insight into growth needs. For example, a team may know how to develop effective student contracts individually, but have difficulty in getting jobs done collaboratively. The result of an interview might be to plan for several workshops on group dynamics and communication skills. Interviews can be useful to uncover

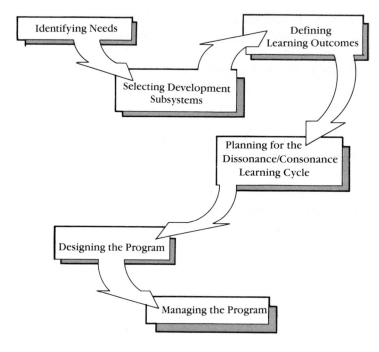

Figure 11.4. II. Program Development

group problems that relate secondarily to the group's action plan and that need to be addressed.

Questionnaires provide information to planners without the time constraints of interviewing. For example, a questionnaire, or a series of questionnaires, might be sent to all work groups for the purpose of identifying perceived growth needs. Some needs that seem obvious to planners, may not exist or seem important to work groups themselves. To illustrate, a pooling of staff talents may elicit sufficient resources to conduct training in diagnostic procedures. The skills required for "planning diagnostic based programs," may be related more directly to cooperation than to diagnosis. A questionnaire may also produce a finding that indicates team leaders want training and coaching in their leadership functions. Or, teachers may want workshops on personal counseling to assist them in their new student advisory role. Worker perceptions of needs must be addressed either directly or indirectly.

A *questionnaire/dialogue* series of activities may be useful in enabling the *staff* to prioritize development needs and to select those that hold the greatest promise for facilitating their total development. The process listed here is a combination of personal reflection, small group dialogue, and whole staff dialogue, and is a useful procedure for prioritizing staff learning needs.

```
┌─────────────────────────────────────────────────────────────────────┐
│                        Needs Assessment                              │
│                    (Group or Individual Staff)                       │
│                                                                      │
│                                                                      │
│ Circle a number from 1 to 5, indicating your level of professional   │
│ growth needs.                                                        │
└─────────────────────────────────────────────────────────────────────┘
```

Category	Scale				
The Learner	No need				Great need
1. How to diagnose and prescribe programs on the basis of cognitive and affective needs	1	2	3	4	5
2. How to develop programs based on					
a) student goals	1	2	3	4	5
b) parental goals	1	2	3	4	5
c) teacher assessment	1	2	3	4	5
3. How to report to parents on individual levels of mastery	1	2	3	4	5
4. How to meet the needs of gifted and talented learners on the team	1	2	3	4	5
5. How to develop classroom management procedures for an effective learning environment	1	2	3	4	5

Figure 11.5.

personal analysis of schoolwide staff needs
team analysis of individual assessments and selection of priority
school analysis of priority team concerns and group selection of priority
    development needs
leadership plan for staff development in areas of greatest concern

A *categorical questionnaire* provides a staff with topics for responding to questions. Such categories may include questions relating to learners, teachers, team leaders, parents, and/or program. An example taken from part of a questionnaire we used with a staff is presented in Figure 11.5.

Goal analysis provides the most direct indicator of needs in relation to the school improvement process. The goals provide the context for staff selection of development needs. Each teaching team selects growth needs as they relate to their particular work group objectives for the year. A summary of all work group development needs for the four school improvement goals outlined previously might be as follows:

(All School) Staff Learning Needs

elements of mastery learning and
quality instruction
observation technology
diagnostic procedures
developing weekly news sheet
developing student planning and
contract system
developing an inventory for
determining effective goals
advisory system processes
record-keeping systems
developing an audiovisual public
relations program

planning for instruction on a
teaching team
organizing vertical curriculum
teams
organizing a student council
organizing student task forces
leadership training for group work
devising plans for involving
students in program planning
planning for team productivity
communication skills for group
work

The staff development model presented here takes into account several dimensions of staff growth: *input* (training), *coaching* (supervision), and *output* (organizing and producing). An analysis of a list of identified needs such as the preceding one enables the leadership team to plan for training needs, supervision needs, organizing activities, and production activities. Based on this list, the staff development program content might appear as follows:

Be Trained in:

elements of mastery learning
and quality instruction
observation technology
advisory role
diagnostic procedures

Clinically Supervise:

learning and instruction
team planning
vertical teams
task forces
leadership council
in-service and materials
development
team leaders
training follow-up

Produce:

weekly news sheet
record-keeping system
reporting system
audiovisual program for public
relations
student planning and contract
system
team teaching model
affective student inventory

Organize:

vertical curriculum
development teams
student council
student advisory system
student input into team
program
student task forces

Learning Objectives

Many in-service programs are directed only to needs in the cognitive domain (new knowledge), while many others focus on the behavioral domain (things to do). It is important in designing staff development programs to consider all three levels of need: cognitive, affective, and behavioral. Workers must be equipped continuously with new personal knowledge, conceptual understandings, and new or refined skills.

A number of bad habits dominate practice for many in-service program planners. One habit is to assume that teachers need only to *hear* about new ideas in order to become motivated to develop new skills. Another bad habit is to assume that theory, conceptual models or ideas, and research findings are irrelevant to teachers and administrators. Teachers probably would not select a physician who ignored emerging theory, concepts, and research findings about his or her specialty. New knowledge about learning, instruction, management, organization, and growth productivity are as essential to teaching performance as to the fields of medicine. One other bad habit is to ignore the needs of the affective domain. Successes with new behaviors result from a personal motivation or drive to make a new behavior effective. By ignoring personal goals, motivations and self-concept, the entire staff development program will yield far less than anticipated. Programs must build on staff motivation and commitments as new knowledge is introduced and skills are learned.

Effective planning in all four staff development clusters involves addressing the needs of all three learning domains. A program may emphasize one domain over others (for example, observation methods versus knowledge about adult learning), but the inclusion of all three domains influences the total learning of a concept or skill. Figure 11.6 outlines the learning outcomes that can be expected if domain needs are addressed in staff development cluster programs. To change a behavior requires a combination of techniques, new concepts, perceptions of what is possible, and personal commitment.

An analysis of the four school goals and of work group objectives suggests that the following learning outcomes are reasonable to expect if programs are designed with cognitive, affective, and behavioral needs in mind.

General Learning Outcomes

Cognitive
> mastery learning and quality instruction concepts
> knowledge of different observation processes
> problem solving for team planning
> advisory system formats
> reporting and record-keeping system options

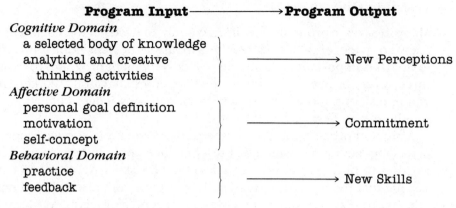

Figure 11.6. Program Design

Affective
   motivation for goal attainment
   satisfaction from group planning
   commitment from shared decision making
   healthy self-concept from producing in a team context
Behavioral
   skill in methods of student diagnosis
   skill in team planning
   communication skills
   skill at facilitating effective individual student planning
   teaching processes that facilitate mastery
   skill in program development

The Learning Cycle

The dissonance/consonance cycle (Figure 11.7) is a description of the "probable" route from learner question (problem) to learner answer (resolution). The program planner's task is to anticipate which kinds of activities are likely to facilitate growth to each next stage. The model shown here is not viewed as an absolute guide to planning activities, but rather as a conceptual guide for resolving particular learning problems. Hence, the model is descriptive, rather than prescriptive.

   Some skills may emerge after all five stages have been experienced, while some may require three stages for a few students and all five stages for other students. Moreover, some teachers may require a significant amount of time at the trial (practice) stage prior to shaping. Others may require a longer period

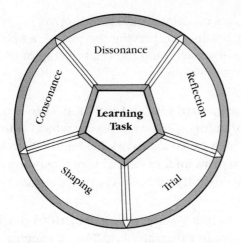

Figure 11.7. Dissonance/Consonance Cycle

in the reflection stage with concepts and then proceed quickly to consonance. The cycle should be viewed as a general guide for planning and actual teaching and learning activities.

In the following simulation, the dissonance/consonance cycle illustrates the process of learning to sail. By recognizing that staff development and mastery occurs in various stages over time, rather than from a single event, the principal can make productive use of learning concepts. Learning is a continuous process that can be reinforced and managed to yield increasingly more effective staff behaviors.

A Simulation

Dissonance Stage.　I live on the coast of Maine now, and want to learn how to sail. I have never sailed before, and in fact only once have I been on a sailboat. Yet, I want a summer sport; the bays and lakes are too cold for swimming; I dislike fishing; I like the challenge of the sea. Therefore, I want to learn how to sail.

Reflection Stage.　During initial sailing lessons I reflect often on past experiences that have prompted me to consider sailing over motorboating. My personal motivations for learning how to sail are many: I love to travel; I am intrigued by the challenge of changing weather conditions; the peace and calm of working with the wind and waves on calmer days is seductive; my reflexes and judgments in driving, skiing, tennis, and playing the piano can be transferred to learning how to sail; and I am learning the relationship of old skills to the new ones that I am learning in sailing.

Trial Stage.   Several sailing behaviors are selected and others discarded as I begin to practice setting the sail or sailing with or against the wind. I learn from experience and from a coach, which behaviors work best and which do not work at all, all of which is based on principles of sailing. I am beginning to gain a sense of what it's like to sail successfully, to be in charge of a sailboat.

Shaping Stage.   I am beginning to enjoy some sailing situations more than others. I enjoy sailing with others rather than alone; sailing in rough water is a more enjoyable challenge than sailing on a very calm day; sailing for pleasure is more satisfying than entering a sail race. It is time to develop the skills needed for collaborative sailing, rough-water sailing, and cruising for pleasure.

Consonance Stage.   After considerable practice and coaching I am ready to plan a short cruise around the islands in Penobscot Bay. I anticipate that in another year or two I will be ready to sail down the East Coast and back. I feel increasingly confident about my ability to learn to sail well and to enjoy the satisfaction that sailing provides.

The task in program planning is to design activities so that *growth* occurs cognitively, affectively, and behaviorally. The dissonance/consonance cycle can function as a conceptual guide in planning. Learning activities are to be designed so that potential problems/concerns/questions are resolved and lead to clear, self-confident actions. Cognitive, affective, and behavioral activities are to be included in each stage, although one domain may be emphasized. For example, resolving dissonance about diagnostic procedures can begin by practicing a new diagnostic technique (behavioral), followed by reflection and information-gathering activities (affective and cognitive). Another approach would be to introduce new information (cognitive) followed by practicing (behavioral) new techniques. The selection of activities depends on your judgment of what is most likely to produce desired results in each situation.

Table 11.1 demonstrates the utility of the cycle by addressing design implications, context, and activities for each stage. We have selected the "mastery teaching" staff training focus to illustrate planning for the learning (dissonance/consonance) cycle.

TABLE 11.1 Planning for the Learning Cycle

Concept	Program Design Implications	Goal/Context	Activities
Dissonance			
Confusion, concerns, questions regarding a given task or problem	Define task-related concerns, presentation of problem/task	Introduce concepts of mastery teaching	Request each staff member to select something they have mastered and not mastered. Identify what caused them to be not *cognitively* ready, and *affectively* ready. Identify the element of instruction that was present (or not) to facilitate mastery
Reflection			
Attempted linkage between personal experience and new knowledge and behaviors	Presentation of related new knowledge and behaviors. Discussion/simulation/role play activities linking new knowledge to problem focus	Mastery learning in the classroom	Reflect and discuss the ways in which the three mastery learning factors can be translated to the classroom, and the problem likely to be encountered
Trial			
Exploration of new concepts and behaviors to determine their potential for problem resolution	Additional learning tasks that provoke reflection and exploration on cognitive, affective and behavioral learning levels	Techniques to use in implementing mastery learning principles	Identify ways to diagnose *cognitive* and *affective* readiness. Identify ways to provide instructional *directives, reinforcement, student participation* and *correctives/feedback*

Table 11.1 (cont.)

Concept	Program Design Implications	Goal/Context	Activities
Shaping			
Development of skill in relation to new knowledge and behaviors	Practice and feedback on activities requiring the utilization of new knowledge and skills	Numerous observations and critique sessions on actual instruction	Watch videotapes of instruction, and critique teaching and learning using mastery learning principles
Consonance			
Resolution of concerns, new personal knowledge, attitudes and behaviors	Probing of residual concerns, planning for ways in which new knowledge and skills will be employed. Assessment of learning outcomes	Planning for mastery teaching	Plan for ways to improve diagnostic procedures and instructional procedures to facilitate greater student mastery

The following list of possible learning activities can be used in any cycle stage.

Learning Activities

Workshop activities	*Non-workshop Activities*
large group listening/reacting	participation on task forces
small task groups	participation in a professional conference
conferences	
programmed instruction	participate in a study group
seminars	demonstrate a skill to others
debates	personnel exchanges of ideas and methodologies
panels	
discussions	conduct/attend a workshop or seminar
creative problem solving	
simulation	symposium
role-playing	attend a learning institute
projects	visit
case study	seek task-related consultations
individual reading	engage in independent study

independent work materials
skill practice/feedback
interviewing
research
data collection
comparative analysis
personal/group planning:
   task analysis
   training analysis
lecture
videotape
audiotape
computer programming
filming
books

participate in on-the-job training
participate in a retreat
attend resource center

Program Action Planning

It is time to develop the entire action plan for staff development. It may appear that identifying three domains of learning outcomes and five stages in the learning cycle is a bit cumbersome to consider for regular planning activities. The two sets of decisions should be viewed as a way of thinking (a guide) about planning staff growth programs. For those situations in which planning for learning seems not to be an obvious or simple procedure, breaking activities into several stages can be useful. The cycle may provide a helpful lens following a program to examine those problem and success factors that made the program particularly successful or less than successful.

The action plan presented in Chapters 6 and 7 provides a useful example of why and how a goal-based development program is designed. The following sample format provides guidelines for "thinking about" and planning for effective programs.

School Goal: Instructional skill development
Staff Development Subsystem(s): Training for skill development

Learning Outcomes

Cognitive: Knowledge base for mastery learning and teaching

Affective: Commitment to improving teaching skills for mastery

Behavioral: New diagnostic, planning, and teaching skills for altering practices to facilitate more mastery

Learning Cycle Activities

Dissonance: Personal application of mastery learning principles

School Goal   Instructional skill development
Task Force Objective   To conduct workshops on mastery learning
Work Group   In-service on mastery learning teaching

Chart all key events and time lines on this calendar for quick referral throughout the year.

Key Events	Sept.	Oct.	Nov.	Dec.	Jan.	Feb.	Mar.	Apr.	May	June
1. Study basic concepts	X									
2. Identify trainers	X									
3. Identify and gather references	X									
4. Identify practice		X								
5. Contract with trainer		X								
6. Plan program			X							
7. Gather equipment				X						
8. Reserve facilities				X						
9. Develop learning activities			X							
10. Make videotapes			X	X						
11. Provide training sessions					X					
12. Conduct evaluation					X					
13. Provide feedback						X				

Figure 11.8.

Reflection: Discussion: how to apply concepts to the classroom

Trial: Identify ways to diagnose; provide quality instruction

Shaping: Observe and critique videotaped instruction

Consonance: Plan for ways to alter teaching practice to incorporate mastery principles

The sample task force made decisions to engage in 13 clusters of activities, which are planned to occur from September through February (see Figure 11.8). For those same key events, they identified resources for each event from a variety of district and other agencies and individuals (see Figure 11.9). Re-

Identifying Details			

Work Group _____

School Goal _____ Program Design For _____ Subsystem

Key Events	Resources	Responsibility	Deadline Date
1. Study basic concepts	1. University, library	Joan, Jim	Sept. 15
2. Identify trainers	2. Service center	Bill, Ann	Sept. 20
3. Identify and gather references	3. Service center	Bill, Ann	Sept. 20
4. Identify practice	4. Central office; Service center	Joan, Jim	Oct. 10
5. Contract with trainer	5. —		Oct. 20
6. Plan program	6. Task force	Entire	Nov. 10
7. Gather equipment	7. Media center	Alex, Ernestina	Dec. 15
8. Reserve facilities	8. Media center	Alex, Ernestina	Dec. 15
9. Develop learning activities	9. Task force materials	Task force	Nov. 20
10. Make videotapes	10. Media center	Jose, Rose	Dec. 20
11. Provide training sessions	11. Trainer	Trainer	Jan. 15
12. Conduct evaluation	12. Task force		Feb. 10
13. Provide feedback			

Evaluation Methodology   Questionnaire: ratings and open-ended responses
                          Observation of practice
Follow-Up Procedures   Structured peer and leader coaching sessions
                        Group reflection and planning sessions
                        Task force objectives to be identified later

Figure 11.9.

sponsibilities were divided so that the task force worked in pairs on only two of the 13 events. Deadline dates were identified for each event, and the evaluation and follow-up procedures were anticipated in advance. The two-page plan is sufficient to guide the task force activity in pairs, and also to provide information to management that can guide the supervision of the task force.

The staff next decided to devote one entire week during the summer in training and team planning; one hour per month in training; one hour per month for task force meetings; and one hour per month for developing materials for the new reading lab (all on school time). Since the staff prioritized its growth needs, they were eager to devote planned hours to meeting their growth needs.

Program Management

Central to the success of a school-based staff development program is the principal's effective leadership and management. Goal-based leadership guides the school's development process, while a management system controls activity to ensure effective results. Elements of the management system for the staff development program include the following management tasks:

> task force action planning
> individual goal setting and action planning
> periodic reporting and planning
> performance supervision and monitoring
> resource management
> performance evaluation: group and individual

Looking at Management Another Way

Bloom's four instructional variables are useful for facilitating the staff learning process. The principal, team leader, supervisor, peer, or consultant can all provide quality instruction and guide the staff's development process.

Cues and Directives

Provide guidelines, planning systems, benchmarks, expectations

Teach through in-service, observation feedback, and participation

Participation

Involve staff in multilevels of participation and decision making regarding performance improvement

Reinforcement

Provide coaching to teams and individuals in relation to goal sets and action plans

Provide resources

Conduct continuous evaluation and replanning

Feedback/Correctives

Classroom observation

Team meeting observation

Monthly monitoring

Program Output: School Development

If a staff development program has been designed around school goals and plans, and is prepared to foster adult learning of identified concepts and skills, then the school ought to realize products from staff development activity. Figure 11.10 outlines the basic areas in which results can be planned for and expected.

Direct Program Outcomes

The ecological process and progress of school improvement are enhanced by linking staff development programs to school goals. Each staff development subsystem plays a function in school and individual growth. Training impacts on the existing knowledge and skills base of the staff; clinical supervision impacts on actual teaching and learning practices; production impacts on instruction and management practices and materials; and organization impacts on communications, relationship patterns, and effective group performance.

In analyzing the four school goals we have used throughout this exercise, along with staff development plans, the school leadership may identify the following observable and measurable outcomes of school productivity.

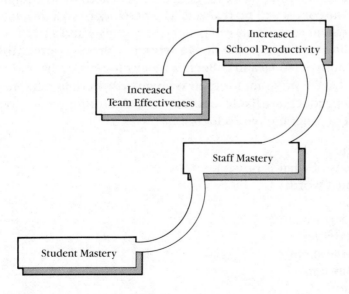

Figure 11.10. III. Growth Outcomes

School Productivity

communications network
interdependent teams: specialized
    and integrated
outcomes-based curriculum
"mastery" record-keeping and
    reporting system

Team Effectiveness

planning systems: organization
    and program
observation/feedback system
peer supervision
student planning and advisory
    program
diagnostically based program

Staff Mastery—Skills

team teaching
team program planning
task force participation
student/teacher planning
quality instruction
diagnostic procedures
interaction

Student Mastery—Skills

program objectives
assuming responsibility
social interaction
planning
group participation
leadership

Indirect Program Outcomes

In addition to the direct outcomes expected from staff activity in completing goals, additional outcomes will be realized. The network of staff projects and increased involvement of students can generate synergism and a healthy ecological growth climate. When professionals work in a group context toward goals that reflect both personal and collective beliefs and concerns, and when, in addition, they have a program for their own growth, certain personal and organizational by-products are likely to result. Consider the following possible indirect outcomes (program by-products):

new knowledge
new perceptions of what is possible
sense of personal worth
improved skills
effective role performance
goal-related activities
collective commitment
dynamic equilibrium
critical reflection

Conclusion

Learning is the daily experience of teachers, principals, and students as they engage in the tasks of instruction, management, and exploration. The goals of the school and the curriculum provide the standard measure of growth, whereas the context of a specific school dictates certain work parameters. Learning is the basic activity of staff and students in an attempt to alter achievement norms.

The instruction system guides planning, action, and coaching as principals seek to make teaching more effective. The curriculum, learner diagnosis and evaluation, program planning, classroom management, teaching, and learning are interdependently linked to influence achievement gains. The school's staff learning program is guided by the school goals and workers' needs, and provides for staff growth in four clusters of activities: training, supervision, organization, and production. The staff and student learning programs are the primary focus of school development and are the reasons for the existence of the other school systems.

The systems approach to staff development enables the local school to plan an effective professional growth program. We have come to understand more fully the nature of staff growth in a collaborative school context, recognizing how a staff can become energized to work collaboratively toward agreed-upon priorities. Moreover, the systems model recognizes that existing professionals possess a great deal of knowledge, skill, and creative ability that, when tapped, can influence the growth and quality of results. Deficiencies in staff performance are addressed within the context of achieving common goals and making contributions to the school's success. By welding together school improvement plans with staff development programs, a school staff can more effectively achieve the results they envision.

Commitment to an ideal, shared plans and dreams—in combination with strong leadership—can enable a staff to function at a higher level of performance. Management must keep the hopes and dreams alive continuously, reinforce and recognize the successes of staff and students, and guide the daily simultaneous processes of staff and student learning.

12

The Management Subsystem:
Influence Systems

The primary function for any management role is to increase the job results of other people. Management is concerned primarily with the behavior and results of workers as they relate to organizational purposes and to current priorities. The traditional management functions of supervision, planning, controlling, and evaluating take on new meaning within the systems context of organizational growth and group productivity. Given a set of role standards and a certain thrust for school improvement, the principal's major tasks are to provide the organizational structure for work group planning and action, and subsequently to direct the cluster activities of teacher development, monitoring, and evaluation for school success.

The *efficiency* issue in managing performance focuses on the results of teacher efforts rather than activities per se. The *effectiveness* issue focuses on the congruency between teacher activity and work results as they relate to school goals. Management engineers the work climate for efficient and effective worker performance, with accountability for staff performance as the objective of the management job.

A recent study of 165 middle managers (Kanter 1982) reveals salient characteristics of innovative managers who make a significant contribution to their company. Kanter's findings tend to dispel prevailing myths about productive management and, further, provide clear direction for effective school management in particular. She observes that innovation flourishes in companies where territories overlap; where people have contact across functions; where information flows freely; where excess funds are available in budgets; where man-

414

agers are in open-ended positions; and where reward systems look to the future, not to the past.

The overarching condition required for productive management, according to the Kanter study, is that *managers must envision an accomplishment beyond the immediate scope of their job.* They must be able to acquire the power they need to carry out their idea easily; that is, they find the additional strength it takes to carry out new initiatives. Innovative accomplishments are categorized by Kanter as (1) effecting a policy change of orientation or direction; (2) finding a new opportunity or developing a new product; (3) introducing new process procedures or technology for continued use; and (4) reorganizing the structure of the organization.

The process of management itself reaffirms the reports about excellent American companies and productive Japanese industries. Effective managers achieve their success by persuading more than ordering, by building a team and seeking input from others, by acknowledging others' potential stake in the project, and by sharing rewards and recognition willingly. "Clearly there is a strong association between carrying out an innovative accomplishment and employing a participative-collaborative management style" (Kanter 1982, 102).

The principal as school manager first must envision the characteristics of a more effective school in relation to learning and instruction, and then build within the organization the capacity and the conditions to share effectively the planning, supervising, controlling, and evaluating school improvement tasks. Productive and innovative management is a shared function today, with a flat view of organizational decision making and action. Change is normal and constant in the organization that is decentralized and matrixed. Information flows freely in productive organizations; the culture favors staff initiative; pride and a team feeling dominate; and rewards are abundant, visible, and provide a chance to do more challenging work in the future. Clearly, this view of management does not resemble the maintenance paradigm of school management, and points to a qualitatively different style, one that is necessary for managing productive schools.

The concept of management itself has been grossly misinterpreted. To illustrate, the debate in the early 1970s over role emphasis of the principal called for either a management focus or an instructional leadership focus. The first was conceptualized as a school-building maintenance (administrative) function; the second was viewed as an intervention function into the school's education process. Management has been interpreted as a cluster of tasks and responsibilities for administering budgets, buildings, buses, and the like. Nowhere in the new management literature, however, is there reference to "thing-management" functions. Rather, management theory has a "people-development" focus, and is concerned primarily with enabling people to accomplish what has not yet been accomplished in their organization. The purpose of management is not to maintain a well-oiled organization, but rather to enable an organization to develop continuously through its workers. Consequently, *management in this volume is viewed* not as a function for maintaining healthy building operations, but rather, *as the influence and coaching system that enables a staff to develop new norms of school productivity.*

Surprisingly, for the last century management functions have been identified similarly to the conceptualizations initiated by Fayol in 1929: planning, organizing, motivating, supervising, controlling, and evaluating. Those same functions of management are essential under the systems approach; however, the nature of management tasks has changed. Today emphasis is placed on organizational goals as a primary work context, combining the needs of both the organization and workers. Moreover, the management function is collaborative in style, rather than authoritarian. There is greater staff involvement in *planning, controlling,* and *evaluating* work group performance. *Supervision* also is a shared function between and among workers and management. The principal's management function is to provide leadership for and to initiate co-involvement efforts, and then to direct staff efforts through continuous engagement with staff throughout the school development process.

We devote this and the next two chapters to the management subsystem. We open this chapter with a discussion of the influence systems of power, authority, and leadership. In the following chapters, the "people-management" functions are developed from the perspective of the principalship: supervisory influences (Chapter 13) and quality control influence (Chapter 14). Many scholarly lists of management functions also include "organizing" and "motivating workers" which we have already examined in Chapters 6, 7, and 9.

Throughout the following discussion the reader is encouraged to consider ways to reorganize personal work patterns so that the majority of management time and effort is spent working with teachers. Administrative responsibilities such as buses, lunches, and building maintenance will continue to require attention. Our hope is that the reader will develop strategies for spending less time on these functions personally so that "people management" can take place effectively.

Jerry Kramer, a onetime football star, has developed a film entitled *The Habit of Winning,* describing Vince Lombardi's approach to managing the Green Bay Packers. While Lombardi was ruthless in many instances, his people-building philosophy is worth noting. The beginning questions for building a winning team are relatively simple and straightforward: "What do you want?" "How badly?" and "What do you have to do to get it?" The following Lombardi guidelines are useful in developing the skill for a people-management orientation:

1. Make sure you're prepared.
2. Expect the best; pressure comes from risk and brings out the best in people.
3. Remain on course and consistent with your goals.
4. A good salesman won't take "no."
5. Review, evaluate, and go back to the basics.
6. A professional gives more to the job than the job gives to him or her.
7. Set your own deadlines.
8. Know who to kick in the seat of the pants and who not to.
9. There is a winner's circle and loser's circle.
10. Play the little games 100 percent; it makes the big games easier.
11. Winning is personal pride.
12. Don't give up.
13. Winning is not a sometime thing, it is an all time thing.
14. Desire is what turns the game into a win.
15. Establish the habit of winning.
16. Totally commit and prepare yourself and others for your goals.

Management, basically, is a people-movement function and has been cited as one of the three hot executive careers looming up fast, according to the *Nashville Banner* (October 26, 1979). The three most important executive careers for the future are (1) management information systems executives, (2) human resource executives, and (3) logistics executives, those with skills for the distribution of goods and services. Preparation for these roles requires foundational knowledge in business management and in technical or scientific fields.

Consider the challenge of a people-development approach to managing schools. Recent rapid advances in school learning and instruction suggest that the instructional techniques that most teachers learned in preparation programs are outdated. Continuous teacher development is essential for meeting the student achievement challenge as it is currently being defined.

To continue managing schools as they are now managed not only ignores the research on the decline of schools and outdated organizational and instructional practices, it assumes a level of teacher proficiency that does not exist. Scholars in the fields of management, motivation, and learning all describe worker skill on some low to high continuum. Operating on an assumption that teachers already are or ought to be the best they can be (without continuous assistance) assumes a naive position. To continue the practice of letting teachers do what they think is best requires that a principal perceive that all teachers now

1. provide optimal quality instruction

2. are fully mature in their teaching skill (Hersey and Blanchard—maturity level 4)
3. function as self-actualized persons (Maslow)
4. are all "motivators," not "hygiene seekers" (Herzberg)
5. are all "Y" or "Z" workers (not "X") (McGregor; Ouchi)
6. work in Type 4 school organizations (collaborative decision making) (Likert)
7. function continuously as "adults," not "children" or "parents" (transactional analysis)
8. are themselves "conscientisized" (critical shapers of their destiny) (Freire)
9. self-confident persons (Rogers)

An analysis of a teaching staff through the series of lenses noted above will quickly identify those teachers who are the most mature workers, those who are the least mature, and those who are somewhere in between. The function of management is to develop individuals and groups of workers to become increasingly knowledgeable, skillful, confident, and competent; essentially an adult growth process that must be managed.

The challenge of people development for principals is, without a doubt, the central job task. However, a research study on educational governance and finance at Stanford University (*Education USA,* January 28, 1980) reported that principals in schools that they studied seemed to be floundering about without the knowledge of coordination strategies and the kinds of supervision necessary to solve the problems of educational technology. Without the knowledge and controls necessary to respond to new complexities, the management skills of principals are questionable at best and perhaps even primitive.

Management Practice Revisited

The history of management was explored briefly in Chapter 1; however, it seems important here to elaborate our definitions of management for effective school performance. Under scientific management, emphasis was given to the physical limitations of the body in job performance. Wages were paid in terms of dollars for piecework production, which included management authority over workers for their efficient accomplishment of tasks. Management set work parameters and assessed worker value.

Barnard (1938) was the first management theorist to suggest that worker cooperation and involvement was important for the successful achievement of organizational goals, a factor which he observed had the potential to offset low levels of production. The challenge for management was to provide a system of communication, promote efforts, and formulate and define organizational purpose. McGregor (1960) espoused that if workers could incorporate their personal goals into the work setting, more effective organizational production would occur. Management shifted from defining all work parameters to inviting worker input into decisions. Nevertheless, management in both the scientific management and human relations movements assumed a distinct separation of management and worker roles.

The contingency, or systems, theorists, in more recent years, have urged that effective management requires coinvolvement *with* workers. Hersey and Blanchard (1977, 13) define management as working with and through individuals and groups to accomplish goals. Kast and Rosenzweig (1974, 369) view management as a process of converting information into action through problem solving and decision making. Some theorists focus more on managing people and their relationships, others on decision making as it relates to goals. All models, however, assume a coinvolvement of management. Naisbitt (1983, 200) contends that there will continue to be enormous pressure from younger, well-educated, rights-conscious workers to participate with management in decisions regarding the future. There is a growing disdain, he observes, for the old-fashioned hierarchical structures in favor of a networking approach and more participatory management. The new leader is a facilitator, not an order giver.

Table 12.1 illustrates the nature of the shift in management practice from traditional to co-involvement patterns in planning, supervising, providing quality control, and evaluation.

The basic question for principals is how to adopt a more participative management style. An effective shift in management practices from unilateral decision maker to participative decision making depends on the staff involvement history of each school, the professional maturity levels, and prevailing beliefs about the nature of work in schools. Likert (1967) studied various types of management and categorized management behaviors into four systems, with system 4 being the most effective for increasing organizational productivity. Likert illustrated the progression from unilateral to participative decision making in organizations. The management task is to assess the current norm in decision making, and teach a staff to function effectively and productively in a participative norm. The four systems are useful for analyzing current norms in school management and for planning strategies that will enable school management to grow toward system 4. Likert's theory recognizes that a Cinderella-type change in management (simply adopting system 4 style) is not realistic but requires a growth process over time. Let us look, then, at each of the four systems described by Likert.

System 1: Management assumes virtually no confidence or trust in sub-

TABLE 12.1. Management Subsystem

Activities	Maintenance Paradigm	Productivity Paradigm
Supervision	Inspection visits by principal that provide data for teacher evaluation	Regular and systematic in-class coaching of teachers by peers and administrators/supervisors. Facilitates skill development
Planning	Staff/student assignments, facilities maintenance, supply and equipment inventory and budget	Goal focus for the school; task assignments to work groups; strategies for supervision and control
Control	Problems are addressed as needed: crisis orientation	Regular assessment of progress toward goals by work groups and administration. Feedback utilized
Evaluation	Staff evaluation by the principal. Judgment about teacher cooperation with administration and ability to control students	Assessment by work groups and administration of progress toward goals; of achievement gains; of program effects on performance

ordinates; workers are seldom involved in any aspect of organizational decision making. The bulk of the decisions are made at the top levels of management and issued down the chain of command. Subordinates work in a climate of fear, threats, and punishment with occasional rewards. Superior–subordinate interaction typically is boss initiated and perpetuates fear and mistrust. The control process is highly concentrated in top management. However, an informal organization generally develops, which opposes the goal of the formal organization and keeps the organization in tension.

System 2: Management is condescending to subordinates, such as a master to a servant. Major decisions of the organization are made at the top, but many decisions also are made within a limited framework at lower levels. Rewards and actual or potential punishment are used to stimulate workers. Superior–subordinate interaction perpetuates fear and caution. Although the control process is still concentrated in top management, some decisions are delegated to middle and lower work levels. An informal organization usually develops, but it does not always resist formal organizational goals.

System 3: Management places substantial, but not complete, *confidence and trust in subordinates.* Broad policy and general decisions are kept at the top, but subordinates are permitted to make more specific decisions at lower levels. Communication flows both up and down the hierarchy. Rewards, occasional punishment, and some involvement are used to motivate workers. There is a moderate amount of superior–subordinate interaction, which generates a fair amount of confidence and trust. Significant aspects of the control process are delegated downward with a feeling of responsibility at both higher and lower levels. An informal organization may develop, which will either support or partially resist the goals of the organization.

System 4: Management has complete confidence and trust in subordinates. Decision making is widely dispersed throughout the organization, although well integrated. Communication flows not only up and down the hierarchy but across work groups among peers. Workers are motivated by participation and involvement in developing economic rewards, setting goals, improving methods, and appraising progress toward goals. There is extensive, friendly superior–subordinate interaction with a high degree of confidence and trust. There is widespread shared responsibility for control processes, with the lower units fully involved. The informal and formal organizations are often one and the same. Thus, all social forces support efforts to achieve stated organizational goals.

In summary, system 1 is a task-oriented, highly structured, authoritarian management style; system 4 is a management style based on teamwork, mutual trust, and confidence. Systems 2 and 3 are intermediate stages between these two extremes. Hersey and Blanchard (1977) have selected several characteristics of each system, which are shown in Table 12.2.

The concepts of planning, supervising, controlling, and evaluating can be applied to management in any of Likert's four systems. However, discussion of each management function in this chapter assumes that principals will build the staff organization toward a system 4 approach, toward that stage of organizational maturity. The task of developing an organization toward system 4 requires knowledge of factors that stimulate workers to grow. An overview of the performance research indicates a number of factors that can serve as a catalyst. The following studies illustrate the range and complexity of motivation in the work setting. Likert (1967) observed that high levels of performance goals influence organizational success. Freedom, responsibility, and self-understanding promote personal growth for adults (Rogers 1973). Incorporating personal goals into the work setting facilitates productivity (McGregor 1960). Job autonomy, variety, identity, and knowledge of results are positively related to productivity (Hackman and Lawler 1971). Supervisor praise, skill variety, task identity, autonomy, and feedback all relate to worker satisfaction (Locke 1974; Luthans 1981). Behavior directed at contributions rather than

TABLE 12.2. Examples of Items from Likert's Table of Organizational and Performance Characteristics of Different Management Systems*

Organizational Variable	System 1	System 2	System 3	System 4
Leadership processes used				
Extent to which superiors have confidence and trust in subordinates	Have no confidence and trust in subordinates	Have condescending confidence and trust, such as master has to servant	Substantial but not complete confidence and trust; still wishes to keep control of decisions	Complete confidence and trust in all matters
Character of motivational forces				
Manner in which motives are used	Fear, threats, punishment, and occasional rewards	Rewards and some actual or potential punishment	Rewards, occasional punishment, and some involvement	Economic rewards based on compensation system developed through participation; group participation and involvement in setting goals, improving methods, appraising progress toward goals, etc.
Character of interaction–influence process				
Amount and character of interaction	Little interaction and always with fear and distrust	Little interaction and usually with some condescension by superiors; fear and caution by subordinates	Moderate interaction, often with fair amount of confidence and trust	Extensive, friendly interaction with high degree of confidence and trust

* (*Source:* Paul Hersey and Kenneth H. Blanchard, *Management of Organizational Behavior: Utilizing Human Resources,* 3e [Englewood Cliffs, NJ: Prentice-Hall, 1977], 75. Reprinted by permission of the publisher, © 1977.)

effort, is a key to worker productivity (Drucker 1982). Participation in decision making increases the level of work group productivity (Morse and Reiner 1956). Team development activities increase staff productivity (Schmuck, Runkel, and Langmeyer 1969). Collaboration is the organization's energy exchange system (Mink et al. 1979).

A school management system must address the concepts of worker goals, participative decision making, development, supervision, control, and evaluation. These variables act as a job context either to inhibit or to stimulate exemplary performance. Worker planning, development, and evaluation function interdependently with management planning, development, and evaluation to create the conditions for transforming performance norms.

Management Influence Systems

The management functions of supervising, planning, monitoring, and evaluating are required to facilitate and ensure organizational productivity. The processes of influence within each of those functions, however, require a perception of the power, authority, and leadership that is required to influence workers in varying situations. As was discussed in Chapter 9 under "learning," motivation is a personal response to an influence or stimulation; the ability and skill to influence is the management responsibility.

In this section we discuss selected conceptualizations of authority, power, and leadership that have particular potential for stimulating effective management behaviors. The art (not the tasks) of moving people to new performance norms emerges from a critical analysis of the situation, a reflection on past experiences, and a selection of specific actions to influence future work behaviors. Sound principles of human behavior enable a manager to make educated guesses as to which influence strategies are most likely to work, and why, in a given situation.

Authority

Power and authority are conceptualized as separate systems of influence on organizational behavior (Weber 1946; 1947). Authority is the right to influence; it is the legitimate power of one role or person over another. Typically, authority is delegated to a role from a higher level within an organization, state, or nation.

Actual authority, however, is formally administered or functionally provided, and is not necessarily tied to a role hierarchy. Peabody (1964) identified four different kinds of authority that function for groups and which are useful in a cooperative management schema. *Legitimate* authority is demonstrated through code and policy administration; legitimate authority is controlled through organizational standards. *Position* authority is delegated from a higher to a lower role. Position authority has higher level organizational support for decisions made at the delegated level. *Competence* is the kind of authority that rests within an individual and is neither controlled nor delegated. Competence is personally developed and becomes authority when the competence is recognized by others in a way that influences their behavior. *Person* authority lies within personality and other characteristics that function as an influence over others.

To illustrate the functions of authority in a school: A principal may have the *legitimate* power to institute mastery learning throughout the school, but may *delegate* authority to the teaching teams after training to develop their own mastery learning programs. Further, the special-education teachers in the school may have the *competence* to teach the staff the necessary knowledge and skills for successful mastery learning programs. Various other teachers or team leaders may have the *personal* qualities to assist the teams in becoming successful.

Peabody's model of authority is in keeping with cooperative management concepts. Authority in effective schools is a combination of legitimate power, delegated authority, individual competence, and personal influence. An effective school manager identifies individuals and groups with influence capability and enhances the natural influences to function as legitimate behavior stimulators. Each influence system functions for specific needs and works interdependently with the others as a general influence on school productivity.

Power

Another source of influence is the force or control that functions as a primary influence on people through a one-way communication effort. Field theory (French and Raven 1968, 259–269) identifies five different types of power that a person may use to exert primary influences on others: (1) reward, (2) coercion, (3) referent, (4) expert, and (5) legitimate. Workers can be influenced through *rewards* for specific behavior. The function of a reward is to influence a repetition of the desired behavior (a one-way influence). Management can influence workers through *coercive* and intimidating practices. Coercion has the power to influence certain desirable responses through fear tactics. *Referent* power is a collaborative influence between group members and the legitimate organizational authority. To the extent that workers avoid discomfort or gain satisfaction by conformity, regardless of legitimate organizational responses, the power is referent.

Expert power is a primary influence on the cognitive structure of others. The content of an expert's knowledge is not the power factor, but acceptance of the validity of that content signifies the power. The influence is in altering the cognitive structure of others and establishing an initial dependency relationship that dissolves with the passage of time.

Legitimate power is perhaps the most complex form of power. Inherent in legitimate power is the evaluation of the behaviors of others. Legitimate power stems from internalized values, which suggests that one person has the right to influence another, and the other has an obligation to accept this influence. Job descriptions are examples of the bases for legitimate power in organizations.

Comparative studies on the French and Raven categories report that "expert" power has the greatest total amount of control or influence on others. The implication for principals is to become expert in instruction and management, and through a solid knowledge base influence the behaviors of staff members. Managerial motivation has been useful as a predictor of leadership effectiveness (McClelland 1975). It has been learned over a period of time that effective managers in large organizations have a strong need for power. These same managers have a "socialized-power orientation," and exercise power to build up the organization by making subordinates feel strong and responsible. Because of an orientation to building organizational commitment, the effective manager is more likely to use a participative coaching style of management, and less likely to be coercive or autocratic (Yukl 1982).

The key to effective management power and authority in schools derives not from absolute control over others, but rather from the involvement of others in "reorienting" experiences (Spady 1977). The nature of influence is delicate and subtle. Charismatic power and authority, observes Spady, begins with leader awareness of subordinate needs, followed by empathy and sensitivity. The power to influence evolves from a response to needs which is perceived as stimulating, exciting, and engrossing. Charismatic appeal emerges from the spontaneous and intimate authenticity of an encounter. The subordinate's experiences of attraction and intimacy are likely to stimulate further openness and sharing.

Leadership

Leadership is generally defined as the ability to influence the behavior of others in a certain direction, usually in a two-way interaction. We will discuss several selected theories of leadership that we perceive to be of particular use to school leaders.

Focus on Great Men and Their Traits

The literature on leadership is exhaustive and indicative of the endless search for definition in the art and skill of influencing others. In the early days of leadership study, the biographies of "great men" were analyzed to identify factors that enabled some men to rise and hold significant influence over others. Due to a growing perception that greatness cannot be decoded, measured, and/or predicted, the great-man theory of leadership gave way to a new focus in leadership study. With attention given specifically to the personality of great leaders, scholars (such as Barnard 1930) began to examine the traits of great leaders that enabled them to elicit a following. Initial studies examined the one-way influence of leaders that induced compliance in followers (Stogdill 1974, 85). The clarity of certain characteristic traits of leaders led to the study of particular behaviors within those traits.

Stogdill (1948) reviewed the results of 124 traits studies conducted between 1904 to 1948 and concluded that individual traits failed to correlate with leadership effectiveness in a strong or consistent manner. In 1971, Stogdill, Nickels, and Zimmer analyzed 136 research studies and were able to categorize traits of effective leaders into three categories: self-oriented traits, task-oriented traits, and socially oriented traits.

Focus on Leader Behaviors

Likert (1967) observed strong differences in the behavior patterns of effective and ineffective managers. Effective managers usually concentrate on planning, coordinating, and facilitating the work, without neglecting interpersonal relations with subordinates. More effective managers are likely to set high performance goals for subordinates, to use group methods of supervision, and to serve as a "linking pin" with other groups and with higher management.

In their early study of leaders in Air Force flight squads, Halpin and others at Ohio State University began to perceive two different and complementary sets of behaviors that were operational by effective leaders: personal consideration and initiating structure (Halpin 1959, 79). Halpin went on to replicate his studies among school superintendents and found virtually the same patterns existing.

Initiating structure was defined as the degree to which a leader provides psychological clarity and unambiguous direction, such as assigning tasks, providing schedules, and clarifying expectations. The leader plans, organizes, directs, and controls. *Consideration* was defined, by contrast, as the degree to which the leader creates a supportive environment for personal welfare. Superintendents who were thought to be most ideal were high in both consideration and initiating structures, each behavior set playing a fundamentally different role in stimulating followers. The four different combinations of consideration and structure behaviors are illustrated in the quadrant in Figure 12.1.

In a study of 27 organizations, Stogdill (1965) verified again that both leader behaviors seem important to organizational life. Consideration tends to be associated with group drive and freedom of action, while structuring of expectations tends to be associated with cohesiveness and support of the organiza-

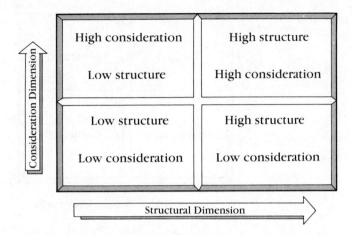

Figure 12.1. Ohio State Leadership Factors

tion. However, subsequent studies (House 1972, 486) bore out that in the case of some workers, particularly those new to a task or job, high relationship behavior caused confusion. What is needed is a high task structure and low consideration. Highly skilled workers, on the other hand, are confined and restrained by high degrees of task structure and consideration; they require low structure and low consideration to be successful. The question then emerged, "How can a leader tell which behaviors are the most appropriate?"

Effective Behaviors. Research studies began to demonstrate that four sets of behaviors (high-low structure; high-low consideration) were appropriate in certain situations, no one being the best in all situations. Reddin began to point the way to a more flexible conceptualization of leadership structure and consideration. In an attempt to address the apparent problems within a fixed view of desired leadership behaviors (consideration and structure), Reddin (1970) added another dimension: *effectiveness.* "Effectiveness," he contends, "is not a quality a manager brings to a situation . . . effectiveness is best seen as something a manager produces from a situation by managing it appropriately." The focus for Reddin was on the results of management behavior, not the discrete behaviors one enacts.

Reddin (1970) renamed Halpin's behavior set for each quadrant (see Figure 12.2), and contended that leader behavior is either effective or ineffective, depending on leader perception of which leadership actions are required in a situation. No one style is always effective.

Reddin defined task, relationship, and effectiveness in such a way that a

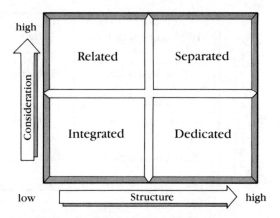

Figure 12.2. Reddin's Four Basic Leader Styles (*Source:* William J. Reddin, *Managerial Effectiveness* [New York: McGraw-Hill Book Company, 1970], 222. Reprinted by permission of the publisher, © 1970.)

leader could act on each concept (high or low), depending on situational variables. The basic behavior definitions in his three-dimensional theory are

> *Task Orientation (TO)*—the extent to which a manager directs his subordinates' efforts toward goal attainment. It is characterized by planning, organizing, and controlling.
>
> *Relationship Orientation (RO)*—the extent to which a manager nurtures personal job relationships. It is characterized by mutual trust, respect for subordinates' ideas, and consideration of their feelings.
>
> *Effectiveness (E)*—the extent to which a manager achieves the output requirements of his position.

Viewing the theory graphically (see Figure 12.3), each quadrant has an effective and ineffective dimension. A leader tends to use one basic style, either related, integrated, separated, or dedicated, in most situations. A leader tends to branch into other styles as conditions dictate. Basic tendencies can be identified with regard to relationship and task (Reddin's terminology for consideration and structure). Furthermore, a leader can identify those specific behaviors that tend to foster either effective or ineffective results within the dominant leadership style.

Reddin has developed a general guide to effective performance within each leadership style (1970, 94). The grid in Figure 12.4 provides clues to effective behavior patterns within each basic style.

Following an identification of personal tendencies in the four leader behavior styles, principals can further identify patterns that are effective in that

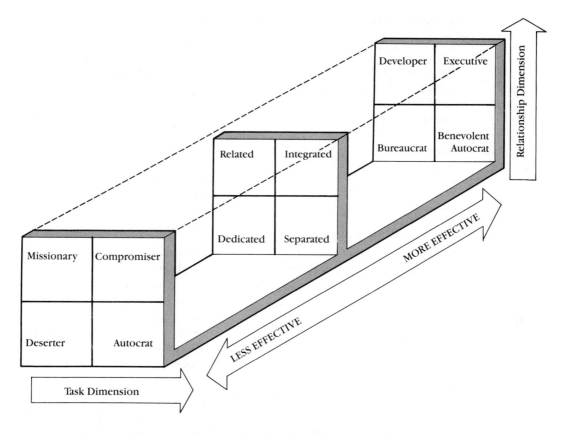

Figure 12.3. Reddin's 3-D Theory of Leadership Effectiveness (*Source:* Adapted from William J. Reddin, *Managerial Effectiveness* [New York: McGraw-Hill Book Company, 1970], 230. Reprinted by permission of the publisher, © 1970.)

mode and those that are less effective. Note Reddin's descriptors listed in Table 12.3.

Follower Maturity.   Hersey and Blanchard (1977) expanded on Reddin's 3-D Theory by examining situational variables for applying either high or low task structure, or consideration behaviors. What evolved from their studies was situational theory which is based on a curvilinear relationship between task structure, relationship behavior, and worker maturity. Leader perceptions of follower maturity, they hypothesize, determine the appropriate leader behavior (see Figure 12.5).

Maturity is defined in situational theory in relation to three worker conditions: (1) achievement motivation (the ability to set high but attainable goals), (2) responsibility (willingness and ability), and (3) experience (education of

TABLE 12.3 Effective and Ineffective Leadership Behavior Styles*

More Effective	Less Effective
Bureaucrat Indicators follows orders, rules, procedures reliable, dependable maintains system watches details, efficient rational, logical, self-controlled fair, just, equitable	*Deserter Indicators* works to rules, minimum output, gives up avoids involvement, responsibility, commitment gives few useful opinions or suggestions uncreative, unoriginal, narrow-minded hinders others, makes things difficult resists change, uncooperative, uncommunicative
Developer Indicators maintains open communication channels—listens develops talents of others—coaches understands others—supports works well with others—cooperates trusted by others—trusts	*Missionary Indicators* avoids conflict seeks acceptance of himself, dependent makes things easier avoids initiation, passive, gives no direction unconcerned with output, standards, controls
Benevolent Autocrat Indicators decisive, shows initiative industrious, energetic finisher, committed evaluative of quantity, quality cost, profit, sales conscious obtains results	*Autocrat Indicators* critical, threatening makes all decisions demands obedience, suppresses conflict wants action, results immediately downward communication only, acts without consultation feared, disliked
Executive Indicators uses teamwork in decision making uses participation appropriately induces commitment to objectives encourages higher performance coordinates others in work	*Compromiser Indicators* overuses participation yielding, weak avoids decisions, produces gray acceptable decisions emphasizes task and relationships when inappropriate idealist, ambiguous, distrusted

* (*Source:* Adapted from William J. Reddin, *Managerial Effectiveness* [New York: McGraw-Hill Book Company, 1970], 205–234. Reprinted by permission of the publisher, © 1970.)

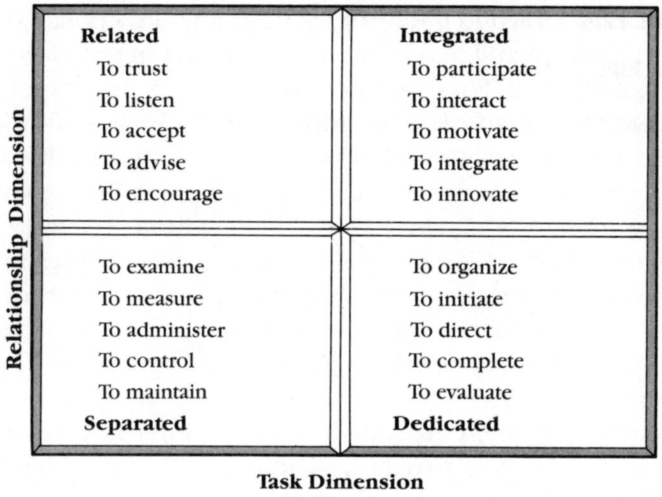

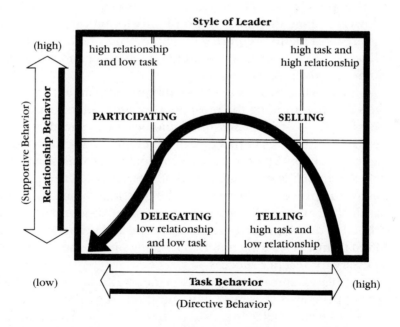

Figure 12.4. Reddin's Task and Relationship Behaviors

Figure 12.5. Situational Leadership (*Source*: Adapted from Paul Hersey and Kenneth H. Blanchard, *Management of Organizational Behavior: Utilizing Human Resources,* 3e [Englewood Cliffs, NJ: Prentice-Hall, 1977], 246. Reprinted by permission of the publisher, © 1977.)

the individual/group). Maturity in this sense does not focus on a worker's overall self-concept and psychological maturity, but rather on maturity as it relates to a specific task. For example, a teacher who has taught for 15 years may be professionally mature in developing a behavior modification program for 6- to 8-year-olds, but relatively immature in planning an individualized reading program for low-achieving 13-year-olds. A leader working with the teacher in the former situation (high maturity) would delegate the task (developing a behavior modification program), providing guidance and resources only as needed. In the case of the latter situation (low maturity), the leader would need to sell the teacher on the rationale for developing a reading program for 13-year-olds and then define specified task parameters, resources, expectations, and time lines.

For those who are least mature in relation to a given task, leader behavior provides a high degree of task structure and a low amount of consideration or relationship behavior. As the group/individual becomes more confident and skillful, the leader maintains the high structure and raises the degree of consideration, which adds a support dimension. The situation between the leader and follower then changes to a "selling" mode. As the follower(s) assume still greater responsibility and skill with a task, the relationship shifts to more of a "participation" mode. The leader continues a high degree of support while the followers assume the major responsibility for task structure. Those followers who are most mature require only a bare structure for task expectations; they will be able to assume responsibility for structure and consideration needs in completing the task effectively.

A situational approach to leadership provides an important clue (maturity levels) for determining the most appropriate leader posture and subsequent behavior. To illustrate, a seasoned middle school social studies teacher, who was having problems with a task of developing a social studies scope and sequence, finally pleaded with her principal to explain again the rationale for such, and to define more clearly what was expected and provide some direction for the process to be used. While listening to her, the principal realized that she had made an inappropriate judgment about the teacher's knowledge and skill in developing a curriculum scope and sequence. The principal then shifted from a delegating mode to a selling mode, and provided the structure necessary for teacher success.

In further examination of situation theory, Kunz and Hoy (1976) found patterns of principals that raise new questions regarding structure and consideration of leader behaviors. They found that "initiating structure" was the overriding factor that influenced the teachers' willingness to accept decisions of superiors. Structure, not consideration (although a minimal level was maintained) was found to be the most important dimension of the leader's style. These findings suggest that principals who are strong in initiating structure are more successful in gaining acceptance for their directions than those who concentrate on consideration.

If a principal's objective is to stimulate the entire work culture, a careful analysis of current worker maturity levels will lead to a variety of leader involvement patterns. Moreover, no one work culture is all productive or all unproductive. In some schools, at any point in time, a principal necessarily will use a balance of telling, selling, participating, and delegating. In other schools the leader necessarily will participate with, and delegate changes for, most work groups. In other schools, a successful leader necessarily will tell and sell the changes to most groups. An understanding of maturity levels within a particular work context will enable principals to respond appropriately to different levels of involvement. If success is the leader's objective, providing appropriate involvement opportunities is likely to stimulate worker cooperation.

Focus on Path to Goal

One of the most promising leadership models to emerge in recent years is House's Path-Goal Theory (1973, 285–286). He examined the problems relating to inappropriate leader behaviors, examining the functions of leader behavior and worker motivation. The central concept in the Path-Goal Theory is of utmost importance for managing productive schools. The leader's primary task is to assist workers along the path toward the achievement of their work goals. The concept implies that active leader intervention prevails in effective organizations in terms of management direction, resources, rewards, and support, which are calculated to foster worker success.

Actual worker behavior is a function of two variables: (1) expectation that a certain behavior will result in a specific desired outcome, and (2) belief that satisfaction will be derived from that outcome. Performance results from motivation and ability ($P = M \times A$). House explored both the extrinsic (outcomes) and intrinsic (satisfaction) motivation variables in performance, both of which guide path-to-goal leadership.

The motivation functions of the leader are twofold. The first is to increase the satisfaction associated with the task outcome, thereby increasing the personal payoff for the work goal. Second, the leader must provide necessary assistance (path instrumentality) required for goal attainment, by clarifying, reducing road blocks, and increasing opportunities for success.

An effective leader provides subordinates with essential coaching, guidance, and performance incentives that are not otherwise provided by the organization or work group. Situational variables determine subordinate preference for a particular pattern of leader behavior, thereby influencing the impact of the leader on worker satisfaction.

House and Mitchell (1974) proposed that four kinds of leader behavior are useful in different path-goal situations. *Supportive* leadership focuses on worker welfare; *directive* leadership emphasizes task expectations; *participative* behavior involves subordinates in decision making; and *achievement-oriented* leadership emphasizes worker goals, performance improvement, high expectations, and recognition.

Despite the mixed research results to validate the theory, the model provides insights into the relationship between the leader, moderating work variables, and worker motivation. The leader clearly provides continuous facilitative support, using situation-defined behaviors.

Principals must provide clear role expectations of each staff member, which are continuously reinforced by worker goals and leader coaching. The primary task of the principal is to emphasize the function of *effective* teaching, and to provide multiple opportunities for teachers to participate in development activities and to offer feedback. The coaching/counseling function is critical to developing a climate for effective worker growth and achieving work goals.

The path-goal theory provides a conceptual framework for managing increasingly competent teachers as they work collectively on school goals. Leadership occurs continuously to make the path to the goal both easier and more satisfying. Increased levels of performance will result from the extent that satisfaction increases and is associated with the goal-directed effort.

Conclusion

The influence systems of authority, power, and leadership describe the intangible ways of stimulating certain work behaviors. *Authority* influences work at a number of different levels. Legitimate and position authority control work behaviors through organizational role-related standards. Competence and person authority provide the more informal influences that guide task-related work behaviors. Shared authority is the strongest approach to work influence.

Power is assumed and maintained in a variety of task-specific dimensions. Legitimate and reward power generally are provided from established leader roles, whereas expert and coercive power can emerge from either formal or informal roles. Referent power is that which is equally shared by management and workers. Of all types of power, *expert power* is the most influential.

Leadership theory today focuses on situational variables and identifies salient features among individual workers that tend to guide leader behaviors in varying situations. High and low task structure provide a general framework within which to analyze situations and necessary leader behavior. Perhaps the most important leadership theory is path-goal theory. The concept of leader assistance in a worker's progress toward goals, has within it the power to transform school leadership in general, and teaching performance specifically.

In the following chapters we address concepts of and methodologies for management supervising, planning, monitoring and evaluating. The influence systems of authority, power, and leadership permeate each management function and provide a psychological perspective on influencing others.

13

The Management Subsystem: Supervisory Influence

The Changing Context for Supervision

Especially in the professions, there are few, if any, roles in which those engaged in the work can expect to reach and maintain an ideal level of performance. On the contrary, one of the characteristics of true professionals is that they are constantly searching for new skills and solutions, and occupying the role of advanced learners. Perfection in human activity is rare, even unimaginable, not only because of human limitations but because each new accomplishment opens up the possibility of higher level accomplishment and defines new limits. Even in fields such as music or sports, the world's greatest composers, singers, and athletes are typically restive in their awareness of unmet challenges and unbroken boundaries. *Striving* for perfection seems more significant in life experience than do the attainments along the way. The continuous condition of everyone who works is, or should be, a search for improvement.

In this volume, there is a basic assumption that those who engage in highly complex human-service tasks such as teaching have two needs: thorough and intensive preservice preparation; and continuous assistance through supervision and other in-service growth opportunities. A related assumption is that there are now available procedures and technologies that make it possible for supervisors and even for peer-level colleagues to provide guidance to human-service professionals as they seek to perform more effectively in their roles.

Within the field of education, administrators have an obligation to monitor the quality of services and to make certain that clients are well served. Early

436

in the history of the public schools and their nonpublic equivalents, administrative and inspectorial roles were created to accomplish such purposes. Over the years there evolved not only postsecondary institutions to prepare educational workers, but also statutes and bureaucratic mechanisms to enforce certain standards and expectations. Simultaneously, there emerged attitudes and policies that accepted the need to provide continuing assistance to employed personnel. As probably in many other professions, teaching became a role within which those in superordinate capacities (principals, department heads, directors of instruction, and superintendents) sometimes engaged in evaluative (judging) tasks and sometimes engaged in supervisory (helping) tasks, all justified by the acknowledged need to ensure that pupils were being well served. Unfortunately for the children and their well-being, however, neither the judging nor the helping functions were performed with consistent skill or often enough to have a significant beneficial effect upon actual teacher performance. In sum, both the amount and the nature of evaluative/supervisory activity within schools fell short of what was needed. This situation remains true today.

The complexities of educating all sorts and conditions of children have never been well enough understood even by educators, and the legal and financial provisions for teacher education and for school operations in all fifty of the states remain geared to simplistic perceptions and expectations. This has become dramatically apparent the past decade or so, during which American society has been under a very great strain and the schools have suffered a disproportionate share of abuse, criticism, and neglect. Even as these pages are being written, public schools are being permitted to close down for lack of funds and teachers are either deserting the profession or resorting to protests because of uncompetitive salaries. Book censors and other pressure groups are attacking school officials, and a disastrous shortage of qualified teachers is on the horizon.

Paradoxically, these discouraging developments are taking place at a time when educators are at the brink of a potentially golden era. In many ways, education has reached the stage that medicine reached earlier in the century. Not very long ago, physicians were poorly trained and far less appreciated for their skill than they have been in recent years. The twentieth century has seen remarkable advances in mankind's understanding of the human body, of disease control and health maintenance, of pharmaceuticals, and of countless technologies that have made it possible for medical practitioners to succeed, a remarkable percentage of the time, in their work with patients. For these reasons, medical education has become a lengthy, expensive, and respected enterprise. There is virtually no public debate about the cost or the nature of medical training. Similarly, medical service costs are very high, and doctors are among the best compensated and the most respected of persons in the society. Funds for the support of medical research are generously provided not only by private donors, but also by the federal government, by industry, and by thousands of private foundations.

Much of the knowledge that undergirds medical practice also relates to educational practice, and many of the aforementioned technologies have either direct or indirect applications in educational research and procedure. In addition, advances in other "hard" sciences, in the social sciences, in the humanities, and within various branches of education itself, have provided an enormous reserve of theory, information, technology, and other resources upon which educators can call. Furthermore, many new educational theories have been introduced, new instructional approaches have been tested, better materials have been developed, and many lessons have been learned about how to educate all types of children.

Pedagogical scholarship, across many dimensions, has also become increasingly productive; and within a historically mediocre literature there are now appearing more and more top-flight materials about human learning and how to advance it. The significant intervention in educational research and development by wealthy foundations and by the federal government has permitted some quantum leaps into an era of more effective theory as well as practice. The tremendous impact upon the schools of civil rights legislation, of Public Law 94–142 (The Education for all Handicapped Children Act), and of various controversies such as school busing, has placed schools in a much more central (and basically uncomfortable) societal role than they had ever occupied, and also spurred some overdue and courageous changes. Increased attention in the press to school effectiveness, while often embarrassing to school people, has spurred research and raised provocative questions about educational tests and measurements and their limitations. These and other forces have obviously put educators on the spot, but in the aggregate they have set the stage for what *could* be a period of educational development equivalent to the medical revolution to which previous reference was made.

Supervision: A Brief Commentary

If a golden age in education is to come about, one of the first reforms will have to take place in teacher education. Because their training is so brief and incomplete, today's newly certified teachers, even though we believe they are better prepared than were their own teachers, begin with only a fraction of the information, insights, and techniques they need in order to function competently. Extended and more extensive preservice preparation could provide them with a more nearly adequate background. Even so, we perceive that every highly trained teacher will forever be faced with the need to know more and to control more skills. Another reform must therefore involve a significant stepping-up of the supervisory services in the schools as well as the more general provisions that are made for professional study and growth while in service.

The very term *supervision* is one that has muddied the water of education for a long time. Often in professional workers' minds, it refers to the unwelcome intrusion into their lives of persons who inspect their work, make judgments about it, and then commit those judgments to personnel records in ways that could have negative consequences, such as outright dismissal or a denial of promotion and/or salary increments. The stereotype of a harsh and arrogant evaluator, sampling only a tiny segment of the professional's work and providing virtually no useful feedback, probably has historical validity and is a hard one to ignore or forget. In the golden era for which we long, this stereotype would vanish altogether, and in its place would be an arrangement so fair, so thorough, and so helpful that teachers and other professionals would regard supervisors as the most valued associates in their lives.

One of the main reasons that the stereotype persists is that the various school officials who carry the responsibility for the *helping* function generally have the additional responsibility for *evaluation.* This might not seem unreasonable if the amount and the quality of helping activity were sufficient. Unfortunately, however, in most schools or other professional settings, the helpers (usually administrators) tend to neglect their helping functions and allow themselves to become immersed in administrative tasks. For these persons, skill in supervision develops slowly at best, and greater psychological rewards seem to come to them from activities where their success or accomplishment is more apparent. On the relatively rare occasions when they *do* visit the work setting, therefore, their observations lack historical depth and their relative inexperience in data gathering may lead to superficial conclusions.

Another reason for the persistence of an uncomplimentary supervisory stereotype is that professionals have long been encouraged to value their privacy and their independence. Even though it no longer has much theoretical support, and collaborative alternatives are slowly gaining ground, the familiar "self-contained classroom" has dominated the teaching scene for hundreds of years. Protected by four soundproof walls plus the belief that it is better, or at least more comfortable, to work alone in one's own classroom, many teachers are literally annoyed when someone else, perhaps especially an evaluator-on-the-prowl, opens the door and invades their space. As a result, teachers probably spend less time actually collaborating with each other, and in exchanging advice and ideas about specific classroom practice, than do all other kinds of professionals. In fact, much research about the teaching career suggests that teaching is a particularly lonely existence. The lively interchange that has become increasingly typical in law, medicine, engineering, corporate management, and other vocations is not yet a familiar mode in schools.

There are two ways available to school districts for promoting the growth of their certificated employees. One is to sponsor rich and varied in-service programs, and to offer incentives and rewards for postgraduate university study. Most school districts offer salary adjustments to teachers who pursue advanced course work or degrees, although these adjustments tend to be nominal. Few, on the other hand, elect to offer substantial in-service training programs on their own initiative; and most seem content to allow their staff to participate in the generally low-level meetings and conferences that are sponsored periodically by professional associations. The result is that the very term *in-service education* is in low repute, and only in rare situations are teachers exposed to truly meaningful in-service growth opportunities in the course of performing their duties.

The other means available to school districts for inducing teacher growth is the *supervisory program.* Building principals, department heads, directors or supervisors (both general and specialized), and consulting teachers share in this function. In most districts, however, budgetary and other constraints are such that the amount of such assistance available to teachers is quite small. Building principals, as line officers, also carry the responsibility for evaluating teachers and making administrative decisions about tenure, promotion, and the like. Often, though, their preoccupation with these and other administrative functions causes them to neglect the *helping* activities with which we in this volume prefer to associate the term "supervision." Our general argument is that the helping aspects of supervision, especially in a clinical context, need to be increased at least threefold or fourfold in the years that lie ahead, if teachers are to overcome their severe deficits of knowledge and skill and if schools are to evolve into truly professional environments.

Supervisors, especially principals, are caught in a very real bind. They are accountable for the performance of teachers, and therefore must be able to document not only teacher performance patterns but also their own involvement in efforts to influence and improve them. Yet their training has generally failed to provide them with adequate definitions of optimal teacher performance and with the necessary intervention and helping skills. Therefore, fears that administrators have about accountability may well be the motivation behind the renewed interest in acquiring what Sullivan (1980) referred to as "inspection" skills, such as those associated years ago with scientific management.

Clinical Supervision

Since the late 1960s there has been increased interest in the general topic of supervision, with *clinical* supervision receiving the most attention. Cogan first applied this adjective to that form of supervision that focuses on providing in-class assistance (or in other words, perceives the classroom as a clinic). Cogan was the major developer of what came to be called the clinical supervision cycle when he and others (including Anderson) at Harvard University were engaged in the supervision of student teachers in the 1950s and sought ways to make the process more powerful and effective. Goldhammer's (1969) volume on the topic grew out of the same environment, and a second edition (Goldhammer, Anderson, and Krajewski 1980) is among the several recent contributions to the literature. Acheson and Gall (1980), whose interest in clinical supervision stemmed from work in the early 1960s at Stanford University, concentrate upon techniques and applications of clinical supervision. Sullivan (1980) reviews the history, the status of research, and the potential for clinical supervision in the years ahead. Characteristic of these and nearly all other commentaries (including Cogan's 1973 volume) is that this thoroughly professional in-class, data-based, hands-on, analytical approach has enormous potentiality to improve the teaching profession; but, alas, it is all too seldom practiced to any significant extent.

Over the past 30 to 40 years the general field of supervision has outgrown its primitive origins and has emerged as a major subdiscipline of education. Sometimes as a function related to curriculum development (as reflected in the name of the Association for Supervision and Curriculum Development), sometimes as an aspect of administration (as in university departments of educational administration and supervision), and sometimes as a sister activity with counseling, supervision has received more and more attention in the literature and has generated a growing body of basic research. Especially important is the fact that it has become in many ways a "clinical" specialty, focusing upon deliberate intervention based upon episodes of professional performance that have been observed by the intervener at first hand. For many years, the writers of supervision textbooks underplayed this clinical dimension, which calls for the supervisor to "roll up his sleeves" and commit significant blocks of time to direct observation. They cluttered up their textbooks with references to all sorts of assisting and coordinating activities which, however meritorious they may have been as services to teachers or to the school district, had little if any direct impact on the teachers' classroom behaviors. When clinical supervision, a term that has been in common use for only about 15 years, came to be acknowledged as the most central aspect of supervisory work, the field emerged from its adolescence into maturity.

The context of clinical supervision requires elaboration for it to influence the performance of teachers significantly. The expertise of teachers today is fairly sophisticated when compared to that of the 1940s and 1950s. Yet, teachers remain only minimally knowledgeable about the fields of learning, teaching, organization, management, and group production. In fact, teachers resist supervisory visits to facilitate professional growth. Blumberg (1980, 20) summarized various research studies on teacher and supervisor attitudes about supervision. He found that teachers place little value on traditional supervision, while supervisors say their work has much value. Supervisors want to spend more time at what teachers regard as useless. The context of supervision requires major redefinition in function, emphasis, and methodology.

Drucker provides an important clue to this dilemma. He refers to professionals in organizations today as "knowledge workers," and asserts that knowledge workers demand responsibility to overcome irresponsible and arrogant behaviors (Drucker 1982, 113). Sergiovanni (1982, 108–118) notes in the same spirit that schools are bureaucracies with professional workers who require a different kind of supervision than nonprofessionals. He proposes that supervision be conceptualized and practiced as "mutual adjustment," as a coordinating mechanism for operating teams of teachers. Given group responsibility for achievement of a certain number of students, teachers are more likely to engage in higher level dialogue about the nature and effects of their instruction. Consequently, we believe that teachers today will benefit from clinical supervision and they will realize far more professional growth if clinical supervision not only becomes a supervisor's task, but is shared among teachers as a mechanism to help them alter their teaching and learning norms.

Although teachers see little benefit in supervision as it now exists, they perceive a need for supervision (Cooper 1982, 11). Teachers prefer a combination of direct and indirect approaches to supervision. In clinical supervision settings, many studies confirm that desirable changes actually occur in teachers' classroom behavior (Garman 1971; Kerr 1976; Krajewski 1976). Clinical supervision facilitates positive attitude changes and high levels of openness among teachers and increased numbers of effective teaching behaviors (Shuma 1973). Teachers tend to seek assistance from other teachers far more often than from supervisors (Blumberg 1980). The central target in clinical supervision, which stimulates growth, is self-confrontation; feedback on performance with a focus, fosters change (Fuller and Manning 1973). So powerful is the feedback element in clinical supervision that 98 percent of teachers are able to adopt new concepts and practices if role coaching is practiced (Joyce and Showers 1980). Research tends to confirm that systematic observation and feedback on classroom events enables teachers to alter their teaching patterns significantly.

Wherein lies the power of clinical supervision to transform teaching behaviors? Garman asserts that inquiry and theorizing are the primary proclivities in clinical supervision; reflection about teaching can lead to new kinds of action. Schön (1983) describes reflection-in-action as "on-the-spot surfacing, criticizing, restructuring, and testing of interactive understandings of experience phenomena; often, it takes the form of a reflective conversation with the situation." Sergiovanni (1982, 17) proposes that at least three interdependent relationships within the coaching process should receive *reflective* attention:

1. the relationship between teaching and the mentality of the teacher
2. the relationship between teaching incidents as parts and the totality of teaching
3. the relationship between teaching and its cultural context

Dialogue about teaching today focuses on what is known about effective teaching; significant direction can be drawn from research for improvements in teaching. Research and theory provide the standard for reflection, dialogue, and action in clinical supervision.

During its early stages of development, clinical supervision was concerned primarily with helping teachers with classroom climate factors. A five- or eight-stage methodology, in the form of an observation cycle, was developed to assist teachers in improving instruction, with particular attention given to classroom climate. The past several decades, however, have generated considerable certainty about the learning process. Supervisors can focus on climate factors, and move beyond to examine learning objectives, diagnostic procedures, program planning, and classroom management decisions as well as the substance of teacher/pupil interaction during instruction. The selection of a general focus for supervision springs from school and individual goals; the particular focus is teacher/team specific. Thus, clinical supervision provides a coaching dimension for the school/teacher improvement process.

In this volume we view clinical supervision as the most important and potentially the most useful of all management technologies. We perceive that neglect of supervision has in the past made it very difficult for new ideas and new practices to take hold in American schools. Further, we believe that the systems approach to managing productive schools is likely to fail or to succeed in direct proportion to the use that is made of clinical supervision practices by supervisors and among peers.

A Systems Approach to Supervision

A systems approach to school management assumes that organizational and personal staff needs can and should be woven together for the purpose of producing anticipated patterns of school growth. An example from the sports world comes to mind. The Dallas Cowboys football organization has sometimes been criticized as a kind of inhuman machine. However, when its great quarterback, Roger Staubach, announced his retirement and was being questioned by television reporters (April 1980) he said the system (Dallas Cow-

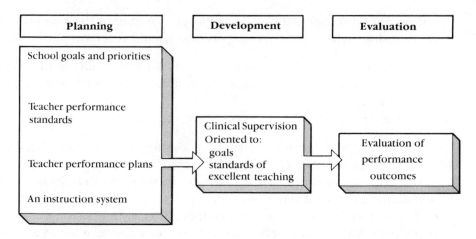

Figure 13.1. Clinical Supervision Linkage System

boys) isn't inhuman—it's a bunch of people who know what they're doing. Goals and means are specified and are pursued by people who know what they are doing.

Within a systems context, clinical supervision does not function as an isolated practice. It is directly linked to school goals, to performance standards, to individual goals and evaluation, and to a clear definition of instruction and learning (see Figure 13.1). If schools develop the capacity to link these schooling practices together, clinical supervision has the power to alter instructional norms. Given a mechanism that deals tough-mindedly *and* humanly with both growth and evaluation, principals and supervisors can become catalysts in transforming schooling. If clinical supervision with its comprehensive and systematic data collection technology, is not viewed within a systems context of schooling transformation, the practice could become little more than a sophisticated inspection system.

School Goals and Priorities

The performance of teachers occurs within the context of a school's social system, which has its established norms and priorities. In order to survive, a school needs to become increasingly aware of its own ecology, and to define its growth priorities each year. Strong school leadership, a healthy climate, and flexible organization all impact significantly on actual teaching and on learning. Consequently, school improvement priorities each year must reflect more than the deficiencies of the curriculum or of individual teachers; and they must relate to all dimensions of school life that impact on instruction.

If a school decides, for example, to develop a personalized reading program for all students, then teacher performance goals, clinical supervision, and evaluation will focus on improving instructional effectiveness with regard to desired reading program results.

Teacher Performance Standards

General job descriptions for teachers will yield to more comprehensive categorical definitions of teacher role performance outcomes. Satisfactory teaching performance will be defined in several clusters: instructing students; developing programs and materials with colleagues and by one's self; and being trained and supervised to improve teaching skills. Known effective practices will guide the direction of teacher planning, development, and evaluation.

Teacher Performance Plans

Personal goal setting and planning will become viewed as essential to ensure that school goals are achieved and that performance standards actually guide practice. No longer can we expect teachers merely to "get in gear." Teachers must work within specific parameters to ensure that performance facilitates school development. Studies of performance systems in business and industry continue to rate goal-based systems as far superior to the more familiar rating and ranking performance systems (Cummings and Schwab 1973, 97). The key to goal-based performance lies in involvement of workers in defining personal as well as organizational priorities, and in defining the focus for their professional contributions, growth, and subsequent evaluation. In fact, goals are an important determinant of performance (Locke 1968, 157–189). The guessing games that plague traditional teacher evaluation systems can be eliminated through a planning system that involves the professional in the organizational decision-making process.

Teaching Decision Sets

The instruction system described in Chapter 10 (Figure 10.1) becomes the framework for teacher coaching (Figure 13.2). Link one addresses teaching decisions regarding curriculum selection and the ways those decisions influence the instructional program and student achievement. Link two includes the diagnostic and testing procedures that are used to identify levels of student readiness, interest, and learning styles. Link three relates to specific program plans as they incorporate curriculum objectives and assessed needs, and provide the specific guide for instruction. Link four addresses decisions necessary for managing an effective classroom activity system to facilitate learning. Link five focuses on actual teaching and learning interactions and changes while plans are implemented. In link six, clinical supervision provides coaching for teachers as to the effectiveness of their plans and their teaching patterns during classroom experiences. Clinical supervision provides feedback on the specific effects of their teaching decisions.

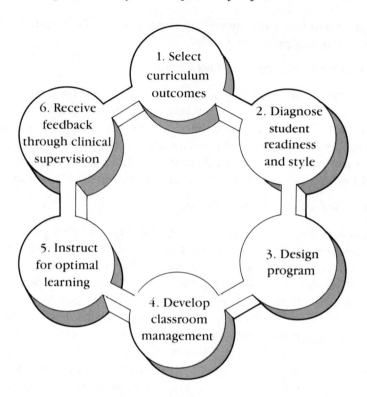

Figure 13.2. An Instructional Delivery System

Clinical Supervision

Anderson and Krajewski (Goldhammer et al. 1980, 1–11), in their recent revision of Goldhammer's landmark book, observed that preoccupation with the stages of the classic observation cycle is now giving way to a larger concern for underlying concepts. Clinical supervision was conceptualized by them (1980, 26–27) as

  a technology for improving instruction
  a deliberate intervention into instructional processes
  goal oriented, combining school and personal growth needs
  a working relationship between teachers and supervisors requiring mutual trust
  a systematic process that requires a flexible methodology
  an approach that generates productive tension

assuming that the supervisor knows more about instruction and learning than teachers*

a system that requires training for the supervisor

These nine concepts are foundational for effective clinical supervision today. The concepts enable us not only to understand and practice observation processes more effectively, but, perhaps more importantly, to develop a mind-set or belief system about a goal approach to coaching teachers.

Given this conceptual framework, the specific clinical supervision methodology known as the observation cycle becomes a useful guide for supervisory practice. Briefly stated, the classic observation cycle includes the following five stages:

1. *Pre-observation conference*—a briefing conference that results in a contract between a teacher and observer regarding the purpose of the specific observation
2. *Observation*—actual collection of data concerning events in the classroom as they relate to the contract topics
3. *Analysis and strategy session*—review and interpretation of collected data as they relate to the contract and to pedagogical theory and research
4. *Conference*—provision of feedback to the teacher on the observed teacher/learning segment; preparation for "next steps"
5. *Postobservation critique*—joint analysis of the usefulness of the foregoing observation cycle activities

Each cycle should be viewed as one of many successive events, all geared to both long-range and short-range goals and all interconnecting in a developmental process.

Concluding Comments

Clinical supervision offers promise when viewed as a part of a comprehensive teacher development system that aims at ambitious goals (especially for learners) and assumes that teachers have need for continuous extension and refinement of their skills in goal setting, diagnosis, program design, organization and management, instruction, and responding to supervisory assistance. The linkage system presented provides a context for an effective clinical supervision program.

---

* A current rewording of this statement might be: assuming that the supervisor knows more about critiquing and analyzing instruction and learning than do teachers.

Coaching Teachers

The championship football team is usually applauded by its fans for results of the combined coaching/playing efforts during the season. No fan questions that the coach is responsible for tapping the skill potential of the players and training them relentlessly prior to and throughout the season. The winning coach continuously assesses performance strengths and gaps in individual players and devises numerous strategies for eliciting more effective performance. The coaching process is strenuous, unending, and results oriented. In many respects, individual player failure reflects coaching failure and results in lessened team status. Thus, coaching tasks throughout the season determine in large measure team status at season's end.

Tom Osborn, the head football coach for the University of Nebraska reported his coaching philosophy to an audience at a sports banquet at Texas Tech University (April 27, 1982). He intentionally turns losses into wins by focusing on what works and moving with that. Further, the only way to have a good team is to have team players. No matter how much individual talent is on the team, unless players all have a team sense, the team cannot be a winning team.

Clinical supervision methodology has the potential for enabling supervisors and principals effectively to coach teachers to win the teaching game (causing sufficient student learning to occur). A spot judgment, twice a year, will rarely alter a teacher's performance. However, coaching throughout the year toward winning performances can eliminate ineffective patterns, and also instill new practices.

Research on the practice of teacher coaching has yielded impressive results. Joyce and Showers (1982) report from repeated research studies that on-the-job coaching is the practice that enables 98 percent of teachers to master new skills and transfer those skills to classroom use. In fact, coaching is so powerful that without follow-up, only 25 percent of the teachers (at the most) attending an exemplary workshop will transfer to their classrooms the skill that was taught. However, with systematic coaching following a workshop, 98 percent can master the new skill.

It now seems that the presence of an ongoing coaching system for teachers is the central organizational function that will enable teachers to transform instructional norms. The context for teacher coaching includes a supervisor and/or principal, but goes far beyond the limitations of a unidimensional relationship. A growing body of research reveals that teachers working together on supervisory matters are often more satisfied and more effective in their instruction. Goldsberry, who has coined the term *collegial assistance,* reports that practice in clinical supervision can influence teacher performance posi-

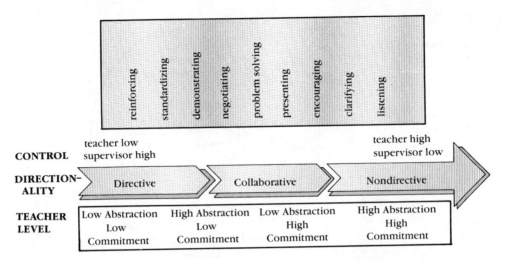

Figure 13.3. Developmental Match and Directionality of the Supervisory Behavior Continuum [*Source:* Carl D. Glickman, *Developmental Supervision: Alternative Practices for Helping Teachers Improve Instruction.* (Alexandria, VA: Association for Supervision and Curriculum Development, 1981), p. 49. Reprinted with permission of the Association of Supervision and Curriculum Development. © 1981 by the Association of Supervision and Curriculum Development. All rights reserved.]

tively, and that collegial assistance fosters leadership development, direct classroom support, and increased colleagueship among teachers (Goldsberry 1980). Teachers can be trained to use clinical techniques with each other and to provide useful feedback. Blumberg observes (1980) that teachers actually seek assistance from other teachers more often than from supervisors, when given an option.

Teachers, however, are at varying stages of development as professionals. Glickman (1981) defines three kinds of supervisory behavior for the various levels of teacher development (see Figure 13.3). *Directive* supervision assumes that teachers need a low level of abstraction about teaching and are themselves low in commitment. A higher level of supervision, *collaborative,* assumes that teachers have a need for high abstraction about learning, ranging from high to low levels, which correspond to levels of low to high commitment. *Nondirective* supervision, the highest level, assumes a high level of abstraction about teaching; it is the most effective level due to a high level of teacher commitment to growth. While the focus in the model is on supervisory behavior, levels of teacher maturity with regard to levels of abstraction about teaching and commitment to growth guide supervisory decisions about the nature of the coaching relationship.

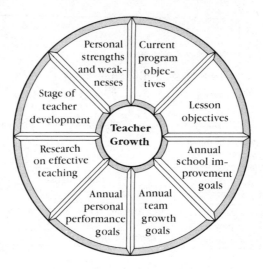

Figure 13.4. Variables Influencing Teacher Coaching Sessions

Diagnostic supervision provides a framework within which to plan for supervision during each developmental stage. Diagnostic supervision includes several dimensions: (1) a recognition of a need; (2) a problem statement; (3) an agreement on performance objectives; (4) an assessment of teacher attitudes, skills, and concepts; and (5) strategies for developing concepts and skills (Seager 1979).

The context of coaching is complex and therefore requires that it be both personal and school oriented in its focus. Figure 13.4 delineates the variables that come into play when teachers coach each other and are coached by supervisors. The *goals* of the school, the work group, and the individual teacher provide a particular annual emphasis for clinical supervision. *Research* on effective teaching serves as a general direction finder for any and all coaching sessions. Stages of *teacher development* provide general guiding principles for diagnostic supervision within a given year and enable a teacher better to master a new skill. *Personal strengths* and weaknesses are viewed within the context of goals, exemplary practice, and development stages. A particular instructional program and the objectives of the lesson observed provide an observation context for identifying salient teaching behaviors. Recommendations for growth, then, relate to teacher needs within a goal structure and in relation to the natural developmental stages of professional growth.

In several workshops, we have invited principals to identify concepts inherent in the terms *coaching, monitoring,* and *supervision.* Listed here are many of their ideas, which further embellish the concepts and provide a clearer understanding of the context and the nature of the coaching function.

When principals are asked to explain the functions of monitoring, they tend to equate it with traditional supervision linked to inspection, periodic checking, critiquing, correcting, reviewing, and observation of records, plans, and performance. The functions of coaching are seen as optimum utilization of personnel, using strategies to get the players going, inspiring top performance, providing examples and demonstrations, helping everyone to know the rules, constantly studying the fine points of the game, developing effective game plans, and similar activities geared to performing as well as possible.

Principals refer to *supervisory feedback* as sharing important information, offering positive reinforcement, offering suggestions, reinforcing desired learning and behavior, creating understanding, furthering planning and goal setting for future needs, inviting self-improvement, increasing awareness, and utilizing effective communication skills. In one seminar, a group of principals was asked to draw analogies from their actual coaching experience in sports or the arts to coaching teachers. Six suggestions were made:

1. set high expectations
2. convey expectations
3. analyze performance
4. adjust game plan to teacher needs
5. practice, practice, practice
6. break instruction into small, "defendable" bits

Coaching assumes a tough-minded intent to foster growth in teaching performances. It is a continuous feedback mechanism provided by peers, supervisors, and principals with the intention of intervening into instructional practices. The focus for coaching stems from goals and relates current patterns to standards of excellence. Coaching is the agent that has the power to transform teaching into a facilitating function in the student mastery process.

Observation Cycle Methodology

On the following pages, each of the five observation stages (see Figure 13.5) will be discussed in relation to key behaviors. However, it should be noted that five discrete phases do not themselves comprise the observation cycle. Rather, certain key behaviors are central to the coaching cycle: contracting, observing, data collecting, data analysis, and conferencing/feedback.

To illustrate the centrality of key behaviors, one regular five-stage cycle may be followed by a variety of follow-up supervisory activities. The contract for

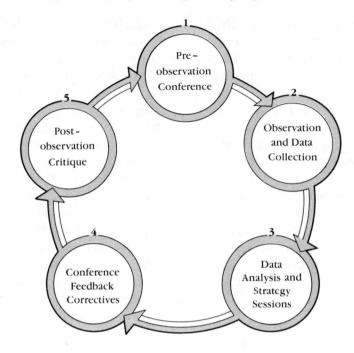

Figure 13.5. The Observation Cycle. The Goldhammer Model

the *next* observation is established during a feedback conference. A teacher may plan to develop a certain skill; the next observation then will focus on that skill. The strategy session and conference, however, may not occur separately but may be merely a sharing of the data collected by the observer. In a work context where the observer and observee have a mutual understanding of teacher goals, observations and data feedback may provide the necessary feedback on progress. At the end of the projected period, however (several weeks or months), a formal conference is held during which progress is assessed summatively. Observation cycles should become flexible mechanisms designed to provide feedback and correctives to teachers on their progress toward specific goals.

Stage 1.   Contracting: Preobservation Conference

In all discussions of supervision, especially in its clinical aspect, one of the most frequently mentioned needs is for the supervisor and the teacher to enjoy good *rapport.* Teachers are naturally apprehensive about supervision, partly because supervisors seek an intense, highly personal interaction with another adult. It is important for the supervisor to understand and deal sympathetically with the hesitant posture that teachers are likely to adopt at the beginning of a supervisory relationship. They must be prepared, for example, for a teacher's reluctance to invite criticism of very *basic* and value-laden aspects of his or her work: at the outset, the topics proposed by teachers for supervisory review are likely to be "safe" areas in which the teacher does not feel inadequate or vulnerable. Supervisors must therefore make certain that the way they deal with each teacher nurtures rapport, helps the teacher to feel safe within the supervisory framework, and causes the teacher to volunteer contract items that relate to real and perplexing (rather than superficial) problems.

The contract or agreement can be built around a simple problem or question, or it can involve several different problems. If more than one observer will be involved, in a supervision team approach, it is of course easier to handle several different data-gathering approaches simultaneously. For example, a teacher may be concerned about two of the students in a given class, whose responses to the teacher and to the class activities have been very muted and apathetic. As a result, the teacher may have planned tomorrow's lesson in such a way that these two students will be given certain responsibilities and opportunities designed to capture their interest and attention. This is only one aspect of the lesson as planned, however, and the *main* thing the teacher wants the observer(s) to focus upon is the general social-emotional climate. If there are two observers, it could be agreed that one of them would seek to collect as much data as possible about the two reportedly apathetic students, while the other observer would use an instrument such as Withall's index. If there is only one observer, presumably he or she would agree to use the SECI and would *also* seek to keep an eye on, and record some pencil notes about, the two students.

It is important during the preobservation conference to ask enough questions so that there results a thorough understanding of the objectives of the lesson, of the relationships of this particular lesson to the overall learning program being implemented, of the specific activities to be observed, and of other factors that will be involved, such as handouts to be provided, materials to be used, and the physical setup of the classroom. The items or problems on which the teacher wants feedback should be carefully defined, and the exact nature of the teacher's questions should be spelled out. "How do I come across?" is far too ambiguous a question, and it should be modified and expanded until what the teacher means by "come across" is quite explicit. Also at this stage, the two or more adults should consider what types of data or information will be needed in order that the question(s) can in fact be answered. For example, what sorts of behaviors on the part of the two apathetic students would convince the teacher that his or her plan to activate them was a success? More frequent volunteering of responses? More smiles and expressions of enthusiasm? Increased willingness to produce and turn in assignments? Often as such questions are raised, the teacher's definition of both the problem and the solution will become clearer.

The contractual agreement usually also includes reference to such details as the time and length of the observation, the place where the supervisor-observer should sit, the interaction (if any) that should occur between the students and the observer, and the most convenient time and place for the postobservation conference to take place.

During this discussion, and again during the postobservation conference, a good rule of thumb for the supervisor is to try to operate within the teacher's psychological comfort zone, and not to try to press beyond the teacher's apparent willingness to explore dangerous questions. As time goes by and each successive observation cycle increases the rapport and trust that is felt, teachers will become more willing to ask for help with complicated and delicate questions. A related rule is that supervisors should be careful to stay within the agreed contract, and not to stray into other topics or problems that come to his or her attention while in the classroom until they are sure that the teacher will be able to deal objectively and comfortably with such problems. If the contract calls only for collecting information about time-on-task, and the supervisor subsequently starts talking about the teacher's apparent rudeness to certain children, rapport could disappear. At some point in the future, as the contracts move more into social–emotional climate and other such realms, it will become possible to assemble and share information that helps to describe how, if at all, the teacher deals differently with some of the children.

Sometimes there is ample time for the preobservation conference, but at other times it may be necessary to hurry. To hurry can be manageable if the situation is clear cut or if the two people have a reasonably long history of working together, but it can also be disastrous if it leads to a poor understanding of the intended lesson and/or a fuzzy contract. In the latter case, it may be smarter to cancel or postpone the observation than to proceed unprepared.

Prior to showing up at the appointed hour, the supervisor should always feel that he or she is indeed well prepared, has a clear and explicit contract, has selected an appropriate observation instrument or approach, and is confident that the assembled data once analyzed can provide a solid basis for productive discussions of the contract problem(s). This makes for a healthy supervisory situation.

Stage 2.   Observation and Data Collection

Most of the time teachers are obliged to collect data about learning as best they can on their own, but this is usually difficult and often impossible to do with any kind of accuracy. An observer who is not preoccupied with the management of the classroom and who is equipped with appropriate data-gathering instrument(s) can do a far more accurate and comprehensive job of discovering the actual extent of pupil attention to the designated task, and the nature of teaching behaviors and their influence on the learning process.

Two principles involved in data collection are important. The observer is recording a *sample* of behavior; that sample needs to be gathered in a scientific fashion. First, *data are to be collected systematically.* In some situations, a decision needs to be made to count and record observations every three minutes, or every minute, and so on. For example, in documenting the numbers of students on task, the observer records behaviors at regular intervals. In other situations, the observer records virtually every behavior. For example, *each* teacher comment is recorded for a certain period, when assessing classroom climate on the social-emotional climate index. For other situations, the observer selects one situation and analyzes it in relation to certain criteria. In decoding the degree of effectiveness in directives provided by a learning station, for example, the observer checks for the presence or absence of certain characteristics.

Data are gathered not by the whim of an observer (a subjective approach), but by systematic recording of words, behaviors, tallies, characteristics, and so on. Subjective analysis occurs in the analysis session of the observation cycle. The intent in clinical supervision is to analyze and critique an objective sample, a snapshot, of what occurred in the classroom, so that the actual happenings can provide a basis for assessing instructional strengths, weaknesses, and next steps for the teacher.

The second principle in data collection is that *the observer uses any means possible to collect desired data.* For example, the teacher may be interested in student results regarding a particular teaching strategy. The observer would document the strategy (record behaviors systematically), and then collect and analyze student projects, papers, and so on. Or, the observer may record student interactions in work groups on audio or video recorder. Or instant-print photographs may capture observable data that will be useful to the teacher.

In many situations the observer will have selected a particular instrument for gathering specific data, only to find that instrument useless in a particular observation. In order to collect data relating to the agreed-on purpose of a cycle, the observer will select another instrument during observation, or perhaps, and more probably, will invent an instrument on the spot that will lend itself more to the purpose of that particular observation (see Descamps and Hernandez 1981).

Most instruments require the observer either to tally specific observations or to check certain characteristics of the instructional setting. The observer should also feel free to diagram a situation to illustrate certain patterns. The teacher may want to know if there are bottlenecks or problems associated with space design and student work patterns. Or the teachers may want to learn the amount of talk each student contributes in a small group setting. Maps and codes can be especially helpful in situations such as these.

Stage 3.   Analyzing Data: Preparing For the Conference

We have indicated our belief that the analysis stage in the cycle challenges the intellectual and professional skill of the observer more than other stages. After a lesson has been observed for about 20 minutes, sufficient data have been gathered to "sample" the teacher's overall behavior patterns. The observer can assume that these salient behaviors guide this teacher's instruction all day every day, and therefore are a proper subject for exhaustive analysis.

Having recorded the events that occurred in the classroom, the next task is to arrange and rearrange the data so that they shed light upon the contract questions or problems. How can these data and insights be linked with prior knowledge of this teacher's professional behavior and with excellent pedagogical guidelines and standards? What strengths have been noted that can be reinforced in the teacher? What weaknesses, problems, or difficulties have been unearthed or confirmed? Especially with respect to problems, how can the matter be discussed with the teacher in a way that does not do unintended harm to the teacher's well-being or to the supervisor/teacher relationship?

Fairly well accepted in the supervision literature, of which the volume by Goldhammer, Anderson, and Krajewski (1980) is especially relevant here, is that teachers function within well-established patterns that (1) tend to be repeated over and over again and (2) are very difficult to change. Principals and other supervisors need to be very perceptive, and also very patient, as they work with teachers over the weeks, months, and years. Analysis of the *content* of data from each classroom observation can be time consuming. Often the supervisor must ignore, or at least postpone reflection upon, some of the collected information in order to concentrate upon the data that relate more clearly to the contract question(s) or that appear to be more manageable at this point in time.

It is important for the supervisor to allow enough time for the analysis phase. If several observers are serving as a team, our experience suggests that at least 45 minutes will be needed, and it may be prudent to reserve a full hour. Happily, this is certain to be an hour well spent, because in addition to making the necessary preparation for meeting with the teacher, the observers often get into enlightening discussions of pedagogy and of supervisor technology, which helps the observers/supervisors to grow in professional skill and knowledge. Even when one works alone, however, there is opportunity for growth through the reflection that takes place.

Several guiding principles exist for the analysis stage. The first is that all data are to be reported first (for example, 21 teacher statements versus 3 student statements; climate index of .9; 15 negative reinforcers and 2 positive reinforcers). After the observation team has reconstructed the classroom events through objective data summaries, the next task is to analyze the data.

Data analysis is a subjective task in which observers attempt to link the meaning of numbers and behavior patterns to the goals of the lesson and to the purpose of that particular cycle. During analysis the observers consider several bodies of personal knowledge; what research and theory can contribute to understanding the data; personal experiences with similar situations; personal feelings and emotions about the classroom events; and general knowledge among observers that relates to the situation. All of these elements of knowledge are tools for analysis as the team identifies which teaching behaviors were effective, which were ineffective, and which need to be replaced.

The outcome of the analysis session is for the observers to be able to identify *what worked* in the classroom and why; what *did not work* and why; and *next steps* in the teacher's growth process. Answers to these three central questions enable the observers to prepare for the teacher feedback conference (stage IV).

Once the reflections and analyses have been completed, the supervisor(s) must plan for the conference. In effect this is the strategic phase of the cycle, because it involves developing a strategy for approaching the interview: Which issues can appropriately be discussed? In what order should they be approached? Should we try to balance the positive (strengths) items with the negative (weaknesses) items? How can we check along the way to see if the teacher is comprehending our messages? How much, and what types of data should be brought forward? How should the conference be opened? What end product goals are we shooting for? These and other questions must be answered in advance, so that the conference can proceed with minimum confusion or difficulty (see Goldhammer et al., op. cit., 117–141 for detailed suggestions).

Stage 4.   The Supervisory Conference

The quality of advance planning, which in turn is influenced by the clarity of the contract questions and the adequacy of data collected, will greatly influence the nature and the effectiveness of the postobservation conference. The purposes of the conference are several: (1) to provide feedback, geared to the teacher's contract questions, on the teacher's classroom behavior and activities; (2) to provide reinforcement and increase the satisfactions of the teacher; (3) to stimulate higher level thinking about critical issues in teaching; (4) where necessary, to provide didactic helps to the teacher; (5) to help the teacher to perceive how data analysis and reflective thinking can lead to self-improvement; and (6) to develop incentives for more intensive professional self-analysis. Although many teachers are, at least at the outset, fearful of supervision, we believe that most teachers are not only willing but eager to evaluate and improve their teaching. When good clinical supervision services are made available to them, teachers will overcome their fears and welcome the help and stimulus that are provided.

One of the keys to successful staff development is supervisor skill in conferencing. This applies to the preobservation conference as well as the postobservation conference, although the former is mostly in the control of the teacher and has less emotional loading than does the latter, during which there is the possibility of receiving disappointing, embarrassing, or even painful messages. How to conduct conferences in a manner that is comfortable for the teacher, especially with respect to negative messages, is therefore a critical talent in the supervisor's repertoire.

One of the greatest advantages of using observation instruments that produce quantified data is that they are "emotionally neutral" and make the news available to both the supervisor and the teacher without editorial comment and/or accusatory implications. If a supervisor says "my impression is that you talk too much, and provide too little reinforcement," the message comes across as a personal judgment and threatens to contaminate the teacher-supervisor partnership. If a data collection instrument shows that teacher talk occupies 91 percent of the time, or reveals only three reinforcements against 26 correctives, the data speak for themselves. Nor, we might add, is the teacher likely to hold a grudge against the instrument.

Most textbooks on supervision include advice about conferencing, and several recent references are available (for example, Warner 1981; Kindsvatter and Wilen 1981). However, most principals are former teachers and all teachers are well experienced in conferencing technology because of their continual interactions with students and frequent meetings with parents. Therefore, there are not many aspects of postobservation conferencing that are literally strange or unfamiliar to the participants. All the same, a few comments and suggestions may be useful.

The opening moments of each conference are especially important, and the observer's words and actions ought to be based on a deliberate plan that takes into account the probable reaction of the teacher to the opening message. Sometimes it is appropriate to open the conference by recapping the preobservation agreement and then to deal, one by one and in the order in which they came up, with data pertaining to each of the contract questions. At other times, it may seem better to open the conference with a request for additional information ("What happened after I left? Did the two girls complete their project?") or to ask the teacher how she felt about the lesson in relation to her stated intents.

During the conference, the observers need to be mindful of time constraints and see that the discussion does not stray off course or focus too long on particular points, especially minor ones. Some observers develop real skill in wrapping up each piece of the conference and effecting a transition to the next part. The same is true about knowing how and when to wrap up the entire conference and bring it to a successful close.

It is sometimes useful, with the teacher's permission, to tape-record a conference so the supervisor can play it back later and either learn from his or her mistakes or confirm the success of procedures that were followed and phrases that were used. Such a recording can also be useful to both the supervisor and the teacher during the postobservation critique.

One of the most crucial tests of a conference is whether or not each party was really hearing what the other party was saying, or trying to say. It is often a good idea to stop and say something like, "If I understand you correctly, you are saying . . . ," or "I'm not sure if you and I are seeing these data in the same way. My interpretation is . . . ." At the end, too, it is often good for each party to state, in two or three sentences, what he or she considers to be the main message or conclusions of the conference. Does the teacher now understand what worked and why? What didn't work and why? Is the teacher now able to report probable next steps to the observation team?

Equally important, of course, is to be sure that the conference ends with an agenda for the future: "We are agreed, then, that I should return twice next month to use the same instrument, so we can see if the [new procedures] will make a difference." "My plan is to put my desk over in a corner for a while, and try not to depend on it so much." "We'll each try to put together a list of phrases, other than okay and good, for reinforcing positive pupil behaviors . . . ," and so on. The process of teacher self-improvement never ends!

Stage 5. Postobservation Critique

It is very useful, once the four prior stages of the clinical supervision cycle have been completed, for the two parties to spend a few additional moments together in an assessment of the experience just shared. Were each of the two conferences conducted in an effective and professional manner? Were the physical and psychological conditions comfortable and appropriate? Did we come up with an important and valid contract agreement? Did the principal/supervisor(s) select pertinent data collection procedures and/or instruments? Was the observer's behavior during the visit in keeping with the plan? Did the cycle lead to new and useful insights into professional problems? Do we now have a clearer sense of next steps to be taken, and does it seem that in the next cycle we can move forward even more confidently? Are we both becoming more skillful in our professional roles? Pursuit of these and related questions can help to put everything into healthy perspective, and make long-range professional-growth goal attainment all the more probable.

Getting Started

The observation cycle we have outlined here is highly structured and systematic, and it is obvious that to conduct such cycles frequently would be very expensive in terms of time and energy for teachers and supervisors alike. As the reader may surmise, the authors have a strong preference for cycles conducted by a *team* of observers, as opposed to the far more common practice of one-on-one observation, and such a practice further exacerbates the problem of time and energy. However, in their experience, both the depth and breadth of analysis (and, for that matter, of data gathering) is so much greater when there are several observers, that a teacher who is observed once by three colleagues might well gain more from it than from being observed three (or more) times by just one observer. Furthermore, in our experience, a team of observers probably gains even more from a cycle than does the observed teacher, because of the aforementioned quality of analysis.

We recommend, as an ideal arrangement toward which every school might strive, that every classroom teacher (except beginning teachers, for whom at least twice as many observations should be planned) should be observed under clinical conditions at least once per week, and that the *full* cycle as described should be experienced at least once per month. Ordinarily we would assume that the principal or other designated supervisors will be essentially involved in the supervisory activities, but we propose that *peers* be involved regularly so that each teacher's personal-professional growth is a matter of collective ambition. A corollary of these proposals is that every teacher, including beginners, should serve on a peer observation team *at least* once per month, in order to have systematic experience with data collection, with conferencing, and with the analysis of professional behaviors. Service on observation teams also helps teachers to look at pupils' needs and behaviors in more detached and objective ways, and it causes them to raise questions about curriculum, about materials, about school policies, and about the overall school environment that might not occur to them in the relentless "daily grind" from which there is often no detachment.

Supervision implies a subordinate-superordinate relationship, and under ordinary circumstances we are not uncomfortable with such a notion. In virtually all fields of endeavor, there are persons with special skills and knowledge who, by virtue of their greater expertise and perspective, can legitimately offer advice, criticism, or even punishment to other workers in that field. We perceive that many such persons exist in education, and that it is not only appropriate but necessary that some of them (if willing) be placed in roles where they can assist and, as necessary, evaluate others. In healthy and well-managed school districts, principals and supervisors do (with rare exceptions) have excellent experience and knowledge on which to draw, and are indeed qualified to serve as helpers and judges. Usually, too, their training and their orientation enable them to work with teachers in a friendly, constructive, and professional manner. In healthy situations such as this, a feeling of mutual trust develops and teachers are very receptive to the supervisory services that are made available. A reasonable analogy is that the supervisor/teacher relationship, at its best, may in several ways resemble the teacher/pupil relationship at *its* best.

When pupils are sufficiently mature and skillful, often the teacher's best option is to "get out of the learner's way." When pupils are immature and unable to give much direction to their learning program, the good teacher provides necessary guidance and structure. The good teacher's goal is for the learners to become as self-sufficient as possible, yet there is never an abdication of the guidance functions when need arises. Furthermore, teachers exist in part to be sure the learner is in a state of productive tension, between the reality of now and the possibility (ideal) that exists for the future. What has just been said about good teaching, we believe, holds also for good supervision.

Just as classroom instruction should be goal oriented, so should supervision. One thing we especially value in the observation cycle is that under usual circumstances the teacher and the supervisor are both aware in advance of specific instructional goals or objectives toward which the lesson is directed, and also of technical–professional skills and behaviors the teacher is seeking to acquire or to improve. This is not to deny the value of impromptu supervisory visits, but rather to emphasize that a supervisor can usually be of greater help when he or she has advance knowledge of the planned experience and has therefore prepared himself or herself psychologically and tactically to deal with probable events or situations.

Within the school, counselors are another major group whose work can be examined with the help of clinical supervision technology. The nature of their training, as well as their orientation to analysis, causes counselors to be somewhat more amenable to clinical supervision than some other types of education professionals. Furthermore, they have usually had a great deal of experience with data collection and with the analysis of verbal behavior. It is not unusual for them to make use of one-way mirrors or tape recorders as a way of protecting the privacy of counseling sessions while making observation and analysis possible.

In the central office of school districts, every role occupant including the superintendent of schools can, subject only to willingness, profitably submit to observations by other professionals. For example, many of the situations suggested for the high school principal occur in the daily lives of directors, supervisors, coordinators, and other administrators.

Clinical supervision is not necessarily, or even preferably, a one-on-one activity. The cycle just described evolved originally in the Graduate School of

Education at Harvard University, where groups of preservice teachers-in-training conducted cycles on each other, three or four observers sharing the responsibility for responding to the student-teaching performance of a classmate. Professor Morris Cogan, working with these students, found that by sharing their observation data and working out a group reaction to the observed events, the observers benefited as much from each cycle as did the observee. Later, when the cycle was used for the purpose of training supervisors, again it proved expedient to use a *team* of observers and again the benefits of sharing the responsibility proved to be very great. A strong recommendation to all professionals is that clinical supervision should be done two-on-one, three-on-one, or four-on-one whenever possible. Cycles can also be done on groups of persons, for example, a committee whose members are seeking to improve upon their ways of meeting and working together.

Helping Versus Evaluating

As can be seen in the foregoing discussion of clinical supervision, a high value is placed on the dignity and the judgment of the worker to be observed. We did not say that in the preobservation conference the observer calls the shots or determines the purpose or the focus of the cycle. On the contrary, we left those decisions to the teacher. This is not to preclude that the observer may offer suggestions or even request that a particular question be examined. However, it seems important that each set of observation contract items grows out of the concerns and values of the teacher, for whom the cycle promises to have more utility and meaning than it would if the observer's agenda predominated.

Over time, it is to be expected that the supervisor–observer who has been playing a helping role will come to be regarded by the teacher not only as a professional, and perhaps even personal friend, but also as a highly knowledgeable and skillful critic. Furthermore, the principal or team leader will have been witness to a great many different situations in which many aspects of the teacher's talents and tendencies will have been revealed. This means that the observer is therefore especially well qualified to describe, and to assign some sort of a value or rating to, the typical strengths and weaknesses of that particular teacher. In the overwhelming majority of cases, we are convinced that the principal's summary judgment or opinion will be more positive and complimentary than negative or uncomplimentary, and that whatever negative statements there might be would probably not surprise the teacher involved or seem unwarranted. If this is so, then a teacher will probably be much more willing for that supervisor to participate in formal evaluation activities than to be, instead, at the mercy of an administrator whose only evidence has come from occasional evaluation-only observations.

It may, in fact, be an oddity of the education profession that there has customarily been resistance to the idea that superordinates can legitimately be both helpers and evaluators. In most other occupations the two functions reside in the same persons and the *extent of familiarity* with the worker's usual behaviors is seen as a key to the legitimacy of those persons' assessments. In education, probably the main reason for the prevailing resistance is that the evaluators have *not* been sufficiently familiar with worker behaviors, and therefore there is a strong feeling that assessments cannot be trusted. Our hope is that significant increases in both the amount of supervision provided, and the caliber of supervisory service will cause those supervised to become more trusting and accepting.

In any event, improvements in the technology of supervision promise to enhance the value of the supervisory function. The more skills possessed by the observer, the more likely that his or her work will be productive of a congenial supervisor-supervisee relationship. Among the most important are those skills related to data collection. We contend that efficient means and a wide range of instrumented formats are available toward this end. We feel that the data-collection technology we advocate can be used for both "helping supervision" and evaluation purposes, although our conviction is that helping is by far the most important and most useful reason for supervision as well as the most frequent activity. Therefore we assume that most of the time the ideas and techniques contained within our approach will be exploited within a helping framework.

Prior to schoolwide implementation of clinical supervision, it is essential that the principal, team leaders/department chairpersons, and selected teachers practice the skills involved in each of the five stages. Skill proficiency with the methodology is a prerequisite to making clinical supervision a useful mechanism for teacher growth schoolwide. Listed here are various options for developing skills in observation technology.

Select exemplary teachers for initial practice in data collection.
Select a few exemplary teachers on whom to practice the five stages of the observation cycle.
Include volunteer teachers as observers in initial observation cycles.
Videotape observation cycle stages and critique performance.
Select only a few observation items for initial practice (for example, time-on-task).
Learn from teachers those techniques that facilitate learning.
Build a bank of data collection instruments.
Build a bank of effective instructional practices.
Build a bank of helpful conference/feedback techniques.
When you feel confident in the observation cycle techniques, plan a clinical supervision program for your staff as defined in the CS Linkage System.

In addition, you may want to consider working with other principals prior to launching a clinical supervision program. We gave the following advice to one group of principals several years ago.

Here is a modest and workable training proposal. Find at least two, but not more than five, other principals who are similarly motivated. Insist that everyone read both Cogan and Goldhammer in advance, and meet in a seminar two or three times to be sure you have at least some common understanding and vocabulary. Hold these meetings alternately in your respective schools, as much in the open as you dare to be so that teachers will recognize what you are seeking to do. Share as much as you can with each other about supervision as you have experienced it, and some of the skills, problems, satisfactions, worries, and tricks-of-the-trade you've gathered over the years.

When you feel ready, find a courageous teacher in one of your schools with whom you will conduct an O Cycle. Allow a full half-day for the observation. The following week, go to the next school and conduct another cycle on another courageous teacher. The following week, yet another. Take turns being the observation team leader. When you've done it in all five or six schools, take all the courageous teachers out to dinner in some private dining room and ask them to help you evaluate the training experience through which, with their help, you have just gone. Then hold another seminar series to gear yourselves up to a higher level, and find five or six more courageous teachers with whom to refine your skills.

In all probability, you'll have a waiting list of would-be observees before the second cycle of observations has been completed. Another probability is that you'll not only begin to be more comfortable with each other and with the cycle, but also to feel that in some respects you're now an administrative-supervisory team whose collective turf includes the five or six schools you represent.

Principals in Greensboro, North Carolina, suggested to us the following ways to begin clinical supervision in their schools.

1. Start with one teaching team, then swap teams
2. Principals teach a class while teachers observe someone else
3. Provide in-service to the entire school leadership team
4. Begin with two trained teachers, then ask for volunteers
5. Require each teacher to observe before being observed
6. Use simple instruments at first
7. Share data collection instrument ideas with each other
8. Have a monthly emphasis, such as student motivation
9. Conduct sharing sessions about clinical supervision experiences

10. Share videotaped lessons
11. Invite central office staff members to participate as observers
12. Start with one grade level, hopefully a volunteer group
13. Ask for volunteer teachers, and train them in clinical supervision methodology
14. Have the workshop-trained teacher train his or her team members
15. Principals select teachers to be trained
16. Establish a clinical supervision focus for the month: time-on-task, classroom management, cues, reinforcement, feedback
17. Have teachers practice a particular new data-gathering instrument each month
18. Data-gathering instruments can be shared regularly with staff members and modified for individual needs. Copies can be shared with staff
19. Suggest that volunteer teachers select a peer with whom they would be comfortable learning and practicing the process
20. Involve team leaders first
21. Discuss in-school progress with clinical supervision regularly on the leadership team
22. Invite others to participate regularly

Full Implementation of Clinical Supervision

Since this volume on managing school productivity is group oriented, it should come as no surprise that our orientation to implementing clinical supervison schoolwide is also group oriented.

Consider the possibility of each teacher being involved in clinical supervision as an observer or the person being observed once a week, with the principal being involved in the same practice with *all* staff members each week. If teachers work in a group context around team plans, then clinical supervision provides a natural mediating resource into the work norms of each working team.

Each team or department selects an observation focus for the week, depending on their goals and needs. A teacher is selected on rotation to be the teacher observed. The team defines its goals for supervision each week and invites the principal to participate on the observation team along with the team members of their team or other teams. Each four to six weeks each teacher is observed, but that same person participates on some school observation team for most of the other weeks. The principal has the opportunity to enter into each team's work life through the clinical supervision mechanism each week. In so doing, the principal, in addition to learning about instruction norms, observes the results of team plans, group dynamics, problems, and strengths. Discussion about a particular teacher observation not only provides an opportunity for coaching that teacher, but also provides openings to learn about and to facilitate development of the context of that teacher's performance.

Team observations permit the principal to stay in meaningful contact with the goal progress of each team or department each week. Discussions with the team leader may naturally follow a teacher observation, in which leaders engage in dialogue about observed concerns and successes, and also engage in problem solving about particular problem patterns. Team observation, in this sense, permits a regular meaningful exchange between the principal and team leader. Leadership challenges are shared and delegated schoolwide as a result of continuous attention to the pulse of team-based instruction and team work life. The team provides a meaningful context for teacher coaching, which is likely to facilitate team as well as teacher growth. An observation may occur only once a week, but as teachers work together throughout each day, a natural setting exists for practice and feedback and also for informal reinforcement of patterns that are beneficial to team success that were realized in systematic clinical supervision.

In summary, clinical supervision provides a mechanism for principals, team leaders, and teachers to sample instruction and to shape norms regularly. The observation cycle, when used regularly and systematically, has the power to eliminate outdated and nonproductive practices, to develop, alter, and refine potentially useful practices, and to reinforce those that are productive stimulators of student mastery. In fact, clinical supervision enables a staff to engage in its own behavior modification through regular schedules of reinforcement and through managing the effects of instruction. The principal's most powerful tool is clinical supervision.

14

The Management Subsystem: Quality Control

R ecent reports on schooling confirm that schools are highly complex
organizations in which people and activity are loosely coupled to purpose
(Meyer, Scott, Deal 1977; Weick 1982). Principals tend to bounce from one
set of interactions to the next in a continuous stream of brief planned and un-
explained events designed to keep the ship afloat. The labor intensity of running a school has been confirmed through various anthropological studies
(Morris et al. 1982; Greenfield 1982). However, the existing art form of the
frenetic principalship is called into question upon consideration of studies of
productive management in the corporate world (Peters and Waterman 1982)
and in effective schools (Purkey and Smith 1982). Altering the learning and
work norms of schools may well depend on how well the norms of school management are transformed.

Management, essentially, is moving people toward organizational goals. If
this is the central concept of management, then principals necessarily must
become more occupied with the school's planned development process. Concerns for the maintenance of the school's plant, program, and personnel are
important, but only for the purpose of maintaining a productive work climate.
Concerns for the school's development, however, will precipitate movement
toward transforming outdated practices and will more likely result in resolving learning problems. Maintenance tasks must be delegated, while production
tasks become the central job focus for the principal.

What about the labor intensity of the principalship? It is our contention that
we must move beyond crisis management and assume a new posture for leading a productive school: planned management. Effective management is born

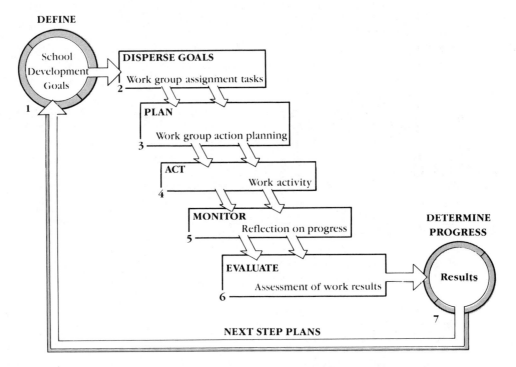

Figure 14.1. Managing School Productivity: A Task Linkage System

out of a vision of what a school can become, and is capable of transforming staff attitudes and behaviors toward cooperative ownership of new schooling plans, practices, and results.

Schools *can* develop the capacity over time to become tightly coupled around goals and goal-related tasks. Principals can and must plan for the school's development with their staff and then act as a facilitating force as well as control function.

Managing a Tightly Coupled Process

A management task linkage system is outlined in Figure 14.1, identifying the key tasks between school goals and new schooling results. The model assumes that a school must have specific development *goals* each year which are then divided into *multiple tasks.* The staff works cooperatively in multiple kinds of groups on selected tasks toward manageable results. Each work group *plans* how it will achieve its expected results.

During the planned period of staff productivity, each group reflects period-ically on its progress. *Self-monitoring* allows each group to correct, reinforce, and/or replan the next stage of work. *Evaluation* becomes an assessment of results as they relate to task assignment and to overall goals. Accounting for work activity is important only to the work group; the results of their work are of concern to the principal and to the entire school staff.

The principal's management tasks are far more than getting things going and helping in general terms. Productive management requires a discrete set of tasks at each benchmark of the school year. These tasks require the principal periodically to separate himself or herself from the school development proc-ess, and to reflect and plan strategies for guiding all seven phases of the school development process. The school development tasks relate directly both to instruction and to those production activities that are designed to influence the results of instruction.

The Principal's Tasks

Defining School Development Goals

State and district expectations provide a context for envisioning next steps in a school's growth process. Likewise, parent and staff concerns stimulate plans for the specific nature of a school's growth within its political context. The principal synthesizes these multiple concerns and defines both the long-range (5-year) and short-term (1-year) growth targets for the school. The goals that result become the guiding light for the principal's involvement of staff in school development planning.

After specific growth targets are identified, the principal then engages the entire staff in planning goal parameters for each target by defining observable, measurable results. The staff develops ownership of the school development process as they analyze test data and parent, staff, and student surveys to specify the focus of their planned productivity. The resulting school goals then are communicated to parents, students, staff, administration, and board, indicating school commitment to growth each year. Goals might include specifics relat-ing to school climate, the math program, parent involvement, or to coopera-tive teaching and learning.

Assigning Goal Tasks to Work Groups

A basic principle of organization is to identify groups of people to accomplish certain *permanent functions* (for example, middle school math instruction) and *temporary tasks* (for example, designing a school learning program with a local textile industry). Permanent work groups plan for and achieve their ongoing purpose at increasing levels of productivity, while temporary schoolwide tasks grow out of the school's new goal set.

The next management task is to divide each goal into achievable tasks and to assign tasks to temporary work groups. The objective is to break each goal into manageable-size tasks and to get a group working toward a specific result. The principal involves representative staff members in decision making about goal tasks and work group assignment.

For example, one school goal might be to develop a comprehensive diagnostic approach to math instruction. Several discrete tasks might include procedures for diagnosing

math readiness levels
learning styles
cognitive styles
affective characteristics
student interests

Each task area (objective) is assigned to a work group (either within or across grade and subject area specialization). Expected results of the group are communicated along with the task assignment. In this way, the principal plans for goal accomplishment in specific ways. Groups of teachers are the workers of discrete tasks, while the principal manages task definitions and task assignment to groups.

Work Group Action Planning

The task of a specific work group is to reflect on and to plan for the task assigned. An example might be to "develop procedures for diagnosing student interests and their relationship to the math curriculum program." Given the objective, the work group then develops a general one-page plan of action. The plan includes essential clusters of activities (key events), individual *responsibilities* for selected activities, *resources* available and needed, and a *time line* of events.

Plans are negotiated between the work group and principal before work begins. A conference permits ideas to be reinforced, altered, or changed as the group seeks to plan for the most effective and efficient plan for achieving assigned results for the school.

Work Group Action

Each staff member works on specific tasks that relate to planned school development. Rather than all staff members working toward general improvement on all goals areas, each person is linked tightly to a specific group and to specific tasks. By defining tasks, and assigning tasks to work groups, new schooling results can be planned and controlled for in a manageable and productive pattern.

While groups work on plans, the principal's task is to coach, reinforce, develop, recognize, and correct staff behavior. Tight management of work groups will alter the disastrous effects of "innovation breakdown" that has become the norm in schools. Through careful task assignment and work management, the principal enables a school to alter static work patterns.

When group work begins, a new set of principal behaviors is required. The tendency is to assume all is well; the group has a plan. To alter the pattern of implementation breakdown, the principal needs to remain a constant source of energy, enabling each group to succeed with its assigned task. Work groups remain vital and productive to the extent that they are managed through reinforcement, feedback, and correctives.

Monitoring Work Activity

Schools are tumultuous organizations that exist within environments marked by increasing complexity and changing expectations. Consequently, each work group, and the school as a whole, must respond to conditions while it works on planned activity. Several times a year it is important for each work group, with the principal, to stop work and to reflect on progress toward results. Perhaps plans need to be refined or altered to reflect changing conditions. Perhaps the behavior of some individual workers or groups needs to be corrected. A time for corporate periodic self-correction is necessary within a changing and dynamic political and social context.

Reinforcement and recognition are stimulators to productive work. The monitoring periods provide opportunities for principals and groups to applaud and recognize small successes. Moreover, reinforcement provides a standard of high expectations for results. Periodic recognition enables a principal to keep a staff "built up" and to keep the goals central to work activity. The staff receives new stimulation and becomes motivated to proceed with plans within a context of cooperation, success, and expected results.

Evaluating Results and Determining Progress

Assessing results of school development involves far more than analyzing student achievement patterns. To be certain, these patterns are the ultimate measure of productivity. School evaluation also assesses the results (not activities) of each work group. Did each group produce what was set forth in their task objective? Next comes a critical question: Did the results from each work enable the school to achieve its anticipated goal?

The productive work ecology in a school is more than the listing of results for certain tasks performed. The organization as a unit is more than the sum of its parts. If there are six permanent work groups and five temporary task groups, then assessing a school's productivity includes adding the results of six groups and five groups. Measuring the school's success always includes an additional question: Did all of these results produce the major outcome anticipated?

Asking both the additive questions and the question of gestalt generates the answers to a school's productivity in a given year. Moreover, answers to these questions provide direction to the most obvious "next steps" in a school's development process. Hence, evaluation measures the results of organizational productivity at a given moment in its growth process, and at the same time signals the beginning of the next development phase.

Managing a productive school requires primary attention to the school's developmental process. Several management tasks are critical between goal definition and evaluation. The principal must assume responsibility for *identifying tasks* embedded in the school's goal statements; engaging task groups in *action planning,* which is results focused; *coaching and assisting* groups in their activity; managing corporate quality control through various forms of work group *monitoring*; and, with the staff, *assessing* the results of work groups and of the school's total productivity.

Attending to purpose is the central challenge for principals; stimulating a staff to work productively on goal-based tasks is the primary job task. The principal continues to keep workers built up by reinforcing and applauding small successes and by invigorating the work culture with a preoccupation with shared purpose.

Management: Planning

How does a principal prepare for cooperative school planning, and then plan for monitoring and evaluating in ways that keep staff energy high and produce results? In this section of the chapter, we present a model for personal planning. In a sense, the model suggests *a way of thinking about planning,* rather than a structured methodology.

Planning is a sorting activity that enables a school manager to behave in a *goal-focused* way for organizing, motivating, supervising, controlling, and evaluating staff performance. "Planning is the key managerial function which provides the means by which individuals and organizations cope with a complex, dynamic, everchanging environment" (Kast and Rosenzweig 1974, 436).

Planning also is decision making under uncertainty, which requires a mechanism for adapting the plan to unexpected developments (Kast and Rosenzweig 1974, 451). In this sense planning is a continuous sorting and selecting process for keeping a staff on a goal attainment path. Planning also initiates certain behaviors as a staff adapts to a changing environment. Management planning is *the* activity by which principals continuously guide staff behavior in a new direction.

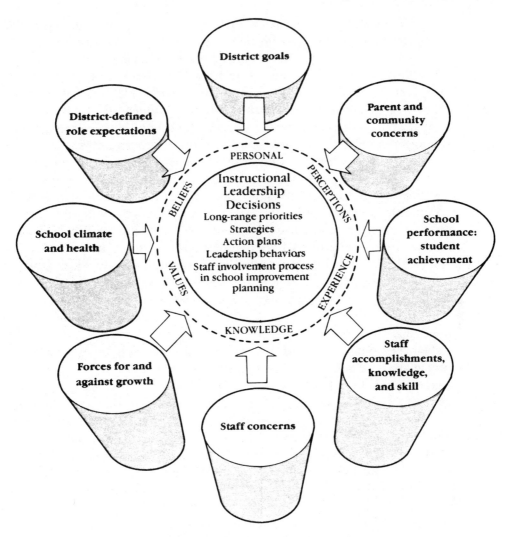

Figure 14.2. Influences on Instructional Leadership Decisions

While the principal might have certain visions about what is optimal in a given school, so also do the state, the local school board, and the central office, each providing schools with certain sets of expectations. The principal's responsibility is to enable the school organization to move in the direction of combined expectations and visions in an effective and efficient manner.

Various contextual influences impact on management perceptions of what is *necessary* (either politically or educationally), *appropriate* (for a particular school), *available* (in terms of resources), and *feasible* (in relation to your judgment). Figure 14.2 describes those variables that influence leadership/

management decisions regarding priorities, methods for leading the staff, current forces, specific leadership behaviors, and a plan of action.

Role expectations or definitions of the principalship typically are determined formally by central administration, which assesses a principal's relative effectiveness in serving a school and the district. Selected district goals provide considerable direction for the principal. Parent and community concerns about a school also are indicators of priority school improvement needs. The school's performance record, both in terms of student achievement and staff accomplishments, is the strongest signal for selecting improvement priorities. Moreover, the health of the school as an organization dictates the kind of leadership task structure and consideration that are necessary for success. Various community and district forces, for and against growth, need to be assessed in order to design a school improvement game plan. Finally, all seven influence factors noted in Figure 14.1 are distilled through the principal's belief system and perceptions about ideal schooling. Perceptions of "what is most needed" and "how the game can be won," determine in large measure the success of the school manager. The magic of success, if there be any, lies in a continuous commitment and attention to goals and to leadership perceptions of what most is needed at the moment.

Management planning as it is presented in this section is similar to the natural analysis/selection process that people use every day. A planning process has been developed here as a guide to thinking about and planning for school growth. The principal's planning process guides the analysis of various influences on the school as well as on the goal accomplishment process. For example, one goal might be to involve representative staff members, parents, and students in setting schoolwide goals. How will the principal plan tasks that address such questions as: Who will represent each group? What will be their first task? How will every staff member participate in the process? What sequence of events is necessary? Which teachers and parents are most likely to be responsive? What about dissonant staff members? Analysis of the context and decisions about cooperative planning are critical to the successful orchestration of the school's improvement activities.

Personal Planning

External pressures for change need to pass through a filter in each school. How the pressures for changes are addressed depends on the internal needs of the school organization and the professional maturity levels of the staff. A careful analysis of the school's subsystems provides a useful structure for analysis. A sample is provided in Table 14.1 in which a principal has been able to identify

TABLE 14.1. Analysis of a School's Subsystems

Systems	Strengths	Weaknesses	Improvement target
Organization subsystem	Age group teachers enjoy working together, although activity is mostly spontaneous	No organization exists for teachers to teach or work together	Organize formal work groups in the school for teaching and for working. Assist teams in planning
Goal subsystem	We've set five-year school goals	School goals only suggest activity; they do not guide it	Decide who will be responsible for which goals
Performance subsystem	Teachers are motivated to improve, although improvement is not a formal process	Teachers are fearful of evaluation. Their growth is unrelated to school improvement goals. No formal individual goal setting exists	Involve each teacher in setting annual growth goals that reflect responsibility for school goals and for personal growth needs
Program subsystem	The curriculum defines learning outcomes in math and reading. Districtwide staff development programs involve all teachers	No system for teacher accountability for student progress exists Staff development is not linked to the school's goals	Develop a record-keeping system for student progress in math and reading Plan a staff development program that relates to school improvement goals
Management subsystem	The evaluation dimension is strong Planning occurs as needed	No use of adult motivation, controlling, or coaching dimensions to management	Identify staff goals and needs and help them achieve their goals Coach teaching improvements through clinical supervision Institute a teacher planning and reporting system
Personal development	I'm not afraid to make tough decisions I can organize activities easily	I need to learn how to lead groups in planning I want training in clinical supervision I need to develop a control system for teacher performance	Get training in planning, clinical supervision Develop a control system and teacher planning system

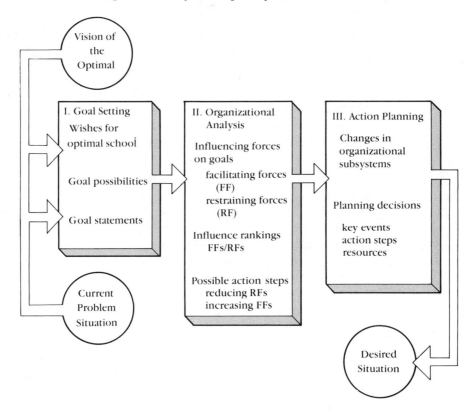

Figure 14.3. Planning for Action

strengths and weaknesses for each subsystem and subsequently to select "next-step" improvement targets.

The personal planning task now requires a synthesis of various external pressures and internal improvement targets. In the next several pages, a planning model is presented that shows a way of thinking about personal planning. The model draws upon a combination of techniques for stimulating both the creative and the rational thinking processes.

The personal planning model is described in three steps: (1) goal setting, (2) organizational analysis, and (3) action planning (see Figure 14.3). The reader will recognize techniques and concepts presented earlier in this volume. The first step involves a goal selection and refinement process. The second step makes use of force field analysis to examine variables that influence the select goals. The third step focuses on decision making about future actions, filtering decision making through a school system lens.

Step 1: Goal Setting

Selecting improvement targets requires an examination of present conditions in relation to an ideal. Given an image of the ideal school, questions can be entertained that relate to closing the real-ideal gap. The Rand Corporation study on change in education supports a comprehensive approach to management planning. Their studies show that "the more carefully planned and the more complex an innovation is, the more likely it is to succeed," (Mann, no date).

The following questions are springboards for reflection during the principal's planning process.

1. What is my educational mission as a school leader?
2. What are the glaring gaps between the real and ideal practices and outcomes in my school?
3. Where do I want my school to be next year? In five years?
4. What are my leadership strengths?
5. What kinds of assistance do I need?
6. What is the relative maturity of my staff?
7. What are the primary activities necessary for moving my school forward?

The goal-setting steps presented in Figure 14.4 include wishing, identifying goal possibilities, and finally, selecting actual goals.

Wishes are explored as they relate to the school organization, instruction, staff performance, and learning norms. Then goal possibilities are entertained by listing concerns and then rank-ordering stated concerns. Out of this analysis emerge personal school development goals.

The first task is to wish and dream about the ideal school, for *wishing* enables the planner to move psychologically beyond perceived restraints, and to entertain new possibilities.

An analysis of current conditions is the next step. An analysis of things as they really are provides a perspective for "wishes" and enables the planner to perceive more clearly apparent gaps between the ideal and real work worlds in a school.

The second task is to translate dreams and real conditions into tentative goal statements by assessing what is necessary in order to begin closing the gap between ideal-real worlds.

The tentative goals are critically analyzed in terms of potential problems that may prevent actual goal attainment. Concerns about accomplishing a particular goal must be identified in order to anticipate potential stumbling blocks to its success.

Concerns about some problem areas are greater than others. By

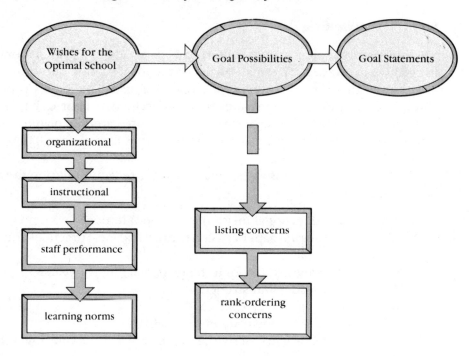

Figure 14.4. I. Goal Setting

rank-ordering your concerns and giving a possible value to each concern, the greatest potential stumbling blocks are identified. Consequently, less energy is spent altering a particular condition. After goal areas are ranked, the indicators for accomplishing a particular goal are identified. Often the indicators are defined in terms of specific attitudes and behaviors.

After wishes have generated general goal categories and concerns have been identified, the manager is ready to define specific personal goals for school development. Refine each goal so that it reflects a revised perception of that goal. Goal wishing to goal refinement is a sorting process that takes into account your perceptions of what best can be accomplished in relation to your perception of the need and the ideal.

The following story illustrates the goal sorting/goal setting process. The principal's goal for school development results from a combination of wishing and critical analysis.

Situational Analysis

Mrs. Peterson's school seemed to be going through the same patterns year after year. Very little new ever seemed to happen, and little improvement in achievement or organizational health had occurred in any recognizable fashion in years. In fact, the place had settled into a kind of sleepy lull, and achievement scores had actually declined. The superintendent insisted that something be done to generate movement among the teachers, students, and parents. After talking with other principals and reading a few articles on school improvement, Mrs. Peterson decided she needed to involve all of her staff as well as interested students and parents in planning for ways to improve the school. She had come to recognize that if more people were involved in deciding what needed to occur, perhaps greater participation and commitment to new actions would follow.

The Principal's School Development Goal

To include all 37 teachers, representative students, and parents in setting goals and in planning for school improvement.

Step 2: Organizational Analysis

Accomplishing goals in a school organization is becoming increasingly complex due to the multiple outside and inside forces that influence organizational activity. Lewin (1936, in Bennis 1969, 62, 98–107) developed a diagnostic technique for decoding confusing and complex social situations called force field analysis that provides a useful technique for envisioning what actions are most likely to lead to the accomplishment of even the most difficult goals. Rather than looking at simplistic causes of problems (we can't do X because of S, V, and B) another problem-solving approach can unlock tough problems perceptually. Lewin suggests that the multiple forces at work in our environment can be analyzed in such a way that we can perceive more clearly how forces interact and influence what actually occurs. Those forces that work for us Lewin called "facilitating forces," and those that work against us he named "restraining forces."

The organizational analysis process described in the following pages is an *optional* activity in management planning. It is presented here as a tool to use when actions are not obvious and when the situation is confusing or even binding. The examination and problem solving of forces is useful in breaking down perceptual barriers so that a clearer way can be envisioned to achieve certain goals. By identifying *restraining* forces, plans can be made more easily to circumvent them, whereas the influences of *facilitating* forces can be enhanced through analysis and planning. Figure 14.5 outlines the three stages in organizational analysis: identifying influencing forces on goals; rank-ordering the influences; and selecting action steps for altering the force of influences on goals.

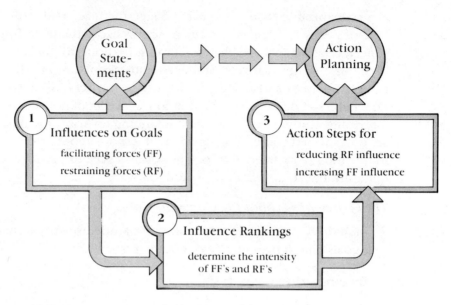

Figure 14.5. II. Organizational Analysis

Restraining Forces on Schools

Morrish (1976) identified many barriers to growth in schools, awareness of which may be helpful in organizational analysis. He notes that creative changes occur in schools in spite of restraining forces. A healthy school organization can develop a capacity for creative change in spite of, and in fact even because of, resistance. Note Morrish's list of factors influencing growth in schools.

Factors that retard change in schools

1. resistance from community
2. incompetencies of outside agents of change
3. overcentralization of the district
4. teacher defensiveness to new developments
5. absence of educational extension agents
6. insufficiently developed conceptual linkages between theory and practice
7. incomplete science base
8. schools' historical conservatism as public institutions
9. professional invisibility and isolation of teachers in their daily work

Factors preventing change from being developed and energized from within the school or district

1. confused or unagreed-upon goals

2. few tangible rewards for innovation
3. uniformity of instructional approaches
4. school as a public monopoly
5. low investment in research and development
6. low technological and financial investment
7. difficulties in diagnosing weakness
8. problems of validly measuring outcomes
9. emphasis on being accountable to present commitments
10. low investment in organizational and personal development
11. a lack of entrepreneurial models
12. a psychological passivity among professionals

Factors retarding the diffusion of ideas

1. separation and isolation of members and units
2. hierarchy and differential status
3. lack of formal procedures and planned training for change (Morrish 1976, 56–78)

By identifying both positive and negative forces, a principal can increase the likelihood of developing workable and even creative solutions to tough school problems. After forces have been identified, it is important to determine which forces have the greatest influence on the problem or goal. The strongest forces at work are those that deserve primary attention; others literally can be ignored.

After the forces have been prioritized, the next task is to develop strategies for altering their negative and positive influence. This step is essentially a problem-solving activity. Consider the following strategy options as you think about ways to resolve tensions between the effects of restraining and facilitating forces upon your goals:

Add a force (for example, add additional planning time through flexible scheduling of staff responsibilities)

Eliminate a force (for example, assign angry parents to a task force to plan with teachers)

Strengthen a force (for example, offer leadership responsibilities to teachers who are receptive to the change process)

Weaken a force (for example, require all teachers (teams), including apathetic and dissonant staff members, to identify areas of their own instruction that need improvement)

Experience with goal analysis has shown that while increasing the effect of facilitating forces is useful, reducing the negative effect of restraining forces has a greater overall effect on goal accomplishment. For example, by requiring *all* teachers to identify areas in which they will improve their instruction, while providing the necessary coaching, the school may realize more lasting effects than by merely assigning additional responsibilities to teachers who are already responsive.

During the next stage in organizational analysis, it is helpful to generate various options for decreasing or increasing the influence of active forces on goals; this is a problem-solving activity. Focus on those forces that most influence selected goals. List strategies for reducing the restraining forces. Many facilitating forces will be strengthened as restraining forces are eliminated or weakened. Allow strategy ideas to flow freely, and suspend all judgment about feasibility. During the action-planning phase decisions are made regularly for the most promising strategies.

The last task in organizational analysis is to decide on those actions that hold the greatest promise for resolving problems and creating opportunities for the attainment of the selected goals. As the various facilitating and restraining forces are identified, variables within each school subsystem may provide clues to potential resources.

Sources of Influence on Subsystems

   Educational Leadership Subsystem
Educational vision, mission and purposes
Contingency leadership
Instructional leadership
   Goal Subsystem
Collective values and beliefs
Internal and external goal sources
Goal focus
Goal-setting process
   Organization Subsystem
Organizational teaming—interrelationships and interdependencies
   leadership teams
   instructional teams
   vertical program development teams
   task force production teams
   team dynamics, cohesion, and productivity
   Performance Subsystem
Performance expectation issues
Performance expectations for
   principals
   unit leaders and department chairpersons
   teachers
   student teachers

Program Subsystem
Learning theories
Staff development program
Student learning program
Management Subsystem
Organizational planning
Problem solving and decision making
Staff supervision
Monitoring and controlling
Organizational evaluation

A change in any one schooling practice is likely to alter all subsystems to some extent. The kinds of changes that will be required or are inevitable within each subsystem need to be anticipated. If changes are anticipated and planned, the goal activity is much more likely to be successful.

Upon completion of the organizational analysis process, the leader will have identified the forces working for and against new practices. By engaging in the problem-solving activity of altering force influence, the principal comes to perceive more clearly the ways in which the new project can be successful. The negative influences are minimized and the positive influences enhanced through problem-solving activities. Further analysis of the school subsystems provides an avenue for gaining new perspective on the complexity of the goal and the decisions necessary for success.

The goal-setting and organizational analysis processes presented thus far may be too cumbersome to use on a continuous basis. The detailed steps, however, provide the reader with a way of thinking about a school organization and how to "explode" the problem in order to understand complex organizational factors more clearly. These management techniques can be useful in making sound professional judgments and action plans for improving the quality of school life.

We return to the simulation presented earlier, of Mrs. Peterson's goal setting. The organizational analysis process that she used prior to action planning is presented in the following.

Organizational Analysis

Mrs. Peterson began to study the various factors that might work for and/or against her plans in an attempt to determine the feasibility of this goal. In the course of her assessment, she identified the following *facilitating forces* in her school environment:

a handful of interested parents
five teachers who generally respond enthusiastically to new ideas
an existing team teaching structure

central administration's expressed concern for the general lack of
interest and commitment to growth among the staff

Mrs. Peterson identified the following *restraining forces* in her school
environment:

a teacher contract limiting the number of after-school staff meetings
teacher resistance to altering established patterns of instruction
parental complaints about "unapproachable" teachers
declining test scores
general apathy and lack of evident creativity among students

In an attempt to *resolve the problems* with the restraining forces, Mrs.
Peterson decided she needed to include the following events in her
action planning:

link teachers and parents on various task forces
offer leadership roles to "responsive" teachers
involve all teachers and willing parents in the goal-setting process
require each teacher to identify areas for his or her own instructional
improvement and professional growth

Step 3: Action Planning

Action planning assumes a professional commitment to accomplishing specific organizational goals, and is the key task in management planning. Figure
14.6 illustrates the steps in the action-planning process, focusing on decision
making for planning, monitoring, and evaluating the accomplishment of school
goals.

Plans are guidelines to assist people in setting a course and for keeping track
of their progress in realizing certain goals. Plans are not laws, however.
Changes naturally occur regularly in schools because of the complex nature
of human interaction and the changing environmental conditions. Consequently, human activity can be planned only to a certain extent, and as work

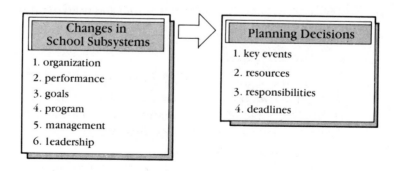

Figure 14.6. III. Action Planning

progresses and new needs surface, plans need to be modified. As action plans are implemented and monitored, continuous judgment of the current situation is critical in determining whether to follow the plan as it was defined or to modify it to be more responsive to a new situation. A fine line exists between responding to every whim and making little progress, and responding to changes in the situation in appropriate ways to permit success.

Moreover, to ensure that goals are met, the school staff must be held accountable for fulfilling its selected or delegated responsibilities. Linking organizational goals to performance is the means by which managers control work behavior and the quality of schooling outcomes. The manager must analyze each goal to determine how best to link goals to staff performance, to professional improvement, and to evaluation.

As each work group develops its own action plans, the principal prepares a plan for how best to design, organize, and assist in the school's goal activities. Management is a facilitating cluster of activities. The principal's action plan defines key events, resources, responsibilities, and a time line for guiding staff progress toward the goals. Without a plan, the staff is likely to veer from their course easily. With planned management guidance, however, success is likely.

As we return to the simulation, we observe that Mrs. Peterson was able to identify a set of actions for stimulating organizational response to selected areas of school development.

Action Plan

Mrs. Peterson's *action plan,* which was listed in her organizational analysis, reflected the concerns in specific plans for involving teachers, students, and parents in goal setting and planning for school improvement. Her action plan spelled out the following objectives:

goal setting at the teaching team level

team representatives (staff, parent, student) to form the school coordinating council

council discussion of all team goals and selection of those that could function as school goals

council action planning

implementation of plans by the council and teams

monitoring of plans by the council

formative and summative evaluation of plans by the council

As the coordinating council proceeded through its series of tasks (goal setting, planning, implementation, monitoring, and evaluation), Mrs. Peterson continuously reviewed her own action plans, controlling all events so that the goal of collaborative goal setting and planning for school improvement could be accomplished most effectively and efficiently.

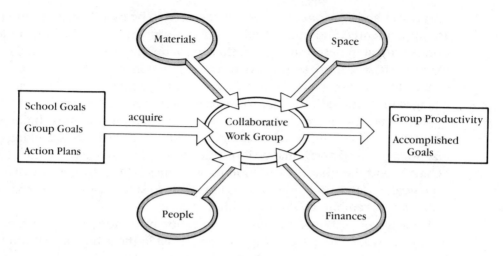

Figure 14.7. Resource Management

A detailed example of the three-step personal management planning process is found in the appendix to this chapter.

Resource Planning for Work Groups

Management resource planning anticipates the needs of work groups and specifies the types of resources that will facilitate group productivity. Figure 14.7 outlines the nature of resource planning and management. The *tasks* of acquiring tangible resources function symbiotically to assist work groups in successful accomplishments.

The model suggests that after a school has defined its goals, work groups are formed to implement various parts of each goal. Each group then develops an action plan to carry out the work. Resources are identified, gathered, and utilized. Each work group explores resource alternatives; the questions include:

"Who else can assist in the task?" (people)
"What else can we use for our tasks?" (materials)
"What kinds of locations are necessary?" (space)
"What funding is necessary?" (finance)

The principal facilitates the tasks of acquiring and allocating resources. Questions include:

"How can I keep the groups on task?"
"How can I provide resources?"
"How can I increase the probability of the group accomplishing its goals?"

The process skills of communicating, focusing, decision making, problem solving, and assessing enhance the group's productive activity, while the task of acquiring resources contributes to the quality of work results. This view of resource planning allows the manager to facilitate the work process of the staff while it ensures a goal-driven use of resources.

Facilitating the Task

The principal continually keeps groups focused on goal activity and also defines resource clusters so that each group will have a broader sense of the available possibilities. The following are expanded definitions of people, material, space, and finance resources.

People resources include persons with skills, talents, and interests, or who have access to other resources. By systematically exploring the resource possibilities, principals can begin to establish a "people bank" for work groups. A few possibilities include names of the following:

School	District	Community
students	other faculties	business people
faculty	other staffs	professional organi-
staff	fellow principals	zations
parents	resource persons	service organizations
neighbors	central administration	public agencies
friends	consultants	state departments
	support persons	university people

Material resources include all "things" used to accomplish the goals. Things are best acquired by knowing where things are, and also by having contact with people who know how to acquire certain resources. The use of informal networks is crucial to productive resource management. The principal opens communication channels with a wide variety of outside persons, in order to identify quickly the materials that are needed by groups. Free, available, inexpensive, stored, stockpiled, and forgotten materials are examples of resources that are often available through various channels. Knowledge of materials in school bookrooms, closets, storerooms, and other places can make available much valuable material. Students' homes and neighborhoods are also potential resources to consider, along with numerous district resources. An awareness of locations, distribution points, and access privileges for materials is needed in resource management.

Space resources are the locations where tasks are accomplished. A school space utilization chart showing activity type and frequency of use is helpful for decision making. Turf squabbles and "squatters' rights" conflicts are minimized if space is assigned for well-understood purposes centering around goals. Information about available district space can be helpful to groups. Utilizing public facilities outside the school, either for specific educational purposes or to collaborate with public agencies, offers other alternatives.

Financial resources include the several categories of funds assigned to the school. The use of finances entails planning, programming, budgeting, and evaluation. With the school goals in mind and the tasks and outcomes clearly delineated, finances can be acquired, disbursed, and then evaluated to measure the impact. This type of budgeting is important if goals and outcomes are to be accomplished effectively. Knowledge about the criteria involved in allocating funds, plus the official cycle for financial allocations can be useful. Often funds can be redistributed into other categories through an analysis.

There is a growing need for schools to secure funds from the private sector, which can be accomplished either through district foundations or by applying to agencies directly, using district guidelines.

Financial planning includes knowledge of funding categories, time allocation selection, criteria, private sources, and a goal-based budget planning and evaluation system. The principal then becomes a manager of resources rather than a conduit for funds.

Conceptualizing resources for school improvement activities, in terms of resource acquisitions, enables the principal to realize a significant amount of psychological and material energy in the school's development activities. The staff is the most significant resource; facilitating its productivity enhances the likelihood of success and it also draws out resources continuously from group members for the task at hand. The tasks of acquiring other people, materials, space, and financial resources enhance the productive capability of the work group and add to its capacity to produce what the school requires. Management resource planning is a vital key for work productivity.

Management: Quality Control

The concept of controlling behavior generates a wide range of emotions among educators, from rejection to enthusiasm. In recent years, however, school officials have come to understand more fully the relationship between program success and control. Quality control practices in organizations function as a strong influence on success (Likert 1967). Moreover, the amount of control operating is directly related to an organization's success (McMahon 1972). In the absence of control, individuals tend to stray from plans or orders (McFarland 1974).

Let us look for a moment at potential sources of fear regarding control practices in schools. The concept of controlling worker behavior emerged during the scientific management days when regard for worker well-being was virtually ignored. Management told and controlled. The practice of coercive control was based on assumptions of worker ignorance, lack of product knowledge, and a lack of self-motivation and control. Sadly, vestiges of that perception and that kind of control still remain in some school organizations today.

As management practice shifted over the years to concern for the worker (human relations era), the practice of coercive management control was rejected by many, especially in service organizations. Workers were given responsibility for tasks and expected to apply self-control. School organizations function largely on the same assumption about staff: administrators delegate self-control. However, as organizational productivity in general failed to keep up with rising expectations throughout society, the concept of control was reassessed. As organizations shift to a specific goal and results focus, control of some sort is viewed as necessary for accomplishing specific predetermined outcomes. The systems era introduced the concept of "collaborative control" to guard against coercive control and yet to ensure that organizational outcomes were met.

The concept of control also will need to be reestablished as schooling practices progress from a maintenance orientation of management to a production mode, but in an altogether new way. Management control shifted in the past from a top-down style (scientific management) to bottom up (human relations); and it now requires both a bottom-up and a top-down style (systems approach) to provide an effective function for organizational productivity.

Effective control practices in schools will become collaborative. An effective control system includes a combination of self-control, team control, and management control practices. The basic issue at stake is whether or not control restricts human freedom or fosters more productive performance. As we discuss the management function of control, we shall first of all establish more fully the purpose of an organized control function and then explore various models of control. The purpose of this section on management control is to present an open systems collaborative control model.

Purposes of Control

Many problems arise in organizations due to the diversity of worker interests, skill, knowledge, and behaviors. Control is the management function that orders diversity and ensures that organizational goals are accomplished. Thus, control provides order to the organization so that workers can be creative and productive in their specific ways.

The original application of control to business organizations derives from the French usage meaning "to check" (Tannenbaum 1973, 522). Fayol's definition of control, established in 1916, set precedent for years and today commonly guides control practices in organization, although practices are cooperatively managed. He proposed that control should include verifying that everything occurs in conformity with the plan adopted, the instructions issued, and the principles established. The object of control is to point out and rectify weaknesses and errors. It operates on everything: things, people, and actions (1949, 107).

The basic concept of control contains the essential elements necessary for managing modern organizations. Various viable approaches to control are listed here, all of which contribute to systems thinking.

1. Control maintains organizational activity within allowable limits (Kast and Rosenzweig 1974, 467)
2. Control standardizes performance and the high quality of services. It also limits the amount of authority at various levels (Hellriegel and Slocum 1974, 245)
3. Control regulates the process of growing in a moving organization (Kast and Rosenzweig 1976, 253)
4. Controls are a means of contributing to goal accomplishment (Albanese 1975)
5. To make knowledge workers productive requires constant attention to assignment control; that is assigning capable workers to the right job (Drucker 1982, 115)
6. Managerial control involves measuring progress and performance and, when necessary, taking corrective action to ensure that objectives are achieved (Raia 1974, 82)
7. The control cycle helps managers anticipate and master the change process (Michael 1981, 322)

Upon analysis of these various purposes for control, it seems clear that control allows modern organizations to build in self-regulating mechanisms so that purposes, whether formal or informal, reported or observed, provide information for decision making. In fact, control is maintained by decisions about future actions that are based on varieties of information. Without a control function, anything within a range of legitimate action can occur. With a control function, selected growth targets can be realized; they are the staff's blinders to prevent seduction into other activities.

Types of Control Mechanisms

The automobile industry has numerous control mechanisms, for example, to ensure that Cadillac Sevilles are Sevilles and not Buicks. Sony TVs are built under a tightly controlled environment to ensure that each television set measures up to the standard design. Industry has necessarily developed numerous work control mechanisms to ensure quality production according to a design. Even service organizations, such as hospitals, have developed high quality control measures for performance to ensure the future health of patients.

Control in organizations takes on many patterns so that purposes are realized. A unique feature in Japanese industry is that quality control measures of work, product, and evolving technology have all been delegated to the work level, to quality circles. Worker participation is redistributed power not only in the planning and organization of work, but also in the control of products.

Luthans (1981, 499–501) affirms the Japanese approach to control by noting that the control unit is defined not by budget, but by responsibility. Standards, he observes, emerge from goals, plans, programs, policies, procedures, and budget allocations, all of which are controllable. Basic management control elements in Luthans' view are (1) standards and goals to guide performance; (2) measurement of performance against standards and goals; and (3) decisions to change standards and goals, tighten up and develop new motivation techniques, or maintain current deviation from plans.

Hellriegel and Slocum (1974, 260–261) observe that five strategies of control already operate within most organizations: (1) *human input* is accomplished through selection and training; (2) *reward and punishment* systems provide both intrinsic and extrinsic measures to workers; (3) formal *job descriptions and assignments* announce general performance expectations; (4) *policies and rules* regulate behavior within general guidelines; while (5) *budgets* control expenditures and therefore limit performance to a degree. All five strategies ensure general stability and adaptability in open organizations. However, organizations need more than general control; they also need specific controls to realize specific new kinds of results.

Michael et al. (1981, 264) propose a rather novel approach to control. They observe that most established control mechanisms function on the basis of "feedback" within real time parameters. Rather than controlling for prior decisions only, organizations today depend heavily on anticipations made about the future (for example, next year; five years from now). They recommend adding the concept of "feedforward" to management control practices, that is, to plan for the future through knowledgeable anticipation—not reaction.

It is suggested that three kinds of control systems can operate, each for a unique purpose (see Table 14.2). The *homeostatic approach* provides feedback on performance within fixed job parameters. This approach is used for controlling operations that are expected to remain unchanged for some time (for example, student behavior in assemblies). The *adaptive feedback* approach assumes more flexible parameters and describes real time results (for example, a teacher observation on March 4). The *feedforward* approach an-

TABLE 14.2 Types of Control Systems

Types of Feedback		Feedback Focus	Control Focus	Control Outcome
Homeostatic	→	Fixed job parameters (over time) (such as student behavior management in assemblies)	= Established policies →	Smooth operations
Adaptive	→	Flexible job parameters (present time) (such as student learning opportunities)	= Current conditions →	Refined practices
Feedforward	→	Changed job parameters (future time) (such as new student record-keeping system)	= Prepares for future →	Planned changes

(*Source:* Adapted from Stephen R. Michael et al., *Techniques of Organizational Change* [New York: McGraw-Hill Book Company, 1981], 264. Reprinted by permission of the publisher, © 1981.)

ticipates the future and prepares for necessary changes (for example, a reporting system to match a new mastery approach to math instruction). Parameters are open and rely on short- and long-range planning mechanisms to guide the direction of control.

To summarize the three approaches, the first model controls for what was established in the past (established behavior patterns in assemblies). The second approach controls for present needs (three students are off task and appear confused; two other students need to be on a higher level in the math program; all other students appear on task and productive). The third method controls conditions and prepares for future needs. (The reporting system task force may visit three college professors and two school systems to study available reporting system options.) Often, the feedforward system (the future plans) are superimposed over the adaptive system (the now) to address current and future realities simultaneously.

Upon analysis, the feedforward approach (control cycle) does not appear to be very different from practices in many organizations. Let us examine the model more closely. The control cycle includes three parts: (1) the goals and action plans, (2) implementation practices and results, and (3) evaluation of results. In the past, either management blueprints or worker daily movement tended to guide control patterns. In the feedforward control cycle, worker plans about the future are the first signal of *what* is to be controlled. Second, the implementation process and results (where innovation success typically turns to failure) provide insights into what is or is not working, and guide decisions regarding future actions, either reinforcement or correction. Evaluation, the third element, measures not only results, but the plans themselves and also the implementation processes. All three stages are integrally linked and controlled so that desired future results can be realized.

As a school plans for control systems, it will be managed for goal clarity, goal commitment, goal conflict resolution, role and task match, goal-directed training and skill implementation, obstacle removal, feedback and correctives, performance rewards, and consequences.

Quality Control for Productive Schools

As schools grow and adjust to changing times, many levels of regulating devices will be necessary to control performance toward goals. In complex and demanding situations, a school staff relies on signals to assist them in clarifying which activities require priority attention. A multilayered control system is useful for worker self-correction. That is, individuals, teams, team leaders, specialists, and principals all need to assess their own progress regularly. Simultaneously, all roles will benefit from feedback from others, and from feedforward procedures for correcting and applauding progress.

Teachers require information and feedback and recommendations from parents, peers, team leaders, and principals regarding their performance results. *Team leaders* require corrective feedback from students, parents, teachers, peers, and principals. Likewise, *principals* need to self-correct and simultaneously receive feedback from many role groups within the school, as well as from their peers and supervisors.

Wide distribution of control is central to our discussion of a school as a self-regulating and correcting organism. No longer is the principal the holder of all management power, decision making, and responsibility for tasks; these functions are dispersed and shared among many groups within the school organization. By distributing power and control throughout the organization, a sense of involvement and creativity is created in schoolwide functions, and ultimately in decisions that affect individual instruction.

Teacher influence within the school organization may be a more important concept than previously has been imagined by administrators. Likert (1961) examined worker/supervisor/management *influences* to examine their relationship to control and to productivity. He found that the top one-third of most productive groups were those who had the greatest amount of influence within their organization. His findings support the concept of shared management control with groups of teachers.

Tannenbaum's (1973, 530) more recent studies have confirmed the earlier results of Likert. He found that workers who have a greater sense of control in their organizations are more positively disposed to their supervisors. Changing patterns of influence are integrally linked to control redistribution in schools. The power to produce, as well as some of the controls for production will shift to small work groups.

The Quality Control System

The school's quality control system has four active dimensions: (1) team regulation, (2) individual regulation, (3) management control, and (4) external review (see Figure 14.8). All four cycles act as a feedforward and a corrective mechanism to teams, each mechanism viewing team activities and results from a different and therefore unique perspective.

Goals and Work Group Plans

School improvement activities are planned by work groups and subsequently controlled to ensure staff energy remains focused on achieving specific results. Figure 14.9 outlines the basic school improvement process. Plans precede action, which then directs development activities; evaluation summarizes the results of planned action.

The control process acts as a monitoring, reinforcing, and corrective function during the implementation and development stage. Figure 14.10 outlines

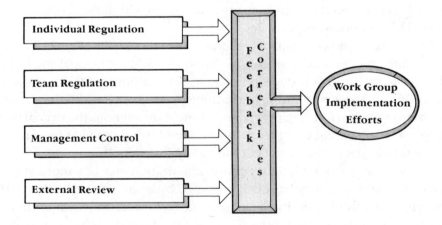

Figure 14.8. Dimensions of a Quality Control System

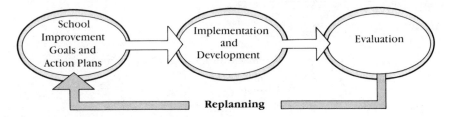

Figure 14.9. School Improvement Process

the generic control cycle, illustrating its continuous problem-solving relationship to the implementation of plans, as well as to the refinement of plans. The control cycle reviews implementation behaviors as they relate to either initial or revised plans and anticipated results.

Work Activity and Correction

The interrelationship between worker activity and correction and adjustment is established to control cycles throughout the year. Work groups are assigned to task objectives and proceed to develop their action plan. During the three work stages (planning, implementation, and development), results are supervised and monitored (by various roles) continuously. At three benchmarks during the year, all school actors (team members, team leaders, principals) stop work in order to reflect on their experiences and perceptions, and to make specific affirmations, corrections, or adjustments in the next short-range plan (see Figure 14.11). Work correction is a productive rather than punitive ac-

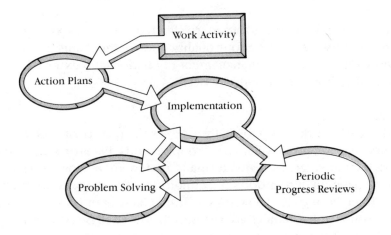

Figure 14.10. Basic Control Cycle

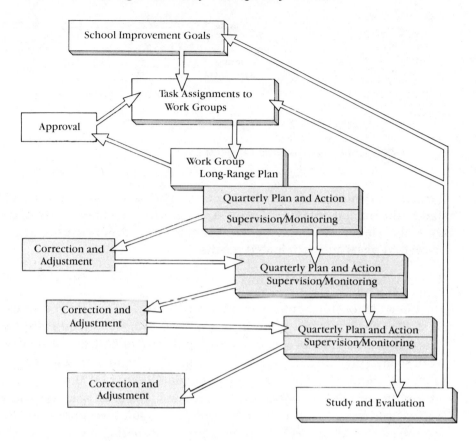

Figure 14.11. Work Activity and Correction Process

tivity, one that enables a team to act more effectively in the next work period. Let us consider how each of the four quality control mechanisms—team regulation, individual regulation, management regulation, and external review—is integrated into both of these processes.

Team Regulation

Periodically, each work group formally assesses the quality of each member's performance in the team as well as the group's results. Plans often are changed during a reflection stage, as teams formally review their work in relation to goals and to changing perceptions and conditions. The work context changes regularly, either from external factors or from changes in growth conditions within the group itself. Changes are realities that need to be addressed as new challenges and opportunities. One way a group can regulate itself is by adjusting and revising its own plans.

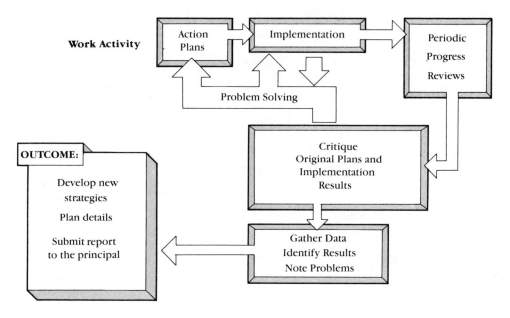

Figure 14.12. Team Regulation Cycle

During each team's regulation session (held, for example, monthly or quarterly), the group reviews original plans and critiques progress. The reflection process involves gathering and analyzing performance data, reflecting on experiences, sharing perceptions, and identifying results. Refined or affirmed plans will guide work flow during the next months (see Figure 14.12).

A team self-regulation control cycle is a variation of the basic cycle. Team self-regulation requires members to assess all three work stages and to plan for work activity in the next period. Self-regulation activities include gathering data, assessing results of activities, refining plans, and developing new strategies for the next phase of activity. A team progress report to the principal includes essential information in relation to the results of planned activities and to future plans. A team might assess its progress and plan for the next month as is shown in the sample, Table 14.3.

Individual Regulation
Teachers in effective schools tend to work in the context of a group. Each teacher defines personal goals and action plans as they relate to team (and task force) goals, responsibilities, and also to personal growth needs. Figure 14.13 outlines the individual staff member's self-regulating cycle. Note that the self-criticism process occurs as a teacher analyzes work patterns and outcome re-

TABLE 14.3. Quarterly Report

Key Events	Progress Results	Report November Plans
Identify instruments	Cognitive inventory instrument selected Learning style inventory selected	Develop own interest inventory
In-service diagnosis		Need to identify trainer for administering instruments
Diagnose students		Administer learning style inventory
Record-keeping systems	Four books located Math professor's system	Need to locate other systems; service centers; other school districts
Data translation; programs		We need help to learn procedures
Develop manual for teachers		(March)

sults. Personal regulation affirms plans and/or makes modifications that address emerging conditions.

Individual monitoring enables corrective measures to be made regularly (three times per year) to enhance the probability of quality results. Let us again

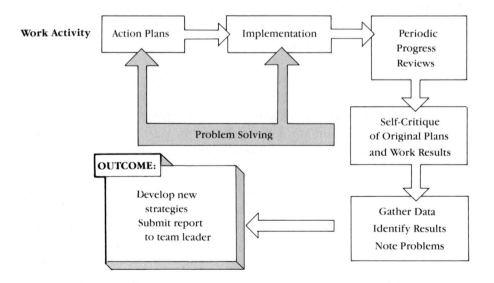

Figure 14.13. Individual Regulation Cycle

use as an example Donna Morris's progress report and her new plan (see Figure 14.14) for the first work period (the second quarter).

Management Regulation

The primary function of school management is to ensure that the school's goals will be realized in the most effective and efficient manner. The principal bases control decisions on a combination of factors: (1) each work group's *progress report,* (2) personal *observation* and other feedback, (3) *conferences* and problem-solving meetings, and (4) feedback from the *external review* team. The control task is to synthesize all data collected and to plan for reinforcement, problem solving, and corrective feedback to each working team.

During each stage of school work activity (organizational goal setting, team planning, implementation efforts, and team reviews) the principal provides specific leadership functions (see Figure 14.15). During goal setting (I), the principal directs and negotiates schoolwide goal-setting activities. After tasks have been assigned to work groups (II), the principal reacts to and finally approves plans. During the implementation stage (III), the principal observes activity, supervises, guides teams, and collects data on performance patterns. The principal then analyzes and assesses past management activities and the progress of each team through periodic progress reviews (IV). The outcome of this management control cycle is to periodically (three times annually) identify problems and successes, and to plan for correcting and reinforcing team behavior.

External Review

An annual outside study provides a unique perspective on team progress that is different from that of team members and principals. Teachers, supervisors, and administrators who have no responsibility to the team observed are eligible for service on an external review team. Their task is to ask questions and to observe behaviors as nonparticipants in the goal achievement process. Often work patterns will surface for external observers that team members may overlook. External observation data provide a team with additional information data on work patterns and their results. Unbiased feedback tends to help work groups correct patterns in a fresh way.

Figure 14.16 illustrates the relationship of the external review team to the observed work group's action plans, to implementation activities, and to the data analysis process. Team plans and reports are reviewed, and interviews are conducted with sample students. All data are analyzed by the review team to determine the group's relative success in achieving its goals. Work patterns are identified and recommendations are made for correction and reinforcement. The critique of team progress is reported to the team and to the principal simultaneously, outlining perceived achievements and areas in need of corrective action.

Teacher Progress Report
Teacher: Donna Morris
Quarter: First
Subsystem 1: Quality Instruction
Objectives: Develop Proficiency in Demonstrations and Learning Centers
Activities 1. Observed 3 teachers in demonstrations and 1 in learning centers 2. Developed criteria for demonstrations 3. Read 2 books on learning centers
Outcomes 1. I have a sense of an effective demonstration but need to develop more clear cues about next steps and to involve learners in problem solving re: demonstration concept/skill 2. I am having a difficult time locating effective learning centers in action

Figure 14.14.

Following the external team's report, the work group synthesizes the feedback and subsequently plans for corrective action. A revised team action plan may be presented to the principal for approval prior to action, as a synthesis

Quarter:

Subsystem 1: Quality Instruction

Objectives: Develop Proficiency in Demonstrations, Learning Centers, Contracts

DEMONSTRATIONS

1. Work on cues and student problem posing

2. Involve 2 teachers in classroom observation-feedback

LEARNING CENTERS

1. Locate 2 more effective learning centers to observe

2. Study learning center books and select 1 curriculum area in which to begin a learning center

CONTRACTS

1. Browse the bookstore and library for readings on contracts

2. Locate professors at universities who use contracts

Figure 14.14. (continued)

may be incorporated into a team's own regulating progress report. It should be noted that the team and/or principal may elect not to address all areas of an external team's recommendations. External feedback should be viewed as additional perceptions that can stimulate team action to become more productive in the long run. The external observation is, in a sense, a bonus feedback

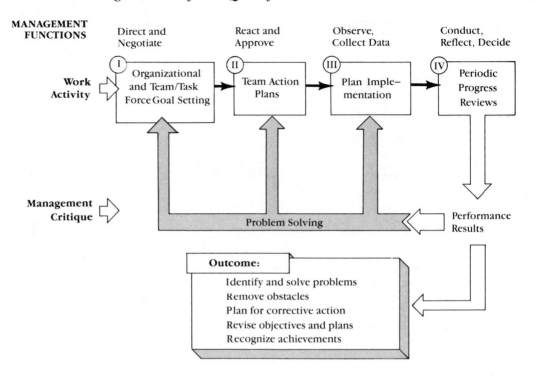

Figure 14.15. Management Control Cycle

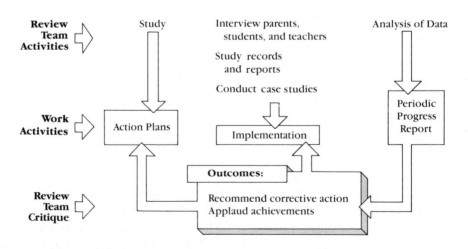

Figure 14.16. External Review Cycle

mechanism that offers a team additional opportunities for increasing productivity.

To develop an external review process, a school leadership team reviews the school goals and work group objectives, and develops an external review sequence of events. Listed here are a few considerations.

1. List procedures for determining the group composition of external review teams
2. Select work groups for external review
3. Outline responsibilities, tasks, procedures, and a time line for the review team
4. Define reporting procedures and follow-up activities
5. Define how you will guide the review team's examination of quality
6. Develop a plan for implementing a review cycle in your school/district

Feedback and feedforward systems provide clues and recommendations to the work group for adjustment to work patterns; thus additional information assists the group to plan more effectively for future actions. A multilayered system of control allows the school to grow with a steady state of dynamic growth. In the process, all professionals grow in their ability to observe, collect, and analyze data, and to critique a situation for group commendation and correction. Thus, control within an open systems model not only allows for directed and effective growth, but it also enables a staff to become more adept at critiquing and refining work processes in schools. The overall benefit to the school is that cooperative control mechanisms weld together various groups and further enhance the ecology of a school and the shared sense of purpose.

Next Steps

The principal's quality control task is to determine team and management control processes to be introduced in the school. The quality control measures selected are likely to influence directly the quality of schooling results produced by work groups. Several decisions for designing and implementing quality control cycles are as follows:

1. assign specific objectives to certain work groups
2. introduce an action planning process for all groups to use
3. negotiate and approve team plans
4. designate due dates for team action plans
5. assign to teams the task of individual planning and periodic reflection
6. designate due dates for periodic team reflection, with reports and new short-range plans being sent to you
7. observe your teams planning or working, or individuals working on team plans

8. conduct conferences for performance feedback, reinforcement, and correctives
9. provide resources to teams in terms of ideas, materials, experts, and dollars
10. recognize exemplary performance publicly
11. plan your supervision for each team, providing helpful on-the-job coaching
12. plan the school evaluation procedures to include the following feedback and assessment of results:
    a) team self-assessment
    b) client assessment (students, other teachers)
    c) principal assessment
    d) preparation of a final report to be shared with the staff, parents, and central office administrators

Concluding Comments

A quality control system is vital to a school's productivity. The management task is to design a system where control processes are shared throughout the staff. A multilayered system provides a variety of feedback and feedforward information for ensuring organizational success. *Team regulation* permits each work group to control its own patterns in order to succeed in specific ways. *Individual regulation* allows teachers to critique their own progress within the context of a work group. *Management control* provides organizational feedback to work groups, so that the group continues on a path in keeping with management expectations. An *external review* permits work groups to gain fresh new insights into their patterns from a team that studies work patterns and results. Together these four regulating mechanisms enable the school to function at its potential capability. Control data are the lifeblood for each new phase in a school's development.

Management: Evaluation

Evaluation determines the value of school productivity. Schoolwide evaluation in a multiwork group school is a qualitatively different practice from evaluation in other schools. In keeping with a bottom-up/top-down pattern of school decision making, evaluation processes require several layers of activity for examining the effectiveness of school performance. Following an engagement in several control cycles of planning/acting/reviewing during the year, the school's performance processes and results are judged in light of measured achievement gains. The task in evaluation is to measure the degree and the value of behavioral changes, processes, and products as they relate to criteria set forth in the school's goal sets. The focus of the management evaluation task is the design of levels of evaluation that are necessary for effective schoolwide assessment of productivity.

The purpose of evaluation is to assess the results of work performance against standard expectations and against annual organization goals. Consequently, schoolwide evaluation is viewed as a four-layered set of evaluation activities, each layer interdependent with the other, yet examining a discrete subset of school life. Team leaders, principals, and teachers are all partners, each playing different roles in the school improvement process. Consequently, schoolwide evaluation requires several layers of assessment activity for the examination of performance results.

Figure 14.17 outlines the evaluation model for schools that function in collaborative arrangements. The *school goal set* and subsequent work group action plans provide the annual context for work and for evaluation. *Individual performance* is assessed in a work group context and reviewed in relation to work contributions. *Student achievement,* the primary school product, is analyzed in relation to team objectives and results. Finally, the various functional and operational *subsystems of the organization,* such as programs and technology, are analyzed in relation to their assistance to the staff in all school and team school improvement efforts.

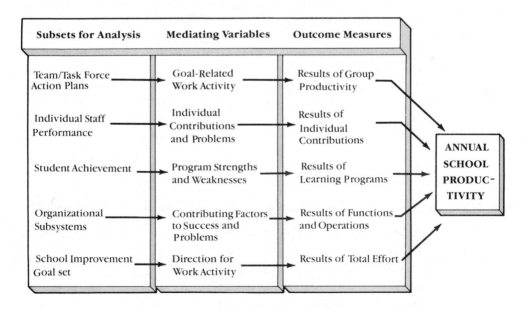

Figure 14.17. A Production Model of School Evaluation

Assigning Values to Goals

School goals provide the general measure and value for school productivity within any given year. The first task in school evaluation is for the leadership team to weight each goal in terms of its relative value for a given year. Using 100 as a total, a percentage value is assigned to each school improvement goal. Table 14.4 illustrates the goal weighting task.

The second task is to assign a value (weight) to each work group's objective. A task value provides perspective as to the relative importance of the team work objective; that value will guide team assessment. This task is outlined here using the five goals in Table 14.4.

TABLE 14.4. Weighted Goals

Weight (%)	School Goals
20	1. To develop a schoolwide *communication system* to foster greater organizational effectiveness, increased cross-team collaboration, and enriched program development and implementation
20	2. To develop a continuous improvement process whereby *teachers improve their skills* in providing instruction for mastery
15	3. To develop a *system for student involvement* in school organizational life and in personal program development
25	4. To plan team-taught, *personalized learning programs* that are based on diagnosed mastery level; affective needs/ interests, learning style and cognitive processing style
20	5. To increase math scores by 15 percent over last year

School Goal 1—Communication System (Total Weight: 20)

Leadership Council Objectives	*Task Weight*
To produce a weekly news sheet of events, needs, responsibilities, re- sources, etc., related to the activities of the following: leadership council, three teaching teams, and task forces	3

To organize vertical curriculum teams to develop a schoolwide outcomes/mastery-oriented curriculum	10
To organize task forces to develop three identified products: record-keeping system, reporting system, and audiovisual public relations program	4
To coordinate schoolwide in-service programs and materials development workshops based on needs	3

School Goal 2—Instructional Skill Development (Total Weight: 20)

In-service Task Force Objectives

To conduct workshops on peer supervision, observation technology, the four elements of quality instruction, and mastery learning	6
To videotape segments of instruction for staff analysis and improvement recommendations	

Teaching Team Objectives

To observe each other, collecting data on the four instructional variables	3
To plan for the four instructional variables in team program plans	
To critique each others' instruction plans as they relate to quality instruction variables	

Principal's Objectives

To formally observe each teacher four times and informally assist teachers in developing quality instruction expertise	3

School Goal 3—Student Involvement (Total Weight: 15)

Teaching Team Objectives

To develop a team student council to organize student task forces as they relate to team life	5 Team A 5 Team B 5 Team C

To develop a student advisory system to ensure personal growth and well-being

To develop a planning model for regular student input into program focus, design, and learning alternatives

To develop a contract system for individual planning and evaluation in each program area

School Goal 4—Diagnostic-based Instructional Programs (Total Weight: 25)

In-service Task Force Objectives

To conduct workshops in diagnostic procedures including learning style, program interests, cognitive processing style, mastery level, and motivation	7

Leadership Council Objectives

To develop a planning model for teaching teams to use in linkage diagnostic data with curriculum parameters and available resources	7

Teaching Team Objectives

To diagnose all team students in the following areas by March 1: learning style, interests, self-concept, and mastery in major curriculum areas	5

Inventory Development Task Force Objectives

To develop an inventory for teachers that diagnoses student interests, strengths, motivation, and self-concept; success history	6

School Goal 5—Increase Math Scores by 15% (Total Weight: 20)

Teaching Team Objectives

To increase math scores 15 percent
above last year

5 Team A
5 Team B
5 Team C
5 Team D

In preparation for evaluation activities, it is important to gather sufficient evidence for making an objective assessment about results. Management considerations include the results of planned school products, organizational designs, training, and supervising. The following list illustrates indicators for assessing the sample goals used throughout this text: (1) communication system, (2) teacher skill development, (3) student involvement system, and (4) team-taught learning programs.

School Productivity Measures

New Products
a set of weekly news sheets
curriculum revisions
a record-keeping system
a reporting system
a public relations audiovisual program
a videotape of instruction
planning model for student input
a student contract system
teacher planning model to link diagnostic data to instructional planning
diagnostic instruments

New Organization Designs
vertical curriculum teams
leadership council
task forces
school-based in-service
teacher observation teams
student council—team based
student advisory system
student contract system
team-based student diagnosis

Training Elements
peer supervision
quality instruction

mastering learning
diagnostic procedures
   In-Class Coaching Elements (Observe)
instruction—Bloom's model
effectiveness of plans for "quality instruction"
contract system
evidence of plans based on diagnosis

Work Group Assessment

The next task is to consider the overall effect of the work group task assignments and results on the goal itself. Individual group goals may have been accomplished in general terms, whereas the overall results may not have satisfied the goal. Or, team work results may have been less than expected and yet the school goal was accomplished. Evaluation is a judgment call that links perceptions about the relative value for desired results with actual outcomes. Consider the following analysis.

Goal 1

Communication Objective 1—Production of a *weekly news sheet*. A management review of monitoring activities provides a certain perspective on goal attainment. Feedback from teachers on the *value* of the news sheet serves as another indicator of success. Dialogue sessions or surveys might yield additional kinds of feedback. A leadership team analysis of the process of producing the news sheet, along with team uses of the information would add additional data regarding effectiveness. Questions to address might include: Was the sheet produced weekly? Did all teams share news? What were team responses to increased information? What evidence exists of increased coordination and cooperation as a result of the news sheet? The leadership team analyzes all types of feedback and determines whether or not the weekly news sheet fostered organizational effectiveness, increased cross-team collaboration, and enriched program development and implementation.

Following a careful analysis of the data, the leadership team assigns a numerical value to the objective. Analysis of all four objectives for goal 1 would proceed in a similar fashion, followed by a total value ascribed to results. Twenty points is the maximum total value for goal 1.

Goal 2

Teaching Skill Development—Work analysis requires data from the in-service task force, each teaching team, and the principal regarding work results and their value. In addition, teacher feedback provides clues to the effectiveness of training and follow-up observation and feedback. The result of each school objective is assigned a weight and subsequently totaled to determine a total weight for the goal. The bottom-line question for assessing each objective is: "Were teacher skills improved in providing 'quality instruction'?" What is the evidence?

Making a Judgment

Each report needs to be assessed in the same pattern. The goal is to be considered along with work progress throughout the year in combination with coaching. Did the group exceed expectations, fall far short, or did they achieve what was hoped? For each assigned objective, assess results within the work context and assign a value. The total value for each goal should not exceed the weight assigned, except in cases of unusual productivity.

Listed here is an example of a team's self-assessment. Note the prose critique as well as a brief listing of goal outcomes.

Team A's Assessment

Team A, upon assessment of goal results, perceives that a large portion of our goal was achieved. The learning styles and interests of all students were assessed. However, we were able only to assess the mastery level of all students in math. The task of diagnosis resulted in much more data than we were able to translate into programs. Consequently, we decided that by limiting mastery level diagnosis to math for this year, we could study our process and refine it for use in other areas of study.

As we began to translate the learning style, interest, and mastery level data into programs we became bogged down. The implications of the data are much broader than we anticipated. Consequently, we imagine that skillful translation requires additional staff knowledge and skills. We expect this to become a major focus for our work next year.

The manual on diagnosis that we developed for other teams primarily reflects the knowledge we gained this year about different types of diagnosis. We eagerly await staff feedback on the first draft, as well as their suggestions for how the manual can be used throughout our school.

Key Events	*Goal Outcomes*
1. identify instruments	six located
2. in-service: diagnosis	training in learning style inventory; designed interest inventory

3. diagnose students	interest inventory given in November; learning style inventory given in December; math pretest given in January
4. record-keeping systems	Workshop in January; March product complete
5. handbook for other teachers	First draft in April, ready for dissemination

School productivity is judged in relation to goals and the results of goal-related activity. Suppose the final score for a 29-point goal is 10. The goal may have been too broad; or the team/task group may have been unproductive. The score suggests a relative value of productivity and provides a context for determining next steps in the school improvement process.

Suppose a 29-point goal was assessed at 29. Each work group would deserve recognition for its achievement as well as for the members' ability to work together productively. Suppose a goal were assigned 15 points out of 30. Recognition would be important for results that led to the 15, while plans would need to be made for refining the goal-setting process or for providing skill building to a team in its work habits. Assessment of work group results leads to three possible outcomes

1. recognition for achievements
2. plans for corrective action
3. plans for next steps in the improvement process

Individual Performance Assessment

Each role set is analyzed in relation to their contribution to school productivity. Teacher, team leader, and principal are the essential role sets to examine.

Level 1: Teacher Evaluation

Until such time as the courts assign teacher evaluation responsibilities to team leaders or department heads, only principals will be involved in the evaluation process. We propose, however, that both team leader and principal conduct a shared leadership conference with each teacher.

Preparation (Principal and Team Leader).   The teacher's goals, reports, and monitoring activities are all reviewed. Results and responses to supervisory directions are reviewed in order to identify teacher strengths, weaknesses, and potential next steps. The teacher in preparing for the conference reviews the same cluster of materials and prepares a personal summary assessment of the result of each performance goal. Data, reports, and artifacts are all gathered to support the self-assessment process.

Conferencing patterns will be different for each individual but will seek to elicit concensus regarding the results of each goal. Reports, analysis, and data are reviewed together by teacher and supervisor(s) to identify performance strengths, weaknesses, and recommendations for the following year. The evaluation process is a collaborative discussion of performance, based on available evidence. Final judgments are made, however, by the principal regarding the effectiveness of individual performance.

Evaluation: A Systems Approach.   Viewed within the school's growth context, evaluation becomes a measure of success as it relates to specific goals. Evaluation is an assessment that springs from goals, results, formal data, informal observations, reports, problems, deviations, and needed improvements. In a sense, evaluation is a stepping stone to the future that follows an assessment of the past and an interpretation of what is needed. Rarely does performance evaluation dwell on personality, punishments, or reprimands, and only then as it relates to the results of goal attainment.

Note the evaluation of Donna Morris on the results of goal 1 (see Figure 14.18). Her accomplishments are noted as reported from a wide variety of sources: classroom data, informal conversations and observations, and an analysis of various reports. The area mentioned to be in need of attention resulted from many observations. Recommendations for next steps grew out of an evaluation.

Level 2: Team Leader Evaluation

Following a performance review of the individual teachers on each team, each leader is assessed by the principal. Goals, work activity, monitoring, and supervision results are all analyzed to identify strengths, weaknesses, and potential next steps. The team leader reviews the same goals, reports, data artifacts, and notes to prepare a personal assessment of goal results. During the conference the two parties strive for concensus on assessing the value of performance progress. The principal has the final word in determining team leader effectiveness in providing leadership for team student achievement gains or losses.

Level 3: Principal Evaluation

Typically the principal is evaluated by a central office administrator. Feedback from teachers, specialists, and team leaders on the effectiveness of the principal's performance is important in the school's assessment process. The principal might distribute his or her goals to the staff and request goal-based feedback. Following an assessment of the principal's performance results, it is

---

FORMATIVE/SUMMATIVE EVALUATION

Name _____ Donna Morris _____   Date ____ 4/8 ____

Evaluator ___*Jerry Willis*_____

Subsystem 1 _____ Instruction _____

Goal
To develop proficiency in 4 techniques:
       Demonstration
       Learning centers
       Contracts
       Peer teaching

Accomplishments
Donna was successful in developing minimum proficiency in 3 of the 4 techniques: demonstration, contracts, and peer teaching; and developing criteria of effectiveness for each technique.

Areas in Need of Attention
Donna's cues and corrective mechanisms in all three areas need further attention.

Recommendations
1. Due to her particular success with demonstrations, Donna should be listed as exemplary and serve as a model for other teacher observations.
2. Due to the extensive involvement in 3 techniques, it is recommended that skill in learning centers be postponed until next year.

Figure 14.18.

important to identify skill strengths and weaknesses. Do team leaders represent their teams or only themselves? Do teachers seek out team leaders first with a problem? Does the principal provide sufficient coaching and intervention into team/task force work life? Do specialists carry their responsibilities adequately in response to team needs? Answers to these questions are among the indicators of a principal's effectiveness.

Schoolwide Student Assessment

Measures of student gains in achievement are the bottom-line measure for determining a school's success. Debate continues on the inadequacy of both norm-referenced and criterion-referenced measures of achievement. The pub-

TABLE 14.5. Analysis of Achievement

Subject	Gain or Loss (%)
Team A	
reading	+4.0
math	−0.3
science	+3.1
language arts	+.09
Team B	
reading	+9.5
math	−0.4
science	+7.5
language arts	+1.2
Team C	
reading	+3.3
math	+0.2
science	+3.7
language arts	−1.7

lic at large, however, believes that achievement tests measure something important about student achievement and about the local school's capability to ensure certain levels of growth. Schools have only begun to sample the ways in which they are acccountable for the growth they produce or do not produce.

The task in measuring student achievement schoolwide is twofold: team level analysis and schoolwide analysis.

Team-level analysis includes several activities. First, a comparison is made between the team goal (predicted score) for achievement in each area tested (for example, CTBS, IOWA-TBS) and the actual gains or losses. Note the example in Table 14.5.

Upon analysis, Team A showed gains beyond what was predicted in reading and science especially, and achieved slightly above what was predicted in language arts. However, the score in *math* was slightly less than predicted, a loss worth noting. The target for particular attention in the next school year for Team A must be its math program.

Team B showed unusually high gains in reading and science, with a slight increase in language arts. Math achievement, however, was slightly lower than expected; a target for improvement is the math program.

Team C showed high gains in reading and in science, with math showing a little better than predicted. Language arts scores, however, were lower than predicted. A target for improvement is the language arts program.

When analyzed as a group, two of the three math programs need attention, along with the language arts program. The reading programs in all three teams are quite successful, especially on Team B. The science programs on all teams are also noteworthy, especially on Team B. The language arts programs are producing achievement results as predicted, with the exception of Team C. The overall achievement score predicted for the school was a mean gain; however, test results showed a net gain of +29.2 above the predicted score. The actual gain above that which was predicted was 2.9 standard deviations above the district norm. An overall judgment suggests applause for the teams in their efforts to facilitate student achievement in the areas tested.

Recommendations to each team include continuing to practice the programs that produced effective results, modifying them as the need arises. Particular efforts are to be directed at the programs that showed losses, and toward improving diagnostic, program design, and instructional practices.

School Subsystem Assessment

An assessment of organization variables provides clues regarding the facilitating forces in the school's goal attainment process. A careful analysis of each subsystem as a unit, and also of its impact on all other subsystems, will help to identify sources of system weakness. This fourth step in the school evaluation process enables the staff to identify potential factors in goal success, or lack of success, and also in achievement gains. Without this second level analysis, successes and failures will be identified but the causes for such may go unnoticed.

The first level for analysis is a teaching team assessment of school subsystems. A composite picture is synthesized by the leadership team as it addresses staff perceptions and incorporates leadership analysis to point out schoolwide productivity (see Table 14.6).

Each subsystem is analyzed in terms of strengths and weaknesses, and general recommendations for improving the school's various subunits of performance are made. A summary sheet for communicating bottom-line results to the staff, parents, and to central office administrators is an effective planning device for principals. The summary sheet (such as the one in Figure 14.19) records "wins" and "losses" as related to the complex dimensions of school activity.

Concluding Comments

A four-phase process for school evaluation has been described, which includes individual staff performance, school goal results, student achievement gains, and subsystem analysis. Each phase provides certain information regarding the effectiveness of schooling productivity. Individual evaluation identifies individual staff contributions and problems; school goal assessment identifies the values of staff activity; student achievement measures point out program strengths and weaknesses; and school subsystem analysis provides useful clues for directing reinforcement or corrective staff action. Each layer, examined

TABLE 14.6 School Subsystem Analysis

Subsystem	Strengths	Weaknesses	Recommendations
Leadership	Provided staff with a sense that we could produce effectively if we work cooperatively	Started the year with a strong sense of purpose but did not continue to lead well enough throughout the year	Participate in team planning sessions and in teacher observation
Goal	Organized entire staff to define school goals	Some staff concerns did not appear in final goals	Repeat the goal-setting process until all concerns are built into goals or are recognized
Organization	Teaching team organization went smoothly with almost everyone participating well	Team leaders need special training. Task forces need help in group dynamics and planning	Staff development plans to include programs for team leaders and sessions on group processes. Principal should intervene more often
Performance	All roles established personal goals and plans	Not all goals were linked to team priorities, nor were they measurable. We had a difficult time at evaluation	Develop in-service programs on goal setting and planning
Program	Staff development was linked to school goals. We revised the school language arts and reading programs	Not all in-service programs were useful to everyone; too much time was wasted. Many operational problems exist and need to be resolved	Design in-service programs for different needs: only attend what is personally important. Assign a task force to resolve operational problems
Management	Planning processes are working effectively	Monitoring and supervision were weak areas	Prioritize activities so that goals can be monitored and staff activity supervised and coached
School District Supra-system	Supported school goals	Required meetings outside building; often had little to do with our goals and responsibilities	Have principal negotiate for use of staff nonteaching time

| Assessment Target | Global Assessment | | | |
	Indicators of Effectiveness	Assessment Process and Means	Results	Next Steps
School Goals Communication system	Productive staff exchange	Survey staff feedback	Productive beginning to connect people	Team newsletters
Instructional skill improvement	Increased co-operative learning	Student feedback	Enthusiasm	Train student leaders
System of student involvement	Increase in quality of projects	Observation	Productive beginning	Expand to social studies classes
Diagnostic-based math and language program	Achievement tests	District tests	Gain 5.0	Train all teachers in diagnostic skills
Team and Task Force Goals	Influence on instructional program	Observation survey	Moderate	Training in communication skills
Individual Goals	Contributions	Feedback	Moderate	Recognition strategies
Student Achievement	Increase in active student participation	Observation	Moderate	Enhance student involvement patterns

Figure 14.19.

collaboratively by the staff groupings, provides useful indicators of successes and problems, and points to directions for the next school improvement targets.

In planning for school assessment, check these elements presently included in your evaluation system.

Elements of an Evaluation System

☐ A school goal set
☐ Values assigned to school goals
☐ Evaluation of work groups
☐ Evaluation of individual performance

☐ Evaluation of student achievement
☐ Evaluation of the school's organizational subsystems

Of those performance system elements that exist in partial form, consider which parts need further to be developed.

Conclusion

In this chapter we have sought to complete the discussion of management tasks that have been introduced and developed throughout the text. The book is about school management, which we define as coaching people toward new norms of school productivity. Said in another way, this entire book has been about staff management and the nature of cooperative leadership and work in an ecologically sound school context.

In conclusion, let us examine the generic management skills as they relate to the 10 competency sets introduced in Chapter 3 and developed throughout the text.

TABLE 14.7. Overlap of Management Skills and Functions

10 Competency Sets	Generic Management Skills								
	Plan-ning	Organ-izing	Moti-vating	Teaching	Coach-ing	Decision making	Communi-cating	Monitor-ing	Evalua-ting
Schoolwide goal setting	X	X	X	X	X	X	X		
Work group organization	X	X	X	X	X	X	X		
Individual performance planning	X	X	X	X	X	X	X		
Staff development	X	X	X	X	X	X	X	X	X
Clinical supervision	X	X	X	X	X	X	X	X	X
Quality control	X	X	X	X		X	X	X	X
Work group development	X	X	X	X	X	X	X	X	X
Instructional management	X	X	X	X	X	X	X	X	X
Resource management	X	X	X	X	X	X	X	X	X
Schoolwide evaluation: school, team, teacher, student	X	X	X	X	X	X	X	X	X

Table 14.7 shows how the skills of planning, organizing, motivating, teaching, coaching, decision making, and quality control relate to each of the 10 management competencies that direct school development. Note that each management skill is embedded in each of the competency functions. Furthermore, the management skills are used by principals in each competency, and they are used equally by the staff.

Management therefore is a shared function in a dynamic school organization. When a principal shares power with a staff, the responsibility for success is shared as well. The principal who risks co-involvement of staff creates the conditions for more stimulating professional and intellectual involvement in schooling. In return, the school becomes transformed over time as the staff learns from each experience, shares in the failures as well as successes, and develops the capacity to alter norms.

Metamorphosis occurs over time. The stages of transformation from a caterpillar to a butterfly, for example, require careful nurturing and rejoicing in incremental successes. The monarch butterfly emerges from successive stages of development, each of which occurs in an optimal growth environment.

As a principal leads the school development process, careful, caring, and yet highly demanding behaviors are critical. Otherwise the process will be aborted. Success depends on careful attention to goal-related needs and a firm belief that the staff working together can transform schooling norms. Success will come to those intent upon winning and doing what it takes to succeed.

APPENDIX

Personal Management Planning: A Simulation

Step A: Goal Setting

WISHING

We often limit our sense of what can occur by reminding ourselves of existing constraints on our goals. For a moment, suspend all restraints and dream about your organization functioning at optimal performance. What do you envision? What do you wish for in relation to the following:

Your organizational environment

> I wish that every staff, student, and parent felt that the school was a kind of learning home, one in which they could create, risk, develop the untried, and work together in numerous configurations to create the impossible.

Your instructional program, process, and methodologies

> I wish that the program would reflect a high energy system in which students and teachers were working together congnitively, affectively, and behaviorally in numerous kinds of groups, activities, and throughout the community to learn what we announced through the curriculum.

Your staff performance and working relationships

> I wish the staff would develop patterns for continuous examination of their instruction and planning by observing in each others classrooms and providing useful feedback.

Your resources

> I wish we could involve the university professors and students and the regional service center staff in our growth process on a regular basis.
> I also wish every teacher had a computer terminal to record student data and for making program decisions.

Your organizational outcomes (student learning, staff performance)

> My wish is for all students to be on grade level with 30% above; for the staff to be able to learn and transfer all they need into effective instruction and peer collaboration.

WHERE WE ARE

Think in broad general terms about the gap between where your school is and where you want to be in relation to your goals. Describe the following.

The current condition

> The staff seems eager to move ahead and explore alternative and potentially more useful patterns of organization planning and teaching. They seem hesitant, however, to drop any of their existing practices and therefore perceive that

anything new will require additional time and energy.

Teachers, for the most part, are still teaching groups of students rather than personalizing programs around diagnosed needs and selected outcomes. They need help in shifting from "what I'm teaching" to "what each is learning."

Reading and math scores are quite low; 50% of the students are below grade level, 35% are on grade level, and 15% are above. Parents want significant improvement.

Last year several incidents of vandalism led us to explore student attitudes. Students perceive that the school is primarily for the teachers, not them.

RANK-ORDER CONCERN

Identify Indicators for Success

Summarize your key areas of concern in a phrase for each goal. Next to each area of concern, describe how you will judge if your concern has been resolved and your goal has been met. Be as specific as possible while recognizing that not all indicators of accomplishment can be quantified.

Key Areas of Concern	Indicators of Goal Accomplishment
Goal 1	
1. training	1. Teachers using more effective diagnostic and planning procedures

2. record keeping/reporting 2) A teacher-developed/
selected system that
links to the
curriculum

3. fear   Teachers will adapt
and invent alternative
methods for fostering
student mastery
enthusiastically

Goal 2

1. teacher isolation   1) Teachers willing to
plan and teach
collaboratively

2. Scheduling   2) Teachers determining
schedules as needs
arise

3. textbook programs   3) Teachers will develop
programs geared to the
curriculum and
diagnosed needs
using textbooks
as one of many
resources

Goal 3

1. fear of observation   1) Teachers soliciting
peer observation

2. focus for observation 2) Teachers selecting focus for instruction in relation to group definition of instruction and to immediate concerns

3. data collection 3) Teachers developing instruments that provide specific useful feedback to peers

Goal 4

1. outdated professors 1) Professors teaching staff new concepts and methodologies

2. willing outside participation 2) Professors, students and service center staff initiating ways to be involved

3. low teacher self-concept 3) Teacher self-concept improvement on a scale

Goal 5

1. how to raise scores 1) Group strategies for raising scores based on principles of learning

2. failure possibilities 2) Raised school norms 10% each year

Step B: Organizational Analysis

GOAL POSSIBILITIES

Reflect on your wishes. Are they representative of your values and beliefs? Now analyze these in relation to the current situation. Perhaps you can accomplish some of your wishes by transforming them into goal statements. Think in terms of long-range desirable outcomes.

My Goals

1. To provide instruction in my school that is geared to learning outcomes and to the diagnosed needs and interests of my students

2. To provide learning options for students through a wide range of activities, teachers, resources, and peer interaction

3. To involve the staff in continuous observation and criticism of their own instruction as well as of their peers' instruction

4. To involve university and service center persons in school improvement activities

5. To raise learning norms for the school by 10% each year

KEY AREAS OF CONCERN

Analyze each goal and state your concerns for its fulfillment in relation to the following questions:

1. Will parents accept the plan?
2. Will school board policy permit it?
3. Can activities be supervised adequately to facilitate optimal learning?
4. How can teachers best be helped?
5. Will significant learning actually occur?

Reflect on your own goals and state the concerns you have for accomplishing these in your school setting.

Goal 1
Concerns   teachers aren't adequately trained
reporting and record-keeping systems
are inappropriate
teachers are fearful of
changing their practices

Goal 2
Concerns   teachers want to teach
themselves
the schedule prevents peer
planning
teachers believe the textbook
is basic

Goal 3
Concerns   teachers are fearful of being observed
teachers don't know what to observe
teachers don't know how to collect
data
teachers believe they can do
their job best alone

Goal 4
Concerns   teachers feel university professors
are outdated
professors and students won't
want to participate
involvement of outsiders would lead
to retrenchment for the staff

Goal 5
Concerns

teachers' self-concepts will go down
if we bring in outside help

we won't know how to raise
scores

we won't be able to determine
appropriate changes in practice
we will fail or even
reverse scores if we alter
practice

GOAL REFINEMENT

Restate your goals now so that they more clearly reflect your desired outcomes.

Goal 1   To enable teachers to diagnose
students and plan programs
more effectively

Goal 2   To organize teachers into teams of
4-6 teachers to foster greater
choices and options for
mastery

Goal 3   To enable teachers to critique
themselves and each other
for the improvement of
instruction

Goal 4 *To provide additional resources to the staff through the university and service center*

Goal 5 *To raise student achievement by 10% this year*

INFLUENCING FORCES ON GOALS

Goal 1 *To enable teachers both to diagnose each student and to plan learning programs effectively in all learning areas.*

Using the chart below, identify all facilitating forces and restraining forces, writing them opposite each other where they appear to be opposing forces.

Facilitating Forces ⟷	Restraining Forces
Four teachers are trained in special education	Teacher don't believe different approaches than they already use will improve learning
A consultant is available to train teachers in mastery learning	The schedule permits only three in-service days a year
Achievement scores went down last year	The textbook in most subjects is the real curriculum for teacher
A district goal is to raise math and reading scores by 10% this year in each school	Teachers believe they know how to diagnose learning. Teachers teach generally to the group learning norm
The newspaper gave the school bad press in reporting test scores	Little money exists for staff training

INFLUENCE RANKING

Review each goal and rank-order the facilitating and restraining forces in terms of the strength of their importance to your goal.

Goal 1

Facilitating Forces	Restraining Forces
1. Achievement scores went down	1. Beliefs about diagnosis
2. District goal to raise scores	2. Textbooks diagnosis
3. Trainer available / specialized staff	3. Planning schedule limits training

Altering Influences

Goal 1: Restraining Forces.   Possible actions for decreasing force influence.

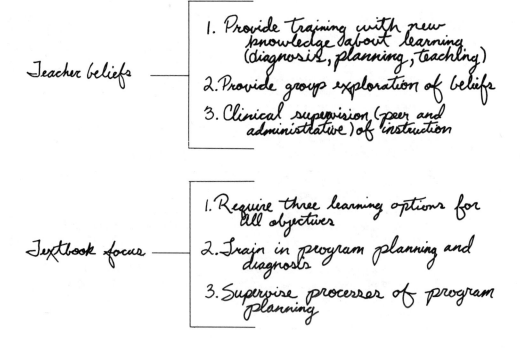

Teacher beliefs —

1. Provide training with new knowledge about learning (diagnosis, planning, teaching)
2. Provide group exploration of beliefs
3. Clinical supervision (peer and administrative) of instruction

Textbook focus —

1. Require three learning options for all objectives
2. Train in program planning and diagnosis
3. Supervise processes of program planning

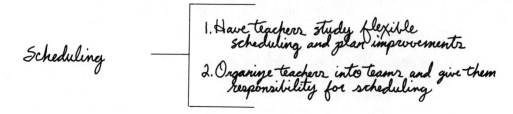

Scheduling
1. Have teachers study flexible scheduling and plan improvements
2. Organize teachers into teams and give them responsibility for scheduling

Facilitating Forces.   Possible actions for increasing force influences.

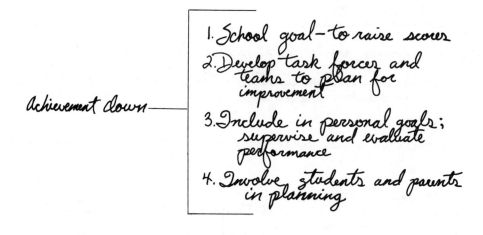

Achievement down
1. School goal — to raise scores
2. Develop task forces and teams to plan for improvement
3. Include in personal goals; supervise and evaluate performance
4. Involve students and parents in planning

Trainers/staff
1. Provide training for staff in diagnosis, planning, teaching
2. Provide coaching observation using special education teachers
3. Conduct monthly group discussions about progress

Step C: Action Planning

CHANGES IN ORGANIZATIONAL SUBSYSTEMS

Goals provide the raison d'être for the local school organization. As you make decisions regarding the events and activities for accomplishing your goals, consider each subsystem within your school organization's ecosystem, and the changes that are likely to occur if you progress toward your goals. List the potential effects in each subsystem.

Effects on the Organization
1. Teachers will work in teams.

2. Task forces will be organized to develop products (e.g., record-keeping systems).

3. Observation teams of teachers will coach each other.

Effects on Performance
1. Teacher goals will include diagnostic and planning skills.

2. Observation cycles will provide feedback on performance.

3. Learning and instruction options will reflect district curriculum and diagnostic data.

Effects on School Goals
My five goals will become part of the school's goal.

Effects on the Program Subsystem
1. Teachers will learn to translate the curriculum into mastery programs.

2. Staff in-service will equip teachers with necessary knowledge and skills.

Effects on Technology
The instructional delivery system and the supervision system will have greater definition and link more closely to diagnosis, planning, and teaching.

Effects on Your Management Subsystem
I will need to develop a school planning and monitoring system to keep the staff on course toward our goals.

DECISION-MAKING TASKS

You are now ready to make decisions that will enable you to accomplish your goals. For each goal identify the key events, resources, responsibilities, and time line that will best enable you to achieve your desired outcomes.

Goal 1: To enable teachers to diagnose students and plan programs effectively

Key Events	Resources	Responsibility	Deadline Date
Provide 3 Training sessions diagnosis/program planning teaching for mastery observation technology	Consultant " " "	Staff development Planning task force	September November January
Conduct monthly rap sessions	Special ed. Teachers	Principal	October – May
Conduct peer observation cycles	Selected Teachers	Team leader	December – May
Team critique of plans	All staff Special ed. teacher	Team leader	October – May
Teachers set personal growth goals or contribution efforts	Training sessions	Principal	September

533

BIBLIOGRAPHY

Acheson, Keith A., and Meredith Damien Gall. *Techniques in the Clinical Supervision of Teachers: Preservice and Inservice Applications*. New York: Longman, 1980.

Ackoff, R. L. *Redesigning the Future, A Systems Approach to Societal Problems*. New York: John Wiley, 1974.

Adizes, Ichak. "Teamwork is the Key to Management Success." *New York Times*, September 16, 1977, IV, 5:1.

Albanese, Robert. *Managing Toward Accountability for Performance*. Homewood, Ill.: Richard D. Irwin, 1975. See also Third Edition, 1981.

American Association of School Administrators. *Time on Task: Using Instructional Time More Effectively*. Arlington, Va.: AASA, 1982. Note that a videotape on the topic is also available from AASA.

Anderson, Linda M., et al. "Principles of Small Group Instruction in Elementary Reading." East Lansing, Mich.: Institute for Research on Teaching, College of Education, Michigan State University, Unpublished paper, 1982.

Anderson, Robert H. *Teaching in a World of Change*. New York: Harcourt Brace and World, 1966.

———. "The School as an Organic Teaching Aid." In *The Curriculum: Retrospect and Prospect*, edited by Robert M. McClure, pp. 271–306. Seventieth Yearbook of the National Society for the Study of Education, Part I. Chicago: University of Chicago Press, 1971.

———. *Opting for Openness*. Arlington, Va.: National Association of Elementary School Principals, 1973

———. "Improving Your Supervisory Skills." *The National Elementary Principal* 58 (June 1979): 42–45.

Araki, Charles T. "Leadership Study in Hawaii—How Characteristics of Principals Affect the Schools." *NASSP Bulletin* 66 (October 1982), 88–96.

Argyris, Chris. *Integrating the Individual and the Organization*. New York: John Wiley, 1964.

Armor, David J., et al. *Analysis of the School Preferred Reading Program in Selected Los Angeles Minority Schools*. Santa Monica, Calif.: Rand Corporation, 1976.

Armstrong, David G. "Team Teaching and Academic Achievement." *Review of Educational Research* 47 (Winter 1977), 65–86.

534

Aspy, David N., and Flora Roebuck. "From Humane Ideas to Human Technology and Back Again Many Times." *Education* 95 (Winter 1974), 63–172.

Austin, Gilbert R. *Process Evaluation: A Comprehensive Study of Outliers*. Baltimore: Maryland State Department of Education, 1978.

———. "Exemplary Schools and the Search for Effectiveness." *Educational Leadership* 37 (October 1979), 10–14.

Bair, Medill, and Richard G. Woodward. *Team Teaching in Action*. Boston: Houghton Mifflin, 1964.

Bales, Robert F. *Interaction Process Analysis: A Method for the Study of Small Groups*. Cambridge, Mass.: Addison-Wesley, 1950.

Barnard, Chester. *The Functions of the Executive*. Cambridge: Harvard University Press, 1964. Originally published in 1938.

Barsky, H. "The Political Style of an Urban Principal: A Case Study." Ph.D. dissertation, University of Pennsylvania, 1975.

Becker, G., et al. *Elementary School Principals and Their Schools*. Eugene, Oreg.: Center for the Advanced Study of Educational Administration, University of Oregon, 1971.

Benne, Kenneth D., and P. Sheats. "Functional Roles and Group Members." *Journal of Social Issues* 4(1948), 41–49.

Bennis, Warren. "Leadership: A Beleaguered Species?" *Organizational Dynamics* 5 (Summer 1976), 3–16.

Bennis, Warren, Kenneth D. Benne, Robert Chin, and Kenneth E. Corey, eds. *The Planning of Change*. 2nd ed. New York: Holt, Rinehart & Winston, 1969. 3rd ed., 1976.

Bentzen, Mary. *Changing Schools: The Magic Feather Principle*. New York: McGraw-Hill, 1974.

Berkowitz, Leonard. "Social Motivation." In *The Handbook of Psychology*, Volume 3. Reading, Mass.: Addison-Wesley, 1954.

Berliner, David. "On Improving Teacher Effectiveness: A Conversation with David Berliner." *Educational Leadership* 40 (October 1982), 12–15.

Berliner, David, and William Tikunoff. "The California Beginning Teacher Evaluation Study: Overview of the Ethnographic Study." *Journal of Teacher Education* 22 (Spring 1976), 24–30.

Berman, Louise M., and Jessie A. Roderick, eds. *Feeling, Valuing and the Art of Growing: Insights into the Affective*. 1977 Yearbook. Washington, D.C.: Association for Supervision and Curriculum Development, 1977.

Berman, Paul, and Milbrey W. McLaughlin. "Federal Programs Supporting Educational Change." Vol. 1–8 (R-1589/through R-1589/8) Santa Monica, Calif.: Rand Corporation, 1978.

———. *Federal Programs Supporting Educational Change*. Vol. 8, *Implementing and Sustaining Innovation*. Santa Monica, Calif.: Rand Corporation, 1978.

———. "Factors Affecting the Process of Change." In *Schools, Conflict and Change*, edited by M. Milstein. New York: Teachers College Press, 1980.

Bertalanffy, Ludwig von. *Problems of Life*. New York: John Wiley, 1952, p. 201.

———. "The History and Status of General Systems Theory." In *Academy of Management Journal* 15 (December 1972), 417.

Bessent, E. Waylan, Ben Harris, and Michael P. Thomas. *Adoption and Utilization of Instructional Television*. Austin: University of Texas, 1968.

Bigge, Morris L. *Learning Theories for Teachers*. New York: Harper & Row, 1971.

Block, James H. "The Effects of Various Levels of Performance on Selected Cognitive, Affective, and Time Variables." Ph.D. dissertation, University of Chicago, 1970.

Bloom, Benjamin S., ed. *Taxonomy of Educational Objectives: The Classification of Educa-*

tional Goals. Handbook I, Cognitive Domain. New York: Longmans, Green and Co., 1956. Handbook II, Affective Domain. New York: David McKay Company, 1964.

Bloom, Benjamin S. "New Views of the Learner: Implications for Instruction and Curriculum." *Educational Leadership* 35 (April 1978), 563–576.

———. *Human Characteristics and School Learning*. New York: McGraw-Hill, 1976.

———. "The New Direction in Educational Research: Alterable Variables." *Phi Delta Kappan* 61 (February 1980), 382–384.

Blumberg, Arthur. *Supervisors and Teachers: A Private Cold War*. 2nd ed. Berkeley: McCutchan, 1980.

Blumberg, Arthur, and William D. Greenfield. *The Effective Principal: Perspectives in School Leadership*. Boston: Allyn & Bacon, 1980.

Bossert, Steven. *Tasks and Social Relationships in Classrooms*. Cambridge: Cambridge University Press, 1979.

Bossert, Steven J., David C Dwyer, Brian Rowan, and Ginny Lee. "Instructional Management Program." San Francisco: Far West Laboratory, 1981. Mimeographed.

Boyan, Norman J., and Willis D. Copeland. "A Training Program for Supervisors: Anatomy of an Educational Development." *Journal of Educational Research* 68 (November 1974), 100–116.

———. *Instructional Supervision Training Programs*. Columbus, Ohio: Charles E. Merrill, 1978.

Boyatzis, Richard E. "The Human Resource Management Cluster." In *The Competent Manager: A Model for Effective Performance*. New York: John Wiley, 1982, pp. 121–141.

Bragg, J. E., and J. R. Andrews. "Participative Decision Making." *Journal of Applied Behavioral Science* 9 (1973), 727–735.

——— (1973), as reported in "The Role of Team Development in Organizational Effectiveness: A Critical Review," by Richard W. Woodman and John J. Sherwood. *Psychological Bulletin* 88 (July 1980), 166–186.

Brookover, Wilbur B., and L. W. Lezotte. *Changes in School Characteristics Coincident with Changes in Student Achievement*. East Lansing, Mich.: Institute for Research on Teaching, College of Education, Michigan State University, 1979. (ED 181 005).

Brookover, Wilbur B., and J. M. Schneider. "Academic Environments and Elementary School Achievement." *Journal of Research and Development in Education* 9 (1975), 82–91.

Brookover, Wilbur B., Thomas Shailer, and Ann Paterson. "Self Concept of Ability and School Achievement." *Sociology of Education* 37 (1964), 271–278.

Brookover, Wilbur B, Charles Beady, Patricia Flood, John Schweitzer, and Joe Wisenbaker, *School Social Systems and Student Achievement: Schools Can Make a Difference*. New York: Praeger Publishers, 1979. (First published in 1977 under title *Schools Can Make a Difference*.)

Brophy, Jere E. "Advances in Teacher Effectiveness Research." Occasional Paper No. 18. Institute for Research on Teaching. East Lansing, Mich.: College of Education, Michigan State University, April 1979.

Brophy, Jere E. *Recent Research on Teaching*. Occasional Paper No. 40. East Lansing, Mich.: Institute for Research on Teaching, Michigan State University, November 1980.

Brophy, Jere E. "Classroom Organization and Management." Paper presented to National Institute of Education, Warrenton, Va.: February 25–27, 1982.

Brophy, Jere E. and Thomas L. Good. *Teacher-Student Relationships: Causes and Consequences*. New York: Holt, Rinehart & Winston, 1974. See Chapters 2 and 3, pp. 30–70.

Brophy, Jere E., and Joyce G. Putnam. "Classroom Management in The Elementary Grades." Research series no. 32. Institute for Research on Teaching. East Lansing, Mich.: College of Education, Michigan State University, October 1978.

————. "Classroom Management in the Elementary Grades." In *Classroom Management*, edited by D. L. Duke. Seventy-eighth Yearbook of the National Society for the Study of Education, Part 2. Chicago: University of Chicago Press, 1979.

Brown, George Isaac. *Human Teaching for Human Learning: An Introduction to Confluenct Education*. New York: The Viking Press, 1971. See Chapter 3, "Some Affective Techniques."

Bruner, Jerome S. *The Process of Education*. Cambridge: Harvard University Press, 1960.

————. *Beyond the Information Given: Studies in the Psychology of Knowing*. New York: W. W. Norton, 1973. See Chapter 23, "Readiness for Learning," pp. 413–425.

California State Department of Education. *Report on the Special Studies of Selected ECE Schools with Increasing and Decreasing Reading Scores*. Sacramento, Calif.: Office of Program Evaluation and Research, 1980.

Callahan, Raymond E. *Education and the Cult of Efficiency*. Chicago: University of Chicago Press, 1962.

Carnegie Council on Policy Studies in Higher Education. *Giving Youth a Better Chance*. San Francisco: Jossey-Bass, 1980.

Carroll, John B. "A Model of School Learning." *Teachers College Record* 64 (1963), 723–733.

Cartwright, Dorwin, and Alvin Zander. *Group Dynamics*. New York: Harper & Row, 1968

Cawelti, Gordon, and Charles A. Reavis. "How Well Are We Providing Instructional Improvement Services?" *Educational Leadership* 38 (December 1980), 236–240.

Clauset, Karl H., and Alan K. Gaynor. "A Systems Perspective on Effective Schools." *Educational Leadership* 40 (December 1982), 54–59.

Cogan, Morris L. *Clinical Supervision*. Boston: Houghton Mifflin, 1973.

Cohen, E., J. Intili, and S. Robbins. "Task and Authority: A Sociological View of Classroom Management." In *Classroom Management*, edited by D. Duke. The 78th Yearbook of The National Society for the Study of Education. Chicago: The University of Chicago Press, 1979, pp. 116–143.

Cohen, E., and R. H. Miller. "Coordination and Control of Instruction in Schools." *Pacific Sociological Review* 23 (October 1980), 446–473.

Cohen, Michael. "Effective Schools: What Research Says." *Today's Education* 70 (April/May 1981), 48–G.

Cohen-Rosenthal, Edward. "Participation as a Pedagogy." Quality of Working Life and Adult Education, *Convergence: An International Journal of Adult Education* 15 (1982), 5–16.

Coleman, James S. "Differences Between Experimental and Classroom Learning." In *Experimental Learning: Rationale Characteristics and Assessment*, edited by Morris T. Keeton and Associates, pp. 49–61. Washington, D.C.: Jossey-Bass, 1976.

Collins, Paul. "Very Model of a Middle School." *National Elementary Principal* 59 (June 1980), 18–23. See also *Education USA*, April 28, 1980.

Cook, Ann, and Herb Mack. *The Head Teacher's Role*. Informal Schools in Britain Today. New York: Citation Press, 1971, p. 11.

Cook, Michael H. "Quality Circles—They Really Work, But . . . " *Training and Develoment Journal* 36 (January 1982), 4–6.

Cooper, James M. "Supervision of Teachers." In *Encyclopedia of Educational Research*, 5th ed., edited by Harold E. Mitzel. New York: The Free Press, 1982, pp. 1824–1834.

Corwin, Ronald G. *Reform and Organizational Survival—The Teacher Corps as an Instrument of Educational Change*. New York: John Wiley, 1973.

Coulson, John E. "Overview of the National Evaluation of the Emergency School Aid Act." Santa Monica, Calif.: System Development Corporation, July 1977.

Craig, Dorothy P. *Hip Pocket Guide to Planning and Evaluation*. Austin: Learning Concepts, 1978.

Croghan, John H., Dale C. Lake, and Harry M. Schroder. "Identification of the Competencies of High Performing Principals in Florida." Document prepared for the Florida Council on Educational Management. Tallahassee: Florida State Department of Education, December 1983.

Crosset, R. J. "The Extent and Effect of Parents' Participation on the Children's Beginning Reading Program: An Inner-City Report." Doctoral dissertation. University of Cincinnati, 1972. In *Dissertation Abstracts International* 33:3148 A; 1973, University Microfilms No. 72–31, 922.

Cruickshank, Donald R., Betty Myers, and Tham Moenjak. "Statements of Clear Teacher Behaviors Provided by 1,009 Students in Grades 6–9." Unpublished manuscript. Columbus, Ohio: College of Education, Ohio State University, 1975.

Cummings, Larry L., and Donald P. Schwab. *Performance in Organizations Determinants in Appraisal*. Glenview, Ill.: Scott Foresman, 1973.

Cunningham, Luvern L., Walter G. Hack, and Raphael O. Nystrand, eds. *Educational Administration: The Developing Decades*. Berkeley: McCutchan Publishing Corporation, 1977.

Davies, Ivor K. *Instructional Technique*. New York: McGraw-Hill, 1981.

Deal, Terrence E., and Allan A. Kennedy. *Corporate Cultures: The Rites and Rituals of Corporate Life*. Reading, Mass.: Addison-Wesley, 1982.

DeGuire, Michael. "The Role of the Elementary Principal in Influencing Reading Achievement." Ph.D. dissertation, University of Colorado at Boulder, 1980. In *Dissertation Abstracts International*, p. 1299 in Vol. 41/04-A.

Denham, Carolyn, and Ann Lieberman, eds. *Time to Learn. A Review of the Beginning Teacher Evaluation Study*. Washington, D.C.: The National Institute of Education, 1980.

Deutsch, Karl W., John Platt, and Dieter Senghaas. "Conditions Favoring Major Advances in Social Science." *Science* 171 (February 5, 1971), 450–459.

Dewey, John. *Experience and Education*. New York: Macmillan, 1916.

Doll, Ronald C. *Leadership to Improve Schools*. Worthington, Ohio: Charles A. Jones Publishing Co., 1972.

Dollard, John, and Neal Miller. *Personality and Psychotherapy*. New York: McGraw-Hill, 1950.

Doss, D., and F. Holley. "A Cause for National Pause: Title I Schoolwide Projects." Austin: Office of Research and Evaluation, Austin Independent School District. ORE Publication No. 81.55, 1982.

Doyle, Walter. *Classroom Management*. West Lafayette, Ind.: Kappa Delta Pi, 1980.

———. "Making Managerial Decisions in Classrooms," Ch. II, pp. 42–74. In *Classroom Management*. The 78th Yearbook of the National Society of the Study of Education, edited by D. Duke. Chicago: University of Chicago Press, 1979.

———. "Student Mediating Responses in Teaching Effectiveness" (Final Rpt. NIE-G-76-0099). Denton, Tex.: North Texas State University, 1980.

———. "Accomplishing Writing Tasks in the Classroom." Paper presented to the American Educational Research Association, Los Angeles, 1981.

———. "Research on Classroom Contexts." *Journal of Teacher Education* 32 (November-December 1981), 3–6.

Drucker, Peter F. *The Practice of Management*. New York: Harper & Row, 1954.

———. *Managing in Turbulent Times*. New York: Harper & Row, 1980.

———. *The Changing World of the Executive*. New York: Truman Tally Books, 1982.

Duffy, Gerald G. *Teacher Effectiveness Research: Implications for the Reading Profession*. East Lansing, Mich.: The Institute for Research on Teaching, College of Education, Michigan State University, 1980.

Duffy, Gerald G., and Lonnie D. McIntyre. "A Naturalistic Study of Instructional Assistance in Primary-Grade Reading." *Elementary School Journal* 83 (September 1982), 15–23.

Duke, Daniel L. *Managing Student Behavior Problems*. New York: Teachers College Press, 1980.

Duke, Daniel L., J. Cohen, and R. Herman. "Running Faster to Stay in Place: Retrenchment in the New York City Schools." *Phi Delta Kappan* 63 (September 1981), 13–17.

Dunkin, Michael J., and Bruce J. Biddle. *The Study of Teaching*. New York: Holt, Rinehart & Winston, 1974.

Dunn, Rita, and Kenneth Dunn. *Educator's Self-Teaching Guide to Individualizing Instructional Programs*. West Nyack, N.Y.: Parker Publishing Co., 1975.

Dunn, Rita, Thomas DeBello, Patricia Brennan, Jeff Krimsky, and Peggy Murrain. "Learning Style Researchers Define Differences Differently." *Educational Leadership* 38 (February 1981), 372–375.

Edmonds, Ronald R. "Effective Schools for the Urban Poor." *Educational Leadership* 37 (October 1979), 15–27.

———. "Some Schools Work and More Can." *Social Policy* 9 (1979), 28–32.

———. "A Report on the Research Project 'Search for Effective Schools and Criteria of the Designs for School Improvement' that are Associated with the Project." East Lansing, Mich.: The Institute of Research on Teaching, College of Education, Michigan State University. Unpublished Report prepared for National Institute of Education, 1981.

———. "Programs of School Improvement: An Overview." *Educational Leadership* 4 (December 1982), 4–11.

Edmonds, Ronald R., and J. Fredericksen. *Search for Effective Schools: The Identification and Analysis of Schools That are Instructionally Effective for Poor Children*. Cambridge: Harvard University Center for Urban Studies, 1978.

Educational Research Service, Inc. "School Staffing Ratios: Update 1978–1979." *ERS Research Memo*, Highlights. Arlington, Va.: ERS, Inc., 1979.

Educational Leadership (Journal of the Association for Supervision and Curriculum Development) 41 (September 1983) Theme issue, "Preparing For the Future," pp. 3–69.

Education Research Service Management Operations Information Exchange. Report from Kettle Falls School District 212, Washington (Fall 1982), p. 10.

Eisner, Elliott W. "Future Priorities for Curriculum Reform." *Educational Leadership* 37 (March 1980), 453–456.

———. "The Role of the Arts in the Invention of Man." *New York University Education Quarterly* 11 (Spring 1980), 2–7.

Ellett, Chad D., and Herbert J. Walberg. "Principal's Competency, Environment and Outcomes." In *Educational Environments and Effects* edited by H. J. Walberg. Berkeley: McCutchan, 1979.

Emmer, Edmund T., and Carolyn M. Evertson. "Effective Management at the Beginning of the School Year in Junior High Classes." Paper presented at Meeting of American Educational Research Association, Boston, 1980.

———. "Synthesis of Research on Classroom Management." *Educational Leadership* 38 (January 1981), 342–347.

Emmer, Edmund T., Carolyn M. Evertson, and Linda M. Anderson. Effective Classroom Management at the Beginning of the School Year." *Elementary School Journal* 80 (May 1980), 219–231.

England, George. "Personal Value Systems of American Managers." *Academy of Management Journal* 10 (March 1967), 53–68.

Erickson, Donald A. "An Overdue Paradigm Shift in Educational Administration, or, How Can We

Get That Idiot Off the Highway?" In *Educational Administration: The Developing Decades*, edited by Luvern L. Cunningham, Walter G. Hack, and Raphael O. Nystrand. Berkeley: McCutchan Publishing Corporation, 1977, pp. 119–143.

Fantini, Mario. "Community Participation: Alternative Patterns in their Educational Achievement." University of Massachusetts, 1979.

Fayol, Henri. *Administration Industrielee, Et Generale*, 1916. Translated into English in 1929 by Constance Storrs, as *General and Industrial Management*. London: Pitman & Sons, 1949.

Fendley, Jeffrey, and Ben M. Harris. "Research on Staff Development in Texas Schools." In *Staff Development: A Texas State of the Art Review*, edited by Karolyn J. Snyder. Palestine, Texas: Texas Association of Supervision and Curriculum Development, 1980, pp. 15–23.

Festinger, Leon. *A Theory of Cognitive Dissonance*. Stanford, Calif.: Stanford University Press, 1957.

Fiedler, Fred. *A Theory of Leadership Effectiveness*. New York: McGraw-Hill, 1967.

Filby, N. N. "How Teachers Produce 'Academic Learning Time'; Instructional Variables Related to Student Engagement." Paper presented to the annual meeting of the American Educational Research Association, Toronto, 1978.

Fisher, Charles W., Nikola N. Filby, Richard S. Marliane, Leonard S. Cahen, Marilyn M. Dishaw, J. E. Moore, and David C. Berliner. *Teaching Behaviors, Academic Learning Time and Student Achievement: Final Report of Phase III-B, Beginning Teacher Evaluation Study*. San Francisco: Far West Regional Laboratory, 1978.

Fosmere, Fred R., and Carolin S. Keutzer, 1971, as reported in "The Role of Team Development in Organizational Effectiveness: A Critical Review." By Richard W. Woodman and John J. Sherwood. *Psychological Bulletin* 88 (1980), 166–186.

Freer, Mark. "Clinical Supervision: Verifying a Strong Training Model." Unpublished study, College of Education, University of Idaho, 1983.

Freire, Paulo. *Pedagogy of the Oppressed*. Translated from the 1968 Portuguese manuscript by Myra Bergman Ramos. New York: Herder and Herder (Continuum), 1976.

French, Jr., R. P. John, and Bertram Raven. "The Bases of Social Power," In *Group Dynamics*, 3rd ed., edited by Cartwright and Zander, pp. 259–269. New York: Harper & Row, 1980.

Friedlander, Frank, 1974, as reported in "The Role of Team Development in Organization Effectiveness: A Critical Review," by Richard W. Woodman and John J. Sherwood. *Psychological Bulletin* 88 (1980), 166–186.

Fullan, Michael. *The Meaning of Educational Change*. New York: Teachers College Press, 1981.

———. "Implementing Educational Change: Progress At Last." Paper presented to a conference on the Implications of Research on Teaching for Practice. Washington, D.C., National Institute of Education, February 25–27, 1982.

Fuller, Frances T., and Brad A. Manning. "Self Confrontation Reviewed: A Conceptualization for Video Playback in Teacher Education." *Review of Educational Research* 43 (1973), 487–493.

Gage, Nathaniel L. *The Scientific Basis of the Art of Teaching*. New York: Teachers College Press, 1978.

Gapport, Gary. "Does Educational Administration Need a Revolution in Training?" A Policy Resource paper prepared for the HEW Conference in Training Educational Administrators. Philadelphia: Research for Better Schools, Inc., May 1979.

Gardener, R. W., and R. T. Schoen. "Control Defense and Concentration Effect: A Study of Scanning Behavior." *British Journal of Psychology* 53 (1962), 129–140.

Garman, Noreen B. "A Study of Clinical Supervision as a Resource for College Teachers of English." Unpublished doctoral dissertation. University of Pittsburgh, 1971.

Georgiades, William D., and Nancy Guenthar. "Guess Who's Not Hiding Behind the Classroom Door." *Record in Educational Administration* 2 (Fall, 1981), 19–22.

Gephart, William J., Robert B. Ingle, and Frederick J. Marshall, eds. *Evaluation in the Affective Domain*. Bloomington, Ind.: Phi Delta Kappa, 1976.

Getzels, Jacob W. "Educational Administration Twenty Years Later, 1954–1974." In *Educational Administration: The Developing Decades*, edited by Cunningham, Hack and Nystrand. Berkeley: McCutchan Publishing Corporation, 1977, pp. 3–24.

Gigleotti, Richard J., and Wilbur B. Brookover. "The Learning Environment: A Comparison of High and Low Achieving Elementary Schools." *Urban Education* 10 (1975), 256–257.

Gil, Doron. "The Decision-making and Diagnostic Processes of Classroom Teachers." East Lansing, Mich.: Institute for Research on Teaching, Michigan State University, March 1980.

Gil, Doron, Ruth M. Polen, John F. Vinsonhaler, and Joel Van Roekel. "The Impact of Training on Diagnostic Consistency." East Lansing, Mich.: Institute for Research in Teaching, Michigan State University, January 1980.

Ginnell, Sherman K. "Collaboration: A Vital Factor in Group Practice." *Dental Clinics in North America* 16 (April 1974), 358–375.

Glenn, Beverly C., and Taylor Mclean. *What Works? An Examination of Effective Schools for Poor Black Children*. Cambridge, Mass.: Center for Law and Education, Harvard University, 1981.

Glickman, Carl D. *Developmental Supervision: Alternative Practices for Helping Teachers Improve Instruction*. Alexandria, Va.: Association for Supervision and Curriculum Development, 1981, p. 49.

Glines, Don. "Futures in Education." Paper presented to the Texas Association of Supervision and Curriculum Development Convention, Corpus Christi, Tex., November 1978.

Goldhammer, Keith. *Elementary Principals and Their Schools: Beacons of Brilliance and Potholes of Pestilence*. Eugene: University of Oregon, 1971.

Goldhammer, Robert. *Clinical Supervision: Special Methods for the Supervision of Teachers*. New York: Holt, Rinehart & Winston, Inc., 1969

Goldhammer, Robert, Robert H. Anderson, and Robert J. Krajewski. *Clinical Supervision: Special Methods for the Supervision of Teachers*. 2nd ed. New York: Holt, Rinehart & Winston, 1980.

Goldsberry, Lee F. "Colleague Consultation: Instructional Supervisor Augmented." In *Critical Policy Issues in Contemporary Education: An Administrator's Overview*, edited by Louis J. Rubin. Boston: Allyn & Bacon, 1980.

Good, Thomas L. "Teacher Effectiveness in the Elementary School." *Journal of Teacher Education* 30 (March 1979), 52–64.

Good, Thomas L., and Jere Brophy. *Looking into Classrooms*. 2nd ed. New York: Harper & Row, 1978.

Goode, William J. "A Theory of Role Strain." *American Sociological Review* 25 (1960), 483–496.

Goodlad, John I. *The Dynamics of Educational Change*. New York: McGraw-Hill, 1975.

———. "An Ecological Approach to Change in School Settings." Abraham M. Weckstein Memorial Lecture, New York University, March 8, 1975.

———. *A Place Called School: Prospects for the Future*. New York: McGraw-Hill, 1984.

Goodlad, John I., and Robert H. Anderson. *The Nongraded Elementary School*. New York: Harcourt, Brace & World, 1959. Revised Edition 1963.

Goodson, Barbara, and Robert Hess. *Parents as Teachers of Young Children: An Evaluation Review of Some Contemporary Concepts and Programs*. Palo Alto, Calif.: Stanford University Press, 1975.

Gordon, Ira, J. "The Effects of Parent Involvement on Schooling." Chapter 2 in *Partners: Parents and Schools*, edited by Ronald S. Brandt. Alexandria, Va.: Association for Supervision and Curriculum Development, 1979.

Gordon, Richard, and Kenneth E. McIntyre. *The Senior High School Principalship. Vol. II: The Effective Principal*. Reston, Va.: National Association for Secondary School Principals, 1978.

Gottfredson, Gary, and Denise Daiger. *Disruption in Six Hundred Schools*. Report 76 289. Baltimore: Center for Social Organization of Schools. Johns Hopkins University, 1979. See also *Education USA*, January 28, 1980, p. 1

Graicunus, V. A. "Relationship in Organization." In *Papers on the Science of Administration*, edited by Luther H. Gulick and Lydall Urwick, pp. 183–187. New York: Institute of Public Administration, 1937.

Greenfield, William D. "Research on Public School Principals: A Review and Recommendation." Final Report to the National Institute of Education, June 1, 1982.

Gregorc, Anthony F. "Learning/Teaching Styles: Potent Forces Behind Them." *Educational Leadership*, 36 (January 1979), 234–236

Griffin, Gary. "Staff Development." Paper prepared for a conference on Implications of Research on Teaching for Practice, Arlie House, National Institute of Education, February 1982.

Gross, M. J., et al. "Combined Human Efforts in Elevating Achievement at the Wheatley School, Washington, D.C." Ed.D. Practicum, Nova University, 1974. ERIC Document Reproduction Service ED 102666.

Gross, Neal, and Robert Herriott. *Staff Leadership in Public Schools*. New York: John Wiley, 1965

Guditus, Charles W. "The Pre-Observation Conference: Is It Worth the Effort?" *Wingspan*, A Pedamorphosis Communique, 1 (1980), 7.

Guilford, J. P. *The Nature of Human Intelligence*. New York: McGraw-Hill, 1967. See pp. 213–214.

Hackman, J. Richard, and Edward E. Lawler. "Employee Reactions to Job Satisfaction Characteristics." *Journal of Applied Psychology*, 55 (1971), 259–286.

Haefele, Donald L. "How to Evaluate Thee, Teacher—Let Me Count the Ways." *Phi Delta Kappan*, 61 (January 1980), 349–352.

Hall, Gene, and Howard Jones. *Competency-Based Education*. Englewood Cliffs, N.J.: Prentice-Hall, 1975. See pp. 29–30.

Hall, Gene E., and Susan F. Loucks. "Teacher Concerns as a Basis for Facilitating and Personalizing Staff Development." *Teachers College Record*, 80 (September 1978), 36–53.

Halpin, Andrew W. *The Leadership Behavior of School Superintendents*. Chicago: University of Chicago Press, 1959.

Harris, Ben M. *Improving Staff Performance Through Inservice Education*. Boston: Allyn & Bacon, 1980.

Harvey, O. J., D. E. Hunt, and H. M. Shroder. *Conceptual Systems and Personality Organization*. New York: John Wiley, 1961

Heathers, Glen. "Overview of Innovations in Organization for Learning." *Interchange*, 3 (1972), 47–68.

–––––. "Theory and Strategies of Planned Change in Education." Unit 2 in *Training for Leadership in Local Educational Improvement Programs*. Philadelphia: Research for Better Schools, 1975.

Hellriegel, Don, and John W. Slocum, Jr. *Management: A Contingency Approach*. 2nd ed. Reading, Mass.: Addison-Wesley Publishing Co., 1974.

Hemphill, J. K., and A. E. Coons. "Development of the Leader Behavior Description Questionnaire." *Leader Behavior: Its Description and Measurement*. Columbus: Ohio State University, 1957.

Herbart, Johann Friedrich. *Outlines of Educational Doctrine*. New York: Macmillan, 1904.

Hersey, Paul W. "The NASSP Assessment Center Develops Leadership Talent." *Educational Leadership*, 39 (February 1982), 370–371.

Hersey, Paul, and Kenneth H. Blanchard. *Management of Organizational Behavior: Utilizing Human Resources*. Third Edition. Englewood Cliffs, N.J.: Prentice-Hall, 1977.

Herzberg, Frederick, Bernard Mausner, and Barbara Snyderman. *The Motivation to Work*. New York: John Wiley, 1959.

HEW Safe School Study. IRC Monograph Series (Robert J. Rubel, ed.). College Park, Md.: Institute for Reduction of Crime.

Hilgard, Ernest R., and Gordon H. Bower. *Theories of Learning*. 3rd ed. New York: Appleton-Century-Crofts, 1966.

Hill, Winfred F. *Learning: A Survey of Psychological Interpretations*. Novato, Calif.: Chandler & Sharp Publishers, 1971. See pp. 123, 125, 126.

Hines, Constance. "A Further Investigation of Teacher Clarity and the Relationship Between Student Achievement and Satisfaction." Doctoral dissertation. Columbus: Ohio State University, 1981.

Hoban, Patrick. "Citizens Take Part in Long Range Planning." *ERS Management Operations Information Exchange*, Fall 1982, p. 10

Hobson, Phyllis J. "Structured Parental Involvement: An Analysis of a Title I Summer Parent Guided AT HOME Project." Doctoral dissertation, George Washington University, 1976. See pp. 80–81.

Hoover, Mary Rhodes. "Characteristics of Black Schools at Grade Level: A Description." *Reading Teacher* (April 1978), 757.

House, Robert J. "A Path Goal Theory of Leader Effectiveness." *Administrative Science Quarterly*, 16 (September 1971), 321–338. Reprinted in Scott and Cummings, *Readings in Organizational Behavior and Human Performance*. Homewood, Ill.: Richard D. Irwin, 1973.

House, Robert J., and Terence R. Mitchell. "Path-Goal Theory of Leadership." Reading Number 26 in *Organizational Behavior: A Book of Readings*, edited by Keith Davis. New York: McGraw-Hill, 1974 and 1977, pp. 140–152.

House, Robert J., and J. R. Rizzo. "Role Conflict and Ambiguity as Critical Variables in a Model of Organization Behavior." *Organizational Behavior and Human Performance*, 17 (June 1972), 467–505.

Houts, Paul L. "The Changing Role of the Elementary School Principal: Report of a Conference." *National Elementary Principal*, 55 (November/December 1975), 62–73.

Hoy, Wayne K., W. Newland, and R. Blazousky. "Subordinate Loyalty to Superior Esprit, and Aspects of Bureaucratic Structure." *Educational Administration Quarterly* 13 (Winter 1977), 71–85.

Hull, Charles L. *Principles of Behavior*. New York: Appleton-Century-Crofts, 1943.

Hyman, Joan S., and Alan Cohen. "Learning for Mastery: Ten Conclusions After 15 Years and 3,000 Schools." In *Educational Leadership*, 37 (November 1979), 104–109.

Ingram, John E., Jr. "School Community Relations and Student Achievement." Paper presented to the American Educational Research Association, San Francisco, 1979.

Institute for the Development of Educational Activities. *Learning in the Small Group*. Dayton, Ohio: /I/D/E/A/, 1971.

Ivancevich, J. M., J. H. Donnelly, Jr., and J. L. Gibson. "Evaluating MBO: The Challenges Ahead." *Management By Objectives* (Winter 1976), 15–24.

Janis, Irving L. "Groupthink." *Psychology Today*, 15 (November 1971), 43–46 and 74–76.

Johnson, David W. "Student-Student Interaction: The Neglected Variable in Education." *Educational Researcher* 10 (January 1981), 5–10.

Johnson, David W., G. Maruyama, R. Johnson, D. Nelson, and L. Skon. "Effects of Cooperative, Competitive, and Individualistic Goal Structures on Achievement: A Meta-Analysis." *Psychological Bulletin* 89 (1981), 47–62.

Joyce, Bruce R. *Selecting Learning Experiences: Linking Theory and Practice.* Washington, D.C.: Association for Supervision and Curriculum Development, 1978.

Joyce, Bruce, and Lucy Peck. *Inservice Teacher Education Report II: Interviews.* Syracuse, N.Y.: National Dissemination Center, Syracuse University, 1977.

Joyce, Bruce, and Beverly Showers. "Improving In-service Training: The Messages of Research." *Educational Leadership* 37 (February 1980), 379.

———. "The Coaching of Teaching." *Educational Leadership,* 40 (October 1982), 4–8.

Joyce, Bruce R., and Marsha Weil. *Models of Teaching.* Englewood Cliffs, N.J.: Prentice-Hall, 1972. See also Second Edition, 1980.

Kagan, Jerome. *Developmental Studies of Reflection and Analysis.* Cambridge: Harvard University Press, 1964.

Kanter, Rosabeth Moss. "The Middle Manager as Innovator." *Harvard Business Review,* 6 (July–August 1982), 95–105.

———. *The Change Masters.* New York: Simon and Schuster, 1983.

Kast, Fremont E., and James E. Rosenzweig. *Experiential Exercises and Cases in Management.* New York: McGraw-Hill, 1976.

Keefe, James W. "Learning Style: An Overview." Chapter 1 in *Student Learning Styles: Diagnosing and Prescribing Programs.* Reston, Va. National Association of Secondary School Principals, 1979.

Kennedy, John J., Donald R. Cruickshank, Andrew J. Bush, and Betty Myers. "Additional Investigation into the Nature of Teacher Clarity." *Journal of Educational Research* 72 (September/October 1978), 3–9.

Kerr, B. J. "An Investigation of the process of using Feedback Data Within the Clinical Supervision Cycle to Facilitate Teacher's Individualization of Instruction." Unpublished doctoral dissertation. University of Pittsburgh, 1976.

Kimbrough, Ralph B., and Michael Y. Nunnery. *Education Administration: An Introduction.* New York: Macmillan 1976.

Kindsvatter, Richard, and William W. Wilen. "A Systematic Approach to Improving Conference Skills." *Educational Leadership* 38 (April 1981), 525–529.

King, L. H. "Student Thought Processes and the Expectancy Effect." (Research Rpt. #80-1-8). Edmonton, Alberta: Center for Research in Teaching, University of Alberta, 1981.

Klausmeier, Herbert J. "A Research Strategy for Educational Improvement." *Educational Researcher* 11 (February 1982), 8–13.

Klein, M. Frances. "State and District Curriculum Guides: One Aspect of the Formal Curriculum." Technical Report No. 9. Study of Schooling Series. Los Angeles: University of California, Graduate School of Education, 1980.

Knezevich, Stephen. *Management by Objectives and Results.* Arlington, Va.: American Association of School Administrators, 1973.

Kohler, Wolfgang. *The Task of Gestalt Psychology.* Princeton, N.J.: Princeton University Press, 1969.

Kounin, Jacob. *Discipline and Group Management.* New York: Holt, Rinehart and Winston, 1970.

Krajewski, Robert J. "Clinical Supervision to Facilitate Teacher Self Improvement." *Journal of Research and Development in Education* 9 (1976), 58–66.

Kuhn, Thomas. *The Structure of Scientific Revolutions*. 2nd ed. Chicago: The University of Chicago Press, 1970.

Kunz, D. W., and W. K. Hoy. "Leadership Style of Principals and the Professional Zone of Acceptance of Teachers." *Educational Administration Quarterly* 12 (Fall 1976), 49–64.

Land, Michael L., and Lyle R. Smith. "The Effect of Low Inference Teacher Clarity Inhibitors on Student Achievement." *Journal of Teacher Education* 30 (May/June 1979), 55–57.

LaPorte, R. E., and R. Nath. "Role of Performance Goals in Prose Learning." *Journal of Educational Psychology* 68 (1976), 260–264.

Lasley, Thomas J. "Helping Teachers Who Have Problems with Discipline—A Model and Instrument." *NASSP Bulletin* 65 (January 1981), 6–15.

Lathan, G. P., and G. A. Yukl. "A Review of Research on the Application of Goal Setting in Organizations." *Academy of Management Journal* 18 (1975), 824–845.

Lawler, Edward E., III. *Pay and Organizational Effectiveness*. New York: McGraw-Hill, 1971.

Letteri, Charles A. "Cognitive Style: Implications for Curriculum," pp. 64–69. In *Curriculum Theory*, edited by Alex Molnar and John A. Zahorik. Washington, D.C.: Association for Supervision and Curriculum Development, 1977.

Levin, Tamar, and Ruth Long. *Effective Instruction*. Alexandria, Va.: Association for Supervision and Curriculum Development, 1981.

Levine, Daniel U., and Joyce Stark. *Extended Summary and Conclusions: Institutional and Organizational Arrangements and Processes for Improving Academic Achievement at Inner City Elementary Schools*. (Mimeo) Kansas City: University of Missouri-Kansas City, School of Education, Center for the Study of Metropolitan Problems in Education, August 1981.

Lewin, Kurt. *Principles of Topological Psychology*. New York: McGraw-Hill, 1936.

———. "Field Theory and Learning." In *The Psychology of Learning*, Part II, edited by Nelson B. Henry. The Forty-First Year Book of the National Society for the Study of Education. Chicago: University of Chicago Press, 1942, pp. 215–252.

———. "Group Decision and Social Change." In *Readings in Social Psychology* edited by E. F. Maccoby, T. M. Newcomb, and E. L. Hartley. 3rd ed., New York: Holt, Rinehart and Winston, 1958.

———. Cited in *The Planning of Change*, 2nd ed., pp. 62, 98–107, edited by Bennis, Warren G., Kenneth D. Benne, and Robert Chin. New York: Holt, Rinehart and Winston, 1969.

Lezotte, L. W., et. al. *A Final Report: Remedy for School Failure to Equitably Deliver Basic School Skills*. East Lansing, Mich.: Department of Urban and Metropolitan Studies, Michigan State University, September 1979.

Lieberman, Ann, and Lynne Miller. *Introduction to Staff Development: New Demands, New Realities, New Perspectives*. New York: Teachers College Press, 1978.

Likert, Rensis. *New Patterns of Management*. New York: McGraw-Hill, 1961.

———. *The Human Organization*. New York: McGraw-Hill, 1967.

Lipham, James M. *Effective Principal, Effective School*. Reston, Va.: National Association of Secondary School Principals, 1981.

Lipham, James M., and Marvin J. Fruth. *The Principal and Individually Guided Education*. Reading, Mass.: Addison-Wesley, 1976.

Lippitt, Gordon. "Forward." For O. Mink, J. Schultz, and B. Mink, *Developing and Managing Open Organizations: A Model and Methods for Maximizing Organizational Potential*. Austin, Tex.: Learning Concepts, 1979.

Little, Judith W. *Schools Success and Staff Development: The Role of Staff Development in Urban Desegregated Schools*. Boulder, Colo.: Center for Research, Inc., 1981.

———. "The Power of Organization Setting: School Norms and Staff Development." Report for National Institute of Education, 1981.

————. "Norms of Collegiality and Experimentation: Workplace Conditions of School Success." *American Educational Research Journal* 19 (Fall 1982), 325–340.

Locke, Edwin A. "Toward a Theory of Task Motivation and Incentive." *Organizational Behavior and Performance* 3 (1968), 157–189.

————. "The Nature and Causes of Job Satisfaction." pp. 1297–1349. In *Handbook of Industrial and Organizational Psychology*, edited by M. D. Dunnet. Chicago: Rand McNally, 1974.

Lorsch, Jay W. "Introduction to the Structural Designs of Organizations," pp. 1–16. In *Organizational Structure and Design*, edited by G. W. Dalton, P. R. Lawrence, and J. W. Lorsch. Homewood, Ill.: Richard D. Irwin and The Dorsey Press, 1970.

Lortie, Dan C. *School Teacher: A Sociological Study*. Chicago: University of Chicago Press, 1975.

Loughheed, Jacquelene, Linda Lentz, William Moskal, and Richard Rarter. "Meaningful Collaboration on Behalf of Troubled Youth: The Farmington of Oakland University Youth Advocacy Program '78 Case Study." In *Stating the Case: Six Approaches to the Election of Community Councils*, edited by Anglin and Patton. Minneapolis: University of Minnesota Press, 1979.

Love, Ruth, reported in Joseph M. Cronin, "Parents and Educators: Mutual Allies." *Phi Delta Kappan*, 59 (December 1977), 243.

Luthans, Fred. *Organizational Behavior*. New York: McGraw-Hill, 1981.

Luthans, Fred, and Robert Kreitner. *Organizational Behavior Modification*. Glenview, Ill.: Scott, Foresman, 1975.

Lysakowski, Richard, and Herbert J. Walberg. "Classroom Reinforcement in Relation to Learning: A Quantitative Analysis." *Journal of Educational Research*, 75 (1981), 69–77.

————. "Instructional Effects of Cues, Participation and Corrective Feedback: A Quantitative Synthesis." *American Educational Research Journal*, 19 (Winter 1982), 559–578.

McBer and Company. "Principal Differences: Excellence in School Leadership and Management." A study conducted for the Council of Educational Management, Department of Education. Tallahassee, Fla., 1982.

McCarthy, Bernice. "Brain Function and Learning Styles." *The School Administrator*, 38 (June 1981), 12–13.

McCaskey, Michael B. "An Introduction to Organizational Design." pp. 84–94 in *Readings in Management: Contingencies, Structure and Process*, edited by Henry L. Tosi. Chicago: St. Clair Press, 1976.

McCleary, Lloyd E., and Scott D. Thompson. *The Senior High School Principalship*, Vol. 1: *The National Survey*; Vol. 2: *The Effective Principal*; Vol. 3: *The Summary Report*. Reston, Va.: National Association of Secondary School Principals, 1979.

McClelland, David. *Power: The Inner Experience*. New York: Irvington, 1975.

McFarland, Dalton E. *Management Principles and Practices*. Fourth Edition. New York: Macmillan, 1974.

McGregor, Douglas. *The Human Side of the Enterprise*. New York: McGraw-Hill, 1960.

McLaughlin, Milbrey W., and David D. Marsh. "Staff Development and School Change." *Teachers College Record*, 80 (September 1978), 69–94.

McLaughlin, Milbrey W. "Implementation as Mutual Adaptation: Change in Classroom Organization." *Making Change Happen*, edited by Dale Mann. New York: Teachers College Press, 1978.

McMahon, J. T. "Management Control Structure and Organizational Effectiveness." Paper presented at the 32nd Annual Meeting, Academy of Management, Minneapolis: August 15, 1972.

Madden, J. V., et al. "School Effectiveness Study: State of California." Paper presented to American Education Research Association, San Francisco, 1976.

Maier, Norman R. F., and Ayesha A. Maier. "An Experimental Test of the Effects of Developmental vs. Free Discussions on the Quality of Group Decision." *Journal of Applied Psychology*, 41 (1957), 320–323.

Maier, Norman R. F. "Assets and Liabilities in Group Problem Solving: The Need for an Integrative Function," pp. 422–428. In *Readings in Organizational Behavior and Human Performance*, edited by Scott and Cummings. Homewood, Ill.: Richard D. Irwin, 1973.

Manatt, Richard P., Kenneth L. Palmer, and Everett Hidlebaugh. "Evaluating Teaching Performance with Improved Rating Scales." *NASSP Bulletin*, 60 (September 1976), 21–24.

Mann, Dale. "The Politics of Staff Development," p. 10. In *The Field Evaluation Programs for Educational Change*. Santa Monica, Calif.: Rand Corporation.

———. "An Introduction to the Rand Corporation's Study of the Change Agent Programs Sponsored by the U.S. Office of Education." In Rand Corporation, Field Evaluation of Programs, 2. Santa Monica, Calif.

Mann, F. C. "Studying and Creating Change: A Means to Understanding Social Organization." *Research in Industrial Human Relations*, edited by C. Arensbert, et. al. New York: Harper and Row, 1957.

Marcus, Alfred C., et. al. "Administrative Leadership in a Sample of Successful Schools from the National Evaluation of the Emergency School." System Development Corporation. Santa Monica, Calif. Paper presented at AERA Convention, April 14–16, 1976

Marien, Michael, and Warren L. Ziegler, eds. *The Potential of Educational Futures*. Worthington, Ohio: Charles Jones Publishing Co., 1972.

Martin, Gary S. "Teacher and Administrator Attitudes Toward Evaluation and Systematic Classroom Observation." Ph.D. Dissertation, University of Oregon, 1975.

Martin, William J., and Donald J. Willower. "The Managerial Behavior of High School Principals." *Education Administration Quarterly*, 17 (Winter 1981), 69–90.

Maslow, Abraham H. "A Theory of Human Motivation." *Psychological Review* 50 (1943), 394–395.

———. *Toward a Psychology of Being*. Princeton: D. Van Nostrand Co., 1962.

———. *Motivation and Personality*. Second Edition. New York: Harper and Row, 1970.

Mayhew, Katherine Camp, and Anna Camp Edwards. *The Dewey School: The Laboratory School of the University of Chicago 1896–1903*. Introduction by John Dewey. New York: D. Appleton-Century Company, 1936.

Mayo, Elton. *The Human Problems of an Industrial Civilization*. New York: Macmillan, 1933.

———. *The Social Problems of an Industrial Civilization*. Boston: Harvard University, Graduate School of Business, 1945.

Merton, Robert K. *Social Theory and Social Structure*. Revised edition. New York: The Free Press, 1957.

Messick, Samual, and N. Kogan. "Differentiation and Compartmentalization in Object-Sorting Measures of Categorizing Style." *Perceptual and Motor Skills*, 16 (1963), 47–51.

Meyer, John, W. Richard Scott, and Terrence Deal. "Research on School and District Organization." In *The Structure of Educational Systems: Exploration in the Theory of Loosely Coupled Organizations*, edited by Davis et al. Stanford, Calif.: Stanford Center for Research and Development in Teaching, 1977.

Michael, Stephen R., Fred Luthans, George S. Odiorne, W. Warner Burke, and Spencer Hayden. *Techniques of Organizational Change*. New York: McGraw-Hill, 1981

Miles, Matthew B. "Planned Change and Organizational Health: Figure and Ground," pp. 18–21. *Change Processes in Public Schools*. Eugene, Oreg.: University of Oregon, Center for the Advanced Study of Educational Administration, 1965.

———. "School Innovation from the Ground Up: Some Dilemmas." *New York University Education Quarterly*, 11 (Winter 1980), 2–9.

Miller, L. "BYTES: Implications for Staff Development." *Time to Learn*, edited by C. Denham and A. Lieberman. Washington, D.C.: U.S. Department of Education, 1980.

Miller, L., and T. Wolf. "Staff Development for School Change: Theory and Practice." In *Staff Development: New Demands, New Realities, New Perspectives*. Edited by A. Lieberman and L. Miller. New York: Teachers College Press, 1978.

Mink, Oscar G., James M. Schultz, and Barbara P. Mink. *Developing and Managing Open Organizations: A Model and Method for Maximizing Organizational Potential*. Austin, Tex.: Learning Concepts, 1979.

Mischele, Harriett N., and Walter Mischele. *Readings in Personality*. New York: Holt, Rinehart & Winston, 1973.

Molnar, Alex, and John A. Zahorick, eds. *Curriculum Theory*. Washington, D.C.: Association for Supervision and Curriculum Development, 1977.

Morris, Monica B. "The Public School as Workplace: The Principal as a Key Element in Teacher Satisfaction." Technical Report #32, *A Study of Schooling*. Los Angeles: Graduate School of Education, University of California, 1981.

Morris, Van Cleve, Robert L. Crowson, and Cynthia Porter-Gehrie. *The Urban Principal: Discretionary Decision-Making in a Large Educational Organization*. Chicago Circle: The University of Illinois, March 20, 1981.

Morris, Van Cleve, Robert L. Crowson, Emanuel Herwitz, Jr., and Cynthia Porter-Gehrie. "The Urban Principal: Middle Manager in the Educational Bureaucracy." *Phi Delta Kappan*, 63 (June 1982), 689–692.

Morrish, Ivor. *Aspects of Educational Change*. New York: John Wiley and Sons, 1976.

Morse, N. C., and E. Reiner. "The Experimental Change of a Major Organizational Variable." *Journal of Abnormal and Social Psychology*, 52 (1956), 120–129.

Murnane, John W. *The Impact of School Resources on the Learning of Inner City Children*. Cambridge, Mass.: Ballinger Publishing Co., 1975.

Myers, E. C., and S. S. Koenigs. "A Framework for Comparing Needs Assessment Activities." A paper presented to the annual meeting of the American Educational Research Association, San Francisco, Calif.: April 1979.

Naisbitt, John. *Megatrends*. New York: Warner Books, 1982. Paperback, 1984.

National Association of Secondary School Principals. *Study of the High School Principalship*. 3 Vols. Reston, Va.: NASSP, 1979.

National Commission on Excellence in Education. *A Nation at Risk*. Washington, D.C.: U.S. Government Printing Office, 1983.

Newman, F. M. "Reducing Alienation in High School: Implications of Theory." *Harvard Education Review*, 51 (November 1981), 546–564.

Newman, William H., Charles E. Summer, and Warren E. Kirby. *The Process of Management Concepts, Behavior, and Practices*. Second Edition. Englewood Cliffs, N.J.: Prentice-Hall, 1967.

New York State. "School Factors Influencing Reading Achievement: A Case Study of Two Inner-City Schools." Office of Educational Performance, Review, State of New York, Albany, March 1974.

Niedermayer, G. C. "Effects of School to Home Feedback and Parent Accountability on Kindergarten Reading Performance, Parent Participation, and Pupil Attitude." Doctoral dissertation, University of California at Los Angeles, 1979. Dissertation Abstracts International, 30:3198A, University Microfilms No. 70–2240.

Nolan, Robert R., and Susan S. Roper. "How to Succeed in Team Teaching by Really Trying." *Today's Education*, 66 (January/February 1977), 54–61, 105.

Odiorne, George S. *MBO II: A System of Managerial Leadership in the 80's*. Belmont, Calif.: Fearon Pitman Publishing, 1979.

O' Leary, K., and S. O'Leary, eds. *Classroom Management. The Successful Use of Behavior Modification*. Second Edition. New York: Pergamon, 1977.

O'Neil, Harold F., Jr., and Charles D. Spielberger. *Cognitive and Affective Learning Strategies*. New York: Academic Press, 1979.

Ouchi, William. *Theory Z—How American Business Can Meet the Japanese Challenge*. Reading, Mass.: Addison-Wesley, 1981.

Ourth, J. "Have the Universities Failed Us? *National Elementary Principal*, 59 (March 1979), 80.

Parker, Barbara. "Bud Scarry: This Fiesty Superintendent Thrives on the Tough Decisions." *The Executive Educator*, 3 (May 1981), 12–15.

Peabody, Robert L. *Organizational Authority*. New York: Atherton Press, 1964.

Peters, Thomas J., and Robert H. Waterman, Jr. *In Search of Excellence: Lessons from America's Best Run Companies*. New York: Harper and Row, 1982.

Peterson, K. "The Principal's Task." *Administrator's Notebook*, 26 (1978), 1–4.

Peterson, Penelope L. "Direct Instruction: Effective for What and for Whom?" *Educational Leadership*, 37 (October 1979), 46–48.

Peterson, Penelope L., Terence Janicki, and Susan R. Swing. "Ability X Treatment Interaction Effects on Children's Learning in Large Group and Small Group Approaches." *American Educational Research Journal*, 18 (Winter 1981), 453–473.

Pharis, William L. "The Principalship: Where Are We?" *National Elementary Principal*, 55 (November/December 1975), 12–17.

Pharis, William L., and Sally Banks Zakariya. *The Elementary School Principalship in 1978: A Research Study*. Arlington, Va.: National Association of Elementary School Principals, 1979.

Phi Delta Kappa, Inc. *Educational Goals and Objectives*. Administrator's Manual. Bloomington, Ind.: Phi Delta Kappa, no date given.

Phi Delta Kappa Study of Exceptional Urban Elementary Schools. *Why Do Some Urban Schools Succeed?* Bloomington, Ind.: Phi Delta Kappa, 1980.

Phi Delta Kappa Newsletter. *Practical Applications of Research*. Bloomington, Ind., 3 (March 1981), p. 3.

Pitner, Nancy J. "Administrative Training: What Relation to Administrator Work?" Paper presented at the annual meeting of the American Educational Research Association, April 1981, Los Angeles, Calif. Mimeographed.

Pool, Jonelle. "Compilation of Competency Statements for School Administrators as Derived from Literature." Research Report No. 1, Project R.O.M.E. University of Georgia, Athens, Ga. February 1974, ERIC ED088839.

Popham, James. A paper presented to the Multi-state consortium on Performance-Based Teacher Evaluation, New Orleans, February 25–28, 1973.

Popham, W. James. "Customized Criterion-Referenced Tests." *Educational Leadership*, 34 (January 1977), 258–259.

Porter, Lyman W., and Edward E. Lawler, III. *Managerial Attitudes and Performance*. Homewood, Ill.: Richard D. Irwin, 1968.

Prince, George. *The Practice of Creativity*. New York: Collier Books, 1970.

———. "Mindspring: Suggesting Answers to Why Productivity is Low." *Chemtech* (May 1976), 290–294.

Purkey, Stewart C., and Marshall S. Smith. "Effective Schools: A Review." Paper presented to a conference on implications of research for teaching. National Institute of Educators, Warrenton, Va.: February 25–27, 1982.

Raia, Anthony P. *Managing by Objectives*. Glenview, Ill.: Scott, Foresman and Company, 1974.

Rand Corporation. *Organized Teachers in the American Schools*. Santa Monica, Calif.: Rand Publications, 1979.

Reagan, Billy. Reported in Joseph M. Cronin. "Parents and Educators: Mutual Allies." *Phi Delta Kappan* 59 (December 1977), 243.

Reddin, William J. *Managerial Effectiveness*. New York: McGraw-Hill, 1970.

Roe, William H., and Thelbert L. Drake. *The Principalship*. New York: Macmillan, 1974.

Roehler, Laura R., and Gerald G. Duffy. "Classroom Teaching Is More Than Opportunity." *Journal of Teacher Education* 32 (November/December 1981), 7–11.

Rogers, Carl. *Freedom to Learn*. Columbus, Ohio: Charles E. Merrill, 1969.

————. "Toward A Modern Approach to Values: The Value Process in a Mature Person." In *Readings in Personality*, edited by Mischele and Mischele. New York: Holt, Rinehart and Winston, 1973.

Rokeach, Milton. *Beliefs, Attitudes and Values*. San Francisco: Jossey-Bass, 1968.

————. *The Nature of Human Values*. New York: Free Press/Macmillan Publishing Company, 1973.

Rosenshine, Barak. "Content, Time and Direct Instruction." In *Research on Teaching; Concepts, Findings and Implications*. Edited by A. Walbert and P. Peterson. Berkeley: McCutchan Publishing Co., 1979.

Rosenshine, Barak, and Norma Furst. "The Use of Direct Observation to Study Teaching." *Second Handbook of Research on Teaching*, edited by Robert M. W. Travers. Chicago: Rand McNally, 1973.

Rosswork, S. G. "Goal Setting: The Effects on an Academic Task with Varying Magnitudes of Incentive." *Journal of Educational Psychology* 69 (1977), 710–715.

Rotten, Elizabeth. A personal correspondence, 9 December, 1927 (quoted in *Locarno—and What Next*) Jenaplan F., Netherlands.

Rowe, David L. "How Westinghouse Measures White Collar Productivity." *AMACOM Management Review*, 70 (November 1981), 42–47.

Rutherford, William L. "Questions Teachers Ask About Team Teaching." *Journal of Teacher Education* 30 (July/August 1979), 29–30.

Rutter, Michael, Barbara Maughan, Peter Mortimore, and Janet Duston. *Fifteen Thousand Hours: Secondary Schools and Their Effects on Children*. Cambridge: Harvard University Press, 1979.

Sagotsky, Gerald, Charlotte Patterson, and Mark Lepper. "Training Children's Self Control: A Field Experiment in Self-Monitoring and Goal Setting in the Classroom." *Journal of Experimental Child Psychology*, 25 (1978), 242–253.

Saily, Mary. "Teachers Team to Cope with Complex Materials." *Educational R&D Report* 2 (Winter 1979), 1–5. St. Louis: CEMREL, Inc., 1979.

Sarason, Seymour B. *The Culture of the School and the Problem of Change*. Boston: Allyn and Bacon, 1972.

Schein, Edgar H. *Process Consultation: Its Role in Organizational Development*. Reading, Mass.: Addison-Wesley, 1969.

Schmuck, Patricia, Susan Paddock, and John Packard. "Management Implications of Team Teaching: A Summary Report of the Findings." Project MITT, Center for Educational Policy and Management, University of Oregon, Eugene, Oreg., 1977.

Schmuck, Richard A., and Philip J. Runkel. *Organizational Development in Schools*. Eugene, Oreg.: Mayfield Publishing Company, 1972.

Schmuck, Richard A., Philip J. Runkel, and D. Langmeyer. "Improving Organizational Problem Solving in a School Faculty." *Journal of Applied Behavioral Science* 5 (1969), 455–482.

————. "Using Group Problem-Solving Procedures." In *Organizational Development in Schools*, edited by R. A. Schmuck and M. B. Miles. Palo Alto, Calif.: National Press Books, 1971.

Schmuck, Richard A., Philip J. Runkel, Jane Arends, and Richard I. Arends. *The Second Handbook of Organizational Development in Schools*. Palo Alto, Calif.: Mayfield Publishing Company, 1977.

Schön, Donald A. "Leadership as Reflection in Action." In *Administrative Leadership and Organizational Culture*, edited by T. F. Sergiovanni and J. E. Corbally. Urbana, Ill.: University of Illinois Press, 1983.

Scott, W. A. "Conceptualizing and Measuring Structural Properties of Cognition." In *Motivation and Social Interaction*, edited by O. J. Harvey. New York: Ronald Press, 1963.

Scott, W. E., Jr., and L. L. Cummings. *Readings in Organizational Behavior and Human Performance*. Revised Edition. Homewood, Ill.: Richard D. Irwin, Inc., 1973.

Seager, G. Bradley, Jr. "Diagnostic Supervision. A Branch of Instructional Supervision." A paper presented to the Council of Professors of Instructional Supervision. Athens, Ga.: December 6–8, 1979.

Sergiovanni, Thomas J. "Factors Which Affect Satisfaction and Dissatisfaction in Teaching." *Journal of Educational Administration* 5 (May 1967), 66–82.

————. "Supervision and Evaluation: Interpretative and Critical Perspectives." A paper presented to the Council of Professors of Instructional Supervision. Knoxville, Tenn., November 12, 1982.

Sergiovanni, Thomas J., ed. *Supervision of Teaching*. ASCD 1982 Yearbook. Alexandria, Va.: Association for Supervision & Curriculum Development, 1982.

Sergiovanni, Thomas J., and Fred D. Carver. *The New School Executive: A Theory of Administration*. First Edition. New York: Dodd, Mead and Company, 1973. Third Printing 1975.

Sexton, William P. *Organization Theories*. Columbus, Ohio: Charles E. Merrill Publishing Co., 1970.

Shaplin, Judson T., and Henry F. Olds, Jr., eds. *Team Teaching*. New York: Harper and Row, 1964.

Sharon, S. "Learning in Teams: A Critical Review of Recent Methods and Effects on Achievement, Attitudes, and Race/Ethnic Relations." *Review of Educational Research* 50 (1980), 241–272.

Shaw, Marvin E., and Philip R. Costango. *Theories of Social Psychology*. New York: McGraw-Hill, 1970.

Shuma, K. Y. "Changes Effectuated by a Clinical Supervisory Relationship which Emphasizes a Helping Relationship and a Conference Format Made Congruent with the Establishment and Maintenance of this Helping Relationship." Doctoral dissertation, University of Pittsburg, 1973. Dissertation Abstracts International, 35:729A.

Singer, Robert N., and Richard F. Gerson. "Learning Strategies, Cognitive Processes, and Motor Learning." pp. 215–247 in *Cognitive and Affective Learning Strategies*, edited by Harold F. O'Neil, Jr., and Charles D. Spielberger. New York: Academic Press, 1979.

Sizer, Theodore Ryland. *Horace's Compromise: The Dilemma of the American High School*. Boston: Houghton Mifflin, 1984.

Skinner, B. F. *Science and Human Behavior*. New York: Macmillan, 1953.

————. *Contigencies of Reinforcement*. New York: Appleton-Century-Crofts, 1969.

————. In *U.S. News and World Report*, November 3, 1980, p. 79–80.

Slavin, R. E. "Cooperative Learning." *Review of Educational Research* 50 (1980), 315–342.

Snyder, Karolyn J. "The Implementation of Clinical Supervision." *ERIC* Clearinghouse on Teacher Education. July 1982, ED 213 666.

Spady, William G. "Power, Authority and Research on Schools: New Perspectives on Leadership and Control." Vice Presidential Address. Division G. American Educational Research Association Convention, New York City, April 1977.

————. "The Concept and Implications of Competency-Based Education." *Educational Leadership* 36 (October 1978), 16–22.

Spady, William G., and Douglas E. Mitchell. "Competency Based Education: Organizational Issues and Implications." *Educational Researcher* 6 (February 1977), 9–15.

Springer, Judy. "Brain/Mind and Human Resources Development." *Training and Development Journal* 35 (August 1981), 42–49.

Stallings, Jane. "Allocated Academic Learning Time Re-Visited, or Beyond Time on Task." *Educational Researcher* 9 (December 1980), 11–16.

Stock, D., and H. A. Thelen. *Emotional Dynamics and Group Culture*. New York: New York University Press, 1958.

Stogdill, Ralph M. "Personal Factors Associated with Leadership: A Survey of the Literature." *Journal of Psychology* 25 (1948), 35–41.

————. *Individual Behavior and Group Achievement*. New York: Oxford University Press, 1959.

————. *Manual for the Leader Behavior Description Questionnaire*. Columbus: Ohio State University, 1965.

————. "Basic Concepts for a Theory of Organization." In *Organization Theories*, Willis P. Sexton, ed. Columbus, Ohio: Charles E. Merrill Publishing Co., 1970.

————. "The Trait Approach to the Study of Educational Leadership." In *Leadership, The Science and the Art Today*, edited by Luvern L. Cunningham and William J. Gephard, pp. 83–107. Sponsored by Phi Delta Kappa and The National Society for The Study of Education. Itasca, Ill.: F. E. Peacock Publishers, 1973.

————. *Handbook of Leadership: A Survey of Theory and Research*. New York: The Free Press, 1974.

Stogdill, Ralph M., W. G. Nickels, and A. Zimmer. *Leadership: A Survey of the Literature on Characteristics, Attitudes and Behavior Patterns*. Unpublished report. Greensboro, N.C.: Smith-Richardson Foundation, 1971.

Sullivan, Cheryl Granade. *Clinical Supervision: A State of the Art Review*. Alexandria, Va.: Association for Supervision and Curriculum Development, 1980.

Swing, Susan R., and Penelope L. Peterson. "The Relationship of Student Ability and Small Group Interaction to Student Achievement." *American Educational Research Journal* 19 (Summer 1982), 259–274.

Tannenbaum, Arnold S. "Control in Organization: Individual Adjustment and Organizational Performance." In *Readings in Organizational Behavior and Human Performance*, edited by Scott and Cummings. Homewood, Ill.: Richard D. Irwin, 1973, p. 521–531.

Taylor, Frederick W. "The Finest Type of Ordinary Management" Chapter 1, pp. 6–11. In *Organization Theories* by William P. Sexton. Columbus, Ohio: Charles E. Merrill Publishing Co., 1970.

Thelen, Herbert A., and Watson Deckerman. "Stereotypes and the Growth of Groups. In *Group Development*. Washington, D.C.: National Training Laboratories and National Education Association, 1961, pp. 73–80.

Thomas, Stephen B. "The Dismissal of Incompetent Teachers: A Legal Perspective." *Texas School Business* 26 (September 1980), 14, 27.

Thompson, J. D. *Organizations in Action*. New York: McGraw-Hill, 1967.

Thompson, Patricia, Deana Finkler, and Steve Walker. "Interrelationships Among Five Cognitive Style Tests, Student Characteristics and Achievement." Paper presented at AERA in San Francisco, Calif., April 1979.

Tikunoff, W., B. Ward, and G. Griffin. *Interactive Research and Development on Teaching*. Far West Laboratory for Educational Research and Development, 1979.

Trisman, D. A., M. I. Waller, and C. Welder. *A Descriptive and Analytic Study of Compensatory Reading Programs*. Final Report, Vol. II (PR-75-26), Princeton: Education Testing Service, 1976.

Tursman, Cindy. *Good Schools: What Makes Them Work*. Arlington, Va.: National School Public Relations Association, 1981 (no date given). (In ERS Bulletin March 1981, vol. 8.)

Tye, Barbara Benham. *Multiple Realities: A Study of 13 American High Schools*. Lanham, Md.: University Press of America, 1985

Tye, Kenneth A. *The Junior High: School in Search of a Mission*. Lanham, Md.: University Press of America, 1985.

Tyler, Ralph W. *Basic Principles of Curriculum and Instruction*. Chicago, Ill.: The University of Chicago, 1950.

————. "Desirable Content for a Curriculum Development Syllabus Today." *Curriculum Theory* (Molnar & Zahorik, editors). Washington, D.C.: ASCD, 1977, pp. 36–44.

Vallina, Salvatore A. "Analysis of Observed Critical Task Performance of Title I-ESEA Principals of Illinois." Ed.D. dissertation, Loyola University, 1978, pp. 156–166.

Vanezky, Richard L., and Linda F. Winfield. "Schools that Succeed Beyond Expectations in Reading." *Studies in Education*. Newark, Del.: University of Delaware, 1979. (ED 1977 484).

VanWagenen, R. K., and R. M. W. Travers. "Learning Under Conditions of Direct and Vicarious Reinforcement." *Journal of Educational Psychology* 54 (1963), 356–362.

Vroom, Victor H. *Work and Motivation*. New York: John Wiley and Sons, 1964. For discussion of expectancy model see Hellriegel and Slocum, 1974, pp. 320–322.

Ware, B. A., "Second Chance for High School Dropouts." *Journal of Home Economics* 67 (January 1975), 17–20.

Warner, Allen R. "Conferencing: The Heart of the (Supervisory) Matter." In *Improving Classroom Practice Through Supervision*, edited by Robert H. Anderson. Dallas, Tex.: Texas ASCD, November 1981, pp. 27–33.

Watts, G. H., and R. C. Anderson. "Effects of Three Types of Inserted Questions on Learning from Written Materials." *Journal of Education Psychology* 62 (1971), 387–394.

Weaver, W. Timothy. "The Delphi Forecasting Method: Some Theoretical Consideration." See *The Potential of Educational Futures*, edited by Michael Marien and Warren L. Ziegler. Worthington, Ohio: Charles Jones Publishing Co., 1972, pp. 29–30.

Weber, George. *Inner-City Children Can Be Taught to Read: Four Successful Schools*. Washington, D.C.: Council for Basic Education, 1971.

Weber, Max. *The Theory of Social and Economic Organization*. Edited by Talcott Parsons, translated by A. M. Henderson and T. Parsons. New York: Free Press of Glencoe, 1947.

————. "Bureaucracy." See p. 41 in *Organization Theories*, by William P. Sexton. Columbus, Ohio: Charles E. Merrill Publishing Co., 1970.

Weick, Karl. "Educational Organizations as Loosely Coupled Systems." *Administrative Science Quarterly* 23 (December 1978), 541–552.

————. "Administering Education in Loosely Coupled Schools." *Phi Delta Kappan* 63 (June 1982), 673–676.

Weiss, Iris R. Report of the 1977 "National Survey of Science, Mathematics & Social Studies Education." National Science Foundation Stock #038-000-00364-0.

Williams, Richard, Charles C. Wall, Michael W. Martin, and Arthur Berchen. *Effecting Organizational Renewal in Schools*. New York: McGraw-Hill, 1974.

Withall, John. "Classroom Learning: Group and Social Factors." In *International Encyclopedia of Psychiatry, Psychology, Psychoanalysis and Neurology*, edited by B. B. Wolman. Vol. III, CA-CZ, pp. 167–169. New York: Van Nostrand Reinhold; Aesculapius Publications, 1977.

————. "Problem Behavior: Function of Social-Emotional Climate?" *Journal of Education* 161 (Spring 1979), 89–101.

Withall, John, and Fred H. Wood. "Taking the Threat out of Classroom Observation and Feedback." *Journal of Teacher Education* 30 (January/February 1979), 55–58.

Witkin, H. A., C. A. Morre, D. R. Goodenough, and P. W. Cox. "Field Dependent and Field Independent Cognitive Styles and Their Education Implications. *Review of Educational Research* 47 (1977), 1–64.

Wolcott, Harry F. *The Man in the Principal's Office: An Ethnography*. New York: Holt, Rinehart and Winston, 1973.

Wood, Fred H., and John F. Neil. "A Study of the Effects of an /I/D/E/A/ Clinical Workshop: Report Two." Dayton, Ohio: Charles F. Kettering Foundation, 1976.

Wood, Fred, and S. R. Thompson. "Guidelines for Better Staff Development." *Educational Leadership* 37 (1980), 374–378.

Wood, Fred H., Frank O. McQuarrie, Jr., and Steven K. Thompson. "Practitioners and Professors Agree on Effective Staff Development Practices." *Educational Leadership* 40 (October 1982), 28–31.

Woodman, Richard W., and John J. Sherwood. "The Role of Team Development in Organizational Effectiveness: A Critical Review." *Psychological Bulletin* 88 (July 1980), 166–186.

Wright, Joyce. *Teaching and Learning*. Technical Report No. 18. A Study of Schooling. Los Angeles: UCLA Graduate School of Education, 1980.

Wright, R. J. and J. P. DuCette. "Locus of Control and Academic Achievement in Traditional Educational Settings." *ERIC* (1976) ED 123 203.

Wynne, Edward A. *Looking at Schools: Good, Bad and Indifferent*. Lexington, Mass.: D. C. Heath, 1980.

Yukl, Gary. "Managerial Leadership and the Effective Principal." A paper prepared for the National Institute of Education, October 20, 1982.

Zahorik, J. A. "Classroom Feedback Behavior of Teachers." *The Journal of Educational Research* 62 (1968), 147–150.

Zirkel, Perry A. *The Legal Memorandum*. Reston, Va.: National Association of Secondary School Principals, 1978.

NAME INDEX

SUBJECT INDEX

Numbers in *italics* denote figures; numbers followed by "t" denote tables.

A 6
B 7
C 8
D 9
E 0
F 1
G 2
H 3
I 4
J 5